MW00777560

Empire of Ecstasy

Helmi Nurk, Bremen, 1926, from RLM, plate 54; Gertrud Leistikow dancing, Amsterdam, 1917, ink drawing by Jan Sluijters, from *Jan Sluijters 1881–1957* (1981), 115.

Empire of Ecstasy

Nudity and Movement in German Body Culture,
1910–1935

Karl Toepfer

UNIVERSITY OF CALIFORNIA PRESS
Berkeley   Los Angeles   London

This book is a print-on-demand volume. It is manufactured
using toner in place of ink. Type and images may be less
sharp than the same material seen in traditionally printed
University of California Press editions.

University of California Press
Berkeley and Los Angeles, California

University of California Press, Ltd.
London, England

© 1997 by
The Regents of the University of California

Library of Congress Cataloging-in-Publication Data

Toepfer, Karl Eric, 1948–
    Empire of ecstasy : nudity and movement in German body culture, 1910–1935 / Karl
Toepfer.
        p.   cm.—(Weimar and now ; 13)
    Includes bibliographical references and index
    ISBN 0–520–20663–0 (alk. paper)
        1. Physical education and training—Germany—History—20th century.   2. Dance—
Germany—History—20th century.   3. Nudism—Sociological aspects—Germany—History—
20th century.   4. Nudity in dance—Germany—History—20th century.   5. Body image—
Germany.   I. Title.   II. Series
GV251.T64r   1998
    613.7′0943—dc20   96-34015

Printed in the United States of America

The paper used in this publication meets the minimum
requirements of ANSI/NISO Z39.48-1992(R
1997)(Permanence of Paper)

for Carlos Tindemans

CONTENTS

ILLUSTRATIONS

Frontispieces. Helmi Nurk, 1926; Gertrud Leistikow, 1917

(following p. 96)

ABBREVIATIONS

AI	*Archives Internationales de la Danse*, No. 3 (15 July 1934)
DG	Dorothee Günther, *Der Tanz als Bewegungsphänomen* (1962)
DS	Dirk Scheper, *Oskar Schlemmer, das Triadische Ballett und die Bauhausbühne* (1988)
ESG	Eva van Schaik, *Op gespannen voet. Geschiednis van Nederlandse teaterdans vanaf 1900* (1981).
EST	Emanuel Siblik, *Tanec, mimo nás i v nás* (1937)
FGK	Fritz Giese, *Körperseele* (1924)
FGW	Fritz Giese and Hedwig Hagemann, *Weibliche Körperbildung* (1924)
FP	Frank-Manuel Peter, *Valeska Gert* (1985)
HB	Hans Brandenburg, *Der moderne Tanz* (1921)
HFH	Hans W. Fischer, *Hamburger Kulturbilderbogen* (1924)
HFT	Hans W. Fischer, *Das Tanzbuch* (1924)
HK	Horst Koegler, "Tanz in den Abgrund" (1981)
HM	Hedwig Mueller, *Mary Wigman* (1986)
LF	Lothar Fischer, *Anita Berber, Tanz zwischen Rausch und Tod* (1984)
LF	Lothar Fischer, "Getanzte Körperbefreiung" (1989)
LS	Lothar Schreyer, *Expressionistisches Theater* (1948)
JJ	Joe Jencik, *Anita Berberova* (1930)
KT	K.Toepfer, "Speech and Sexual Difference in Mary Wigman's Dance Aesthetic" (1992)
KTP	*Konzert, Tanz und Presse* (1920–1921)
MS	H. Mueller and Patricia Stöckemann (eds.), ". . . jeder Mensch ist ein Tänzer" (1993)
MWB	Mary Wigman, *The Mary Wigman Book* (1973)
OG	Otto Goldmann, *Nacktheit, Sitte und Gesetz* (1924)
OS	Oskar Schlemmer, *The Theater of the Bauhaus* (1961)
OSI	Oskar Schlemmer, *Idealist der Form* (1990)
PS	Patricia Stöckemann, *Lola Rogge* (1991)

RB   Rudolf Bode, *Expression-Gymnastics* (1932)
RL   Rudolf Laban, *Die Welt des Tänzers* (1920)
RLM   Rudolf Lämmel, *Der moderne Tanz* (1928)
VP   Valerie Preston-Dunlop and Susanne Lahusen (eds), *Schrifttanz* (1990)
WBD   J. W. F. Weremeus Buning, *Dansen en danseressen* (1926)
WBT   J. W. F. Weremeus Buning, *Tooneel en dans* (1925)
WS   Werner Suhr, *Der künstlerische Tanz* (1922)

ACKNOWLEDGMENTS

A book of this magnitude appears because many people in many ways participated in its development and production. They participated, often with lavish generosity, because they were eager for a history of German body culture to be told on a larger scale than previously attempted. They wanted a history that revealed the contributions to German body culture of people whose achievements were much more significant than their obscurity in archives would indicate. The adventure of producing this book therefore brought me into contact with numerous people who made extraordinary efforts and sometimes great personal sacrifices to help me solve problems, answer questions, or excavate valuable but barely accessible evidence.

Professor Anton Kaes at the University of California, Berkeley, showed tenacious faith in the project from the beginning, when I participated in his 1991 NEH summer seminar on the Weimar Republic, "Modernity and Its Discontents." Tony has been a decisive figure in getting this story told. I have never met anyone in academia who has been so successful in motivating me to exceed all expectations of myself and to reach my potential as a scholar. Ed Dimendberg, humanities editor for the University of California Press, also made a powerful contribution in shaping the book. With a bit of help from Tony, he wisely, patiently, and gracefully got me to shape a much stronger and sharper book.

Numerous institutions and organizations provided very important support for the project. These include the National Endowment for the Humanities, the American Council of Learned Societies, the German Academic Exchange Service, and the Houghton Library of Harvard University (a Rothschild Fellowship). A sabbatical granted by the College of Humanities and the Arts at San Jose State University allowed me to spend several months in European archives. The dean of the college, Jack Crane, also aided the project by approving a grant for photo reproductions. I owe a great debt to several libraries at which I spent many exciting days: the New York Public Library, the New York Public Library for the Performing Arts, the Library of Congress, the San Francisco Public Library, the Bancroft Library at UC Berkeley, the Research Library at UCLA, the Sutro Library in San Francisco, and the library of UC San Francisco. Through interlibrary loan at San Jose State University, I received many valuable publications from so many libraries across the nation that I cannot possibly list them all, even if I could remember them all. Hjordis Madsen and Shirley Miguel of ILL at San Jose State University displayed a delightful exuberance and persistence in obtaining extremely elusive publications.

Much of the source material in this book resides only in European archives. These treasure troves include: the great Deutsche Bücherei in Leipzig, the Deutsche Bibliothek in Berlin, the Leipzig Tanzarchiv, the Deutsches Tanzarchiv in Cologne, the Academy of Arts in Berlin, the Hamburg University library, the University of Cologne Theatre Museum Library, the *Freikörperkultur* library in Kassel, the Czech National Library in Prague, the Polish National Library in Warsaw, the Estonian Theatre Museum Library in Tallinn, the Swedish Theatre Institute in Stockholm, the Netherlands Dance Institute, the Netherlands Theatre Institute, the Center for Netherlands Music, the Donemus Foundation in Amsterdam, the Gemeente Museum in The Hague, the Flemish Cultural Library in Antwerp, the Belgian National Library in Brussels, the Flemish Theatre Institute in Brussels, the Arsenal Library in Paris, the Austrian National Library in Vienna, the Austrian Theatre Museum and Library in Vienna, and the Museum of Modern Art in Vienna. My work in several of these institutions was especially productive because of the wonderful attention paid to the project by particular persons: Onno Stokvis, Arjan Bokelman, Arne van Elk, and Maartje Wildeman (Netherlands Dance Institute), Christine Boonstra and Maike Hendriks (Netherlands Theatre Institute), Monika Faber (Museum of Modern Art in Vienna), Ronald Vermeulen and Mariëtte Borghouts (Center for Netherlands Music), Jeanne Newlin (Harvard Theatre Collection), Uwe Schöne (Deutsche Bücherei), Gabriele Ruiz and Jenny Metz (Leipzig Tanzarchiv), Josef Kroutvar (Museum of Applied Arts in Prague), and Lilian Kirepe (Tallinn). Frank-Manuel Peter, director of the Deutsches Tanzarchiv in Cologne, provided generous, decisive assistance in getting me to shift perspective or direction in the gathering of documentation. In addition, Dr. Ingrid Eggers, cultural affairs director of the Goethe Institute in San Francisco, and Barbara Bernhardt, librarian for the institute, provided me with opportunities and materials that proved significant during the writing of the book.

Outside of these institutions, a number of individuals did much to make the book a reality through their knowledge, curiosity, insights, suggestions, gifts, hospitality, or enthusiasm. I mention these names with great affection:

Dominika Vogt (Berlin), Ina Gutzeit (Berlin), Dorine Lustig (Utrecht), Mathias Zeiniger (Berlin), Chantal LePrince (Tours), Sonja Schonemans (Paris), Gert Opsomer (Ghent), An-Marie Lamprechts (Leuven), An-Marie Torfs (Brussels), Tina Mantel (Zurich), Wilfried van Poppel (Amsterdam), Max Dooijes (Amsterdam), Mina Garman (San Jose State University), Janet Van Swoll (San Jose State University), Russell Merritt (Oakland), and Mel Gordon (UC Berkeley), as well as Maura Shaw Tantillo and John Fout of *The Journal of the History of Sexuality*. During the past few years, Laurence Senelick (Tufts University) has done gracious, friendly things on my behalf that made it possible for me to achieve more with this project than I anticipated. Susan Manning (Northwestern University) was also generous in her support of the research; her comments on a draft of the manuscript were of great help in shaping the final version. Marcia Siegel (New York University) was another reader of the manuscript whose commentary was powerfully inspiring. Sarah Clark (San Francisco) assisted me in a multitude of ways that made it easier to accomplish a huge range of tasks, not least of which was mastering the computer organization of text and data. Tanya Breindl (San Francisco) provided superb help in translating documentation from the Czech. Through the piano artistry of Charles Turn (San Francisco), I was able to hear some of the delightful dance music of Jaap Kool. I have benefited considerably from insights and scholarship offered by several graduate students in my dance history seminars, and these include: Mary Forrest, Pam Otto, Amy Zsadanyi, David Popalisky, Yi-Chun Wu, Candace Ammerman, Sheryl Bergeson, and Kathy White. In Hilversum, Rene Lobo and his wife, Sjouke, extended enchanting and unforgettable hospitality that allowed me to accomplish much more in The Netherlands than I ever expected I could.

I must also thank members of the UC Press staff who have applied such excellent skill in assuring the best possible production of the book: Danette Davis (production), Erika Büky and Nina D'Andrade (editing), and especially Larry Borowsky, whose superb copy editing has given the text much stronger rhythm and clarity than it possessed before I turned it over to him.

My parents, Walter and Hazel Toepfer, deserve appreciation for their contribution to the book, for it was they who instilled in me from the beginning a powerful respect for the beauties of bodily expressivity.

Finally, I dedicate the book to Carlos Tindemans, who for many years guided the theatre research program at the University of Antwerp. Over the years, he and his wife, Grete, have extended to me many kindnesses and opportunities, and these were decisive in shaping my scholarly ambitions. Carlos patiently and dramatically revealed to me the great advantages of a semiotic approach to performance analysis and history, and so I felt his generous, awakening spirit guiding me throughout the project, even if he would have told the story differently.

Figure One

BODY, IMAGE, CONTEXT

Figure 1 projects a distinctly modern image of the female body and, more-over, a peculiarly German attitude toward the modernity of the body. Such an image of the body is impossible to find in photography—indeed, in the whole realm of visual arts—before 1920. The body of the woman seems to have no "context": suspended in a white void, the body demands that the viewer look at nothing but itself as an autonomous force, free of definition by anything external to it. The pose assumed by the woman is complex, dense with contradiction. The brazen nudity of her torso contrasts dra-matically with the veiling of her face by the thrusting elbow. The upward reach of her left arm is in stark tension with the inward coil of her hidden face and right arm. The filmy skirt seems like a skin the woman sheds in her surge toward ecstatic autonomy, yet the choice of a diaphanous mater-ial suggests that the flesh itself is a kind of veil that conceals the "real" iden-tity of the body, no matter how naked. Both the pose and the image ideal-ize the muscular sleekness of the body and proclaim the newness of this quality by situating the body within a pure white zone that contains no con-taminating sign of the past, no attachments to history. The modern body is, one might say, the context, the determining power of the space it chooses to inhabit: perception of the body determines the identity of the world, the reality external to the self. This decontextualization of the body implies that the more naked the body becomes, the more the body dominates per-ception, the more the body assumes an abstract identity. Modernity signi-fies a tendency toward abstractness of form, but this photograph is inter-esting because it discloses a powerful tension between the sensual materialism of the naked flesh and the abstractness of bodily form released by the nudity.

I begin with this image partly because it is a typical specimen of German modernist attitudes toward the body in the 1920s and partly because the historical identity of the image is also typical. The image appears in a book published in 1927, *Tanzkunst und Kunsttanz*, by Max Adolphi and Arno Kettmann, but the photograph is by Alfred Ohlen. The book consists almost entirely of Ohlen's beautiful photo portraits of female dancers from Ida Herion's dance group in Stuttgart. Two of the photos show dancers posing in the garden of a villa, and one depicts a male dancer. The remaining sixty pictures show different dancers in different costumes (or nude) assuming different poses against the white background. None of the dancers' identities is known. Indeed, almost nothing is known of Ida Herion, and Kettmann's four pages of text, completely given over to a glorification of "dance art and art dance" generally ("living body feeling and consciousness"), provide no information about either Herion or the people in the images. The title page merely remarks that Adolphi "supervised" the poses Ohlen photographed. Thus, though the image of dance casts a strong feminine aura through the profuse depiction of female bodies, all linked to Ida Herion's group, the view of dance is largely male. But the superior elegance of the photographs is self-sufficient: the bewitching beauty of the images, bodies, and poses implies that the reader does not need to know anything about the dancers, the image-makers, or even dance itself to find dance a liberating and satisfying vocation. And though female readers are far more likely than males to act upon the impulse to make dance a vocation, male readers can hardly help feeling that a woman's power to dance, to assert herself physically with the complexity of signification I have ascribed to Figure 1, is a modern, self-determined condition of her desirability.

The uniquely exquisite charm of *Tanzkunst und Kunsttanz* should not obscure the realization that the book is but one of a huge, unprecedented multitude of aesthetically distinctive dance and body culture publications produced in Germany between 1910 and 1935. The scale, diversity, and significance of dance and body culture in Weimar Germany in particular has never been adequately recognized, because any serious assessment entails the study of traces left by a great number of people as obscure yet distinctive as Ida Herion and her dancers. The tendency to reduce the Weimar dance culture to the activities of a few major figures—for example, Mary Wigman, Kurt Jooss, and Rudolf Laban—gives a very incomplete view of how dance and attitudes toward the body produced a modern culture within a particular European social context. Indeed, the greatness of someone such as Mary Wigman appears even more mysterious when one views her achievements in relation to the complex spectrum of dance impulses defining the context in which she worked. Much of the powerful Weimar dance culture has been undeservedly forgotten because scholars cannot compile thick dossiers on many personalities and therefore cannot confine their perception of dance to those manifestations (or documentations) of it that produce a life story about which one can write at length. But strong personalities are not always well documented, and in any case part of dance's intense appeal lies in its promise to free the body from modes of documentation that excessively stabilize it. The concept of dance is key to understanding dance culture, not dances themselves, for the vast majority of these have left so little trace that no one can reconstruct them. Even in the 1920s, before anyone could make any serious effort to record dancers, the concept of dance achieved its most pervasive and perhaps most seductive expression through images of dance staged specifically for photographers or other visual artists. Pictures of dancers and images of dance probably intensified public enthusiasm for dance to a much greater degree than did dance concerts themselves, for images of dance provided greater access to the spirit of the dancing body than concert performance permitted. In a 1957 television interview, the American dancer Ruth Page claimed that she taught herself to dance (ca. 1915) by cutting out pictures of dancers from theatre journals, pasting them on the walls of her room, and imitating the poses depicted (Page, *Video Archives*, tape 106).

By dramatic contrast, Anna Pavlova explains in her autobiography that her ultimately suicidal passion for dance resulted from her seeing, at the age of eight, a performance of the *Sleeping Beauty* ballet at the Marinsky Theatre, St. Petersburg, around 1890 (Magriel 1–3). Perhaps no other dancer has ever done as much as Pavlova to awaken love for dance through dance performance itself; certainly no other dancer ever toured as widely, as intensely, or as successfully as she. One can say that with every performance she tried to reconstruct the ecstatic enchantment of the first time she saw the dancing body. This ambition to imbue the dancing body with the innocence of a child made her beloved everywhere. But innocence is convincing to the extent that it appears fragile, ephemeral, momentary; for Pavlova, this magical fragility depended not only on the delicate beauty of her body but also on the cultivation of the exquisite melancholy that made *The Dying Swan* (1907), choreographed for her by Michel Fokine, her signature work. Though Pavlova was extremely photogenic and hardly indifferent to the power of her image to build audiences, she never doubted that the authority of dance to restore innocence to the body lay entirely in the act of watching dance performances.

Moreover, her notion of dance performance was virtually untouched by modernist ideas of bodily movement: the body recovered its innocence insofar as the dancer projected an attitude toward the body which prevailed the first time one had seen, with a child's eyes, the enchanting beauty of the dancing body. The innumerable photographs of Pavlova displayed a more modernist sensibility than did her performances, in which she presented an "eternal," ethereal image of the (female) body hardly modified by any of the modernist currents in movement theory that had emerged since 1900. She was an enormous inspiration, yet few of the multitudes she inspired actually regarded her as a model for their own ambitions in dance (Money; Lazzarini). Her dances suggested that the innocence (and melancholy) of the female body resulted from the dancer's complete submission to nineteenth-century ballet technique, which assumed that the female body, being a highly volatile and unstable force, preserved its magical innocence through an elaborate, powerfully institutionalized set of conventions governing every movement toward the ideal incarnation of feminine beauty. What made Pavlova great was the beautiful poignancy she brought to the pervasive and ambivalent perception of a fundamental tension, provoked by aesthetic movements of the body, between innocence and modernity.

The complex and very seductive body culture emerged in early-twentieth-century Germany questioned, though did not entirely dissolve, this tension between innocence and modernity. The relation between innocence and modernity was more complex (and ambiguous) in Germany than elsewhere because of German tendencies to link innocence with conditions of maturity and evolution rather than to a "lost," childlike state of perception. This ambition to present modernity as a condition of innocence depended on the situating of the body within elaborate philosophical frameworks, a persuasive metaphysical rhetoric. The concept of dance, for example, had to include more than the evidence of mere dances. Thus, the great theorist of bodily movement, Rudolf Laban, spoke of "the dance of flowers," "the dance of constellations," "the dance of peoples" (RL 150). Dance was a cosmic force that was only partially visible in dance performances as such. But when dance assumes this sort of metaphorical identity, its meaning, its power to liberate, derives as much from its image and from ideas about it as from witnessing dance performances themselves.

This point receives some initial support from Figure 2. Like Figure 1, it is of a dancer from the Ida Herion group, but it comes from a different book, *Getanzte Harmonien* (1926), and is the work of a different photographer, Paul Isenfels. The book was popular enough to run through seven editions in one year. It contains 120 photos, and the dancers assume a much wider array of poses and costumes than in *Tanzkunst und Kunsttanz;* the book also contains more nude poses, more group poses (two women and one man; two men and a woman; three women; four women; one man and seven women), and far more images of male dancers. But the major difference between the Isenfels imagery and the Adolphi is that Isenfels views the dancers within a highly specific physical context. In all the images, the dancers pose within the luxurious rooms and garden of a wonderful neoclassical villa. Figure 2 typifies the visual complexity of these images, which present the dancing body as the decisive phenomenon effecting a "harmonious" reconciliation of nature (the garden) and monumentally civilized architecture. The woman opens her body to the sunlit garden yet remains a shadow to the viewer. Isenfels likes setting the bodies against stone or marble-tiled surfaces engraved with elegant geometric designs, as if to blur the distinction between organic and inorganic forms. He photographs the dancers on stone stairways, on stone balustrades, in stone archways, against stone columns, or through stone colonnades, and it seems that the dancers are neither entirely indoors nor entirely outdoors but somehow poised between "inner" and "outer" zones of being. Isenfels intensifies this perception in numerous images, adroitly manipulating delicate shadow effects and making exquisite use of sunshine to create luminous backlighting of the bodies. But in spite of the obvious preoccupation with compositional elegance, the viewer always sees the body as a phenomenon that resists abstraction, that does not need to be seen as anything other than itself. The neoclassical architecture connects the body to a grandiose sign of tradition or history, in great contrast to the Adolphi photos, which establish the modernity of the body by freeing it from any visible historical context.

Yet all of the Isenfels images remain modern precisely because the bodies assume new poses and a bold new authority over the space. These dancers, with their supple gestures and sleek vulnerability, seem to have invaded this "old" space and imposed upon it a daring will to freedom—and the space accommodates them generously, luxuriantly. In all the photos by Adolphi or Isenfels, it is the body itself—through its poses, its nudity, or its relation to other bodies—that casts the controlling sign of modernity. Perhaps the visibility of this corporeal modernity in Figures 1 and 2 is due less to the photographic approaches of Ohlen or Isenfels than to an attitude toward the body absorbed by the dancers from their teacher, Ida Herion, whose identity is only slightly less obscure than that of her students. However, despite the lack of information regarding the people who produced these books, the images are significant for their power to link modernity to the body itself rather than to external signs such as masks, costumes, or decor. The latter is more obviously the case in Figure 3, depicting Ursula Falke in a pose from her dance *The Prince* (1925), or Figure 4, a Bauhaus image of Karla Grosch performing her *Metal Dance* (1929). Moreover, the difference between Ohlen's and Isenfels's ways of seeing the Herion dancers suggests a large degree of instability in the image of dance and of the modernity of the body. Prevailing attitudes toward the body did not create a unified vision of human identity but instead spawned contradictory strands of perception.

A THEORETICAL CONTEXT

My interest in German body culture of the 1910s and 1920s arose from a lifelong curiosity about modernistic representations of the human form in

German theatre, literature, psychology, film, sexology, photography, and art, especially that produced by the expressionists. The latter group's distinctively dynamic and mysteriously distorted images of the human body urged me to explore ever more facets of German culture to understand this powerful and disturbingly modern expressivity ascribed to the human body. The Germanic way of seeing the body seemed aggressively modern, but it was not clear why. Post-1950 scholarship on modernism has not provided convincing answers, guided as it has been by the assumption that modernity implies impulses toward abstraction and a consequent estrangement from the body itself as a source or site (rather than simply a sign) of historical tensions. To construct more persuasive answers, it was necessary to recover a great mass of primary material that previous European cultural studies had either ignored altogether or treated as marginal. This mass of primary material reveals that the scale and complexity of Germanic body culture was far greater than previously supposed, even during the time it unfolded. My main concern in this book is to offer a fairly comprehensive description and interpretation of specific achievements peculiarly associated with Germanic ideas about what makes the body modern. But any comprehensive history of these achievements means accommodating a bewildering variety of contradictory goals, motives, ramifications, strategies, implications, and consequences. As a whole, German body culture was neither a unified nor a unifying force on the European cultural scene. It repeatedly and often brashly declared its intention to be such a force, but in reality it achieved almost the opposite effect: an increasingly crowded and confused cultural space in which the body consistently triumphed as a source of difference rather than sameness. This effect was a much greater achievement than what those responsible for it may have intended. The outstanding legacy of the German body culture is that it showed how modern bodies project an ambiguous historical function: bodies are modern because they create significant instabilities of perception.

German culture between 1910 and 1930 cultivated an attitude toward the body unprecedented in its modernity, intensity, and complexity. This attitude motivated the formation of body culture. But despite the body's apparent finiteness as an object of cultural development, body culture tends to encompass an ever expanding range of activities, including the performing arts, literature, the fine arts, sports, athletics, medicine, sex, sexology, fashion, advertising, labor, ergonomics, architecture, leisure activities, music, physiognomic study, and military discipline. German culture made interesting and often spectacular contributions in all these areas. However, it is useful to observe that a genuinely modern attitude toward the body entails more than a modern attitude toward the representation of the body or toward identities imposed upon the body. Much of what most people consider modern, such as fashion or machines, is external to the body; the body itself remains a constant, even eternal mode of being, far more obedient to pressures of biology than of history. Indeed, much of German body culture may seem to fit this doctrine of modernity. But then one encounters the plenitude of evidence that indicates an ambitious attempt by the culture to physicalize modernity within the body and to view the body itself as a manifestation of modernist desire. Body culture appears as a mode of aesthetic performance that collapses conventional distinctions between mind and body, subject and object, self and world. Of course, other cultures within industrialized countries experimented with modernizing the body, especially in the realm of sports and athletic development. Germans also made prodigious contributions in these fields, but it is difficult to see how these contributions disclosed a distinctly Germanic perception of the body, for they differed little from the techniques, goals, and rhetoric of sport culture pursued by Americans, Italians, Swedes, or Russians during the interwar years. I therefore have not paid a great deal of attention in this book to German sports history, which in any case has already received monumental analysis (Ueberhorst; Diem; Pfister).

The uniquely Germanic construction of the modern body involved two large categories of performance: nudity and physical movement, particularly ideas about movement introduced by the most turbulent dance culture in history. The Germans powerfully emphasized nudity and movement as the decisive elements bestowing modernity upon the body. But the body culture was never able completely to resolve fundamental tensions between these elements, largely because the more dancelike movement became, the more difficult it was to resolve underlying tensions between the sexes. The interweaving of material on nudity, movement, and dance shows the uncertainty within the culture about whether modernity was ultimately an ecstatic condition of nudity or an ecstatic release of movement. I propose that nudism and dance were answers to questions circulating, often unconsciously, within the social reality that created the culture. The questions may be summarized as follows:

How can the body itself assume a modern identity? What are the dominant signifiers of a modern body?

What are differences between normative, ideal, and perverse bodies in a modern context?

How do the sexes differ in using their bodies to signify attitudes toward modernity?

What are relations between modern bodies and mechanized identities?

How does modernity construct a new relation between the body and metaphysical dimensions to identity, such as soul, spirit, consciousness?

What sacrifices are required to achieve a modern body?

How does a modern body function as a sign of tension between individual and social identity?

Nacktkultur, Körperkultur, and dance never gave coherent answers to any of these questions. Rather, the answers became fragmented into a widening domain of competing ideas, personalities, and institutional gestures. I use the term "empire" to designate the scale of this diversity and will to power (or appropriative energy) defining the complexity of the body culture.

Chapter titles identify themes or theoretical categories, such as "Aesthetic Nudity" or "Group Dancing"; each chapter comprises subsections mostly devoted to personalities whose achievements made a difference in the manifestation of the abstract category. The motive for this method of organization is to show how the notion of a modern body provoked numerous categories of difference that achieved their strongest expression through the formation of intensely different personalities. Even by the standards of the Germanic body culture itself, the ultimate value of the modern body lay in its power to designate a distinct personality that established the authority of difference over unity. The emancipatory goals of the culture, its strategies for redefining conditions of freedom, focused on amplifying the power of nudity or movement to promote difference and accommodate further differences.

Related to the use of the word "empire" is my inclination to speak of "Germanic" rather than "German" body culture. I make this distinction because it is necessary to view the body culture as a phenomenon that extended beyond the national borders of Germany. Body culture had serious export value for Germany, and numerous personalities with international careers developed German ideas abroad. Moreover, many people who contributed significantly to the body culture in Germany did not originally come from Germany. The body culture was "German" insofar as distinct personalities regarded Germany as somehow decisive in shaping their ideas and careers, but it did not exist only and entirely in Germany. I therefore make occasional excursions to other countries in following the achievements of several personalities. Indeed, in an earlier draft of this book I included a large section that examined the dissemination of Germanic body culture throughout Europe, the United States, and Japan. However, this section became so large that I have decided to make a separate project of it.

In our time, the following question inevitably arises: to what extent was the body culture responsible for the advent of the Third Reich? The question seems especially significant because of the deep-rooted presumption of the "irrationality" of early German body culture, a prejudice William H. McNeill summarizes very succinctly: "Since World War II, repugnance against Hitlerism has discredited rhythmic muscular expression of political and other sorts of ideological attachment throughout the western world.

Distrust of visceral responses to such exercises prevails" (McNeill 151). In this book, however, I gather a large amount of evidence to show the difficulty of constructing a decisive correlation between particular attitudes toward the modern body and impulses toward fascism or totalitarian beliefs. Some forms of body culture that we might consider irrational failed altogether to interest the Nazis; moreover, the body culture pervasively attempted to anchor itself in theoretical discourse precisely to overcome the widespread suspicion that any aesthetic or pleasurable preoccupation with the body was irrational.

As a manifestation of modernity, the body culture was, like romantic music or precision tool machinery, accessible to a wide spectrum of political positions. Several personalities discussed in this book became ardent supporters of the Nazi cause, and I have tried wherever possible to give an accurate account of how all the personalities of that time responded to the Nazi cultural program. But the mere fact that several people enthusiastic about Weimar body culture also became enthusiastic about National Socialism does not mean that some deep, inherent connection between body culture and Nazism needs to be explained. Arguing as much is like arguing that because Hitler was a vegetarian, a deep connection exists between vegetarianism and Nazism. The evidence presented here suggests that those who embraced Nazism and those who did not acted for uniquely personal reasons rather than because body culture somehow predisposed them to follow one direction or another. People embraced body culture for equally personal reasons rooted in powerful, individuating desires rather than in self-sacrificing devotion to abstract concepts such as nation, state, or class. If anything, body culture strengthened the authority of personalities and individuality and thus dramatized with auspicious and even audacious viscerality the importance of placing the political within the personal.

Related to the question of whether the body culture was "responsible" for Nazism is the more difficult problem of defining the context for the body culture. What caused body culture to emerge? I have avoided the tendency of some cultural histories to cast cultural phenomena as virtually mechanistic responses to large-scale political or social events such as the Great War, the revolution, the catastrophic inflation, or the Great Depression. The body culture did not remain indifferent to such events, but the advantage of gathering evidence from throughout the period between 1910 and 1930 is that it allows us to evaluate body culture in relation to events that might seem to distinguish, for example, Weimar culture from Wilhelmine culture. The evidence indicates a remarkable firmness of purpose across the period; the aims of German body culture in 1914 were fairly consistent with the aims of 1929, and one can observe in it a determination not to let big events undermine its emancipatory ambitions. Yet much of the body culture seems to have entered a period of decline in the early 1930s. The Nazis did express aggressive hostility toward it, but they cannot be entirely blamed for a decline that set in before they assumed power. It was a decline marked more by theoretical stagnation than by diminishing membership rosters.

The context, therefore, must extend further back into history, perhaps deep into German history, if it is to explain the Germanic uniqueness of the body culture. In earlier drafts of the book, I included extensive discussion of theoretical discourses related to bodily identity: the physiognomic research of Carus, Klages, Kretschmer, Stratz; the "characterological" theories of Prinzhorn and Utiz; the race theories of Hertz, Günther, Müller, and Lenk; the eugenic philosophies of Muckermann, Reich, the League for Sexual Reform; the prolific and often monumental messages of sexologists such as Moll, Wulffen, and Stekel. However, effective examination of these and other theorists requires another book in itself. Moreover, these theorists do not answer our primary question: what was the context for this German eruption of theory about bodily identity? I am inclined to propose that general conditions of modernity, perceived more intensely in Germany than elsewhere, urged Germans to look more intensely at the body as a projection of identity. Pure theorists tend to view the body as a hypothetical construct, a generic organism. My focus here is to show how bodily *performance*, through the nudity and movement of specific bodies, strengthens the projection of modern identity. Nudists, dancers, and gymnasts made more insightful contributions to theories of bodily identity than did the pure theorists. The great, unconscious, and untheorized contribution of the pure theorists was to establish the context of body culture in language itself, in a mysterious and unexplained relation between, on the one hand, properties peculiar to the German language that control perception and, on the other, the limited ability of language, as a thing without body, to make the body completely visible. The tendency of the Germans to assign a deep, metaphysical significance to the body suggests serious uncertainty about the extent to which humans can see themselves or each other on the most physical level. Language is deep inside the body, yet no one can see it. In other words, I feel the most convincing context for explaining the emergence of the Germanic body culture is *cognitive,* that historically unique conditions of modernity activated a cognitive condition that focused perception on the body as a source of meanings that hitherto had remained hidden (instead of being created as such by manifestations of modernity). However, it is obvious to me that humanity does not yet possess the resources or the knowledge (especially of language) to discuss how this cognitive notion of context actually works to produce cultural history. I think it is unwise to speculate further about the body culture's origins, which already seem tinged with mysticism.

Germanic body culture was largely the achievement of women who associated modernity with expanded opportunities for freedom of identity and action. These women believed that unprecedented assertions of freedom and power for their sex depended on revised perceptions of the female body and its expressive capabilities. The desire for a modern identity in a modern body entailed a desire for unprecedented expressions of ecstatic experience resulting from a collapse of difference between inner and outer forms of being and metaphysicality. The rhetoric of modernity never detached itself from mystical metaphysics, even among the most rational advocates of the body culture. But ecstasy does not occur without the perpetration of excesses, severe instabilities and ambiguities of perception that attend any collapse of difference and subsequent effort to appropriate minds, bodies, spaces, and institutions on a national scale. Yet every excess exposes a limit or boundary designating a difference. An "excessive" number of women inhabited the body culture only if one assumes that society should have urged them to articulate female desire in some other way than the celebration of the body as an emancipatory, salvational force. But one might just as well complain that men showed greater reluctance to participate in dance or gymnastics than in nudism because society failed to urge them to focus their desires more avidly on the idea of the body as an emancipatory, salvational force. Obviously men felt that the more their bodies moved with dancelike qualities, the more their bodies assumed a feminine identity, for dance endeavors precisely to make the body the dominant sign of instability, or "viscosity," of identity. This sexual difference was at the heart of the problem in reconciling nudity and movement to produce a coherent definition of the modern body. However, this sexual difference was not unique to German culture; it is pervasive in premodern, modern, and postmodern societies. What was unique to the Germanic body culture, in both the Wilhelmine and Weimar eras, was the intensity with which it self-consciously treated modernity as a problem of sexual difference rooted in deep uncertainty about the power of the body, of a biological "destiny," to become a decisive agent of history. The vast outpouring of sexual discourse produced, from increasingly "scientific" perspectives, during the Wilhelmine and Weimar eras testifies to this gathering uncertainty about the relation between modernity and sexuality, though it failed to provide answers that might have lessened our own uncertainty about this relation.

This book focuses on the great outpouring of bodily performance that attempted to resolve the tension between biology and history by ascribing to the body—and especially the female body—an unprecedented power to give ecstatic experience a large public dimension. It hardly diminishes the achievement of the body culture to observe that it created far more uncertainty than it resolved (or than subsequent historical eras have resolved). Thus, another reason I have kept the context of the body culture fairly open is that the value of these achievements does not depend on a specific set of historical conditions, even if the conditions were necessary to produce the achievements. Despite decades of scholarly neglect, most of what the body culture had to say about the relation between the body and modernity still seems as relevant and exciting for people throughout the world as it was for those who transmitted its message.

WOLFGANG GRAESER

Some commentators, several fairly recently, have suggested that the body culture mania of the 1920s was an intense reaction to the excessive rationalization and mechanization of European civilization, whose malignant consequence was the war. Such observers stressed the government "culture film" *Wege zu Kraft und Schönheit* (1925), with its juxtaposition of grim factory-life imagery and bucolic shots of radiantly active bodies in sun-dappled meadows. Stated one, "Every era until the great war had something of a true orgy of obedience to reason. In its complete aridity it could only end in such a catastrophe" (Graeser 12). But, as will become apparent, body culture, especially gymnastics and dance, was hardly lacking in enthusiasm for system, for rationalistic, technocratic, and mechanistic constructions of identity, even if its advocates proclaimed the opposite.

One of the most significant of these romantic metaphysicists of the body was Wolfgang Graeser (1906–1928), whose book *Körpersinn* (1927), remains an engrossing commentary on the body culture of the era. Graeser was a protégé of Oswald Spengler, and he shared the master's vision of apocalyptic transformation in Western civilization: "The evolution of the West now stands in its final stage. The path is prescribed upon which we must move forward" (47). This path "can only come out of those sources of life which gymnastics has rediscovered," for "so long as we feel the red pulse of our bloodstream our being is assured" (47). Graeser's book contained no pictures, no "totems" (as he put it) of body culture, no discussion of any body culture personalities, no discussion of any techniques, specific dances, body types, schools of physical education, or documented achievements; it did not even contain any dates, except for frequent reference to the war as the decisive moment in the awakening of modern "body sense." Although he clearly differentiated the objectives of sport, gymnastics, and dance, Graeser treated them as abstract theoretical categories, which he did not analyze in relation to subcategories or specific manifestations. He specified sport as the most "rational" mode of body culture because of its (unhealthy) attention to records and quantitative evaluations. Graeser sought to reveal the metaphysical significance of the body, but unlike adherents of the "characterology" cult he did not believe this significance resided in the "invisible" cognitive processes, which shifted analytical energy away from objects or forms to the logic of perception itself. For Graeser, no form of sport, gymnastics, or dance possessed the power to produce unique personalities or distinctive expressions of identity. The transformative value of these modes of body culture lay in their power to bring bodies to a more abstract condition of being, one that transcended the oppressive constraints on identity through rationalistic particularization and differentiation. Gymnastics and dance brought people closer to the unconscious identity of life itself, to blood, breath, pulse, rhythm: "Reason and will do not undermine the pulsebeat of our blood, it is completely spontaneous and the most elementary life-rhythm which penetrates our being. In the heart is the central driving motor. . . . But we can only feel the heartbeat indirectly, because it is so overpowering. Breath is different. . . . We feel the breath directly. It vibrates with every feature of our body, the expansion of the chest puts all muscles of the body into play. When we free the breath from constraining will and muscles and submit to it, we feel with all our senses the rhythm of life itself, the 'id' within us" (145).

Graeser compared the psychoanalytic attitude toward the body with the gymnastic attitude. Psychoanalysis hoped to reveal the unconscious source of life through a new sexual discourse on the body, but its ultimate aim was to domesticate the body and adapt it to the life-draining demands of "Faustian" or "Uranian" rationalism. Language was no more capable than numbers of bringing to light the protean creative energies of the unconscious. Gymnastics, by contrast, focused on locating the unconscious foundation of power and being in the irrational, in an abstract pulse over which the rationalizing will exerted no control. But for Graeser, whose other publications were annotated editions of Bach's music, the highest and most abstract form of body culture was dance because of its close attachment to music, the core of which is rhythm (although he insisted that music and dance do not exist in "mutual slavery" to each other) (120). Dance was the superior abstraction of the body rather than an intensified particularization of it, and modern identity disclosed itself through degrees of abstraction: "It is the new dance that mirrors the image of our era in all its qualities. One finds embodied in dance the image of the machine, one finds the eruption of the chaotic ideas of the Bolshevik world as well as the strict forms of fascist hierarchies, but above all an unbridled dynamism, the sensually turbulent ecstasy of movement in the frenzied lunge toward the Immeasurable that is our life" (106). The glamorizing rhetoric of blood and irrational pulse beat is reminiscent of Nazi mythology. Graeser acknowledged that both bolshevism (in the European rather than Russian mode) and Italian fascism "feel the elementary power of red blood" and were "forms of the chthonic-barbaric life-stream which have opened a new path through the petrified crust"—they signaled an impending "revenge of the blood" (148). He did not indicate his preference for one ideology or the other, but, more than any other thinker of the era, Graeser seemed prophetically conscious of a great potential for violence in the effort to recover through dance or gymnastics the repressed "rhythm of life itself."

KARL BÜCHER

Graeser presented the modern impulse to expose the unconscious rhythm of life as an entirely aesthetic phenomenon in tension with the rationalized regulation of everyday life in the socioeconomic realm. But the notion of "life-rhythm" did not originate with him, and perhaps the recovery of the life-rhythm could have greater consequences on the workaday world than Graeser's approach indicated. Such was the message of Karl Bücher's *Arbeit und Rhythmus,* the first edition of which appeared in 1896. Although this encyclopedic book, supplemented with photos, tables, and musical examples, came equipped with a rigorous scholarly apparatus, it went through many revised editions until 1930 and apparently enjoyed an unusually large audience for a work that initially appeared as Volume 17 of the Proceedings of the Royal Saxon Society of Sciences.

Bücher, an anthropologist, sought to uncover an archaic relation between labor and rhythm by analyzing a vast number of work songs and chants as well as performance conditions of premodern societies throughout the world. He also examined work songs of ancient societies in Europe, Asia, and the Middle East. Bücher analyzed songs in relation to the work performed (milling, spinning, plucking, dredging, hammering, digging, lifting, circumcising, infibulating, carrying, piloting, scrubbing, dealing with animals, and so forth); in relation to whether work was performed alone or in a group; in relation to sexual identity of the workers; and in relation to the cultural identity of the workers. He also analyzed the relations between words and work, between rhythms and work, between bodily movement and musical rhythm, and between motives for singing (magic, inspiration, communication of instructions, group dialogue, stimulation of "compatible feelings," and so forth). He then theorized on the origins of song and dance in labor and their separation from labor in most of the contemporary world. Although no single musical rhythm seemed to dominate relations between song and work, one could nevertheless observe an "original unity" in which "labor, play, and art blended into each other" to establish "rhythm as an economic principle of development" (413). This unity was possible to the extent that the worker-singer did not perceive the thing produced by labor as alien to his or her expectations of life: "Labor is for [the worker] no longer music and poetry as well; production for the marketplace no longer brings him personal glory or honor as does production for his own consumption" (441). Machines have their own complex rhythms, Bücher observed, but in machine-driven labor, "the tempo and duration of the labor is detached from the worker's will; he is chained to the dead and yet quite living mechanism" (439). Superficially, Bücher's impressive treatise seemed to carry a message somewhat similar to Graeser's, notwithstanding Graeser's assertion that the war was responsible for the new consciousness of the body. Bücher, however, stressed rhythm as an external (though "organic") unifying economic principle that controlled the relation between body and production, whereas Graeser stressed the body as the source of an internal rhythm that was an end in itself, a purely aesthetic experience, not a mechanism of production, and therefore a much more chaotic phenomenon.

ÉMILE JAQUES-DALCROZE

Bücher's idea of rhythm as an aesthetic-economic principle that tied bodily movement to production was obviously less disturbing than Graeser's more apocalyptic vision of a world rhythm emanating from the pulse beat of blood, and in 1909 he noted with approval the gathering appeal throughout Europe, especially in Germany, of the doctrine of "rhythmic gymnastics" developed by a Swiss pedagogue, Émile Jaques-Dalcroze (1865–1950). But rhythmic gymnastics was to experience a consequence quite remote from what Bücher perhaps imagined. Jaques-Dalcroze came from a well-respected Genevan family; his father was Viennese representative for a watch firm when Dalcroze was born. The family was musical, and Dalcroze was a child when he decided to pursue a career in music. He studied in Vienna, where one of his teachers was Anton Bruckner. The early part of his life he spent striving to establish a reputation in Paris and Geneva as a composer, chiefly of theatrical works and songs. He wrote many of these for his wife, Nina Faliero, who was a splendid singer. Dalcroze composed a huge quantity of music throughout his life, but after about 1910 he designed the bulk of his compositions in direct relation to his pedagogic work.

In 1889 Dalcroze met the Swiss composer Mathis Lussy (1828–1910), who had published theoretical works on expressive values in music, especially the expressive functions of rhythm, accent, and phrasing, somewhat in contrast to the dominant interest of the time in harmony, counterpoint, and polyphonic coloring. Lussy's ideas moved Dalcroze toward the perception of rhythm as a suppressed power not only within music but within the body. The Geneva Conservatory appointed him professor of music in 1892, but it was not until 1904 that he actually conducted a course in rhythmic gymnastics at the conservatory and not until 1907 that he offered (in Stuttgart) any extensive public demonstration of the method. In 1909, as a result of a widely publicized demonstration tour through Austria and Germany, Dalcroze received an invitation from Wolf Dohrn to establish in Germany an institute for the study of rhythmic gymnastics. Before his fatal accident, Dohrn (1878–1914) was secretary for the Deutscher Werkbund, a loose union of workshop artisans dedicated to the reform of urban and industrial culture. He came from a distinguished family of scientists and educators, and his ambition apparently was to become a kind of golden prince of modern art. Dohrn agreed to provide the financial backing to open the institute in Hellerau, a suburb of Dresden. Dalcroze believed the denizens of Hellerau, a Werkbund "garden city," were more sympathetic to his ideas about bodily rhythm than were the Berliners, who, he claimed, put too much emphasis on purely musical applications of his ideas. Dohrn and Dalcroze collaborated with architect Heinrich Tessenow, Swiss scenographer Adolphe Appia, and Russian designer Alexandre Salzmann on the design and construction of an elegant complex of neoclassical buildings with spacious garden zones for open air performance. In 1912 the school had more than 600 students from all over Europe, but Hellerau was by no means the only place offering instruction in the Dalcroze method of rhythmic gymnastics. By this time private schools dedicated to the teachings of the master flourished throughout Germany and in Stockholm, Paris, London, and Geneva. The Dalcroze school in St. Petersburg, promoted by Imperial Ballet impresario Serge Volkonsky, had 800 students in 1912. But Hellerau was, so to speak, the great temple of rhythmic gymnastics, to which the disciples made pilgrimage. It attracted enormous attention from the press, partly because so many famous people in the arts paid visits to it.

Dalcroze inspired extraordinary confidence because of his impeccable cosmopolitanism and eminently rational vision of bodily movement as the foundation of, as his friend Ernest Ansermet put it, a profoundly social art. He corresponded voluminously with important personages in the arts and traveled serenely throughout Europe, and though he continually felt compelled to correct publicly (but genially) what he believed were "misunderstandings" of his theories by his disciples, he never ceased to display a remarkable self-composure and teacherly patience toward obtusity. He suffused the emerging cult of the body with an aura of radiance, linked the discovery of bodily rhythms almost entirely with the experience of joy, and dispelled the anxieties, phobias, and psychic shadows that until that time made the body a supreme sign of irrationality (Figure 5). In 1912 a luxurious yearbook, *Der Rhythmus,* was launched in Hellerau, and it did much to advance the sunlit benevolence of Dalcroze's vision, as did the grandiose festival productions of *Orpheus* (1913) and the Genevan *Fete de Juin* (1914), a single performance of which was attended by 6,000 spectators.

Yet all was not well. Dalcroze faced endless difficulty in persuading public school officials to introduce rhythmic gymnastics into their curricula. Dohrn died in February 1914, and war broke out in July, leaving Dalcroze in no position to maintain funding of the institute. The Hellerau experiment came to an end after only three glorious years. Dalcroze returned to Geneva, and there in 1915 he established the Institute Jaques-Dalcroze in conjunction with the Geneva Conservatory. He continued to coordinate an international network of schools and became closely attached to the Dalcroze Center in London. In 1919 the ballet of the Paris Opera, of all places, began instruction of rhythmic gymnastics under its director, Jacques Rouche. Dalcroze himself thought this idea was premature, knowing well the vehement hostility of the ballet world (including the powerful ballet critic André Levinson) toward his teachings. (Indeed, when Rouche departed in 1925, the Opera forbade its members to study rhythmic gymnastics.) But Dalcroze's influence in Germany waned considerably with the collapse of Hellerau. True, a Dalcroze-Bund remained quite visible in Germany until the mid-1930s, and many of the Hellerau students—most notably Mary Wigman, Henny Rosenstrauch, Valerie Kratina, Suzanne Perrottet, Hilda Senf (who taught in the Paris school), and Elfriede Feudel—became significant figures of Weimar body culture. In 1915 a group of Germans took over the Hellerau complex and gradually converted it to a school-company devoted to expressionist dance; in 1925 the company accepted an invitation to move its entire operation to the castle of Laxenburg in suburban Vienna. But the Hellerau-Laxenburg school of the 1920s, like nearly all other schools of dance or physical education in Germany, paid little attention to the discourse then issuing from Geneva, even if the Germans accorded Dalcroze himself enthusiastic receptions on his visits to Frankfurt, Hamburg, and Berlin in 1929. The war had undermined German confidence in the neoclassical optimism of the Dalcrozian ideology of rhythm; to a defeated nation struggling to recover its competitive cultural identity, Dalcroze's method appeared too Gallic in its reasonableness and perhaps too imbued with a Rousseauian belief in the innate innocence of bodies. The Germans now offered a body culture that showed less fear of the very shadows, the dark, "inner" impulses, that Dalcroze tried so hard to pretend were merely mythical illusions.[1]

Dalcroze wrote many occasional articles on rhythmic gymnastics, but he lacked the temperament to produce books, which might have presented his manifold thinking in a sustained, systematic, and comprehensive manner. The semi-improvised lecture-demonstration was his ideal medium, but it also led to numerous misperceptions of his program. It was (and still is) not altogether clear what the "method" of rhythmic gymnastics entailed, for the success of the method depended as much on unique personal qualities of

[handwritten marginalia: Interesting difference of Freud + Germans ideas abt the body]

1. The major sources of information about Dalcroze appear in Bachmann; Berchtold; Gagnebin; Dutoit-Carlier; Stadler, "Jaques-Dalcroze"; Jaques-Dalcroze; and Appia, Vol. 3. In addition, Dominika Vogt of Berlin, who teaches rhythmic gymnastics, supplied me with numerous details about the Dalcroze method in conversations held in 1987 and 1992. Unlike his disciples and nearly everyone else who taught gymnastics, Dalcroze never personally performed any of the exercises he devised. He theorized without embodying his theories.

the teacher as on the governing set of general principles that Dalcroze published. That was both the appeal of the method and its primary limitation. Dalcroze was a great teacher, not a great scholar, artist, or philosopher. He loved being in the classroom more than anywhere else and believed that the most intense learning occurs through immediate, physical application of ideas as managed by a teacher, not a book. Dalcroze hoped that rhythmic gymnastics would eventually become accessible to all people, regardless of age or class. The aim of rhythmic gymnastics was to create a heightened condition of individual freedom as well as a stronger sense of social unity by "establishing rapid communication between the brain which conceives and analyzes and the body which executes" (Dutoit-Carlier 346). The expression of individuality required the disclosure of a "unique rhythm." But rhythmic gymnastics, ostensibly at least, did not prepare bodies for professional careers as performers; it embraced all bodies, regardless of talent, aptitude, or intelligence. Dalcroze persistently attacked ballet training as a tyranny that intimidated people into thinking they had no business exploring their bodily expressivity if they lacked rare physical gifts. He proposed that people become conscious of their bodily rhythms by *listening*, especially to music. In the Dalcrozian system, the development of bodily awareness never occurred independently of music, a point of contention among many German physical educators.

Awareness of bodily rhythms began with the heartbeat. A body's unique response to different rhythms was the result of a distinctive heartbeat. Then a drumbeat and eventually piano tunes would permit the students to explore different rhythms: 4/4, 3/4, 3/8, 5/4, 2/2, 6/4, 9/8, 3/2, and so forth. Students moved in relation to different rhythms and different tempos; they moved only the left hand or only the right hand; they moved only the head; they moved only the left hand and the head; they moved the left hand in 4/4 while the right hand moved in 3/8. They marched, they hopped, they skipped, they stamped, they crept, they undulated; they moved in unison, in a line, in a column, in concentric circles, in parallel circles; they moved in a canon; they mirrored each other's rhythms in duets, trios, quartets, and so forth. They introduced accents and syncopations, then added expressions into the movement, displaying anger or delight when the teacher so instructed. Eventually students would add their own voices to the movement and construct "rhythmic dialogues" within the group (rhythmic gymnastics, unlike ballet training, is always a group activity). The exercise trajectory was always from the simple to the complex, so that rhythmic mastery nearly always implied a capacity to express multiple rhythms within the body simultaneously. The variety of such exercises was practically infinite, and Dalcroze liked nothing better than to compose hundreds of them, for he believed that the exercise, not the lecture or reading, was the key to effective learning.

But for Germans, a Gallic rationalism pervaded this approach. Dalcroze's idea of rhythm was too metrical, too mathematical. He linked all movements of the body to note values to produce synchronization of body and music; he had no concept at all of body movement performed *against* the rhythm of the music. Moreover, he showed far too little consideration for the relation between movement and musical values other than rhythm, such as tonality, harmony, and dynamics. And Dalcroze all too easily reduced the notion of expression to a simple correspondence between a vague, one-word category of emotion—such as fear—and a generic set of movements. The great weakness of exercise-driven instruction is that it makes students masters of fragments but hinders them from structuring actions in relation to a culminating point. In spite of his many compositions *short-comings* for the theatre, Dalcroze had little understanding of dramatic action; he *drama* understood parts but not the whole, and he really did not understand how *space* a body could display mastery of ideas in movement without displaying much mastery of rhythmical movement. Moreover, Dalcroze scarcely considered space as a material value effecting bodily rhythm; space for him was pretty much an abstract category, a thing in a schematic diagram rather than a particular place for the body. In *Der moderne Tanz* (1921), Hans Brandenburg complained of an aesthetic that even before the war was losing adherents "through an evermore tortuous metricality, evermore convoluted and entangled rhythms, wherein neither the body nor music moves forward" and neither the body, nerves, nor mind acquires any strength (107). Brandenburg also criticized the use of archaic Grecian costumes in rhythmic gymnastics, and he denounced the excessively austere auditorium at Hellerau and the "pretentious" obsession (due to Appia) with lighting and luminosity at the expense of dramatic effects. For Dalcroze, what happened in the classroom tended to be far more interesting than what happened on the stage, but this attitude was not helpful in enhancing the public value of either dance or physical education.

Such criticisms were surely significant in urging Dalcroze, upon his return to Geneva, to focus his energies on the rhythmic education of children, which was also the focus of the Dalcroze-Bund in Germany. Yet Dalcroze was and remained a decisive, deeply respected figure in Germany, precisely because he showed how the teaching (perhaps more than the learning) of bodily movement was an intensely liberating expression of individuality. This was no small achievement, for it quickly became obvious that it was extremely difficult to pursue a life devoted to expressionist dance without also being a teacher. More than anyone before the war, Dalcroze established a pervasive didactic credibility for activities that, from a social (if not particularly public) perspective, even long after the war, might otherwise have seemed excessively aesthetic, mere narcissistic body worship.

Dalcroze looms over the relation between modernity and carnality in Germany before and after the war. Perhaps more than any other figure, he made it possible for modern dance to become the most powerful contribution of Weimar body culture. I have hardly provided a comprehensive analysis of the intellectual-cultural context in which peculiar manifestations of body culture, especially dance, emerged, for I have ignored much evidence from psychology, sexology, race theory, physiognomic theory, feminism, eugenics, medicine, social hygiene, literature, painting, graphic arts, film, fashion, sculpture, theatre, and music. I intend to use some of this evidence in analyzing the German modern dance culture, but I do not want an obsessive preoccupation with the context of German body culture to deflect attention away from a major consequence of that context. A new view of modern German perceptions of the body and identity requires examination of hitherto neglected yet revelatory sources of information. These sources lead us to four principal conclusions. First, a powerful dance culture emerged in German society during the modernist era because that society displayed an unusually intense preoccupation with the body as a redemptive sign of a deep, or metaphysical, identity. Second, they show that the cognitive-cultural context that made such preoccupation possible was not reducible to a single or dominant set of ideas, personalities, or events. What dominated the body-consciousness of modernist Germany was the notion of modernity in relation to carnality. Many ideas about the body never intersected with each other or achieved universal circulation, and many fascinating and influential theories about the body came from people who are today quite obscure but whose thinking was readily accessible to audiences of that time. Third, the continuity between Wilhelmine and Weimar body culture was much stronger than one might suppose when one interprets, as so often happens, Weimar culture almost entirely in relation to a set of immediate, violent political events, such as the war, the November Revolution, and the turbulent adventures of the state. The continuity between Wilhelmine and Weimar body culture was actually much stronger than the continuity between Weimar and Nazi body culture. The war, of course, was by no means irrelevant to the production of body culture, but people in Germany thought about the body, regardless of whether the state thought about it. The Wilhelmine and Weimar states, more than any other, *let* them think about it, whereas the Nazi state emphatically did not. Fourth, the scale of the German discourse on modernity and carnality was vast, both in quantity of documentation and ideological ambition, and it involved an extraordinarily diverse range of participants, even if the driving force of the body culture was essentially middle class. A peculiarity of the personalities I have discussed so far was their determination to integrate body consciousness into a larger cultural framework: they crossed disciplines, ignored borders between art and science, sought to transcend clearly defined identities, and were especially curious about zones of experience that were "between worlds." If anything is clear, it is that as one examines the body as a configuration of identity, identity becomes more ambiguous than authentic.

But the context, as I have presented it, does not explain why Germany was a favored site for such an immense discourse on the body. The answer does not depend entirely or even mostly on analysis of historical events; one can as well argue that attitudes toward the body are responsible for historical events as vice versa. It requires a semiotic analysis of distinctive features of the German language, features that bestow a unique power of perception (and a distrust of perception) with regard to forms, bodies, and appearances. Great anxieties and ecstasies must seem embedded in the need to name "authentic" forms or form "authentic" names, the need to produce an ecstatic unity of internal and external conditions of being in which, as Novalis remarked, "the world-state is the body." The problem is primarily cognitive, and I do not think we should remain excessively skeptical of the many German theorists of body culture who kept insisting that the value of their subject actually lay deep within the body. But such an analysis of language and its power to construct identities is not within my skill and demands a much deeper mind than mine. My chief concern is to show how dance was the most powerful, complex, and memorable manifestation of German body culture. It is not possible for dance to achieve such unprecedented vitality outside of such a convoluted and, indeed, dark context. Dance offers perhaps the most startling and revelatory challenges to a culture's perception of the body. Moreover, the context, as a cognitive-cultural phenomenon, is primarily synonymous with theories of body culture, and it seems largely devoid of participation by women. But this perception is misleading. One may lament the marginalization of women's contribution to Weimar film, literature, music, philosophy, fine arts, architecture, medicine, law, and science; but in the realms of dance and physical education women achieved such a large measure of expression, both theoretically and practically, that it is necessary to argue that a deep preoccupation with the body as the secret of identity is not altogether a feminine mode of being. That women overwhelmingly chose these disciplines over others may have to do with a great desire, shaped by gender politics, to expose the limitations of language and signification governing those disciplines. These women responded to a context that was not entirely of their own making, and their success in shaping that context means that they were by no means content to regard their insights or their identities as a fate determined either by sex or by gender.

Early *Nackttanz*

In the years immediately after World War I, several factions within the German modern dance movement attempted to present the nude body as a sign of a modern, liberated identity in the age of mechanical reproduction. Concurrent with the appearance of *Nackttanz,* or nude dancing, was the discovery, one might say, of modern relations between desire, the body, and the gaze. But whereas the use of nudity to signify modernity occurred at a time of quite complicated experimentation in formulating a modern attitude toward relations between desire and the body, these relations were never remote from erotic significance. Attitudes toward the modern, nude, and especially female body exposed more complex and recessed attitudes toward danced performances of sexual difference, in which nudity symbolically equated modernity, with the assertion of a more naked identity.

Shortly before World War I, several female dancers acquired fame in Central Europe by performing solo dances completely in the nude. Knowledge about these dances is obscure, highly unreliable, and dominated by the notion that their artistic significance merely rests upon their having been performed in the nude. However, it also suggests that nude dancing actually had the effect of producing significant differences between performers in their attitudes toward modernity.

ADORÉE VILLANY

Adorée Villany apparently performed a kind of refined striptease that unveiled her body as an artwork. Nude dancing was, for her, movement toward a pose; total nudity apparently brought the movement of the body to an end. Complete nakedness therefore stabilized both the body unveiled and the gaze of the spectator. Villany began performing nude dances in

public around 1910. All were versions of works she had been performing
since at least 1905, and it appears that she performed nude dances for photographs as early as 1906.

Born in Rouen, she became enamored of theatre as a child, though she
had almost no firsthand experience of it. Alone in her bedroom, she performed little plays of her own composition, despite stern opposition from
her mother and aunt. She was completely self-taught as a performer, blessed
as she was with an astonishingly rich imagination and sense of enterprise.
She first captured public attention in 1905 with a Salome dance in which
she not only performed the *Dance of the Seven Veils* but simultaneously spoke
(in French) Salome's final monologue from Wilde's play. From then on she
continued to experiment with what she called "spoken dances." As an exponent of new dance, however, she displayed a curious fondness for archaic,
mythical, historical, and Oriental themes: *The Assyrian Dance, The Dance of
Esther, Dance of the Roman Woman, The Old Egyptian Dance, The Old Hebrew
Dance, The Old Persian Dance, The Dance of Phryne, The Babylonian Dance, The
Pre-Raphaelite Woman,* and *Death and the Maiden,* all of which involved pantomimic and intricately narratived movements. She combined these performances with "silhouette dances" (Turkish) and dances of a more abstract
quality, such as *Dance of Anger, Visionary Dance, The Seduction,* and *Dance of the
Blind.* In all these works, she exhibited a brilliant skill at manipulating costumes (which she designed herself) and scenographic effects; apparently
she favored archaic themes because these provided greater opportunities to
employ daring, even lurid, costumes that generously revealed her flesh. In
1909 she performed her morbid one-act femme fatale play, *La Panthere,* in
which the heroine, in a spotted leotard, performs a strange panther dance
for the man she loves before strangling him; the panther woman "strokes—
then scratches." Supplementing this repertoire with dances that interpreted paintings by Stuck, Böcklin, and other contemporary artists, Villany
performed in Prague, Paris, Ghent, Berlin, Rotterdam, Vienna, Brussels,
and numerous spas, such as Marienbad and San Sebastian. But it was in Germany that she found her largest audience.

Villany's nude performances were attended largely by upper-class aes-
thetes and held in private homes or in spaces Villany rented for the purpose
of entertaining members of a specially formed dance society. Munich police
found these strategies distressing and prosecuted her for obscenity in 1911.
The following year, she responded to her conviction by publishing *Tanz-
Reform und Pseudo-Moral,* a huge and wonderfully entertaining book—one
of the most entertaining books on dance ever published—in which she
argued that reform of dance was equivalent to reform of morality.
Undaunted by condemnation of her as a narcissist and exhibitionist, she
perceived that to overcome a pervasive fear of the female body one had to
gaze at it with the same seriousness that one applied to the contemplation

of artworks. She felt that being beautiful was a right and that the assertion of this right entailed displaying her own beauty, which in itself did not transgress any healthy idea of the good. Of persistent fascination to her audiences was the slenderness of her body, which contrasted dramatically with the "softer" ideal of feminine beauty that prevailed at that time. Besides reprinting much of the sensational press coverage of her performances and trial, she made extensive, unprecedented use of photography to document her aesthetic and link her dances to the lofty zones of consciousness occupied by the visual arts. (Apparently she made some films of her dances, too.) But some of the nude images self-consciously show facial expressions that betray a measure of anxiety toward either her nakedness itself or toward the gaze focused upon it. Villany also included abundantly illustrated chapters on her stylized dances, on her costumes—"The reform of dance is as much a question of costume as it is a question of dance technique" (79)—on "dance language and body culture," and on her life; she condemned ballet as an oppressive, obsolete art form; she denounced her imitators; she presented witty interviews with herself and included quite humorous cartoons satirizing her notoriety; she presented the views of her critics; and she offered a series of comic fantasy sketches of nude dances she proposed to perform in public, at the Frankfurt Zoo, before government ministers, painted entirely black so that she looked Negroid, and so forth. She even imagined the creation in 1950 of a museum dedicated to her memory and wrote humorous tour-guide commentary for it.

Tanz-Reform und Pseudo-Moral is a maddeningly complicated book, and it therefore seems that Villany's nude performances must be seen in the context of a rather ambitious vision of freedom. The author's nakedness motivates a wild and monumentally generous release of discourse and imagery that allows her to shift suavely, if somewhat manically, from luxuriant tragedy and theory to exquisite comedy and affable memoir ("I have no idea what headaches are," 121). But above all, Villany linked the reform of dance (and morality) not to reform of movement, music, nor even law but to reform of the body and its image. For her, reform of the body involved not just looking at it but displaying it with unapologetic narcissism. However, it is quite difficult to determine what happened to her after 1912. In 1915 she performed, as a "special attraction," a nude dance at the Oscar Theatre in Stockholm in an operetta, *Solstrålen*, set in a "dance cafe" on the planet Mars (Jannario 21). After that, I find no trace of her.

MATA HARI

By contrast, Mata Hari (Margarete van Zelle) (1876–1917) offered both public and "members only" concerts that included dances in which she displayed her nudity from beginning to end. But even before she gained notoriety for her espionage activities, the public seemed to regard her style of dancing, with its emphasis on exotic, Oriental effects, as the product of a courtesan personality whose chief objective was to bewitch wealthy, influential male spectators.

Mata Hari began doing nude dances for private audiences in Paris in 1905, then in Vienna and Berlin, but shortly before the war broke out her appeal started to wane, especially in Paris after the immense success of the Ballet Russes. Like Villany she was interested in photography, and she produced numerous images of herself in nude dance poses, some of which were even available as postcards. But the femme fatale image she projected through these pictures (rather than performances) was powerful enough to preclude any serious study of her dances themselves, which to this day commentators tend to dismiss as vulgar, presumably because the image she constructed conformed entirely to expectations defining the male gaze. Biographies of Mata Hari invariably teach an archaic moral lesson that more modern innovators in nude dancing were anxious to discredit: that naked dancing actually *hides* something, a "secret" life whose treacherous desires can have disastrous consequences for entire nations.[1] With Mata Hari, then, we encounter an extravagant manifestation of the myth-bound perception that nudity urges us to inquire about the life of the dancer rather than about the significance of the dance itself. Moreover, the life Mata Hari constructed was such a dense web of lies, fabrications, and deceptions that it was difficult to equate her nude performances with superior honesty of identity.

GERTRUD LEISTIKOW

A German dancer whose career unfolded largely in Holland, Gertrud Leistikow (1885–1948) was also familiar to German audiences before and during World War I. She, however, displayed less confidence than Villany or Mata Hari in photography's ability to produce a satisfactory image of her art. Photographs of her nude dances are extremely difficult to locate, although Brandenburg published one (an ecstatic leap in a meadow, with face obscured) in *Der moderne Tanz* (Figure 6). Instead, she placed the documentation of her image in the hands of gifted painters, for her face lacked charm, and her reputation as a dancer stemmed primarily from her innovations in grotesque dancing, which sometimes entailed the use of bizarre

---

1. Of the many biographies of Mata Hari, the most complete and scholarly is Waagenaar's, although even he does not examine her dances very seriously. But his book contains much intriguing photo documentation. The "diary" of Mata Hari is also an interesting document, but its authenticity and even its authorship are questionable, and in any case it, too, devotes more pages to the dancer's lurid private life than to her dance aesthetic.

costumes and masks. It is not clear where or when she performed nude dances. She debuted in Berlin in 1910, but nearly all references to her nudity in performance seem to date from the war years. In 1917 the Dutch artist Jan Sluijters did a mysterious, expressionistic painting of Leistikow in nude performance (he also did a very similar print of the painting) (Juffermans 96, 100; Bakker and Trappeniers 72, 115). Her flesh glows out of a dark, curtained background and through a diaphanous, veil-like negligee; lurid flowers blossom behind her. The pose captures her in a moment of voluptuous bodily undulation while she turns her face, with eyes shut, away from the spectator. This tension between revealing and withholding, expressed in a single movement, effectively dramatizes an attitude of deep (and by no means unpleasurable) uncertainty in her regarding the consequences of performing the nude dance.

Leistikow brought an unprecedented complexity to the image of nude dancing. Hans Brandenburg (HB 157–173) discussed Leistikow at length as a "tragic," "Dionysian" dancer but devoted only one page (167) to her nude performances. In her case, he explained, nudity served to expose movements concealed by costume and mask; more important, it revealed the "thousand-fold play of muscles" in the body. He did not analyze any particular dance but identified general features of Leistikow's aesthetic defining all her dances. Because "the painful tension between the personal and suprapersonal sets her body in action" (161), Leistikow was the "envoy of a new tragic culture" rather than some sort of savior who linked women's emancipation (*Frauenemanzipation*) to "women's movement" (*Frauenbewegung*) (173). The book included Dora Brandenburg-Polter's collagelike sketches of Leistikow in nude performance; these ascribed to the body of the dancer a freedom that was much less evident in those sketches of Leistikow performing in costume. In other words, the sketches did not entirely support the text's contention that nude dancing is the sign of a tragic, rather than emancipated, condition of female identity. What was evident in the images of both visual artists was the stark expressionistic quality of her nude performances. Unlike the many prewar female dancers who linked the performance of graceful movements to the signification of an elevating spirituality, Leistikow favored a hard, convulsive, ecstatic, even violent type of movement. The "thousand-fold play of muscles" disclosed by her nudity made her body a radical sign of power and freedom, contradicting traditional inclinations to inscribe female bodily strength in theosophic, exotic, and spiritual terms. Moreover, Leistikow was in her mid-thirties when she had artists document her nudity; it seems quite possible that, because she did not depend on photography to transmit her image, she succeeded in making nudity a sign of modernity without imprisoning that sign within the image of virginal youthfulness pervading female nude dancing in the 1920s.

The discussion of these three pioneers of nude dancing raises a contradiction. The evolution of modern dance generally (not just nude dancing) depended on the still image of the dancer projected by the visual arts, chiefly photography; yet modern dance, with its stress on the liberating effects of movement, sought quite consciously to release the body, especially the female body, from the imprisoning images of it dominating premodern consciousness. Not surprisingly, many dancers, particularly those involved with nude performance, entered into an ambivalent relation with those who wished to produce images of them. Images of dance were obviously necessary to expand public interest in dance, but it was also necessary for the image to project enough complexity to indicate something withheld from it and given only in performance. Nina Hard, a Swiss expressionist, is a peculiar example of this ambivalence. She enjoyed posing nude for photographers and painters, especially (1921) Ernst Ludwig Kirchner, but apparently did not want her nude dances documented photographically (Kirchner 241, 259, 270, 281; LFg 110, 118). Yet she did not mind photodocumentation of her transvestite performances (Holtmont 205).

OLGA DESMOND

Somewhat more complex was the aesthetic of Olga Desmond, an English woman whose career developed almost entirely in Germany. In her prewar work she used photography to blur distinctions between dance and posed tableaux, so it is not quite clear whether the images documented a performance or functioned as a mode of performance in themselves. In 1910 she produced a luxurious folio that featured narratively sequenced nude photos of her as she assumed statuesque, classical Greek poses of a heroic character. She even treated her hair to give it a sculpted look. Thus, the sense of movement was cinematic rather than corporeal (Figure 7). Furthermore, she dramatized her nudity in a manner that was extremely rare in nude dance: in partnership with a nearly nude male, Adolf Salge. Fear of obscenity prosecution perhaps compelled her to confine such presentation of the body to a Berlin photography studio. Dance, nevertheless, was where she wanted to manifest her enthusiasm for nudity. In 1919 Desmond published a pamphlet, *Rhythmographik*, that linked the self-study of dance to the study of her own system of dance notation. For her, as for so many other modern dancers, the new image of dance actually implied a new method of *writing down* dances, of transcribing the movements into a special grammar of symbols. Yet the pamphlet's frontispiece is a photograph of Desmond dancing in a see-through diaphanous gown. The little book, obviously intended for female readers, also prefaced chapters with ornamental arabesque designs that showed nude women dancing within floral or arboreal patterns. For Desmond, nothing was more significant than nudity in calling attention to the problem of seeing the movement of the body itself.

But in spite of her close connection to the nudist movement (she was for a while the wife of Karl Vanselow, the editor of the nudist magazine *Die Schönheit*), after the war she avoided nude dancing and photography altogether, perhaps because she felt she was too old. A review of a 1920 Berlin dance concert (*KTP* 4, 115) suggests that she projected a sibylline aura of "great artistic consciousness" signified chiefly through movements of extreme precision and delicacy (rather than voluptuousness or wildness): a "convincing, lovely self-absorption which makes one forget for a moment that her elegance and cosmetic as well as dance- technical aesthetic cannot dispel her age and her weariness." In reporting her suicide attempt in 1937, *Der Tanz* (10/11, 8–10) associated her dance aesthetic with that of Anita Berber, Lucy Kieselhausen, and Cleo de Merode, all of whom delighted in flamboyantly theatrical, artificial effects rather than unity with "nature." In 1925 *Der Blitz* (2/50, 1) published a photograph of seven women at Desmond's Berlin school wearing tiny bikinis, constructing a very complicated tableau for a "ballet." Yet an anonymous 1924 mimeograph deposited in the Fritz Böhme Collection of the Leipzig Tanzarchiv, "Olga Desmond" (apparently a lecture by Desmond herself), urged students to keep focused on simple movements (stepping, breathing, bending, turning, plucking, springing, hopping) and then to incorporate the movement of insects, birds, and animals. Thus, for Desmond, nudity appears to have been an early phase in an evolution toward greater and greater uncertainty concerning her aesthetic and identity.

BAREFOOT MODERNISM

Before all these dancers gained renown, Isadora Duncan had made modern dance virtually synonymous in popular consciousness with barefoot performance, and in 1903 she even went so far as to appear nude in a performance at the Kroll Opera in Berlin. Barefoot dancing may have signified the modernity of a body liberated from external (social) constraints (for which clothing is the most obvious sign), but efforts to extend nudity in performance beyond bare feet or beyond the solo performer always seemed to produce an enormous, quite unliberating anxiety. Barefoot dancing introduced a logic of signification that teased the spectator with a promise of liberation, which the dance world then hesitated to fulfill. Perhaps for this reason, the grotesque dancer Valeska Gert, who apparently never danced nude, asserted that "one should dance barefoot only when naked or simply covered with a shirt" (VP 13–16). Moreover, because all the early nude dancers were women, the European public seemed to regard nude dancing as a mode of erotic performance capable of sexually exciting its spectators.

Occasionally, German courts had to determine the legality of some of these dances (OG 49–73).

But it was clear even before the war that the legal ambiguity of nude dances did not stem entirely from a perceived threat to the female body posed by the male gaze, for audiences of nude dancing were as much female as male. Moreover, it became obvious during the 1920s that female nude dancing was inspiring many women to participate in modern dance culture. The degree to which nude dancing transgressed moral norms depended on the relation, in performance, between nudity and the signifi-cation of erotic desire. This relation apparently achieved transgressive power when a nude dance included both male and female bodies (with either gender dancing nude), for we encounter great difficulty in finding manifestations of such combinations of bodies. However, male interest in nude dancing did not confine itself to spectatorship. By 1910 Emile Jaques-Dalcroze had incorporated nudity into his ambitious program for the liber-ation of European bodies through systematic study of bodily movements and musical rhythms. "Nudity," he remarked,

> provides not only a medium of control indispensable for purposes of physical expression, but is in addition an aesthetic element inducing the respect for the body that animated the great Greek philosophers. In proportion as the idea of sex subsides in the fervour of the artist, and in the passion for com-plete absorption in beauty and truth, so our bodies take on new life, and we feel lack of respect for nudity to be a sin against the spirit (Jaques-Dalcroze, 207; Appia, *Oeuvre Complètes*, III 14).

Dalcroze hoped that as erotic interest in nude movement waned, rhyth-mic gymnastics would gain wider support from the state and the public. An implication of his argument was that a linking of nudity to erotic significa-tion produced a profound anxiety toward the body, impeding the hygienic or therapeutic, rather than aesthetic, significance of movement studies. But after the war, Dalcroze's linking of nudity to an idealized classical antiquity seemed an inadequate sign of modernity; indeed, nudity was modern to the extent that it *avoided* classical models. Of greater significance by far in shap-ing German attitudes toward the relation between nudity and dance was the strange and complex world of *Nacktkultur* (free body movement). However, by 1930 *Nacktkultur* had not succeeded at all in changing the conditions under which nude dance had been possible in 1920. Getting men involved with nudism was hardly a problem, but getting them to perform modern dances was, and getting them to perform nude dances was practically impossible.

Nacktkultur

Free body movement
Nudity

German *Nacktkultur,* or *Freikörperkultur* (free body movement), refers to a network of private clubs that promoted nudism as a way of linking the modern body more closely to nature, giving it a freer presence in the great outdoors. Heinrich Pudor (Heinrich Scham, 1865–1943) supposedly coined the term *Nacktkultur* around 1903. His book *Nacktende Mensch* (1893) and the three-volume *Nacktkultur* (1906) established an enduring, if not accurate, link between *Nacktkultur,* vegetarianism, social reform, and racial hygiene (including anti-Semitism). However, Rothschuh (113) claims that *Nacktkultur* first appeared in Germany in the 1870s, along with the animal protection, vegetarian, and natural healing movements. Nudity was an important feature of *Freikörperkultur* well before World War I, and the idea of nudity as a healthful activity apparently owed something to the medical profession's efforts to combat such diseases as tuberculosis with what before the war was called *Luft und Licht Therapie* (air and light therapy) or *Heliotherapie* (cf., Dorno; Bernhard; Rollier). As late as 1922 a Munich filmmaker, Robert Reinert, released a film (*Nerven*) that concluded with scenes of nude bodies in the mountains finally cured of neurasthenic ailments contracted in a decadent urban environment (OG 78).

Nudity to combat disease

Membership in the more than two hundred German nudist clubs seems to have appealed equally to men and women. The documentation and imagery of *Freikörperkultur* nudity was prodigious, perhaps because human nudity had such a complicated impact on perception that it was impossible to have enough documentation or "explanation" of it. The movement produced numerous journals, and by the late 1920s books on the subject of *Nacktkultur* were only slightly less numerous than all those devoted to sports and dance.[1] Yet *Nacktkultur* had no unified ideology, and one finds within it all sorts of differences.

Nacktkultur was a constellation of subcultures, each of them pursuing values that were not always or even usually common to the constellation as a whole. Indeed, one might even say that, for each subculture, the naked body functioned as a sign of ideological difference rather than as a universal identifier in relation to the alienating pressures of modernity. The tendency to read *Nacktkultur* as an anti-intellectual, proto-fascistic (or, at least, conservative) response to the problems of urbanization and rationalization results from an overemphasis on two issues often associated with the phenomenon: (1) the use of racial and eugenic theory to justify nudism; and (2) the idea that "natural" nudism was antierotic and did not disturb conventional sexual morality. But *Nacktkultur* was actually much more complex than we might suppose from such a focus. Something deeper is at stake in critiques of *Nacktkultur* that seek to bestow a stable political identity on the constellation of subcultures and in the subcultures that seek to bestow a stable political identity on the naked body itself. *Nacktkultur* was too mysterious to project any clear political identity. Far from being anti-intellectual, it spawned a considerable philosophical discourse that ascribed deep metaphysical significance to the human body. In his insightful book *Körpersinn* (1927), Wolfgang Graeser gave perhaps the most direct articulation of this preoccupation with constructing a metaphysics of the body: "The dark, chaotic side of Western technocracy has damned the body, branded it with hell and sin. But in the luminous side, the body stands anew in unconcealed clarity. Exposed and naked is our thinking. Now we comprehend the body, uncaged and without veiling insinuations. Radiant bronze skin mirrors the light of the Olympian sun with the same pure sobriety as the sparkling pistons of clearly formed machines" (47). An even deeper thinker, Martin Heidegger, made a relevant contribution to theories on the metaphysics of the body when, in his masterwork *Sein und Zeit* (1927), he linked the mysterious concept of "unveiling" simultaneously to the construction of truth and to the manifestation of being itself (51–61). *Nacktkultur* consistently presented itself as a sign of modernity and an aspect of modernism rather than as a reaction against both.

1. *Nacktkultur* journals of the 1920s included: *Asa; Amarosa; Barberina; Eos; Figaro; Das Freibad; Freie Körperkultur; Freikörperkultur und Lebensreform; Die Freude; Geist und Körper; Kraft und Schönheit; Körperbildung Nacktkultur; Lachendes Leben; Leben und Sonne; Die Lebensreform; Der Leib; Lichtfreude; Licht Luft Leben; Licht-Land; Der Mensch von Morgen; Nacktsport; Die neue Sphinx; Die neue Zeit; Orplid; Pelagius; Die Schönheit; Skarabaus; Soma; Sonne ins Leben.* Andritzky and Rautenberg (97) present a list of from the late 1920s of nearly two hundred *Nacktkultur* societies in cities throughout Germany.

Confusion about the political identity of *Nacktkultur* therefore may derive from an excessive inclination to regard abstraction as a controlling sign of modernist aesthetics. Perceptions and images of human bodies are apparently the source of the most powerful and disturbing emotions people can experience. Perhaps this relation to perception is due to the fact that bodies (their flesh, at any rate) for the most part remain hidden by clothes. Similarly, the flesh itself hides an intricate and mysterious field of invisible activities whose material identity no microscope can yet reveal, activities we designate by such terms as "emotion," "desire," "drive," "consciousness," "memory," "mind," "soul," and "the unconscious." The invisibility of these activities is itself evidence of a dark, formless, or metaphysical dimension to the body. But if we associate modern identity with an antimetaphysical belief system that achieves its strongest expression through antifigural abstraction, then we do not need to see the body itself as a relevant sign of modern identity: all that matters is a modern mind. By pushing representation and performance toward ever greater intensities of abstraction, much of modernist culture attempted to demystify the body and liberate people from the deep—hence, dark—controls over perception emanating from the body or its image. "No more nudes," demanded the futurists, for they understood well that memory structures emotion, and nothing stirs emotion so profoundly as the sight of the naked body. Thus, the liberation of people from memory, from the past, depended on their being freed from the emotions they attach to the body (Chipp 293). Much of modernist cultural history until recently has avoided dealing with strands of modernism that focus perception on the body rather than away from it, perhaps because modern identity seems less difficult to achieve or comprehend when it is aligned with a constant idea of the body that lies beyond the grasp of those conditions of perception and signification that make identity modern. *Nacktkultur* projected an ambiguous political identity because it treated the body as a double sign: on the one hand, it presented nudity as a return to an eternal primeval; on the other hand, it regarded modern identity as an unprecedented condition of nakedness.

Because male nude bodies were so conspicuously absent in the evolution of nude dance yet so pervasive in the realm of *Nacktkultur,* the unhelpful possibility emerges of a gendered partition resulting from the contradictory political values assumed by the double sign of the body, with nude female bodies in dance signifying an emancipatory energy and nude male and female bodies in *Nacktkultur* representing a conservative notion of the unveiling that is the basis of a modern identity. But the relation between *Nacktkultur* and *Nacktkultur* was so complex that an adequate explanation for the absence of nude male bodies in nude dance must also explain the relation between nudity and the erotic.

HANS SURÉN

Perhaps the most popular promoters of *Nacktkultur,* at least among men, were Adolf Koch (1894–1970) and Hans Surén (1885–1972), both of whom were Berliners. *Nacktkultur* was an invention of the big city, with Berlin providing by far the largest number of club members, and it is obvious that the phenomenon had little interest for people who lived in the countryside or were attached to *volkisch* cultural values. Surén's book *Der Mensch und die Sonne* (1924) was so popular it ran through sixty-eight editions (250,000 copies) in its first year of publication. Surén became a Nazi in May 1933 and made changes in subsequent editions to accommodate Nazi ideology; apparently the book remained in print until the end of World War II.

Though the numerous photographs of nude bodies no doubt enhanced the appeal of the book, the main attraction was the radiant mythic apparatus Surén constructed to justify a new culture based on "naked living." From Surén's perspective, it was necessary to detach nudity from the association with sickness it had acquired through its use in *Luft und Licht Therapie* and from its stigmatization by anxiety-ridden forces of "prudery" that were poisoning modern civilization. Open nudity, for Surén, was a sign of health, strength, and beauty; the text implied that people do not "open" their nudity to the world unless their bodies possess all three qualities. Of course, we now know that healthy bodies are not necessarily beautiful, and beautiful bodies are not necessarily healthy; healthy bodies are not necessarily strong, nor are strong bodies necessarily healthy; bodies are not necessarily beautiful because they are strong, and strong bodies are only occasionally beautiful. Such complexities, however, did not trouble Surén, who saw nudity as the key to achieving a convergence of health, strength, and beauty. As long as people remained remote from their own bodies, as long as they were unable to see their own bodies, they could not possibly enjoy health, strength, or beauty. The urge to be naked, he believed, lies dormant within us, yet it is as strong as the urge to feel the light of the sun.

Because nudity was a natural condition, the proper setting for its manifestation was the great outdoors. Almost all the photos in *Der Mensch und die Sonne* showed nude bodies in flower-speckled meadows, sun-drenched beaches, grassy flatlands, tranquil marshes, and snow-bright alpine slopes (Figure 8). Nudity was not only a daytime event for Surén but also primarily a summertime affair; despite the fact that Germany is for most of the year a cold and cloudy country, Surén did not find interesting any image of nude bodies set against clouds or even shadows. He perceived nudity above all as a matter of the body's relation to sunlight, of its power to see and be seen in a great, open space in which nothing hides the horizon. The "friendship" between sunlight and flesh motivated activities that strengthened and

beautified the body. The primary activity was gymnastics, with hiking, swimming, and noncompetitive sports (such as archery) assuming subordinate
significance. Not surprisingly, Surén promoted his own gymnastic method,
which stressed the use of medicine balls, weights, and throw-thrust exercises. Naked exercises achieved maximum effect when performed in groups
rather than alone. Yet he separated nude gymnastics from competitive
sports, which could have unhealthy consequences for the body. And though
he accepted nude dancing as an agreeable component of *Nacktkultur,* he
clearly regarded it as an activity for women. The profound freedom offered
by the conjunction of nudity, sunlight, and open space depended on the
perfection of self-discipline resulting from gymnastic training. Despite his
emphasis on group performance, Surén saw nudity and gymnastics as
modes of self-discovery and will formation. A former army officer and son
of an officer, he displayed a lifelong disdain for the regimented, "command
and drill" methods of discipline employed by the military, for these undermined the capacity of men to act on their own in relation to any problem of
modern life.

That men were the target audience for the book was obvious from the
use of male models to demonstrate all the gymnastic techniques. But the
book left a deeper problem only partially resolved. Surén realized that *Nacktkultur* could become a sign of national strength only by involving large numbers of men. But he also realized that the involvement of men depended on
the involvement of large numbers of women, so he included numerous photos of nude women and described the significance of *Nacktkultur* for women.
This material, however, worked to assure men that *Nacktkultur* enhanced
their attractiveness for women. Surén had to deal with the fact that erotic
desires achieve fulfillment above all through some condition of nakedness,
and that it is very difficult for images of group nudity to escape association
with the fulfillment of an orgiastic or at least communal (rather than couple-
contained) erotic desire. Therefore, he insisted that the sexes remain seg-
regated in the performance of their nude activities, and nowhere did he
include a photo of men and women naked together. But such segregation
left *Nacktkultur* vulnerable to the insinuation that it was attractive to men
with homoerotic desires. Surén reminded his readers that in earlier, Teutonic times, men and women bathed together and indeed explored opportunities to live naked together. He even introduced the possibility that labor
of all sorts could become more efficient and productive by being performed
naked. But this naked utopia would emerge only after the entire sphere of
education itself collaborated with nudity to shape the will of every citizen
from a very early age. Consequently, Surén advocated allowing children
under twelve to play naked together in the streets of big cities.

However, the gender politics of *Der Mensch und die Sonne* apparently both-
ered Surén, for in his next book, *Deutsche Gymnastik* (1925), he presented a

much narrower vision of the ideal male body. Here he distanced himself emphatically from the "feminine" dance schools, the gymnastic schools, and the nudist movement. "My gymnastic views," he wrote, "find their origin in the terrible breakdown of our time," which lacked the self-discipline that gymnastics, far more than "mass compulsion and drill," could develop (54). Surén had been an instructor at the Army School of Physical Education, but when he introduced his gymnastic methods, the army became alarmed and dismissed him. Only when gymnastics operated "in the home," as an everyday activity accessible to anyone, he proposed, could it become a uniquely German mode of self-discipline and restoration of national strength. Surén integrated nude gymnastics with vegetarianism and a sensibly ascetic lifestyle, but most of the book consisted of numerous exercises a man could perform alone. All of the photographs showed Surén himself, lavishly bronzed and nearly nude (wearing only a tiny jock strap), before a totally uncontextualized white background, neither indoors nor out, neither in nature nor in a domestic interior. Though he devoted a chapter to praising the benefits of nudity, he did not treat nudism as an activity for signifying communal unity but rather as the ultimate image of individuality and self-discipline. The ideal male appeared alone and nude, not especially vulnerable in his nudity but not brought closer, through nudity, to other men or women.

ADOLF KOCH

Surén's thinking about *Nacktkultur* was not entirely original, for he relied on some arguments made before World War I. What was original (and popular) about his presentation was the ingenious way in which he made *Nacktkultur* attractive by implying that the problem of erotic desire was not a matter for *Nacktkultur* to solve—that problem was the responsibility of those who did not know their bodies. But Surén by no means spoke for everyone involved with *Nacktkultur*. Adolf Koch, for example, never placed such heavy emphasis on the connection with nature. A former schoolteacher, he saw nudity as a pedagogical activity that integrated the study of the body and the study of culture to create a kind of athletic intellectual. But because he favored the integration of the sexes in nudism, which he regarded as a necessary component of sexual hygiene, it was even less clear to what extent his approach met or neutralized the expectations raised by erotic desires. That he accepted this erotic ambiguity was evident from the beginning (Figure 9). In 1921, as a public school teacher in a proletarian section of Berlin, Koch introduced open-air nude exercises to male and female children suffering from the effects of vitamin deficiency. The state was sympathetic to his program until a woman visitor to the school made a loud public complaint against "nude dancing" in a state institution. School authorities forbade him from doing anymore nude exercises, so he decided to form his own school in 1926 (Koch, *Nacktkulturparadies*, 37; Merrill 146).

Koch was unique in that he did not merely form a nudist organization; he founded a nudist *school*. Naked students attended classes on all sorts of subjects and participated in gymnastics, group movement exercises, nude theatricals, and outdoor activities. Unlike Surén, Koch was enthusiastic about drills and group coordination exercises (Merrill 134–148). He also aggressively recruited proletarian men and women into nudism. His success was considerable, partly because all members paid the Koch organization 5 percent of their income; if they were unemployed, as many were after 1930, the school carried them until they found a job. Meanwhile, Koch found friends among mainstream socialists, although he acknowledged that *Nacktkultur* alone could not dissolve class differences and was not sure that nudism was a reliable model for a new, socialist society (Koch, *Nacktheit*, 126). Nevertheless, by 1930 he had schools in Berlin, Breslau, Barmen-Elberfeld, Hamburg, Ludwigshafen, and Mannheim, with a total enrollment of 60,000; the same year, Koch revealed that the total enrollment in all German nudist organizations was more than 3 million. The Koch schools offered four-year teaching certificates accredited by the government.

In 1929 the Berlin school hosted the first International Congress on Nudity, with participants from twenty-three countries. In Berlin, Koch also presided over a busy publishing program and edited the nudist journal *Körperbildung/Nacktkultur* (1928–1932), which, unlike the majority of the ever-expanding number of nudist magazines reaching the public, stressed the idea of nudism as an indoor, classroom activity. An American documentary film, *This Nude World* (1932), containing English commentary by Koch's daughter, presented a mysterious image of a community, not entirely young, in which nudism not only created a powerful feeling of social unity but was the basis for an even more profound unity between intellectual development and appreciation of nature. Koch was clearly a rationalist, but he had little interest in Dalcrozian rhythmic gymnastics, for his sense of nude group dynamics was too complex for the harmony pursued by Dalcroze's metricalism. Koch wanted people to move to *ideas*, to pedagogical dialogues, not just music. But his thinking was too complex for the Nazis as well, for they shut down his operations in 1933.[2]

2. Some of the most vivid descriptions of Koch's activities and of *Nacktkultur* in general appeared in American publications. Frances and Mason Merrill's *Among the Nudists* (1931) and Maurice Parmelee's *Nudism in Modern Life* (1927) gave enthusiastic autobiographical accounts of experiences in German nudist camps, and both books enjoyed several editions, with Parmelee's book reaching a new edition as late as 1940 after a protracted battle with puritanical censors in various states. The 1940 edition includes detailed documentation of the Supreme Court deliberations on the moral-legal decency of the book.

RICHARD UNGEWITTER

With Richard Ungewitter (1868–1958), the relation between nudity and culture assumed an intensely reactionary expression. Ungewitter, one of the foremost spokesmen for *Nacktkultur* before the war, promoted communal nudity as a powerful sign of racial purity in such books as *Nacktheit und Moral* (1906) and *Nacktheit und Kultur* (1907). He saw *Nacktkultur* as preparation for and an extension of married life, for healthy marriage was the key to preserving racial purity. No other promoter of nudism made such an explicit and narrow connection between *Nacktkultur* and marriage. Of all the theorists of nudity, Ungewitter disclosed the deepest (actually fanatical) commitment to spartan, military ideals. After the war, when it seemed to him that Germany had sunk into an abysmal state of degradation, he argued that the "pure," naked body must signify an "armored spirit" in a nation deprived of military power. Though like Surén he regarded nudity as a natural condition, he was quite unique in believing that nudity could not achieve complete significance until it became a compulsory element in daily life, a duty integrated into a specifically German lifestyle that also included a vegetarian diet and communal ethic. In 1919 he edited a monumental anthology, *Der Zusammenbruch: Deutschlands Wiedergeburt durch Blut und Eisen,* in which he incorporated compulsory nudity into a gigantic, Nibelung-scale plan for renewing German cultural, political, and economic power.

Nudity was for Ungewitter the projection of human identity uncontaminated by capitalism and socialism, the two forces most responsible for the corruption of Aryan racial beauty. Recovery of this beauty, he argued, was a much more strenuous matter than people such as Surén or Koch would have us believe, for one *must* pursue nudity daily, year-round, doing nude exercises at six or so in the morning, at noon, in the late afternoon, and just before bed. The communal environment in which Aryan nudity operated was as insulated from the rest of society as a military camp. It was obvious that for Ungewitter, resident in Stuttgart, *Nacktkultur* could not remain confined within a club or association—it must become an

---

In Germany, such puritanism on the part of official custodians of morality was unthinkable before 1935.

Another, perhaps even more interesting American book on German nudism was Jan Gay's *On Going Naked* (1932), which touchingly described a libidinous young woman's journey from a suffocatingly repressive Midwestern milieu to the ecstatic freedom of outdoor German nudism. Gay collaborated on the film *This Nude World* (1932). By contrast, a grotesquely misnamed pamphlet, *Facts about Nudism,* by Hugh Morris, published in the mid-1930s, hysterically warned Americans that Naziism was synonymous with homosexuality, vegetarianism, and nudism.

expression of a complete, purified community, as he explained at length in *Nacktheit und Aufstieg* (1920). Nevertheless, Ungewitter aligned his views with those defining the strange cult surrounding the Viennese journal *Die Ostara*, whose membership excluded all but blond males of "Aryan-aristocratic" beauty. *Ostara Nacktkultur* strove to embody a "blond, heroic manliness," an ideal physicality manifesting a superior synthesis of science, art, and Christianity and free of all "feminine" decadence, which, for Unge-witter, was synonymous with racial impurity.[3] Nudity within this cult was not only a paramilitary activity but a cosmic political adventure involving com-mitment to an elaborate, fantastically reactionary program for reforming the whole of European society around an archetypal, premodern image of male identity. Ungewitter displayed a much deeper concern than Surén with the inclusion of (Aryan) women in *Nacktkultur*, prescribing in great detail nude activities to prepare them for the heroic role that awaited them on the journey to utopia; but that role always remained limited, by nature, to the "world of feeling and beauty," which had no connection with the "morbid" and "degenerate" proposals of feminism (*Zusammenbruch*, 293).

3. For information about Ostara, see Ungewitter, *Deutschlands Wiedergeburt*, 408, and two pamphlets: *Ostara: Nackt-und Rassenkultur im Kampf gegen Mucker-und Tschandalkultur* (1912); Jörg Lanz-Liebenfels, *Ostara: Einführung in der Sexual-Physik oder die Liebe als odische Energie* (1913).

Feminist *Nacktkultur*

BESS MENSENDIECK

A major sector of *Nacktkultur* regarded nudism as an aspect of feminism and as a force promoting a new, modern identity for women. Many among this sector adapted the body pedagogy doctrines of American physician Bess Mensendieck (1864–1957), whose book *Körperkultur der Frau* (1906) exerted a pervasive influence over German women gym instructors into the 1930s. Mensendieck, based in Vienna, believed that nudity was fundamental in enhancing women's body consciousness, which motivated all activity that made the female body strong, healthy, and beautiful. She quoted Nietzsche to her students: "Beauty is not a mere accident. . . . [A] mere discipline of the senses and of the thoughts alone amounts to almost nothing. Therein lies the great mistake of German teaching, which is entirely illusory. One must first discipline the body. . . . It is important for the destiny of nations and of humanity, that one should start culture from the right point—not the soul, as was the fatal superstition of priests and half-priests, but the body" (*It's Up to You,* 37). In 1909 Maria Lischnewska, an officer of the feminist League for the Protection of Mothers, contended that the "new woman" expected not only legal equity but also opportunities for nude gymnastics and nude sunbathing in the public schools, a position more radical than that assumed by any other major apologist for *Nacktkultur* (Soden 45). Mensendieck herself worked to create a network of disciples who would form private schools that transmitted her ideas in a kind of summer-camp environment; indeed, it was in just such an environment that feminist nudism flourished, although it was not until after the war that this peculiar manifestation of feminism achieved a powerful hold on the imagination of bourgeois girls. The publications of the Mensendieck cult were much less grandiose in their ideological

39

program than those of male *Nacktkultur,* but their attitude toward nudity was much more complex.

Mensendieck was a student of the American physical culturalist Genevieve Stebbins, who developed a feminine mode of physical expression patterned on the body semiotics of the French theorist Francois Delsarte (1811–1871). But Mensendieck departed from this "classical" tradition of bodily education by linking the cultivation of a woman's personality to the efficient and beautiful performance of ordinary, practical actions. More than any other physical educationalist, Mensendieck tied nudity and the beautiful image of the body to commonplace tasks and objects in daily life. She urged women to think scientifically about their bodies as "machines" of liberation; the expressive power of the body as a whole depended on the strengthening of different parts of the body, from head to toe, in ways that were specific to their functions. Accordingly, in her 1906 book, which remained virtually unchanged in its ninth edition (1925), she introduced fifty-three exercises, each designed to strengthen a particular part of the body, with all movements controlled by a "correct" posture of equilibrium. A peculiarly feminine feature of Mensendieck's system was what Artus (9) calls a "principle of reserved strength": a woman signified bodily power not through demonstrations of strength or muscle-flexing but through economy of movement—for example, by completing an action or signifying an attitude by moving only an arm rather than her whole body. The total strength of the female body was difficult to measure when its movements remained localized in relation to an optimum state of equilibrium.

Mensendieck relied on photography to develop in her students a comparative analytic approach to bodily performance. Photos showed a woman performing the same task incorrectly, correctly, and then (sometimes) wearing clothes. Her English-language book, *It's Up to You* (1931), provided a good example. The same young woman posed nude for all the photos (although prudish American censorship laws required the publisher to paint a skimpy bikini over her body). Facing each photo was an elaborate caption analyzing the image and the mechanics of the bodily action. These actions included, to name but a few, standing, standing while talking on the phone, washing one's face at a bathroom sink, reaching for an object on a shelf, stooping, ironing, reading while sitting, leaning forward at a desk, carrying a tray, lifting a baby, and looking over one's shoulder. Although she strongly contextualized the nude body by comparison with Surén—who in *Deutsche Gymnastik* had depicted nude male gymnastics "in the home" in relation to an empty white background—Mensendieck consistently presented the nude woman alone or before mirrors. Nor did she associate nudity much, if at all, with nature or outdoor activity; indeed, she displayed a very confined ,or perhaps excessively immediate, perception of the relation between movement and space. Her hostility toward drill techniques also betrayed a limited perception of relations between time and movement. Music had no function in her system: "Physiologic rhythm is not, however, to be confused with musical rhythm. It is the outcome not of an adaptation of bodily rhythm to musical rhythm, but of an intelligent obedience of the body to its own inherent laws of movement" (*It's Up to You,* 35). It is therefore somewhat surprising that her work held peculiar fascination for women who wanted to become dancers. But Mensendieck revealed how "everyday" movements could possess a strange, poetic expressive power quite as compelling as anything in ballet.

Mensendieck succeeded in establishing an elaborate network of schools in Germany, Austria, Holland, Denmark, and Czechoslovakia, the Mensendieck-Bund. But when war broke out she had to return to New York City, where she coordinated the introduction of her method into finishing schools in several U.S. cities and promoted the International Mensendieck League. On her return to Europe in 1921, she discovered that the women she had taught to teach her ideas had modified them, even though they claimed to be teaching the "Mensendieck system." She reestablished herself in The Hague; then, in 1926, a Copenhagen newspaper published an interview with her in which she accused the Germans of misusing her ideas and name. She reiterated her attitude during an unannounced visit to Hamburg, where she denounced educator Hedwig Hagemann. But at a lecture in Berlin, she changed her tone and blamed the widely reported "misunderstandings" on the press. Closer questioning of her, however, revealed her bitter sense of betrayal, although none of the people she denounced believed they had done anything to discredit or misuse her system (Hilker 48–54). Mensendieck had not introduced any significant changes in her system since 1896, but her students modified it to accommodate social-cultural realities that had changed for them, if not for Mensendieck. Her Berlin lecture seemed to them to disclose a "cold" attitude toward the body, and after 1926 her influence in Germany steadily waned. According to a 1926 article in the impressive journal *Gymnastik,* body culture pursued "work whose aim is not the most perfect or painfully exact performance of exercises, but the development of a person to his purest and freest form" (Hilker 54).

FRITZ GIESE AND HEDWIG HAGEMANN

Major propagandists for the Mensendieck cult included Fritz Giese, Hedwig Hagemann, Dorothee Günther, Maja Lex, Ellen Petz, Lisa Mar, Jarmilla Kröschlova, and Dora Menzler, and her disciples operated schools in numerous cities throughout Germany. Giese (1890–1935) was a highly cultivated Social Democrat and labor psychologist who published extensively in the area of "psychotechnics" and educational psychology. He collaborated with Hagemann, director of a Hamburg body culture camp for girls, on a very successful book, *Weibliche Körperbildung* (1922), which also contained essays by physicians, dancers, and art historians to establish the wide-ranging implications of the Mensendieck system.

Like Surén, Giese and Hagemann assumed that nudity was the key to producing a bodily convergence of strength, health, and beauty; but they grounded nudist discourse in the rhetorics of science, history, and aesthetic theory rather than in the rhetorics of myth, nature, and national will. In one of his essays, Giese asserted that the purpose of nude gymnastics was not to produce a woman who embodied a state ideal or communal will but rather to develop in each woman a distinct personality, a highly unique identity that could adapt well to the complexities and instabilities of a modern reality driven above all by technology (108). Giese was not a utopian dreamer in the manner of Surén, Ungewitter, or even Koch; he was a rationalist for whom nudity was an element of technological mastery over the construction of identity at a historical moment in which differences between humans and machines were growing increasingly blurred. He therefore regarded the body not as a machine but rather as a mysterious organism needing constant exposure in order to find a distinct identity in the world. Peculiar to the whole Mensendieck cult was the perception of nudity as a sign of difference rather than unity between bodies. Difference operated above all through gender: basic anatomical differences between male and female bodies necessitated a difference between *Weibliche Körperbildung* and *Männliche Körperbildung* (1924), with sport and dance exemplifying the major distinction between the objectives of male and female body cultures. Yet a large contradiction between image and inscription complicated the ideology of *Weibliche Körperbildung*. Though Giese repeatedly stressed how *Nacktkultur* transformed bodies into unique personalities, the numerous photo illustrations showed nude women performing "correct" and "incorrect" daily activities, such as picking up objects from the floor, combing the hair, standing, breathing, walking, bending, arching, kneeling, stretching, holding schoolbooks, and assuming "graceful" poses. In other words, the photodocumentation did not demonstrate how nudity makes one different—it showed "correct" modes of performance that *all* female bodies should emulate. In another essay Giese linked feminist *Nacktkultur* to Taylorism (American time-motion industrial labor studies); the implication, apparently, was that differences in personality emerged not from a "correct" image of the body but from the enhanced productivity and efficiency of a body that performs actions "correctly."

Giese, however, reached more deeply when he suggested that anatomical differences were responsible for differences in drive structures and always worked toward the assertion and fulfillment of erotic desire: "All body culture is full of eroticism, especially that for women" (111). Whereas the eroticism of the male body found its dominant metaphor in athletic prowess, the key metaphor for the eroticism of the female body was dance, as explained by Frank Thiess (79–102). The book reinforced this point by including several photographs (some nude) of dancers Clotilde von Derp and Ellen Petz, a brief essay by Petz, and repeated reference to dance by other contributors. The book as a whole intimated subtly but clearly that nothing exposed the structure of feminine erotic desire more powerfully than nude dancing and that the highest aim of feminist nudism was nude dancing, yet none of the contributors dared to answer any of the questions that made nude dancing more powerfully controversial than any other mode of performance. Where does nude dancing take place, and for whom? If nude dancing inevitably objectifies erotic desire, to what extent does objectification fulfill such desire for either the performer or the spectator? What happens when nude dancing transcends solo performance and begins to include partners or even groups of nude bodies? How does the erotic desire of a unique personality maintain itself when the performer dances nude with a nude male or, indeed, with another nude female? Can nude dancing ever transcend an idealizing of the body and achieve the grotesque, satiric form that Rita Aurel, Grit Hegesa, or Valeska Gert created for non-nude dances? In other words, does nude dancing occur only when the body of the performer conforms to a spectator-determined, normative image of beauty that does not provoke a strong tension between the erotic desire of the performer and that of the spectator? What relations between body, dancelike (aesthetic) movement, and erotic desire are "exposed" by nude dancing? In one of his ecstatic 1922 letters to dancer Niddy Impekoven, Fred Hildenbrandt stated flatly what the vast majority of dance photo imagery merely implied: a dance is beautiful because the dancer is beautiful (*Briefe*, 29).

After the acrimonious events of 1926, when Mensendieck denounced the misuse by the Germans, particularly Hagemann, of her name and system, Hagemann produced another book, *Über Körper und Seele der Frau* (1927), in which she clarified differences between the "old" and "new" "Mensendieck gymnastics." Though still quite respectful of her teacher, Hagemann was in no sense repentant. She declared that the needs of the postwar woman required that the "analytic, dissective approach of Bess Mensendieck dissolve into a synthetic, constructive working method" emphasizing the "totality of the body in relation to space" rather than the isolated perfection of individual body parts and muscles (47–48). Hagemann devised her own system of whole-body swinging exercises and introduced many dancelike movements, although she remained opposed to the use of music ("external stimuli") to motivate bodily movement. A peculiar feature of Hagemann gymnastics was the performance of movements on tiptoe to intensify contraction-and-release rhythms. Moreover, she insisted

that some nude exercises be performed outdoors in an idyllic natural setting, a requirement she felt further transformed Mensendieck gymnastics
from a "luxury for privileged girls" into a liberation for "the woman wearied
by the exertions of daily labor" (46).

Many of the photos in the book, taken by Olga Linckelmann and Gerhard Riebicke, showed a lone nude woman performing one of the numerous swing or spiral movements, but other photos showed nude women performing dancelike exercises in duos, trios, quartets, and one quintet,
producing a distinctly homoerotic image of unity that was completely lacking in Mensendieck's iconography. Hagemann also suggested that mothers
should be willing to appear naked before their children, for if they did not
they perpetuated the oppressive sense of shame associated with the body
and exacerbated by the glorification of errorless bodies in movies and mass
media photographs (35–37). However, for the indoor photos of her own
book, Hagemann set nude bodies against an uncontextualized black background, as if to emphasize the whiteness of the body (whereas Surén, using
white backgrounds, had emphasized its bronzeness). But whether indoors
or outdoors, the nude body in Hagemann's imagery appeared as a much
more abstract form than in Mensendieck's task-oriented scenography. A
more abstract image clearly was the object of Hagemann's program, as evi-
denced by the inclusion of schematic diagrams that provided highly
abstract and exhilaratingly dynamic views of the whole-body swing movements guiding the exercise system (Figures 10 and 11). With the diagrams,
rather than the photographs, one sees more clearly how modern movement
toward abstraction is movement toward ecstatic freedom.

DORA MENZLER

Nude dance in *Weibliche Körperbildung* emerged more as a figment of romantic fantasy than as a serious mode of performance that modern society could
accommodate. The intensifying eroticism resulting from the nude performance of dance or dancelike movements could well jeopardize the innocence feminists wished to ascribe to their *Nacktkultur*. A more sobering view
came from Dora Menzler, whose Mensendieck-influenced school in Leipzig
went into operation about 1908. *Die Schönheit deines Körpers* (1924) linked
her teaching to feminist efforts to construct a "new ideal of woman." Menzler thought too much nakedness could dissipate the physical vitality that
feminist body culture sought to cultivate: "Nakedness must not lead to apa-
thy" (41). Therefore, it was not necessary for women to perform all gymnastic activities in the nude. Though she did not specify what activities
require nudity, the implication, derived largely from the photodocumentation, was that nudity was appropriate only in solo or group stretching exercises. By contrast, Surén, Koch, and Giese linked nudity to performance in

sports (such as archery, javelin, rowing, wrestling, and weightlifting) as well as dancing.

Menzler, however, asserted emphatically that "dances and dancelike movements which result in heightened emotion should in no case be performed naked." But who felt this ominous "heightened emotion"?—the performer? the (female?) spectator? or both? And what sort of dancelike movements actually heightened emotion? Was the power of these mysterious movements independent of the music that normally accompanied them? Virtually all *Nacktkultur* theorists implicitly assumed that dancelike movements projected a potent erotic significance independent of the narrative or musical contexts that motivated them. Yet the identity of these movements remained obscure, veiled in a rhetoric of ambivalence toward the unnamed consequences of nude dance. On the one hand, the theorists claimed that body culture reached its highest manifestations through dance and through nudity; on the other hand, they discreetly worried that any convergence of dance and nudity would lower the authority of either to construct a modern, liberated identity for humanity. A few representatives of feminist *Nacktkultur* resolved the paradox by blurring distinctions between dance and gymnastics, and even the photodocumentation in Menzler's book did not make clear the difference between gymnastic and dancelike movements. Although the bodies she depicted performed in untheatricalized, outdoor spaces, the actions were aesthetic in that they focused attention entirely on the bodies performing them, not on the movements themselves (Hagemann's abstractionism) nor on intragroup dynamics (Hagemann's homoeroticism). However, Menzler did include separate photos of men performing the same exercises as the women, suggesting that gymnastics was a way to resolve differences between men and women associated with feminism. With this strategy, nudity, dance, and gymnastics were subordinated to a peculiar image of a healthy, beautiful body that was desirable without being "seductive," without being a calculated assertion of desire, without being an invitation, a promise, a challenge, or a dare. It was a strategy that completely deflected the burden of desire away from the performer and onto the spectator. More precisely, it intimated, in spite of a ceaseless ambition to document it visually, that *Nacktkultur* innocence needed no spectator, that those who engaged in it were oblivious to the presence of a critical other.

But Menzler understood that artistic dance is always the embodiment of a powerful desire, a great "must." Giese and Hagemann called this desire erotic, but Menzler preferred to designate it as a "complete surrender" to one's own "bodily form" (42). For her, dance marked the division not only between male and female body culture but also between "healthy" and "dangerous" nudity, for dance, not nudity, was the controlling sign of desire in modern culture. All body culture, she proposed, strove toward the highest phase (dance, not nudity) because (female) desire was much more complex (vulnerable to misunderstanding) than any condition of nakedness could signify. Thus, "nudity is only a means to an end," and that end was a state of liberation embodied above all by "artistic" dance: "We use nudity for the sake of body culture, but do not pursue body culture for the sake of nudity" (41). But this attitude did compromise the perception of modern identity as a condition of nakedness, unveiling, complete disclosure, fearless objectivity. When nakedness failed to become an end in itself, then all movement served an end that was "mysterious" because it was "hidden" from others. Such a compromise, however, implied a submission to the premodern notion of femininity as a "veiled" construction of identity.

ALICE BLOCH

Alice Bloch was much more technical yet more muscular in her approach to feminist *Nacktkultur* than either Hagemann or Menzler. Before the war she had studied with Mensendieck and, in Berlin, with Hedwig Kallmeyer, but her method also borrowed from Nils Bukh's "Swedish gymnastics" theories, which were highly popular in Germany before and after the war. Like Mensendieck, Bloch was a physician, specializing in orthopedics. After the war she founded the Alice Bloch Institute for Gymnastics, and in 1926 she published *Harmonische Schulung des Frauenkörpers*. Like Mensendieck, Bloch favored a medical-analytical approach to physical education, in which different exercises strengthened individual parts of the body. One chapter described in great detail the effects of gymnastic exercise on specific organs, physiological functions, and inner structures of the body. The descriptions of the more than one hundred exercises were likewise detailed in terms of performance and physiological effect. Bloch did not describe the emotional, pleasurable, or aesthetic experiences of the performer, nor did she discuss the impact of her method upon the image of the female body, but these matters were nevertheless relevant to a reading of her book. Whereas Hagemann made the whole-body swing the controlling principle of her method, Bloch grounded her program in a push-pull-thrust-twist principle of bodily strengthening. And whereas Mensendieck's "principle of reserved strength" required that each exercise strengthen a single part of the body, Bloch devised unusually complex exercises that strengthened different parts simultaneously. Her series of crawling exercises, for example, strengthened the back, the shoulders, the neck, the thighs, and the chest; the performer must not bend her back, must sometimes advance herself on her elbows instead of her hands, must sometimes advance herself with her hands perpendicular to her chest instead of in front of her, and must sometimes keep her head up and forward no matter how deep she bows on her elbows.

Complex as they were, none of Bloch's exercises was difficult to perform. She displayed a fertile imagination for bending exercises, and, unlike Mensendieck, Hagemann, Menzler, Surén, or Koch, she cultivated a large image of relations between bodily movement and space, constructing clever running, leaping, jumping, marching, climbing, throwing, and skipping exercises. Bloch also employed gymnastic wall bars, which were quite effective in revealing the muscled look of her students. Even more significant, some of her exercises worked only when performed in pairs or trios, supporting the idea that the strengthening of a body depends upon another body. But it is difficult to look at the numerous photographs (all taken by Willy Balluff), some of which show as many as six nude girls closely intertwined, without supposing that such gymnastics awakened in the performers an erotic affinity for each other, or at least an erotic excitement derived from not being afraid of this implication. Most of the nudity occurred outdoors, in a woodsy, parklike milieu; the interior poses took place in relation to the wall bars or before an uncontextualized white background. Despite her reluctance to explicate the emotional-aesthetic impact of her method, Bloch definitely pursued a dancelike vision of feminine movement. Though not as abstract or perhaps even as ecstatic as Hagemann's, her vision nevertheless manifested a greater diversity and strength of elasticity in the female body than that of any other theorist of *Nacktkultur.*

Erotic *Nacktkultur*

Menzler warned that "good-looking women posing on the beach, water fairies bending over reeds, fruit-grasping daughters of Eve, as one sees in so-called beauty-pictures, have nothing to do with healthy and serious body culture" (*Schönheit,* 41). In this statement she was criticizing not so much a false or romantic attitude toward the body as the idea of nudity as an end in itself. The belief that nudity did not depend on any disciplined activity (sports, dance, gymnastics) for its justification characterized yet another sector of *Nacktkultur* and perhaps represented the most open acknowledgment within the movement that *Nacktkultur* was an exploration of eroticism. Major propagandists for this sector included Hamburg photographer Lotte Herrlich and the clusters of writers and photographers associated with two publishing firms: Schönheit in Dresden and Parthenon in Leipzig.

LOTTE HERRLICH

Lotte Herrlich (1883–1956) seems to have inherited the prewar perception of *Nacktkultur* associated with the north German artist colony of Worpswede and with the neoromantic paintings of communal nudity in nature produced by Worpswede artist Heinrich Vogeler (1872–1942), who subscribed to an unorthodox, mystical vision of communism.[1] Though photography was Herrlich's medium, her pictorialist imagery retained perceptions of nude bodies that Vogeler achieved through painting. Photography, how-

1. For the most comprehensive examination of the romantic-utopian art produced by the Worpswede cult, to which Herrlich seems indebted, see Bernd Stenzig, *Worpswede Moskau* (1989), and Bernd Küster, *Das Barkenhof Buch* (1990) and *Kunstwerkstatt Worpswede* (1989). However, the Worpswede artists showed little interest in photography as a medium for expressing their idyllic visions.

ever, verified what painting only imagined. Herrlich's interest in nude photography emerged after the birth of her son, Rolf, and all of her publications of the 1920s, beginning with the three-volume *Edle Nacktheit* (1920–1921) and continuing with *Neue Aktstudien* (1923), *In Licht und Sonne* (1924), *Seliges Nacktsein* (2 vols., 1927), *Der Kinderakt und Anderes* (1928), and *Das Weib* (1928), presented nudism as a familial activity—she constructed images of nudity permeated by an aesthetic of domesticity. She detached the image of nudity from images of labor, exercise, physical dexterity, athletics, or tests of strength. The nude body did not need sports, gymnastics, or dance to justify its manifestation. Very simple actions performed by nude bodies fascinated her: walking through woods, bending over streams, reading a book, leaning against a doorway, kneeling before a sandpile. She suffused the image of nudity with a gentleness and tranquility that was in tension with the vitality, power, and sublimated erotic excitement that other *Nacktkultur* propagandists ascribed to the naked body. For Herrlich, nudity was a restful, pleasurable, and—especially in relation to children and youths—playful phenomenon (Figure 12). Moreover, although nature was the scene for most of her pictures, she did include images of nude bodies (mostly women) reposing (rather than posing) comfortably in conventional bourgeois interiors.

Recent commentary tends to see in Herrlich's work a "naive," antimodern impulse because her images lack anticipated signs of modernism (Schmidt-Linsenhoff 49–51; Köhler 342–349). Yet the apparent passivity idealized in her imagery does exert an enduring command over perception. The gentle strategy Herrlich employed did not divide perception between body and movement or establish the value of each through the other—it focused perception entirely on nudity as the source of aesthetic experience. The dominant activity performed by the nude body in Herrlich's imagery was letting others see it as nakedly as possible, something we do not really see when other activities performed by the body (sex, athletics, exercises, dance) command our attention simultaneously. This attitude toward nudity was actually much more modern than we might suppose if we do not see in the image the obvious signs of modernism we expect with the disclosure of activities we consider modern. In her interior shots, Herrlich avoided altogether the secretive atmosphere of the studio, the pose, and the cosmetic artifice, with the result that the naked body appeared as an extension of nature into the timeless bourgeois home. The effect was rather startling: Herrich's photography implied that modern identity did not depend on surrounding oneself with modern objects or locating oneself within a modern scene; it depended on being comfortable (at rest) with one's nakedness before the modern spectator (the camera) and in even the most archaic and traditional settings (nature, the prewar bourgeois interior).

One of Herrlich's most interesting productions was *Rolf: Ein Lied vom Werden in 30 Natur-Aufnahmen* (1924). In this book, Herrlich selected thirty nude photographs she had taken of her son, Rolf, to document his evolution from boyhood to manhood. The preface, by Magnus Weidemann, claimed that "we nordic souls of light . . . are not just 'becoming,' but are 'Becoming' itself" (16). The idea that identity is more an expression of "becoming" (*Werden*) than of being, he asserted, is a Nordic trait (15), and children "become more" not through the acquisition of wealth or social rank but through a "fine and noble humanity" achieved by naked living (17). Herrlich chronicled the "naked becoming" of her son, beginning with photos of Rolf as a small boy playing naked in idyllic natural settings or assuming exaggerated boyish poses in a studio. Plates 10 and 11 showed Rolf and another nude boy playing pipes and flutes. Subsequent images depicted Rolf as an adolescent and young man posing alone with a sword, a skull, a bow, a violin, a wreath, a staff, a shotput, and sometimes without props at all, in pensive or heroic poses. Plates 17 to 20 presented the adolescent Rolf with a nude woman in images that showed him writing, aiming a bow, dancing with her, and playing pipes with her. In the final image of the book, the nude Rolf advanced toward the camera in a heroic pose, with uplifted face. An aura of primeval, Teutonic mystery pervaded this female iconography of male beauty, yet the book was unmistakably modern, not only in its ambiguity and irony but also in its documentation of a woman's seeking to know the limits of her power to look at her own child.

In the 1930s Herrlich focused on photos of nude children for calendars, some of which reappeared on calendars of the 1950s. Her son became a gifted photographer himself in the late 1920s, and many of his images appeared in nudist journals published by Parthenon. But unlike his mother, Rolf displayed little enthusiasm for nude bodies in woods, meadows, and beaches. He liked the studio, creating complex, dramatic scenes with eerie and glamorous chiaroscura lighting designs. His nude models were always female. Photography was for him an art of capturing, dramatically, an abstract or emotional state. Many of his images bore allegorical titles: "Joy," "Devotion," "Melancholy," "Sleep," "Pain," "Dance," "Fear," "Vice," "Vision," "Shadow Love," "Pride" (*Asa*, No. 2, 1931; *Das Paradies des Körpers*, 1929); *Sonnige Welt: Asa Sammelband No.4*, 1928). In "Ecstasy" (1931), he presented a blurred image of a nude woman on her knees arching backwards with her eyes closed. He used a very similar pose to represent "Despair" in 1928, yet the two images were not the same. The difference between ecstasy and despair lay not in the pose or body of the model but in the blurring of the image of "Ecstasy" by technical-chemical processes. In other words, the allegorized emotion lay in the act of seeing rather than in the thing seen. Other images were more blatantly theatrical or illustrative: "In the Harem," "The Cigarette," "Venetian Woman," "Dancing Bird," "Living Bronze," "Resting

Venus," and the stunning "Kimono" (Ibid.; *Asa*, No. 3, 1931). "Lucretia" (1931) plunged a dagger into her breast; in "Footlight" (1931), the model, kneeling, aimed a bow and arrow before an ominous, luxurious curtain. In "The Saint' (1931), she wore a black nun's gown but exposed her breasts. Apparently, then, for Rolf Herrlich the nude body provoked a wider and more contrasting range of emotions than for his mother, and the revelation of these emotions depended on images that did not neutralize the body within illusions of nature or naturalness.

Magnus Weidemann (1880–1967), the author of the preface to *Rolf,* developed an aesthetic similar to Lotte Herrlich's. Weidemann, a former pastor in a suburb of Hamburg, abandoned his religious vocation in 1919 for *Nacktkultur,* art, and participation in the youth movement. He worked with Herrlich, Hagemann, and Menzler; some of his images, appearing in *Kunstgabe 4* (1921), *Wege zur Freude* (1926), and *Deutsches Baden* (1927), therefore stressed the vitality of the naked body to a greater extent than Lotte Herrlich's, although none of his images ever achieved the almost hypnotic serenity of hers. In 1925 he published probably his most interesting work, *Körper und Tanz,* which contained photographs of nude dancers. With these images he sought to free nude dancing from a "bourgeois atmosphere" of perfume, cigarettes, wine, money, and intoxication (11). The true nude dance, however, was "not a matter for just anyone. Anyone can learn social dances. But the rhythmic personal dance must come from an inner drive and therefore only from those who experience life. That is frequent in children. With them, the desire for life pulses in leaping and spinning, bending and stretching, and play becomes rhythm, then dance" (25). Many of Weidemann's images depicted solo female dancers, whose hair was always braided in a traditional *volkisch* style; he also presented pairs of nude female dancers in images with allegorical or impressionistic titles such as "Surrender" or "Seabreeze." He included no pictures of nude male dancers because man is "active in contrast to the passive-intuitive character of women. His entire bodily education points and strives toward 'das Werk'; the object is more with him than the subject" (25). Although this attitude could explain why it was so difficult to find nude male dancers in the Weimar *Nacktkultur* iconography, it left unexplained why dance was less of an expression of *das Werk* than popular imagery of nude men hurling javelins or playing tug-of-war.

NUDISM, DANCE, AND EROTICISM

Lotte Herrlich's work occupied an ambiguous zone between an activist strand of *Nacktkultur,* which strove to free the body from unhealthy constraints imposed upon it by industrialized civilization, and a contemplative strand, which saw the nude body as the manifestation of a cosmopolitan, aesthetically advanced civilization. The contemplative strand valued nudity as an end in itself, but nudity was an end in itself only to the extent that the desire to be nude consciously modeled the desire to see nudity. This strand, defined by the conscious exchange of desire through nudity, bestowed a more overt erotic aura on *Nacktkultur* than did the activist strands. Erotic signification is always theatrical, a matter of scenes, enactments, pretenses, masks, dramatic pressures on perception. Though the contemplative strand found pleasure in the performance of the nude body in nature, it did not shun the bodily beauty created by the urban studio, the carefully staged pose, the narrativized "mood," the decorative detail, or the cosmetic supplement. But, of course, a consequence of this eclectic attitude was that it conveyed the impression that nudity in "nature" was just as much a pose or theatrical gesture as everything contrived in the secret, exclusive realm of an artist's studio in the big city. The contemplative strand aligned itself more with theatre, film, dance, and art photography than with sports, gymnastics, or communal hygiene. Nude dancing, however, made it difficult to maintain a neat division between activist and contemplative strands of *Nacktkultur*.

In *Der nackte Tanz* (1927), Werner Suhr declared that "dance in itself is erotic. Dancing is eroticism. And not just since the illusion-destroying claims of Sigmund Freud" (11). He contended that nude dancing "works most strongly in open nature" (30) and that in its strongest form nude dancing signified an intense critique of the modern mechanization of human identity: "The machine has certainly made hundreds into heroes, but millions into neurasthenics. The machine means nothing to artistic dance" (31). Yet Suhr did not believe that modern nude dancing benefited much from absorbing nude dance rituals of "primitive" peoples (*Naturvölker*), especially African or African-American dance: "The Negro plays the role of the oppressed excellently, but in reality it is merely a question of [displaying] physical potency" (37). An unknown writer for the Darmstadt nudist journal *Orplid* (4/5, 1925) acknowledged that "erotic nude dances" among some *Naturvölker* led to violent ecstasies and "wild orgies," compared to which all forms of modern and social dancing seemed tame; but the author also observed that constant nudity and even nude dancing among "many" other *Naturvölker* did not lead to uninhibited eroticism nor to an absence of moral controls (63). He therefore concluded that responses to the naked body, including nude dancing, were not innate but rather conditioned by attitudes toward the body, a "feeling of shame" (*Schamgefühl*) introduced by religious doctrines to preserve the authority of marriage as an economic, rather than aesthetic-erotic, institution: "The weaker the feeling of shame, the more marriage becomes the expression of free love, not the pressure of economic considerations and cares" (61). "A person does not acquire the feeling of shame from God or nature" (63). Another anonymous writer in the same issue of *Orplid* decided that "true *Nacktkultur* is not only a healthy pursuit but an intensifying necessity born of a deeply religious feeling. . . . The faith in light is pure German religion" ("Lichtglaube," 54). This author proposed that movements of the nude body in nature signified the recovery of a primeval, pre-Christian, and supremely redemptive mode of Nordic "sun worship," the opposite of the death-darkened anxiety about the body inherent in Christian ideology.

But Christian sentiment and nude dancing were not entirely antithetical during these years. In 1925 Suhr commented uncertainly on Charlotte Bara's nude performance at a concert (not at a school or camp) of her *Hymnis* ("Der entfesselte Tanz," 243). By no means a pagan, Bara suffused this dance, like many others in her repertoire, with a romantic, Gothic-Christian piety—without, however, depriving her image of erotic glamor. In the Hamburg *Nacktkultur* journal *Die Freude* (5/6, 1928), Suhr stressed again the necessity of performing nude dances in the open air, where they would emerge "organically" from a specific environment (256). He insisted that the open-air dancer resist the use of any makeup or theatrical devices, and he denied the relevance to open-air performance of dancers such as Anita Berber, Grit Hegesa, and Jenny Hasselquist, whose styles of movement were too worldly and nocturnal to survive exposure to the sunlight. These dancers were "exotic hot-house flowers," "artistic products, whose art only seldom ignites interest outside of themselves and never glows in real sunlight" (257). The open-air dancer, he observed, is anonymous, has no need to affix names to the naked body. Heavy intellectuality, such as pervaded the work of Mary Wigman, was also alien to Suhr's concept of nude dancing: "[O]ne follows only 'the call' that comes out of the heart of nature and the human body." He felt only Edith von Schrenck possessed the "double nature" to dance in the open air and on the stage, because her eyes and style of movement revealed a strange connection to the earth and to a subterranean feel for theatre.

But in an earlier issue of *Die Freude* (5/4, 1928), Lotte Neelsen, who in 1924 had published a small book containing twelve photographs of a nude female dancer in an austere studio, complained that open-air nude dancing was a kind of artless folk dance that associated freedom with only one emotion: joy. Artistic dance, however, was not always the creation or expression of joy; art dominated space to produce concentration in a critical spectator ("Tanzkunst," 184). The real problem with nude dancing, she contended, was that dance lacked its own unique architecture. "It is not in the open air, with its incessant weavings and rushes, but in silent halls and ceremonial temples that the elements of the neo-classical dance will unfold as a great, sacred flame" (185). Her vision of nude dance was much more Hellenic than Nordic and more severe than exuberant. In a 1924 article for the Essen *Jugendkultur* journal *Hellweg*, Neelsen asserted that dance was most naked

(and "cold") when stripped of music. She had tried dances in which she
moved to the accompaniment of her own speech instead of music, but these
experiments failed; she therefore sought a way in which dance, through
nudity, could become musical without depending on music ("Wohin," 399).
But once nude dancing became more than or other than an expression of
primordial joy, the motive for it, even when it manifested artistic ambition,
remained shadowy. An unsigned editorial in *Licht Luft Leben* (23/6, 1925),
a Dresden *Nacktkultur* journal, announced that nude dancing "must be a
service to God, as in India and other ethnic cultures." Moreover, "the nude
dancer must be above all an artist," for "as long as the danger exists that she
can be confused with the demimondaine," the (female) nude dancer must
continue to hide behind some final veil. This danger existed because "it
comes naturally to the nude dancer," who is "an international type" from
Rumania or Sweden as much as from France or Germany, that she charms a
man with her presence and beauty. "But what use is a beautiful body if its
owner is unable to show beautiful movement?" ("Die Nackttänzerin," 88).
In other words, one could take nude dancing seriously only when it offered
a mode of performance (movement) that was too complex and educated to
serve as a nightclub "enticement of the mass audience."

Willi Warstat somewhat echoed this attitude in his excellent treatise on
nude photography, *Der schöne Akt* (1929). He wrote that "educated" dancers
of both sexes were "very valuable models" as long as they understood that
they appeared before a camera, not on stage, and therefore avoided always
putting forth their "best" poses, avoided putting powder or cosmetics on
their bodies (43–44). To avoid "kitsch" effects in nude dance photography
and reveal the essence of bodily movement, Warstat recommended, dance
poses should occur in an uncontextualized "ideal space [i.e., a studio] without any motivating or situation-determined connection to a recognizable
environment," as exemplified by the nude dance images of Danzig photographer W. Kernspecht (53). Nude dancing appeared far more frequently in
photography than in theatrical performance. Claire Bauroff's wide reputation as a nude dancer seems to have derived entirely from the exquisite
nude photographs of her taken in Vienna (1925) by Trude Fleischmann
(Schreiber 117–119) (Figure 13); in theatrical performance, she was, if
anything, innovative in her use of mysterious, androgynous costumes. Perhaps her motive in making nude images of herself was not much different
from that of the famous "waltz queen" of 1910 Vienna, Grete Wiesenthal,
whose then husband, Erwin Lang (1886–1962), published a book of his
woodcuts glorifying her. Several showed her performing in the nude dances
that she never performed nude on a stage: she wanted an idealized, symbolic image of dance, not a document of her dances (Figure 14). (Indeed,
no one during the Weimar era used photography to look at dances them-

selves as innovatively as Adorée Villany had back in 1908–1911.) In any case, although Warstat disapproved of theatrical effects in nude models, his preoccupation with lighting problems, control over the camera apparatus, and manipulation of chemical processes defining the image indicated that nude photography was not far removed from theatre in being the sign of a "nature-estranged, preeminently intellectual culture, which has transplanted us into the stoney deserts of the big city and left us to perceive our bodies through fashion" (13).

A more skeptical position appeared in a 1927 comment on "Tanz und Nacktheit" in *Die Tat*, a cultural-political journal published in Jena. Adam Kuckhoff argued that pornographic images of nude dance were misleading, in spite of their pervasiveness, for the nude dances in nightclub revues were actually antierotic, schematic, mechanized *tableaux vivants*. However, he did not think nude *Ausdruckstanz* (expressive dance) would change the situation, because *Ausdruckstanz* glorified individualism through the "strongest possible physical individualization" of bodily movement itself. But "to European humanity, nudity outside of the individual erotic sphere is simply unbearable." Thus, nudity in performance did not intensify expression—it merely superimposed an expression that movement itself should already have made naked. But because *Ausdruckstanz* was too "sentimental" to accommodate adequately the relation between nudity and the "individual erotic sphere," revue dance nudity remained closer to the reality of the future (644). This view, however, could hardly have seemed modern to anyone who saw, even if only in the dance photographs, how "new" the body looked when it performed *Ausdruckstanz* movements in the nude.

Even though nude *Ausdruckstanz* was not much of a reality in a theatrical context, it was definitely alive in schools and clubs where the physical expression of "inner," individualizing drives depended on blurring distinctions between gymnastics and dance, between the active and contemplative strands of *Nacktkultur*. Some of these schools included those of Gertrud Volkenesen (Hamburg), Trude Hammer (Berlin), Ellinor Tordis (Vienna), Hertha Feist (Berlin), Helmi Nurk (Bremen), Lucy Heyer (Munich), Ida Herion (Stuttgart), Jenny Gerz (Halle), Elisabet Estas (Cologne), and the Loheland school (Fulda). But much of the evidence for nudity at these schools comes from photographs intended to document neither the dances nor the pedagogical methods associated with the schools. The nude photographs give a strong idea of the ultimate, idealized image of dance to which students should aspire, but they do little to clarify relations between nudity and movement or between nudity and circumstances of instruction. In *Der moderne Tanz* (1928), Rudolf Lämmel published several beautiful photographs of a nude dancer at the Elisabet Estas School of Movement in Cologne; these pictures made imaginative use of backlighting in an uncontextualized space to heighten the abstraction of bodily pliancy and suppleness of movement (Figure 15).

In a fascinating section of the text, Lämmel unfavorably compared the teaching methods of the Berthe Trümpy school in Berlin with those of the Estas school. Estas's background was actually in ballet, but in Vienna she became a disciple of *Ausdruckstanz*. As a member of an examining board, Lämmel described the day-to-day process of instruction at the school. He found impressive the very efficient use of classroom time, as well as the superior seriousness of the students, all female. Instructors required students to verbalize responses to the body and to movements; to physicalize ideas with their own bodies; to watch the teacher physicalize ideas with *her* body; to articulate movement choices in relation to general functions and specific expressive significance; to respond briefly to questions in writing; to explain rhythmic and musical ideas on the piano or with drums; to lead group movement studies; to critique their own movements orally and demonstrate corrections; to present improvised and prepared dances or exercises with different pieces of music, different combinations of bodies, and different aesthetic-gymnastic goals; and to display current progress in the mastery of lecture material and exercise categories of bodily movement (188–200). Like Mensendieck, Estas favored an analytical attitude toward the body, with different exercises designed to strengthen the physical and expressive power of individual body parts. Lämmel found her students much more confident, imaginative, and accomplished than those in the relaxed atmosphere of the Trümpy school, even though students in the Estas school did fewer exercises (but in greater depth) and covered far fewer themes and historical-philosophical topics. But he did not indicate where, if at all, in the Estas curriculum nudity took place. Yet even if nudity was merely a publicity image for Estas (which seems unlikely, given the all-female environment of the school and Lämmel's status as an examining male "outsider"), it was evident that one could associate nudity in dance as much with analytical rigor and refined self-consciousness as with a mystical, intuitive "call from the heart of nature."

DIE SCHÖNHEIT

Publications of the Verlag der Schönheit (Dresden), perhaps the largest of all *Nacktkultur* publishing houses, concentrated on linking nudism with a modern aestheticism, with an art of bodily display and expression. In *Revolution und Nacktkultur* (1919), Hugo Peters announced that in postwar Germany the nudist movement must move beyond the ambitions of the Wilhelmine era and pursue goals having more concrete national ramifications than did the goals guiding the pioneers of *Nacktkultur*. He conceded the difficulty of achieving the ultimate goal: a nation in which any well-behaved citizen could appear naked anywhere, without reproach, a nation where it was possible for a man and a woman to stroll nude in the zoological gardens on a Sunday afternoon. In the short run, however, some goals seemed quite feasible. These included the expansion of public space available for nudist activity, an improvement in the quality of public space for nudism, the abolition of male and female sectors for unmarried nudists, the transformation of all nudist zones on public lands into "family zones," the formation of an effective network of influential individuals for the acquisition of private lands, and the promotion of *Nacktkultur* through performance media, especially nude dancing, for "painting, sculpture, and literature alone cannot quell the hunger for a beauty that belongs only to real, living human bodies" (9–39). Peters's largest goal, however, was to unite all nudist societies into a single, powerful force with the influence of a major political party, for "in a democratic time such as the present, the individual personality . . . in its uniqueness appears less frequent than earlier," and "only people in their collectivity" could achieve goals that would bring individual lives to a higher plane (10).

On this point, however, Peters's power of prophecy failed him. The idea of a great, unified nudist movement proved as much of an illusion as the idea of a great national consensus in mainstream Weimar politics. On the contrary, during the 1920s *Nacktkultur* became increasingly diverse, fragmenting into a vast subculture capable of absorbing ever stranger and more virulent forms of individuality. Josef Seitz's *Die Nacktkulturbewegung* (1923) therefore characterized nudism as an evolutionary (rather than revolutionary) movement toward a modern aesthetic identity, and he explained how different political parties, religious ideologies, and racial groups had responded to it and myths about it since the beginning of the century. With its many illustrations, this was perhaps the most popular book published by Die Schönheit. Die Schönheit also produced such compilation picture books as *Ideale Nacktheit* (9 vols., 1920–1928), *Ideale Körper Schönheiten* (1923), and *Körper Schönheit im Lichtbild* (1924), as well as Otto Goldmann's entertaining book on law and nudity in the arts, *Nacktheit, Sitte und Gesetz* (1924). But perhaps its most significant publication was the journal *Die Schönheit,* founded in 1903 by Karl Vanselow (1876–1959), the husband of Olga Desmond. From its beginning, *Die Schönheit* presented nudism as an extension of modernism in the visual and performing arts. In prewar issues of the journal, which Vanselow edited until 1914, symbolist and *Jugendstil* paintings of nude bodies, particularly the immensely popular illustrations of mythic primeval Nordic nudity by Fidus, appeared almost as models for dramatic poses assumed by nude bodies of both sexes in photographs. The journal pioneered in the publication of photographs that depicted men and women nude together, often enacting a scene that previously was merely imaginable through painting, such as *The Judgment of Paris.*

After the war, however, *Die Schönheit*'s editors placed much more confidence in photography's ability to establish its own themes. Images from film, theatre, and especially dance filled many of the journal's pages, along with photographs devised by artists quite conscious of modernist currents in that medium. *Die Schönheit* published photographs by Lotte Herrlich and Magnus Weidemann, but it consistently perceived the power of nude modern dance to intensify the aesthetic significance of nudism and the artistic exposure of the body. An entire issue (1926) was devoted to the group movement studies of Rudolf Laban, the only major dance theorist or dance writer of the 1920s to take any serious interest in nude male dance. Other issues celebrated the solo nude dances of Claire Bauroff or of the female members of the Loheland, Menzler, or Hagemann schools; however, these images, deprived of analytical commentary, revealed very little about what movements, music, or narrative contexts were appropriate for nude dancing and much about what constituted a "beautiful" image of woman. In the late 1920s, the journal introduced complex photocollages of nude bodies interacting with images from diverse times and places, but these hardly repudiated the impulse on which the journal was founded. From its beginning, *Die Schönheit* saw dance not as the object of nudism but as a metaphor for a movement of history, a motion of consciousness caused by a desire to see the body more nakedly, from a modern perspective. The body was ultimately naked when the desire to see it, a completely aesthetic phenomenon, was also naked. By the late 1920s, this intersection between the desire to be naked and the desire to see nudity entailed, for *Die Schönheit,* a collage mode of signification that superseded the power of any single image or narratively sequenced movement to represent the historically evolved power of nudity to make us see many things "at once," besides the nude body that is the kinetic source of collage perception.

The activities of Die Schönheit expanded significantly in the 1920s. It published numerous books on marriage, sexuality, eroticism, physical education, nudism, and art, including a huge series devoted entirely to the works of Fidus; it packaged slide-show lectures on *Nacktkultur;* it marketed its own lines of stationery and art supplies; it operated a large bookstore, printing plant, and mail-order business in Dresden controlled by Richard Giesecke; it maintained branch offices in Vienna, Berlin, Munich, and Leipzig; and in 1925, partly because of the great success of the film *Wege zu Kraft und Schönheit* (and partly because this film did not give an entirely satisfactory view of modern body culture), Die Schönheit began to finance motion picture productions with the Emelka Studio in Munich. In 1925, under the direction of Dr. Friedrich Möhl and with the advice of Dr. Paul Lissmann, leader of a Munich *Nacktkultur* society, Emelka released three films—*Licht, Luft, Leben; Die Grazien—Blüten der Körperkultur und Frauenschönheit;* and *Insel der Seligen,* an adaptation of Wilhelm Heinse's 1787 novel, *Ardinghello,* about a Mediterranean beauty utopia—and then launched a series of "Körperkultur im Film" books.

However, Die Schönheit did not rely entirely on imagery to transmit the emancipatory message of *Nacktkultur*. The monthly journal *Licht Luft Leben* (1904–1932), edited by Otto Goldmann, contained few pictures and many, many words, in Gothic print, densely crammed into double-column pages. The journal featured essays on nudist theory, ethnography, anthropology, sexuality, race hygiene, birth control, bathing, gymnastics, sports, and cosmetology; reports on nudist activities throughout Germany and in other countries; reports (often satiric) of legal and moral challenges to nudism throughout the world; reviews of books, films, lectures, gymnastic demonstrations, dance concerts, and art exhibits; summaries of reports from other journals; advertisements for books, photography supplies and services, vitamins, hiking shoes, rare-edition erotica, spas, cosmetics, chocolates, art objects, dance and gymnastic schools, the Breitkopf und Härtel complete edition of Richard Wagner's works, and the nude dance photography of Germaine Krull; and heaps of personal advertisements: "Christmas Wish. Music-loving worshipper of beauty (female), 32, seeks exchange of thoughts with ideal-inclined friend of beauty (male). Write 'Beethoven,' 4189 Verlag der Schönheit." *Licht Luft Leben* still makes fascinating reading, not least because of its bibliographic data and commentary on the avalanche of German books on body culture produced in this period but also because of its highly compressed presentation of information, indicating the huge dimensions of the *Nacktkultur* movement, and its appropriative range of historical, philosophical, cultural, commercial, and aesthetic interests. The political identity of German modernism generally, not just nude dance, evolved out of the value constellation and cultural perspectives articulated by Die Schönheit and publishers similar to it rather than out of the party-driven utopianism defining more overtly political media, which tended to detach human identity from any serious focus on bodies.

PARTHENON

The ideology of Die Schönheit obviously acknowledged *Nacktkultur* as an expression of eroticism, but it presented eroticism in terms of an idealized code of beauty that filtered out "dark," highly enigmatic, or melancholy relations between desire and nudity. The Parthenon publishing house in Leipzig was perhaps the most daring and erotically conscious promoter of *Nacktkultur* until 1933. The controlling personality at Parthenon was Ernst Schertel (1884–1956), one of the really fascinating figures of Weimar cultural history. *Nacktkultur* interested the Parthenon cult insofar as nudism was an aspect of its central obsession, the exposure of erotic desire and pleasure. Schertel gathered photo images of the nude body from a wide array of sources: the nature worshippers, the dance world, the sport and gymnastic cults, sexual medicine, the Mensendieck movement, the film industry, and the theatrical milieu of the art photography studios. The complicated book series issued by the publishing house thematized the imagery in relation to various social, historical, religious, aesthetic, and, above all, psychological issues raised by nudity.[2] But, unlike other *Nacktkultur* propagandists, the Parthenon cult seemed to accept that nudity could never transcend its association with "unnatural" desires, perverse pleasures, and secret activities. Thus, a number of books in the various series purported to show relations between particular images of the nude body and distinctly "demonic" desires and "strange" drives.

Psychoanalytic theory made a deep impression on Schertel, and he more than any other *Nacktkultur* theorist accommodated nudity as an expression of perversion and deviancy. Nakedness for him was neither a natural nor an unnatural condition but a projection of fantasy with a great power to surprise regardless of its context. But this power of surprise depended on the perception that nudity was the revelation of something more than a consciously formed ideal—it was the revelation of unconscious desires that were hidden from the body that felt them. Schertel understood nudity as the exposure of a complex, primal exchange of power between seen and seeing bodies. Nudity was not will formation, as Giese proposed, but a mode of communicating deeply ingrained structures of domination that manifested themselves through comparative pleasure relations between bodies. In the journals *Skarabäus, Pelagius, Sonnige Welt,* and *Soma* and in the *Asa* albums, Schertel published, in addition to erotic drawings by artists such as Rudolf Schlichter, Christian Schad, and Helga Bode, nude photographs by, among others, Frantisek Drtikol, Rolf and Lotte Herrlich, W. Kernspecht, Trude Fleischmann, Kitty Hoffmann, Wolf Haarhaus, Madame D'Ora, Manasse, Hilde Kupfer-Meyer, Edith Barakovic, Richard Giesecke, and Marta

2. These titles included Herbert Cohen, *Nacktheit und Sexuality* (1929); *Ethik der Nacktheit* (1927); Friedrich Hartung, *Mensch und Sonne* (1929); Walther Gran, *Nacktbaden* (1928); Claus Groot, *Sollen wir nackt gehen?* (1927); Rudolf Salten, *Mehr Nacktheit!* (1928); Albert Kunkel, *Nacktzauber* (1927); Jose Bernard, *Evangelium des Leibes* (1928); Kurt Steffan, *Schönheit oder Unzucht?* (1928) and *Scham und Laster* (1928); Franz Scott, *Erotik und Kultur des romantischen Weibes* (1930); Gordon Du Four, *Das Aktbild als Kunstwerk* (1926) and *Dämon Weib* (1929); Karl Weingarten, *Spielarten des Weibes* (1928); Baron Moeller Dubarry, *Das Luxus-Weib* (1928); Max Brünning, *Der Backfisch* (1928); Ludwig Sandel, *Das gefesselte Weib* (1930); Stanislaw Prezeminewsky, *Leib, Weib und Satan* (1928); Johann Ferch, *Die Welt der Erotik* (1929); and the birth control manual *Geburtenregelung* (1929). Schertel himself wrote so many titles that it's difficult to account for all them, especially since he repackaged so much of his own writing as well as others under different titles in two-, three-, or five-volume "luxury editions" in the early 1930s. Especially interesting, aside from the gigantic treatise on sadomasochism, are *Die Eroberung des weiblichen Körpers* (1926), *Tanz, Erotik und Bessessenheit* (1928), *Geheimwege der Unzucht* (1932), and *Masochismus* (1932).

Vietz, whose bizarre imagery of dancers has only recently been rediscovered. The stress on the revelation of unconscious (fantasy) significations meant that nudity blurred distinctions between fictive, or imaginary, signs and verifiable signs; thus, the journal *Asa* published novels as well as "scientific" works, and Parthenon as a whole appropriated imagery of nudity from an enormous range of sources, including artworks that depicted bodies in ways that photography could not or dared not.

The success of Parthenon was such that the firm pursued a project far larger in scale than anything attempted by its numerous book series or by any of the encyclopedic luxury editions of eroticism introduced by other Weimar-era publishers: Schertel's gigantic, four-volume *Der Flagellantismus als literarishes Motiv* (1929–1932) and its equally vast supplemental volumes, *Der erotische Komplex* (1932). Ostensibly an analysis of sadomasochism in literature, these volumes actually constituted a colossal obsession with articulating the history and aesthetics of relations between pleasure and domination originating in infantile "complexes." The volumes contained a vast number of photos and paintings by male and female artists, and many of these still retain considerable power to shock (Figure 16). For Schertel, the sight of nudity penetrated deeply into the psyche and incited a dark urge to transgress a limit on pleasure imposed by some assertion of otherness. Transgression invariably entailed violence, or, more precisely, manifestations and magnitudes of pleasure that always surprised the body that experienced or witnessed them. The sadomasochistic activities performed by nude bodies did not verify any ideal; rather, they were symbolic enactments or models of a power dynamic, an inescapable cognitive reality that unconsciously controlled all difference between bodies and thus constructed identity itself. From this perspective, nude dance was always a sublimation or fetishizing of a repressed power-pleasure relation—which can achieve ever more naked and dominant forms of expression—between seen and seeing bodies. Schertel made this point somewhat more overtly in *Tanz, Erotik und Bessessenheit* (1928).

In a sense, then, Schertel's project signified a profound disillusionment with *Nacktkultur* as it was pervasively and diversely represented to the late 1920s. Only immense, relentless, and luxurious documentation of the sadomasochistic basis of pleasure and identity could penetrate the illusion that nudity was a sign in tension with repression rather than a melancholy sign of it and of a largely tragic struggle to see what the mask of nakedness hides: the "complex" of desires (to dominate, to submit) that begins the formation of power and identity. Of course, a society on the verge of embracing Nazi fantasies of utopia would hardly find such an intense, sobering view of the body helpful in recovering a long-absent sense of innocence and certainty about the nature of otherness and difference. But what other society has even produced, let alone tolerated, such a monumentally serious exploration of why the naked body can never escape provoking a highly ambivalent emotional response?

ERNST SCHERTEL

Schertel's involvement with dance was an element of an astonishingly diverse career, but he had already identified his ambitions before the war. In his 1911 doctoral dissertation on *Schellings Metaphysik der Persönlichkeit*, paraphrasing Schelling, he articulated a theoretical perspective that detached the concept of personality from rational empiricism:

> [T]he causation of the infinite (absolute) self cannot be constructed as moral-ity, wisdom (in the sense of rules to live by), and so forth, but only as absolute *power*—moral law has meaning and significance only in relation to a higher law of being . . . and the highest law of infinite being is accordingly: be (or rather, become) absolute—identical with your self (no longer separated into ideal and real). . . . Strive to be absolutely free . . . strive through free-dom to expand your freedom to its absolute, uncircumscribed power (54–56). . . . The single, punctuated self, which as such indicates no personality in a higher sense, is merely an empirical median point of a finite, empirical world-sphere (77).

For Schertel, however, it was clear that, in relation to a modern person-ality, concepts such as the absolute and the infinite are above all obsessions, exhaustive accounts of labyrinthine "erotic complexes." After receiving his doctorate from the University of Jena, he apparently traveled on archaeo-logical or ethnographic expeditions in Africa and the Near East. His first book, *Tanz und Jugendkultur* (1913), is now incredibly difficult to locate. In 1917 he published a "novel of contemporary Egypt," *Die Katakomben von Ombas;* at that time, he ran a publishing house in Munich, Wende, which also produced his *Weltwerdung* (1919), a sort of cosmic-expressionist poem; *Die Sünde des Ewigen* (1918), a horror thriller; and *Magie der Leiber* (1921), a study of occult properties ascribed by different cultures to the body. In 1922 Wende got into the movie business by producing Schertel's script for *Das Blut der Schwester,* an "occult sensations film" with a macabre story combin-ing horror, incest, science fiction, and crime-thriller imagery. Meanwhile, he pursued his interest in erotic photography and dance and published his hauntingly erudite book, *Magie: Geschichte, Theorie, Praxis* (1923). Soon dis-enchanted with the fortunes of Wende, he moved to Stuttgart, where in 1925 he formed an expressionistic dance company, Traumbühne Schertel, which gave performances, as far as I can determine, in Stuttgart, Munich, Nuremburg, Zurich, Vienna, and Hamburg until 1927, when his work for Parthenon perhaps absorbed all his energies. In Stuttgart, he was appar-ently a friend of the Ida Herion dance school.

Schertel cultivated a monumentally ecstatic vision of modernity: "The tendency of all living power is expansion, absorption, appropriation across all possible limits . . . borderlessness" (*Bedürfnis*, 84). But he linked ecstatic experience to an encounter with an occult aura of the body pervaded with erotic sensations. "Ecstasy, the transcendence of profane representations of the world," he claimed, "is the foundation of all magic, for only in ecstasy does one gain contact with one's demons, which signify the source of all magic capabilities" (*Magie: Geschichte*, 107). By magic, however, Schertel meant that "we must perceive our bodies as seismographs of a cosmic dynamic" and realize that "there is no consciousness without a body" (60–61). But sport and gymnastics were "not equivalent" to occult dancing, for these failed to develop the "deeper regions of the inner body structure" or the "demonic" dimension (93). His 1911 dissertation on Schelling's metaphysics had persuaded Schertel that the development of a powerful, unique personality depended on a presence that dissolved conventional differences between ideal and real forms as incarnated by a blurring of distinction between the physical and metaphysical in human actions. "At the moment of ecstasy, the self and its environment are transformed—the self becomes a cosmic player on a cosmic stage" ("Traumland," 2). Such a presence obviously implied a distinctive perception of the body.

Contemporary religious ideologies were no longer capable of disclosing the metaphysical significance of identity because of their devaluation of the body. "All religions are a tyranny of spiritual complexes. Complex-free people have no religion. Religion is a form of great hysteria. . . . Woman and religion flow together in unity" (*Das Weib*). From the occult perspective, "the goal is not release from the body, but transfiguration of the body and bodies—it is then that the blue flower of romanticism—the symbol of world mystery—blooms out of the wild garden of bodies" (*Irrgarten*), for only "when the realm of the body achieves a new spirituality [Beseelung] and the realm of the soul a new carnality [Körperhaftigkeit] is the ground prepared for a new religion on its old basis" (*Nacktkultur*). For Schertel, dance was the optimum medium for the occult expression of bodily presence, but by dance he meant an "Ur-Kunst," or primordial, art that induced and was the result of a deep erotic trance. "All ur-dances are trance dances" ("Tanz Erotik Okkultismus," 7), and such dances occurred to the extent that the body moved according to completely unconscious energies: "What we call the self or personality or the soul is nothing but the conscious disclosure of transactions and displacements of tensions enacted inside our bodies. It is only a limited set—a so-called complex—of these transactions which reach our consciousness in conditions of waking life or achieve perceptible materialization in movement. But the great majority of these transactions abide in the so-called unconscious or subconscious and become manifest only through conditions of somnambulism or ecstasy" (4). The most powerful forms of ecstatic trance, he proposed, result from the expression of repressed erotic love. Sexual attraction arose from illusions, fantasies, and "what we call love is only a special form of trance or rapture" (8); moreover, "every love is a sucking out of blood, a nurturing from the flesh of the beloved: every love is the devouring of a person" (*Sünde*, 87).

Art was the supreme manifestation of fantasy or unconscious energy and therefore the most complex form of trance, with dance being the primordial art. A superior unity of dance, eroticism, and occultism produced a grander, unified projection of "art, love, and religion, the highest values humanity can represent" ("Tanz Erotik Okkultismus," 8). "We live in an era which has rediscovered the body," Schertel asserted; in his case, rediscovery was practically synonymous with the initiation of a new religion of the body nakedly and unashamedly suffused with eroticism. That his Dionysian aesthetic creed might become confused with pornographic hedonism did not trouble him much, "for art is from the beginning amoral and even antimoral, since it represents the breakthrough of the cultured self ["Kultur-Ich"] over the civilized self. At its root, all art is pornography and serves the glorification of 'indecency' and the stimulation of 'desire'. . . . The pornographic moment signifies the origin and axis of all cultural values" ("Pornographie," 69, 71). More specifically:

> [O]ur culture is a labor-culture, not a luxury-culture, in spite of all the not insignificant luxuries acquired through labor and produced by it. Our excitation-center has been displaced and we no longer experience a cultic-fantasy but a technical-constructive imagination. . . . Our culture is technical-innovative; old cultures were cultic-imaginative. Even the rococo belongs to the cultic, to the aesthetic-theatrical in the form of an open lasciviousness. It is a luxuriously narcotized culture. . . . The rococo is, like all orgiastic cultures, aristocratically oriented. This results from the nature of orgasm, for the orgiastic person always needs a given material basis to make orgasm live and to create an object out of his rapture (*340 mal*, 34, 39).

But the objectification of these ideas into a specific dance practice remained shadowy, to put it mildly. In 1904 a woman named Madaleine enchanted audiences in Munich by performing dances under hypnosis while Hans Pfitzner accompanied her on the piano. Although she had no dance training at all, she moved as if "a magical command had released her body from earthly laws and gravitational powers" and created an apparition "without will" yet strangely compelling (WS, 104–109; Schrenck-Nötzing; Brandstetter). At that time, Schertel resided in Munich, so it is possible that he saw Madaleine perform and derived some inspiration from her. But his idea of trance dancing was hardly so genteel. He apparently had no systematic dance training, yet by 1919 he had begun to initiate an eleven-year-old

Finnish girl, Inge Frank, into his method of dance instruction (*Soma* 5, 1926, 132). It is not clear at all, however, what this method was. In 1926 he remarked vaguely that "in the modern dance, the body speaks its most puzzling and darkest language" and "is an offering of the body under the radiance of a magic sun which orbits beyond daily consciousness and arises out of the dark sea of bodily depths" ("Der neue Tanz," 22). Later the same year, he observed that the dance technique that releases the "irrational depths of the unconscious" is "not identical with traditional gymnastics, which in spite of its commendable value still over- stresses the development of particular muscle groups" ("Tanz und neue Bildung," 106). A few months later, he repeated his claim that dance, "the most primordial and mysterious of all arts," brings dark vibrations of the unconscious into an "ecstatic light" ("Tanz und Ueberschwang," 272). Then, in 1927, he explained that trance dancing involved a total aesthetic environment, mysterious deployments of light and color, a "twilight or darkness through music and exciting noise, through fantastic costume, through the introduction of narcotics" ("Tanz Erotik Okkultismus," 8).

Schertel's failure to articulate with any precision the actual movements, structure, or pedagogy for his dance aesthetic was hardly unusual for the dance discourse of his era. He nevertheless was unique in supposing that the otherwise ineffable mysteries of ecstatic dancing revealed themselves through photography. Between 1919 and 1925, he made many photographs of Inge Frank and other dancers, only a few of which he dared to publish in the quasipornographic journals he edited for Parthenon. Schertel did not believe one could induce the trance state through a revival of archaic, incantory, sarcedotal rituals; rather, he supposed that the elaborate process of photographing dances produced the conditions of trance, which were more difficult to obtain on a stage. Away from the conventions of live-audience approbation but before the critical scrutiny of the camera, dancers were free of the inhibitions operating in the theatre or even in nature. All of his dance photography took place in a studio, where he presided as a kind of Svengali, inspiring his performers to explore the orgiastic dimensions to bodily movement. For Schertel, who otherwise did not employ any techniques of hypnosis, bringing dance into an ecstatic light entailed photographing the bodily expression of desires that become visible only through the peculiar circumstances of having one's picture taken. The image of the dance itself was less significant than the intricate and somewhat clandestine process of making the image. Male and female dancers often displayed much nudity, but Schertel also delighted in the use of bizarre, ornamental costumes, veils, expressionistic decors, and chiaroscura lighting effects. Moreover, he worked with several photographers in constructing his dances and experimented with purely photographic techniques, such as superimpositions, to represent the trance.

Another technique for dissolving inhibitions was to have nude dancers move in relation to each other with their eyes closed.

The Traumbühne Schertel (1925–1927) contained eight dancers: Hermann Gross, Wanda Roder, Billy de Lares, Inge Frank, Helga Baur, Toni Erick, and two unidentified female dancers. So far, the most detailed description of a performance by this group comes from Hanns Heinz Rosmer, who reviewed a Munich performance for *Der Blitz* (7 September 1925, 4). Rosmer indicated that what he saw was neither a ballet nor a program of discrete little dances but a "ballo furioso" composed of "curious feelings, manic impulses, and excitations," which released "pulsations of the darkest and most incendiary manner." In other words, quite unusual for the time, the company performed a single, large work unified not by a story or characterizations but by an abstract emotional structure. At first, the dancers moved "as if asleep, quite naked," in glaring green spotlights. A strange, unknown music vibrated: "a music like sounds of nature, like wind rustling through the forest, like distant moaning, like sweet curls of color. And suddenly a climax, a thunder, a shaking, a voluptuously tortuous shrieking and clanking. Gongs roar and drums rattle. The bodies hurl themselves into a fantastic intoxication, crawl over each other, actually suck each other, their eyes wide open like dark holes . . . primeval wildness, stormy upheaval, and a violent red glaring on the bodies." A "powerful drumroll" abruptly produced "the deepest silence"; then a "gentle white light" began to "flow over the bodies. The music sounded like an organ and sobbed like a nightingale's song." The female dancers rose and appeared to hover over the stage, their bodies glittering with diamond droplets and silver tassels.

Although Rosmer was enthusiastic about the piece, Schertel seems not to have cared much about gaining the interest of conventional dance audiences or critics, for most performances of the Traumbühne Schertel occurred in rented theatres before invited audiences. Schertel regarded the company as a completely experimental unit, more useful in developing an audience for Parthenon publications than in building one for modern dance itself. But even if he was simply an aristocratic dilettante cultivating an expensive and perhaps prurient hobby, Schertel's dance cult was significant as an expression of a virulent, redemptive irrationality associated with both dance and modernity. It is difficult to imagine dance in any other era inspiring the magnitude of pure experimentation achieved by Schertel, who attempted large-scale abstract projects with an ensemble of eight dancers (including at least two males) and integrated dance performance into an ambitious cultural enterprise involving photographic "trance," nudism, startling musico-scenographic effects, the dissemination of pornography, and the construction of an ecstatic, paganistic religion of the body. And he pursued all this without a school, a clearly identifiable style of movement, or a conventionally understood audience for dance.

IDA HERION

In early Parthenon publications, Schertel made friendly reference to the dance school of Ida Herion in Stuttgart, which had been operating since 1912, but his relation to this institution remains very obscure. Indeed, knowledge of Ida Herion herself seems confined to two books of photographs featuring her students, Adolphi and Kettmann's *Tanzkunst und Kunsttanz* (1927) and Isenfels's *Getanzte Harmonien* (1926). Although the books presented the work of quite dissimilar photographers, both displayed some of the most elegant images of dance produced in the Weimar Republic, and the credit for this elegance was due in no small degree to the dance aesthetic itself. But despite her enthusiasm for nudity, Ida Herion cultivated a concept of dance that differed significantly from Schertel's.

Of the sixty-four photos taken by Adolphi and Ohlen, only two were taken outside, and only one depicted a group; the rest showed unidentified solo dancers before an uncontextualized white background. The order of the images appears arbitrary, without obvious narrative significance. Although total nudity occurs fairly often, the most peculiar aspect of the image series is the posing of dancers in costumes of a theatrical nature: diaphanous or veil-like skirts and dresses, satiny tunics, metallic bikinis, flamboyant pajamas, shiny or feathery headbands (Figures 17–19). Only two images show a male dancer, and he wears a strange, side-slit gown, neither a robe nor a dress but a kind of glamorous, sleeveless toga. The pictures indicate how costume shapes the identity of movement, for every movement in every image could just as well accommodate another costume on a different dancer. The costumes project a purely ornamental effect that does not readily signify a particular sociocultural context. Yet neither do the costumes signify the conventional exoticism found in the work of dancers who sought to incorporate decorative elements from other cultures, such as China (Grit Hegesa), Egypt (Sent M'ahesa), Bali (Gertrud Leistikow), Korea (Anita Berber), Persia (Yvonne Georgi), ancient Greece (Lotte Neelsen), and Arabia (Joachim von Seewitz). Nor do the costumes assume the futuristic, robotic abstractionism associated with some "machine" dances by, for example, the Bauhaus, Vera Skoronel, and Gertrud Bodenwieser. Nevertheless, the costumes are uniquely modern in their elegant sleekness and sensuality, their luxurious pliancy, their subordination to the supple contours of the body. The beauty of the bodies is considerable and completely independent of the costumes: both nudity and movement work to produce the perception that it is above all the beauty of the body that justifies the dynamic impulse toward dance.

All 120 photos in the Isenfels book situate dancers within a specific context: namely, a luxurious neoclassical villa and garden. The number of groups shots is quite large, and the number of pictures including male dancers is much greater than in *Tanzkunst*. The same sorts of costumes appear, as do the same sorts of undulant movement tropes. But now the image of dance seems cultically aristocratic, partly because of the dramatic organization of group shots; partly because of the effort to contrast radiant bodies against hard, stoney surfaces, tiled floors, or lush foliage; and partly because of the photographer's desire to observe the dancers from unusual angles or distances, thus establishing for the bodies a dynamic, expansive relation to space. Photos show dancers tight against stone walls, on stone stairways, before large stone doorways or arches, along colonnades, in vast ballroom interiors, beside pools, on stone ambuscades, in garden paths or meadows, around pillars, and on hillsides (Figures 20–22). Chiaroscura effects are largely absent, as are any concessions to the grotesque, but ambiguity of sexual identity pervades several images of male dancers, who occasionally wear the strange togas and assume only poses that are not exclusive to them. That the dancers, rather than the photographer, determined this seductive imagery of bodies in space is evident by examining Isenfels's other book, *Gymnastik als Lebensfreude* (1926), which depicted children and young women at the Zopport school in Osterstrand on the Baltic seacoast. Here the imagery of health and joy is much more generic and submissive to the beachfront authority of nature.

Both the Adolphi and Isenfels books indicate that, unlike Schertel, Herion linked nudism and ecstatic dance not to the recovery of an atavistic, primordial state of freedom but to the achievement of an aristocratic freedom or remoteness from any familiar place, be it wilderness, the bourgeois studio, or the conventional theatre stage. Ecstasy resulted from the elegantly poised beauty of the dancing body, its ability to create its own beautiful world. Hers was an intensely eroticized image of dance. The Isenfels book went through seven editions, so we may assume that this dance eroticism appealed to a much larger audience than the one Schertel reached or, indeed, than that reached by the great majority of dance books.

PROBLEMS OF *NACKTKULTUR* DANCE

This account of *Nacktkultur* is hardly comprehensive, but it does indicate the range of attitudes toward the naked body circulating in early-twentieth-century German culture. *Nacktkultur* was not a monolithic or unified ideology but a constellation of choices about the meaning a nude body could project within German society. Having a tenuous pedagogical relation to particular strands of *Nacktkultur,* modern dance easily tended to situate itself within this constellation whenever it employed nudity. In other words, the relations nude modern dance constructed between bodies derived more from the choices embodied by *Nacktkultur* than from those embodied by other modes of representing nudity, such as painting, anthropology, or even erotic behavior itself. The choices embodied by *Nacktkultur* regarding the meaning of nudity controlled the presence of nudity in modern dance in several ways: 1) aesthetic nude modern dance for a critical audience was overwhelmingly *solo* dancing, with group nude dancing confined to a private milieu of pedagogic exercises that prepared bodies to fulfill an ideal that was more than a condition of nakedness; 2) nude dancing in the private milieu, though documented abundantly and aesthetically by photography, emerged above all as a therapeutic benefit to the dancer rather than to the spectator; 3) the therapeutic value of nude dance depended on denying the serious erotic significance it rather obviously possessed, so that the motive for dancing nude was free of a more complex desire to see nude dancing; 4) in relation to the hygienic and eugenic ambitions of *Nacktkultur,* nude dancing consistently appeared as a feminine activity, as a choice for (young) women, not men; and 5) nude dancing projected an enigmatic image of the body that was different from that projected by nude gymnastics or athletics because dancing in itself blurred distinctions between "natural" and "theatricalized" ("unnatural") conditions of bodily activity.

Of course, one may find examples outside this range of controls over nude dancing, but they are so unique that they demonstrate the stability of the controls. More significant, such controls perhaps better explain why nude dancing did not occur more frequently than why it emerged at all. In any case, the result was a confused and highly compromised perception of how the relation between nudity and dance created a modern, liberated identity. The high-society arts and literary magazine *Der Querschnitt* (Berlin), for example, promoted modern culture by publishing, often without any commentary, images of nude women dancers side by side with pictures of sports, theatre, film, and society personalities, modernist paintings of nudes, stills from theatrical and film productions, photos of people from exotic or primitive cultures, scenes of modern urban life, and dancers who were not naked. Readers apparently appreciated the idea that both nudity and dance operated within a constantly recombinable montage of modern images; but, then, both nudity and dance remained subordinate to the authority of the image to define modernity.

MARY WIGMAN AND ERNST LUDWIG KIRCHNER

Ambivalence toward the image of the nude dancer assumed a curious expression in Mary Wigman, the most significant German dancer and choreographer of the 1920s. Though she apparently had some experience of the obscure nude dance experiments conducted by her mentor, Rudolf Laban, at his Ascona colony during World War I, Wigman had no illusions about the potential of nude dance to produce regressive misperceptions rather than a modern, liberated identity; from 1918, when she achieved her first major success, none of her dances included nudity. For her, nudity did not signify modernity. Governing her aesthetic was a complicated expressionistic metaphysics that implied that movement, not flesh, makes the body naked (and therefore modern)—movement reveals contradictory energies hidden within the body. To call attention to movement, Wigman was fond of veiling bodies through the use of masks, hoods, capes, gownlike costumes, and bold contrasts between light and shadow; then, by favoring entirely percussive sounds, she limited the power of music to weaken visual perception of movement. Yet she does not seem to have minded at all that between 1926 and 1932 the great expressionist artist Ernst Ludwig Kirchner (1880–1938) did a number of beautiful watercolor sketches of her students rehearsing dances nude or in transparent garments, although Wigman never rehearsed in this manner (Ketterer 100–102). As an expressionist, Kirchner painted more what he felt than what he saw, and he felt that dance made the body naked in such a way as to make his own desire naked, but it was a desire to see dance rather than the bodies of dancers. As Ketterer puts it, Kirchner's numerous dance images from this period constituted "efforts to free himself from the actual model and arrive at a more geometric abstracted" perception of the body (Kirchner 212).

Nude dancers were a subject of Kirchner's art as early as 1911, but perhaps his most ambitious statements on this subject were the numerous sketches he submitted between 1928 and 1937 for a monumental, but never implemented, mural complex in a section of the Folkwang Museum in Essen. In the early phase of the project, Kirchner envisioned a portion of the mural complex containing a large triptych of sport, dance, and bath, with many male and female figures, all nude, in panoramic, alpine, or Rhenish landscapes fermented by the eerie glow of blue, purple, white, and pink suns. He planned to integrate the triptych into a mural that presented large images of, perhaps, labor, revolution, the past, the future, the will. But around 1930 his interest focused more and more, and then exclusively, on a monumental image of dance, with male and female dancers, all nude, in powerfully abstract contexts, moving entirely through sunlight itself or, rather, through vivid spectrum bands of refracted light (Froning). These "Color Dance" sketches amplified ideas the artist had pursued in his images of the Wigman dancers: the colors of the light meshed with the colors of the dancers' bodies so that, for example, blue, purple, or orange bands of light "reflected" the blue, purple, or orange flesh of the dancers, as if their bodies were translucent, dynamic vessels of light. The bodies themselves were mere black outlines, hardly individuated by line or even movement, a point Kirchner further reinforced by depicting dancers in pairs performing identical, mirrored movements (Figure 23). In a couple of sketches, he set off the colors dramatically with large patches of black or gray wash. He never completed the project because of the museum director's failure to commit to it. It is not clear why, although the director (Gosebruch) did not treat the work of other artists for the museum with such protracted caution. Kirchner regarded dance as an expression of ecstatic nudity. By nudity, however, he meant not just the display of flesh but the display of light within the body and the display of otherwise invisible color hidden within light. The nude body was a kind of prism that refracted light, and dance was the optimum expression of this kinetic interaction of light and flesh. Color, not movement or physiognomy, was what ultimately individuated bodies and differentiated them from each other.

Wigman's enthusiasm for Kirchner's work obviously transcended a major contradiction between her own and the artist's perception of relations between movement, nudity, and light. But this contradiction was perhaps more apparent among her students than one might expect. A Dutch woman, Letty Thom, was a student at the Wigman school in Dresden between 1925 and 1930. Her extensive scrapbook-diary of this period is now in the possession of Wilfried van Poppel of Amsterdam. The diary contains extensive notes on her school work, many clippings and photos, as well as personal reflections on dance and art generally. From Wigman she learned such creeds as "Without ecstasy, no dance! Without form, no dance!" and "Out of the 'too much' comes gradually a simple, clear 'only so'" (1930). She made no mention of nude dancing in the classroom or on the stage, but she did paste in numerous photos of nude women clipped from dance, gymnastic, and art journals, and she included one uncaptioned photograph of herself nude, kneeling in a woodland grove and smiling at the camera. The student was occasionally critical of her "demonic" teacher and other dancers, but the images of nudity constituted a very subtle criticism: movement is not enough to construct or signify an ecstatic identity—nudity is necessary.

RUDOLF LABAN

Wigman's mentor, Rudolf Laban, perhaps the most significant teacher of bodily movement in this century, cultivated a more obscure attitude toward the relation between nudity and modernity. It is obscure largely because we understand his attitude through the vague documentation done by his disciples. We know that he made efforts to link nudity and eurhythmic "development" of the body at his workshops for men and women at Ascona (1913–1917) and, to an even less adequately documented degree, that these experiments coincided with experiments in erotic experience (Wolfensberger 102–117). After the war, however, Laban became preoccupied with detaching movement from the bodies that performed it. He realized that an expanded value for dance depended on theorization of human movement, not on theorization of dances or dancers. His great task, then, was to construct an elaborate vocabulary, a movement grammar (Labanotation), that enabled one to identify the signifying potential of the body, the total range of signs the human body was capable of making.

Meanwhile (1925–1930), his disciples in various German cities absorbed the new doctrines of the master without abandoning the *Lebensreform* impulse of the Ascona period. In Hamburg, Albrecht Knust conducted movement exercises with all-male groups of nude dancers, and in Berlin, Hertha Feist, a *Nacktkultur* enthusiast, was utterly unique among women dance instructors and choreographers in exploring nude movement with all-male ensembles, although she avoided such nudity in her ambitious dance concerts for the public. In Hamburg, Jenny Gertz supervised nude group, or "choir," exercises involving male and female children aged five to fourteen. Naked, the children improvised or created solo and group dances meant to imitate the movement of flowers, snowflakes, insects, birds, sunbeams, clouds, storms, grotesques, and forest rustlings; the instructor herself was nude, and sometimes nude dancing lasted all day long and into the night. These nude dances always took place outdoors because, "unfortunately," children were not permitted to perform nude in the exercise studio of the public school where Gertz taught (Gertz, "Tanz und Kind"). Gertrud Schnell, Toni Vollmeyer, and Martin Gleisner apparently also introduced nudity at the Laban schools in which they taught. Perhaps some of the Laban disciples were even more radical in their practice of nudity than was Adolf Koch, but the documentation of these adventures is insufficient to produce a serious understanding of them.

Public consumption of these nude performances remained largely confined to photographs, some of which appeared in *Die Schönheit*. In *Gymnastik und Tanz* (1926), Laban included numerous photos of nude men and women taken at various Laban schools (and at the Menzler and Hagemann schools), but he did not even mention nudity in this lengthy discussion of method in bodily education. Nevertheless, it seems that Laban and his disciples, in dramatic contrast to Wigman, considered the detachment of movement from the body dependent upon the nakedness of the body that performed the movement. This was a startling observation only because it implied that movement lost its power to signify gender when the gender of the body performing movement was exposed. For Laban, the problem of labeling dance as a feminine activity derived from the perception (or misperception), by both sexes, that female bodies veil a unique mystery that aesthetic movement reveals or expresses. However, the genderless vocabulary of Labanotation suggested that the greatest source of mystery was actually movement itself, which bodies of either sex could appropriate without compromising sexual difference. Nude performance of dance ostensibly proved this point. But a problem with Laban's system was that, although it provided a comprehensive vocabulary of movement, it did not theorize syntactic relations between movements. Therefore, it was still not clear if sexual difference controlled specific relations between movements or if aesthetic syntactification in itself was a feminine activity.

Nacktballett

Nude performance in theatres for critical, paying audiences seeking entertainment and artistic excitement was an altogether rarer phenomenon than all the nude dancing pervading the realm of *Nacktkultur*. Theatre culture treated the idea of nude performance with great caution, and most of the attempts to introduce nudity in drama came from writers, whose thinking about what was possible on the stage was generally much more radical than that of actors and directors. After all, even the *Nacktkultur* societies sometimes had difficulty with the police when they wanted to present public slide-show lectures and films about their activities (OG 73–76). In the script for Arnolt Bronnen's *Die Geburt der Jugend* (1914), a large, antiphonal chorus of nude (but unnamed) male and female youths, some riding horses, trample down the older generation in the final scene and announce, in an orgiastic, expressionist hymn, the advent of a new, ecstatic community of naked bodies in the forest. All that differentiates the bodies from each other is their location in one of several choruses dancing and recombining across a vast space: "those in the forest," "those at the edge," and so forth. But when the play finally appeared on the stage in Berlin in 1925, nudity was conspicuously absent. With *Die Exzesse* (1923), a comedy and one of the most daring and innovative European plays of the twentieth century, Bronnen wrote three scenes involving nudity. Again, however, productions of the work, involving well-known Berlin actors, failed to put any naked bodies on stage. Among its numerous perversities, Hermann Essig's *Ueberteufel* (1918) featured a bizarre nude scene, but in Leopold Jessner's 1920 Berlin production the actress was not nude. In *Die Schwester* (1916), an even wilder drama of lesbian passions, Hans Kaltneker included a startling dance scene (with film) as well as a hymnic nude scene of lesbian prisoners receiving God's blessing. Curt Corrinth's *Die Leichen-schandung* (1918) featured a dead prostitute walking nude, a Madonnalike

74

vision, among soldiers on the battlefield. But these two plays never had any performance.

All these nude scenes appeared in expressionist dramas, for by this time no one believed that realism had anything to do with nudity, and even films such as *Opium* (1919) and *Von Morgen bis Mitternacht* (1920) presented images of nude women as figments of a drug-induced dream or hallucination. As early as 1907, a Munich opera company planned to have Salome in Richard Strauss's opera perform the *Dance of the Seven Veils* completely naked, but the police intervened and forbade this choice. In 1924 the Vienna Volksoper dared to produce a pantomime, *Adam und Eva,* with nude performers, but the conductor, Felix Weingarten, refused to rehearse it and canceled the show. Nevertheless, in Hamburg in December 1922, Hugo Hillig (1877–?), a promoter of socialist hygiene policy and author of books on painting technology, staged his pageant *Sonnenweihe* for an audience of two hundred invited spectators, and several scenes contained completely unclothed men and women (OG 52). Adolf Koch staged a similar sort of pageant at the Volksbühne in Berlin in November 1929 (Merrill 187).

But, aside from these examples, nudity in the theatre was manifested through dance. From 1918 onward, impulses emanating from ballet culture moved toward an ever stronger identification of nudity with eroticism in dance. Berlin was the center for these developments, but the performance arena was largely the nightclub or music hall rather than the theatre or concert hall. Here nude dancing prospered in a strictly commercial environment in which artistic enterprises depended entirely on audiences rather than subsidies, enrollments, and memberships. As the war came to an end, James Klein (1886–ca.1940), manager of the Apollo Theatre, apparently introduced "nude ballets" within a revue format resembling the lavish glorification of the female body cultivated by the Ziegfeld Follies (Jansen 42–44). By 1921, when Klein moved his operations to the Komische Oper, these nude ballets had become main attractions and inspired vigorous competition from nude ballets elsewhere, especially those of Herman Haller (1871–1943) and Erik Charell (1895–1973). The scale of these productions escalated to the point that by 1924 Klein could offer a revue, *A Thousand Naked Women,* that offered twenty-two separate scenes, twelve songs, and as many as twenty-five women performing nude (topless, at least) in a single ballet (Jansen 45–50; Kothes 67–71).

CELLY DE RHEYDT

In 1919, with managerial help from her ex-army-officer husband, Celly de Rheydt (Cäcilie Schmidt) produced nightclub acts that featured a small ensemble of nude women ballet dancers. (She actually launched her career by making a film of nude dances, which she apparently used as a promotional device.) De Rheydt's ballets exuded an aura of seriousness, even perversity, that was quite lacking in bigger productions, and because she avoided the revue format, her dances were more strictly balletic. She does not seem to have used more than five women in a single dance, which means she did not experience the pressure to build dances out of the mechanically synchronized, chorus-line movements used in revues. But her aesthetic created legal problems, and so she performed most of her ballets in private studios and clubs. *Die Schönheit* praised her 1920 performance in a large Berlin theatre: "It is the dancing of an idealist . . . in [whom] a strong artistic will dominates." Her program included a waltz in diaphanous veils, a "wild bacchanal" in purple light with bare breasts, a czardas in Hungarian tunics but bare legs, a pantomime called *Opiumrausch* with all dancers topless, and *Die Nonne,* in which de Rheydt and her ensemble removed nun's habits and danced completely naked in a gorgeous light. This last dance was especially annoying to the police. In 1921 the Munich Bund für Kunst, Wissenschaft und Natur used Celly de Rheydt and her dances as models for a series of idealized paintings of the body. By 1922, however, with numerous cabarets and clubs presenting lurid menus of nude dances, de Rheydt accepted an offer to perform at the Black Pussy (Schwarzer Käter) Cabaret, where her *Salome Dance, Whip Dance,* and *Harem Ballet* promptly inspired obscenity charges from the city prosecutor. Though the police had little success in forbidding her enterprise, it was clear that a nude erotic performance was somehow more daring if authored by a woman rather than a man.

In 1922 Otto Goldmann saw her perform in Leipzig. He felt her dancing was not as skillful as that of the teenage girls in her ensemble, nor was she as pretty as he expected. Yet he praised her acting ability, which excelled in a piece about vampirism. For this she wore a huge, fiery wig, and her face was deathly white, "full of merciless, enigmatic expressions." Her breasts were bare, but she wore blood-red gloves and tights, her hands like claws. In a green light, the vampire sought the blood of naked girls. "The creeping and gliding toward the victims, the leap at the throat of the victims on the ground—not a disgusting performance, as the material might indicate, but a highly theatrical performance in a modern style." However, he criticized the cabaret atmosphere in which de Reydt presented her dances, "with its alcohol flow and cigarette fumes, the stage so close to the first table that it could be the next table. And when a dancer steps onto a table of alcohol-befogged guests, the thought arises that she's eliciting something definite." "Whoever lets naked girls dance in public must make a sharp distinction between the here acceptable elf-like undulation and gliding and the typical cabaret dance with stamping and leg kicks. . . . Of the first sort too little is offered, and of the last, too much." Goldmann would much prefer to see

Celly de Reydt and her girls dance in "a sun-radiant forest meadow or by full moonlight . . . as forest witches, nymphs, and sylphides," for then he would not have to endure the vulgarities and prejudices of the cabaret audiences. But by 1924 de Rheydt's dances no longer seemed daring enough for the public, and she entered a new phase with a new marriage, this time to a theatrical producer.

GIRLKULTUR

Some nude ballets, especially those in the semilegal clubs, reveled in pornographic sensations, whereas others, particularly Charell's, drifted toward an accommodation of the machinelike synchronization of moving bodies found in American-style pageants such as the Ziegfeld Follies (although the initial site of the nude ballet was prewar Paris, not New York). Figure 25 is a photograph taken in 1919 of a revue-type dance in a Berlin nightclub, well before the rise of enthusiasm for things American, which began after the inflation period and with the infusion of American investment capital. Swedish dancer Rigmor Rassmussen, whose nude image appeared in various arts magazines in the mid-1920s, was unique in migrating from modern dance to revue ballet, but the dances she performed interested the public much less than did the sleek image of dance she projected in photographs, and these eventually were successful enough to make her popular on Broadway. But the image of nude dance in a couple of modernist literary works from Berlin was perhaps more sensational than any visual art could verify. Curt Corrinth's *Potsdamer Platz* (1919), a wildly experimental novel, presented an apocalyptic nocturnal image of Berlin in which hundreds of thousands of people dancing nude and orgiastically signified a "borderless world of love." A decade later, a disillusioned Yvan Goll published *Sodom Berlin* (1929), in French, and this memoir sarcastically described the milieu of the expressionist nightclub culture in the early 1920s:

> The word "freedom" is a stronger explosive than dynamite. The formula for "Universal Brotherhood" soon became dangerously expanded. Every compulsion should be abolished, and the intellectuals preached against every repression. The logical and natural consequence of a general orgy, with the gods as well-wishing witnesses. After midnight, everyone gathered in the temple of "Universal Brotherhood." The women undressed to destroy the seed of [commodified] voluptuousness, they pretended that ultimately the veiling of the body was responsible for the mysteries of sexual aberrations and that complete nudity would lead humanity to a condition of purity and nobility such as Adam and Eve had known. . . . Better than any sermon or profound theory, the dance proved that the human body had a soul (80–81).

In *Sittengeschichte der Inflation* (1931), Hans Ostwald reinforced this retrospective detachment by referring to a "dance frenzy" that swept the nation in the early 1920s, led by young women hungry to know the limits of pleasure (134–150). In numerous illustrations by such artists as Max Beckmann, Otto Dix, Hugo Scheiber, George Grosz, Jeanne Mammen, Christian Schad, and Rudolf Schlichter, nude erotic dancing appeared as a lurid, inflammatory sign of social upheaval, with the unveiled, provocative body of woman as its vortex (Figure 24). This perception stood quite in contrast to the expressionistic, primeval-idol view of nude dancers found in the work of Emil Nolde, Ernst Ludwig Kirchner, and Otto Mueller.

METROPOLIS

Perhaps the most spectacular Berlin effort to align nude dancing in the nightclubs with violent social upheaval appeared in Fritz Lang's monumental science fiction film, *Metropolis* (1927). One scene in this film overloaded with excesses featured the robot Maria (Brigitte Helm), nearly nude, performing a modern erotic dance atop a giant globe-turntable supported by naked musclemen. This voluptuous dance, performed in a luxurious club, precipitates a frenzied pandemonium in the audience of male spectators (investors in robot manufacturing), who all end up as a surging mob, with arms upreached toward the machine-idol perched elusively above them. This frenzy infects the slave workers inhabiting the subterranean depths of the city; they destroy the machines that have mechanized their lives, not realizing that the robot Maria who incites them is herself a machine, programmed by the mad scientist Rotwang to lead the masses to extinction.[1] In the dance scene, dance not only links social upheaval to the glorification of the erotic (feminine) body but also links erotic desire to the machinelike perfection of the human body: nude dance dissolves distinctions between human and machine, and out of this dissolution emerges an explosive mass of humanity, blind to its own destruction. In the nightclubs and cabarets of Berlin, interest in erotic nude ballets implied a capacity to see life and the feminine without illusions, without the desexualized naiveté with which the eurhythmics movement and modern dance tended to define the modern body. As Felix Salten remarked in 1924, "An era that has no illusions makes a public spectacle of the unveiled female body" (LF 25). But it was hardly surprising that many modern dancers, confronted with so many fantastic images of dance, felt that even mildly erotic themes merely contributed to the vulgarized image of dance purveyed by the entertainment industry, which, from a Marxist perspective, simply reduced the body to a fetish or commodity. This vulgarization was considered symptomatic of people's fundamental alienation from a higher value to existence than that supplied by primal drives.

1. For further commentary on *Metropolis,* see Huyssen; Böhm; Combes; and Kaes.

CRITIQUE OF *GIRLKULTUR*

In *Girlkultur* (1925), Fritz Giese regarded the erotic element in dance as an ideological problem that German modern dance should transcend. The appearance after 1923 of American *Girlkultur* in Germany was for him an example of how capitalism produced decadent, vulgar attitudes toward dance and the body (Figure 25). According to Giese, the mechanized chorus-line dances of troupes such as The Tiller Girls (which was, in fact, an English enterprise operating in Germany) and the Amazonic Hoffmann Girls were grotesque efforts to emulate an absurd American obsession with measuring beauty. It was a delusion of men. To measure beauty by comparing and quantifying the bodies of women in a line in relation to a stable rhythm was to succumb to mass culture's unliberated perception of the body, the American notion of "collectivity," which treated all values quantitatively. Within the mass culture created by capitalism, dance always functioned to construct an image of the body freed from labor. The erotic interest of these mechanical dances therefore merely sustained the illusion of action that had no meaning or value as labor, work, or compulsion. For Giese, then, any modern dance must project a higher, transcendent attitude, detaching the moving body from the illusions of mass culture and from the mechanized obsession with measuring beauty cultivated by American capitalism.[2] As a labor psychologist, however, Giese displayed a vast preoccupation with measuring, as precisely as possible, almost every aspect of bodily performance that had no pleasure value. Seen in relation to his enormous "psychotechnical" works, his critique of *Girlkultur* indicates that the chorus line challenges rather than exemplifies efforts to measure pleasure. In his book *Girlkultur* he provided plenty of illustrative photos but none of the enormous array of labor-analyzing statistical devices, tables, and techniques used in *Handbuch psychotechnischer Eignungsprüfungen* (1925) and *Methoden der Wirtschaftpsychologie* (1925); he never discussed techniques for measuring pleasurable activities or aesthetic experience.

By contrast, physicist Rudolf Lämmel, in *Der moderne Tanz* (1928), contended that rhythm itself is precisely what allows us to perceive the body as a machine. Freedom, movement toward ecstasy, he suggested, is not a release from metronomic rhythm or ballet-type regulation of the body; on the contrary, freedom entails the capacity of the body to synchronize itself with mathematical laws governing the structure of music and movement (139–143). Lämmel sought to link new modes of dance to the dominance of science and technology in modern life. But what set him apart from so

---

2. An argument similar to Giese's came from Siegfried Kracauer in a 1927 essay on "The Mass Ornament." More recently the argument has appeared in Klooss and Reuter, *Körperbilder* (1980).

many other dance thinkers of the era was his assertion that the chief attribute of dance movement was eroticism. Whenever the body called attention to itself through aesthetic movement, questions of sexual identity and erotic motive were not only inescapable but fundamental: scientific understanding of the body and movement as machine (dance) compels us to perceive modern being as an unveiled mode of erotic signification. Nevertheless, Lämmel was not enthusiastic about either *Girlkultur* or ballet, and he believed that *Ausdruckstanz* was the medium for the most serious and revelatory significations of erotic feeling. Despite their contradictory attitudes toward the eroticizing of the body through dance, both Giese and Lämmel linked eroticism in dance to mechanization, measurement, and rhythmic regulation of the body.

But these attitudes contrast emphatically with those of Paul Leppin in his article on "Tanz und Erotik" for the first issue of the semi-*Nacktkultur* journal *Das Leben* (1917, 7–11). Leppin argued that eroticism manifests itself most powerfully in conjunction with the expression of intense religious feelings, for ecstasy is always a response to an immanence of the divine. Dance offered the strongest potential for signifying and experiencing ecstasy, but Judeo-Christian dogma had smothered dance in its determination to separate eroticism from great religious feeling. As a result, European dance culture could present nothing more than the feeble, "sweet and decayed" eroticism of the waltz. "That we have nothing from the lives of the great modern erotomanes indicating a preference for dance has its basis in the violent and brutal drives of the masses, who always seek to resolve their differences through a normative form, while individuality means losing oneself in the formless and the immense without even remembering one's limits. . . . The time must come which shakes us, which revitalizes the dormant evil and splendor within us, tremendous powers, doubts, which rumble in our hearts like the thunderstorms of romanticism, oaths, hate, anticipations." Leppin did not explain what sort of dance would accommodate this rhetoric, but the accompanying illustrations of Salome dancers and a female sword dancer, along with such phrases as "a glowing fanaticism of the flesh," "extravagant power which resounds in our blood," and "overflowing pleasure," implied that serious erotic dance entailed both nudity and rhythmic motions simulating orgasm and sexual intercourse. It was these movements more than any other, we are to understand, that undermined the mechanization of identity imposed on the body by Judeo-Christian dogma and its ambassador, the French-Italian ballet tradition. Leppin did not acknowledge any of the multitude of Salome dances that had already saturated European theatres by this time, so presumably all of these fell short of the cultural upheaval he ascribed to religiously grounded erotic dance. Although the accompanying pictures showed only female dancers, Leppin made admiring reference to the orgiastic dancing that followed the sermons of the sixteenth-century Anabaptist heretic John of Leiden, whose congregation glorified the nudity of the community and the repeal of clerical constraints on erotic feeling. But one could hardly say that Leppin was a prophet of *Girlkultur,* which in its balletlike regimentation of the body— all kicks, stamps, salutes, twirls, and bobs—would never permit anything so "formless" as the simulation of orgasmic movement.

By 1930 nudity in theatrical dance ceased to enjoy the strong presence it had achieved by the mid-1920s, even though *Nacktkultur* in general continued to grow in popularity. The heyday of the nude commercial ballet in Berlin was between 1923 and 1926. By 1927, however, Berlin audiences seemed to have grown weary of the lack of innovation or daring in nude performance; forces of censorship, managing at last to mount successful legislation (or appoint more aggressive prosecutors) against its targets, established a threshold of daringness in performance, which theatre producers felt little inclination to test. A problem with linking nudity to eroticism is that interest in nudity wanes if its erotic aspect does not escalate or intensify from performance to performance. Producers sought to accommodate this process of escalation by introducing larger, more elaborate production numbers. But with nude erotic performance, as Celly de Rheydt apparently understood when she quit the game in 1924, the escalation of erotic significance does not depend so much on production values as on the introduction of newer and stranger erotic actions. These, in turn, create more highly specialized audiences. The period 1925–1932 was supposedly the golden age of semiclandestine cult clubs catering to very specialized sexual tastes— homosexuals, lesbians, transvestites, bisexuals, sadomasochists, fetishists of all sorts, pedophiles, female mud wrestlers, and other gross or grotesque entertainments described, rather politely, by Curt Moreck in his underground guidebook, *Führer durch das lasterhafte Berlin* (1931). In Piel Jutzi's film *Mutter Krausens Fährt ins Glück* (1929), a young worker takes his new girlfriend to a club for a wrestling match between a runty little man and a ferocious fat lady, who throws him all over the stage; this spectacle so offends the worker that he insists his date leave with him, although she seems to find the entertainment amusing. In a 1923 issue of *Die Nachtpost* (1/24, 2), a squalid Hamburg tabloid sanctimoniously dedicated to the eradication of smut and prostitution, Hermann Abel complained loudly about a Hamburg theatre in which a master of ceremonies invited male patrons to suggest lewd poses and dances to several nude women and to masturbate while watching them for twenty minutes. Lavish revue-type productions were simply too tame to sustain the interest of audiences for such clubs. Yet the audiences were never large enough to justify high production values or investment in superior talent. Indeed, in such clubs it was more likely the patrons who danced with each other (social dancing), and serious nudity was not a significant feature of their erotic performances. As a result, cult clubs often exuded an atmosphere of sleaze, as represented, for example, in Josef von Sternberg's famous film, *The Blue Angel* (1930). However, the permissive activities of the sex clubs were not entirely a product of the purported Weimar decadence following the war nor of the inflation period, as Ostwald made clear in his five-volume anatomy of this pre-Weimar subculture, *Das Berliner Dirnentum* (1905).

In her admittedly unreliable diary, Mata Hari included an entry from about 1906 describing her visit to a bisexual club in the vicinity of Potsdamer Platz in Berlin; there she saw male and female transvestites, dancing pairs of male and female homosexuals, men and women who allowed persons of either sex to fondle and disrobe them, and a beautiful male dancer in female costume who concluded his voluptuous performance by lifting his dress to reveal his erection, a gesture Mata Hari found intensely arousing (217–221). Nor did these sorts of displays disappear entirely with the advent of the Third Reich. The Kattenberg Archive in the Harvard Theatre Collection contains the correspondence of a Chilean corporate executive, Eduardo Titus, whose great obsession was contortionist acts. On 12 December 1939, Titus wrote to a fellow contortion fan, Burns Kattenberg, of his visit to Berlin cabarets, where he saw female contortionists perform for groups of women who seemed more nude than the performers.

> I often found in Berlin a table in a cabaret with four or five women around completely naked under their gowns, smoking and drinking and giving little attention to the men. They were heavy in their applaud [sic], making a lot of noise when a woman was contorting. When I saw senorita Carmara at the Zoo cabaret, three women that were seated at a first row table got so excited when Miss Carmara got her head through the thighs in a headstand, and placed the back of her head against her cache-sexe, that one of them jumped over the platform and started to kiss and caress the body of the acrobat and had to be taken away by the waiters.

Nevertheless, few can doubt that the Weimar era, especially during the inflation period, provided unprecedented and perhaps unsurpassed opportunities for underground and perverse erotic entertainments. The Swedish poet Bertil Malmberg, who was close to the aristocratic dance circle cultivated by Beatrice Mariagraete in Munich during the war, wrote in 1953 that Germany in 1919 seemed overwhelmed by a vast "social orgasm," of which the woman-driven craving for dance was the most obvious sign and from which Munich was no more immune than Berlin. "Munich in the 1920s signified a public procession of licentiousness [in the dance cafes]. . . . Indeed, there reigned a kind of mass sexuality, which was actually narcissism, fantastic excesses, camoflouged behind a curtain of ambiguities and obscurities . . . a taste for infantile polymorphous perversity." Adolf Hallman, another Swede in Malmberg's circle, described "the other Munich" of the dance halls attended by a "degenerate public," where "on the dance floor sleek youths in pageboy haircuts and undershirts and girls with boyish heads, clad in smoking jackets, danced with each other in a convulsive mass, then suddenly stood still . . . their eyes blank with cocaine, their nostrils trembling . . . and everything [occurring] in a lurid decor of German expressionism, choked with cubism." Malmberg believed that the "pornographic scenes" available in Bavarian dance clubs disclosed a new form of "revolution" dominated by "strong narcissistic-erotic impulses" (Bergman 200–203).

ANITA BERBER

In spite of its persistent hesitation to deliver any serious statement about nudity and modernity, the Berlin nightclub culture of the early 1920s produced, in the work of a bizarre exponent of expressionism, Anita Berber (1899–1928), what was perhaps the most complex, significant, and memorable relation between nudity and dance to emerge between 1910 and 1935. Because of the sordidness of Berber's life, few dance scholars take seriously her contributions to German modern dance. Yet the perversity of her approach to dance is worth extended attention here precisely because she took risks; she staged more overtly than any other Weimar dance figure the dark (erotic) complexity governing perceptions of relations between modernity and nakedness. No one of the era has been more closely associated with nude dancing than Anita Berber. She made numerous nude photos of herself in poses from her dances, although it is not at all clear where or when she actually danced naked in public. In a comment for *Das Stachelschwein* (2, 2 February 1925, 46), a writer with the initials "K.S." claimed to have worked with Berber for more than a year and asserted that "she has never danced naked." But this pronouncement is probably as exaggerated as many of the scurrilous fantasies about her. Berber deepened the notion of nakedness in dance by making her dances so intensely autobiographical—and the life she made naked in her dances was very messy.

Berber came from a bourgeois family that was a textbook example of dysfunctionality. She studied under Jaques-Dalcroze at Hellerau (1913) and ballet in Berlin under Rita Sacchetto from 1914 to 1916, but she had no affiliation with the *Nacktkultur* societies. A brief dance scene in a film she made in 1919, *Unheimliche Geschichten,* shows a body well trained in ballet technique, able to move from decorative, on pointe delicacy to explosive lunges, but Berber's use of ballet technique was always subordinate to an expressionistic aesthetic that relied more on theatrical effects than on a refined sense of movement. Berber pursued an eclectic career as a concert and cabaret dancer, high fashion model, fine artist's model, and film actress, appearing in twenty-five films between 1918 and 1925. By 1917 she was a star fashion model for the mass circulation women's magazine *Die Dame,* and in 1919 she posed for a number of pornographic drawings by Charlotte Berend, some of which appear in Fischer (53–59). She made her debut as a solo dancer in Berlin in 1917, introducing her Korean dance wearing an exotic, silken pajama-type costume with a fantastic headdress. According to *Elegante Welt* (6/3, 31 January 1917, 15), she was already a mature artist, full of "daring" presence, "remote from all sweetness," and "always a little boyish." Berber experienced powerful bisexual passions that urged her into a promiscuous, perverse lifestyle and compelled her to push dance into dark, violent regions of feeling. As her dances became more lurid and apparently enticing, she displayed an increasingly haughty, disdainful attitude toward her audiences, who tended to show little appreciation of her as an artist, regarding her as a totem of the freakish era in which they lived. As the gifted modernist Czech choreographer Joe Jencik (1893–1945) accurately explained, "Both men and women feared her creations, which showed the trash and extinction of bourgeois bedrooms and barbarous marriages. . . . The public never appreciated Anita's artistic expression, only her public transgressions in which she trespassed the untouchable line between the stage and the audience. . . . She sacrificed her person to a self-vivisection of her life" through dance (JJ 8–9).

As a dancer, she achieved notoriety through her use of flamboyant costumes and her skill at representing a variety of attitudes toward romantic music. In 1919 she introduced Berlin to her ambitious *Heliogabal,* a complicated piece of bisexual eroticism inspired by a passage from a Dutch novel by Louis Couperus, *De Berg van Licht* (1905). She performed the role of the perverse Roman emperor Heliogabulas, the high priest of a Syrian sun-worshipping religion. "Exquisite, entirely attired in gold, her metallic body lured the sun, while two Moorish boys effectively manipulated the decor.—Another image. A mask interlude during the Saturnalia, with music by Delibes. A silver mask, including a stylish headdress, was pulled back just a little to reveal the mysterious face under it. Roses, red silks and scarves, pants a la Chanteclair. It is plainly a mask ritual. Serious, very worldly, seductive, imperial, full of daring contrasts is this dance" (*Elegante Welt,* 8/2, 1919, 5).

It is not known when Berber first performed nude dances, but presumably it was around the same time (1919–1920) she became interested in nude photography. Yet most of her dances involved bizarre expressionistic costumes and scenographic devices. In *Astarte* she was the cold moon goddess who rejects the lascivious advances of the men and women who lust after her. With *Salome* she explored an unusual perspective: "from below." "From a place where the legs are distorted and look like mammoth columns marbleized with veins, where the thighs look like ecstatic girders carrying the terrible sex on a shameless balcony; over it the canopy of a swelling stomach—this was Anita's perspective. Everything else is insignificant, the head is small, like an unripe plum. . . . This perspective allowed [Berber] to see somebody in love boundlessly obsessed by sex, without a head and breasts . . . love concentrated only in the lower part" (JJ 25–26). Attired in a purple cloak, she began this dance rising, undulating, out of a huge urn filled with blood. But then she froze and, with closed eyes, inhaled the blood, dipped her hands in it, while her face produced an expression that "could have been lust or torment." When she stood up, her arms crossed, blood dripped from between her legs as if she were menstruating. She discarded the robe and was naked, panting orgasmically; she masturbated with bloody hands, yet she "did not cease to be royal." Then she started to move to the music of Richard Strauss. Berber pivoted elegantly, executed ballones, arched back, then shot up straight with each violent chord. Her blood-stained hands floated in the air as she performed *port de bras*, "like in a beautiful exercise." She also introduced *caprioles*, spinning *tours en l' air*, and graceful *tombes* (falling to the knees), in what must have been one of the most astonishing travesties of ballet technique ever imagined. Finally she crawled about the urn, making undulating movements with her belly, then spiraled up triumphantly before kissing the blood and sinking back into the urn.

In Debussy's first *Arabesque*, a more abstract mood prevailed, as Berber adjusted her body to the "maze of rhythms" in the music. Her arms and hands developed a rhythm that contradicted the rhythm of her legs and feet, while her head followed yet another rhythm. She found a way to physicalize every notation in the score, incorporating abrupt jerking movements with gossamer rippling motions to produce, in spite of its technical density, a dance as luminous as the music. In *Morphine*, however, she was back in a gloomy narrative mode, and her vocabulary of movement was much more economical. Clad in a black dress, she sat in a huge armchair and injected herself with a syringe. She sat deathly still for a moment; then, according to Jencik, "she thrust her body in an incredible arch, like a morbid rainbow." Her movements appeared broken, incomplete, as the drug-induced visions arose before her; finally the drug "stabbed" her, and she contorted into the beautiful arch again and died in the chair.

One of her most unusual pieces was a "love dance" in a sadomasochistic vein, set to a waltz by Brahms. Here she had a male partner. They entered the stage dragging each other, she all in white, he in black. As the gentle waltz flowed on, the pair engaged in a violent struggle in which passionate embraces were asphyxiating and kisses—to the neck, the chest, and the thighs—appeared predatory, cannibalistic. Exhausted, the lovers sank into a stupor, but the pretty music streamed on, oblivious to the violence it motivated. Then the music revived the energies of the dancers, and they renewed the attack with even greater ferocity; their arms, legs, and torsos became intertwined, and they exerted "the force of a lion and lioness," without rationality or even feeling, "only the senses remain[ing]." The man now dominated the dance, while the woman "groan[ed] with her knees and incredibly bent spine." A sort of rape occurred, but the music just floated on serenely. The dance ended before the music did: on their knees, the dancers let their arms hang limply as they bent their heads backward, as if to ask a question of the sky but unable to formulate it. Then they stood facing each other without even touching. Here, as in *Salome*, the dance made sophisticated use of ballet technique: the male executed chasses, glissades, low jetés, and degages, while Berber performed chasse glisses, ballones, arabesques, attitudes, fouettés, and *port de bras* to create a "true poetry of power" that did not rely on mimicry. Jencik noted the significance of the dancers' bodies: "one had female beauty in a male body, the other male grace in a female body." Another strange partner dance was *Shipwrecked*, in which Berber used a gramophone on stage to play ragtimes, fox trots, and Charlestons. But the marooned and naked husband and wife did not dance with each other; instead they wallowed in narcissistic, masturbatory movements, as if the other was only an untouchable mirror of the self. As the ragtime kept playing, the dancers kept "moving in the belief that the dance would kill them." On the whole, though, Jencik did not think Berber was as strong in partner dances as in solo dance. Works such as *Lotusland*, devised by Sebastian Droste (Willi Knobloch), struck him as hopeless kitsch glorifying the decorative, passive, masochistically submissive woman of prewar Orientalist fantasy.

In 1918, after touring Germany, Vienna, and Budapest, Berber became involved in a homosexual scandal at the Hotel Bristol in Vienna. She returned to Berlin, married immediately, and began making movies until 1922, when she fell in love with a woman and divorced her husband. But the affair did not work out; the same year, she met and then married Droste, a somewhat unsavory opportunist who became her partner as a dancer and transformed every "real feeling" of Berber's into a "sensation" (Lania 153–154). As Willi Knobloch, he published some interesting experimental poems and a quite bizarre little "visionary" drama of family salvation in the Dresden expressionist journal *Menschen* (2/7, 1919, 14–24), but otherwise he spent his life in shady enterprises and sleazy homosexual subcultures. He and Berber went to Vienna in 1922, where he soon was accused and then imprisoned for fraud. Berber paid his debts, and he went to Budapest; then Berber was arrested for trying to steal the objects she had put up as collateral to pay the debts. The police told her to stay out of Austria for five years. In 1923 the marriage broke up, and Droste fled (with Berber's jewels) to New York to start a new career as a representative of avant-garde counterculture, appearing, for example, in a startling experimental film by Bruguiere in 1925 (Enyeart 29–48). Droste apparently succeeded in interesting D. W. Griffith in a movie script he had written about his life, but ill health compelled him to return home to Hamburg, where he died in 1926.

Meanwhile, Berber continued with another male partner she met in Munich, the American Henri Chatin-Hoffmann, whom she married within fourteen days of making his acquaintance. The couple traveled throughout Europe, creating scandals almost everywhere because of her perversity on stage and off—sometimes she would go out into the streets wearing only her fur coat; she conducted orgies in her hotel rooms; she danced lasciviously with other women. The couple visited Breslau, Cologne, Leipzig, Hamburg, Dresden, and Prague, but in Zagreb she went too far during a performance by insulting the King. For this she went to jail. Henri finally managed to obtain her release, and in 1927 the couple embarked on a tragic tour of seedy nightclubs in the Middle East: Athens, Cairo, Baghdad, Damascus, Alexandria, Beirut. Soaked with drugs, Berber became progressively ill and barely made it to her deathbed in a Berlin hospital, where she died of the same disease, tuberculosis, that had claimed Droste. As Jencik put it, her dances carried with them the "scent of bedrooms, hospitals, asylums, and morgues." The central focus of her artistic existence was "not the studio, but the boudoir," which she treated as a luxurious laboratory-temple for the exploration of sensual pleasures of all sorts. She surrounded herself with a huge collection of idols and religious images, and she collected sexual partners as if they, too, were part of her icon collection.[3]

DANCES OF VICE, HORROR, AND ECSTASY

In 1922, Berber and Droste published (in Vienna) a strange book of poems, photographs, drawings, and semitheoretical statements (by Leopold Wolfgang Rochowanski [1885–1961], a Viennese cultural historian, expressionist poet, and promoter of radical expressionist art and dance) related to the

3. Henri tried to establish himself as a dancer in New York in 1929–1930 but was not successful because, apparently, he was "so persistent in strangling his own potentialities for the sake of an ideal only visible to himself and a little group of similarly attuned spirits" (*The Dance*, 14/1, August 1930, 60). By far the most complete account of Berber's life and art is Jencik, *Anita Berberova* (1930). Fischer's *Anita Berber* (1984) does not examine her dancing with any specificity, nor does Leo Lania, *Der Tanz ins Dunkel: Anita Berber* (1929), both of which concentrate on the sensational aspects of her messy life. That is also the case with Rosa von Praunheim's sleazy 1987 film *Anita Berber—Tänze des Lasters und des Grauens*, a campy story about an old woman who imagines that she is Anita Berber. In Amsterdam in March 1990, Ute Dörner choreographed and danced in a piece called *Tanz ins Dunkel* about Berber's life with Droste. An even more outrageous desecration of Berber occurred in San Francisco in March 1994, when Mel Gordon, in collaboration with the Goethe Institute and punk rock singer Nina Hagen, staged *The Seven Dances of Lust*, a garish, absurdly "decadent" bio-drama at Bimbo's 365 nightclub.

Die Tänze des Lasters, des Grauens und der Ekstase, which they had performed in Berlin (Figure 26). Fischer claims the couple made a film of the same title in Vienna in 1923, but if so it has disappeared. The relation between the poems and particular dances is not clear from either the book or descriptions of the performances. Berber and Droste staged dances bearing the titles of the poems; it is not known if anyone spoke the poems before or during the performances, but the structure of the dances apparently corresponded to the "voice" of the poems. Berber's writing style differed from Droste's in that she linked words together to represent, rather conventionally, the rhythms of sensory perception that form a complex image in the mind, as these lines from "Orchids" indicate:

> For me they [orchids] are like women and boys—
> I kissed and tasted each until the end
> All all died on my red lips

Droste, by contrast, isolated words and phrases so that they called attention to themselves as discrete energies that did not depend on an action (a verb) to establish intense emotional relations to each other, as appears evident in "Kokain" (Berber was a cocaine addict):

> Walls
> Table
> Shadows and cats
> Green eyes
> Many eyes
> Millionfold eyes
> The woman
> Nervous scattered cravings
> Inflamed life
> Swollen lamps
> Dancing shadow
> Little shadow
> Great shadow
> THE SHADOW
> Oh—the leap over the shadow
> It tortures [me] this shadow
> It martyrs [me] this shadow
> It devours me this shadow
> What desires this shadow
> Cocain
> Outcry
> Animals
> Blood
> Alcohol
> Pains

Many pains
And the eyes
The animals
The mice
The light
These shadows
These terrible great black shadows

According to Jencik ("Kokain"), Berber interpreted this poem as a dance with the aid of some unidentified piano music by Saint-Säens and ominous scenery by Harry Täuber featuring a tall lamp on a low, cloth-covered table. This lamp was an expressionist sculpture with an ambiguous form that one could read as a sign of the phallus, an abstraction of the female dancer's body, or a monumental image of a syringe, for a long, shiny needle protruded from the top of it. Light emanated from a beacon in the middle of the sculpture and allowed the dancer to cast a powerful shadow, requiring her to perform movements that made the motion of the shadow as interesting as the motion of her body. It is not clear how nude Berber was when she performed the dance. Jencik, writing in 1929, flatly stated that she was nude, but the famous Viennese photographer Madame D'Ora (Dora Kalmus) took a picture entitled "Kokain" (included in the book) in which Berber appears in a long black dress that exposes her breasts and whose lacing, up the front, reveals her flesh to below her navel. Because Berber performed other dances in the nude, and because nudity in dance is a persistent theme of the book, it is possible that Berber sometimes performed *Kokain* completely nude and sometimes performed it wearing her costume, depending perhaps on the moral climate wherein the performance occurred.

In any case, according to Jencik, she displayed "a simple technique of natural steps and unforced poses." But though the technique was simple, the dance itself, one of Berber's most successful creations, was apparently quite complex. Rising from an initial condition of paralysis on the floor (or possibly from the table, as indicated by Täuber's scenographic notes), she adopted a primal movement involving a slow, sculptured turning of her body, a kind of slow-motion effect. The turning represented the unraveling of a "knot of flesh." But as the body uncoiled, it convulsed into "separate parts," producing a variety of rhythms within itself. Berber used all parts of her body to construct a "tragic" conflict between the healthy body and the poisoned body: she made distinct rhythms out of the movement of her muscles; she used "unexpected counter-movements" of her head to create an anguished sense of balance; her "porcelain-colored arms" made hypnotic, pendulumlike movements, like a marionette's; within the primal turning of her body, there appeared contradictory turns of her wrists, torso, ankles; the rhythm of her breathing fluctuated with dramatic effect; her intense dark eyes followed yet another, slower rhythm; and she introduced the "most refined nuances of agility" in making spasms of sensation ripple through her fingers, nostrils, and lips. Yet, despite all this complexity, she was not afraid of seeming "ridiculous" or "painfully swollen." The dance concluded when the convulsed dancer attempted to cry out (with the "blood-red opening of the mouth") and could not. The dancer then hurled herself to the floor and assumed a pose of motionless, drugged sleep. Berber's dance dramatized the intense ambiguity involved in linking the ecstatic liberation of the body to nudity and rhythmic consciousness. The dance tied ecstatic experience to an encounter with vice (addiction) and horror (acute awareness of death).

Movement toward ecstasy (and utopia) entails the convulsion or fragmentation of the body and (as the form of the poem implies) language. The ecstatic body vibrates with multiple rhythms. But an acute sense of rhythm is simultaneously an acute sense of time arising out of an acute intimation of death, of finality, of stillness and silence. The dancer's ecstatic rhythm is in fact a struggle to transcend rhythm itself: ecstasy is an anesthetic state, a condition of being drugged, free of bonding emotions. Rhythm signifies not liberation but repetition, addiction, craving for balance in a world of shadows; it is the mechanization of time and feeling, that which makes of the body a marionette. Thus, mechanization does not exist in tension with ecstatic experience; it *is* the drive toward ecstasy. It is the aesthetic correlate of addiction, of dependency on surrogate sources of pleasure (drugs, music). And, just as ecstasy is within vice and horror, so the healthy body is within the poisoned body. The nude body is the site of contradictory rhythms, of conflict between drugged and erotic drives toward ecstasy. But the healthy body can triumph over the poisoned one only through the voice, speech, language, the cry—which, however, the dancer cannot produce.

Droste's words, the language of the other, the male partner, inspire complex movements but remain unspoken. Missing are the actions (verbs) that define the relation between the identities listed. Dance does not translate the words into movements; rather, it supplies the movements the language motivates. Nudity here signifies a state of heightened aloneness before the shadow-other, before an anonymous audience, before "millionfold eyes," before the "devouring" image of death. The death-suffused words of the (male) other motivate nude dance, which in turn exposes the relation between the body, modernity, and ecstasy. Cocaine is not a source of ecstasy but a sign of modernity; ecstasy entails a performance of the nude body before an anonymous audience, without fear of appearing ridiculous, of disclosing masochistic dependencies on drugs, mechanized rhythms, or men, of the "horror" of narcissism provoked by being the only one naked. Such performance of nudity is in effect a mode of ecstatic confession, an intense pleasure in showing people how utterly alone and different one is in a modern world of addictions and mechanized rhythms.

Giese, Hagemann, and Menzler implied that the most powerful sign of a unique personality is nude dance. Berber's dance did not contradict this implication, but it was "more naked" than nude dance elsewhere in constructing a perception of uniqueness as a condition of stark aloneness, estrangement, and perversity. Nude dance was no cure for cocaine; it was not modern because it had any therapeutic effect. For Berber, nude dance *aestheticized* her sickness, and by doing so, by aestheticizing the addictions, compulsions, and mechanized rhythms defining the modern body, her dance anticipated postmodern sensibility; it was an almost satiric critique of the pretentions to a healthy, modern identity that both eurhythmic consciousness and *Nacktkultur* sought to achieve. Pleasure for the modern audience (not just the dancer) depended on aestheticizing, through nude dance, the symptoms of an incurable aloneness that makes the body modern.

However, the meaning of *Kokain* should not be detached from the context of its presentation (as a "dance" of vice, horror, and ecstasy) in the strange book Berber and Droste published. It is difficult to imagine, let alone find, a more bizarre and complex relation between dance, writing, speech, nudity, and image than that found in this little book. Berber wrote only four of the twenty-six poems in *Tänze des Lasters, des Grauens und der Ekstase*, and none of these inspired a dance. Droste wrote all sixteen of the poems the couple danced. He was the solo dancer for four of the poems, and Berber was the solo dancer for another four. The couple danced as a pair for seven of the poems, and one poem, which apparently never reached live performance, required three distinct "persons"—a "murdered woman," a "murdered boy," and a "hanged man"—as well as an "accusatory mob" and a "hundred thousand corpses."

Some poems are quite tiny; others run on for three or four pages. The mood of all the poems is consistently morbid and decadent, with pervasive references to death, phantasmal figures, tortured flesh, narcissistic sensuality, and narcotic visions. Droste juxtaposes allusions to artworks and artists with images of archaic cultures: Byzantium, ancient Egypt, imperial Rome, the sinister world of the Borgias. He also decorates his poems with mention of exotic sensations and materials: gold, diamonds, pearls, amethyst, silver light, perfumes, wax, powdered skin, distant organ tones, glass objects, silken pajamas, lurid lampglow, blue mist: "Woman/Red-haired/Gold net/pearls on the forehead." But the most disturbing references are to bodies (living and dead), parts of bodies, and body metaphors: "fingers like blood," "powdered thighs," "gold on the naked body," "green eyes," "screaming green," "boyish arms," "white head," "flaming hair," "ecstatic hands," "painted like a whore," "glassbright cry," "sibling corpses," "yellow-green desires," "the trembling steps of woman," "Oh she is an orchid/And seven heads." All these rhetorical devices construct an image of the dancer, male or female, in which the glamor of the body arises out of its morbidity. It is a variant of Wigman's perception of dance as ecstatic movement toward death.

But in Wigman's case, a different relation between writing and movement prevailed. With Wigman, writing preceded dance in the form of dense notebook collages of words and drawings whose meaning was often indecipherable. For her, dance was a phenomenon that freed the body from inscription, from containment within a text (or supertext). Berber and Droste apparently treated this belief in moving from writing to dance as incomplete, even naive. Though each individual poem may have motivated the dance that bears its title, the calculated aesthetic effect of the book (which extends to the typography and luxurious paper) suggests a more complete movement, from writing to dance back to writing. For these authors, dance performance continued beyond the moment the body made movement synonymous with life. The lurid, seductive book included some documentation of dance performance (as if to convey that documentation allows performance to live on after it is over); more important, it presented *itself* as a collection of dances, constructing the perception that dance is complete only when dancers become authors and transform their dances into poetic inscriptions. Whereas Wigman saw dance as life that emerges out of writing, Berber and Droste understood dance as an art that emerges out of writing and completes itself through publication in the form of a book. The writing was only one element of a performance that included an assortment of images and codes. For Berber and Droste, the body had to free itself, not from words or images, but from the all-too-brief moment in which it lived through performance. However, the dominant sign of this freedom was not words nor writing as such but rather the perverse book, which attempted to blur distinctions between writing and movement by obscuring relations between poems and dances. One might say, then, that insofar as the book represented a further state of nakedness for the dancer, the desire for nakedness entailed a desire to construct a highly ambiguous rather than ultimate perception of identity.

Consequently, it is almost impossible to determine the extent to which the dances translated into movements the words, syntax, or rhetorical devices of the poems. Theoretical statements by Droste and Rochowanski provide some clarification. These also appear as poems. In "The Dance as Form and Experience," Droste, asserting that "form is the expression of an inner experience" that ballet is incapable of embodying, concluded that the dances he and Berber performed constituted an "unconscious, sacred movement to the sounds/of an alien world" (16). Perhaps, then, the poems were supposed to project the emotional effect of this alien sound world rather than to encode specific correlations between bodily movements and particular words, syntactic structures, or rhetorical devices. Even so, it is probably impossible to detach the morbid and ecstatic effect of the poems from their referents or semantic values. Indeed, the whole book constituted a fantastic network of referentiality. Poems referred to dances, and dances referred to poems. Both poems and dances referred to both art and the lives of the dancers/authors. In the theoretical (that is, undanced or undance-able) poems, Berber and Droste referred to each other with narcissistic intensity. But all these layers of referentiality became so convoluted that ref-erentiality itself became a sign of morbid doubt over the authenticity of what was written or written about. The incessant, gaudy references to nudity, the body, and the decoration or masking of the body disclosed an inclination to believe that neither nudity nor the body were signs of authen-tic being; they were signs of fantasy, hallucination, upon which the inter-section of horror, vice, and ecstasy were predicated.

Droste developed this perception most overtly in one of his theoretical poems, "Der Lasterhafte und der Nackte" (The Vicious and the Naked), which is actually a violent kind of allegory. In his apartment, a man powders, perfumes, and ornaments his nude body. Having completed this ritual, he dons a cape and visits a bar in a Roman piazza frequented by homosexual boys and prostitutes. He has a drink, leaves without paying, and goes to another lonely piazza, where he removes the cape and stands naked, "smil-ing at his slender powdered thighs" and apparently masturbating. "A cry went through the streets/Out of the alleys streamed" singing fascists, "slen-der boy bodies," and frenzied women, all of whom sink to their knees before him, as if he is an idol. "Only the vicious one stood smiling in the crowd." This figure wears a dark coat and dark glasses, but he also powders his face and paints his lips. He approaches the naked one and kisses his navel, fright-ening away the crowd. The vicious one proceeds to strangle the naked one "with scientific precision," then decapitates him.

> Then he took the painted head of the naked one back home
> Placed it in a glass baroque vitrine
> And sank trembling to his knees

None of these extreme actions involves any speaking (except for the anony-mous cry provoked at the moment of the man's disrobing). This poetic lan-guage produces a scenario for bodily movements that possess the voiceless authority of a perverse, violent dance. The poem presents nudity as a silent yet public performance that awakens unspeakably turbulent emotions in crowds, classes of persons, and one "vicious" individual. Nudity appears as the obverse condition of viciousness, a monstrous desire to torture and mutilate that body that puts its nudity on public display. The murderer reduces the naked body to a part, which he fetishizes, a part (the head) that one normally exposes anyway.

Most significant, public nudity here signifies a feminization of the male body, in the sense that powdering, painting, and bejewelling the body are signs of a feminine attitude. The poem suggests that it is not the nude female body but rather the feminization of the nude male body that gives rise to intensely turbulent emotions in public performance. Male nudity is feminized when it becomes an element of an aesthetic performance, of a dance. The act of exposing the genitals, in public and for aesthetic effect, is feminine, regardless of whether the genitals are male or female. For this reason, perhaps, it is very difficult to find examples of total male nudity in German modern dance. Droste sometimes performed in a loincloth (as in his St. Sebastian dance) but never completely nude, as Berber sometimes did.

Despite the shocking effect of this poem, it is the image of Berber's body that dominates the book. Even the body of the male nude in "Der Lasterhafte und der Nackte" impersonates the powdered, orchidaceous body projected by Berber in the other poems/dances. The brief, theoretical poem immediately following "Der Lasterhafte und der Nackte," titled "Versuchung," is "dedicated to Anita" and purports to describe Berber's body. The poet identifies her "slender naked boy thighs," her "slender purple petals," her whiteness, her fullness, her "clouds of powder," with particular actions or movements: the spreading of "countless raptures," the breathing of the wind, the pressing of desires, the quivering of flesh and the clinging of things to it, the veiling of lights, the gleaming of glass, the undulating of tassels, the waving of the arms, the pulling of "immeasurably wide spaces," the entwining and winding of circles. These movements, ascribed to the nude female dancer as a set of events devoid of narrative context, awaken male desire over and over again, in "circle and circle," and create "temptation," which threatens to destroy or corrupt the male body. It is movement performed by the female body, not anything spoken, that tempts the male poet.

But what does it mean for feminine movement to tempt the male poet? Because Droste wrote the great majority of the words in the book, including all the poems made into dances, it would seem that temptation implies a kind of fatal submission to language, an urge to write, to speak, to disclose morbid desires, the exposure of which addictively enslaves him to the one person who understands him, his partner, the female dancer. In spite of the lurid implications for nudity in male aesthetic performance theorized by "Der Lasterhafte und der Nackte," the riskiest, "most naked" manifestation of male vulnerability is apparently not nudity in performance but writing and speech that motivate performance. The relation between language and bodily movement is as symbiotic as the relation between Berber and Droste.

Narrative-free movements of the female body motivate the male body to write, to speak, to inscribe, to narrate the female body as a dance. But in seeking union with the female body through dance, the male body becomes female insofar as it impersonates the feminine signs of the powdered, painted body. At the same time, the female body displays signs of masculinity: "slender naked boy thighs," "boy arms," a knifelike form. The relation between language and movement is ambiguous, interpenetrating, with the result that *neither language nor dance nor nudity can lead to greater authenticity of being*. For Wigman, movement constructed authenticity of being, and language (writing) was an initial manifestation of movement. For Berber and Droste, however, modern dance and the language that motivates it undermine secure categories of sexual difference, and in doing so they also expose narrative itself, in language and in dance, as morbid, decadent, a pathological mode of signification. Modernity itself then refers not to any condition of inauthenticity but to consciousness of the idea that the authenticity (and therefore the inauthenticity) of signs is a myth. The pleasure of the modern body derives from the supposition that narrative can no longer contain the body to which it refers, that performance does not contain enough signs to signify the unspeakable aspects of desire and identity.

The book amplifies the ambiguity of the relation between language and dance by its use of illustrations. These call attention to the problem of establishing the authenticity of the language that defines the modern body. Droste and Berber present sixteen photos of themselves taken in the Viennese studio of Madame D'Ora. Of these, only five include Droste, and only two feature him alone—the rest are of Berber alone. The photos bear no captions. Though the poses and costumes Berber and Droste adopt are from their dances, the photos are in no sense documentations of their dance performances; rather, the poses give the photos their own lurid, glamorous value. The sequence of pictures constitutes an artwork that shows the female body's capacity to exist independently of either its partner or its "original" performance. Berber undermines the authority of this glamor by including three of her own drawings, grotesque caricatures, of her head alone in profile. In two of them she appears bald-headed and wears outrageously huge earrings on her tiny ears, and in all three her heavily mascared eyelids vanquish any view of her eyes themselves. Yet each profile gives her a different identity: the first (bald-headed with small turban), fantastically Asian; the second (bald-headed with halo), a sort of monk wreathed in cigarette smoke; and the third, a sleek cosmopolitan with short-cropped black hair (she was actually a redhead).

These crude self-portraits give way to performance documentation: seven paintings, in color, by Harry Täuber of scenery and costumes employed in specific dances. These, preceded by Täuber's short prose preface, contain captions briefly describing the actions meant to occur within the contexts depicted. Here Berber and Droste are neither glamorized nor caricatured but rather are given a tortured, "demonic," expressionistic look. Whereas the photos glamorize the dancers after having performed their dances, the paintings present the images the dancers strove to achieve through performance. These are stark, violent images, saturated with gloomy shadows, glaring light, and distorted perspectives. The small, anguished bodies of the dancers appear imprisoned in monumental spaces of terror and pain. Yet are these images any more authentic than the others?

Berber and Droste preface their book with two more images of themselves, drawings by the Viennese artist Felix Harta (1884–1967), who did many sketches of theatrical personalities. These are done somewhat realistically, with Berber and Droste, facing each other in profile, presented as debonair, even cute, embodiments of brash youth. But the very sketchiness of the drawings suggests a quite incomplete perception of the subjects. Altogether, the illustrations fail to stabilize perception of the author-dancers, reinforcing the governing idea that neither language nor movement nor music nor image nor nudity nor any complete unveiling that allows us to "see everything" has any special power to establish the authenticity of the modern body, to affirm that modernity is a progression toward authenticity of being, or to persuade us that liberation depends on achieving authenticity. Nevertheless, the complicated aesthetic of Anita Berber is as modernist as eurhythmics, *Nacktkultur,* and *Nacktballett* in linking modern identity to a more naked condition of being than premodern consciousness ever contemplated. Obviously, being naked in itself is not modern; yet it is difficult to imagine modernity reaching more extreme or controversial expression than through nude dance, than through the desire of a naked body to be seen making purely aesthetic movements that render both desire and the body more naked.

Figure 1. Dancer at the Ida Herion School in Stuttgart. Photo by Alfred Ohlen, from Adolphi and Kettmann, *Tanzkunst und Kunsttanz* (1927).

Figure 2. Dancer at the Ida Herion School in Stuttgart. Photo by Paul Isenfels, from Isenfels, *Getanzte Harmonien* (1926).

Figure 3. Ursula Falke in a pose from *Der Prinz* (1925). Photograph by Richard Luksch (Hamburg), from Hamburg Museum für Kunst und Gewerbe.

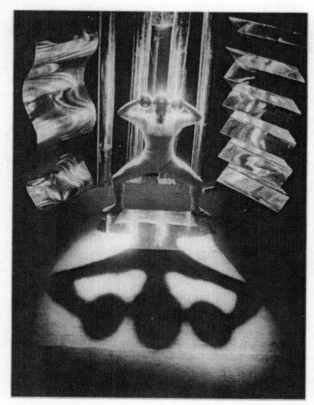

Figure 4. Karla Grosch performing *Metalltanz* (1929) at the Bauhaus experimental theatre studio in Dessau, from OS, 93.

Figure 5. Open-air rhythmic gymnastic exercises at the Dalcroze school in Hellerau around 1913. From a contemporary postcard.

Figure 6. Gertrud Leistikow performing in a meadow near Ascona, 1914. From HB, plate 68.

Figure 7. Olga Desmond in "classical" (sculpted) nude tableau, Berlin, 1910. From Andritzsky and Rauthenberg, *"Wir sind nackt und nennun uns Du,"* 52.

Figure 8. Male nudists surging toward the sun. From Hans Surén, *Der Mensch und die Sonne* (1924).

Figure 9. Male and female nudists exercising together indoors at the Koch school in Berlin. From Adolf Koch, *Körperbildung/Nacktkultur* (1932).

Figure 10. Students of the Hagemann school in Hamburg. From Hagemann, *Über Körper und Seele der Frau* (1927).

Figure 11. Woman gymnast of the Hagemann school. From the Joan Erikson Archive of the Harvard Theatre Collection.

Figure 12. Brother and sister nudists. Photo by Lotte Herrlich, from Herrlich, *Seliges Nacktsein* (1927).

Figure 13. Claire Bauroff, Vienna, 1925. Photograph by
Trude Fleischmann, from Pastori (1983), 44.

Figure 14. Grete Wiesenthal performing *Pantanz*, Vienna, 1910. Woodcut by Erwin Lang, from Lang, *Grete Wiesenthal* (1910).

Figure 15. Dancer at the Elisabeth Estas school in Cologne, 1927. From RLM, plate 91, photographer unknown.

Figure 16. Drawing by Hata Deli. From Ernst Schertel, *Der erotische Komplex* (1932).

Right: Figure 17. Dancer at the Ida
Herion school in Stuttgart. Photo by
Alfred Ohlen, from Adolphi and
Kettmann, *Tanzkunst und Kunsttanz*
(1927).

FACING PAGE:
Left: Figure 18. Dancer at the Ida
Herion School. Photo by Ohlen,
from Adolphi and Kettmann.
Right: Figure 19. Dancer at the Ida
Herion School. Photo by Ohlen,
from Adolphi and Kettmann.

Figure 20. Dancers at the Ida Herion school in Stuttgart. Photo by Paul Isenfels, from Isenfels, *Getanzte Harmonien* (1926).

FACING PAGE:
Top: Figure 21. Dancers at the Ida Herion School. Photo by Isenfels, from Isenfels. *Bottom:* Figure 22. Dancers at the Ida Herion School. Photo by Isenfels, from Isenfels.

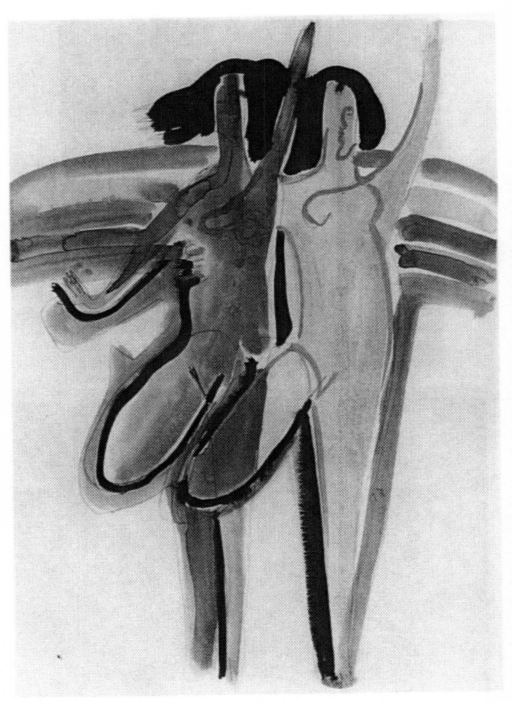

Figure 23. Watercolor study by Ernst Ludwig Kirchner for the "Color Dance" mural in the Folkwang Museum, Essen, ca. 1932, from Froning (1991), 97.

Figure 24. Social dancing in a sleazy Berlin bar. Watercolor by Jeanne Mammen, ca. 1929, from *Jeanne Mammen 1890–1976* (1978).

Figure 25. Chorus girls in a Berlin nightclub, 1919, before the advent of *Girlkultur,* with spectators and performers in a puzzling relation to each other. Photographer and source unknown, reproduction from postcard.

Figure 26. Anita Berber and Sebastian Droste in a pose from their St. Sebastian dance, Vienna, 1922. Photo by Madame D'Ora, from Anita Berber and Sebastian Droste, *Die Tänze des Lasters, des Grauens und der Ekstase* (1922).

Figure 27. Outdoor movement choir performing Laban improvisation exercises, ca. 1924. From Laban, *Gymnastik und Tanz* (1926).

Figure 28. A sketch, ca. 1924, by Rudolf Laban attempting to describe human movement as a dynamic geometric form. From Ullmann (1984), 34.

Figure 29. Mary Wigman's *Zweitanz (Studie)* (1927); Wigman is the figure on the left. Photo by Charlotte Rudolph, from Rudolf Bach, *Das Mary Wigman-Werk* (1933).

Figure 30. Masked solo figure from Wigman's *Totentanz*
(1926). It was quite unusual
for a Wigman dancer to perform on a carpeted rather
than polished wood surface.
From Rudolf Bach, *Das Mary
Wigman-Werk* (1933).

Figure 31. Image of the
"prophetess" section of Wig-
man's *Frauentänze* (1934).
Photo by Charlotte
Rudolph, from Wigman,
Deutsche Tanzkunst (1935).

Figure 32. Female Loheland (Fulda) student projecting ambiguous sexual identity, ca. 1920. From Fritz Giese, *Körperseele* (1924), plate 31.

Figure 33. Page 323 of the *Základy rytmického telocviku sokolského* (1929), one of hundreds of exercises in this huge manual on the Sokol system of movement education, probably the most comprehensive account of Dalcrozian movement pedagogy ever published.

Obr. 129.   Obr. 130.   Obr. 131.

34.

Hmitání.

Hudební skladba č. 45.
Rytmus: C ♩♩♩♩♩♩♩♩ | atd.
Útvar: Zástup.
Základní postavení: Stoj zánožný levou, tyč rovně před prsa.
   I. 1.–4. čtyři hmity dolů a nahoru (celkem 8 hmitů) tyč před prsa, v hmitu as 20 cm. Současně osm skoků běhových vpřed. Posledním hmitem tyč nad hlavu rovně.
   II. 1.–4. čtyři hmity vodorovně, vpřed a vzad, tyče rovně nad hlavu (s každým skokem jeden hmit), hmity se dějí do mírného prohnutí kříže. Současně osm skoků běhových vpřed.
   III.–IV.   I.–II.
   V. 1.–4. zvolna předpažit, tyč rovně před prsa a současně čtyři hmity rovné vlevo a vpravo stranou, osm běhových skoků vpřed.
   VI. 1.–4. zvolna tyč dolů rovně a čtyři hmity tyče rovně vlevo stranou, osm běhových skoků vpřed.
   VII.–VIII. Opáčnou cestou tyč rovně nad hlavu s osmi hmity vlevo a vpravo stranou, osm běhových skoků vpřed.

Figure 34. Interaction between male bodies performing Swedish gymnastics. Leipzig, ca. 1926, from a contemporary postcard.

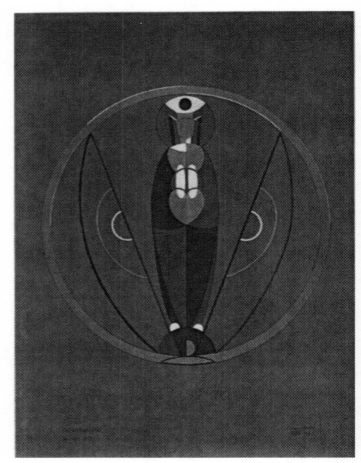

Figure 35. Design by Lothar Schreyer for *Maria im Mond*, Weimar, 1923, with robot female idol perched on "dance shield." From DS 70.

Figure 36. Image from Schlemmer's *The Triadic Ballet,* ca. 1925. Photo source unknown.

Figure 37. Experimental dance at the Bauhaus, Dessau, ca. 1927. Photo by Lux Feininger, Copyright The Oskar Schlemmer Theatre Estate, 79410 Badenweiler, Germany, Photo Archive C Raman Schlemmer, Oggebbio, Italy.

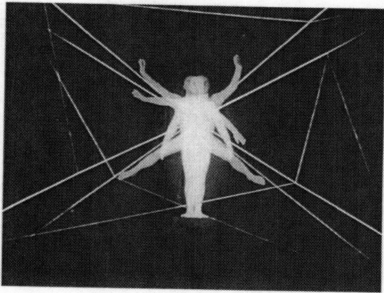

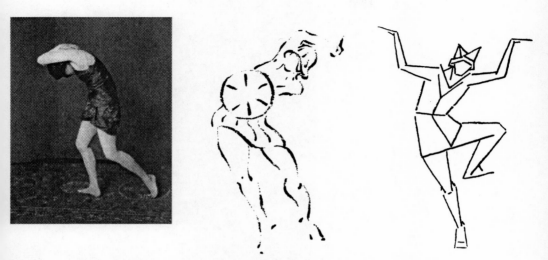

Left: Figure 39. Edith von Schrenck. Photograph by Hanns Holdt. Compare with Figures 40 and 41.

Center and Right: Figures 40 and 41. Edith von Schrenck's *Kriegertanz* and *Polichinelle* (1919). Lithographs by Ottheinrich Strohmeyer, from (left) Buning, *Dansen en danseressen* (1926), and (center and right) Schrenck (1919).

FACING PAGE:
Figure 38. Image of the *Staff Dance* (1928–1929), performed by Manda van Kreibig at the Bauhaus, Dessau. Copyright The Oskar Schlemmer Theatre Estate, 79410 Badenweiler, Germany, Photo Archive C Raman Schlemmer, Oggebbio, Italy.

Figure 42. Grit Hegesa perform-
ing *Groteske,* Rotterdam, 1917.
Etching by Herman Bieling, from
Netherlands Theatre Institute.

Figure 43. Grit Hegesa dancing,
Rotterdam, 1918. Painting by
Herman Bieling, from Nether-
lands Theatre Institute.

Figure 44. Grit Hegesa, Berlin, ca. 1925. Painting by Emil van Hauth, from *The Studio*, 92/401, 14 August 1926, 134.

Figure 45. *The Dancer Charlotte Bara,* Worpswede, 1918. Painting by Heinrich Vogeler from Küster, *Das Barkenhof Buch* (1989), 113.

Figure 46. Sent M'ahesa in a pose from an Egyptian dance, Munich, ca. 1915. Photographed by Wanda von Debschitz-Kunowski, from HB, plate 24.

Schools of Bodily Expressivity

DANCE AND DANCES

As the most complex and distinctive manifestation of German modernist body culture, *Ausdruckstanz* deeply stirred the imagination because it unfolded within a dynamic system of signifying practices whose emancipatory potential appeared limitless. But this system did not establish its credibility chiefly through a canon of discrete works that can be read as closely as literary pieces, artworks, plays, or films. Perhaps the emancipatory appeal of dance depended on its reluctance to leave behind concrete evidence of its forms. In any case, one cannot construct much of a history of *Ausdruckstanz* by analyzing particular dances of particular "authors," because the documentation simply does not exist to produce any sustained analysis. But this absence of documentation does not mean that German dance culture failed to produce a substantial body of works worth documenting. Many dancers resisted documenting their pieces in any detailed form, such as notation or film, because they feared that others, in an intensely competitive market, would steal their ideas or that audiences' desire to see the dance in a live performance would evaporate. Yet the most obvious reason for the lack of documentation was great uncertainty about how to document a dance. Movements of the body produce such complex impact on perception that they challenge the power of language to describe them accurately, especially in relation to their meaning, which bestows value on signifying practices. Even today, the great majority of writing about movies, which are much more similar than dances to conventional texts, focuses on issues of narrative and character and completely subordinates to these issues the analysis of performance elements whose value often does not depend on narrative context: acting, set design, lighting, costume design, cinematography, musical score, and editing. Signifying practices migrate across performances and therefore across narrative contexts; one sees performance by detaching signifying practices from narrative contexts and placing them within a larger context, within a range of choices open to performers to signify a specific narrative situation.

German commentators on dance during the Weimar era seemed to view the art from this perspective. They wrote prodigiously on dance but rarely described specific dances in detail. They repeatedly announced that dance was the greatest expression of individuality, of the repressed or dormant "inner being," of national identity, yet they did not regard dance culture as foremost a repertoire of specific dances or even dance forms. The major dance chroniclers of the era—Hans Brandenburg, Fritz Böhme, Hans W. Fischer, Werner Suhr, Fritz Giese—did not describe dances so much as they described personalities associated with habits of signification used in dances. As the chief manifestation of the profound metaphysical significance the Germans sought to ascribe to the modern body, dance could not be reduced to dances or to highly concrete forms. To preserve the metaphorical, symbolic, and political integrity of dance, it was necessary to construct a discourse that shifted perception away from material incarnations to the embodiment of a stirring—indeed, ecstatic—spirit that transcended the limits of materialism and sensory perception in even quite modernist sensibilities.

Before the advent of the Third Reich, no country was more active in the development of modern dance than Germany, but even then German dance culture self-consciously regarded itself more in relation to an expanding potential than to the solid establishment of practices that one could eventually call traditions. The motive for the metaphysical perspective seems reinforced when one examines recent attempts in Germany, the Netherlands, and the United States to reconstruct, on paper or in performance, dances by Mary Wigman, Harald Kreutzberg, Gertrud Leistikow, or the Bauhaus. These reconstructions always seem a little disappointing, even when a huge amount of money and time is expended on them, as in the Joffrey Ballet's 1988 effort to reconstruct Nijinsky's *The Rite of Spring* (1913). As long as reconstruction primarily entails the recovery of movement, music, sets, and costumes, it will always tend to disclose the inadequacy of past performances, for the appeal of past performances depends less on those elements than on the bodies and personalities of dancers, as well as on historically unique factors that are not easily recovered. For example, if one compares Marja Braaksma's 1990 reconstruction of Mary Wigman's *Hexentanz* (1926) with Wigman's own version of it in a 1930 film clip, one sees two entirely different dancers performing the same movements to the same music in practically the same costumes to produce two quite different images of witches, with Wigman appearing far more spooky and Braaksma far more voluptuous. We cannot reconstruct the vast majority of dances produced between 1910 and 1935, but we can recover the system that enabled German dance culture to achieve such immense productivity and to make dance central to a modern perception of the body.

RUDOLF LABAN

No figure of the German dance culture enjoyed a greater reputation for treating dance as an abstract system than Rudolf Laban (1879–1958), and no figure left more abundant documentation of his ambitions. In the 1920s no one wrote more on dance, no one had more students, no one had more schools devoted to his teachings, and no one seemed to have such a huge slate of enterprises devoted to dance than Laban. His life teemed with so much activity and he left behind such a vast archive of documentation in several countries that no one, least of all himself, has yet been able to construct a coherent, comprehensive biography. His memoirs, *Ein Leben für den Tanz* (1935), gave a remarkably reticent and unengaging account of a life that was apparently too complicated for the author to examine with sufficient patience. Laban fabricated a powerful mystique, and his disciples have perpetuated an aura of mystery surrounding him with a rhetoric that is sometimes even murkier than his own. But once one penetrates the cloud of reverence enshrouding him, one sees that Laban began far more projects than he could possibly complete and that productivity does not necessarily equal concrete achievement. Like Emile Jaques-Dalcroze, Laban was neither a great artist nor a great theorist; he was a great teacher who possessed a powerful gift for motivating people to exceed their own expectations of themselves and to pursue ideals that are not easily understood.

Laban came from the Hungarian nobility, and after studying art in Paris he decided to pursue a career in dance, against the wishes of his family. He received ballet training in Paris, performed with different companies in North Africa, Germany, and Vienna from 1906 to 1910, then started his own school in Munich. When war broke out, he migrated to Zurich and then to Ascona, where he established an experimental school that integrated dance into a larger, countercultural lifestyle that included nudism, sexual adventurism, and nature worship. A great deal of legend surrounds the Ascona period, perhaps the least adequately documented phase of Laban's life. It was during this period that he perfected his strategy of insuring the legacy of his pedagogic ideas by cultivating powerful erotic-physical relations with his female students. He formed a kind of harem of devoted women, demonstrating that *Ausdruckstanz* involved the construction of a mysterious personality with an almost hypnotic control over the dynamic, liberated body. From then on, Laban's relations with women were so complicated that one must conclude he had a rare gift of making them feel utterly unique without allowing himself to feel possessed by them (although he does seem to have needed, in the erotic sense, numerous women to sustain his sense of purpose).

After the war he returned to Germany, where he established institutes in Nuremburg, Stuttgart, Mannheim, Hamburg, and Würzburg. By 1926 he had schools dedicated to his teachings in all these cities, plus Leipzig, Basel, Munich, Salzburg, Tübingen, Berlin, Budapest, Vienna, and Nordhausen. All were run by women except the schools in Jena (Martin Gleisner) and Hamburg (Albrecht Knust). In 1928, at the Essen Dance Congress, he introduced his method for notating dances, subsequently known as Labanotation, which has since become the most widely used system of dance notation. The same year he helped launch the journal *Schrifttanz* (1928–1932), published by Universal Edition of Vienna, with Alfred Schlee as editor and Laban's perspective as an editorial principle. Between 1930 and 1934 he directed the ballet of the Berlin State Opera, and in 1936 he coordinated the dance productions for the Berlin Olympics. Because of the Nazis' "hostility toward dance as an art and cultural language," Laban decided that the Third Reich lacked sufficient opportunities for him, and in 1938 he migrated to England, where he spent the rest of his life, much of which he devoted to the study of bodily movement in industrial production, asserting that the most aesthetic movements were also the most efficient.

During the 1920s, Laban produced numerous public dance performances, including *Die Geblendeten, Himmel und Erde, Tannhäuser Bacchanal* (Mannheim, 1921), *Der schwingende Tempel, Lichtwende, Prometheus, Gaukelei, Komödie* (Hamburg, 1923), *Agamemnons Tod, Dämmernde Rhythmen* (Hamburg, 1924), *Narrenspiegel* and *Die gebrochene Linie* (Berlin, 1927). His most ambitious choreographic project was the enormous three-hour ballet *Don Juan,* produced in Berlin in 1926. But in spite of his obsession with documenting dance accurately through his notation system, information about his dance productions is astonishingly meager, and none was intensely successful either commercially or critically. In an article for the *Deutsche Allgemeine Zeitung* (9 February 1925), Fritz Böhme, commenting on Laban's experiments with "musicless" dances, remarked that Laban's sense of bodily movement was "more choreographic than musical," by which he meant that Laban devised movements without paying much attention to musical motivation—without, in effect, listening to rhythms or harmonies in dialogue with bodies. But Laban's idea of dance was too complex to achieve its strongest or most lucid expression through dances. He saw dance as a mode of action that transcended the borders of institutions and conventional distinctions between nature and civilization.

In 1922 in Hamburg, he began his most serious experiments with the notion of "movement choirs." In these exercises, conducted both indoors

and outdoors, large groups combined and recombined in numerous variations to dramatize the power of dance to accommodate difference within
the struggle for communal unity. Although the movement choirs appeared
in theatrical productions such as *Faust II* (1922), their expressive value was
much more evident in improvised or appropriated contexts (Figure 27).
Throughout the 1920s, the exercises for movement choirs attained an ever
greater complexity and intricacy that was specific to the moment and too
difficult to duplicate or rehearse for the purposes of theatrical dance performance. However, the movement choirs were merely one element in a
grandiose ambition to liberate the value of dance from its dependence on
dances. Laban's true medium was not the theatre but the school, and his
most congenial form was not the dance nor even choreographic activity but
the lesson, the lecture, the demonstration, the act of instructing. Laban
hoped to release dance from its institutionalized confinement within the
theatre and the business of touring, which he hated, as is evident from his
correspondence in the Leipzig Tanzarchiv regarding the ill-fated tour of
Poland in February 1928. His plan was to construct a large network of
schools throughout Europe as an alternative production and performance
system operating independently of conventional, tradition-bound theatre
culture.

To achieve this objective, Laban had to detach a cosmic notion of dance
from its material manifestation in performances; he had to establish a powerful, alluring value for dance more through writing about dance than
through performance. But a potent aura of mysticism pervaded his writings on dance. He rarely, if ever, analyzed actual dances or bodies but constantly introduced hypothetical models and examples of movements. This
antiempirical attitude almost suffocated his most theoretical and popular
book, *Die Welt des Tänzers* (1920), which was more a meandering collection
of notes than a cogently argued theory of bodily expressivity. He did not
analyze dances or dancers, nor did he refer to any other thinkers on dance;
rather, he presented a vast constellation of categories of analysis. The
world of the dancer consisted of this seemingly endless labyrinth of categories: "Dance as Gesture" (13), "Tonality as Gesture" (14), "Thought as
Gesture" (15), "Harmony of Gestures" (20), "Body Sense and Sense of
Tension" (25), "Symmetry and Asymmmetry of Gestures" (32), "Becoming
Conscious—a Symbolic Action" (34), "Appearance of Duality" (38).
"Appearance of Triality" (38), "Desiring, Feeling, Knowing" (40), "Movement, Stupefaction, Instruction" (44), "Dance of Inorganic Nature" (59),
"The Self as Source of Recognition" (66), "Language of the Hand" (94),
"Activity and Passivity of the Spectator" (169), "Periodicity" (233), and so
on. Laban introduced several hundred theoretical categories, none of
which he defined for more than a few paragraphs before moving on to the

next category. His writing style was majestically aphoristic and even a little oracular:

> Like the ecstasies of terror and hate, the ecstasies of joy and love will indicate the same contradictory signs. Whispering and calling, high and deep tones interact. With broken voice, turbulent motives, in which stammering and poetic soaring become reconciled, the movements of surrender and the gestures of the pressing toward the thing in itself [An-sich-Pressen] are performed (179).

> The solo dance is a duet between dancer and environment or dancer and inner world. In the first case subjectively real, in the second case subjectively ideal. More concrete is the group or mixed movement in which rhythms of fleeing and following or inclination and repudiation enter simultaneously and with greater potency. . . . The battle dance, the fertility dance, and the temple dance are the most pervasive kinds of art dance (208).

> Rites are symbolic actions. Their educational value and their aim is the inner vision and outer expressive capacity in the sense of a demanding and testing of plastic experience. The context of ritual is the festival. . . . Every ritual arises out of dance, tonality, and word. Definite movements, gestures, steps are bound to audible rhythms, imagined and spoken words (54).

Laban's writing hardly ever became more precise or analytical than in these passages from *Die Welt des Tänzers,* yet his language stirred a great many people. By introducing such a multitude of theoretical categories, none of which he actually applied to any concrete manifestation of dance, Laban implied that dance itself defined the limits of analytical rationality by usurping and dissolving all stable distinctions between forms. For Laban, dance was a transcendent, cosmic force that imbued everything with erotic rhythm and tension: "[I]ndeed, in all life, in all being is dance: dance of the constellations, dance of natural forces, dance of human actions and feelings, dance of cultures, dance of the arts" (156). One could even observe the power of dance in stones, for "the crystallization process is excitement and movement" (59). The uncaptioned photographs in the book, most of which showed himself and his lover, Dussia Bereska, were merely decorative illustrations with no direct relation to anything in the text. They depicted the two dancers in uncontextualized studio poses, with Bereska consistently wearing bizarre, rather mythical costumes. The photos created the impression that dance inhabited its own strange world, an immense, bewildering system of phenomenal relations detached even from the language that tried to explain it.

In *Gymnastik und Tanz* (1926), Laban's rhetoric was less awe-inspiring but also less overtly theoretical. Here he did not associate dance so much with a transcendent, cosmic rhythmic principle; instead, he presented it as the superior sign of a modern expression of communal unity and social transformation—dance appeared as a historically unique force of liberation within European civilization. Whereas gymnastics focused on purely quantitative evaluations of bodily strength and health, dance made the body a field of expressivity possessing emotional qualities that eluded quantitative measurement. As in *Die Welt des Tänzers,* Laban's analysis of the body paid no attention to typologies or physiognomic categories, even between the sexes: he presented both the body and its movements as hypothetical constructs, reinforcing the perception of dance as a unifying phenomenon capable of accommodating manifold differences. He examined numerous parts of the body, from head to toe, in relation to their movement potential, although even here he was not altogether precise about what movement signified as opposed to what the body part in itself signified. Dualism permeated Laban's thinking about dance. Every movement entailed a countermovement; thus, breathing was the complement of the pause, symmetry the complement of asymmetry. Bending unfolded against arching, the swing against the turn, the flight against the fall, the spiral against the lateral profile, stamping against tiptoeing, stretching against coiling, advancing against retreating, the ring against the line, the left hand against the right, the head against the torso. The tension between symmetrical and asymmetrical movements led to further complexities: both arms could move symmetrically while the legs moved asymmetrically; the heads and legs of six bodies could move symmetrically while their legs moved asymmetrically, pulling them in different directions; all bodies could adopt a swinging motion, but some bodies might arch while others spiraled; the left leg could tiptoe while the right stamped, the outstretched arms trembled symmetrically, the head tick-tocked, and the torso arched, then bent, then swung. The major effect of this recursive dualism was to release dance from popular identification with *steps,* with formulaic phrases, with a focus on lower-body activity. Laban showed that any part of the body could dance and that all were essential to a modern idea of dance. The expressivity of modern dance depended on tensions between body parts and movements, between symmetrical and asymmetrical significations. This concept of bodily "harmony" was alien to ballet, in which the ideal body moved ideally because it was free of contradictory tensions.

However, Laban's discussion of rhythm and temporality was, as usual, exasperatingly vague. He said nothing insightful about the relation between bodily rhythm and musical rhythm; having so little understanding of the power of music to control emotional responses to movement, he tried to present bodily movement as an autonomous expressive field whose meanings remained stable regardless of the total sensory context. Nor did he think it worthwhile to explain the impact of costume, masks, lighting, or scenography on perception of bodily movement. The main point was to free the expressive body from overcontextualization and excessive institutionalization so that it could inhabit or appropriate completely new contexts. The abundant photo illustrations helped support this task considerably, for they showed many male and female dancers, some perfectly nude, from Laban schools throughout Germany, performing indoors and outdoors, in forests and in stadiums, as if all belonged to a pulsating, universally triumphant community or social movement.

Laban was so uncertain of the appropriate context for modern dance that he became obsessively preoccupied with the relation between movement and spatiality. Theoretically, at least, he regarded space as being as dynamic as movement. In a little dialogue published in *Die Tat* (14/9, December 1922), Laban had a dance lover ask, "But how should one present the form and content of the dance artwork?" to which a dancer replies, "An empty space organized through manifold gestures of solo dancers and great and small dance groups. . . . A world bound and structured by the discharge of those powers which reveal themselves only through human gestures and of which word and sound know only silence" (679). In an article for *Die Schönheit* (22/2, 1926), he announced that dance required its own distinct performance spaces and that the configuration most favorable to dance was the amphitheatre. In this setting spectators could watch the dance from all sides and from different perspectives, as "every dance composition builds itself as much through depth as through breadth." Dance performance should occur before great tapestries or curtains, not behind them, because "dance is not an art of illusion" but "such a strong stylization of natural movement that an illusionary stage environment only has a corrupting effect." In northern lands, open-air theatre was not feasible year-round, so he suggested the construction of cupolas over the amphitheatre in the belief that great cathedrals offered the best models for the new "dance temples." He also insisted that lighting should illuminate the "plasticity of movement" and not distract through "complicated color-effects." Every dance temple should have different-sized performance spaces for monumentally or intimately scaled occasions.

In another article for *Die Tat* (19/8, November 1928), he reiterated that "dance can serve the opera, the theatre, the festival, the celebration, and many other situations," but "today the dancework still has no venue in which it can be effectively presented to the spectator. Perhaps in the circus. In any case, not on the proscenium stage. . . . Dance theatre is first of all: a space; secondly: a suitably modelled ensemble which can technically and spiritually realize the composition of the dance poet; more remotely: the audience with a cultivated sense of form and movement." (591). That Laban regarded space (not music) as the dominant source of energy for dance became evident from his thousands of drawings of moving bodies and then of movement alone in its most abstract images. The Leipzig Tanzarchiv contains several hundred of these drawings, but they are so cryptic that it is probably impossible to figure out what they mean. It is clear, however, that he sought to represent movement as an abstract, geometrical force struggling with or against space, emptiness, as he emphasized in a lecture at Berlin University on 16 April 1928, when he finally concluded that movement is "not natural, but abstract."

Laban created drawings on all kinds of paper, in different colored inks and crayons, as if color or shading revealed the emotional quality of the movements, but in the vast majority of the sketches he put some sort of geometric frame—a circle, a square, a triangle, a hexagon, a star, intersecting trapezoids, "the crystal"—around the often fantastically arabesque movement, often giving the impression that the frame controlled or determined the limits of the movements (Figure 28). From these drawings emerged Laban's curious notion of the *ikoseheder,* a transparent cubospherical contraption that supposedly would reveal different zones of energy associated with different parts of the body and different movements, depending on the direction of the movement within a section of the *ikoseheder.* He made photographs of dancers moving in the *ikoseheder,* and he explained his space-body theory in almost pedantic (though not lucid) detail in *Choreographie* (1926), but the impression nevertheless remained that he had imagined a cage that contained the moving body rather than a serious map for exploring dynamic relations between body and space.

Moreover, in spite of his demand for a dance performance space that allowed audiences to see the body from different perspectives, all of his images of movement viewed the dancing body from the front in a proscenium frame. All of the dance photographs of himself and of his students were taken from the front at eye level. Unlike Isenfels, the Bauhaus photographers, Schertel, Villany, Drtikol, or Rolf Herrlich, Laban never saw photography as a way to portray dance from an unusual angle or distorted distance. His visual sense was actually much stronger in the use of bizarre or fantastic costumes than in the exploitation of space, a fact that is especially clear from photographs of his simultaneously abstract and medieval "dance tragedy" *Gaukelei* (1923). In his choreography, Laban tended to press bodies close to each other in complicated rhythms, so that the spectator perceived a dense mass of activity without shifting focus or turning the head. He did not see movement as an extension of space, nor did he see space as an opening for movement, as indicated by his remark in an unpublished paper on "Das chorische Kunstwerk" that large public spaces give no joy when occupied by only one or two dancers (MS 88).

Although Laban avoided any sort of empirical discourse on dance and certainly on dances, he nevertheless was responsible for introducing the most successful method of recording dances, Labanotation, which he unveiled at the Essen Dance Congress of 1928. No notation system was so comprehensive in its capacity to accommodate the numerous variables of dance performance: part(s) of the body that moved; direction, weight, duration, force, rhythm, and tempo of the movement; rhythm of the music; relations between two or more moving bodies; number of movements; multiple rhythms within a movement or body; spatial relations. Laban devised a complex code system for marking each performance variable, with the result that a sheet of Labanotation looks as abstract as a sheet of a score for large orchestra, except that Labanotation is actually more difficult to read.

A law of 19 June 1901 declared that dance works enjoyed copyright protection as long as they existed in a written form, as a text. In theory, Labanotation would thus protect choreographers from pervasive plagiarization; it would also offer choreographers the capacity to create dances on paper the way composers write music, and it would ensure that dances did not die with their makers but survived as historical artifacts. As it turned out, however, Labanotation fell far short of achieving any of these objectives. Labanotation was an expensive, time-consuming process that attracted very few students and that even fewer dancers could afford to subsidize, and it was not until Laban had long established himself in England that serious training in the method finally began. In Germany he lectured vigorously on the subject with slide shows, and around 1929 he even contemplated making a *Schrifttanz* (written dance) film of his method, but he never applied Labanotation to any of his own dances. The main task, he decided, was to construct a comprehensive set of symbols for recording all possible movements of the human body. Albrecht Knust (1896–1978) coordinated this unexpectedly gigantic project, which he completed only in the 1970s, when the entire 200-volume *Kinetographie Laban* was deposited in only ten dance libraries around the world. Despite its arcaneness and typically Labanesque obscurities, Labanotation was significant for two reasons: 1) it revealed that the overwhelming majority of dances confined themselves to a tiny range of the total movement possibilities of the human body, that choreographic imagination was incredibly blind to a huge, unexploited expressive potential; and 2) it showed that the dancing body produced such complex disturbances of perception that empirical analysis of dance was much more difficult than almost everyone realized. It was not at all easy to describe accurately bodily movements, let alone their meanings. Labanotation was like an immense dictionary; it provided the letters and words to describe discrete movements, but it was powerless to explain the meaning of the movements it described, nor could it relate variations in movement sequences to semantic variations. By 1930 the meaning of dance seemed in desperate need of a more lucid, persuasive articulation than Laban had supplied.

It was in 1930, as economic conditions for dance culture deteriorated rapidly, that Laban became ballet master for the Berlin State Opera. He hoped an official position might consolidate his influence within government circles responsible for subsidies of the arts. Although he had many well-trained and gifted dancers at his disposal, his productions achieved only modest success, partly because of ballet politics and partly because his choreography seemed indifferent to musical value. His great love was the movement choir, performed by passionate amateurs. For the 150th anniversary of the Mannheim National Theatre in 1929, he staged, in the municipal stadium, a huge piece for movement choirs and speech choirs consisting of 500 men and women; the same year, in Vienna, he produced an even larger spectacle, with 10,000 performers. But the Nazis distrusted his complex, highly contrapuntal sense of rhythm and his close association with a left socialist motive for the movement choir, as exemplified in the work of his former student, Martin Gleisner. The 1930s were a glorious period in the history of mass movement spectacles, with fascists even more than the Soviets displaying considerable imagination in this form; but after 1933 the movement choir as Laban envisioned it blossomed most congenially outside of Germany, in the Netherlands, Belgium, and Czechoslovakia, especially among the Catholic-socialist organizations.

Laban obviously possessed titanic ambition. If his achievements seem less than one expects of titans, it is probably because he could never resolve a great conflict within himself between theory and practice. He saw that creating a higher value for dance depended on treating it as a huge, abstract system that functioned independently of dances and even bodies, just as language operates independently of speakers and texts. Indeed, he spoke of dance as a language and choreography as writing in movement (*Tanzschrift*); Labanotation (*Schrifttanz*) was a monumental effort to find a way to write down movement. Yet he associated language not with lucid systematic communication but with mystical crypticity. His rhetoric inspired plans rather than executed them. But by building an abstract system out of cryptic language and esoteric symbolism, he also demonstrated the completely contradictory power of dance to produce the unique, mysterious personality that appealed equally to his many students. Perhaps he best summarized his ambiguous conception of dance as an enigmatic language in a lecture on the subject given with Ruth Loezer at the Volksbühne in Berlin on 8 February 1925, when he claimed that dance was a form of runic inscription: "If we want to understand dance, we must learn to understand the law of the rune.... The whole history of dance is simultaneously the history of the encirclement of dance as writing [Tanzschrift]" ("Tanzsprache" program).

MARY WIGMAN

Laban's most famous student was Mary Wigman (1886–1973), who became the greatest dance artist Germany has yet produced. Much has been written about her, and I feel no need to cover the enormous terrain already traveled in Hedwig Mueller's excellent biography of Wigman and Susan Manning's wonderfully detailed reconstructions of her dances in the 1920s.

Wigman matured rather slowly as a dance artist. After receiving unsatisfying instruction under Dalcroze at Hellerau, she studied with Laban in Munich, then in Zurich and Ascona, where she became friendly with the dada circle around Hans Arp, Raoul Hausmann, and Hugo Ball (Melzer 103–104). But dadaistic nihilism was not compatible with her disposition toward heroic gestures. She produced her first program of dances in 1914 at the Laban school in Zurich, and she contributed dances to various Laban programs until November 1917, when she presented, again at the Laban school in Zurich, a solo program of *Ekstatische Tänze.* By this time she felt she had nothing more to learn from Laban, but her next move was not clear. She retreated into monastic solitude in the mountains; with writer Felix Moeschlin, she made an alpine fantasy movie, *Der Tanz um die Tänzerin* (1919), which has disappeared (Dumont 53–54); and she put together solo dance programs in Davos and Zurich. The acclaim these received inspired her to test what she believed was a more demanding audience in Germany. The break with Laban had major repercussions, for over time the two came to represent opposing tendencies in German modern dance. By the mid-1920s, Laban perceived her as the dominant threat to his own ideology and worked subtly to discredit her, largely by omitting her achievements from his prolific pronouncements on dance and by building within German dance culture powerful political blocs that opposed her. The tensions were still evident at the dance congresses in Magdeburg (1927), which Wigman refused to attend when Laban managed to prevent her and her students from performing, in Essen (1928), and in Munich (1930).

A successful tour of north German cities in 1919 brought Wigman back to Dresden, where audiences displayed the most gratifying enthusiasm. With another Laban student, the Swiss Berthe Trümpy, she founded a school in that city, acquiring as students young women stirred by her bold dance performances. During the 1920s her performing ensemble expanded from four to eighteen dancers; she produced nearly one hundred solo and group dances, and her school prospered so much that by 1927 she had 360 students enrolled at Dresden and more than 1,200 enrolled at "Wigman schools" operated by former students in Berlin, Frankfurt, Chemnitz, Riesa, Hamburg, Leipzig, Erfurt, Magdeburg, Munich, and Freiburg. In 1931, Hanya Holm went to New York to establish a Wigman school there.

Once she had left Laban and completed her first tour in 1919, Wigman enjoyed a meteoric rise to fame. By 1924 no German dancer was as widely known outside of Germany as she, even though she had yet to make any of the great solo tours of central, eastern, and northern Europe that would later confirm her as the most important artist of modern dance on the continent. In 1921 Hans Brandenburg announced, "She is now herself a phe-

nomenon, and in her style perhaps the greatest the art of dance offers."
She did not merely dance—rather, "with magic-demonic objectivity," she
made the "absolutes" of dance, "space and movement, visible in themselves . . . for [in her] the dance impulse has become cosmic, movement an
eternal hieroglyph and rune, the self an encircling center" (HB 202). The
same year, Ernst Blass commented rapturously that Wigman was "a wilderness, barbaric and fecund"; her "path leads into the nordic-prehistoric, into
wild intertwinings with dragon heads, horses' skulls. . . . Something nocturnal, black remains the most significant element of her consciousness. In her
leaps and wild hurlings, she is often formless and consuming, inaccessibly
remote" (34). In 1922 Werner Suhr, comparing her to Thomas Mann and
Hans Pfitzner as representative of a "classic" German artist, explained that
"Mary Wigman surrenders in the wildest frenzy to entirely explosive, overflowing movements, her arms fall with power through space, her hands are
clenched, her feet stride and glide to the inner pulse, her body trembles—
a swirling, unquenchable line!—in a singular, delirious forwards-upwards-
push, uninhibited and untamed, for this apparent lawlessness of her dance
reveals a higher law of the soul—her dance is a *dionysiac* festival, sensual-
spiritual joy, ecstasies of body and brain" (WS 102). Nor was this sort of
rhetoric confined to German commentators. In 1924 the Spanish weekly
picture magazine *La Esfera* (11/538, 26 April, 11–12) described Wigman
and her students in Dresden from a more classical-Mediterranean perspective: "The last drama of Wigman's performance . . . possessed something of
the sacred drama of the Passion and of the Suppliants, as well as the
Eumenides . . . the divine simplicity of Aeschylus . . . a terrific impression of
the chorus of Furies."

By 1929 Wigman had reached a creative impasse with her performance
group, so she disbanded it, returned to a cycle of solo dances entitled
Schwingende Landschaft, and collaborated with Albert Talhoff on the largest
and possibly most controversial production of her entire career, the huge
multimedia spectacle *Totenmal,* which premiered at the Munich Dance Congress of 1930. Then she embarked on the first of two grandly acclaimed solo
tours of the United States (1930–1931 and 1931–1932). However, a third
(1933) U.S. tour, this one with an ensemble, was not so successful. She
resumed creating new choreography for groups with *Frauentänze* (1934)
and *Tanzgesänge* (1935) and participated in the organization of the mass
Olympic dances of 1936, but otherwise all of her choreography until after
World War II consisted of solos for herself. Her last public performance, of
Abschied und Dank, took place in 1942.

In 1930, Wigman sought a respected outsider who could serve on the
board of directors for her school and reinforce its credibility with potential
funders. Hanya Holm introduced Wigman to her boyfriend, Hanns
Benkert, an executive engineer with the Siemens electric manufacturing

corporation. Not only did Benkert serve on the board, he and Wigman became lovers for over a decade. As a high-level industrial planner, he exerted serious influence among the Nazi elite. Benkert could protect Wigman from Nazi distrust of her, but he could not overcome Goebbels' emphatic distaste for her aesthetic, and by 1942 she found herself alone, without a company, without a school, and without her home in Dresden. After the war she attempted to revive her school in Leipzig, but she sensed that West Berlin offered a more congenial atmosphere for her art, and there she remained from 1949 until her death, teaching, choreographing opera performances (including *The Rite of Spring* in 1957), and gradually becoming more remembered than anticipated.

Unlike Laban, Wigman believed that a superior value for dance depended on the ability of dance performances to move audiences, not on a theoretical perspective that transcended dancers and dances. She had no interest in establishing an alternative system for institutionalizing body culture, and pedagogical objectives for her always remained subordinate to the task of discovering and perfecting her own artistic expression. She did not question the spatial contexts designated for dance before World War I, even in such a complicated production as *Totenmal;* indeed, all her dances fit well on the most conventional municipal stages. They also toured comfortably because Wigman did not favor elaborate scenographic effects, although her powerful dramatic sense entailed a very imaginative use of costumes. But she and Laban did have some beliefs in common. Like her former teacher, Wigman linked a superior value for dance to a heightened condition of abstraction established through movement, not body type, music, or narrative convention. She shared with Laban an inclination toward mystical signification, but she did not veil her feelings, as he did, in foggy crypticity. Wigman was great because she brought to dance an unprecedented magnitude of tragic feeling. For her, modern dance had to go well beyond the naive expressions of joy, innocence, and decorative idealism the public had come to expect since the heyday of Isadora Duncan: she tied conditions of ecstatic liberation to conditions of heroic sacrifice. The dance art of Anita Berber explored dark and violent regions of feeling, but Berber lacked the capacity or concentration to cultivate a tragic aesthetic, for her sense of dramatic conflict never extended beyond the image of innocence lost or desecrated in an inescapably sordid world. Wigman could appropriate the domain of the tragic because her morality was ambiguous. She saw the body as the site of great, conflicting urges, neither good nor bad but equally redemptive and equally strong: the experience of ecstasy entailed the sacrifice of conventional notions of life, communal unity, and bodily harmony. For her, dance was not a release from death but an exposure of it. As Hedwig Mueller has observed in relation to *Ekstatische Tänze* (1917), movement toward freedom implied for Wigman a tragic "transformation of the physical into the metaphysical," a heroic condition that achieved its most dramatic signification through the power of bodily movement to represent the immanence of death, "the unity of desire and destruction" (*Mary Wigman* 186). Movement made us see what was otherwise hidden: namely, that life is *in* death rather than opposed to it.

To amplify the tragic expressivity of bodily movement, Wigman linked movement to more concrete significations of feeling than either Dalcroze or Laban had. She moved the center of kinetic energy from the legs, thighs, and hips to the torso, which had the effect of dramatizing a struggle with gravity rather than an ethereal escape from it. Indeed, she often brought the body close to the dancing surface: one could dance while kneeling, sitting, crawling, reclining, or squatting. Arms and hands, she believed, should dance as much as the legs and feet. Much of the "Seraphisches Lied" section of *Schwingende Landschaft* has the dancer lying on her side with only her right arm and hand (and fingers) moving arabesquely (see also Bach, plate 9). A favorite device of hers was to have one arm reaching, imploring, or summoning while the other arm clung to the body, caressed it, or moved in a contrary direction to indicate energies withheld at the very moment they are released. A similar effect might occur when the dancer crossed her arms over her breasts while advancing toward the spectator but spread out her arms while turning her back to the audience; or both arms might beckon or implore but the hands remain inwardly cupped. She would make much of rotating the hands from palms straight down to palms straight up—or palms pressed against the air and the audience before her. No one better understood the dramatic potential of exposing the palm or the back of the hand or concealing the hand altogether in the armpit, behind the back, or under the other hand. The hand shifted from being clawlike to featherlike; it swept out from the body, then clenched into a fist; it hovered, then soared or plunged. Sometimes arms and hands burrowed into the belly or breasts, as if digging out a recalcitrant strength. Wigman also made unusually expressive use of the head, especially the eyes. She frequently danced with her eyes closed or half-closed, then opened them suddenly, briefly, in a deep stare generally cast to her right or left (rather than forward) and away from the direction in which she moved, as if the moving body were drawn to what it could not see rather than to what it did. Wigman (1929): "The dancer's glance is a visionary gazing. . . . The eye is the focal point of the dance event" ("Der Tänzer," 12–13). She liked having the head at an odd tilt, with the chin up, not vertically perpendicular to the ground, as in ballet.

She did not neglect the feet and legs. She loved slow arcing, gliding steps, which she might integrate with slow march steps on tiptoes while the rest of the body remained statuesquely poised. Nearly always barefoot, the dancer very often signified both caution and boldness by having one foot solidly planted on the sole and the other on tiptoe, moving in this fashion by shifting the solid foot to the tiptoe position with each step. Wigman was fond of having the dancer advance toward the spectator in small steps, on tiptoe usually, with each step directly in front of the previous and with the body dipping on the step. She liked to bend and coil the body and seems to have appreciated curvature as much as angularity, but she avoided the balletic tendency to straighten out or elongate the body. Her dancers shifted abruptly from small, stalking steps to lunging strides and glides. Wigman also made dramatic use of sways, teeters, and tremblings, especially in relation to rhythms of inhalation and exhalation. Although she tended to favor slow, groping, or sometimes languid tempos, the dancer constantly surprised the spectator by shifting rhythms within movements, so that even the steadiest configuration of movement contained within it unexpected discharges of energy. Wigman was a master of stillness and the pause. In the first part of *Hexentanz II* (1926), for example, the dancer crouches on the floor, head sunk between her knees, in stillness; suddenly an arm shoots straight up, then down; the head rears up and stares, immobile; then the whole body rocks from side to side before the head sinks again between the knees—pause!—then one foot stamps, then the other; then in a great, cyclonic whirl, the dancer spins around stamping and stops. Movement was unstable, unpredictable, as if the body coiled within it circulating springs of "convulsion," as some commentators put it. Death manifested itself partly through degrees of stillness, languor, gravitational pull, inclination to the ground.

Wigman believed that dance must free itself from music to establish its unique expressive power. Her first full-length concert of dances, in 1914, contained no musical accompaniment at all, and she produced several other unaccompanied dance cycles, including *Ekstatische Tänze* and *Die Feier* (1921). Thereafter she integrated silent dances into larger structures involving accompaniments. Like many other dancers of the era, Wigman preferred an orchestra of percussion instruments—drums, gongs, and cymbals, usually handled by a single player—and all the sound composed specifically for her dances until 1939 was written for percussion instruments by Klaus Pringsheim, Willi Goetze, and Hanns Hasting, the last two being her resident music directors from, respectively, 1923 to 1929 and 1929 to 1939. By employing percussive sound, Wigman stripped music of its power to destroy or weaken visual perception of movement and at the same time showed the authority of movement to provoke emphatic auditory response to it, for the percussion followed the dancer rather than the other way around. She did produce some dances to conventional romantic music (Bizet, Granados, Dvorak, Saint-Säens, and especially Liszt), but modernist developments in music apparently had little impact on her perception of either the body or movement.

In costumes, she persistently displayed a taste for archaism and exoticism. She swathed herself in flowing capes, mantels, and shawls; she delighted in bizarre hats and headpieces, austere hoods and cowls. She mostly performed in long dresses of shiny gold or a strong monotonic color, but she seldom appeared in black (the "Schicksalslied" section of *Tanzgesänge* [1935] and *Niobe* [1942] are interesting exceptions), and she seemed much more hesitant to bare her legs than her arms, although her legs were quite as beautiful. She liked occasionally to appear in silky, luxuriously patterned Oriental gowns for grotesque-macabre pieces (*Hexentanz II*) or more melancholy works (*Szenen aus einem Tanzdrama* [1924], *Tanz der Brunhild* [1942]). In *Tanzmärchen* (1925) she experimented with a bizarre intermingling of clownlike, or *zanni*, costumes: extravagantly exaggerated skirts, gold wigs, and romantic dresses. Eerie masks appeared on dancers in *Totentanz* (1926), *Hexentanz II,* and *Totenmal,* for these were instances, she explained, when the "formal transformation of the dancer demands of the dancer an effacement of the personal in favor of the typical and the intensification of the typical to the superpersonal" (HM 131). In *Totenmal,* Wigman was the only figure to appear without a mask; all the other dancers, large male and female speech-movement choirs, wore, as in *Totentanz,* masks bearing practically the same ominous expression. All the costumes for her dances strongly evoked a medieval or biblical atmosphere, and she never employed costumes that clearly situated the dance within the present. Yet images of her dances always seem modern, for it was the movement, the positioning of bodies, that placed the image within the context of modernism. With the body veiled in archaic costumes, its movement became more visible but also more abstract; and, of course, abstraction was the most pervasive sign of modernity (Figures 29–31).

Wigman introduced further abstraction into the structure of her dances. She did not produce a program of discrete dances designed to show the diversity of her technique and expressiveness; she produced cycles of dances that explored in depth a particular emotional state, metaphor, or allegorical vision. Thus, *Ekstatische Tänze* was a cycle of six dances: "The Nun," "The Madonna," "Idolatry," "Sacrifice," "The Dervish," and "Temple Dance." *Die sieben Tänze des Lebens* contained dances of "Longing," "Love," "Desire," "Sorrow," "The Demon," "Death," and "Life," whereas *Szenen aus einem Tanzdrama* entailed "Summoning," "Wandering," "Circle," "Triangle," "Chaos," "Change," "Vision," "Encounter," and "Greeting." *Opfer* (1931) comprised "Swordsong," "Sun Dance," "Death Call," "Earth Dance," and "Lamentation." In *Die sieben Tänze des Lebens,* she impersonated a single character who moved expressionistically through different phases of life, but in other cycles she incarnated a powerful feminine spirit that resisted confinement within the notion of "character." One may say that these incarnations were simply different, archetypal aspects of her personality—but the perception remains that she built narrative unity out of formal abstractions of emotions rather than out of psychologically motivated logic. Her narrative sense was more musical than literary; emotions generated distinct movements and actions, regardless of their context in a particular character or body. Dance cycles therefore became structured around dramatic contrasts between light and dark dances, between quick and slow, grotesque and monumental, cool and warm, lyrical and geometric, and various combinations therein. By exposing abstract relations between mood and movement and by freeing the body from the conventions of characterization, Wigman helped push dance into the realm of montage sequencing of action, which defined much of modernist film and literature of the 1920s. She was by no means alone among dancers in pursuing this strategy.

In her group dances, she applied on a larger scale the devices with which she had expanded the expressivity of the dancing body. Her perception of group and community was more complex than Laban's, for although she liked to press bodies together in polyrhythmic, tangled clumps, as he did, she was much more imaginative in developing dynamic spaces *between* bodies. She allowed the group to cover a larger portion of the performing space, and she displayed a strong sense of the group's spreading out, encircling, and converging on the solo dancer (inevitably Wigman herself): she saw communal movement as a dynamic force that explodes and implodes around the magnetic ambitions of a leader. As Manning has repeatedly · observed, Wigman revealed considerable ambivalence about the relation between group and leader. Dancers often disclosed greater individuality or expressivity within the group than when they briefly stepped outside of it for a solo, a suggestion of tension between individual and community. Yet the leader rarely came out of the group, was always identifiable within it, and was never seriously challenged or confused with anyone else for the role. In *Frauentänze* (1934) and *Tanzgesänge* (1935), Wigman made elegant, monumental use of abstract geometric group symmetry, with spacious, cinemascopic choir movements built around uniform gestures of prayer, invocation, imploration, and offering. But in some of her group dances, perhaps especially *Im Zeichen des Dunklen* (1927), the dancers seemed unaware of each other, were wrapped up within themselves, moving to different rhythms, gazing in different directions or even keeping their eyes closed, yet they remained within a group insofar as they followed the leader.

Although Harald Kreutzberg and Max Terpis studied briefly under Wigman (and she had several other male students), all of her performing groups contained only female dancers. Only after the war, when she began working with opera companies, did she really start thinking about the male dancer, most notably in *The Rite of Spring* (1957). Apparently she experienced some sort of intense anxiety toward the male body; in any case, she felt no inclination to explore the expressivity peculiar to it. In *Tanzmärchen*, women impersonated explicitly male figures, and in *Totenmal,* which memorialized soldiers killed in the war, the members of the male choir were all zombielike figures of the dead, and the only male dancer, masked, was Death.

As a teacher, Wigman exerted tremendous influence in the classroom. But she was not much of a theorist, and her authority outside of the classroom depended on her success in dance performance. Her great appeal for students lay in her promise to maximize the individuality of the student through dance: "The longing for self-expression so characteristic of our age is driving today's girls to seek satisfaction through dancing" (MWB 104). However, this attitude had significant limitations. Her first, and possibly best, ensemble broke up in 1924 because Berthe Trümpy, Yvonne Georgi, and Gret Palucca had developed such strong personalities that they had to leave in quite separate directions to fulfill their ambitions. Moreover, the improvisational "technique" Wigman used to accommodate diversity of personalities was difficult to transfer outside of the cultic atmosphere in the Dresden studio, with its gold and red walls and with Wigman, swathed in luxurious gowns, veiled in cigarette smoke, gazing with hawklike intensity and presiding on a throne in the corner as a mysterious priestess. Trümpy's effort to establish a Wigmanesque pedagogy in Berlin encouraged Rudolf Lämmel to compare the discipline and accomplishments of her faculty and students unfavorably with those of the Estas school in Cologne.

Occasionally Wigman published brief articles in dance journals. In these pieces her language remained consistently metaphorical and polemical rather than analytical. Her views on dance composition (1925) and dance curriculum (*Deutsche Tanzkunst* [1935]) were even cloudier than Laban's at their most cryptic: "Whether the dancer moves as a soloist in his own creations, or plays his instrument in the orchestra of moving bodies, he always is, above all, servant to a work of art. This is the only and eternal law under which the dancer lives his entire life" (MWB 129). Yet language, both written and spoken, was very important to her in creating her dances and her cult. She wrote out scenarios for her dances and incorporated into the manuscripts sketches, marginal comments, and cryptic movement notations, sometimes employing different colored inks and pencils. She was fond of drawing pictures that included words in the imagery; for example, a sketch she did of New York City in 1931 consisted entirely, in collage fashion, of words from signs she saw in the streets of the city (HM 173–175). She kept extensive diaries and was definitely at her best when she wrote autobiographically, when she connected attitudes toward dance to specific events in her life. Apparently she "saw" the dances and dance cult she created through a process of inscription. The image of language gave her the image of movement (KT). In rehearsal and in the classroom, she was not content to watch and comment nor even to interpret the performance by her commentary; she liked to talk to the dancers while they danced, telling them, in highly metaphorical language, not what movements to make but what feelings they should release, what effects they should produce. The urge to speak compelled her to enter the dance, but she would shout out isolated words and phrases rather than complex or even complete sentences (film documentation in Snyder). But even though her own language to explain the meaning or theory of dance remained enshrouded "in the sign of darkness," so to speak, never reaching much beyond stern and somber exhortation, she differed strongly from her teacher, Laban, in supposing that the real "language of dance" was not an elaborate system operating independently of dancers or dances but a physicalization, a supreme materialization or extension of language as the controlling phenomenon constructing difference, identity, personality. But the key to her system was not her attitude toward language; it was the idea that the student does not ultimately succeed until she confidently differs from her teacher.

LOHELAND

Laban and Wigman represented the most dramatic and politicized antipodes regarding the conditions for establishing the value and modernity of *Ausdruckstanz*. But Wigman obviously understood that although dance performances may determine the value of dance, they hardly established a life in dance. Dance performances increasingly depended more on schools than on audiences, and by 1925 being a modern dancer pervasively entailed teaching dance. Before 1925 a rather large number of dancers pursued entirely artistic careers on the stage, but by the middle of the decade very few enjoyed such an exclusive focus of their energies. The economics of performance discouraged full-time dancing careers. The German "dance frenzy" actually signified a situation in which the supply of dancers quickly exceeded the demand for dance performance. As Laban realized, audiences for dance performance, as for opera, would expand only through a large-scale process of education and theoretical indoctrination in which masses of people learned to appreciate dance without feeling the desire to do it. However, the education of audiences occurred much more slowly than the education of dancers, not so much because of weak critical institutions within cultural media but because educational institutions, including dance schools, stressed participation in dance rather than serious analytic discourse on the meaning of it all. Dancers relied excessively on a mystical rhetoric to explain themselves—ecstatic appeals to good health, national revitalization, or cultured idealism—which, frankly, even quite mediocre performers could appropriate. When the "voice" of dance begins to sound everywhere the same, audiences become distrustful and apply ever greater pressure on dancers to supersede all thresholds of expectation—but

fewer and fewer can muster the imagination to meet these rising expectations. Thus, the desire to dance continues to grow, but the desire to watch
dance remains static.

Both Laban and Wigman intuitively grasped that language constituted
the mysterious core of a deeper understanding of dance, but they themselves lacked the language to unravel it. It was easier to recruit students,
whose understanding of dance was intuitive rather than theoretical, than
viewers, who depended on a complex aesthetic rationale to sustain their
interest. Schools flourished everywhere. Berlin alone had 151 dance
schools in 1929 (Freund 83–84), and by 1933 Germany had 5,122 professional dancers, over 30 percent of whom lived in Berlin (MS 33). But the
number of dance performances scarcely matched the number of schools.
To expand enrollments, dance schools formed closer alliances with gymnastics, but a practical result of this strategy was that by the late 1920s
dancers began to look more and more alike: gymnastics had the effect of
conventionalizing the image of dance, freedom, modernity, ecstasy. The
strangest, most expressionistic, and most experimental period of German
modern dance came between 1918 and 1925; the decade between 1925
and 1935 was hardly dull, but a greater sense of disappointment seemed to
afflict it. By 1929 the market for schools had obviously reached the satura-
tion point, and the following year, when another severe economic crisis
began to grip the nation, modern dance culture launched a determined
campaign to gain control of the subsidized opera ballet companies throughout the land, with the schools suddenly embracing ballet technique (HK
30–32). However, it is not clear whether other strategies would have yielded
greater success, partly because the dominant objective of dance was not
sharply in focus. Was it to produce serious works of art or to signify a new,
redemptive mode of living? These objectives were incompatible, for one
cannot produce serious art without taking risks that are often painful and
unhealthy. Moreover, the dance world lacked the knowledge—the science,
one might say—to identify the difference between the desire to dance and
the desire to see dance.

The Loheland school in Fulda presented a curious example of the anti-
art, dance-as-life cult. Hedwig von Rohden and Louise Langgaard founded
the school in 1912. In 1910 they were students in Berlin of the mysterious Hedwig Kallmeyer, herself a student of the Delsarte technique taught
by the American Genevieve Stebbins. Rohden-Langgaard, as they were
known, also incorporated Mensendieck ideas into their school, whose students were exclusively female. Loheland integrated gymnastic dance into
a craft-centered, cultic lifestyle: daily performance of aesthetic bodily
movement was part of a peculiar moral education that included garden-
ing, physical labor, pottery, weaving, cooking, nudism, drawing, singing,
agricultural activity, and household management. In the early 1920s,

Rohden-Langgaard began to introduce the anthroposophical ideas of Rudolf Steiner. Hans Brandenburg remarked that both faculty and students conveyed an "image of cloistered austerity and purity" (HB 135), and Fritz Giese observed a pronounced "anti-masculinist" attitude (FGK 115) (Figure 32). *Gymnastik* (3/5–6, 1928, 15–21) published a letter from a Loheland student, Ita Röst, who concluded, "Today I know I see the beginning of the path which earlier had led us to the construction of a high and powerful culture. 'Movement' is the first step on this path" (21).

But the study of bodily movement did not lead to an art of bodily performance. The Loheland milieu distrusted the cosmopolitan artificiality of theatre, distanced itself from all professionalism, and denied that serious dance could have anything to do with the expression of eroticism. Few of the Loheland students made dance a vocation (Niddy Impekoven was a major exception), and none of them assumed that dance was rich evidence of a unique personality. Right after the war, Loheland had a small ensemble of dancers, no more than four or five girls, which put on such things as the "silver cult play" *Omnia ad majorem Dei gloriam* (1920). But by 1924 the school refused to produce anything for the public, although lovely photographs of unnamed Loheland women, some nude, continued to appear in books and journals. Eva-Maria Deinhardt, Bertha Buschor, Emmi Heiner, and Edith Sutor attracted some individual attention in 1921. With *Ariel* and *Legende,* the sleek and supple Deinhardt moved as if her arms were feathers or branches in the breeze, her whole body a glowing "transparent ornament"; Sutor, in *Farben* and *Urasima,* preferred broad wavy movements, muscular turns, Amazonic glides, and undulations on bent knees; Buschor, in a shiny, satiny, dark pajamalike costume, did something called *Strömungen* using quick, convulsive movements; and Heiner "loved fast round curves" (HFT 106; HB 136). These women soon faded into oblivion, but Loheland continued to prosper as a pious, nature-worshipping community.

In 1928, Rohden-Langgaard published *Gymnastik, Sport, Schauspiel,* which outlined the Loheland principles of bodily movement. Five core modes of action governed the body as an expressive sign: running, leaping, encircling, ball-tossing, and spear-throwing. Liberating and ecstatic experience emerged out of variations on these modes. Deinhardt (*Gymnastik,* 3/5–6, 1928, 7–12), citing Novalis, asserted that "music sets everything in movement," but Loheland maintained a strict attitude toward the relation between dance and music: absolutely no percussion sounds and (contradicting Dalcroze) no emphatic submission of the body to the rhythm of the music—melody, not the beat, moved the body. Mozart therefore made the best dance music. Yet in spite of the reactionary atmosphere of this school, Rohden-Langgaard's book contained images of startling modernity. These were highly abstract diagrams of movement possibilities issuing from the five core actions. The authors used colored pencils to describe the trajectories of the movements in a manner that exceeded the level of abstraction in Hedwig Hagemann's diagrams; nor were these drawings at all cluttered, as were Laban's sketches. The text hardly explained the diagrams, but they nevertheless gave a powerful image of movement itself (not the body), with emotional values of movement encoded through the color of the pencil, degree of shading, and thickness or intensity of line. What dance "left behind," so to speak, was not a more vivid image of the body but a starkly wild (though human) geometric abstraction, a kind of strange, bold writing in space.

HELLERAU-LAXENBURG

Although the influence of Dalcrozian rhythmic gymnastics waned considerably during the war, disciples of the Swiss educator did not disappear entirely. In 1915 the building complex at Hellerau came under the management of Christine Baer-Frissell, Ernest Ferand, and Valeria Kratina, advocates of the Dalcrozian approach. But Mensendieck ideas also entered the curriculum insofar as the school assumed a significant difference between male and female anatomies, which motivated the need for a completely feminine gymnastics. All students at the school were female. The atmosphere was free of the mysticism that pervaded so many other schools, which was not surprising, considering how carefully Dalcroze had planted his method in Gallic rationalism. Hellerau sought to free the female body without exhausting or depleting it. The school therefore condemned gymnastic acrobatics, dance virtuosity, and a focus on the perfection of movement: the female body possessed a different strength than did the male, and one measured it not by feats of acrobatic prowess but by an ability to move truthfully, confidently, and with adroit intelligence. To achieve this objective, Hellerau teachers had to modify Dalcroze's system to accommodate greater improvisation and greater independence between bodily and musical rhythms. Nevertheless, improvisation at Hellerau was a far stricter matter than with Laban or Wigman.

In 1990, Ilse Losch, a former student, published several examples of Hellerau "improvisations" (31–50), and these show the extent to which music controlled movement and movement unfolded according to an ideal of precision (though not one of "fatiguing" complexity). With the upbeat of a quiet piece of music in 4/4 time, the right leg rises a little, bending slightly at the knee. On the first beat of the bar, the left leg bends somewhat while the right foot, with gentle, intensifying pressure, touches the floor on tiptoe, then sinks onto the full sole, with the right knee bending lightly. On the second beat the left leg stretches to the knee while the right leg curls upward. On the third beat the right leg performs the gesture as in the first beat but more heavily, with the knee bending lightly. On the final beat the left leg copies what the right leg initiated on the upbeat while the right leg stretches easily to the knee. The second measure of the music repeats these movements on the left leg, but the dancer never moves from the initial standing position (35). Each measure—indeed, each beat—introduces a new variation. Other exercises mobilize the arms, hands, and other parts of the body, shift rhythms (such as 3/4 to 5/8 to 2/4), and incorporate group interactions between bodies, but Dalcroze's obsession with synchronizing movement with the beat remains firmly in place.

Movement in this context was precise without being fatiguing, complex without being oppressively intimidating (for the performer). What made dance fatiguing was not increasingly complex synchronization of movement with the musical rhythm but movement that unfolded against the beat, the body in dialogue with the music rather than in harmony with it. As mentioned previously, this failure to acknowledge tensions between bodily and musical rhythms was a great weakness of the Dalcrozian system and hampered it from producing dances that went beyond the expression of a bright, sunny joy. The system did not establish any serious emotional connection between music and movement and made it all too easy for a mechanical sterility to dominate the exploration of bodily expressivity. But the detailed pedagogy, the exactness of the lesson plans, and the precisely measurable accomplishments offered by the exercises were quite appealing to some students, especially those planning to become teachers. In 1934, Hellerau-Laxenburg even gave courses in Paris at Studio Corposano under the guidance of a Finn, Maian Pontan, who had directed courses in Vienna, Berlin (at Diem's school), and Stockholm (AI 16–17). In 1925 the Hellerau school accepted the invitation of the city of Vienna to relocate to Laxenburg Castle, which was its home until 1938, when the Nazis annexed Austria. Between 1921 and 1924 the outstanding Czech choreographer Jarmilla Kröschlova, who had studied under Dalcroze in Geneva, taught at Hellerau before returning to Prague, where her career blossomed. The connection to Prague eventually proved significant for the fate of the Dalcroze system. In 1921 another Czech, from Brno, Rosalia Chladek (b. 1905), studied under Kröschlova and became so successful as a dancer, choreographer, and teacher (Basel) that in 1930 Hellerau-Laxenburg appointed her to manage the dance activities of the school, which she did until 1938.

Under Valeria Kratina, the Hellerau performance group had attracted international interest for its German premieres, in 1923, of Bartók's *The Wooden Prince* (1916) and Milhaud's *L'Homme et son desir* (1921) and, more important, for its open-air productions (the genre so loved by Dalcroze) in ancient Sicilian ruins in 1925, 1926, and 1927. Chladek continued this tradition by choreographing open-air productions at the Greek Theatre in Syracuse of Euripides' *Iphigenia in Aulis* (1933) and Sophocles' *Oedipus at Colonus* (1936) and *Ajax* (1939). Her enthusiasm for themes of classical antiquity extended to her solo choreography for herself in *Mythologischen Suite* (1936), with its separate sections devoted to Narcissus, Daphne, Pythia, Penthesilea, and Agave; to her opera choreography for Glück's *Orfeus und Euridyke* (1940); and to the dance suite *Apollon und die Amazone* (1940). Like Kratina, Chladek displayed a very international taste in subject matter and music, working as comfortably with modern music (Stravinsky, Malipiero, Medtner) as with Handel or Dvořák. As a soloist, she traveled widely throughout Europe and as far as Indonesia in 1939. Indeed, a peculiarity of the Hellerau-Laxenburg school was its cultivation of dance as a sign of both internationality and modernity. Probably no other dancer after 1930 received as many offers to appear outside her homeland (both Germany and Austria) as Rosalia Chladek, but she did not have strong appeal for German audiences, even before the Nazi takeover. Wherever it operated in Europe, the Dalcroze system appeared as a *foreign* doctrine, and (like Dalcroze himself) one became a successful product of the doctrine by accepting the identity of a stranger to it and, quite often, to one's audiences. Certainly this was the case with Chladek, coming as she did from Czechoslovakia.

But as director of dance activities at Laxenburg, she succeeded in opening up the doctrine to the more expressive and improvisational features of "the free dance," as she firmly preferred to call *Ausdruckstanz* (Welziel 19, 22; Klingenbeck 15–16). And she brought male students into the lay course in Vienna. In 1931 she choreographed a large-scale, open-air dance spectacle for the Vienna *Festwoche* in the Rathausplatz, performed before 15,000 spectators. Twenty-five women, ten "youths" (performed by female students), and five men danced to the music of Bizet's *L'Arlesienne Suites* (1872), yet the effect was neither Gallic nor Teutonic nor even socialistic but peculiarly "European." The male dancers, clad in rust-brown tunics, wielded long staffs; the female group, in flowing orange gowns, carried gold shields; and the youths wore red tunics. Chladek made dramatic use of the huge space: the three groups developed a monumental counterpoint on different planes and at great distances from each other, then converged, employing vigorous swinging, rotating, or lunging movements—movement-counter-movement in parallel lines, canon-countercanon, diagonal-counterdiagonal, round-counterround, concentric circles coiling centripedally, concentric circles spreading centrifugally. In the adagio section, the women sat in a half-circle and danced entirely with their upper bodies, moving the shields in "lyrical," undulating fashion so that the sunlight flashed off them; meanwhile the men, deep in the background, made hoeing, threshing movements with the staffs. In the carillon section, the youths usurped shields from the women while the men advanced employing scything movements. Then the soloist (Chladek herself) appeared, in a red and gold cloak, and her swirling dance brought all the groups together into a great whirlpool of "dionysiac-ecstatic vibration," concluding what Ferand suggested "not unfairly could bear the name of 'Eleusinian Festival'"(Alexander 49–51). Yet the piece was actually an elaborate application of the same principle governing the two-bar exercise described above—left leg–right leg; movement-countermovement; diagonal-antidiagonal; clockwise circle within counterclockwise circle; male group–female group—with all movements exactly synchronized with all dynamics of the music (accelerando, crescendo, ostinato, and so forth). The realization of a unified, ecstatic community that transcended divisive pressures of sexual difference depended on large-scale deployment of the symmetricality-synchronicity principle introduced in the rudimentary exercise.

During the 1930s Chladek devoted much of her time to performing solo dances. In these she displayed her preference not only for stark, monumental movement but also for abstract theatrical props such as a staff, a great disk, a hoop, or a cape, as well as glamorous period costumes and archaic garments (*Tanz mit Stab* [1930]; *Jeanne d'Arc* [1934]). Her body was powerfully muscled, like an athlete's, and she sought bold gestures that heightened its muscularity (*Penthesilea*); but she contrasted this quality with a flowing, exaggerated femininity, as in *Die Kamelliendame* (1938), in which she swooned and soared in a luxurious white romantic dress. Unlike Wigman, Chladek enjoyed displaying her powerful legs and introducing mysteriously androgynous touches (*Narcissus; Luzifer* [1938]; *Michael* [1938]). After World War II, she continued busily on the international dance scene, receiving commissions, honors, appointments, and students well into the 1990s. "Strength is the source of movement," she remarked in 1935 (Alexander 95). But Dalcroze himself worked from almost the reverse perspective, that movement is the source of strength. Thus, although Chladek showed the power of the Dalcroze system to produce a compelling artist, she was not quite as faithful to her teacher as were the great majority of his disciples, whose mission was to strengthen ordinary bodies easily fatigued by the rhythms of the modern world.

After World War I, Dalcroze disciples worked primarily in the public school system, where they often faced difficulties no less great than those afflicting dance artists. The Dalcroze Bund constantly struggled against bureaucratic inertia and the pervasive assumption that rhythmic gymnastics was not as practical as the study of the arts and sciences. An important figure in the rhythmic gymnastics movement, Elfriede Feudel (1881–1966), studied under Dalcroze at Hellerau and taught at the Dortmund Conservatory from 1927–1935 (Peter-Fuhr 26–27). Her *Rhythmik: Theorie und Praxis der körperlich-musikalischen Erziehung* (1926) was an impressive collection of essays that coolly addressed the chief criticisms and misperceptions of rhythmic gymnastics, put Dalcroze's method into a historical perspective, clarified its aims, differentiated it from other approaches to bodily education, and provided (as usual) detailed examples of "lead and follow"–type exercises. She denied that, because it did not wallow in the undisciplined, irrational pathos of *Ausdruckstanz*, rhythmic gymnastics was too intellectual; more surprising, she criticized the Mensendieck system for being antierotic (62), and Hedwig Nottebohm attacked arch-rival Rudolf Bode for promoting an idea of rhythm that was hopelessly vague (140). This shift from a defensive to an offensive position somewhat strengthened rhythmic gymnastics in Germany. A school opened in 1910 by Otto Blensdorf (1871–1947) in Elberfeldt (Wuppertal) and later moved to Jena (1928) reemerged as a prominent center for rhythmic gymnastic teaching when Blensdorf's daughter Charlotte (already a lecturer at the Conservatory in Mälmo, Sweden) received an appointment from the university to provide instruction in Dalcrozian thinking (Alexander). Students from this school, as well as from Hellerau-Laxenburg and a school in Essen run by Dalcroze student Dore Jacobs (1894–1979), revitalized hope for making rhythmic gymnastics the basis for a national program of physical education. The Nazis, however, were hostile to rhythmic gymnastics, which furthermore attracted many Jewish women, and they put their faith in Bode's program.

The political ramifications of the Dalcroze system become more apparent if we look at the situation of rhythmic gymnastics in Czechoslovakia. Kröschlova had returned to Prague in 1924 because she realized that rhythmic gymnastics "did not lead to dance expression" (EST 135), but the innovative dance work she did in her native city nevertheless seemed to validate the attitude toward the body implanted in her by Dalcroze. Another student of Dalcroze, Anna Dubska, had managed a popular school for rhythmic gymnastics since 1912, and through her the notion emerged persuasively that the Dalcroze system demonstrated its credibility not through beautiful dances but through behavioral changes in individuals. In 1913 the powerful Sokol (Falcon) Organization of physical educators and bureaucrats, which had close ties to the labor movement, began to absorb Dalcrozian ideas into a large-scale plan to create a strong body culture in Czechoslovakia. Under the leadership of Hanna Burgerova-Dubova, Sokol's physical education program expanded ambitiously, propelled by Dalcrozian objectives but also by the ideas of people such as Klages, Bücher, Bode, Mensendieck, and Duncan, as well as native Czechs such as Karel Pospisel and Augustin Ocenasek (EST 142–144; Sokol 33–38). The Sokol body culture program did not define itself entirely in terms of a response to internal, uniquely national pressures, as was the habit in Germany; it treated body culture as an international network of ideas that produced an embodiment of power and identity.

In 1929 Sokol collaborated with the Czech government to produce an immense book, *Základy rytmického telocviku sokolského*, which presented an official, state-sanctioned method for the rhythmic gymnastic education of girls and young women. The book was designed more for (public school) teachers than for students. Professor Karel Weigner announced that men and women have quite different bodily constitutions that respond to different principles of rhythm: "[M]en tend toward a katabolic principle of courage, inventiveness, and change; women tend toward an anabolic principle of conservatism, continuity, and patience, with the most difficult and noble goal of maternity" (vii). But in spite of this somewhat limited view of sexual difference and the fact that all the authors were men, the book was an amazing and certainly luxurious production, testifying to a spectacularly deep concern with how to manage the modern female body. After several chapters of scholarly, pretty solid theoretical-historical overview, the book presented a vast treatise on rhythmic gymnastic practice, replete with more than four hundred exercises, each one described in detail regarding musical rhythm, bodily movement, and function through the use of stick figures, drawings, musical notations, and more abstract diagrams, charts, and tables (Figure 33). The book also contained some wonderful photographs of exercising students, open-air games, and theatrical dance productions and even had a kind of appendix of advertisements for Prague businesses. No German publication on bodily movement was ever as systematic, comprehensive, detailed, and precise as the *Základy*; no German ideology, not even Laban's *Kinetographie*, showed so clearly the extraordinary range of possible human movements.

Of course, the book suffered from the usual objection to rhythmic gymnastics: it did not explain the emotional or expressive significance of all these movements. Instructors assumed that every exercise was valuable because it led to a healthier body, regardless of whether it was aesthetically interesting. But Germans (and not only Germans) strongly resisted this sort of lucid, systematic view of bodily education, partly because the state believed it was too politically risky to identify itself decisively with a particular concept of body culture and partly because Germans tended to believe that the expressive and liberating power of the body remained enshrouded in irrationality, well beyond the control of measurable, external musical rhythms. The Germans had grasped that a healthy body was not necessarily synonymous with an ecstatic body, and that led to greater darkness in the world of German body culture and to a far more complex dance culture than existed elsewhere. The Czechs liked formalistic analyses of aesthetic phenomena because they tended to believe that formalistic "objectivity" was the key to resolving political conflicts. This perspective favored the development in the 1930s of the great Prague structuralism school of literary and theatrical semiotics guided by such figures as Otakar Zich, Jan Mukarovsky, and Jindrich Honzl and exemplified further in the wide-ranging critical commentaries of Karel Teige (1900–1951) and in Irena Lexova's enchanting semiotics of *Ancient Egyptian*

Dances (1935).[1] In Germany, however, formalism emerged as a source of political conflict because of its innate power to estrange or render foreign even the most familiar significations.

Yet Germany was still the chief exporter of the Dalcroze model, even after it almost ceased to exist in Germany in the 1930s, because so many foreign students had studied there. An excellent example is the Finnish dancer Bertta Reiho, who published *Rytmillinen likünta* (1948), a textbook with numerous stunning photographs, for teachers of female rhythmic gymnastics. Though not nearly as ambitious as the *Základy*, it was nevertheless a beautiful elucidation of the Dalcroze technique—though, not surprisingly, it did not mention either him or a German context. But in the 1930s Reiho was a student of the Finnish expressionist dancer Maggie Gripenberg, who had studied under Dalcroze around 1911 (Hällström 200).

RUDOLF BODE

By the end of World War I, Dalcroze's definition of rhythm appeared too narrow and mathematical to satisfy the German appetite for a more radical, ecstatic, and transformative definition of rhythm that yielded a distinctly "German" expression of modernity. But a German definition of rhythm was not the same thing as a German way of moving the body, nor was it to be identified with some peculiarly German physiognomy. Germanness revealed itself in the origin and formation of the definition, not in the bodies that applied or appropriated the definition. In an interesting article for *Der Leib* (2/2, January 1921, 34–53), Fritz Klatt proposed general categories of creative rhythms associated with the body rather than with music, machines, or dance. Blood pulse and heartbeat constituted the primal sources of rhythm: "Everything called love, knowledge, death, everything which reflects the individuality of the individual human, everything that creates unities and eventually demands the sacrifice of the self, has its sensually traceable basis, its reality, in the depths of the human-bonding bloodstream" (35–36). The breath pulse, however, connected bodily rhythm to the will, because the pace of breathing, the relation between inhalation and exhalation, between magnitudes and urgencies of breath, resulted from specific conditions of emotion and consciousness. The creative rhythm of the day evolved out of the microrhythms of blood and breath insofar as it conformed to a complex pattern of alternation between movement and pause, beat and rest. The rhythm of months and years, deadlines and holidays, seasons and ages was but a macrocosmic pulse resulting from the great

---

1. For more information about the captivating achievements of Czech body culture and aesthetic performance in the 1920s and 30s, see Burian, *O nové divadlo 1930–1940;* Obst and Scherl; Teige; Kröschlova 47–90; Vavra 17–27; Vodicka.

bonding power of the blood pulse. Of course, a Dalcrozian might contend that music itself was both the abstract and material revelation of drive rhythms ultimately originating in the heartbeat, but by detaching his argument from any discussion of music, Klatt implied that music did not make people more aware of the great unifying yet individuating power of the blood pulse. Active in the youth movement and in public school teaching, Klatt believed that instructors could create greater rhythmic awareness, at least among the young, by restructuring the rhythm of the school day and year, changing the durations of instructional periods, the relations between play and contemplation, the divisions between outdoor and indoor knowledge, and so forth (see *Die Tat*, 14/7, October 1922, 621–622).

An equally grandiose concept of rhythm came from Artur Jacobs (*Die Tat*, 14/9, December 1922, 641–664), who proposed that the formation of a redemptive proletarian culture depended on "renewal through rhythm." Much less precisely or concisely than Karl Bücher, Jacobs presented the conventional Marxist argument that "the great misery of the worker is not that he receives too little reward, that things go badly externally for him, but that he must live soullessly and without dignity, that he is merely a mechanical beast of labor, that he must produce in stultifying compulsion completely mechanical things, to which he has no connection and whose meaning he does not understand"—that, in short, the worker lived utterly alienated from a despiritualized (*entseelte*) world: "Our bodies are as strange to us as a still undiscovered land" (655). To renew the physical dignity of the modern worker, it was necessary to perceive in eroticism the great source of love for materials and forms, which together produced a culture that bestowed a more authentic value on labor. By eroticism, Jacobs did not mean anything connected to sexual drives; "on the contrary," he meant more general actions of release, giving, expenditure, and self-offering (653). A new notion of bodily rhythm was essential in cultivating the primal strength (*Ur-Kraft*) of Eros. Jacobs acknowledged that rhythm was an image of time but contended that its form was infinite and beyond empirical measurement, for painting, architecture, theatre, and poetry possessed as much rhythm as music or dance did: "Rhythm stands over nature the way reason stands over nature" (662). He regarded rhythm as a deeply irrational phenomenon, for it did not function according to any logic of causality: erotic rhythm was an end in itself. However, the renewal of the worker through a new concept of bodily rhythm was not exactly synonymous with greater participation in games, sports, athletics, gymnastics, or dance, for these refined the mechanization of life without overcoming it (656). But in spite of his appeal to restore the authority of forms, Jacobs himself did not provide a concrete image of the proletarian body culture other than to echo Klatt in proposing, vaguely, a "complete transformation of the entire contemporary school life" (663). He simply announced the need for a "Copernican turn" in education. With this metaphor, the implication emerged, albeit cryptically, that the rhythm of Eros remained inarticulately embedded in the form of revolution as simultaneously a physical and a historical phenomenon.

In the next issue of *Die Tat* (14/10, January 1923, 755–764), Wilhelm Hagen provided a much clearer image of the definitions of rhythm proposed by Klatt and Jacobs. He supposed that the answer to the question of what is the best school for gymnastics depended on the relation between rhythm and bodily education. He denied that rhythm referred to patterns of repetition, regularity, or automaticity. The study of music theory revealed that the source of rhythm was movement, not the other way around. Thus, the study of bodily movement depended not on musical rhythms but on motives for action, relations between will and object. Rhythm referred to dynamic structural relations between being and becoming. However, Hagen contended that men and women experience different essential rhythms and therefore require different modes of bodily education. He claimed that a woman feels she bears a weight, whereas a man feels he lifts a weight; the woman treats action as a state of being, whereas the man treats it as a state of becoming. Dance could well represent the female state but not the male, because for the male, will and object never merge to produce a state of being. For woman, "dance is always a transfiguration of being, not doing. . . . Man must find the bridge to sport. As a dancer he remains a neurotic" (764). The work of Rudolf Bode, Hagen declared, exhibited an attitude toward rhythm firmly grounded in the body and movement, not in music, although he expressed pronounced reservations about Bode's ability or willingness to maintain the principle of sexual difference in movement education.

Bode (1881–1971) was a student of Dalcroze at Hellerau in 1911–1912. By 1913, when he established his own school in Munich, Bode opposed the methods of his teacher and embarked on a pedagogy that developed bodily rhythms independently of music. In *Der Rhythmus und seine Bedeutung für die körperliche Erziehung* (1920), he introduced a "total" concept of rhythm similar to that of Klatt and Jacobs. A major influence was Klages, who asserted that excessive rationality or intellectual analysis was a source of "arhythm," or unnatural, strained, discordant, stifled movement. "In the rationalizing of instincts in our schools, colleges included, lies the final reason for the inner and outer breakdown of Germany" (RB 21). Bode's most popular work, *Ausdrucksgymnastik* (1925), enjoyed considerable appeal in its English translation of 1931. His school in Munich attracted many students, even though Bode had no ambition to produce dancers, athletes, performances, or anything understood as an artwork. For Hagen, Bode seemed to offer a "masculine" approach to movement education that did not rely on dance or dancelike deployments of the body to justify itself; however, the great majority of Bode's students were women. His anti-intellectualism made him susceptible to National Socialism, and during the

1920s he participated in party activities. In 1933 he became director of the Körperbildung und Tanz division of the Kampfbund für Deutsche Kultur and director of the gymnastic and dance section of the Reichsverband Deutscher Turn-, Sport- und Gymnastiklehrer im NS-Lehrerbund. In these capacities he attempted to undermine the rival Deutscher Chorsangerverband und Tanzerbund (established in 1909), which in 1933 was under the leadership of a socialist, the Hamburg ballet mistress Olga Brandt-Knack, a former student of Rudolf Laban. Bode regarded Laban as his most pernicious rival, but Goebbels, grasping Bode's limited understanding of dance, decided not to put the Tänzerbund under his control—instead, he changed its mission statement and replaced its administration (MS 116). By this time, though, Bode had firmly established the identity of a distinctly "German" notion of rhythm and bodily movement.

According to Bode, a "principle of totality" must govern perception of the body and its expressivity. He disapproved of Mensendieck-type efforts to analyze movement in relation to isolated parts of the body, and, of course, he denounced the Dalcroze system of synchronizing movement to musical rhythms. He also expressed skepticism concerning the use of gymnastic apparati such as parallel bars and weights, for these emphasized movement as a struggle against forces external to the body, whereas expression gymnastics was always a struggle of the body against forces internal to it. Bode did not want his method associated with sport competition; rather, the aim of expression gymnastics was to develop bodily movements derived from rhythms in nature, with the view of making the body expressive in the performance of everyday actions. However, a serious defect of Bode's theorizing lay in his failure to clarify what he meant by natural, or "organic," rhythms. Moreover, the gymnastic body offered "no expression of definite feelings like sorrow or joy, or patternlike forms for any feeling; all this is the task of a school of dramatics" (RB 46). What the body expressed entirely was a heightened, "ethical" sense of "vitality" and a triumphant struggle against the mental and mechanical "opposing powers inimical to life" (25). Bode built an exercise program around "natural" movements, "the simplest movements like walking, striding, swinging, pushing, or beating of the arms, bending of the body" (47). Yet nearly all the exercises in *Ausdrucksgymnastik* kept the body in a standing position: different parts of the body could move in swinging, flinging, beating, bending, raising, dropping, turning, rolling, pushing, or stretching motions without the body's going anywhere.

In spite of the book's focus on single bodies—a focus reinforced by photographs depicting solitary male and female models performing all of the eighty or so exercises—Bode earned respect for his skillful management of group exercises, and he obviously believed that the individual body developed its vitality more quickly through immersion in a controlled communal rhythm. But undated (ca. 1927) photographs by Gerhard Riebicke of student activities in Munich deposited in the Joan Erikson Archive of the Harvard Theatre Collection strongly suggest that Bode did not build group exercises around *interaction* between bodies. In this respect, his method differed significantly from so-called "Swedish gymnastics," especially the method of Nils Bukh, which stressed variations in movement within an exercising group and therefore required an individual body to maintain constant awareness of other bodies; the movement of each contributed uniquely to an overall group design that continually changed in relation to a controlling gymnastic objective (Figure 34). Swedish gymnastics was not dance, yet it did invest group exercises and communal rhythm with a strong subsidiary aesthetic effect. But Bode presumably felt that Swedish gymnastics was too rational for a German mass audience—it was exercise for an elite, upper-class, already alert community. Six of the Riebicke photographs show groups of women exercising in a park or on some sort of beach. But whether the group consists of three, six, or seven women, the bodies make the same synchronized movement. One photo shows eighteen women in Peter Pan–type costumes advancing toward the camera with arms upraised, bearing gongs, mallets, and drums; another depicts a round dance of six women surrounded by another round dance of twenty-four women, all being watched by a milling group of sixteen women, although it is not clear who the leader is.

Thus, regardless of group size, Bode apparently did not introduce any of the polyrhythmic convolutions that delighted Laban. Although he rejected the synchronization of movement with music advocated by his teacher, Dalcroze, Bode nevertheless linked the mysterious German concept of rhythm to the phenomenon of synchronicity. Synchronicity was a supreme sign of unity—with nature, with other bodies, with movements external to the body. But synchronicity is frequently a supreme sign of simplicity, and simplicity made Bode's teachings very appealing to people with simple ambitions. Though many of his students found a humble place in the German educational system, few achieved distinction within the world of body culture. In the 1920s this limitation was evident to serious commentators on movement education: "This gymnastic method follows a friendly middle path between extremes, between unleashing and strictness: but for that reason it can at best build a bridge to an acceptable practical art, never to a high art, which always demands something unconditional" (HFK 218).

DOROTHEE GÜNTHER

In the early 1920s, many people realized that competing theories of bodily movement were equally persuasive, even if they contradicted each other. Some students went from Hellerau to Laban or from Mensendieck to Hellerau or from a Wigman school to a Laban school. Dorothee Günther

(1896–1975) introduced a pedagogic approach that attempted to synthesize Mensendieck, Laban, and Hellerau. At first (1913–1916) she studied art in Dessau and Hamburg, and it was while drawing nude and "crooked" bodies in class that she felt compelled to learn about bodily movement (DG 220). She enrolled in a Mensendieck school, then studied the methods of Laban and Dalcroze. After completing her gymnastic teacher exam in 1919, she taught in Mensendieck schools in Berlin, Breslau, Hamburg, and Munich. In 1923 she settled in Munich, where she collaborated with composer Carl Orff (1895–1982) on the production of his Monteverdi opera adaptations, *Orfeus* and *Tanz der Spröden* (1923). The following year, the two of them established a school in Munich, with Orff as music director. It was here that Orff developed the famous "Schulwerk" method, still used around the world for enhancing children's receptivity to music.

Günther formed stronger creative collaborations with two of her students, Gunild Keetman (b. 1904) and Maja Lex (1906–1986). In 1930 she formed the Tanzgruppe Günther, for which she acted as a sort of executive producer, with Keetman composing all the music for Lex's choreography, which emerged from the joint theoretical perspective of Günther and Orff. Keetman was a protégé of Orff and worked closely with him in editing his Schulwerk publications (see Keetman). Nearly all of Lex's choreography before the war was produced in connection with the Tanzgruppe Günther, but she did direct the Munich premiere of Alois Haba's quarter-tone opera *Die Mutter* (1931). Meanwhile, Günther published articles in *Die Tat*, *Gymnastik*, and *Schrifttanz* and wrote two books, *Gymnastik Grundübungen in eigner Zeichenmethode* (1925) and *Einführung in der deutschen Mensendieckgymnastik* (1928). The *Gymnastik Grundübungen* linked the study of bodily movement to exercises in drawing the body; the *Einführung* modified the Mensendieck pedagogy to accommodate the Weimar cultural scene.

All students of Dorothee Günther were women. At the Munich Dance Congress of 1930, where Günther students performed in Wigman's *Totenmal*, the Tanzgruppe Günther achieved instant glory for Lex's *Barbarische Suite*. Until 1943 the dance group received plenty of offers to tour throughout Germany and several European countries, especially Italy, but Keetman, Lex, and Günther (who designed all the costumes) collaborated in a slow, methodical fashion and produced a rather small repertoire of pieces. These included *Miniaturen* (1931), *Klänge und Gesichte* (1934), *Paukentanz* (1935), and *Tänze aus dem 17. Jahrhundert* (1939). The Günther school merged with the Trümpy school in Berlin in 1933, when Trümpy's status as a Swiss citizen made her suspect as the operator of a state-subsidized business in the Third Reich. Since 1931 Günther had completely owned her own school, though she still received state subsidies. She collaborated with Lex on the immense girls' round dance for the 1936 Berlin Olympiad, a work that required 3,500 children and 2,500 girls. So acclaimed was this piece that Günther and Lex published a two-volume account of it the same year. In 1939 Günther choreographed in Berlin Stadium a gigantic waltz for 350 female dancers and musicians. During these years Lex gave numerous solo concerts, which apparently provoked widespread appreciation, aided, no doubt, by her—if I may put it so bluntly—almost overpowering beauty; but the dark, "non-Aryan" quality of her features prevented her from rising to any serious prominence within the Nazi dance culture (Abraham 42). The Nazis closed down the school in 1944 to use it as a military depot, and a bomb destroyed it in 1945.

In 1947 Günther and Lex moved to Rome to live in a villa owned by a former student, and Keetman went to Salzburg in 1949 to teach the Orff theory of musical pedagogy. Wolfgang Wagner invited Lex to choreograph the 1951 Bayreuth production of Wagner's *Parsifal;* in 1953, Liselott Diem offered her an appointment at the new sport academy she and her husband had founded in Cologne. (In 1933 the Nazis had shut down Diem's Hochschule für Leibesübungen, and she had enrolled in the Berlin Günther school.) Lex went to Cologne with her old assistant, Rose Daiber, while Günther remained in Rome, running some sort of school and finishing what was perhaps the most complete statement of her theoretical perspective, *Der Tanz als Bewegungsphänomen* (1962). Continually prone to illness, Lex did no new choreography until the late 1960s, when she formed the student Tanzgruppe Maja Lex, which traveled to a half-dozen countries around the world, performing several dances to American jazz. In this respect she differed from Günther, whose complex notion of ecstatic dance was nevertheless unsympathetic to the influence of jazz or rock 'n' roll (DG 122). But it was clear from her final project, *Der Weg zum elementaren Tanz* (1986), written with her student Graziela Padilla, that Lex still remained quite faithful to the theory and method of movement education established by Günther and Orff.

From Günther's perspective, the synthesis of Mensendieck, Dalcroze, and Laban entailed not only a synthesis of gymnastics and dance but a peculiar synthesis of music and dance. Her ideas were not entirely unique; for example, a Berlin teacher, Lucie Skerl, had anticipated them in her little book *Anleitung für den Gymnastikunterricht in den Schulen* (1926), which used a crude drawing technique, along with photos, to describe procedures for uniting hygienic and aesthetic movement. But certainly Günther linked the notion of synthesis to a stronger sense of discipline than most other teachers; under Lex, dance instruction was pretty strict and demanding. (After working with Wigman in *Totenmal,* Lex believed that her improvisational method was much too chaotic.) Orff's ideas about music education clarified Günther's ideas about movement education and vice versa. With Günther, dancing and music-making became interchangeable, if not entirely synonymous. The unique identity of dance depended not on detaching dance from music but on allowing bodily movement to structure the content of music. Keetman and Orff therefore produced music that was specific to the dance and the dancers and that permitted the dancers to create music while dancing or to exchange places with musicians. A musical work for dance always was a response to a specific problem of bodily movement. Keetman even designed all the musical instruments used to accompany the Günther dancers. The orchestra consisted of wooden flutes (soprano, alto, tenor, bass), various sizes of drums, tambourines, gongs, cymbals, bells, noisemakers, and special xylophones. One dance, *Zweiklang* (1938), apparently involved the unusual accompaniment of only three xylophones. The first, "cheerful" part of *Klänge und Gesichte* contained a dance with cymbals, a dance with flutes, and a dance with bells, with dancers performing on these instruments. Even when the music remained more explicitly confined to the orchestra, Lex and Keetman treated the playing of the music as a visible part of the choreography, as was spectacularly evident in several "kettledrum dances." This peculiar orchestra even provided the music for the gigantic stadium dances of 1936, 1938, and 1939.

In a 1931 article for *Schrifttanz,* Hans Redlich described the music of the Günther orchestra as "Asiatic," because it belonged "conceptually to another planet than say the music of German polyphony," the world of the Burmese gamelan ensemble (VP 75–77). However, Günther and Orff actually reached deep into the premodern European past for their models, medieval and ancient modes of music and movement. Orff stressed the notion of "elementary" musical structures or tropes in forming musical-kinetic consciousness. He built exercises and compositions around a single, elementary musical idea, such as ostinato, recitative, melisma, accentuation, crescendo, accelerando, psalmody, and intensive repetitions of a phrase at different tempos. Melodic material unfolded monophonically or homophonically rather than polyphonically or contrapuntally, even in relation to rhythm; although Keetman did like to experiment (as did Orff) with unusual rhythms for dance, such as 7/8 time, she completely avoided polyrhythmic configurations that appear, for example, in ancient African drumming.

The Mensendieck method of analyzing isolated movements in relation to specific body parts converged comfortably with the Orffian analysis of elementary musical structures. Günther proposed elementary units of bodily movement, including bending, stretching, raising, sitting, standing, falling, rolling, snaking, creeping, crawling, inclining, turning, grasping, holding, gripping, squeezing, lounging, walking, running, hopping, jumping, swinging, rotating, pressing, pushing, pulling, hanging, catching, carrying, bearing, lifting, juggling, tossing, striking, throwing, braking, climbing, balancing, plunging, arcing, gliding, striding, and leaning (DG 31–32). The human body could localize each of these movement elements within a particular body part, or bodily "element." Moreover, these movement elements operated in relation to other, more abstract elements, including the movement's direction, repetition, magnitude, tempo, accentuation, acceleration or deceleration, and crescendo or decrescendo (71–76). When groups of bodies performed, another series of elements came into play: rows, columns, branches, circles, chains, spirals, clusters, pairings, exchanges, reversals, and so forth (66–69). But all these dynamic elements of movement functioned in relation to musical, costume, and scenic elements such as the ostinato, the mask, and the spotlight. Thus, improvisation pedagogy followed Dalcroze's rational model of almost infinite variation on ever new combinations of elements.

However, Günther identified all elements as premodern, universal categories of signification identifiable in children, primitive cultures, and advanced civilizations. Modernity pervaded the physiognomy of dance only through peculiar combinations of elements, but Günther provided little guidance on how to identify such combinations. She realized that the problem with the rational approach was its failure to link elements or element combinations to specific emotional values or meanings: elements in themselves possessed no inherent semantic resonance, and a single element might carry contradictory significations in different narrative orderings of elements. Günther therefore tentatively referred, dualistically, to what we might call "emotional elements" such as affirmation and negation, having and losing, wanting and leaving, here and there; yet these elements nevertheless existed because of spatial relations between movement elements (27, 57). For Günther, movement was always a struggle with space, not (as for Bode) with the body or (as for Wigman) with death. But space was historical as well as physical. Like Orff, Günther and Lex treated archaic or medieval dance forms as elements of a modern dance, so they set pavannes, gavottes, gigues, minuettes, and contra dances against Keetman's strange (archaic) instrumentation to produce an unmistakably modern image of the body. The drawing of bodily movement enhanced one's capacity to identify movement elements, as Lex explained in a letter to *Der Tanz* (10, 1937, 2–3). But it must be said that the process of identifying movement elements depends as much on naming them as on seeing them and that movement forms emanate as much from linguistic as from visual structures. In any case, Günther admitted that categories of elements were not fixed and that even the difference between a gymnastic and a dance element was not always clear, in spite of a functional distinction between a utilitarian movement (gymnastic) and a movement that is an end in itself (dance).

All the principles of the Günther-Orff method manifested themselves in Lex's *Barbarische Suite* (1930). Here, as in other works, Lex adopted Wigman's "cycle" structure. But in this case, each dance in the cycle represented a crystallization, so to speak, of uniquely synthesized musical, movement, and scenic elements. In "Treibende Rhythmen," the emphasis was on the phenomenon of accentuation: six dancers engaged in a "dialogue of move-ment" driven by continually shifting accents, interruptions, and pauses, with "variation answer[ing] variation." In "Tanz mit Stabe," three dancers accompanied a soloist with hand-clapping and beating of bamboo shoots while the soloist manipulated a staff. The "Paukentanz" began with two dancers beating on kettledrums, and their rhythm called into dialogue the orchestra, other dancers, and then other rhythms, as the beat moved from 4/4 to 3/4 time and the dancers became more violent in their movements. This dance led to the "Kanon," in which the 3/4 rhythm coincided, "qui-etly," with triangular formations of the dance group and sound complexes built out of instrumentation in threes: three different flutes, three timpani, three chrome xylophones, and so forth. In the final section, "Sprungtanz," an orgiastic explosion of ever higher leaps was pitted against ever more rapid accelerandos before suddenly being punctuated by a silence from the orchestra; then came a tapping of feet, a tapping of drums, and a resump-tion of leaps, crescendos, and accelerandos (Selden; Losch 328–331). In both bodily and group movements, Lex continually favored crisscross, X-shaped, and A-shaped (triangular) movements; in costumes, Günther inclined toward quasi-Roman or Visigothic-Viking-type tunics or dresses with metal belts or collars.

For Günther, the meaning of dance derived from the revelation of recessed or repressed elements of expression. Dance was a struggle with space because it was a struggle with the past—or rather, a struggle to recover from the past a buried notion of freedom (love and control of space). This perspective inspired her to devote many words to the discus-sion of dance in so-called primitive cultures (DG 139–219), even though she recognized that differing attitudes toward sexual identity and eroticism made a reconciliation between primitive and civilized cultures impossible. Her fascination with primitive dance was not original; Jaap Kool had antic-ipated her quite perceptively in *Tänze der Naturvölker* (1921). Primitive dance was compelling because it presented undisguised musical-kinetic elements. For Günther, the experience of ecstasy depended on the revela-tion of elemental forces (95–122): "Rapture and ecstasy arise *in* and *through* dance. . . . With the child as with the primitive the drive toward rap-ture and ecstasy *always* attaches itself to movement, to dance" (97). But she did not think elemental-ecstatic forces revealed themselves through recov-ery of the superstitions and myths defining primitive cultures. On the con-trary, in the civilized world the only way to expose elemental signs was through rigorous, complex analysis or deconstruction of bodies and spaces. Analytic capacities, however, separated strong dancers from com-monplace dancers and prevented ecstatic dance from being a total, unify-ing, cultic-tribal experience. In a 1930 article for *Schrifttanz*, Günther sub-tly declared that dance education lacked rigor and remained intolerably permeated with teachers and students of Dionysian desires and mediocre abilities who did not recognize their own limitations (VP 50–53). In other words, an elementary discourse on dance did not make dance simple or more accessible. Indeed, the disciplined effort to disclose the repressed elements of musical-kinetic energy ultimately implied that the experience of ecstasy, especially through dance, was the privilege of a gifted elite, not of a culture in a large, inclusive sense.

THE BAUHAUS EXPERIMENTS

The demand, especially among the young, for knowledge about bodily performance and expressivity was very strong during the Weimar era, and even quite provincial cities could boast not one but two or three schools for gymnastic/dance instruction. As early as 1920, the Mensendieck-Bund alone claimed to have 122 academy-trained instructors managing classes in 63 German cities (FGW 219–223). Through the proliferation of media publicity about body culture, students became more worldly and demanding as the decade progressed, and the competition of schools for students became keener. Strong schools tended to attract government subsidies, but by 1927 they could not receive them unless they met accreditation standards established jointly by the various professional organizations representing state-salaried teachers and educational administrators. The effect of accreditation procedures was to make the curricula of many schools look, on paper at least, alike, with so many hours devoted to anatomy, gymnastics, dance, music, theory, group exercise, and so forth.

The Bauhaus school (1919–1932) in Weimar and then Dessau has provoked intense curiosity because of its supposedly extravagant avant-garde attitude toward theatre and dance performance. However, the Bauhaus was a design and fine arts school and, as such, did not have to conform to the pedagogic expectations imposed upon schools more overtly focused on educating the dancing body. This exception allowed the Bauhaus to explore startling possibilities that the dance schools lacked the resources or even inclination to consider. Of course, the Bauhaus had to conform to other expectations—dance objectives always had to remain subordinate to design objectives—and while architect Walter Gropius headed the institution, the Bauhaus theatre program, to the continual frustration of theatre director Oskar Schlemmer and students alike, constantly retained a peripheral status. Nevertheless, the eccentric Bauhaus dance aesthetic has provoked abundant fascination and commentary, most of which Dirk Scheper documented exhaustively, lavishly, and beautifully in *Oskar Schlemmer: Das Triadische Ballett und die Bauhausbühne* (1988). But the complexities of the Bauhaus culture are too complex for any single account and continue to remain more documented than explained.

In Weimar, Gropius planned for the Bauhaus to incorporate theatrical performances into its public activities, although he did not make clear how, if at all, the curriculum should accommodate the study of theatrical art. The Bauhaus, he proposed, would bring to the public the results of research in the form of dances, dance plays, marionette plays, shadow plays, and stage works under the assumption that "the conscious application of laws of mechanics, optics, and acoustics is decisive for our form of theatre" (DS 65). Gropius brought in Lothar Schreyer (1886–1966) to coordinate the Bauhaus theatre program from 1921 to 1923. Schreyer was a hard-core expressionist with a highly idiosyncratic sense of abstraction. In 1915 he began collaborating with Herwarth Walden on the publication of the Berlin radical expressionist journal *Der Sturm,* and in 1918 he formed the Sturm-Bühne for the production of his own strange plays and those of Walden and August Stramm. But Schreyer found Berlin hostile to his experiments and moved to Hamburg, where from 1919 to 1920 he organized the Kampf-Bühne and collaborated with the bizarre dance couple of Lavinia Schulz and Walter Holdt. In Hamburg and Dresden, his hometown, he attracted a small but enthusiastic audience.

Gropius found Schreyer's radical deployment of technology and formal abstraction seductive; indeed, one can regard Schreyer as a kind of prophet of performance art, for he announced that expressionistic performance had "nothing to do with theatre" but was a completely different "stage artwork" (DS 66; Schreyer, *Zwischen,* 7–10). Schreyer, however, was a mystic, deeply fascinated with archaic Christianity, the moment of conversion from paganism in northern Europe. He saw the stage as a mysterious, dynamic beacon, the components of which produced a performance resembling a great, cinematic stained-glass window. Paul Scheerbart's fantastic ideas for comet and astral dances, published in 1903, also stirred his imagination (LS 39–45). Light and color possessed an inherent performative interest and were sources of action in themselves; thus, the "sacral" performance space, closer to an ancient shrine than a theatre, might contain a violet tapestry, black and gold costumes, red masks, and white feathers, all bathed in a deep blue, deep orange, deep yellow, or dazzling silver glow or set against cathedral-like glass reflectors from which emanated powerful rainbow or prismatic transformations of light. Basic colors ("Grundfarben") functioned in relation to basic sounds, forms, and movements. The human figure appeared as a remote idol, moving, in a mechanized, marionette fashion, toward ecstatic transfiguration (Kersting 155–160) (Figure 35). The revelation of the inner, metaphysical condition of being depended on exposing the core of forms, as Brian Keith-Smith has put it (Schreyer, *Zwischen,* 156).

But Schreyer's idea of core movements derived from a perception of rhythm rooted in language, not music: "Through the rhythmic resounding word, the human form of the expressionistic stage artwork materializes as a sound form, a movement form, and a color form," for "in the beginning was the word" (LS 152). Words were the basic source of all movement, but only when their sound values took precedence over grammatical logic. In his little dramas, Schreyer foregrounded the sound value of words by abandoning sentence structure and employing curious repetitions of words, alliterations, verbless phrases, nounless phrases, illogical word clusters, internal rhymes, and words isolated or suspended in space. Choral voices did not sing but spoke according to rhythmic-melodic values ascribed to the words. Music entered the performance through unusual instruments, such as a West African xylophone, a five-foot-wide drum, a glass harmonica, a violin, or glass chimes ("spherical music"). These notions Schreyer introduced in Sturm/Kampfbühne productions of *Nacht* (1916), *Meer* (1916), *Sehnte* (1917), and *Mann* (1917). However, it is not at all clear how bodies moved in relation to the words of the texts.

In *Kreuzigung* (1920), Schreyer "scored" all components of the performance as if it were a piece of music, using his own symbol code to indicate the dynamics. The action unfolded in "measures," and within each measure he designated the appropriate words, movements, intonations, sounds, pauses, and color effects. The words appeared in different typefaces to indicate different intonations (Gordon 89–103). The little play had only three characters, Man, Mother, and Mistress, speaking in an abbreviated, expressionistic manner: "Mother:|in light|my son|is silent|(Noise tones)|Mistress: Men scream| Men go into|battle|I dance|I|." During this exchange Mother moved her right hand on her right breast and Mistress moved her right arm "sideways horizontally." The performers never moved from their initial positions on the red and yellow–draped performance space until the very end, when, after saying, "Awake. World. Awake," they stepped forward and down some stairs. The scoring of the performance created a haunting, glyphic, abstract design on the page, a bold embodiment of the "word artwork" that made up the core of the dynamic performance.

With this mysterium, Schreyer drifted toward a kind of serial organization of performance dynamics such as Schoenberg initiated with the twelvetone technique in music. In *Skirnismól* (1920) he resurrected a primeval image from the Edda to include, in addition to the exploded, fractured language, riding, sword, and scissor dances. At the Bauhaus, Schreyer gathered about him a small cult, including Hans Haffenrichter, Hermann Müller, Gertrud Grunow, and Franz Singer; he also worked with Eva Weidemann, a dancer not officially connected with the Bauhaus. With them he produced *Mondspiel* (1923), which featured a large, highly abstract, idol-like effigy of Mary in the Moon standing on a mysterious shell moved from behind by an invisible speaker. The shell projected a "moon eye," before which moved a masked male dancer. In other words, the male danced with a petrified idol that actually moved through the dance of the invisible speaker, played by Weidemann. A man spoke the part of Mary, and a woman spoke the part of the dancer. Again, Schreyer "scored" all performance components in great detail (Waserka 127). But Gropius and many other members of the Bauhaus found Schreyer's thinking too cultish and esoteric, lacking in the rationalism they wished to define the Bauhaus ideology. The dogmatic, fanatical cult surrounding the mystical painter Johannes Itten had already caused enough tension in the school, so in 1923 Gropius dismissed Schreyer, who then pursued a career combining art history with an archaic, visionary Christianity.

On 30 September 1922, the Stuttgart premiere of Oskar Schlemmer's *Das Triadische Ballett* attracted considerable attention throughout Germany and inspired Gropius to appoint Schlemmer to manage the theatrical activities of the school. Schlemmer (1888–1943) studied art in Stuttgart, his hometown and produced artworks in a range of forms: paintings, wood and metal sculpture, watercolors, graphics, and murals. He had no formal training in either theatre or dance but nevertheless designed stage sets and costumes for several prominent theatres in Germany, beginning with 1921 productions of Hindemith's short operas *Mörder Hoffnung der Frauen* and *Nusch-Nuschi* in Stuttgart. Until 1930 Schlemmer designed sets for theatrical productions in Berlin, Weimar, Magdeburg, and Breslau, but none of these attracted as much attention as his Bauhaus designs, even though he sought to provide emphatically modern (abstract) images for both classical dramas (Shakespeare, Grabbe) and modernist texts (Stravinsky, Bartók, Schoenberg). In his artworks, Schlemmer had dedicated himself since 1915 almost entirely to the representation of the human form, exploring the limits of the tension between abstractness and humanness—"the human as a mathematically, geometrically defined type and representative of a higher order" (DS 8). In 1919 he helped found the strange Uecht circle of Stuttgart artists who pursued a kind of cubo-expressionism to suffuse images of modernity with mysticism, a vision that coincided in no small degree with that of Lothar Schreyer (Mück). But Schlemmer was a stronger theorist than Schreyer, and he cultivated a much more congenial attitude toward academic environments.

He began working for the Bauhaus in 1921 in the sculpture and metal workshops, where he produced *Das Figural Kabarett* (1922), a sort of mechanical cabaret using abstract dolls and doll parts. As head of the theatre workshop, Schlemmer was a popular teacher, partly because of his aggressively experimental attitude toward performance and partly because of his determination to build performance out of design concepts rather than out of texts. Performance at the Bauhaus was inseparable from the production of independently interesting artworks that had strong exhibition value: models of experimental stages and mechanical theatres, figurines, watercolors, drawings, sculptures, and photographs. Many famous examples of this work appeared in Schlemmer's widely disseminated futuristic promotional brochure, *Die Bühne des Bauhaus* (1925). Performances functioned as showcases for student design work and always took place in a workshop environment, as the school never had the resources to construct anything resembling the utopian theatres imagined by Schlemmer, Andreas Weininger, Gropius, or Ferenc Molnár. The arrival of Xanti Schawinsky (1904–1979) in 1924 brought a touch of circus, music hall, and carnival to Bauhaus theatre projects; other students, such as Molnár, Gyula Pap (1899–1984), László Moholy-Nagy (1895–1946), Lou Scheper (1901–1976), Kurt Schmidt, Joost Schmidt, Georg Teltscher, Karla Grosch, Lux Feininger, and Werner Siedhoff brought an extraordinary range of specialization in different areas of the fine arts. Music for Bauhaus productions was often the work of the Bauhauskapelle, a student orchestra employing the usual gongs and drums but also saxophones, wood flutes, banjos, a trombone, a clarinet, a trumpet, an accordion, a piano, and even a revolver.

Though he had a lifelong preoccupation with dance, Schlemmer maintained only very marginal contact with dance culture outside the Bauhaus, and his thinking about bodily movement was neither precise, deep, nor even innovative. He assumed that the interest of a bodily movement depended almost entirely on the visual context, the scenic design. Schlemmer worked with Ellen Petz on an adaptation of *The Nutcracker* in Dresden (1928) but was not at all happy with the result. Gret Palucca visited the Bauhaus for a concert and demonstration in 1928, but this event led to nothing significant. Otherwise, Schlemmer seemed content to work (1927–1928) with Manda van Kreibig (1901–1990), ballet mistress at Darmstadt and student of Duncan, Bode, Laban, and Wigman, on devising movements for dance pieces. In 1928 Gropius left the Bauhaus, and his successor, Hannes Meyer, sought to move the school toward a more overtly left-wing political position. Schlemmer's politically ambiguous "formalism" brought him into intensifying tension with Meyer and many other teachers at the school, so in 1929 he accepted a teaching position in Breslau. When the Nazis came to power, Schlemmer's art faced severe reproach, and he spent the last decade of his life in painful isolation in Stuttgart.

The work most strongly associated with the Bauhaus theatre program, and Schlemmer's most important theatrical project, was *The Triadic Ballet*. The piece underwent several transformations over a period of twenty years (1912–1932), with major revisions or revivals in 1923, 1926, 1929, and 1932, and it was the impetus for numerous subsidiary projects and experiments by Schlemmer and other Bauhaus artists. Yet the piece transcended the Bauhaus, for Schlemmer's work on it preceded his involvement with the Bauhaus by ten years, and when he premiered *The Triadic Ballet* in Paris in

1932, he had been gone from the Bauhaus for four years. However, Schlemmer's association with the Bauhaus was decisive in shaping the identity of the piece; Scheper has expertly described the not always congenial tension between Schlemmer's modernism and that favored by the Bauhaus administration.

The Triadic Ballet began life in 1912 as an experimental collaboration between Schlemmer and a pair of dancers with the Stuttgart Court Theatre, Albert Burger and Elsa Hötzel, who had studied under Dalcroze at Hellerau. It hardly developed independently of established theatre institutions, although developments in modern dance culture apparently had little impact on Schlemmer, judging by the pervasive lack of reference to them in his letters and diaries. But the premiere, in Stuttgart, did not occur for another ten years, with the original pair of dancers as the stars. During the Bauhaus years, the piece mutated under the pressure of new collaborations. Paul Hindemith wrote "mechanical" music for the 1926 production at Donauschingen, and after that the piece appeared in a popular revue format in Frankfurt and Berlin. By then the dance was famous enough to spawn a gallery exhibit in Central European cities. As the piece grew older, it became shorter; once an evening-long event, it wound up featured on a program of modernist works. Finally, in 1932 the piece went to Paris as part of an international dance competition promoting the restoration of elite, high cultural glory to ballet.

In spite of its title, Schlemmer never considered the piece ballet in any conventional sense—it was always for him a modern kind of pantomime. It was modern perhaps because of the mutability of its aesthetic identity; it could migrate from a radical-experimental to a popular to a high cultural institutional context, and this capacity depended on the generic ambiguity of the work. On the one hand, according to a diary entry of 30 September 1922, the ballet "flirted with lightness without falling into grotesquerie" and strove to "dematerialize the body without destroying it through occultism"; on the other hand, it revived the Dionysian ecstatic origin of dance but did so under the terms of a "final form" of "Apollonian strictness" (OSI 96–97). But this vaguely defined generic ambiguity entailed rather specific, abstract formal relations between aesthetic components. And although *The Triadic Ballet* attracted attention throughout Europe, its impact on theatrical practice was very small, confined almost entirely to the tiny Bauhaus program for theatre, although graduates of the school certainly found opportunities in mainstream institutions. Perhaps Schlemmer's greatest contribution lay not in producing any particular piece but in rethinking the process by which dance does its work.

With *The Triadic Ballet*, Schlemmer introduced an unprecedented degree of abstraction into performance aesthetics. More precisely, he sought to invest dance with the same power of abstraction that modernism had discovered was possible for the painted image. For Schlemmer, the meaning of performance depended on an appreciation of formal relations between abstract categories of aesthetic experience, such as color, shape, and pattern; it was not a matter of constructing characters or correspondences between imaginary actions and real conditions outside the theatre. Schlemmer composed "texts" for theatre from lists of formal elements that, when recombined, were the basis of performed action. This aesthetic entailed a perception of the performance space as a grid that could unitize formal elements according to a unique, mysterious system of geometry, a "symphonic-architectonic" ideology, in that the value or meaning of theatrical action derived from "the pleasure in the play of forms, colors, and materials" (DS 35). In *The Triadic Ballet*, for example, a triangular principle of organization dominated: the piece contained three sections, or "series" ("Yellow," "Rose," and "Black"), each requiring three dancers (two men and a woman), whose movements operated in relation to a dynamically structured trinity of costume, dance, and music; this trinity, in turn, functioned dynamically in relation to the spatial trinity of height, depth, and width, which embraced the trinity of basic forms (triangle, circle, quadrangle) and basic colors (red, blue, yellow)—all these relations accommodated by eighteen costumes and twelve dances.

This "geometrization" of performance was an initial step toward a total mechanization of theatre; indeed, Schlemmer, in collaboration with other Bauhaus artists, contemplated plans for large-scale machine theatres and robotized "plays of forms," none of which, unfortunately, ever came to fruition. Diary entry, April 1926: "No whining about mechanization, instead, joy over precision!" (OSI 183). Indeed, the three transformative "emblems of our time" were abstraction, mechanization, and technological innovation (OS 17). For Schlemmer, this optimism in regard to the salvational potential of abstraction and technology was always suffused with mysticism. No matter how abstract the performance became, the human figure (though not the body) remained the central, dominating image in the play of forms, for it was the most powerful and artistic signifier of immediacy (DS 25). Schlemmer consistently treated the human figure as a geometrical phenomenon, not as the site of a "character" or, as he put it, "psychological-literary" values. In a 1915 diary entry, he noted various geometrical properties of the body:

> The quadrangle of the breast cavity,
> The circle of the belly,
> Cylinder of the throat,
> Ball of the elbow joint, knee, shoulder, bones,
> Ball of the head, the eyes,
> Triangle of the nose,
> The line connecting heart and brain, . . . (DS 24)

In 1930 he explained that human figural art lies "in the realm of the doll-like. For the abstraction of the human form . . . creates an image in a higher sense; it creates, not a natural human being, but an artistic being; it creates . . . a symbol of human form—In all early high cultures . . . the human form is remote from the naturalistic image, but close to the lapidary symbol form: the idol, the totem, the doll" (OSI 231). This geometry of the body was exposed above all by mask and costume, not by any system of movement. Whereas Dalcroze strove toward a costumeless, naked identity for modern humanity, Schlemmer perceived that "costume is everything" in modern theatre (DS 27). Many commentators on *The Triadic Ballet* felt that the extraordinary costumes—by turns mysterious, bizarre, and enchanting—were the *only* significant feature of the piece (Figure 36). Some dance critics believed the costumes merely disguised very conventional choreography. Indeed, in spite of Scheper's meticulous efforts to reconstruct the dance from abundant visual and written documentation, it is still quite difficult to see how the piece works as a kinetic event (33–58). Even Gerhard Bohner's 1977 reconstruction seemed to lack a convincing organization of movement. Schlemmer himself thought the greatest problem with the piece was its failure to inspire any music appropriate for it; before Hindemith composed a mechanical organ score for it, Schlemmer had used an eccentric mix of music by several modern and unmodern composers (Mozart, Haydn, Bossi, Debussy), and he even considered circus marches and popular tunes (235). Not even Scheper can explain why Schlemmer's radical image of the human form could not awaken an equally radical complement of music or movement. Perhaps the designs seemed to mock any complementation with music or movement; the human figure made fun of the human body, and dance became a deprecation of the body.

Schlemmer's notion of costume was total insofar as he regarded all aspects of scenography as categories of mask. He strongly resisted the established theatrical practice of treating costume, scenery, and lighting as the work of separate designers. This idea led to an even more modern one: that a designer could initiate theatrical works and become their author. Schlemmer designed many productions of literary works and established ballets, but he was never happier than when he was fashioning his own "text" out of the principles defining his mysterious geometric system, and for this reason he was utterly unique among modern dance creators. To this day, designers everywhere seem to require a text or scenario created by someone else to justify their contribution to performance. Schlemmer, however, saw scenery, lighting, movement, and sound as extensions of costume and the human figure—that is, he saw *all forms as masks* (although, unlike Schreyer, he did not see masks in terms of core forms). It was a tendency of Teutonic mysticism to perceive being itself as something perpetually masked, veiled, enshrouded, without form. No matter how naked the body appeared, it was always a mask, hiding something within it that had no form: an emotion, an experience of the world, a mood.

Expressionism sought to objectify this inner world of emotion. Schreyer attempted to create a modern dance theatre oriented toward a superabstract mysticism, with an utterly strange human form as its core. His image of humanity was no less radical and abstract than Schlemmer's, but the cultic-ritual obscurity into which he and his adepts retreated violently estranged him from the rest of the Bauhaus. Schreyer simply did not believe that technology was the basis for connecting art and spiritual renewal or for establishing an emancipatory condition of modernity. *The Triadic Ballet* indicated to Gropius that Schlemmer understood how technology imposed a classical restraint or sobriety of form on the construction of emotion and abstraction. But Schlemmer was never really happy in the Bauhaus. A theatre curriculum was expensive, and Bauhaus theatre productions invariably stirred up political controversies that made it difficult for Gropius to raise funds and subsidies for the academy. Today one constantly encounters the inclination to regard formalist abstraction as a strategy for transcending politics, but in the Bauhaus era the reduction of theatre to a play of forms and a geometric abstraction of the body awakened extreme intensities of political feeling. Formalist performance may have constructed highly ambiguous, uncertain, "mystical-fantastic" emotions, but it did not fail to produce an impassioned attitude toward its ambiguities. For this reason, theatre education within the Bauhaus never possessed much more than a marginalized, workshop status. In a letter to his lifelong friend Otto Meyer-Amden in December 1925, Schlemmer described his estrangement from the dominant atmosphere of the Bauhaus and his awareness of the limitations of abstractionism:

> The artistic atmosphere here is so cosmically remote from everything that is not actual, not immediate, not trendy . . . Dadaism, circus, variety, jazzband, tempo, cinema, America, airplane, auto. That is the real situation here. In painting: no subjects. "Abstract" = no subjects, quite demanded by the extreme power bloc of Kandinsky and Moholy. Here I am someone from yesterday, or perhaps a dissident, because I paint "classically." The general course of art is "reactionary." . . . The amusing, the dadaistic, the mechanical, cinema, etc. are the reality. One sneers at every feeling, sentiment, indeed at anything really serious (OSI 157–158).

One can now even suggest that the abstractionism pursued not only by *The Triadic Ballet* but by the Bauhaus generally disclosed a profound anxiety toward the body and the irrational, emotional dynamics emanating from deep inside it. Bauhaus abstractionism transcended the body rather than revealing it or developing perception of it. When abstract eccentricity replaces expressivity as the dominant sign of modernity, the resulting image produces many handsome art books but not performances that bear up to repeated viewing.

Nevertheless, within these constraints Schlemmer made a further major contribution to modernist theatre: he proposed a revision of formal theatre education no less radical than his notion of the designer as author of theatrical performances. Schlemmer's Bauhaus curriculum detached the study of theatre from the study of literary drama, theatrical productions, or theatrical artists. It developed within an experimental, laboratory milieu in which abstract, formal elements of theatrical performance were presumed to have a powerful value independent of any specific literary or historical context and thus became the object of systematic investigation. Schlemmer divided theatre curriculum into three general areas of study: 1) scenic composition; 2) scenic technology; and 3) linguistic, musical, and gymnastic-dance studies. Each of these categories contained within it the study of aesthetic devices deemed particular to theatre, and study itself was considered virtually synonymous with experimental performance on specially designed "research stages" (*Versuchsbühne*). For example, the curtain as a visual device peculiar to theatre could become the subject of various experimental performances exposing the variations in meaning signified when the curtain acted in certain ways in relation to particular qualities of light, material, color, sound, or bodily movement before and behind it. Schlemmer and a brilliant group of students and collaborators performed all sorts of experiments to isolate the signifying power of specific theatrical devices—such as costume, gesture, mask, choric movement, shadows, projections, puppets, footlights, props, and ramps—always in relation to the signifying power of a more abstract category of form—material, shape, color, geometric configuration, sound, size. The experimental group did not seek a context (a literary text) to justify this mode of performance; rather, the modern theatre artist constructed a context around a specific device or element of interest.

These experiments culminated in an astonishing series of performances in 1929 of a twelve-piece program that revealed the intrinsic dramatic interest of tensions between forms and materials: *Glass Dance* (solo female), *Metal Dance* (solo female), *Staff Dance* (solo female or male), *Gestural Dance* (three men), *Mask Chorus* (seven men and women), *Screen Dance* (three men), *Box Dance* (three men), *Space Dance* (three men), *Ring Dance* (two women and one man), *Form Dance* (three men), *Sketch* (one women, three men), and *Women's Dance* (three men) (Figures 4 and 37–38). Piano and percussion instruments accompanied the dancers. Schlemmer attempted to "score" the brief dances in the manner of Schreyer, but in their weird mask-costumes, all the dancers had to do was move to stimulate curiosity— a point that did not go unnoticed by critics of the time (DS 206–207). Most interesting in this regard are rehearsal photographs taken of the *Women's Dance* by a Bauhaus student, Naftali Avnon (1910–1977). These give an idea of the eerie, somewhat stilted movement the doll-like "women" (actually men) made in their extravagant masks and costumes, which look like Oriental parodies of nineteenth-century fashions. Even more interesting, the snapshots reveal the power of the dancers to make the photographer move, to make him get closer to and farther from the strange creatures, look at them from odd angles or in different configurations of light. However, Schlemmer did not want the pictures published because they did not give an adequate sense of the space in which the dancers appeared and because they looked spontaneous or amateurish, not like genuine artworks. He preferred the posed photographs of the piece taken by Umbo (Otto Umbehr), which, although quite interesting in themselves, do not convey the idea of a dance (Faber, *Tanzfoto,* 79–83).

For Schlemmer, theatre education was inseparable from the experimental knowledge derived from performance itself rather than from history or dramatic literature. A modern, emancipatory theatre must derive from a new system of theatre education, a system that saw no great value in preparing students to preserve theatrical traditions dominated by reverence for the enduring authority of texts and by humility over the transitory authority of performance. Moreover, Schlemmer's experiments and the documentation on them indicated that modern study of performance did not mean the study of particular productions; it meant the study of the devices and codes that constitute the context for any specific performance (text). From this perspective, dance became a play of forms, an activation of space that ultimately needed no bodies, no dancers. It was the image of a machine-idol.

LILI GREEN

In spite of pervasive complaints after 1925 about the increasing Americanization of German culture, American ideas about bodily movement, so influential before the war (especially in relation to female physical culture), did not receive particularly serious attention in Germany. Of course, the Mensendieck theory had many disciples, but by 1920 her work was more of an inspiration than a rigorously applied system; in any case, Mensendieck seemed much more European than American. The influence of Isadora Duncan (1878–1927) was far weaker than that of Mensendieck, though commentators on dance continued to evoke her name reverently. She opened a school in Berlin-Grunewald in 1904; in 1911, at the invitation of the Duke of Hesse, the school moved to Darmstadt under the direction of Isadora's sister Elisabeth (1874–1948). Throughout her restless, vagabond life, Isadora Duncan opened schools in Germany, France, the United States, Greece, and Russia, but she was a very poor teacher, with no patience for pedagogic detail, systematic organization of experience, or theoretical rigor. She left most teaching duties to faithful (rather than competent) disciples, and in the classroom she favored a tribe of completely worshipful female children eager to follow her every whim and path (Jowitt 96–97).

Elisabeth Duncan wanted a school that was independent of her sister's chaotic personality. With the help of Max Merz (1874–1964), whom she married, she sought to infuse some discipline into Isadora's improvisatory, Grecian approach to bodily movement by incorporating into the curriculum ideas from German body culture (including Merz's enthusiasm for race hygiene). The war compelled her to return to New York in 1915, but by 1920 she was back in Germany; she revived her school in Potsdam, maintaining a branch office in New York. The school operated out of the castle at Klessheim in Salzburg from 1925 until 1933, when she closed her school in New York and moved to Prague (1933–1935) (Stefan 97–98; Heun). Then she lived in Munich before returning to America. Afflicted with lameness, Elisabeth herself never danced, and her school, unlike Isadora's, did not strive to develop bodies for public performance: she wanted to produce imaginative teachers. Nevertheless, the school operated very much in the shadow of Isadora's looming personality. The pseudo-Grecian image of nature and art prevailed. Liberated movement was always a "natural" response to great pieces of classical music. (Merz published a pamphlet condemning jazz as a subversive, antisocial force.) Movement was an evocation of fantasies inspired by the music. Dance created a picture of the emotion inspired by the music; if neither the music nor the emotion stirred within the body, one should not force movement. A unique feature of the curriculum was a set of exercises in which students sang archaic German folksongs while moving (Rochowanski, *Tanzende*, 3). This approach succeeded with (female) children, but students over the age of thirteen or so required a much more powerful notion of bodily expressivity to sustain their interest (HB 76–81; RLM 38). Indeed, by 1920 a historical perspective had set in that made Isadora's and American attitudes toward bodily freedom seem childlike, unhelpfully naive. Still, it was obvious that in Isadora Duncan dance (more than her dances themselves) had produced a spectacular, tempestuous personality that provoked awe in almost anyone excited by the new currents in dance culture. The whole idea of *Ausdruckstanz*, of the body as a powerful instrument of expressivity, seemed to emanate from her.

Duncan's idea of expressivity, of painting emotion in movement, owed much to the semiotic system of Francois Delsarte, and it is therefore worthwhile to relate the curious fate of Delsartian theory in Germany. Delsarte devised a code, for use primarily in the theatre, that assigned particular gestures to signify particular emotions. Giraudet explained this elaborate system of categories and subcategories of signification in *Mimique: Physiognomie et gestes* (1895). The body moved according to the rhythm of emotions it experienced or desired to represent. But the Delsarte system assumed that both gestures and emotions were clearly and immediately readable, as joy or anger or despair or delight, because emotions derived from universally common phenomena external to the body that experienced them. For Dalcroze or Günther, by contrast, a movement element had no inherent signification; one might even suggest that *Ausdruckstanz* as a whole represented an effort to free the body from imprisonment within a kind of semantic grid that sought to make the body "meaningful," to make it "say" things that were easily, clearly, and unambiguously understandable under conventions of "appropriate expression." American theatrical genius Steele MacKaye (1842–1894) studied the Delsarte system in Paris and around 1873 imported it to the United States, where it became enormously popular in theatre training. Its influence on the development of American modern dance was so considerable, even oppressive, that the greatly respected dancer Ted Shawn (1891–1972) felt disposed to publish a textbook on the system as late as 1954.

Genevieve Stebbins (1857–1915) studied under MacKaye in New York. In books published in the 1890s, she modified the Delsarte system by incorporating theories of breathing and rhythmic movement to produce what she called "harmonic gymnastics" for female students. Stebbins's emphasis was not on developing a large vocabulary of expressions for use on the stage but on cultivating an ideal convergence of female hygiene and beauty. It was she who first associated the "natural" female body with the wearing of Grecian tunics and chitons. A student of Stebbins, Hedwig Kallmeyer (1881–?), opened a school for girls in Berlin around 1905, and her students included Dora Menzler and Gertrud Leistikow. In *Künstlerische Gymnastik* (1910), Kallmeyer modified the Stebbins method to accommodate some ideas of Bess Mensendieck, herself a student of Stebbins; flexibility was apparently a feature of her thinking. By this time, however, the connection to Delsarte began to get lost in the more immediate effort to construct a modern—and "correct"—identity for the female body. Kallmeyer's influence was probably greater than the paltry information about her would indicate. After the war, she seems to have moved to Hannover. Several photographs in the Joan Erikson Archive of the Harvard Theatre Collection depict activities at her school in Hannover around 1925. These show groups of children between five and sixteen years old playing outdoor body games. Some of the children are nude. One photograph shows a group of twelve *boys* with two women instructors; in other images, groups containing both sexes play games, and one photo shows a group of six women sculpting clay animals.

Taken together, these photos imply that Kallmeyer had moved some distance both from Delsarte and from the all-female, Stebbins-Mensendieck cult of idealized physical comportment. But why? Perhaps the answer lies in a 1924 statement by Fritz Giese. Discussing Delsarte, Stebbins, Mensendieck, Kallmeyer, and Duncan as representatives of a single system in which gymnastics worked to produce beautiful rather than strong bodies, Giese remarked:

> Mensendieck's thinking leads to a perhaps all too ice-cold aesthetic in the sense of an impartial, sober perspective. Here, where only women fit into the system, we find the hygienic-aesthetic gymnastic purposeful, useful, and at the same time clear in form, comprehensive, physically appropriate, and therefore beautiful. But one can also deprecate this attitude. The feminine, the womanly, moves into the foreground. The spectator is the man, the performer the woman. At least in general: grace and dignity in their old polarity. That is how one learns to understand the methods of Kallmeyer-Stebbins as well as those of the veil-wrapped Duncan school. (FGK 112–113)

The ideals of the Delsarte-Kallmeyer trajectory were "renown[ed] models of *Nacktkultur:* the unclothed, beautiful human," which led one to "a culture of the pose like an antique bronze or marble." "Body spirit here means the soul expressed in the body—but as if it were crystallized, petrified within it, set up for observation rather than experienced" (FGK 112–113). In other words, although a gesture still signified a distinct emotion, as Delsarte intended, the emotion signified was not grounded in experience nor even in the body; rather, it was imposed upon the body by an "objective" spectatorial gaze that actually looked backward, into an idealized, mythical, eternal past, for guidance—not on how to *feel* but on how to *display feelings* that gained the approval of a society (America) that feared the expressive body's power to undermine a fragile sense of social unity and shared capacity to read signs. The Germans, however, were not so worried about crypticity or darkness of expression.

But the Delsarte system was not entirely dead in Germany. In 1929, Lili Green published *Einführung in das Wesen unserer Gesten und Bewegungen,* perhaps the best and most ambitious treatise ever to emerge from Delsarte's notion of correspondences between gestures and emotions. Green so overhauled the notion that she produced an elaborate semiotic analysis of bodily signifying practices, permeated with a transfigurative Germanic aura. Born and raised in Surinam, where her father owned a coffee plantation, Green (1885–1977) began to study piano in The Hague after the death of her father in 1905, but she derived no happiness from it. Then she saw Isadora Duncan perform in Scheveningen and talked with her. Duncan told her that "you cannot learn dance, you have to make dances." In 1907, Green produced her own dance-song fairy tale in The Hague, apparently with considerable success. She tried to advance her career in the London theatre, but when told she needed more training she returned to Holland, where she appeared as Ophelia in Eduard Verkade's popular 1908 production of *Hamlet*. The following year she was back in England to study ballet (ESG 15–18). She assumed the "Russian" name Vallya Lodowska for a few years and began dancing with Andreas Pavley (Henryk van Dorp de Weyer [1892–1931]), who had studied under Dalcroze and in 1909 had staged in Amsterdam a production of Beethoven's *Prometheus* with more than a hundred performers.

With Pavley, Green produced a series of enormously successful dance concerts in London and The Netherlands (1910–1911). These presented Oriental and classical-mythological themes in a decoratively theatrical manner, for the Java-born Pavley strongly typified the prewar perception of dance as a rapturous submission to glamorous exoticism. But Green had her own ideas, especially in regard to the concert program, which always followed the example of her 1907 debut show: she supplemented dance pieces with solo performances by the pianist, a violist, and a singer (her English friend Margaret Walker). In all her dances, she impersonated a character in a little story inspired by the music: *The Murderer's Dance, Death and the Maiden, Anitra's Dance.* For Tchaikovsky's *Songs without Words,* she and Pavley devised a Pierrot and Columbine tale. Newspaper reviews of concerts given in Leiden, Haarlem, and Amsterdam in 1913 consistently and enthusiastically remarked on the pantomimic quality of her dances, and all suggested that she was a much stronger dancer than Pavley. The decorative elegance of her movements, produced by a body of exquisite slenderness and suppleness ("like the ripples of a harp"), established her enduring appeal for critics and large audiences alike, although "*The Murderer's Dance* doesn't suit her" ("Lili Green," G5-G7, G11). Into the 1930s she continued to perform, in cities across Europe, dances she had created before 1913, provoking virtually the same enchanted critical response she had originally inspired (see *Wiener Gesellschaftsblatt,* 3 March 1930).

In 1913, Pavley met Sergey Oukrainsky (1885–1972), a dancer with Anna Pavlova's ensemble. Oukrainsky persuaded Pavley to join the Pavlova group, and when that tour of duty ended, in 1915, Pavley and Oukrainsky stayed in the United States, where in 1916 they founded the Pavley-Oukrainsky Ballet. They subsequently became quite prominent for their promotion of a flamboyantly decorative ballet culture in Chicago (1916–1927) and then in Los Angeles (1927 ff.) (Prevots, *Dancing,* 133–151; *Het Tooneel,* 3/10, March 1918).

Meanwhile, Green opened a school in The Hague and began working with Margaret Walker as her dance partner. In 1918 she produced *Carnaval,* with Schumann's piano cycle as accompaniment and a group of her students in fantasy Biedermeyer costumes. Here she revised the Pierrot and Columbine story to put Walker in the role of Pierrot and a male dancer in the role of Pantalon; the piece enchanted audiences, despite Green's somewhat perverse approach to the material (Lapidoth). In the 1920s she initiated several ambitious projects, including ballets of Dukas' *La Peri*, Ravel's *Daphnis et Chloe*, and Roussel's *Le Festin de l'araignee*. Debussy's music apparently unlocked a recessed inclination toward perversity in her solo dances, judging by several photos of her in the Nederlands Dans Instituut. Wearing an extravagant wig, she did a witch dance that probably represented the limit of her willingness to depart from the decorative, but in several other Debussy pieces she seems to have enjoyed baring her breasts or appearing nude under a diaphanous cloak, even though she was over forty years old. An article in *Spel en dans* (September 1925, 15–16) ranked her with Tamara Karsavina, Anna Pavlova, and Jenny Hasselquist as a world-class dancer. While on tour in Czechoslovakia, Green, "unhindered by labor laws," collected some slum children and brought them back to Amsterdam to perform in her fairy-tale ballet, *Die Verliebten* (ESG 16). Then she was busy with opera and civic spectacles.

In 1933, she appeared in a powerful open-air production at Zandvoort of Wilde's *Salome*. Besides playing the title role, she choreographed two ballets not designated in the text. These, according to one reviewer, were "absolutely justified" and produced a very dramatic effect, but he felt that, as Salome, Green, though "very beautiful," lacked morbid passion and sensuality, her response to the head of Jokanaan being "more the whim of a spoiled princess than of wild lust." However, she performed expertly and with great delicacy, especially at the end, and the *Dance of the Seven Veils*, with Strauss's music, was perhaps "the great moment of the production" ("Lili Green," A11). Green was forty-eight years old when she played Salome. But just as surprising was the publication of her *Verzen* (1934), which contained turbulent erotic poems: "My love is like a burning wound" (36); "I am lonely, beautiful and pale. My body longeth for thine arms to enfold me, my lips are parted with desire" (63). In 1935 she formed around her students Het Nederlandsche Ballet ("Lili Green," A12), and in 1936 she worked on dances for the Berlin Olympics. But she was not sympathetic to the fascist elements within Dutch dance culture that sought to develop nationalist feeling through ballet, and during the war years she led a cautious existence. In 1948, at age sixty-three, she gave her last solo concert, then went to Washington D.C. to create another school, which lasted until 1959. She then returned to The Hague to receive various honors and gave lessons well into her eighties.

Lili Green had a long career as a performer/choreographer in solo dances and stage plays, in opera and mass spectacle, in modern dance and ballet. Though the curriculum in her schools adapted to new trends, the dances she created did not change in their approach to bodily movement from around 1912 until her retirement from the stage in 1948. Yet her dances constantly seemed dramatic and exciting to audiences in Amsterdam, Paris, Vienna, and Berlin. The reason is that she cultivated an attitude toward bodily expressivity that enabled her to interest audiences regardless of differences in media, cultural context, or historical era. This attitude derived from a Delsartian faith in a correspondence between specific gestures and specific emotions and manifested itself through the phenomenon of pantomime, or "plastic dancing," as Green called it. The *Einführung* was an impressively erudite treatise on pantomimic art. Missing from her book was any discussion of rhythm, music, or group movement. Nor did she introduce any reference to hygienic or therapeutic effect. The focus remained strictly on what particular gestures signified. In pursuit of this aim, Green used photography in an imaginative way. She herself was the model for all the examples. A sequence of photographs could show how a series of gestures produced "concentration moments" that culminated in large emotional complexes; for example, an eighteen-photo sequence depicted a girl awakened, puzzled, and drawn by the fragrance of flowers, then conveyed her desire to possess the flowers and weave them into a rapturous bouquet (67–73). The photos posited a difference between the body's reading of a stimulus ("emotion station") and the body's response to the stimulus ("will station").

"Concentration moments" referred to dynamic tensions between qualities of energy and qualities of will. Subsequent chapters explained these relations. Seven "primary impulses" encompassed all relations between emotion and will: joy, fear, pain, struggle, inclination, disinclination, and sex drive. Each primary impulse subsumed distinct categories of emotional signification. Thus, for example, fear entailed terror, suffocating anxiety, helplessness, or horror, whereas disinclination (not the same as disgust) included repulsion, hostility, or aversion. Accompanying the text for each category was a photo of Green performing the appropriate gesture. To signify attraction, a category of inclination, the body stood with one foot forward, arms hanging away from the body with suspended effect, the head tilted and turned in the same direction as the forward foot, with the eyes fixed level to the object of attraction. To signify friendship under the same category, the head should remained turned (in the same direction as the forward foot) but now should be slightly uplifted, with both arms reaching forward and the hands together. To signify erotic desire, the body stood with feet slightly apart and arms hanging close against the body (thighs) while the head cast a level gaze at the object of desire with eyes half-closed and lips pressed into a slight smile. (However, for me, Green's signs of erotic desire might just as well signify "haughtiness.") To signify erotic enticement, the body stepped forward and approached the object of desire at an angle, with arms behind the back, the head sharply tilted, the eyes open, and the lips pressed into a full smile. To signify erotic excitement, the arms moved away from the body, which curved, arc-like, with the torso and groin pushed forward, the head pushed back, the eyes half-closed or closed, and the mouth open.

Of course, the total range of emotions the body may signify far exceeded Green's capacity to represent them or even to clarify distinctions between emotions she discussed and those she did not (such as the relation between erotic desire and haughtiness). Nor did she suppose that men differed from women in their signification of emotions. Furthermore, she did not clarify how the signification of emotions differed, in expressive value, from the performance of abstract categories of action, such as stabbing, kissing, praying, cradling, marching, or kneeling. Green's aim, however, was to demonstrate the decorative signification of emotion, so she left out all kinds of significations that convoluted the reading of bodily expressions. Decorativeness was synonymous with clear, refined readability of signs, but such readability was also synonymous with a filtering out of significations that transgressed anonymous conventions of appropriate expression and complicated the spectator's perception of the body.

In Germany, by contrast, the general mission of modern dance was to challenge the conventions of appropriate bodily expression. Indeed, German dance equated the liberated body not with an enhanced power to signify a wide range of emotions but with the power to signify and/or experience a single, great, supreme emotion: ecstasy. The basis for a free and modern identity lay in that most difficult to feel of all emotions. Green apparently sensed this problem with her approach, for she devoted a special section of her book to that "exceptional emotional condition," ecstasy (38–41). But her discussion of it was excessively conventional. For one thing, she asserted that the Greek meaning of *ekstasis,* "standing outside oneself," was the same as "an absence of the self," by which she seems to have meant an absence of bodily self-control. She associated ecstasy with dream states, with involuntary bodily movements such as those caused by epilepsy and hysteria, and with mystical visions of an archaic and frequently heretical nature. It was obvious that she was not at all sure how the body should signify ecstasy. "It happens with a cry," she remarked vaguely (38). She offered only one photograph of ecstatic signification, and this appeared at the end of a nine-photo sequence, "Amor Dei," that showed her in a medieval dress and cowl demonstrating the signification of revelation, awe, reverence, humility, service, prayer, sacrifice, embrace, and ecstasy (48–49). Ecstasy was manifest when the body thrust the arms upward and outward, with the head thrown way back so that it looked straight up. Ecstasy was a sculpted pose, a panel in an "appropriate" frieze rather than a peculiar condition of movement. Related to this limitation was her failure to trust her own photographic imagination. She came up with a worthwhile innovation: attaching tiny reflectors or battery lights to parts of the body and then photographing movement at slow shutter speeds so that the image recorded the traces left by the lights (63–64). But she failed to apply this interesting device to the analysis of emotional signification. Yet it was exactly this sort of technology that might have proved effective in resolving the problem of signifying ecstasy.

It is easy to assume that Green's theory of pantomime—and the whole Delasartian legacy she sought to preserve—was as marginal to German body culture as Green herself. But the assumption is misleading. Her analysis of conventions for signifying particular emotions was sound. Though her representation of emotions seems somewhat extravagant (melodramatic) by today's standards, the difference is primarily one of degree, not kind. Conventions of signification rigidly control communication with large audiences. To reach the large audiences vital to its economic security, the German film industry relied on performers who followed fairly closely the conventions of signification described by Green. Acting in silent films especially entailed a mastery of pantomimic expression. The music that invariably accompanied silent films was created independently of the screen performances, which meant that actors could not depend on external rhythms or harmonies to shape their bodily expressivity, nor could they rely on the stilted-looking declamatory style appropriate for classical theatre or make elaborate, time-consuming Stanislavskian efforts to build a completely realistic character. They had to employ conventions of physical-emotional "plasticity." Oskar Diehl's *Mimik im Film* (1922) purported to explain the pantomimic conventions of film acting, which he claimed derived directly from dance. But this little book, containing no pictures and no analysis of any particular signifying practice, was worthless as a contribution to pantomimic semiotics. Diehl focused almost entirely on movements available to the face, then merely listed various dramatic situations that required facial expression. However, the book did not signify so much the bankruptcy of pantomimic art as the failure of film culture to grasp the theoretical foundations of bodily expressions appropriate for the screen, for moving images rather than three- dimensional spaces. As pantomime became an art of containing bodily expression within an image, dance became an art of opening space through movement and therefore freeing the body from conventional images of it, which was why dance critics continually displayed skepticism toward performances that were "merely" pantomimes.

Yet the distinction between dance and pantomime was not always altogether precise, considering the complex career of Green herself and considering that several prominent modern dancers became skillful film actors and even stars, including Valeska Gert, Grit Hegesa, Lil Dagover, Leni Riefenstahl, Jenny Hasselquist, Harald Kreutzberg, Anita Berber, Rita Sacchetto. Conrad Veidt (1893–1943), a wonderful actor with no dance training, developed a highly expressive and idiosyncratic pantomimic style that sometimes seemed dancelike in its precision. According to a 7 April 1920 letter in the Leipzig Tanzarchiv, even Laban himself negotiated with the UFA film studio to produce a ten-part fairy-tale dance-pantomime, *Der Komet,* about a dance temple, a dance god, a dance cult, and a female dancer curious to see the invisible dance god. However, an inability to determine the relation between dance and pantomime prevented the film from being made.

Solo Dancing

Germany produced more systems of dance and bodily expressivity during the Weimar era than I am prepared to describe. Little information is available about many schools, but most seem to have subscribed to one or another or a combination of the systems already explained.[1] To survive, schools had to find a place in society for their graduates, which generally meant creating more schools and raising body consciousness on a national scale, making it part of the education of all modern citizens. Finding a place

---

1. Lämmel mentions several schools affiliated with Laban or Mensendieck without apparently having any official connection to either teacher: Helmi Nurk (Bremen), Margarete Schmidts (Essen), Edith Bielefeld (Karlsruhe), the Lucian School (Erfurt), Olga Suschitzky (Vienna), Karin Schneider (Graz), Gertrud Volkersen (Hamburg), Senta Maria (Munich), Marion Hermann (Oldenburg), Anne Grünert (Duisburg), Trude Hammer (Berlin), Frances Metz (Munich). Freund discusses a few of the more than 150 dance-gymnastic schools in Berlin about which information is otherwise very scant, including Lotte Wedekind, Ruth Allerhand, and Berthold Schmidt. The *Internationales Tanz Adressbuch,* published in 1922, listed approximately 720 persons in Germany who claimed to be solo dancers. Dancers affiliated with theatres and opera houses totaled nearly 600, including 560 females and 35 males. Approximately 250 persons worked as dance instructors, 47 of whom specialized in ballet. Most instruction applied to careers in cabarets and revues. The address book listed nearly 500 German cabaret dance acts, including 325 pair dance acts. In 1922, Germany apparently had 57 dance schools that prepared students for concert performances; these included 12 in Berlin, 5 in Hamburg and Frankfurt, 4 in Munich, and 3 each in Leipzig, Stuttgart, and Dresden. These figures compare with other European nations as follows:

England	58 (11 outside London)	Austria	13 (all in Vienna)
France	55 (26 outside Paris)	Rumania	1
Holland	43 (11 in Amsterdam)	Russia:	1 (the Duncan school)
Italy	5	Switzerland	13
Latvia	1	Belgium	3

for students who wished to become artists was considerably more difficult, especially when the demand to see dance did not expand nearly as dramatically as the desire to dance. But many dancers, especially before 1925, had little or no desire to teach. Such dancers depended on performances to establish and sustain their careers. Very few, however, had the resources to create dances that impressed audiences by their scale or their power to supersede ballet in terms of production values. No one in Germany—or anywhere, for that matter, except France and Russia—could assemble the resources that Sergey Diaghilev was able to muster to support the Ballet Russes, and he was successful in part because no one else was able to set up a competitive company on a comparable scale, although Rolf de Mare and the Swedish Ballet (1920–1924) certainly tried.[2] Many small ensembles emerged, especially out of the schools, but the great majority of these formed around a strong dance personality whose power to lead had been established through solo performances.

An amazing number of dancers gave solo concerts between 1910 and 1935. Today it is almost impossible to find anyone giving a solo dance concert, not because audiences are less indulgent and more demanding of dancers but because so few dancers have the intensity of message, the need to say something on their own, that possessed the solo dancers of the Weimar era. The challenge of sustaining the interest of an audience for an entire concert was an extraordinary test of artistic self-confidence and credibility for a dancer. In Berlin and Halle, Leni Riefenstahl (b. 1902) gave a two-hour solo concert that included a dance to Schubert's Eighth Symphony (1825), a feat that smacks of heroic ambition (Schab, in *Hallesche Zeitung*, 12 May 1923). In a video interview, Hanya Holm conveyed some impatience with contemporary (1980s) dancers who live by the motto, "Don't exhaust yourself": "You have to dare, otherwise you never find your approach" (Hauser). Because no European city contained a dance audience large enough to sustain more than a few performances of the same concert, touring was essential in developing an artistic career. Touring pressured a dancer to cultivate a national and international identity, which opened up a continental rather than merely a local market. Indeed, few solo dancers, unaffiliated with a school, could enjoy enduring careers without an international reputation. Apparently the Austrian dancer Gisa Geert and the German dancer Sonja Markus, representatives of a Wigman-Laban tendency toward "aesthetic brutalism" in modern German dance, were better known in Italy (1932–1933) than at home (Bragaglia). One can even suggest that the authority of German dance depended on its exportability, its power to attract foreign interest, for even the schools, especially the

---

2. On Diaghilev and the Ballets Russes, see, among a vast number of publications, Buckle, Percival, Nijinsky, Shead, and Krasovskaya. On de Mare and the Swedish Ballet, see Häger.

Laban institutes and Hellerau-Laxenburg, depended heavily on foreign students. Linguistic and cultural borders did not hem in dance as they did theatre, even though dancers and audiences alike expected dance to expose cultural differences.

SEMIOTICS OF SOLO DANCE

The credibility of German dance ideology depended heavily on solo dance performances, whereas the credibility of ballet and revue dancing rested on techniques and production values associated with ensemble performance. Of course, *Ausdruckstanz* was by no means indifferent to ensemble performance, and most expressionist dance concerts, especially after 1925, integrated solo dances into a program featuring ensemble dances as well. Yet the power of bodily movement to signify a unique, commanding personality seemed most convincingly affirmed when a single dancer demonstrated skills that could sustain the interest of an audience for an entire concert. But Germans were hardly responsible for the authority of the solo concert. Isadora Duncan established an unsurpassed threshold of glory as a solo dancer, inspiring the world of the arts on a scale that still seems amazing and that explains why so many young people wished to emulate her. In 1908 she collaborated with the eighty-member New York Symphony Orchestra in dancing to the whole of Beethoven's Seventh Symphony as well as five pieces by Chopin (the orchestra also played three other pieces). She repeated the feat, to great acclaim, in Paris as late as 1920, although by that time twenty-year-old dancer Elsie Altmann was scarcely impressed, nor was Mary Wigman (Duncan 199–201; Van Vechten 307–309; Altmann-Loos 155–156; Mueller, "Lebenslauf," 23). But other dancers of international stature soon followed in Isadora's wake to reinforce the prestige of the solo concert format.

Probably no dancer was more beloved around the world than Anna Pavlova (1881–1931). An astonishingly photogenic woman, she more than anyone else conveyed the impression of a beautiful creature who literally could not live without dancing. Although not much of an innovator in relation to bodily movement and not even a great virtuoso of ballet technique, Pavlova always seemed to bring great pathos and poignancy to every gesture. It was as if every time she danced she tried to recreate that ever-receding, enchanting moment when, as a child of six, she had first seen the magical splendor of ballet at the Marinsky Theatre with her mother (Pavlova 1–2). Her major achievement was in bringing dance and its image to an immense global audience, in showing that dance could move them with intensities of emotion to which ballet did not even aspire. Pavlova's pathos derived in large part from the haunting aura she projected of fragile beauty moving alone throughout the world.

Exotic dancers fascinated European audiences in a way that, after 1918, made European dancers who attempted to imitate them appear increasingly inauthentic. This trend pressured the Germans to look at bodily movement from genuinely modern perspectives. The Spanish flamenco dancer La Argentina (Antonia Merce [1890–1936]) acquired, from 1908, a huge international audience and, like Pavlova, danced herself to death through excessive touring (Levinson). Other exotic dancers appearing in Germany included the Indian Nyota Inyoka (1896–1971) and the Javanese Rodan Mas Jodjan (1870–1959), who participated in the 1928 Essen Dance Congress. Yet the taste for exotic dance emerged primarily through the prewar work of Westerners such as Mata Hari, Adorée Villany, Cleo de Merode, Maud Allen, Ruth St. Denis, all the Salome dancers, Ida Rubinstein, and, of course, the Ballets Russes. Exotic dance, in its European manifestations, aligned a libidinously uninhibited and somewhat "dangerous" body with decorative affluence, "excessive" materialism.[3] It was hardly a message that died in the war, but its perpetuation required dancers who shaped archetypes around, rather than merely exposed, their personalities. Even American dancers appeared exotic to Germans. Ruth St. Denis (1879–1968), with her repertoire of "Oriental" dances, enjoyed such success in Germany and Austria that her tour of those countries lasted from 1906 to 1908 (Shelton 67–87). In 1925 Paul Swan (1883–1972), "the most beautiful man in the world," appeared in Germany with "Oriental" dances that, if his attempts to "reconstruct" them in Andy Warhol's bizarre 1965 film about him are even vaguely accurate, must have seemed as fantastically campy then as now (Cluzel 1–31). Ted Shawn attracted much attention in 1929 when he presented in Berlin his he-man versions of North and Central American Indian dances; he then worked with Margarethe Wallmann, appearing more like Adonis than Orpheus in her *Orfeus Dionysos* (1930), although Shawn himself was apparently disdainful of German dance culture (Dreier; Shawn 225).

At any rate, particularly in the years 1919 to 1925, solo dance concerts proliferated abundantly, and a great many of them were performed by people about whom hardly anything is known. The pages of the short-lived (1920–1921) journal *Konzert, Tanz und Presse* contained reviews of solo

---

3. Perhaps the most comprehensive survey of exotic, "ethnic" dancers in the 1920s appears in Divoire (142–171); most of these dancers were Spanish. But an examination of the magazines *La Esfera* and *Illustracão*, published, respectively, in Madrid and Lisbon during these years, indicates that Iberian dancers (entirely female) were just as popular in Spain and Portugal as elsewhere. "Oriental" dancers, by contrast, projected a more complex identity, for some of them were not even Oriental but European, and even those who were Oriental modified their "original" dances to accommodate a Western image of Oriental movement. But often dances were "Oriental" simply because the dancers wore Oriental costumes or used music in an Oriental mode. See Buonaventura.

concerts given around Germany by dancers whose names rarely appear elsewhere: Suse Elsler, Lisa Abt, Ruth Schwarzkopf, Annie Lieser, Ilse Freude, Chari Lindis. Paul Nikolaus, in *Tänzerinnen* (1919), briefly described several dancers whose careers apparently did not progress deeply into the 1920s: Solveig Oderwald, Gusi Viola, Lucie Hertel, Erna Bertini, Macka Nordberg, Hannelore Ziegler. He explained that, although most of these dancers exuded plenty of charm, they lacked sufficiently liberating intensity of feeling because they remained too immersed in ballet technique, too devoted to decorative effects of the variety stage, or too restrained in their exploration of bodily rhythms. Other prominent fashioners of dance culture in the underresearched period of 1917–1923 included Hilde Schewior, Beatrice Mariagraete, Hilde Sinoniew, Hedwig Nottebohm, Vera Waldheim, Edith Bielefeld, Nina Schelemskaja (with Ellen Tels), Olga Samsylova, Hilda Hager, Stella Kramrisch, Maria Ley, and the Bulgarian Radeja Vinarova. The significance of most of these dancers lay in the attractive images of dance they projected in widely published photographs. In Munich and Berlin, beautiful (and apparently blonde) Lisa Kresse darkened her skin to perform whole programs of "Hindu" dances and dances related to "mysteries of the cabala" in the years 1918 to 1921, but information about her work remains difficult to find (*Elegante Welt*, 8/24, 19 November 1919, 10).

Solo dance concerts were definitely economical opportunities to establish precedents. In 1920 a local newspaper reported on a "stormily applauded" concert in Kiel given by an eight-year-old girl, Maryla Gremo, "which offered all manner of character dances with a gracefulness never before seen," although "such dances as the nigger dance, even when presented in all possible decency, are not suited for any child" (*KTP* 4, 121). During these years many "modern" dancers seem to have derived their sense of aesthetic movement from folk dances, from harlequinade/fairytale pantomime, or from romanticized forms of dance, such as the waltz or habanera. Suse Elsler received both praise and condemnation for performing old peasant dances rather erotically in a skimpy costume, portraying "a psychosis, the girlishly floral fantasies of a confused generation." Ruth Schwarzkopf received both praise and condemnation for getting "too deep" into the peasant dances, revealing in them something no one had seen before. Hedwig Nottebohm apparently inspired doubt and curiosity with her gymnastic, "masculine" mode of movement, as in her dance following the theme of a marathon runner.

In 1907 the Danish dancer Gertrud Barrison, formerly of the five Barrison Sisters of the music hall world, began performing folk dances and waltzes at cabarets and at recitals in Vienna before moving on to somewhat more complex pieces in which she obscured the genre of the piece by introducing more and more decorative and narrative (pantomimic) details. She was perhaps the first European to establish (in 1920) a school that offered courses in dance for film performance (Weissenböck 74). Another Viennese dancer, Grete Wiesenthal (1885–1972), was, from 1907 to about 1920, the great incarnation of the waltz spirit so closely identified with the city. Wiesenthal's training was in ballet, but she freed the waltz from the remote formality into which ballet had imprisoned it. The waltz provoked in her an unprecedented lyricism in bodily movement; Aurel von Milloss explained that she did not merely excavate or reconstruct some lost, original form of the waltz but "breathed the spirit of the waltz and danced her waltz-like feelings" (Endler 188). Whether in a swirling skirt or a loose tunic, she seemed driven by the 3/4 beat into a state of ecstatic abandonment. And she made very expressive use of her hair, as Rudolf Huber-Wiesenthal remarked: "Grete's delicate body bent over the ground, covered by her flowing mass of gold-brown hair. And then, slowly, timidly at first, she raised her closed hand into a bouquet, opened them, and with this release of the hands, her body rose also, her hair sinking back. Gradually the flow of tones strengthened the slender body until eventually she became entirely overpowered by frenzy, hurling herself, nearly flying, with her arms outspread, the gold rush of hair always a part of the movement, a part of the dance" (189). She also seems to have danced often with her eyes closed and her mouth parted in a smile; the beauty of her face was exquisitely haunting, and she conveyed that elegiac quality that, as Endler observes, is so often missing from choreographed waltzes (200).

Early in her career, Grete danced with her sisters, Else and Bertha. According to Brandenburg, Else's talent was too pantomimic and Bertha's too undeveloped to compete with Grete's, so Grete moved away on her own. Else and Bertha formed a duo (then a trio with Marta, another sister), but it did not last long, as Else moved in a manner that appeared "half puppet, half schoolgirl" (HB 44–47). In 1908, in Vienna, Rudolf Jobst (1872–1952) took a famous series of photographs of Grete, all outdoors and all showing her in motion. These showed dramatically how she had linked the waltz to an expansive, unbridled experience of space. Wiesenthal commanded deep respect from the Viennese cultural-literary elite, especially the circle around Hugo von Hofmannsthal, who collaborated with her on pantomine dramas, as did Max Reinhardt. Her extremely photogenic beauty brought her into motion pictures, with *Die Stumme von Portici* (1913) becoming an enormous success (Fiedler). By 1919, however, Nikolaus complained (with echoes from Suhr and Fischer) that her dancing lacked expressive power and "in no way triumphed over any limits" imposed by the genre (20).

Around 1915 another Viennese, Lucy Kieselhausen (1897–1927), began specializing in performing waltzes. She, too, had evolved out of ballet culture, but her embodiment of the waltz was virtually opposite that of Wiesenthal. She favored luxuriously decorative hothouse costumes and the utmost refinement of movement. For her the waltz was not a lyrical expansion of space into the freedom of nature but an almost perfumed distillation of the stirrings within an opulent boudoir, with its scenography of exquisite privileges and voluptuous secrets. An adroit sense of irony shaded her movements with abruptly "bizarre and jerky" rhythms; "her joyfully flashing temperament did not hover on a smooth surface but over a shadowy abyss from which issued her fool's dance with its slumbering, half-animal rapture" (HFT 47–48). Her curious appropriation of the waltz ended suddenly when she died in a benzine explosion.

Laura Oesterreich, a Hamburg native. began her career specializing in the performance of the polka, a genre of quite limited movement potential to which she brought a strange ambiguity. Brandenburg felt her polkas incarnated a slithery, darting spirit, "motherly," from the depths of the North Sea, "full of the little fear that one's foot, so capable of hovering, will stumble on a stone and glide away at each step, a small, lowering fear, which merely conceals the greater fear, not to have grown beyond a humble objective" (210). She was at her best, as in *Mazurka melancolique* (1917), combining this "little fear" in her steps with a face of ecstatic intoxication, eyes closed and lips parted, so that the dance seemed to reveal a puzzling internal tension. The tension intensified when she tried to appropriate the waltz, but in this endeavor she apparently failed because her body was "painfully" incapable of breathing the rhythms and tonality of this "southern" genre of music (209). Oesterreich had studied with Laban at Ascona in 1914, and in 1920 she worked, always as a soloist, with the Falke sisters on projects for the Münchener Tanzgruppe. In 1925 she gave a concert in Hamburg featuring six dances with nonmusical accompaniments—gongs, bells, horse clopping, hammer blows, buzzers, rattles—but it was not a success. It is not known what happened to her after this time (Stöckemann, "Pionierie," 40–41).

Oesterreich obviously sensed the severe limitations on the capacity of a dance genre to deepen the identity of either the dance or the dancer. Although dancers continued to explore the expressive potential of inherited genres—waltz, polka, sarabande, gavotte, minuet, czardas, tango, pavanne, fox trot, and so forth—after 1920 it was clear that the evolution of modernity in dance depended on freeing the dancer from too close an identification with generically structured responses; these subordinated dance to music, in the now passé manner of Duncan, and prevented dance from constructing personalities stronger than the genres and, indeed, stronger than music itself. Thus, in Hamburg, Gertrud Zimmermann received praise for her "nearly tragic" dance to a prelude by Rachmaninov because in this piece she seemed to get beyond the conventional, affable "sweet femininity" imposed upon her by the genre dances that made up the rest of her program (KTP 13, 1921, 214).

Even within the realm of genre dancing, dancers strove to differentiate themselves, to compete with other dancers for the attention of audiences, by imposing a personal attitude onto the genre. As a result, the aesthetics of the solo concert grew more complex. Programs began to include dances with unusual musical sounds for accompaniment—zithers and harmoniums, bass drum and woodblocks, harps and gongs. They contained mixtures of genre dances—a mazurka followed by a tango, a waltz before a polonnaise. But musical genres did not determine the identity of all the dances. Some dances carried progammatic titles that subordinated the composer's intention to that of the dancer: *Sea Clouds, The Pied Piper, The Amazon, Heart Flame, The Captured Bird, Astarte*. Others signified "genres" established entirely by dancers: sword dance, barbaric dance, marionette dance, demon dance, machine dance, wolf dance, temple dance, celestial dance, death dance. Variety of costume further displayed the complexity of the dancer's personality. A simple, elegant tunic exposed the beauty of the dancer's legs and arms, but romantic moods went best with long skirts, capes, mantels, hoods, or period garments (quite often from 1830–1845); a dance or two might feature an exotic look, appropriated perhaps from the Orient, ancient Egypt, or imperial Rome. And it could not hurt to perform a dance in sleek, decorative pants, although few dancers performed in leotards unless they sought to convey a harlequinesque effect. Performers perfected the expressive authority of their dances with accessories: strange hats, gloves, scarves, sashes, gilded belts, bizarre necklaces and bracelets, ribbons, garlands, veils, masks, fans, stockings, helmets, and feathers. *Ausdruckstanz* was not synonymous with barefoot dancing, and the use of sandals or high-heeled shoes was not at all rare, with Kreutzberg going so far as to employ knee-length boots in a couple of dances. But a dance concert should never turn into a fashion show; Nikolaus, Thiess, and Suhr warned that costumes could distract from perception of movement, although only Nikolaus supposed that nudity did not help to create an expressionist dance (70). Finally, dance concerts offered a range of moods: a solemn, heroic dance, then a melancholy dance, then a grotesque dance, then an exuberant dance, then a "Korean" or "Javanese" dance, then a romantic dance in bluish tones.

Nearly every dance was only as long as the corresponding musical composition; very rarely did a single dance involve the stitching together of several pieces of music. The vast majority of music came from composers who were already long dead or who had written their music without the dancer in mind. Only when the accompaniment included drums and gongs did the dance determine the length of the music. Most dances lasted about four minutes, but one or two in a given concert usually exceeded ten minutes in length; the entire program typically contained about twelve pieces, with various musical interludes to allow for costume changes. Solo dance concerts were never devoted to the performance of a single, ambitious work, such as a sonata, that explored a theme in depth, although Wigman seemed to move toward this goal with her concept of dance cycles. The dance concert followed the model of the musical recital rather than the epic poetry recital, the dramatic lecture, or the Ciceronian political oration. A successful concert should include at least one experimental dance that violated performance conventions: a "silent" dance, a dance with mirror floors and walls, a dance performed entirely while sitting in an armchair, a dance created by shadow projections, a dance with two masks, a dance involving march movement against waltz music, a dance with sword and shield, a dance performed behind a curtain, a dance depicting murder or sexual rapture (*bacchanale*), a dance in which the body moved faster and faster or slower and slower, a dance allegorizing revolution or the body of the marionette/machine or the Idol of Death. The Danish film melodrama *Afgrunden* (1910), probably the most profitable motion picture released in Europe that year, contained a fascinating scene in a music hall in which the great actress Asta Nielsen (1881–1971) performed a kind of polka-mazurka while smoking a cigarette and wearing a Wild West costume (Seydel 41). By using different combinations of all these aesthetic variables, dancers could pursue a montage mode of performance that allowed for considerable flexibility as long as the dancer maintained an expanding repertoire of pieces. Yet by 1920 Mary Wigman had presented concerts that challenged the semiotic conventions described here. She dared to present concerts almost entirely governed by a somber mood and indifferent to variety of decorative effect or charm. As always, she displayed a deep awareness of the dramatic potential of bodily movement—every step, every gesture, every glance laden with tension, conflict between the body and space, the body and time, the body and death, the body and itself.

The solo dance concert revealed above all a unique, compelling personality, not the values associated with a complex of conventions. One did not attend a solo dance concert to see this or that dance but to observe, across a repertoire, the terms under which the movement of a body expressed an utterly unique personality. This ambition was reserved for all but a few dancers and in any case became less imperative after 1925, when dance had become sufficiently institutionalized to allow dancers to shape their identities through teaching or even through a dance company rather than through solo performance.

EDITH VON SCHRENCK

Edith von Schrenck (ca. 1894–?) projected a cool, aristocratic persona. She consistently garnered much praise for the seriousness of her dances, and critics often compared her with Mary Wigman. Of all dancers in the early 1920s, Edith von Schrenck probably came the closest to rivaling Wigman in cultivating seriousness of expression as manifested in complexity of response. She was never as wild or as innovative as Wigman, but she conveyed a disturbing sense of passion, a dark power to stir deep feelings in audiences. This power depended on an intensity of boldness and vulnerability achieved by hardly anyone else (other than Wigman).

Schrenck was unusual in that she started as a teacher, then became a performer. Once she took to the stage, she showed great reluctance to perpetuate her identity through disciples. She was born in Riga of a Russian mother and a German-Latvian father who was a distinguished gynecologist in St. Petersburg, where she took lessons in piano and singing. But after attending a lecture by Dalcroze she decided to study rhythmic gymnastics at Hellerau. She spent two years there (1912–1914), received a diploma, then returned to St. Petersburg to teach at the Dalcroze institute run by Count Volkonsky. Through teaching she met an actress who had left Konstantin Stanisklavsky's company to develop a purely physical approach to dramatic performance. From Claudia Issachenko, Schrenck learned Delsartian semiotics and the Stebbins-Kallmeyer theory of "artistic gymnastics," but it is not clear if she danced with Issachenko's ballet company. She did, however, study ballet during the war years, without any intention of pursuing a career in dance (Buning, "Gesprek," 49). She also became friends with Estonian dancer Ella Ilbak, who described Schrenck's studiousness in her memoirs (Ilbak 71–72, 79–80). Then the revolution struck, pushing her out of Russia and, in 1918, out of Latvia.

Landing in Munich in difficult financial circumstances, Schrenck decided to establish herself professionally as a dancer. She was slow to do so, perhaps because the Dalcroze method as taught to her did not orient students toward professional performance. At any rate, she was always cautious about deciding anything, and her dances made extensive use of slow, "weighted" rhythms. The success of her solo debut concert in Munich led to a tour of German cities (Berlin, Hamburg, Düsseldorf), then to performances in Holland, Riga, Vienna. She worked briefly (1921) with the Hamburg-based Münchener Tanzgruppe and with Valeria Kratina, but group dances did not allow her talent to blossom, and from then on she performed only in the solo concert format (HB 229). Around 1925 Schrenck married Waldemar Bonsels (1881–1952), an enormously successful writer of children's stories and folk tales who had published praise of her since 1921. According to Ilbak, he opposed her collaboration with "strangers," even though he traveled widely and achieved distinction for his vagabond literary identity (Ilbak 172–174). She opened a school in Berlin (1929) and continued dancing until about 1930, but by this time she had completely detached herself from the mainstream of modern dance in Germany (as well as from Bonsels); she did not attend the dance congresses of 1927, 1928, or 1930, nor did she maintain contact with significant dance personalities of the time, and her school does not seem to have flourished beyond 1932 (Freund 49–52). Perhaps by then she had nothing more to say through dance.

Edith von Schrenck was extremely beautiful, but it is very difficult to find an image in which one sees her full face. She consistently and self-consciously withheld a part of herself from the spectator, always projecting a dark aura of aloofness and loneliness—which, indeed, became the subject of her dances. Brandenburg (203) observed that she tended to avoid the corners and sides of the performance space, conveying a sense of "dense closure" to the totality of her presence. This characteristic was represented perhaps most dramatically in *Gefesselt* (1919). In this piece, with music by Chopin, she danced the condition of being fettered, not moving from an initial position within the performance space. In only a tunic, she lunged and lurched with a violent swinging of her arms and turning away of her head; then, in profile, she curved her body into a bowing stance and crossed her arms over head as if her own body were the source of her bondage; she twisted with her back to the audience, pivoted and leaped high with outstretched arm, as if suddenly suspended by a chain, then immediately sank into the scrunched profile position before lunging out again toward the spectator with clasped, swinging hands, as if preparing to hurl a heavy, destructive weight (Schrenck 16–20). She gave an impression of great strength trapped in a body, not knowing where to go.

Delsartian semiotics allowed her to build a "dance architecture" out of dramatic tensions and ironic details. In *Kriegertanz,* later called *Amazone* (1919–1921), using music by Rachmaninov, she appeared in a pleated miniskirt with helmet, shield, and dagger. She constantly moved on tiptoes, first in a high march step with head tilted straight up, shield held level before her, and dagger clenched with straight arm down her side; then, in profile, she thrust shield and dagger behind her and pushed her belly forward, her head level; suddenly she swung around, shield at her belly, dagger raised high, her whole body a sinewy, muscled curve; she stabbed the space not before her but directly at her feet, then arched back ecstatically, dagger and shield raised over her uplifted head. Wounded, she sank to the ground, danced, pulsated on her knees, on her elbows; finally, some strength returned, and she began moving stealthily on her knees, face behind the shield, then surged up on tiptoes again and made a final, fatal plunge with the dagger before sinking to death (Schrenck 1–8). Brandenburg marveled at her skill in combining movements of "attack and flight, triumph and defeat, pounce and rest, kneeling, sinking, reclining, stretching" to produce a dance that was "no imitation of a sculpture" but the "primeval image" (*Urbild*) of the warrior. Buning saw in her a pagan, heroic spirit, and her *Schmerz* (1922) reminded him of a verse by Hölderlin: "[B]ut where danger is the salvational wakes, too." In this piece, Schrenck employed slow, hunched, rocking movements that became increasingly more delicate, slower, and smaller, continuing after the music had stopped (WBT 153).

To Buning it always seemed as if she danced with an invisible partner, and this curious sense of presence and absence of body made all her movements dramatic (WBD 36). Commentators consistently spoke of the "strictness" of her movements, as if she constantly sought to keep in check a great power or pressure within her, even in pieces such as *Wellen* (1922), in which she blended the motion of combing with the movement of sea waves. In *Polichinelle* (1919), with music by Rachmaninov, she began to dance joyfully, with extravagant lunges, leg stretches, leaps, and sways on one leg until, suddenly conscious of a dark, invisible energy surrounding her, she turned her dance into a melancholy image of pathetic loneliness. Her early dances sometimes displayed a serious sense of humor or irony, as when she did a temple dance dressed as a "piquant Jacobin" or presented her goblin dance with Grieg's music (*KTP* 13, 212–214). But in the ensuing years she completely favored dances of a tragic, melancholy, or elegiac character: *Polonaise, Page, Gothisches Lied, Last, Besiegt, Einsamkeit, Abseits, Marsch, Chaconne, Ziguenerin, Kampf.* Even in *Kindheit* (1923), she made the joy of being a child seem tinged with consciousness of a diminishing innocence. Her summer dance, from a 1924 cycle of the four seasons, began radiantly and luxuriously but suddenly turned somber; she performed again all the movements that had begun the dance but now slowly, heavily, as if under a withering heat.

Schrenck liked music in a minor mode (Bach, Rachmaninov, Scriabin). In 1929 she presented a concert in which all the music was serious: five pieces by Scriabin, two by Mussorgsky, one each by Brahms, Bach, and Handel. She was fond of dancing before and on tapestries, and she chose decorative costumes that displayed the great beauty of her arms and legs. Suhr thought she was perhaps too decorative in her approach: she held back some violence, something deep and great in her that she intimated but never really released (WS 46). Very few dancers could make such expressive use of the arms, yet she never seems to have danced fully erect—she loved displaying her capacity to bend, to twist, to hunch, to fold herself up, and remain beautiful all the same. This ability is quite evident in the twenty stark, expressionistic lithographs Ottheinrich Strohmeyer made in 1919 of three of Schrenck's dances: *Kriegertanz, Polichinelle, Gefesselt* (Schrenck) (Figures 39–41). Hans Fischer saw in her art a "visionary enclosure" of power (*KTP* 13, 1921, 213); Schikowski had "the feeling that through unprecedented exertions of strength [Schrenck] subjugates the depths of a boiling volcano. And one expects at any moment a sundering of the cool surface ... " (*Geschichte*, 152). But one may also see in this aesthetic a woman's tragic awareness of music as a great force pressing in upon the body—a sense conflicting sternly with the doctrine of her decisive teacher, Dalcroze, who insisted that, for anyone as sensitive to music as she obviously was, music could only bring the body to a state of supreme liberation.

GRIT HEGESA

Grit Hegesa (ca. 1896–?) remains a mystery. She came from Cologne, but her debut concert occurred in Berlin in 1917, at which time she apparently associated with expressionist artists affiliated with the Secession ("Exp. im Tanz"). In 1917–1919 she was active in Holland, giving concerts in Amsterdam and in Rotterdam, where she associated with a circle of modern artists, mostly expressionists, calling itself De Branding (Brinkman 107–109). At this time she worked with the Dutch composer Jaap Kool (1890–1959), but it is not clear if this collaboration brought her to Holland or began after she had arrived. Hegesa was unique in exclusively using music composed by a modern composer for her dances. Educated in Paris, Kool contended that dance could not seriously develop a modern identity as long as one danced to old pieces of classical music, even those written for dance. Music for dance, he argued, emphasized rhythm at the expense of harmony, which Western classical music did not but which jazz, some forms of popular music, and exotic music from the Orient did (Kool, *Tänzszene*, 1–4). Old classical music lacked a modern sense of rhythm, by which Kool meant not only a complex, dominating sense of pulse but also strange *sounds*. He therefore employed in his music for Hegesa drums, bells, and gongs from his collection of Javanese gamelan instruments and different kinds of glass-timbred instruments. But Kool had eclectic tastes that allowed him to travel comfortably in the realm of commercial popular music. In addition to his Labor Symphony (1924) and concert piece for twenty-eight drums, he composed arrangements for the Erik Charrell Revues in Berlin, operettas such as *Miss Fu* (1924), film music, jazz pieces, and dance tunes. Perhaps his most widely known works were composed for the eccentric ballets *Die Elixir des Teufels* (1925), staged by Ellen Petz in Dresden, and *Der Leierkasten* (1925), choreographed by Max Terpis in Berlin, then by Claire Eckstein in Würzburg (1927) and Anne Grünert in Duisburg (1927).

In 1919, Kool wrote an article about Hegesa for the Dutch art journal *Wendingen* (2/3, 15–21) in which he described her art as "visible music" and "pathbreaking in expressive possibilities" of the body, especially the arms, because of her excavation of archaic, erotic modes of bodily movement. He quoted Hegesa as saying that when she choreographed herself she kept in mind the image of ancient Greek movement choirs such as appear on vases, not the ladylike Grecian dances of Duncan but those "which in our highly developed culture come into conflict with the censor; I think moreover of the splendid nude dances of the youths and girls of the gymnasium. I think of the stylized erotic dances from the island of Lesbos and the satyr plays and faun dances of the Phrygian Dionysian festivals." However, the *Hegesa Tango* (1922), which Kool also scored for full symphony orchestra, was a dark (E minor), lilting, haunting piece, never loud for a single measure, with a melodic theme built out of the letters of her last name. In 1919, while collaborating with Hegesa in Berlin, Kool also worked with Anita Berber, composing for her the music for her Pritzel Doll dance and the piano arabesque *Profane* (1920), which Hegesa actually danced. In other words, collaboration with Kool implied pursuit of an aesthetic that blurred distinctions between high cultural seriousness, exoticism, and the *mondaine* salon.

But Hegesa had her own ideas about blurring the distinctions. She delighted in cultivating a complex, unstable image of dance, which she reinforced through her affiliations with visual artists. She may have been the first modern dancer to wear the *Bubikopf,* or pageboy haircut, adopting it as early as 1917. In Rotterdam the artist Herman Bieling (1887–1964) did a series of etchings of her dancing, one of which now resides at the Nederlands Theater Instituut (Figure 42). This image from 1917 depicts Hegesa performing her *Groteske* and suggests a sort of manic extravagance in her movements, as if the dance had twisted her body into a fantastic, muscled plant with weird blossoms and sprouts, her foot almost violently rooted into the ground. The picture also contains six tiny human figures—homunculi images of different movements of the same dance. The following year Bieling painted a large portrait of the dancer (also deposited at the Instituut), an astonishingly beautiful piece of expressionism, full of powerful colors (Figure 43). However, it shows her on pointe (in ballet slippers), holding a pose, with eyes closed and head turned away, crowned by a large wig. She wears an enormous skirt decorated with a hieroglyphic expressionist design. Deep in the background, which is traversed by abstract geometric shapes and intersecting layers of planes, stand three women in bathing suits, two with their backs turned, the third gazing not at the dancer before her but at something concealed from both the dancer and the spectator. It is a most fascinating portrait because it dramatizes the perception of dance as a highly artificial construction of identity that moves both the body and space toward abstraction: the dancing body transforms space into a kaleidoscopic skewering of geometric order.

But Hegesa did not confine her image to these visions. For photographer Nicola Perscheid she appeared in luxuriously decorative and sometimes exotic-Oriental costumes; for Berlin photographer Ani Riess she posed in a low-cut, expressionist minidress with an extravagant collar, often before backdrops of swirling expressionist arabesques (*Elegante Welt,* 8/11, 1919; Kool, *Tänzszene,* frontispiece). Then she posed for the fashion page: in lush kimono, with legs exposed, reclining voluptuously on a divan before a luminous Oriental screen; modeling a suave afternoon cloak and dress (*Elegante*

Welt, 9/14, 1921, 20). Despite her considerable beauty and her peculiarly large, captivating eyes, one hardly recognizes Hegesa as the subject of these images, so preoccupied was she in disclosing new aspects of her identity. Suhr reproached her (as well as Kieselhausen and Berber) for her eagerness to produce such worldly, hedonistic images of herself, but he did not think they concealed a weak dance aesthetic (WS 37).

In 1920, Hegesa began starring in movies, including at least two tragic melodramas directed by E. A. Dupont, *Der weisse Pfau* (1920) and the two-part *Kinder der Finsternis* (1921), in which she played an American heiress in Italy. She received strong praise for the sophistication of her acting (*Paul Leni*, 266–267, 279–281). *Der weisse Pfau,* an adaptation of a play by Dupont and Paul Leni, described the doomed effort of an English aristocrat to transform a child gypsy cabaret dancer, Maryla, into a lady. Class prejudices prevent the romance from succeeding, so the dancer goes her own way as Marylova and becomes famous, especially for her dying white peacock dance (modeled, obviously, on Pavlova's dying swan). Years later, the aristocrat cannot forget her, but it is too late: she performs the dying peacock dance, then dies herself when the theatre catches fire.

Hegesa later incorporated a white peacock dance into her concert programs, with music by Kool, and this dance, using a feather costume, contrasted significantly with the film version. The concert dance began with the peacock strutting proudly and narcissistically, then confronting a motionless demonic idol. At first the bird expressed belligerence and fury at the idol for its lack of response, then displayed intense fear of a monstrous doom. Seeking to avoid this fate, the bird bestowed affection and worship upon the idol, but when these failed to produce any response the peacock resumed its proud, haughty strut (Kool, *Tanzszene,* 5). The dance appeared on a program Hegesa and Kool brought with them to Holland in 1921, but this time they performed in a theatre entirely associated with cabaret. One reviewer felt her art was too serious for such a context; her dancing, which made the theatre "as silent as a temple," required too much concentration and lacked the casual informality the cabaret patron expected ("Grit Hegesa"). In 1924 or 1925, Hegesa married the painter Emil van Hauth (1899–?), from Cologne but resident in Berlin. In him, she inspired a fascinating, mysterious portrait of "a type of female youth unknown until lately" (*The Studio,* 92/401, 14 August 1926, 134) (Figure 44). But after this point, one loses trace of her.

The final piece of evidence for the dance aesthetic of Grit Hegesa comes from a program for a concert of her expressionist dances sponsored by De Branding in Rotterdam on 1 February 1919. Kool preceded the dances themselves by giving "ideas on modern dance art," and the program itself announced that dance, which did "not provoke sexual stimulation," could offer "the most beautiful expression of all human feelings" and that the

dances of Grit Hegesa would "evoke the dark spheres of the tragic." Florrie
Rodrigo assisted Hegesa in two of the dances. In all but the last two pieces,
Hegesa wore pants of one sort or another. She began with a waltz, then performed a coolie dance in baggy silk pants, silk shirt, and conical hat,
employing symmetrical movements in accordance with the symmetrical
rhythms Kool associated with Oriental music. Next came the grotesque
dance already discussed and the *Leisure Hour of a Page,* an example, apparently, of what Suhr identified as "psychic perversities" in her aesthetic (WS
35). Then, with Rodrigo, she performed a pantomimic Pierrot and Pierette
dance: Pierette (Rodrigo), having returned from a ball, danced a tired,
happy, "harmless" waltz until she sank into sleep. Pierrot (Hegesa) then
entered, pirouetting exuberantly, but abruptly became delicate upon notic-
ing the smiling slumber of Pierette. He took the flower that had dropped
from her hand and danced with it tenderly, joyfully, reverently, then sank
down to kiss Pierette on the neck. In her sleep, Pierette extended her arms
to embrace the lover of her dream, but when Pierrot awoke her to her feet,
her disappointment and fear drove her immediately from the scene, leaving Pierrot to sink back into the pillows. After the intermission, Hegesa performed a "melodrama," *Der Held,* based on a story by Rabindrath Tagore.
She followed this with a "Japanese scene," assisted by Rodrigo: a servant
(Rodrigo) entered, lighting lamps and arranging flowers and pillows. Then
an elegant Japanese woman (Hegesa) appeared, wearing a "splendid headdress" and the red obie of mourning. She sank to the pillows, and immediately an ominous mood pervaded the scene; the face of her dead lover
glowed briefly in the lamplight, calling to her. The image filled her with
great longing. She called for the poisoned flower petals, which she kissed;
then, in silence, she sank to her death on the pillows (Kool, *Tanzszene,* 5). A
samurai dance followed the Japanese scene, and it, like the grotesque
dance, had "nothing to do with feminine beauty or charming gracefulness";
then a scherzo, in which she wore the strange, expressionist minidress, and
a Slavic dance, about which I know nothing other than that it was in a
melancholy vein.

A reviewer expressed dissatisfaction with the Pierrot and Tagore pieces
because Hegesa play-acted too much at impersonating a male and therefore
looked liked a "childish young woman," in sharp contrast to the "powerful
expressiveness" of the other pieces. The reviewer also noted that Hegesa
moved often on tiptoes, which suggests that she had ballet training ("Grit
Hegesa"). Nikolaus thought she was too intellectual to embody expressionist dance: her will to dance, her intensity of concentration, was stronger
than the feeling she constructed (46). And Suhr felt she danced elegantly,
especially with her arms and hands, but "without the trace of a soul" (WS
35). However, these writers were consistently skeptical of dancers who
relied on pantomimic-decorative effects, an aura of luxurious and even per-

verse refinement; they did not deny that Hegesa presented a strong, serious personality and a smooth technique. The perversity of her aesthetic was perhaps most evident in a dance not performed at the Rotterdam concert. She impersonated a Javanese prince, who sat in the lotus position on pillows and decorated himself with jewels and paint in preparation for his wedding. He rose only in anticipation of meeting his bride, and when she did not appear, he returned to the lotus position and sat, motionless, waiting for her, having become, so to speak, the idol that had appeared in the peacock dance. What made Hegesa unique was the extent to which dance mutated her personality. She seems to have relied on the symmetrical technique of movement, whereby one part of the body mirrors another, for almost all her dances. She displayed a distinct style of movement and a distinct taste in costume, yet she delighted in not being "recognizable," of being someone else every time she appeared, a stranger to her own image.

CHARLOTTE BARA

Charlotte Bara (b. 1901) was perhaps an even stronger inspiration for artists than Hegesa, but the image and the aesthetic she projected were also far more stable. She was born in Brussels of German parents and began dance studies there under a woman who had been a student of Isadora Duncan. She took lessons from Alexander Sacharoff in Lausanne in 1915 and gave her first concert in Brussels in 1917, at which time she presented her Egyptian mummy dance, the prototype for her entire dance aesthetic. The war finally compelled her family to leave Belgium for Holland, where Bara studied Javanese religious dance and became fascinated by the mystical dances of Rodan Mas Jodjan. Soon thereafter she and her mother resided briefly at the utopian art colony of Worpswede, near Bremen, where the maverick communist artist Heinrich Vogeler painted two famous portraits of her, "Die Frau im Krieg" (1918) and "Die Tänzerin Charlotte Bara" (1918). As Vogeler himself put it, she projected a memorable expression of the "trust, imploration, and despair" defining the female victim of war—or, more precisely, the sanctification of the feminine by war (Küster 112) (Figure 45). In 1919 she moved to Ascona, where her father had purchased a huge estate with the plan of creating a large park for the performing arts. During the renovation of the estate, however, the family resided for several years in Berlin, where Bara became a celebrated symbol of salvational mystery within the arts community. She appeared (1919) at Max Reinhardt's Kammerspiel; Moissy Kogan produced woodcut images of her; and Christian Rolfs painted her dancing (Meyer). Georg Kolbe published a set of drawings depicting her Egyptian dances, and Ani Riess photographed her (1920) using an expressionist backdrop (as she had with Hegesa) as Bara presented her Gothic dance *Hymnis,* in which she wore nothing but a dark veil. This quite erotic religious image did not appear in the journal *Roland* (23/33) until 1925.

Soon Rochus Gliese filmed *Die gotischen Tänze der Charlotte Bara* (1923), which apparently has not survived, and the artist Hugo Windisch began designing medieval and Renaissance costumes for her dances. She cultivated a friendly association with the new Wigman-oriented school opened in Berlin by Berthe Trümpy and Vera Skoronel in 1924. In 1925 she produced her first group work, *Totentanz,* which provoked much acclaim, although it was actually a revision of a death dance she had performed solo since 1920. Afterward she performed in Paris, where Fernand Divoire spoke warmly of her art (94–95), and in Florence, where she attracted the enthusiasm of Gabriele d'Annunzio and Anton Bragaglia, whose book, *Scultura vivente* (1928), explicated the principles of her dance aesthetic. With Bragaglia, she staged (1925) dances in ancient Roman ruins. But Bara was also busy with productions in Locarno and Ascona for various festive occasions in parks and plazas as well as the Kursaal Theater. In 1925 the great villa Castello San Materno finally became the family home, and there she and her husband, the psychiatrist Carl Rutters, operated a school for dance, theatre, and singing (1927), with a special curriculum in therapeutic dance. Her father built for her a most unusual theatre, seating 180, that could accommodate different modes of performance: dance, cabaret, theatre, lectures, and experimental or classroom activity. The design, by Bremen architect Carl Weidemeyer, allowed structural units to be moved in relation to the objectives of a particular performance; moreover, large glass windows provided spectacular views of the Swiss landscape, and it was even possible to give open-air performances on the rooftop amphitheatre (Wels). From the late 1920s until around 1940, Bara produced most of her many works in this theatre, which also attracted many distinguished guest artists, such as Rosalia Chladek, Valeska Gert, Lisa Czobel, Rodan Mas Jodjan, and Trudy Schoop, as well as numerous cabaret acts, including Erika Mann's Pfeffermühle, Dela Lipinskaya, and Rudolf Nelson. However, financial difficulties plagued the Teatro San Materno in the 1940s, and it was not until 1952 that Bara resumed her dance productions for it. Her final dance concert was in 1958, after which it became increasingly used as a site for experimental or chamber theatre productions (Stadler, "Theater," 130–132).

But despite her exposure to so many diverse artistic currents, Bara's dance aesthetic remained stable throughout her life and almost unchanged from the time of her first concert, *Tanz der Mumie* (1917), presented in Brussels. She produced a huge number of dances, yet such prolific creativity depended on a certainty of purpose and, indeed, upon a facile treatment of bodily expressivity that never encountered any dramatic measure of doubt. Perhaps her dance aesthetic was even less complex than that of the Bode, but it was definitely more grandiose and much more expressive of a unique personality. Bara suffused all her dances with an aura of religious mystery. At first the image of religious idolatry came to her from archaic Oriental or Egyptian iconography, but in Worpswede and Berlin she started adopting Gothic and then Renaissance models of holiness and beatification. Dance commentators consistently referred to her "Gothic dances"; however, after making her film with Gliese (1923) she called them "sacral dances." These were numerous and completely detached from any church or proselytizing objective: *Trauermarsch* (1919), *Aegyptisches Mysterium* (1919), *Madonna* (1920), *Die Büsserin* (1920), *Die Aegypterin* (1921), *Antike Grabschrift* (1921), *Aegyptischen Tanz* (1922), *Muzierende Engel* (1924), *Kreuzzitter* (1924), *Anbetung der Engel* (1926), *Göttertanz* (1927), *Die Visionen der Jeanne d'Arc* (1932), *Das verlorene Paradies* (1934), *Die Versuchung in der Wüste* (1934), *Bilder aus der Passion* (1935), *Mittelälterliche Legende und Visionen aus dem Orient* (1939), *Danza dei Beati* (1952), *Indische Gottheit* (1953), *Judith* (1955), and *Flucht nach Aegypten* (1955).

This hardly complete list suggests that Bara regarded dance as the way to reconcile a basic, lifelong tension in her between archaic Eastern and medieval Christian images of mystery. She identified mystery with an atmosphere of salvational transfiguration, not with a moral doctrine nor with meditations on the existential structures of good and evil. That is to say, her dances derived from images of religious feeling, not from gospel, even when, during the 1930s, she began structuring her dances according to narratives in the Bible. Egyptian and Oriental dances always remained a part of her repertoire, for in spite of its Near Eastern origin, Christianity could never synthesize Western and Eastern modes of mystery—only dance could do that. Seldom did she even use religious music to accompany her dances, preferring instead secular romantic and modern music by composers such as Scarlatti, Franck, Debussy, Grieg, Bartok, and Malipiero. In the 1950s she started dancing to Renaissance music played on authentic Renaissance instruments, whereas in 1920 she performed several dances in holy silence, without any accompaniment at all.

Her dance aesthetic changed little in the intervening three decades. For Bara, dance was ecstatic to the extent that it was *peaceful*, an expression of luminous serenity, exalted tranquility, shadowy resignation. The ecstatic body in her mind transcended violence and struggle; dance was a release from destructive impulses and perhaps even from awareness of danger. Her dances were not naive or harmless, however—they were mysterious; they signified a cosmic remoteness from the modern world and identified innocence with a gentle, graceful movement into an eternal, idealized, crepuscular past. Visual artists admired her because she modeled her dances after paintings and sculptures; spectators saw the body rather than the movement. She never moved with urgency, nor did she move, as Schrenck did, with a plodding sense of burden. When she swung her arms, she conveyed the lilting, pendulumlike motion of a priestess dispensing incense. She moved through a sequence of obviously "pious" categories of bodily signifi-cation—prayer, invocation, supplication, meditation, imploration, annun-ciation, baptism, annointment, sacrificial offering, reverie, lamentation, adoration, resignation, and ascension. Such were the bodily dynamics des-ignating mystery, all performed with the same eternal rhythm signifying transcendence of temporal discontinuity. Humility pervaded every move-ment; she neither smiled nor frowned but projected a visionary gaze of serene concentration fixed upon the image of God. Fear rarely entered into the aesthetic, neither fear of God nor fear of Satan—most peculiar in work of a religious nature, which usually depicts harrowing sacrifice as a prereq-uisite to redemption. Even in her grotesque religious dances, she avoided the iconography of devils or demons and focused on strange incarnations of idolic femininity: art deco Isis. Yet seldom did she employ recognizably religious costumes such as cowls, monastic habits, or ecclesiastical robes. Instead she danced in long, flowing smocks, diaphanous veils, and elegant nightgowns, often appearing less like an austere holy woman, or sibyl, than a good princess prepared for a good night's rest. On only one occasion (1932) did she ever employ masks. Many images from the 1920s show her in headbands and long silky hair, looking startlingly like a hippie flower child of the late 1960s.

In 1921 Blass noted that her sense of movement seemed dominated by the image of procession (38), and the dance critic for the *Deutsche Allgemeine Zeitung*, Fritz Böhme, complained in 1922 (7/2) and again in 1923 (10/2) that Bara displayed a painterly style, derived from images by Grunewald and Breughel, but no dance technique; in her *Madonna* she danced the image of a "world without sin, a world without the burdens of human weakness or stumbling into misery or torture over earthly things." Schikowski, in 1926, was more benign: "The Gothic style she pursues has little of the elementary, ecstatic weight of the old Gothic—it is a mild, gentle, bourgeois, modern-ized Gothic and stands nearer to the English Pre-Raphaelites than to the spirit of the Middle Ages. And yet it has its moments which reach deep into the soul to produce a stirring sense of beholding. A convulsive, whirling leap, a powerful uprightness of her figure, a sinking of the head with a fold-ing of all lines, an unresisting, surrendering plunge create images of entirely new and unusually strong expressive power" (151). But he observed that this "abstract style" was not an "expression of bodily form but of the pure language of line and shape. A fist lifts high and spreads the fin-gers; yet one no longer sees the arm and the hand—one sees a shooting white line and something balled up unravels and transmits an ignited radi-ance." Ultimately, however, such an aesthetic of the body and movement did "not penetrate the heart": "[T]he eye enjoys the strict linear rhythms of well-patterned attitudes and movements, but our feeling for the body does not resonate with it" (152).

The exception to these judgments, according to Blass, was her solo *Totentanz* (1920), in which she expressed the strength of desire rather than the bliss of contentment: "Here [dance] hunts, drums, rides, hacks, struggles, sprouts, sprouts so powerfully, so irresistibly that the future of Charlotte Bara seems to lie in the expression of unrest, movement, and questioning of the soul" (40). But Bara returned to the death dance theme only twice. The *Totentanz* of 1924 was her first group work and derived its imagery from the famous woodcut series of Hans Holbein. The 1943 *Totentanz*, done at San Marteno, was also a group work and again followed the medieval model of Holbein: with the original sin of Eve, Death, in processional fashion, takes everyone—king and queen, knight and fool, farmer and courtesan, young girl and money lender, physician, beggar, monk, innocent child. Bara herself danced the role of Death, in the stiff manner of a woodcut, moving in a circle around a medieval bell clock (Stadler, "Theater," 131). But the death dances were clearly not typical of her aesthetic. The compulsion to transcend death was the reason for the absence of fear or desire in her other works and for the need to create a religious body dynamic that was too mysterious for Christian morality alone to explain: the image of the mummy loomed over her entire aesthetic, the frozen, eternalized image of the human body. Thus, in almost direct contradiction to Wigman, Bara treated movement as a sign of rest rather than restlessness and thus, too, as an antidote to the convulsive destruction inflicted by the shadow of death upon a body too eager to submit to the rhythms of its desires.

SENT M'AHESA

Bara obviously constructed a unique significance for Egyptian dances within her sacral dance aesthetic as a whole, even though audiences persisted in associating her with Gothic dances. Such confusion of identity did not apply in the case of Sent M'ahesa (Elsa von Carlberg [1893–1970]), whom audiences persisted in identifying with Egyptian dances (though her dance aesthetic included images from other ancient or exotic cultures). She performed all her dances solo. Born in Latvia, she went to Berlin in 1907 with her sister to study Egyptology but became so enchanted with ancient Egyptian art and artifacts that she decided to pursue her interest through dance rather than scholarship. It is not clear whether she saw Ruth St. Denis perform her Egyptian dances in Berlin in 1908. At any rate, under the name of Sent M'ahesa she presented a program of Egyptian dances in Munich in December 1909 (Ettlinger). From then until the mid-1920s, she achieved fame for her exceptionally dramatic dances dominated by motifs from ancient Egyptian iconography. She was apparently an aristocrat who felt no need to establish a school in which to perpetuate her aesthetic. In the mid-1930s she moved to Sweden, settling in Stockholm in 1938 and becoming a Swedish citizen in 1946. There she did some journalism and worked at the Stockholm dance museum. It is not clear that Sent M'ahesa ever visited the cultures she appropriated; many of her ideas likely came from images she encountered in Germany.

Sent M'ahesa took ballet lessons in Berlin, but she was a barefoot dancer whose debt to ballet rested primarily on her cultivation of an elegant bodily aura. She applied a very scholarly sensibility to her dances, yet she was no pedant and did not subordinate aesthetic power to academic authenticity. Moreover, in constructing her Egyptian dances, she extended her sense of detail almost exclusively to ancient Egyptian images. She did not reconstruct ancient Egyptian dances, unlike Irene Lexova in Prague, whose father was a famous Egyptologist and whose versions of Egyptian dances, in the late 1920s, deliberately contrasted with the common perception of formal stiffness associated with the Egyptian image of the body (EST 100–103; Lexova). But, as Brandenburg observed, Sent M'ahesa did "not want to show Egyptian art, but rather the relation of a modern, European person to this art." In this respect she was significant, not because of her scholarly objectivity but because of her complex subjectivity, her "entirely personal interpretations of [archaic] creations" (56). This point seemed reinforced by her determination not to create an elaborate "illusion" of Egyptian culture, for she performed most of her dances, not all of which were Egyptian, before a tapestry (HB 57). In other words, she consciously strove to present an image of the body that was out of context.

Her dances always functioned in relation to intricate, highly decorative costumes of her own design, so that it appeared as if she chose movements for their effect upon her costume. In her moon goddess (or Isis) dance, she attached large, diaphanous cloth wings to her black-sleeved arms. Around 1915 she wore a large, Pharaonic helmet when she danced this piece, but around 1920, with the choreography unchanged, she wore a short white skirt and a small, tight, cloth tiara, large earrings, and heavily bejeweled top. The 1915 costume produced greater ambiguity of sexual identity, but the 1920 image produced a greater impression of purely feminine power (HB plate 26; Ettlinger 33). Sent M'ahesa often exposed her flesh below the navel, but I have yet to find a picture of her in which she exposed her hair, so keen was she on the use of wigs, helmets, caps, scarves, kerchiefs, tiaras, masks, and crowns. In her peacock dance, she attached a large fan of white feather plumes to her spine. In other dances, she draped herself with tassels, decorative aprons, double sashes, layers of jeweled necklaces, and arm, wrist, and ankle bracelets. Only in her Indian dances did she wear anything resembling pants. In one, her legs simply appeared to move within two

large, voluptuous veils; in another, she wore what look like highly ornamental pantyhose complemented by shoulder-length gloves (Nikolaus 37;
HB plate 21). Her costume for *Salambo* (1919) was especially complicated:
she covered her left arm and left leg in matching decorative sleeves, leaving
the right arm and leg exposed. An ornamental chain was attached to each
ankle—she danced in shackles. She further emphasized the sense of her
body's being reined in by applying a jeweled neckband, a tightly bound ker-
chief, and layers of swirling sashes around her waist. Yet she did not convey
an impression of being oppressed; on the contrary, she appeared to surge
with ecstatic energy, as if her body gave her great pleasure in spite of her
own desire to restrain it. Photographs indicate she may have "bronzed" her
skin to exoticize her body even further.

In 1924 Fritz Giese, though quite enthusiastic about her dances, said that
Sent M'ahesa was "neither beautiful nor young" and that her dance aesthetic was "antierotic" (FGK 174). Such a statement might explain her focus
on decorative costume effects. But I find Giese's comment obscure: her
body was wonderfully svelte, and her face displayed a cool, chiseled beauty.
I think, rather, that she sought to decontextualize female beauty and erotic
feeling from archetypal images of them originating in cultures other than
her own or her audience's; she sought to dramatize a tension between a
modern female body and old images of female desire and desireability.
Ettlinger, in 1910, was perhaps more accurate when he remarked that

> Sent M'ahesa's dance has nothing to do with what one commonly under-
> stands as dance. She does not produce "beautiful," "sensually titillating"
> effects. She does not represent feelings, "fear," "horror," "lust," "despair," as
> "lovely." Her art requires its own style. Her movements are angular, geometri-
> cally uncircular, just as we find them in old Egyptian paintings and reliefs. Nei-
> ther softness of line nor playful grace are the weapons with which she puts us
> under her spell. On the contrary: her body constructs hard, quite unnaturally
> broken lines. Arms and legs take on nearly doll-like attitudes. But precisely
> this deliberate limiting of gestures gives her the possibility of until now
> unknown, utterly minute intensities, the most exquisite refinements of bodily
> expression. With a sinking of the arm of only a few millimeters, she calls forth
> effects which all the tricks of the ballet school cannot teach (33–34).

What is especially peculiar about Ettlinger's description is the perception
that Sent M'ahesa put the representation of feelings in quotation marks, so
to speak, by using a style of movement that was incongruous with expected
significations. Brandenburg felt she subordinated movement to a pictorial
effect and therefore unnecessarily reduced the powerful expressiveness of
her body (57–58; WS 48). She moved primarily in two dimensions and displayed little inclination to develop a sense of depth within the performance
space. Her body consistently moved in profile and often within a very narrow zone close to the tapestry backdrop (Figure 46). Within this restricted

space, her body stirred with tension-laden movements. She carefully coordinated the sinking or lifting of her head, for example, with the precise raising of one arm above her head and the other arm above her waist; the fingers of each hand, pressed tightly together, trembled delicately and somehow caused a leg to rise and bend at the knee, the foot dangling elegantly in a pendulum motion. Sometimes she performed such complicated movements very rapidly, giving rise to the perception that she had a "very well-trained body" (*KTP* 4, 1920, 119–120). Yet she never gave an impression of fragility. In her Isis dance, she knelt down with her great wings outspread, head back, eyes shut, and conveyed a most provocative effect of femininity opening up to a yearned-for power that it will soon enclose; on her feet, she marched, erectly, then in a lunge, with the wings wrapped around her like a mysterious armor, her eyes still closed, as if the wings, driven by a force deep inside her, propelled rather than uplifted her.

Ettlinger mentioned that Georg Capellen composed all the (piano) music for Sent M'ahesa's 1910 concert, and from then on she apparently used only music written specifically for her dances, although it is not clear how long her collaboration with Capellen lasted. In 1920 a reviewer of a Hamburg concert complained that Walter Zaun was not an appropriate accompanist for her, but a year later he praised the sensitivity of a "Director Frisch" at a concert in Nordhausen. In Berlin in 1922 she appeared as the first, "tragic" half of a program on "the tragic and the gay dance" with Ronny Johansson and Ernst Blass, who gave an introductory lecture. Margrit Goetz accompanied both dancers, but although the program (deposited at the Cologne Tanzarchiv) listed composers for all the pieces danced by Johansson, it did not identify the music for any of Sent M'ahesa's five dances or a costume intermezzo. It is possible, then, that she used music so severely modified through various collaborations and adjustments to her bodily movements that its authorship was no longer clear. The music became convoluted because the bodily movement, to achieve dramatic effect in such a confined space, became convoluted, tending toward ever more precise refinements.

Sent M'ahesa was similar to Schrenck in one respect, even though Schrenck never performed exotic dances: both projected an intensely erotic aura while moving within a very confined space. They showed persuasively that convincing signification of erotic desire or pleasure did not depend on a feeling of freedom in space, as exemplified in the conventions of ballet and modern dance, with their cliched use of runs, leaps, pirouettes, and aerial acrobatics. These dancers revealed that erotic aura intensifies in relation to an acute sense of bodily confinement, of the body imploding, turning in on itself, riddled with tensions and contradictory pressures. They adopted movements to portray the body being squeezed and twisted, drifting into a repertoire of squirms, spasms, angular thrusts, muscular suspensions. Contortionist dancing is perhaps the most extreme expression of this aesthetic. But Sent M'ahesa complicated the matter by doing exotic dances—that is, she confined her body within a remote cultural-historical context, as if to suggest that the ecstatic body imploded metaphorical as well as physical space. Perhaps this point appeared most evident in her coral tree dance, given at the 1922 Berlin concert, which contained only Asian dances. She signified the slow, gorgeous blossoming of a coral tree without moving from an initial position in the performance space, employing considerable inventiveness in the ornamentation of her movements. This aesthetic, even when she appropriated Indian, Bedouin, Siamese, or Javanese cultures, derived from her love of Egyptian art, which was the complete distillation of it. But, unlike Bara, Sent M'ahesa did not associate Egyptian art with a sublime aesthetic of death; rather, she saw in it the revelation that images that strongly confined or "froze" the body were ultimately the source of the ecstatic desire to make the body move. The body did not need more space beyond the image for movement: it needed to become itself the space containing movement.

ELLEN TELS AND MILA CIRUL

Perhaps even more than Sent M'ahesa, Mila Cirul (1901–1977) demonstrated the degree to which German dance ideology could suffuse with ambiguity not only its own cultural identity but also that of the dancer. Like Sent M'ahesa, Cirul was born in Latvia. The example of Isadora Duncan inspired her to become a dancer, but she began with the study of classical ballet technique in Moscow under the famous dancer Mikael Mordkin (1880–1944). At the same time, she studied Delsartian semiotics and the early "biomechanics" of theatre director Vsevolod Meyerhold (1874–1940), whose "intention-realization-reaction" theory of physical action incorporated ideas from gymnastics, acrobatics, fencing, sports, circus acts, and *commedia dell'arte* (Braun 197–206; Robinson 133). In 1918 she entered the then influential school and company of Ellen Tels (aka Ellen Rabanek [1885–1944]), the daughter of a German baker in Moscow. Tels pursued a kind of pantomimic dance derived from Delsartian principles, although she, too, had studied with Mordkin. Her "dance idylls" attracted audiences in Germany, Austria, and even England between 1911 and 1914, partly because she aligned pantomimic movement with literary scenarios, as in her *Chrisis* (1912), coordinated with music by Reinhold Glière, which evoked erotic texts by Pierre Louys (Suritz 407).

Tels and Cirul began dancing as a pair, but in 1919 Tels saw no future for her company in Russia and moved to Vienna, taking Cirul and three other women with her. Soon her school-company, which briefly included Ellinor Tordis, was producing dance pantomimes of great refinement and very subtle, delicate bodily rhythms, free of metricality. In 1921, Brandenburg described one of these dance pantomimes, Mozart's *Les petits riens,* as being the "nerve" of rococo without being an academic imitation of it: "It is a series of dainty solo dances, tender gavottes, flirtatious war, erotic cunning, snatching and concealing, carnivalistic processions, masquerade interludes and a pantomime in which the jealousy of a masked girl, stuck in a cage of green silk, enacts her suffering acrobatically and everyone executes their actions stiffly, convulsively, like dancing marionettes—yet it all remains a single flow of movement, in which costume and mask are nothing but a play of light and color that only make the waves livelier. That is no ballet in an antiquated sense of dance craftsmanship." (126). Brandenburg did not think much of Tels herself as a solo performer ("too rational") but hailed her as a rare "symphonic creator" of elegantly pliant group movement (although, he complained, the pantomime approach tended to end every dance in a *tableaux vivants* pose). Tels apparently had a strong gift for what I would call "theatricalized rhythm," a skill of seeing the movement potential of theatrical devices: purple and white–clad dancers bearing baskets set in tension with gold-clad dancers tapping gold cymbals with mallets; an entire ensemble moving while wrapped in a great veil (Rochowanski, *Tanzende* 37–38). A girl might swirl like the wind while other dancers undulated like flowers, but with Tels this sort of narrative premise always led to dances in which "movement became visible" rather than a mere imitation of nature (HB 127). In Vienna, Tels produced nearly fifty dance pantomimes, many for opera productions, and in 1924 she collaborated, as scenarist, with composer Egon Wellesz on the *Persisches Ballett,* which Kurt Jooss actually choreographed and presented at Donaueschingen (Amort 394). In 1927, however, for reasons that are obscure, Tels moved to Paris, where Janine Solane (b. 1912), among others, became her student.

Meanwhile, Cirul's star began to rise. In 1926 she and Tels gave a concert in Frankfurt attended by Mary Wigman. Ensuing conversations with Wigman urged Cirul to rethink her dance aesthetic in relation to submission to unconscious forces, and for awhile she worked in complete solitude (AI 21). Then her career suddenly began to blossom: she became a soloist at the operas in Vienna, Hanover, and Berlin, and in 1930 she performed with Margarethe Wallmann's Tanzgruppe 1930 in Berlin and at the big Munich Dance Congress. Unlike Tels, Cirul liked to dance violent, passionate modes of feeling, often with music (Bach, Handel) seldom associated with violence or passion—as in her *Barbarischer Tanz* (1930), using Bach's music, or *Niobe* (1931), wherein pride, terror, and sorrow struggled within her, or in Wallmann's *Orfeus Dionysos* (1930), set to Glück's music, in which she impersonated the Priestess of Death. In *Russischer Tanz* (1929), "she symbolized the sufferings of revolutionary Russia" through the figure (judging from the heavily buttoned dress she wears in a photo) of an austere middle-class woman, not a peasant. The photo is quite interesting: one foot (wearing high heels) firmly planted, the trailing foot on tiptoe in peculiarly Wigmanesque fashion, the body arcing backward, head tilted back, eyes closed, arms spread wide and flinging a dark mantel. At first glance it looks like a surge of ecstasy, but the face, with its dark eyes and mouth shut, conveys a beautiful tinge of melancholy, reserve, or uncertainty: it is a dark ecstasy, a great pulsation of movement, learned from Wigman, complicated by attention to the delicate detail—the "exact expression," as Cirul put it—learned from Tels.

In spite of her success in Germany, Cirul was seeking something she could not find there, for in 1932 she, too, migrated to Paris. However, she did not resume collaboration with Tels; instead she worked for several years in partnership with the French critic Fernand Divoire, who was immediately captivated by her smoldering temperament and her ability to enlarge every space with her intensity of feeling. She received great acclaim for her version of Strauss's music for *Salome,* presented at the Comèdie Champs Elysèes in 1934. Then her sister Elia began dancing with her in complex duets, of which *Tentation* (1935), with scenario by Divoire, was an example. This piece dramatized the struggle between consciousness, performed by Mila, and the unconscious, performed by Elia—thus, two bodies dramatized aspects of a single persona. Accompanying the dance were two voices, both male, in dialogue not only with each other but with the dancers as well. A stunning photograph suggests the sleek image of the modern psyche she sought to create (Figure 47). But this provocative "association of literature, philosophy, and movement did not make a strong impression on the audience" (AI 21; Divoire 287).

Cirul continued dancing until the early 1940s and taught many significant French dancers until 1962, when she retired to Nice. Though critics tended to consider her an avant-garde dancer, her Wigmanesque submission to bold, "instinctual" movement always remained subordinate to a strong sense of dramatic structure and detail gained from the pantomimic aesthetic of Ellen Tels. Cirul did not embody the unconscious force, as Wigman did; rather, she dramatized, through movement, a struggle within herself between consciousness and the unconscious. Indeed, one might even say that the relation between pantomime and the Wigman aesthetic constituted a major tension between self-consciously and unconsciously driven forms of dance. But the synthesis of the two forms in Cirul produced an identity that was neither German nor French nor Russian but always alluringly foreign, always the restless movements of an exquisite body seeking something more or other than that yielded by the space it occupied. Her image of movement toward death was at once less abstract than Wigman's and more clearly identified with the abstract dramatic structure of the dance, rather than with bodily movements, as in her ironically entitled *Le*

Chemin de la Vie (1947), a collaboration with Divoire, using music by Liszt. In scene after scene, death arrived at the ball, the war, the revolution, the modern city of lovers, and led all the dead in a final, grand procession of death . . . into darkness, somewhere else. No frozen pose to end the scene.

NIDDY IMPEKOVEN

"She would be a great dancer even if she had been born a cripple": such was the judgment in 1920 of theatre critic and producer Felix Hollaender regarding Niddy Impekoven (L. Impekoven 15). Probably no other dancer of the era more strongly evoked an aura of feminine innocence and geniality than Niddy Impekoven, yet she spent much of her career struggling against efforts to mold her body according to an image that conflicted with her desires. She was born in Berlin in 1904; her father was a prominent actor, and her family contained many members involved in one way or another with the arts. She began dancing at the age of three to phonograph records played by her father: "Papa was always entirely absent when he sat at the phonograph; his upper body throbbed up and down to the rhythm of the music, and his gaze was directed toward the waltz which one saw coursing somewhere beyond the glass window. So I did not feel I inconvenienced him at all by what I wanted to do: to dance, in which I had quite a model in his surrender to the music. I always danced what he played" (N. Impekoven, *Geschichte*, 22). Throughout her career, music remained for her the chief motive for dance movement. Her charm and precociousness hardly went unnoticed, and, unlike so many other dancers, she did not have to battle family prejudices to establish her identity as a dancer. On the contrary, she had to battle pressures to meet the demanding expectations imposed upon an artistic prodigy.

She was constantly an object of inspection. At the age of six she posed nude for a sculptor's photographs, a circumstance that struck her as excruciatingly boring because she could not move for long periods of time (*Geschichte*, 23). In 1910 she began ballet lessons with the first soloist of the Berlin Municipal Opera, and the same year she danced publicly for the first time, at which time the press acclaimed her as a prodigy. At the outbreak of the war, her family moved to Munich, where her parents compelled her to continue ballet studies, but these she regarded as painfully constricting and deadening: a collection of postcard photos depicting Anna Pavlova inspired her more than the bankrupt rhetoric of ballet did. During the war she danced for patriotic occasions and suddenly acquired a startling number of fans, not all of whom were children. The great moment in her education came when her father permitted her to study for six weeks at the Loheland school in summer of 1918; there she experienced a freedom and awareness of bodily expression that decisively confirmed her desire to dance (72–75). Her father, however, felt the Loheland approach lacked rigor, so she took some lessons from perhaps the most prominent ballet master in Germany, Heinrich Kröller (1880–1930), who appreciated the uniqueness of her talent.

But her health was always delicate; the arduous ballet training had turned her into a dispirited "skeleton," and at the age of fourteen she decided it was time to test the authority of her painful education. She gave her first solo concert in Frankfurt late in 1918. From then until 1923 she created a new program of dances every year, and these made her an object of enormous adulation throughout Germany. Her exquisite, nubile embodiment of fairy-tale feminine innocence often provoked dark, possessive impulses in her male worshippers, and she became eerily conscious of the power of her seemingly harmless art to produce pathological consequences—or rather, to reveal secret conditions of illness, remoteness from innocence, in others (102–105). Most curious in this respect was a book about her, *Briefe an eine Tänzerin* (1922), written by Fred Hildenbrandt, feuilleton editor for the *Berliner Tageblatt*. The dances of Niddy Impekoven awakened in Hildenbrandt a rapturous, unbridled, incoherent, even fanatical language of glorification:

> She dances the breath of rapid-breathing anticipation, the play of a thousand things gleaming in the daylight, she dances the storm of tenderness, the weariness of all meanings, the blessed languor of the heart, she dances the sun, which creeps through the morning window, and [she dances] the early footsteps on the street which press in on her in her sleep. So she spreads in her arms, her hands, her lips and eyes the shimmering mosaic of love and no one is there who can destroy it with naked eyes. Her body is the chosen instrument of dance, the chosen instrument of love (41).

The book was actually an extravagant, obsessive, and often hysterical love letter, but it obviously indicated the wild convolution of feeling that Impekoven's pretty dances could stir up in male spectators. Hildenbrandt advised her not to find a partner for her dances, for "the man who dances should only dance grotesquely" (85). The very looniness of the book did much to clarify the appeal of Impekoven's dances for a particular kind of spectator, "grey with gloom" and living in a "world of rain": "I cannot love people, Ny, because I do not love myself, and I cannot hate them because I do not hate myself, and because I am bound to this [male] sex as I am bound to myself, the result is a desolate condition of foolish hours" (83). As biographer Hans Frentz put it, "She dances what we have all lost"—namely, a mythical sense of childhood purity of being (*Niddy Impekoven*, 35).

In 1923 she married an immensely wealthy physician, Hans Killian, whom she had known for several years. This event marked a dramatic change in her aesthetic. With gentle seriousness, Killian provided her with a deep appreciation of the music of Bach, and through her love of Bach's music she evolved toward a more "womanly" dance aesthetic, attempting to reach an audience looking for more than a girlish affirmation of innocence. But she was never a tragic dancer nor even an especially innovative or daring one. What she offered was an acute aura of fragility. Her fragile body displayed superb mastery of fragile movements, and yet in this fragile negotiation with time and space there evidently lay a superior strength of will that has allowed Impekoven to live a very long life indeed. It was the aura of fragility (more than the aura of innocence) that allowed her dances to open up the emotional responses of audiences to a greater degree than could many dances with more aggressively modern ambitions. As she herself said as early as 1922: "My aim is constantly to distance myself from 'intellectual' dance. . . . The purest, most natural dance is for me the unreflective surrender to music" (N. Impekoven, *Werdegang*, 31). But the music for her dances was now rarely modern, limited to a couple of pieces by Milhaud and Bartók; otherwise her love for Schumann, Mozart, and Bach prevailed.

In 1928 she embarked on an amazing world tour in which she visited numerous European cities before going on to exuberantly acclaimed concerts in Port Said, Bombay, Bangkok, Singapore, Jakarta, Shanghai, Tokyo, Honolulu, San Francisco, New York, and many, many other cities. The tour made her quite wealthy, and she decided to accept further invitations to tour the Dutch East Indies and Southeast Asia in 1930. In 1933–1934 she presented her last program, which contained the *Drei Engel* cycle of dances to Bach preludes and *Das Fest,* a cycle of sixteenth-century German court and folk dances, and these pieces seemed to appeal to the conservative sensibilities that quite suddenly dominated German dance culture. Impekoven, however, felt no invigorating enthusiasm for the emerging cultural scene, so she retired to Switzerland, which she had regarded as her home since 1923. The great majority of her life still lay before her, but she lived quietly, apparently secure in the belief that she had already accomplished what she was born to do. In 1955 she published her brief and poignant autobiography, *Die Geschichte eines Wunderkinds,* which examined her life only up to the age of fourteen and suggested that the image of childhood innocence pervasively defining public perception of her concealed a measure of suffering, self-sacrifice, and anxiety that one could never really transcend and that in any case hardly affirmed the innocence of her audience.

In 1926, John Schikowski observed that, despite their evolution toward an "adult" phase, Impekoven's dances were "still always the dances of a child" and disclosed "a world of naive feelings": "This world is small, but it is full of beauty and fairy-tale radiance. This child gazes with large, teary, strangely shiny eyes, an aching smile on the lips. A sick child. Even over manic exuberance a little, melancholy cloud hovers. Poignant the droll exaltation, the grimacing gestures. Touching the little desires which strive toward heaven, without soaring, but rather helplessly seek their chains. Tensions and releases of a gentle, sweet softness which appears vacuous when it does not assume a child-like style. A perfectly polished body" (153–154). What made Impekoven's dances childlike was her tendency to equate the signification of innocence and fragility with the performance of delicate, precise, highly nimble movements; it appeared as if she moved in a hostile, treacherous space in which the slightest false gesture could lead to a mishap, a fall, a desecration. She was capable of bold, swinging movements, but these always remained subordinated to a small sense of scale, to a doll-sized world. Even in her "adult" phase, she simply transformed the doll image into the image of a lithe angel. Photographs of her dances suggest that while performing she liked suddenly to gaze directly at the spectator, her large eyes leveling in a haunting and almost questioning way, as if to say, "Are you sure what I'm doing makes you happy?" She often danced on the balls of her feet and occasionally on pointe, with numerous delicate, lilting kicks, hops, and skips, and she liked having outspread arms in motion; she apparently did not favor movements that brought her hands close to her body.

She definitely preferred curvaceousness to angularity in shaping bodily expressivity. Her costumes avoided elaborate ornamentation, yet she loved dancing in a great variety of costumes. In *Schalk* (1918) she wore a kind of trapeze artist blouse that displayed all of her arms and legs, but in *Pavanne* (1918) she appeared in an eighteenth-century aristocratic boy's shirt and breeches. For *Pizzicato* (1918) she donned an elegant white ballet tutu, whereas in the Beethoven *Bagatelles* (1920) she wore a gypsy-style shirt dress with long fringes (Holdt). For her dance concerning "the life of a flower" (1918), she wore a simple, sleeveless dress with an abstract floral design. In later dances, she put on a thirteenth-century gown with mantilla or a buffoonish jacket and pants that, when performed with all sorts of quirky movements, made her look like an intoxicated imp. Her costume for *Dernier cri* (1924) was quite odd: she danced in heels, with a little boa around her neck and a small, feathered hat at a tilt; her dark blouse had very short sleeves, yet she wore gloves extending above her elbows. Her skirt was long, extending to her ankles, quite tight around the waist and thighs but shredded just below the thighs into a long, dense fringe. Toward the end of her career, with her Bach pieces, she went in for long, dark, completely undecorated gowns with thigh-length slits that allowed for freedom of movement and flashing glimpses of her legs. But she exuded an austere, vaguely haloed aura.

One of her most memorable costumes was for *Der gefangene Vogel* (1918 [music: Bruno Hartl]). Here she wore a dark caftan that entirely concealed all the hair on her head; her minidress generously exposed her legs, but its sleeves covered her arms and even her hands. Attached to the sleeves and to the sides of the dress were wings, upon which she had painted brightly colored feathers. Unlike Sent M'ahesa's use of wings in her Isis dance, Impekoven made the wings of "the captured bird" an intimate, indistinguishable part of the dress itself, so that it appeared as if the costume was what allowed the body to soar. Yet Impekoven performed this dance in a completely neutral context, pure space, as though in the sky. Thus, she conveyed the sense of the bird imprisoned by its own wings and the dancer's body imprisoned not so much by its costume as by a peculiar sense of many things tightly attached to it: wings, feathers, cloth. The piece implied that the poignant fragility of creatures was most evident when they moved in a state of captivity; yet it also suggested that a creature's fragility was a motive for capturing it, and no amount of space or freedom could protect the body from its fragility. A cage did not amplify the body's fragility; mere consciousness of space and gravity did that (Figure 48).

In 1918 Impekoven created her curious series of doll dances, which in addition to the "rococo" doll and the *Münchener Kaffeewarmer* included miniatures inspired by the wax or porcelain figurines created by Lotte Pritzel, Erna Pinner, and Käthe Kruse. The Erna Pinner doll dance appeared in the film *Wege zu Kraft und Schönheit* (1925), with Impekoven wearing a delightful polka-dot clown costume with black stockings and gloves. She slumbered in an armchair until the twitching of her sleep and dreams propelled her into whirling, jerky, puppetlike movements that quickly exhausted her and caused her to fling herself back into slumber on the chair. Here she signaled that feminine innocence was but a toy of the unconscious, a windup doll with no discernible motive for its sputtering movement other than to exhaust itself with pleasure in its own absurdity.

GRET PALUCCA

Very few dancers received the pervasive acclaim and prestigious respect bestowed upon Gret Palucca (1902–1993), yet today her work seems perhaps less interesting than that of others of her generation. After spending a couple of years in San Francisco, she grew up largely in Dresden, where between 1914 and 1918 she studied ballet intermittently under Heinrich Kröller. In 1919, Palucca saw Mary Wigman perform in Dresden, and as a result she became a student in the new school Wigman opened in that city. Palucca was a member of the famous "first Mary Wigman group," which included Hanya Holm, Vera Skoronel, Berthe Trümpy, and Yvonne Georgi; with this group Palucca created her first pieces, a drum dance and *Golliwog's Cakewalk* (1922). By 1924, however, she, along with Trümpy, Skoronel, and Georgi, decided it was time to chart her own course. She followed an aesthetic path that gained her many admirers yet prevented her from becoming a complex, influential artist. The same year she married Fritz Bienert, the son of wealthy art collector Ida Bienert, and through the marriage (which lasted until 1930) she came into contact with many prominent modernist artists, including members of the Bauhaus, such as Kandinsky and Klee. In 1925 she opened her own school in Dresden, much to Wigman's annoyance; as it turned out, Palucca lasted much longer in Dresden than Wigman did. She then formed a dance group in 1927 whose members for the most part merely accompanied her on percussion instruments.

Palucca was above all a solo dancer, giving up to a hundred solo concerts a year throughout Germany and Switzerland; unlike many German dancers, she found numerous admirers in Poland (1928–1929). She showed little imagination for group choreography, for she was unsure how to create complex, expressive relations between bodies without succumbing to the mechanized drill formations of the revue dance modes, which she disliked intensely (Palucca). She apparently found the process of collaboration on group pieces oppressively tedious and complicated by the necessity of managing so many unexpectedly significant details. Instead she produced new collections of solo dances every year, year after year, until she retired from performance in 1950.

In spite of her friendly connection with the Bauhaus and in spite of her completely "abstract" image of modernity, Palucca gained the favor of the Nazis, with Goebbels an especially enthusiastic admirer. Purged of Jewish students and teachers, including codirector Irma Steinberg, the Palucca school received strong state subsidies, and Palucca herself enjoyed prestigious appointments. In 1935 she turned down the leadership of the newly formed modern dance section of the German master workshops for dance, not for ideological reasons but because she felt that accepting the appointment would make her complicit in government efforts to discredit her teacher, Mary Wigman. The next year she participated in organization of the gigantic dances for the Berlin Olympics, but because these entailed group choreography on an unprecedented scale she found the experience nerve-wrackingly exhausting ("Palucca," 22–23). When at last, in 1939, it became obvious that her method of teaching paid little attention, if any, to matters of ideological indoctrination, the Nazis removed her from the leadership of her school and then from any position within it. But she continued to present solo concerts in cities throughout Germany and Switzerland during the war years.

The catastrophic firebombing of Dresden in February 1945 destroyed nearly all her possessions. She was, however, as resilient as ever: by June she had started teaching classes again, and these became the basis for a new school, which began receiving state subsidies in 1949. In 1952, during the construction of a new building for the school, she ran into disagreements with Communist authorities, and she declined to teach there until 1954, when Minister of Culture Johannes R. Becher intervened on her behalf.

From then on she and her school prospered. The Communist regime heaped upon her numerous medals, honors, privileges, appointments, foreign invitations, commemorations, and documentary tributes, although the government actually promoted a skeptical, unencouraging attitude toward the whole *Ausdruckstanz* legacy. East German publications on Palucca were almost entirely uncritical testimonials (Krüll; Schumann). Even in West Germany she attracted a fairly strong measure of veneration, simply because she seemed a living link to the thwarted, suppressed modernist potential in German culture generated by the ill-fated Weimar Republic ("Palucca"). But during the cold war years, Palucca's notion of "the new artistic dance" hardly represented a new direction anywhere, even when compared with the dance scene of 1920.

Palucca may have been the most abstract of all expressionist dance artists, including Schlemmer, despite his obsession with robotic dancing bodies. She produced a huge repertoire of solo dances, but she was so prolific because she did not complicate her aesthetic with narrative or thematic ambitions. She was a superb technician who regarded the mastery of technique as the subject of virtually every dance. As she herself explained in 1935: "My dances have no other content and meaning than just dance, natural movement, formed in congruity with the music. It is my wish in my dances to be just so free and so bound [by music] as a musician is. Free of themes and symbols" (Losch 104). Palucca viewed the body as a pliant structure, which movement shaped into endlessly varied arabesque forms. Movement was an end in itself, and as such it did not "express" anything except a "natural" state of freedom and a superior command of space. Her dances projected hardly any of the erotic aura found in the work of so many other modern dancers. Palucca was famous for her extraordinarily high and long leaps; when she was a student at the Wigman school, Wigman, who favored strong contact with the performance surface, had to restrain her from incorporating ever greater leaps into the group dances (HM 89). Hardly any other dancer produced such a variety of leaps as Palucca, but she was also fond of bold strides, high kicking steps, exaggerated stretches, sweeping arm movements, torso-twisting pivots, gliding surges, and precisely balanced turns on one foot (Figure 49). Her body seemed to cut across the performance space in diagonal patterns while constantly striving to spiral upward. Her dances were primarily about the beauty of these devices. She kept adding so many new dances to her repertoire because in themselves none of her pieces left a strong emotional impact; in most cases a new dance was simply a reconfiguration of her favorite devices set to different music and given a different title. Her dance titles were often quite abstract and merely descriptive of the movement she performed, such as "lively"(1925), "light" (1925), "colored" (1928), "distant" (1928), "intense" (1925), "furious" (1931), "sad" (1934), "graceful" (1941), "only so" (1945). Other pieces carried purely musical appellations: *Largo* (1943), *Rondo* (1933), *Lento* (1924), *Capriccio* (1932), *Waltz* (1922, 1927, 1933, 1943, 1948), *Tango* (1923, 1929, 1941). She consistently chose neutral costumes that might fit any number of dances, and her taste in music was quite eclectic, though not particularly adventurous.

Throughout her career she tried to succeed at the performance of dark, somber, or tragic moods, but she could not achieve anything memorable in these dimensions, for at bottom she regarded dance entirely as an expression of joy, an exuberant release of energy. The most appealing photographs of her always showed her smiling radiantly, completely delighted by the sheer sensation of her own movement and unconcerned with its significance. In a sense she was a barefoot ballerina, putting ballet techniques and devices at the service of improvisation. She freed ballet technique from elaborate narrative contexts, and the result was dance that meant nothing other than that freedom and ecstasy depended entirely on the perfect exposure, the unclothing, of technical devices. Palucca's aesthetic transcended the political-historical contexts in which she lived and protected the freedom of the body from competing ideological perspectives about its meaning. However, detaching the display of technical devices from narrative motivations required Palucca to detach herself from any strong emotional response to the world around her; she created a perfectly closed universe that was never any greater than the space in which she could leap. Yet it was her ability to detach technique from intention that made her an excellent teacher, for she knew how to correct movements without disrupting the message the student wanted to convey. Her method of improvisational instruction enabled students to achieve superior technical mastery in relation to desires that were uniquely their own, as is evident from the abundant testimonials compiled by Schumann. Some of her students, such as Lotte Goslar, Marianne Vogelsang, and Dore Hoyer, demonstrated far greater emotional expressivity and depth than their teacher but probably could not have achieved such confidence in their expressive power by studying entirely under a teacher like Wigman, someone devoted to the realization of visions and urgent meanings.

Modernists such as Bertolt Brecht, László Moholy Nagy, Ruth Berghaus, and Wassily Kandinsky liked Palucca's dances because they seemed to deconstruct the vocabulary of abstraction that supposedly invested the body with modernity. In 1925, Kandinsky published his famous *Tanzkurven zu den Tänze der Palucca* (Figure 50), in which he went about as far as anyone could go in constructing an abstract image of a still recognizably human form. The artist reduced the movement of the body to a minimal set of converging or intersecting arcs and lines of varying thickness. The images created a strong impression of purely formal dynamism, as if dance were nothing more than a vigorous conflict between curved and straight lines. What

Kandinsky saw in Palucca's dances were devices of movement, expressions of nothing more than a desire to achieve a completely generic identity as a dancer. The images showed "dance" with geometric simplicity and authority, but one needs a caption to know that the dancer who inspired the artist was Palucca; the device discloses the unique identity of a form (dance), not the unique identity of its user, the dancer.

GERTRUD KRAUS

Virtually opposite Palucca in aesthetic temperament was Gertrud Kraus (1901–1977), who lacked a clear idea of technique and for whom "technical ability grew out of emotion" (Manor, "Weg," 11). Kraus possessed an impulsive personality driven by strong emotional responses to the immediate, peculiar moment. Born in Vienna, she first studied piano at the State Academy of Music. Upon graduation she worked as an accompanist for silent movies and for the dancer Ellinor Tordis (1896–1976), a dark figure whose ambitions included dancing to the music of Anton Bruckner. Initially, Kraus was ambivalent about the possibility of dance as an art: "My suspicion was that dance was only for cabarets" (Ingber, "Conversations," 45). But as she accompanied Tordis, she became aware of dance's great expressive potential. Her impulsive personality registered clearly in the story she told of how she decided to become a dancer. One day Tordis asked if any students were prepared to present a piece for the class. After a brief pause, Kraus jumped from the piano, tossed off her shoes, and improvised a piece, completely unpremeditated, unrehearsed, and, indeed, untrained except for what she had learned from watching the classes given by Tordis. Her performance was followed by a long silence, which Kraus found so excruciating that she grabbed her shoes and belongings and headed for the door. Tordis called after her: "Wait! We must talk about this," but Kraus responded, "The pause was too long," and kept going (Manor, "Weg," 9).

With this action, Kraus decided she was a dancer. She studied for awhile with Gertrud Bodenwieser and even joined her dance company for several months. But Bodenwieser's aesthetic soon struck Kraus as too full of theatrical cleverness and sentimentality, and at the end of 1925 she rented one of the largest theatrical spaces in Vienna and presented her own concert of solo dances. The success of her solo concerts encouraged her to form a school and dance company in 1927. The company toured extensively in Germany, giving many performances for socialist and Zionist organizations. In 1929 she assisted Laban in the creation of festival processions in Vienna, and at the 1930 Munich Dance Congress she and her group attracted much attention by performing a cycle of dances evoking "songs of the ghetto." The following year she gave concerts in Palestine, where she became intoxicated by the sounds, colors, and rhythms of the Middle East. Because she was Jewish, the advent of the Nazi regime completely destroyed all artistic opportunities for her in Germany. However, her decision to migrate to Palestine actually resulted from her impulsive response to communism. While performing in Prague in 1934, a clandestine cell of communists approached her and urged her to become an agent of the party and to make her dances an instrument of party propaganda. Though she adopted vaguely left-humanitarian political values, Kraus sensed that in Central Europe she could not do anything anymore without turning her art into a "placard." "I felt I had no flag and I wanted only to leave Europe behind," she said, although she claimed her life in Vienna was "the most glorious time anyone could ever have had" (Ingber, "Conversations," 48). In 1935 she emigrated to Palestine, where she spent the rest of her life choreographing, teaching, researching Jewish folk dance, and sculpting. In her later years, she produced elaborate sketchbooks in which she continued ecstatically to "dance on paper."

Unlike many modern dancers, Kraus relied heavily on literary sources to shape the identity of her dances and suffuse them with narrative logic. She also grounded her dances in socialist and Zionist political theory. Her dances signified heavy emotions because they were intensely dramatic, but the source of dramatic conflict always lay in her strange, almost alien image of feminine beauty. In her dances, female bodies moved as if they came from a secret, unmapped corner of European culture. An eerieness pervaded all her European dances, which consistently favored a convergence of the bizarre and the melancholy. A wispy, diminutive woman with raven-black hair and large, almond-shaped eyes, she delighted in exaggerating the strangeness of her beauty. Unlike Impekoven, however, she did not make the fragility of the body the basis for the emotional intensity of her dances. Photographs of her European dances depict a phantasmal woman, a Lilith, a creature moving in a dusky glow. Expressionist chiaroscura suited her temperament exquisitely, even though that style, so strong in the visual and performing arts in the years 1919 to 1923, was largely out of fashion by the time she started making dances. Kraus loved rocking or swaying movements that curved the body, the arms often moving more freely than the legs. She seldom danced on tiptoes, and she liked having bodies close to the floor, especially in kneeling positions, which compelled them to make inventive use of head, hand, and torso movements; in 1935 she created a piece in which dancers moved while drumming their hands on the floor (Manor, *Life*, 32). Kraus also borrowed curving, serpentine, and undulant movements from Near Eastern and Indonesian dance cultures. In *Fire Dance* (1930, music: De Falla) she stood with legs spread and performed much of the dance using shaking, trembling, throbbing, gyrating movements of her arms, torso, and head. In *Air on a G-string* (1931, music: Bach), she wore a long, flowing lamè gown with long sleeves and began the dance (as photographed at the D'Ora studio) in a profile kneeling position, eyes closed, while her arms made spiraling movements over her breasts and head until her body seemed coiled up; then she spiraled upward onto her feet and began rocking sideways, back and forth, twisting her whole body so that the tilting of her head appeared to control the balance of her entire body. The movement of her head dominated the body and the dance, yet she never opened her eyes. A footlight effect emphasized the trancelike eerieness of the dance. Few dancers could make the head so expressive because few dancers treated dance as a submission to the elevating power of intellectuality.

Guignol (1929) was even stranger. Here Kraus impersonated a bizarre puppet. She sat on a pedestal in a long black dress with a white stripe from hip to hem and a sort of large white claw stamped onto her chest. Around her neck she wore a large bow; her face was painted white, and she attached to her fingers long brass fingernails of the type used by Javanese dancers. In this case her large dark eyes stayed constantly open and gazing at the spectator. She never left the pedestal; she sat on it, knelt on it, peered from behind it, and stood against it while the rocking of her body and tilting of her head inspired uncanny arabesque swirls of her arms and clawlike brass fingernails. She never smiled. Yet one did not see a body trapped in space; rather, it was as if the freedom of her body depended on its achieving a beautiful alienness through its power to concentrate perception within a highly confined space. Kraus created a haunting image of robotized femininity suffused with a vaguely supernatural aura, as if the key to comprehending the mystery of sexual identity lay in the puppetization of the body. Equally spooky was her incarnation of *The Tired Death* (1930), in which she moved in a long, satiny, purple gown and a great purple cape; her head, however, was covered with a white skullcap, so that she looked bald, while her eyes remained heavily mascared and her lips starkly painted. She moved slowly, stealthily, as if in a predatory trance, sweeping into death all humanity in her path. In *The Beast* (1931), however, she wore a kind of jumpsuit and combined powerful striding, lunging, pouncing movements with the "feminine" curvaturing of rocking and swaying motions. Decorative exoticism appeared in *Oriental Girl* (1929), and in *Russian Folk Song* (1932) she introduced a wild, ecstatic swirling movement seldom associated with "colorful" peasant costumes. With *The Jewish Boy* (1929), she experimented with a mysterious, seductive image of androgyny. Manor claims that Kraus's dances contained no eroticism, perhaps because she consistently covered her legs with longs skirts or dresses and did not seem interested in narrative themes of sexual desire (*Life,* 36). But from my perspective, her preoccupation with producing an alien, melancholy image of her body is evidence of a desire to estrange the spectator from normative, narratively contextualized significations of erotic feeling.

Information about her group dances in Europe is so scanty that it is difficult to say anything about them. Apparently she attracted only Jewish women into her group. She had as many as eight women in the group, but in some dances the women impersonated men. In 1928, Kraus tried to persuade Baruch Agadati (1895–1976), a Russian-Palestinian who performed Jewish folk dances in an expressionist style, to join her group, but he insisted that he was exclusively a solo dancer (Manor, "Weg," 9). Old Jewish narrative ballads and Hassidic tales inspired *Ghettolieder* (1930, music: Joseph Achron), which offered tragic images of the hermetic world of Eastern European Jewry; the dancers wore long, dark, expressionist gowns somewhat similar to the *Guignol* puppet costume, with shawls attached to their heads for some pieces. Rocking and swaying movements dominated the choreographic design, but Kraus developed ingenious variations on this motif: for example, a trio of women deep in the space swayed in a horizontal line, backs to the audience, while a quartet of women in diagonal formation swayed-glided toward the trio. She introduced multiple pairs of dancers performing eerie swaying movements: two dancers in profile on their knees rocked their way across the stage while two pairs of dancers, on their feet, swayed in tango fashion behind them, creating a curious image of sexual ambiguity (only two of the tango dancers had a definitively established sexual identity, wearing shawls to signify their femininity).

Pendulum mechanicality of movement appeared again in *Dream of Happiness* (1932), ten scenes built around a poem by Kraus's friend Elias Canetti; some of the accompaniment included the speaking of Canetti's words. In this work, a monumental machine dance turned into a triumphal procession to signify the "dream of happiness" arising from "a vicious circle of hopelessness" (Manor, *Life,* 30). In 1932, Kraus also worked on a dance inspired by Karl Kraus's (no relation) enormous drama *The Last Days of Mankind* (1921), in which the female dancers were soldiers wearing gas masks. Her last and perhaps most popular work, *The City Waits* (1933), derived from a story by Maxim Gorky: "A boy goes to [a] town and hears how the town suffers" (Ingber, "Conversations," 46). The accompaniment included the speaking, by a woman, of words from the Gorky story as well as music composed for the piece by Marcel Rubin. Kraus herself played the boy, though by this time she had at least one male student, Fritz Berger (aka Fred Berk [1911–1980]) in her group. When Kraus disbanded her group the following year, Berger achieved some success in Vienna as a solo performer of folk dances and political allegories, such as the Pharaonic *The Tyrant* (1932), and as a partner for the Viennese ballerina Hedy Pfundmayr (1899–1966). He emigrated (1939) to Switzerland, Cuba, and finally New York, where he became prominent in the research and preservation of Jewish folk dance traditions (Ingber, "Vienna"). In spite of having such a strong male talent on hand, however, Kraus deliberately welcomed opportunities, provided by narrative situations, for female bodies to appropriate male identities and thereby create a strange, alien image of female beauty. She liked shifting sexual identities, just as she liked shifting impulsively from dancing to accompanying dance on the piano, just as she liked rocking, pendulum movements of the body.

GERTRUD LEISTIKOW

In 1921, before Wigman's genius was fully apparent, Hans Brandenburg regarded Gertrud Leistikow (1885–1948) as the most tragic and "Dionysian" of all German modern dancers, the figure closest to the primeval concept of dance as an expression of an ecstatic body (HB 157–173; Bragaglia, too, *Scultura vivente*, 84–85). But by 1925, Leistikow's significance seemed confined almost entirely to the Netherlands, where she had resided since about 1917, although she kept trying to achieve dramatic comebacks as a dancer until 1939. After attending girls' schools in Metz and Spa, she studied at a school of applied arts in Dresden, where in 1904 she observed a demonstration by Dalcroze. The same year she apparently took lessons in the Delsarte-Stebbins "artistic gymnastic" method of Hedwig Kallmeyer in Berlin. Leistikow gave her first dance recitals sometime between 1906 and 1910, with the earliest known dances dating from 1910 (Lustig). By then her reputation was such that until 1914 she could command sizable audiences for her solo concerts in St. Petersburg, Moscow, Lausanne, Utrecht, and Sarajevo. In summer 1914 she joined Laban's group in Ascona, where she and Mary Wigman assumed the main roles in Laban's large-scale "tragic word and dance drama," *Sieg des Opfers,* by Hans Brandenburg (MS 17). In Ascona, Leistikow also experimented with nude performance of several of her dances, though drawings of her by Dora Brandenburg-Polster indicate she may have performed nude dances for special audiences as early as 1911. But she did not stick with the Laban group; in 1916 she toured Germany and the Netherlands, where she attracted much attention in Amsterdam artistic circles. After her marriage to a Dutch rose dealer in 1921, her contact with modern dance culture outside Holland declined sharply, but her influence in the Netherlands grew stronger. By then she operated three schools, in Amsterdam, The Hague, and Rotterdam; a tour of the Dutch East Indies in 1924 inspired her to open three more schools there. She announced "farewell" tours of the Netherlands in 1929, 1930, and again in 1937, but in 1938–1939, she launched another tour of the Indies. When the war broke out on her return home, she and her family became stranded in Somaliland, and when she finally managed to reach Holland again, she opened yet another school in Amsterdam. However, she distanced herself considerably from the pro-Nazi spirit dominating Dutch dance culture during the war years (ESG 20–21).

Gertrud Leistikow had a slender, supple body, but her face lacked charm, elegance, or mystery. She therefore constantly sought to hide her face, partly through suave manipulation of shawls, veils, or masks but also through movements that called attention to the beauty of her body. This anxiety over exposing her face appeared clearly in various carefully constructed photographs of her and even more conspicuously in Dora Brandenburg-Polster's drawings of her, some dating from 1911. Many of these show her nude but faceless or with concealed face. Her earlier dances tended to project a tragic, melancholy aura, but after she moved to Amsterdam her distinction seemed to lie in her peculiar cultivation of the grotesque. The Dutch dance critic Werumeus Buning thought she was stronger in the performance of waltzes than mazurkas, and he contended that in her pursuit of the grotesque she neglected to develop her greater potential for tragic expression (WBD 31–33). But Leistikow's concept of the grotesque was cosmopolitan, so perhaps her grotesque dances constituted a curious evolution of a controlling tragic aesthetic rather than a break with it. Junk suggested that the grotesque dance displayed "more strength than grace" or, "more recently," substituted "the bizarre for the graceful," as manifested through "unusual positions, deformed body structures, and adventurous leaps and gestures" (98). In other words, grotesque dancing did not necessarily imply a comic mood but perhaps made a calculated challenge to aesthetic conventions of "gracefulness" and bodily composure. Brandenburg thought such a challenge led Leistikow into the realms of the demonic and heroic rather than toward any spirit of parody, frivolity, or malicious travesty.

Yet Leistikow's aesthetic of the grotesque placed less emphasis on displays of strength or "deformed" and "adventurous" movements than on perversities of dramatic structure and decor. For *Faun* (1912) she wore a furry black leotard that left her arms and lower legs exposed; her head was completely covered with a horned, furry black mask, with only two slits for the eyes, and a little black tail was attached to her bottom. Borrowing from the "sylph" movement conventions of ballet, she flitted about rapidly on tiptoe, "with increasing estrangement from her own presence in this world wherein she suddenly found herself" (WBD 33). But the dance, which began with animal exuberance, grew darker and slower as "the faun began to wonder about his own nature" and felt some troubling glimmer of consciousness, an impulse to "discover another world." However, the movements of the dance were not in themselves grotesque; rather, the bizarre costume and the dramatic shift from exuberance to anxiety made the conventional, balletic signification of gaiety and frivolity seem grotesque.

In other cases, Leistikow deformed movements by performing them at flashing speed, as in the *Furientanz* (1912), which began slowly and ended in orgasmic frenzy. Brandenburg-Polster's drawings show Leistikow performing the dance nude, except for a great diaphanous veil. Peering directly into a glaring footlight, she started deep in the space, crouching on one knee, her entire body shrouded in the veil and projected as a great shadow behind her by the footlight. Then she rose, swirled out of the veil, and raced around in spiral configurations with the veil trailing behind her and her shadow leaping across the space. She ran lower and lower, ensnaring herself in the veil, struggling with it in dervish frenzy. Finally she stopped running and starting spinning in place with the veil looped over her head, whirling with legs spread, then on tiptoe, until she collapsed (HB plates 23–25).

Most of her dances observed this simplicity of technique and complexity of dramatic ambiguity. *Totentanz* (1912) also used a footlight-looming shadow effect, but in this case, Leistikow, in one of her usual tight-fitting dresses, stood deep in the space, her face nakedly exposed and her legs pressed together, and moved slowly, in tiny tiptoe steps, toward the light. She made undulating movements with a shawl, and when she tossed it away she seemed terribly naked; because she was closer to the violet footlight, her shadow appeared even larger than before. Her face was a violent glare of fear. Wrote Brandenburg:

> The violet spotlight becomes coldly reflected in the pearl ornamentation of the hair. It makes the head of the dancer, with Medusa-like, wide open eyes, perch over the purple shawl which entwines and strangles her throat. The crass red cloth separates head from body, so that the head seems to float in the air, but through constant transformation the little cloth serves the movement of the dance: now it dips and flows like blood, then it throbs and flutters like lightning flashes, then it spreads like an imperial mantel around the shoulders, then it tightened again like a noose around the neck. And the language of the body discloses just as much fear of death as desire for death (HB 162; also Van Collem 22).

For many of her numerous dances, she appears to have repeated much of the movement of earlier dances, merely changing the costume. For example, in *Haremswächter* (1911) she wore a very short dress with long, drooping sleeves and a bizarre Asian mask with a large, black, Afro sort of wig, but her movements were grotesque. For the entire dance, she moved with her body directly facing the audience; she never turned but drifted laterally in the performance space while facing the spectator. She dipped up and down, on her toes, then on her heels; she squatted, then shot up to make odd shifting movements, with one foot on tiptoe and the other jutting forward on its heel. Meanwhile, her arms in their droopy sleeves extended sideways from her body and made wavy up-and-down motions, like the flapping wings of a strange bird. One could say that this simple dance showed the extent to which one became grotesque in maintaining a sense of balance. But "balance" implied more than physical poise; it included the problem of balancing the body between conflicting signs of cultural and sexual identity, as the harem guard wore a dress yet donned a male mask.

In subsequent years, Leistikow used pretty much the same movements with different costumes. In *Maskerdans* (1914) she wore a white minidress with short, billowy sleeves and a flamboyant blonde wig, as if her hair consisted of a huge mass of plumes; her mask was not Asian but macabre, skull-like, with large dark eye sockets and a gleaming red smile (Velde). In another version of the balancing movements, she wore a black leotard that covered even her hands and feet; indeed, her hands looked like reptilian claws. She concealed her face behind an oversized male mask with vaguely Asian features. In her right hand she dangled an Asian sword (male emblem), and in her left hand she dangled a veil (female emblem), while some sort of knotted chain was attached to both arms (WBD 16). For *Rote Groteske* (1922), the simplest version of all, she wore a red minidress, red stockings, and a red mask of indeterminate sex. But, according to Marja Braaksma's 1991 reconstruction, Leistikow apparently did not retain the crouching or tiptoe movements in this version. What made Leistikow's dances grotesque was her determination to invest the simplest movements with startling dramatic power, an unsuspected intensity of conflict.

This determination was perhaps most mysteriously evident in *Gnossienne* (1924), which used as accompaniment Erik Satie's equally simple and haunting piano melody "Gnossienne No. 1" (1889). Here Leistikow stood in a tight-fitting, shimmering gown and faced the audience in a veiled light. She concentrated the dance almost entirely in the hands and arms, which undulated slowly, like waves, horizontally, then vertically, while her face constantly stared straight ahead with Sphinxlike inscrutability (one had to see the dance more than once to make this observation, so strongly did the arms and hands attract focus). After performing a pattern of arm undulations, the dancer took a step forward and turned into profile to repeat the pattern but raised her right leg slightly and held it suspended for the duration of the repetition. Then she turned and faced the audience again and repeated the pattern. The dancer repeated the initial pattern five times, thrice forward and twice in profile. With each repetition, the dancer merely moved forward a step or, while in profile, suggested a step in another direction without actually taking it (Braaksma). The dance conveyed a sense of a body very slowly and hesitantly moving closer to the audience without, in its trancelike state, even seeming aware of the spectators. Repetition of movements was the key to bringing bodies closer to each other, but in this case it did not induce a feeling of familiarity; rather, the closer the body came and the more it repeated its movements, the stranger it appeared. This was a highly sophisticated form of irony. The spectator gained the impression of watching a body moving underwater, its arms and hands undulating hypnotically like the tentacles of a luminous, aquatic plant, a human anemone. This dance still fascinates audiences today.

Buning (*Dansen*, 32), Van Collem (21), and Brandenburg (HB 169) all remarked that in Leistikow's dances, the body undulated like wind or water. More important, she showed that the expressive power of dance depended not on any virtuosity of technique but on intensity of dramatic purpose. Because she subordinated technique to dramatic effect, she could produce many new dances, without having to devise much in the way of new movement, for what made movement new was a different dramatic or theatrical element, such as costume, mask, lighting, or props. Her taste in music was eclectic but not adventurous. She heavily favored music from the nineteenth-century romantic repertoire and folk songs, although in 1921 she attempted a dance to music that contrasted conditions of "blindness" and "seeing" (Buning did not think it successful [33]). In 1929 she experimented with the accompaniment of two harmonicas, then of an accordion, and further introduced a dance employing jazz music, but these did not resonate well with Dutch audiences. She appropriated folk music from many cultures—Spain, Russia, Ukraine, Java, Bohemia, India, Chile, Hungary—yet her dances never gave an image of the culture from which the music derived. Rather, they created a mysterious image of cultural ambiguity, as in *Gnossienne,* which adapted arm movements found in Javanese dance to produce an atmosphere of accumulating uncertainty regarding the cultural identity of dancer and movement. In *Goldene Maske* (1921) she used a Russian folk song (as she had in *Rote Groteske*), but for Anton Van Collem, "the dark, slender little god with the golden mask" performed a dance reminiscent of an ominous Aztec ritual (24).

In the early 1920s, Leistikow worked with the Dutch sculptor Hildo Krop (1884–1970) on the construction of many of her masks, and her success with them inspired other Dutch dancers to work with gifted artists in creating bizarre dance masks. Whereas Krop's masks tended toward a sleek, constructivist image of the face, Jaap Pronk's masks for Tilly Sylon's group exuded a fantastic primitivism. In 1932, Hein von Essen created masks for dances by his daughter, Dini von Essen, but these were more "realistic" than either Krop's or Pronk's—that is to say, they functioned more as caricatures of Western faces ("social masks") than as cultural estrangements of Western bodies (Lagerweij-Polak; Hein von Essen; Dini von Essen).[4] But no dancer

---

4. Krop's mask designs so impressed W. B. Yeats that he employed them in dance drama productions at the Abbey Theatre in Dublin in the 1920s. Another Dutch dancer, Florrie

seemed as sensitive as Leistikow to the face as a mask and as an object of masking and veiling; she saw in the face the decisive emblem of imperfection and deception, regardless of whatever technical perfection the body as a whole possessed. Perhaps this perception was most obvious in her dance to Weber's *Scherzo* (1914), which apparently she performed in a body-covering veil before a mirror. Van Collem remarked of this dance: "The beautiful woman in the dead little village lives as one estranged from herself" (24).

TRUDI SCHOOP, JULIA MARCUS, AND VALESKA GERT

Grotesque dancing in the 1920s assumed so many curious forms that the term "grotesque dance" came to signify a larger and larger measure of freedom for the dancer, even if it never achieved much in the way of a stable definition. Nevertheless, hardly anyone confused grotesque dancing with comic or "cheerful" dancing, and some dancers established their identities by emphasizing this distinction. Ronny Johansson, for example, consistently put on programs of cheerful ("heitere") dances, with brisk, springy, decorative movements accompanied by lyrical music in a major key. Johansson sometimes performed dances in pretty pants, but her dances exuded cheerfulness because they presented a body radiantly freed of sexual, cultural, or psychological ambiguity. In Vienna, Elsie Altmann (1899–1984) projected a similar image of cheerfulness, reinforced by an elegant taste for Biedermeyer-style costumes. This approach marked her entire career, beginning with her debut concert in 1919, just before her marriage to the famous architect Adolf Loos (1870–1933), and continuing unchanged until at least 1929. Her talent brought her opportunities to choreograph operettas (Altmann-Loos 268–278).

By contrast, the Swiss dancer Trudi Schoop (b. 1903) specialized in comic pantomime. An awkward child, she struggled to achieve elegant physicality through rigorous ballet training and then through the rhythmic gymnastics offered by the Elisabeth Duncan school; but when her own family laughed at her as she performed for them a solemn dance, she decided to devote herself entirely to comic dance, and in this direction she exhibited unprecedented ambition. In 1929 she assembled in Berlin a comic ballet company containing twenty-two members, including several men, although Schoop still employed numerous female impersonations of men. *Fridolin*

Rodrigo (b. 1893), commissioned, during the 1920s and early 1930s, extraordinary expressionist masks from the Dutch artists Erich Wichman, Jan Havermans, and Grietje Kots, all of whom emerged out of the *Wendingen* circle of Dutch expressionists. Rodrigo began her career with Grit Hegesa, who also apparently experimented with masks (de Boer).

(1930, music: Paul Schoop) was a great success and led to performances of the group around Germany and in Oslo, Stockholm, Venice, Paris, Prague, and Amsterdam. This pantomime established the model for her subsequent successes, which followed the episodic structure of the expressionist "journey" drama. *Fridolin*, for example, contained twelve scenes, each depicting Fridolin's encounters with a new set of characters as he wanders eternally and vainly in search of a woman who will return his love. Scenes showed Fridolin achieving distinction as an acrobat, competing for a woman who despises him, joining a secret sect, stumbling into a boring marriage, joining a bowling club, and falling hopelessly in love with a cabaret acrobat. Schoop herself played Fridolin, and her brother Max designed the costumes. The ballet company also produced divertissements, such as *Want Ads* (1933) and *Current Events* (1937), in which Schoop presented satiric views of contemporary social realities, such as unemployment, retail selling, and male sports fanatics, but her strength lay in the ambitious comic pantomime. *Blonde Marie* (1938, music: Paul Schoop), with costumes by Oskar Schlemmer, presented eight scenes describing the absurd journey of Marie (Schoop) from servant girl to waitress to soubrette to diva to rich wife to bored mother to publicity-happy adulteress. *All for Love* (1939, music: Lothar Perl, Schoop's brother) contained six long scenes depicting episodes from the life of Catherine (Schoop) as a schoolgirl, at a nightclub, around the Christmas tree, and on trial, concluding with the grotesque apotheosis of Catherine the Clown in a "super-colossal Diamond Star Revue," in which "dancing and vocal choruses, apaches, clowns, jugglers, with the help of make-believe and blinding spotlights, combine to give the romantic illusion: ALL FOR LOVE" (Hurok).

Schoop's aesthetic seemed driven by a Brechtian inclination to puncture the illusions of socially idealized romantic erotic desire. But she achieved the puncturing through eccentric costumes and pantomimic distortions of conventionalized balletic and functional movements rather than through hauntingly bizarre transgressions of gracefulness. Her success in the United States was considerable, beginning in 1935, and when the war broke out she decided to emigrate there. She could not, however, maintain the large-scale ballet company; in the 1950s and 1960s she therefore (and not altogether unexpectedly) devoted herself increasingly to the realm of dance therapy for both physically and psychologically damaged bodies (Schoop).

Schoop's comic aesthetic relied too much on a complicated theatrical definition of society to achieve her distinction in the realm of solo dance: she showed little inclination to see how the body moved alone, apart from a group. Most grotesque dances, however, operated in a solo mode and emphasized the power of grotesquerie to separate the body from a socially determined identity. In the years 1916–1920, Rita Aurel performed solo parodies of Oriental dances, using her contortionist ability to produce bizarrely distorted serpentine movements of the arms and belly. Aurel did a piece in which she represented a woman injecting herself with morphine, causing Brandenburg to suggest that she had devised a form of aesthetic movement that was neither dance nor pantomime. She was not a dance clown but a sort of freakish dancer. With the Mozartian *Rondo* (1916), she appeared in a child's costume and danced with small balls suspended by strings; then a very large black ball descended, introducing "the demonic into the supposedly naively charming music." Despite such obvious evidence of a strong imagination, this "strange, super-tall, super-slender, hysterical, graceful, and very worldly personality" most regrettably left behind very little trace of herself (HB 58–59).

Even more obscure was Hilde Schewior, who lacked any feeling for danced movement, according to Schikowski (153). But she was a dance clown with a gift for goofy, satiric costumes, and she liked impersonating grotesque types of males, deforming her movements to create an impression of bizarre physiognomy (Holtmont 227). Lotte Goslar, a student of Wigman and Palucca, was also a dance clown in the early 1930s, but she was quite a pretty woman and sought to construct a dance aesthetic in which strong comic ingenuity was not incompatible with a confident display of feminine beauty. How she achieved such a remarkable synthesis remains unclear, but a photograph of her suggests that she may have used the theme of trying to look her best as the basis for various comic misadventures with costumes or movements (MS 95). This approach apparently succeeded best in a cabaret milieu. In 1937, as a member of Erika Mann's Pfeffermühl company, she came to the United States, where she has resided ever since. Like Schoop, she felt her comic talent unfolded most effectively in a company, and she founded her own in Hollywood in 1943.

Julia Marcus (b. 1905), a Swiss student of Laban, Elisabeth Duncan, and Wigman, not only was active in cabaret performance but in 1931 became a member of the unusual Berlin City Opera ballet company under Lizzie Maudrik. She apparently had a gift for dark, dramatic voluptuousness, as in her Mexican-Aztec suite of dances (1930), but her uniqueness was most evident in her radically grotesque parodies of contemporary figures such as Al Jolson (1931), Adolf Hitler (1931), Gerhart Hauptmann (1932), and Gandhi (1933). In these she collaborated with Berlin artist Erich Goldstaub, who created for her oversized, caricatured masks of these persons (with Jolson in blackface). She modeled the movements of these dances on acute observations of the gestural idiosyncrasies peculiar to the famous personalities. In *Der Friedensengel* (1932) she reached a truly astonishing threshold of the bizarre when she donned a creepy, oversized mask of French prime minister Aristide Briand (1862–1932), winner of the 1926 Nobel Prize for Peace. But the mask was hardly all that was strange: she wore a tuxedo shirt and jacket over the upper portion of her body, and these garments clashed dramatically with the white ballet tutu, stockings, and slippers apportioned to the lower half of her body. In this costume she performed a waltz satire on diplomatic gesturing. In *Wälzer* (1933), she danced in a gas mask.

Marcus was a friend of the Communist Party, and for party cabaret entertainments she created dance parodies not only of contemporary political figures but also of social types, such as the symphony conductor, the servant girl, the sewing machine operator. Some of her dances used music by the communist composer Hanns Eisler and strove to construct heroic images of proletarian figures ("Julia Tardy-Marcus"). Of course, the Third Reich severely limited opportunities for Marcus, so she began touring restlessly around Europe, inserting herself into the cabaret culture of Warsaw, Amsterdam, and Zurich. She finally settled (1933) in Paris, where, as usual, she made numerous friends and, even during the war, put on well-received dance recitals, sometimes in collaboration with, among others, Ludolf Schild, Lisa Duncan, and Mila Cirul. In 1937 she collaborated with Schild in the production at the Théâtre Pigalle of a "ballet," *Le Fievre du Temps* (music: Graca), employing a scenario based, intriguingly, on scenes from current movies. As a Swiss citizen married to a French engineer, she remained fairly safe from the Gestapo and helped other dancers escape to safety. After the war, she drifted toward cultural-literary journalism (Robinson 134–136; Jelavich 259–260).

When she first arrived in Paris, Marcus rented a dilapidated little theatre in which, according to her unpublished memoirs, one could see mice scurrying across the stage during performances. She shared this space with one of the most renowned of all the Weimar comic dancers, Valeska Gert (1892–1978). Born in Berlin to a wealthy Jewish family, Gert led a complicated international, interdisciplinary life, which she recounted in four autobiographies (1931, 1950, 1968, 1973) and which Frank-Manuel Peter abundantly documented in 1985. But Gert's dance aesthetic was also complex, allowing her to function in different artistic contexts: dance recital, cabaret, film, theatre, and writing. In the realm of dance, her success remained confined largely to the performance of grotesque caricatures, though she made occasional efforts to explore a wider emotional range. Her strength was also her weakness—an acute distrust of romantic feeling—yet she began her career with one of the more romantic figures of prewar German dance culture.

At first she considered some sort of career in the fashion industry, but in 1915 she started taking acting lessons from Maria Moissi. Through her Gert came into contact in 1916 with the dance school of Rita Sacchetto, from whom she apparently received little guidance on matters of technique. Nevertheless, Sacchetto gave Gert a chance to perform her solo *Tanz in orange* (1916), a parody of ballet movements danced in a curious orange dress with

billowy pantaloons. This piece was appealing enough to appear as an intermezzo item on a program of silent films. Meanwhile, Gert pursued opportunities as an actress, appearing (1917–1919) in small, odd roles—a witch,
a skeleton, a parrot, a child, and so forth—in expressionist dramas and productions in Munich and Berlin. She created cabaret dances and in late 1917
introduced them in Berlin; they were so popular that by 1919 she was a
prominent figure in the Berlin dance culture. Her interest in acting for the
stage faded as her interest in more modernist modes of performance intensified. In 1923 she participated in an unusual production that began with
the showing of an abstract color film by Walther Ruttmann, *Opus 2*, followed
by two grotesque dances performed by Jutta Hertig and then, after the
intermission, Gert's performance in the title role of Salome in Wilde's play.
The program purported to demonstrate, as Gert explained, the difference
between technology-driven and actor-driven forms of performance, with
the *Salome* fragments employing extremely austere scenic elements. Gert
played Salome in a simple red apron-dress, and she created the "head" of
Jokanaan simply through the movement of her bare hands; Herodias and
Jokanaan wore, respectively, green and silver-gray dresses, and Herod wore
blue pajamas. For the *Dance of the Seven Veils*, Ruttmann accompanied her
with "meowing" sounds on a cello, along with the "rhythmic, passionate
howling of some women behind the stage" (FPV 26).

Between 1924 and 1931, Gert appeared with memorable distinction in
several major films of the Weimar era: *Ein Sommernachtstraum* (1925), *Die
freudlose Gasse* (1925), *Nana* (1926), *Alraune* (1927), *Tagebuch einer Verlorenen*
(1929), *So ist das Leben* (1929), and *Die Dreigroschenoper* (1931). In all these
films she played unsavory or rather freakish characters. She always left a
strong impression on the spectator, but her roles remained small, and she
never became a star. Berlin photographer Suse Byk made the first film of
Gert dancing, *Die Küpplerin*, in 1925. Throughout the Weimar years, she
supplemented her comic dances with sketches and songs for cabaret performances in Zurich (1918), Oslo (1919), Munich (1922), and Berlin
(1926, 1931). In 1932 she formed her own cabaret company, but it provoked highly ambivalent responses. She had participated with the great
dramatist Bertolt Brecht (1898–1956) as early as 1922, in Munich, on a
cabaret project, *Der Abnormitätenwirt*, that included appearances by the
grotesque actor Max Schreck, the comedians Lisel Karlstadt and Karl
Valentin, and Brecht himself. In 1929 the Baden-Baden premiere of
Brecht's *Badener Lehrstück* contained a filmed sequence, shot by Karl Koch,
of Gert performing her dance *Der Tod* (1927). Her international identity
expanded with performances in Paris (1926, 1930) and a tour of the Soviet
Union (1929), where she became friends with Soviet film director Sergey
Eisenstein (1898–1948), who regarded her as the most interesting of all
modern dancers.

Unlike most dancers, Gert published many brief articles on dance in major periodicals, often from a critical-satirical perspective, but her ability to understand dances other than her own was quite limited. The triumph of Nazism compelled her to wander internationally and not very successfully in search of a cabaret career, first in Paris (1933), then London (1934), New York (1936), London (1937), Hollywood (1939), New York (1940), Provincetown (1941), Paris (1947), Zurich (1948), and finally Berlin (1949). Her first husband, the physician and Sanskrit scholar Helmut von Krause (1893–1980), had built her a vacation cottage on the North Sea island of Sylt back in the early 1930s, and in 1955 she opened yet another cabaret there; it, too, failed to prosper, because of her excessively austere attitude toward scenic decor and production values. But she was always resourceful, publishing books, making guest appearances, and doing an occasional small, bizarre role in a film—for example, the hermaphrodite in Fellini's *Juliet of the Spirits* (1965) and the Old Bird in Ulrike Ottinger's *Die Betörung der blauen Matrosen* (1975).

Gert's dances appealed primarily to a disillusioned intellectual elite that favored modes of performance embodying a critical attitude toward socially determined conventions of signification. Even in her most serious pieces, such as *Salome* and *Der Tod,* she parodied conventions of signification, in contrast to Marcus, who tended to parody the idiosyncratic movements of personalities. Hers was an art of satiric quotation. Like Niddy Impekoven she always worked on a small scale, but unlike her Gert never confused smallness of scale with childlike naiveté. Moreover, the range of subjects she parodied was fairly wide, although her repertoire of dances as a whole was small. She started by parodying dance itself—first ballet, in *Tanz in orange* (1916), then social dances such as the waltz, fox trot, and Charleston. Her *Japanischer Groteske* (1917) and *Japanischer Pantomime* (1921) parodied not only Kabuki-style movements but also images of male bodily assertiveness that already seemed parodies; Gert stamped, strutted, and grimaced with wildly swinging arms, turning Kabuki into a parody and parodying the parody. She also parodied the conventional Spanish dance, the Negro dance, the gavotte, the minuet, and the expressionistic dance incarnated by Mary Wigman, whose compositions, according to Gert, were "never vehemently released from a central force, but constructed and therefore never unified. Something always remains stiff. She is completely undancerly in a higher sense, because she is physically and intellectually without rapture" (Gert, "Mary Wigman," 362).

In 1919 Gert moved toward the parodying of sleazy social types with *Canaille,* in which she impersonated the movements of a street girl who transformed herself from a "sweet, helpless" waif into a brazen, lewd, vulgar slut (*KTP* 4, 1920, 115–116). This parody of feminine modes of seduction remained in her repertoire until at least 1930. In *Die Küpplerin* (1920) she

SOLO DANCING   *205*

was apparently even more lascivious (and disturbing) in her portrayal of a procuress, but in this case the imaginary object of her extravagantly wanton movements was not a man but a woman she wished to turn into a prostitute (a dramatic situation defining her role as Frau Greifer in the film *Die freud-lose Gasse*); here she parodied the movements she had already used to parody seduction in *Canaille*. More lurid still was *Grüss aus dem Mumienkeller* (1925), in which she presented, through movement above all, the most sordid, depraved embodiment of female desire "greeting" the habitués of the mummy dive, a "hellish vision of misery from the deepest depths" and an excellent example of "pornochoreography," according to a 1926 comment in the socialist journal *Vorwärts* (FPV 39). In the mid-1920s, Gert extended her range of parody subjects to include the boxer, the cabaret singer, the concert singer, the celebrated pianist, the "profane Madonna on the cigarette package," and the circus clown (Figure 51). With *Verkehr* (1926) she parodied the impatient movements of pedestrian, driver, and traffic cop at a busy Berlin intersection, and in *Kino* (1926) she parodied cinematic newsreels and film-star posturing. In the late 1920s, she began doing parodies of abstract emotional conditions, such as "nervousness," "pleasurable despair," and, most interesting, "tragic sorrow." The latter characterization appeared in *Kummerlied* (1928), in which she distorted the movements and sounds of sobbing until she burst into a scream, then subsided into a slow, weak, dry, pulsating sobbing (Gert, *Mein Weg*, 41).

In these strange pieces, she used dance to parody conventions of *acting*, and only a dancer with strong acting talent could produce such entertainingly sophisticated semiotic analysis. Actors tend to conserve rather than complicate bodily movement, preferring to emphasize the transparent function of a gesture instead of its autonomous beauty, although in 1920 a critic complained that Gert's dances suffered from too much superfluous, "restless" movement (*KTP* 4, 116). Gert relied heavily on her upper body to construct parodistic signification, but in *Der Tod* (1927) she went to extremes, wearing a simple black dress and painting her face white. One critic wrote: "She does nothing. She stands and dies." That is to say, she moved only her hands and face; her eyes, mouth, chin, cheeks, forehead, and shoulders did all the dancing to convey the approach of death, presenting a "face which seeks help . . . and already knows that nothing more is possible, no return, no escape." No music accompanied the piece, just the dancer's soft sighing or moaning. The movements of hands and face gradually diminished into a "soft and scarcely perceptible trembling." She became so still and silent, yet with eyes wide open, that spectators could not even hear themselves breathe, so powerfully did the parody of dying intensify rather than dissipate the fear of death (Hildenbrandt 128–129).

Gert always danced to popular forms of music—waltzes, Charlestons, tangos, jazz tunes—for "so-called art music says nothing to me." She claimed her favorite musical instruments were the accordion, the saxophone, the calliope, and the street organ. She contemplated a "new music" derived from the sounds of neighing horses, mooing cows, squeaking birds and frogs, barking dogs, the rustling of wind or waves, the buzzing of airplanes and motorcycles, the pulsation of machines, the scolding of women (Gert, *Mein Weg*, 44–45). She believed, however, that dancing without music was "senseless," for she regarded music as the whole motive for dancing. Thus, for her, *Der Tod* was "no longer a dance" but simply an impersonation of dying and death (Gert, "Der neue Tanz"). Hardly any other dancer appeared so closely identified with the cynical, antiromantic atmosphere of Weimar-era Berlin. Bragaglia thought she was the most vivid incarnation of femininity deformed or demonized by immersion in "modern life, the immensity of the city" and the most perfect example of the "macabre apparition" the dancer becomes when she invests the grotesque with purely modernist qualities (*Jazz Band*, 161–168). But one can just as well say that, through her dance parodies, Gert embodied a highly intelligent femininity, deriving ecstasy from the "brutal," as she put it, deconstruction of semiotic conventions that strangled bodily expressivity with "gracefulness."

One could discuss other dancers who pursued careers in the solo concert mode, including Lisa Ney, Hannelore Ziegler, Tatiana Barbakoff (1899–1944), Leni Riefenstahl, Oda Schottmüller (1905–1943), Ilse Meutdner, and numerous others. However, their contributions to the solo medium still remain inadequately documented or, as in the case of Riefenstahl, less important than their contributions in another vein. As for Meutdner, she did not begin giving solo concerts until the late 1930s; though she was not an especially innovative dancer and did little to expand the expressive power of the solo medium, she was nevertheless significant in preserving a measure of the individuating spirit of *Ausdruckstanz* during a time (1937–1949) of intense efforts to discredit Weimar-era dance. Oda Schottmüller was a sculptor as well as a dancer and created an extraordinarily imaginative variety of self-designed masks of fascinating, exotic beauty; in one dance from 1940 she wore a tuxedo, carried a bowler and umbrella, and covered her head with a mask that made her bald and put strange eyes on her forehead, above her real eyes. She also employed music written especially for her, including a "xylophone dance," and, intriguingly, she constructed dance cycles using the music of different composers. But knowledge of her aesthetic remains obscure; research has focused on her participation in the anti-Nazi resistance and her arrest and decapitation by the Gestapo. Her dances themselves apparently did not trouble the authorities, who permitted her to perform them for troops at the front (Molkenbur; MS 202–203).

Pair Dancing

Although the solo dance was perhaps the strongest medium for projecting a distinctive attitude toward the body, it lacked power to expose insightful attitudes about relations *between* bodies. Such attitudes never escape affiliation with attitudes toward sexual difference, sexuality, and erotic orientation; in spite of occasional modernist efforts (such as the *Triadic Ballet*) to construct an abstract, genderless human body, no convincing justification has yet emerged for the belief that the sex of the dancing body "doesn't matter" in exposing relations between bodies. Modern dance clearly expanded conditions of freedom for the female body, but it did little to undermine the perception that dance was a feminine art and a culture overwhelmingly populated by female bodies. The dearth of male dancers in the art made it almost impossible for many female dancers to explore in a satisfactory manner their unique attitudes toward sexual difference and erotic feeling. The solo format allowed them to dramatize this powerful absence and to disclose the redemptive beauty of moving alone. In a sense, the solo dancer's partner was the spectator, whose sexual identity was often ambiguous—even more so in relation to solo dancers than to many all-female group dances in the schools. The solo dance exposed a relation between the passive, desiring body of a critical spectator and the active, desired body of a performer: the solo dance established the desirability of a body vis-à-vis the desiring body of the spectator.

That the structure of desire entailed greater complexities than the passive-active dichotomy indicated was obvious even to the solo dancers, particularly those who ventured into realms of the grotesque, the bizarre, and the tragic, where desirability asserted itself with less certainty and desire required more active articulation than in conventional contexts. But such ambiguities could scarcely modify the perception that dance was a feminine mode of expression. In a 1913 comment on the "metaphysics of dance," Paul Hatvani claimed that men find their identities through action that builds representation, art, images of ideas, whereas women find their identities, their being (*Dasein*), in "the dance—the only expressive form of womanliness," a form that has no intellectual significance. "I saw a woman dance a dance which signified 'God': a smile lay on her cheeks. . . . For the true woman every movement is dance and in every movement she gives something of herself to a beloved" (24–27). No doubt this sort of thinking, which is as prevalent today as it was in 1913, inspired Mary Wigman to remark in response to a 1926 "question about the dance as an expression of sensuality: 'I envision only our aim. My students must give such an impression that every man should enthusiastically call out: "I would not like to be married to any one of them!"'" (MWB 96). But such comments merely reinforced the perception that dance was a zone of signification wherein women made up all the rules and were free of competition from or even for men. If anything, Wigman's remark called greater attention to the cryptic aura of female homoeroticism emanating from various schools and their groups (including Loheland, Günther, Hellerau-Laxenburg, Tels, and Wigman) that consistently fostered a hostile attitude toward the inclusion of male students.

The strongest attempt to cultivate the idea of the new male dancer came from Laban and his disciples, but the rationale they employed was not altogether persuasive. In *Die Schönheit* (22/2, 1926, 69–81), Wilhelm Burghardt, a Laban disciple, proposed a theory of "Der männliche Tänzer," asserting that, due to physiological differences, serious male dance differed significantly from female dance. He criticized Hans W. Fischer's *Weiberbuch* (1924) contention, very similar to Hatvani's, that dance, as the essence of feminine being, feminized and diminished the unique beauty of the male body. Burghardt pointed out that in other historical and cultural contexts men had dominated the art of dance and that even in many European cultures the construction of a manly, warrior identity depended on displaying skill at dancing. Recent geniuses of German culture, such as Goethe, Beethoven, and Nietzsche, showed no fear of dance, and Beethoven's desire to take turbulent walks during thunderstorms was evidence of a male mode of dancing. As Burghardt saw it, the industrialization of European civilization since the French Revolution had intensified sexual difference in regard to the coding and display of bodily movement. What inhibited men from becoming dancers was the misguided notion that men should move in the same way as women. Rather, men should derive their sense of dance movement from "natural" sources of male action such as felling a tree, pulling a rope, or pushing a wagon. Yet photographs accompanying this and other articles in the special Laban issue consistently showed nude men and women performing the same types of movement and never gave the impression that a presumed sexual identity for movement somehow compromised the sexual identity of the body.

In any case, male dancing within the Laban cult remained confined largely to lay movement choirs, and although some of the Laban schools produced a few memorable male teacher-choreographers (Jooss, Gleisner, Weidt, Keith), one clearly could not get men to pursue serious careers as dancers by arguing that dance could elevate the esteem in which other men held them. The key to getting men to dance lay with women: men were much more likely to dance in response to a desiring voice of women than to some sort desirable or desiring voice of men. Hertha Feist (Berlin), Helmi Nurk (Bremen), and Margarethe Schmidts (Essen) probably enjoyed more success in recruiting male students than any other schools, but on the whole women in the modern dance movement remained quite reticent about expressing a desire to dance with men or to see men dancing with women, and they did little even to acknowledge that the absence of men in artistic performance was a problem. Consequently, men with strong dance talent preferred to pursue opportunities in the admittedly moribund world of ballet, where female dancers responded much more favorably to the presence of male dance prowess.

Male desire to dance manifested itself much more clearly in the realm of social dance, which, especially after the introduction in the prewar years of modernist forms of social dance such as the fox trot, tango, shimmy, samba, turkey trot, Boston, apache, and grizzly, became increasingly a zone of opportunity for aligning the display of sex appeal through bodily movement with expanded social mobility. The fantastic popularity of the tango, introduced around 1907, did much to undermine the authority of the waltz as the optimum dance for idealizing bodily relations between male and female. The interest of the upper class in escaping the nostalgic lyricism and decorative modesty of the waltz precipitated a curious interaction between high and low culture (where most modern social dances originated), a process that rapidly evolved in favor of upper-class tastes. Social pair dancing established codes of conduct that did not feminize the male, who could always expect to "lead" his partner. Even in dances where the woman took the lead, as was sometimes the case with the tango or the fishtail, the man did not suffer stigmatization, for by taking the lead the woman presumably expressed an even stronger desire to dance with a man. Mastery of social dances showed quite dramatically the extent to which a man was sensitive to a woman's body and inspired a woman's sensitivity to a man's body.

Moreover, mastery of social dance skills seemed tied to the cultivation of cosmopolitan masculinity and a modern image of the "gentleman." Koebner and Leonard's *Das Tanz-Brevier* (1913), with an initial run of 20,000 copies, not only explained, with the help of numerous elegant photographs and drawings, the correct execution and semiotic significance of various social dances, it situated social dancing within an elaborate, aristocratic, and sport-tinged code of superior male urbanity and competitiveness. Koebner described this code in even greater detail in *Der Gentleman* (1913), a suave guidebook dealing with the aesthetic of smoking jackets, gloves, valets, monocles, and hand kisses, as well as proper bearing at tea dances or the performance of rags and tangos. These works implied that modern social pair dancing no longer belonged primarily to the somewhat sleazy, desperate, lower-class environment of taverns and dance halls described only a few years earlier by Ostwalt in *Berliner Tanzlokale* (1905) and the fourth volume of *Das Berliner Dirnentum* (1906). Interestingly, impulses toward "sexy" bodily movement and display in that milieu did not allow male and female dancers to get close to each other, or even touch, a situation quite similar to most rock dancing today.

After the war, jazz music increasingly displaced folk music in shaping the identity of social dance forms. Jazz-oriented social dancing took on the characteristics of a sport; according to Heinz Pollack in 1924, a dance, like a doubles tennis match, disclosed not the erotic or social relations between the partners but their compatibility as performers: "[T]he new dances . . . are only dances and not masquerades" of sublimated erotic "wishes and drives" ("Erziehische," 124). Pollack had already designated social dancing as a sign of powerful social transformation in *Die Revolution des Gesellschafts-tanzes* (1922), but Rudolph Lothar insisted that jazz worked to expose rather than sublimate the expression of erotic desire, for "the rhythm [of jazz] is so to speak the iron cage in which the noise of the primeval forest becomes adapted to the salon . . . and the rhythm pulls one into voluptuous depths in which no sound and no light from quotidian life penetrates" (88). The confusion inspired by the erotic ambiguity of social dancing led August Traber-Amiel, previously the author of a comprehensive instruction manual, to propose, in the pamphlet-sized *Der Tanz als Weg zur neuen Kultur* (1924), that anxiety over the erotic significance of social dancing would diminish only when social dancing established itself not as a sport or recreation but as an art in which superior mastery of technique produced a "deep" exploration of the emotional currents binding male and female bodies together. Types of music or movement were always less important than the quality of the partners' responses to each other. Nevertheless, as Leonard aphorized in *Tanzsport Almanach 1924*, people with different tastes in music often marry, but then they are not able to dance together (95).

At any rate, jazz became identified with an unsystematic effort to expand the emancipatory significance of social dance, even if that meant provoking greater and greater uncertainty regarding the extent to which social dances affirmed or undermined sexual morality. Jazz-driven social dancing became an important, ever-expanding sector of the German entertainment industry and probably an even more pervasive sign than modern dance itself of the modern hunger for ecstasy (Eichstedt 37–72). Despite copious efforts to produce their own, unique jazz music, the Germans persisted in viewing both jazz and the new forms of social dance as imports, manifestations of foreign bodily codes. Though German popular composers showed much inventiveness in modernizing older, folk-derived dances such as the tango, the waltz, and the mazurka, their success in producing jazz music that competed well with American tunes was limited, to put it mildly; in the huge "TanzSzene Berlin" series (1925–1934) of recordings compiled by Karl-Heinrich Jordan, for example, numerous dance orchestras professing to offer jazz tunes show a curious inability to escape the relentless "oompah" of march or polka rhythms. The German enemies of jazz were numerous and grandiose in their apocalyptic condemnations of it as a symptom of decadence, addiction, racial impurity, sexual immorality, capitalist amorality, Jewish morbidity, Bolshevik propaganda, or animalistic submission to "low," uncultured instincts (Schröder 329–365). But because its rhythms and harmonies urged the body to display mastery of "sexy" movements, jazz strengthened the perception that social dancing was the most overt expression of female desire to dance with a male, and as long as this desire asserted itself with ever-greater confidence, men had strong incentives to become dancers.

Not surprisingly, then, in the realm of *Ausdruckstanz*, pair dancing between a male and a female amplified the value of the male dancer and dramatized female desire to dance with males. Indeed, expressionist pair dancing showed the power of this desire to produce art worth watching. Pair dancing performances were almost entirely done by a man and woman who formed their own tiny company to produce concerts featuring each other, for men appeared "effeminate" if they danced either alone or in a company overwhelmingly composed of females. Some pair dancers (Isa Zarifah and Fred van Hutten; Jan Trojanowsky and Frida Hess) apparently confined themselves to appearances in cabarets and nightclubs, and their work remains poorly documented. Even the work of more "serious" pair dancers is still frustratingly scant, despite their considerable popularity at the time; these included, in the 1920s, Ernst Matray and Katta Sterna (1897–1984), who later joined Trudi Schoop's company, and, in the 1930s, the ballet-trained Alexander von Swaine (1905–1990) in partnership with Alice Uhlen, then Darja Collin, then Lisa Czobel (b. 1906). Czobel also paired with Karl Bergeest, who eventually became her husband. Equally vague is the partnership between Ruth Abramowitsch and George Groke, which began in Berlin around 1930 and continued in Warsaw after 1933. Pair dancing on the concert stage was extremely rare in Germany before 1914, and hardly any documentation of it exists before that time beyond Pavlova's occasional numbers with a male ballet dancer, whose function was simply to heighten her own idealized desireability. Of course, the pairing of

Olga Desmond and Adolf Salge in Berlin in 1908 provoked much interest because of Desmond's nudity in performing dances inspired by ancient Greek statuary; but, having aroused so much curiosity, the couple declined to continue their partnership.

In Stuttgart, Elsa Hötzel and Albert Burger may have been active as early as 1912, but their work remains completely obscure. In 1913 the German artist Alastair (1887–1969), soon to become famous (or notorious) for his exquisitely lurid illustrations of literary works and contemporary personalities, performed "chimerical" dances with a Russian woman called Katerina in the Paris mansion of Baroness Ilse Deslandes. According to Gabriele d'Annunzio, Alastair performed "Gothic dances" in an "azure tunic brocaded with gold," then moved gravely in the violet robes of a bishop while "bronze antelopes and other nimble animals of the Far East grazed in the carpets." Sinking into cushions, Katerina seemed a figure of wax with enameled eyes, but her legs and ankles moved lightly and delicately, "like a serpent twitching its tail in love or in wrath" (149). It was an eccentric soiree that apparently did not persuade Alastair to develop further his talent in this direction, but the strangely androgynous aura he cast reappeared in the work of other male pair dancers, including Hans Wiener, who was active in Gera (1925–1926) as a modernist theatre choreographer before teaming up (1928) with Ottilie Foy in New York. Photos of his Ethiopian and Hindu dances convey an impression of florid, decorative male beauty (Martin, "New Dance").

Helge Peters-Pawlinin (1903–1981) perhaps displayed an even stronger bisexual aesthetic. He had a long career as a dancer, choreographer, and costume designer, beginning with the Rita Sacchetto ballet company, then moving on to the Lotte Fassbaender company, the Rhea Glus company, and the Ellen Petz state opera company in Dresden (1927) before running his own Romantische Ballett in Munich from 1936 to 1943. After the war he concentrated on choreographing large-scale ballets with dark and somewhat perverse themes, such as Der Student von Prag (1950), with Harald Kreutzberg, the controversial Abraxas (1948), and the rock opera Mixed Media (1973). As a dancer, however, Peters-Pawlinin displayed such ambiguity of sexual identity that he scarcely needed a female partner: often within the same dance he shifted abruptly from "masculine" virility to "feminine" undulation; in 1928 photos of him, both his costumes and his movements are so sexually ambiguous that it seems as if he were his own partner (Peter). Male bisexuality of this sort was not an uncommon feature of pair dancing concerts, for the male and female dancers did not perform all the dances together and did as many solos as they did pair dances. This convention served to accommodate more than costume changes: it allowed the male dancer an opportunity to display a solitary consciousness of his divided sexuality.

LO HESSE AND JOACHIM VON SEEWITZ

Lo Hesse and Joachim von Seewitz were active in Munich and Berlin between 1916 and 1920. Their dances relied heavily on extravagantly exotic costumes designed mostly by the Munich expressionist artist Walter Schnackenberg (1880–1961), who also produced several charming art deco figurines of Lo Hesse (Schnackenberg; Arwas 214–216). The couple favored fantastically Oriental, Venetian, Spanish, or rococo costumes that had the effect of making dance a sign of ultrarefined luxury and exquisitely privileged voluptuousness. This linking of dance to fashion and fashionableness did not escape criticism. Hildenbrandt condemned Lo Hesse for appearing in fashion magazine poses behind the wheel of her Mercedes or with her sleek greyhound, and he deprecated the couple as "female and effeminate mannikins for a refined masquerade wardrobe" (*Briefe*, 50–51). However, *Elegante Welt* (6/1, 3 January 1917, 4–5) praised the "orgy of beauty" and "inclination toward the bizarre" created by the couple, as well as their lack of sentimentality. Seewitz was self-taught as a dancer, but the journal compared him favorably with the great Russian male dancers. In 1920, Ola Alsen, writing for the same journal (9/1, 7 January 1920, 7), maintained that he was "undoubtedly" the greatest of all male German dancers. Virtually all commentaries presented Lo Hesse as the decidedly inferior dancer of the pair. Nikolaus suggested that Hesse's sense of bodily rhythm was too measured and constrained, too lacking in boldness, whereas Seewitz, despite his elaborate costumes, moved with great freedom and showed enchanting skill in shifting abruptly from one rhythm to another, although all his movements seemed suffused with lyrical "boyishness" or undulant femininity; Hesse strove to keep up with Seewitz, but she was incapable of dramatizing any serious idea of "striving" (50, 74–76). Török in 1918 supposed that Hesse disguised her lack of talent behind a luxurious wardrobe, but he lauded Seewitz as an example of "pure fluidity," a dancer who almost seemed not to have a body (11).

Apparently Hesse achieved more satisfactory performance when she danced with Seewitz than when she danced her solos, but the two of them performed only a couple of dances together, the Moszkowski *Masquerade* and Weber's *Invitation to the Dance*, and these never delighted as much as Seewitz's solos. His most significant piece was probably *Heliogabal* (1919), a "terrifyingly beautiful masterpiece of pantomime" in which he evoked the perverse sun-worship ritual of the homosexual Roman emperor (*KTP* 4, 1920, 120). Here he displayed his effeminacy with stunning boldness: he swathed himself in a dark, satiny robe, which he opened up and discarded to reveal a "super-slender, quite lean" body decorated with pearl necklaces, earrings, slippers, bracelets, lipstick, mascara, a glittering blouse, and a gorgeous miniskirt. All of his movements were feminine insofar as they consisted of serpentine undulations and narcissistic basking in his own refulgence. Imperial and cosmic power seemed concentrated in a "terrifyingly" ambiguous image of maleness. Seewitz also performed, in Pierrot costume, the "dancing fool" to Debussy's music and a "grotesque waltz in black" to music by Chopin, but his main achievement was to make the presumed "effeminacy" of the male dancer a more disturbing source of power than the term implies. However, he achieved this effect probably because he chose such a weak female dancer as his partner.

WALTER HOLDT AND LAVINIA SCHULZ

Knowledge of the astonishingly bizarre and tragic art of Walter Holdt and Lavinia Schulz is obscure and largely based on the rediscovery in 1986 of artifacts deposited in a Hamburg museum back in 1925 (Jockel 55–75). The artistic power within this couple apparently lay with the woman, for virtually nothing is known of Holdt. After suffering from a severe ear disease, Schulz (1896–1924) studied ballet, painting, and music in Berlin, where as early as 1913 she came into contact with Herwarth Walden's Sturm circle of expressionists. Through this circle she became friends with Lothar Schreyer, who invited her, "my first student, a genial person with violent passion," to perform, apparently nude, in his wild production of August Stramm's *Sancta Susanna* in 1918 (LS 197). When Schreyer, disillusioned by his struggle to form an avant-garde theatre in Berlin, moved to his native Hamburg in 1919, Schulz followed him. It is not known whether she met Holdt there or whether they had already met by this time. In Berlin Schulz was a costumer and seamstress for Schreyer's early *Kampfbühne* productions, including the 1920, Edda-inspired *Skirnismól;* Holdt played Skirnir in a heavy, robotically abstract costume but seemed to dance in it without difficulty.

Schulz married Holdt in April 1920, and the couple soon drifted away from Schreyer, for, as Schulz explained in a note, "Expressionism is not a solution; expressionism works with machines and industry." Schulz and Holdt led a fanatically austere existence in a bizarre expressionist cellar apartment without a floor, bed, or hot water. They slept on straw and dedicated themselves religiously to the construction of their strange mask dances, wearing gray tights during the day so that they could work on the dances as they worked on the masks and costumes. The couple became obsessed with recovering an archaic Aryan-Nordic identity free of Jewish-Christian contamination. According to H. H. Stuckenschmidt, who was their friend, Schulz craved hardship: "Poverty, hunger, cold, Nordic landscape with snow, ice, and catastrophes: that was her world, and with Holdt she found it" (36). The couple put on only a few dance concerts between 1920 and 1924, but these were among the strangest produced by the whole Weimar dance culture, and although Hamburg audiences responded with bewilderment, critics tended to recognize a powerful imagination. The marriage, however, experienced intense strain. The couple had great difficulty earning any money and longed to find a way to live without it; Holdt apparently possessed a character that was not entirely trustworthy, and Schulz was violently jealous, perpetually terrified that Holdt would betray her for another woman. In 1923 she gave birth to a son, but in this last year of the great inflation she and Holdt suffered from continual hunger. In June 1924 police discovered their bodies in the bizarre cellar apartment, with the baby between them. Schulz had shot Holdt to death, then killed herself.

Husband-wife dance pairs are quite rare on the stage; in the case of Schulz and Holdt the concept of marriage entailed a peculiarly deep implication in that it also referred to a haunting marriage of dance and costume. The couple created dances and costumes together and at the same time, so that bodily movement and the masking of the body arose from the same impulse. Schulz was a highly gifted artist whose drawings and sketches invariably startle the viewer with their hard primitivism and demonic abstraction, but Holdt assumed much responsibility for the design of the costumes and masks; for most of the costumes deposited in Hamburg, it is not possible to assign definite authorship to Schulz. The mask portions consisted mostly of fantastically reptilian, insectoid, or robotic heads, whereas the rest of the costumes comprised eccentric patchworks of design, color, and material to convey the impression of bodies assembled out of contradictory structures. One costume consisted of a white veil draped over a nude female body, topped by a large mask shaped like a triangular birdcage. To develop the "abstract organicism" of the mask-costumes, the couple built their designs out of diverse materials: wood, leather, rope, wire, metal, canvas, cloth, yarn, clay, cardboard, and gypsum. The costumes were often quite heavy and difficult to move in, because Schulz believed that art should be hard, an expression of struggle; however, all of the costumes disclose a quality of cartoonish, demonic grotesquerie rather than frightening ferocity (Figure 52). The couple gave the costumes eccentric names, as if they were mysterious pets: "Tobaggan," "Springvieh," "Technik," and so on. Yet the designs never achieved the level of abstraction reached by Schreyer or Schlemmer, partly because Schulz and Holdt cultivated a zealously ecological consciousness that made them associate abstraction with redemptive organic forms of nature and the animal world but also because the couple had a more refined feeling for bodily movement than Schreyer or Schlemmer did.

Schulz repudiated the ballet aesthetic she had studied in Berlin. In 1921 she published her notation of the dance *Mann und tote Frau*, using a graphic "scoring" technique similar to what Schreyer had done for *Kreuzigung* (1920), although Schulz's scoring was more precise and lucid. This *Tanzschrift* indicated a dance style built out of varying intensities of creeping, stamping, squatting, crouching, kneeling, arching, striding, lunging, and leaping in mostly diagonal-spiraling patterns across the performance space, with both arms thrusting or grasping and the whole occasionally punctuated by pauses. It is not clear what the costumes or music were for this dance, but it is evident that the movement was uniquely expressive in dramatizing the violent struggle of a female body to achieve central, dominant control of the performance space and its emptiness. As for music, the couple worked with H. H. Stuckenschmidt, who composed a "dadaistic" piece for *Springvieh* (1922) and arranged "trivial music" for the ecstatic *Mein Blut* (1922) and *Toboggan* (1921). For *Ungegeheuer vom Sirius* (1922), a contribution to a Hamburg "astral dance show" involving several artists, Stuckenschmidt composed a shimmy; Schulz and Holdt "dashed in wild rotation; between them a star nebula of Loheland girls, swirling to the perimeter, their raised arms a wave full of delicate arpeggios" (Hans Fischer, *Hamburger*, 265). Jockel regards the couple as an example of the self-destructive fate that awaits people who live so completely for their art that they become mortally estranged from life (75). The Schulz-Holdt dance aesthetic does seem to embed a powerful masochism, not only in the marriage between dancers but in the equally passionate marriage of mask and movement. But the dances of this strange couple were also a kind of bizarre, expressionist demonization of marriage itself, the most grotesquely touching critique of pairing to appear in the whole empire of German dance culture.

THE FALKE SISTERS

Female pair dancing enjoyed special appeal because it dramatized competing models of femininity and exposed conditions under which one model of femininity dominated or achieved equilibrium with another. The homoerotic dimension to this sort of pair dancing was not negligible in supporting its appeal. For this reason, perhaps, it is extremely difficult to find any examples of male pair dancing, although Kurt Jooss did experiment with male duets in larger dances. Female pairs appeared more frequently in the period 1916 to 1921, and Mila Cirul danced with her sister Elia in Paris as late as 1935. The three Wiesenthal sisters were popular in the prewar years, but when Else and Berta formed a separate pair (1908–1914) they achieved only modest success. Ruth Schwarzkopf (1900–?) danced with her sister Isabella (1899–1918) before turning to the solo mode, and in Vienna, Mila Cirul formed a pair with Ellen Tels in 1919–1920. During the premiere exhibition in Berlin of two movies in 1916, Valeska Gert and Brigitta Riha, wife of the artist Erich Heckel, performed an intermezzo pair dance to Debussy's *Golliwog's Cakewalk* in which one dancer wore white and the other, clad in black, moved in "snakelike" fashion around her (FPV 29–30).

Perhaps the most interesting of the sister pairs was that comprising Gertrud (1890–1984) and Ursula (1895–1981) Falke. Their father, Ham-

burg poet Gustav Falke (1853–1916), encouraged them to pursue artistic
vocations and introduced them to prominent figures of the Hamburg cultural elite. After studying with Dalcroze in Hellerau (1911–1912), Gertrud
established her own Dalcroze-oriented school in Hamburg in 1913 and the
same year presented, with her students, her first public concert, which
received much acclaim. Ursula remained uncertain of her artistic direction,
drifting tentatively into music, painting, and sculpture, and she was grateful
when her sister invited her to study dance at the new school and eventually
become a director of it. For some time the Falke family had experienced
intensifying financial difficulties, which exerted great pressure on the sisters
to alleviate the situation.

At Hans Brandenburg's suggestion, the sisters went with Laura Oesterreich to Ascona in summer 1914 to study Laban's ideas about bodily movement, but they found the atmosphere there uncongenial ("too technical").
Not until 1916, after the death of their father, did the Falkes begin performing dances together. They enjoyed considerable popularity between
1917 and 1919, making fifty appearances in ten German cities, but the critical response never escaped the tentativeness and reserve emanating from
the sisters themselves. They consistently gave the impression of never giving
more than enough to please, as if they danced entirely in response to a
momentary external pressure rather than out of a powerful inner drive.
They were beautiful women, tall, slender, and dark, and they made much of
undulant, linear body movement, often on tiptoe, but they avoided any
technical complexity and cultivated a restrained romanticism that reminded Brandenburg of the "nordic" music of Brahms (132). Peculiarly, they
never attempted any productions with their students. In the solo portions
of their concerts, Gertrud was apparently a more expressive dancer than
Ursula, but they seemed strongest in the dances they performed together;
in spite of Brandenburg's preference for their solo dances, their pair dances
provoked far greater pleasure. In these they embodied a "ghostly life." For
example, in *Versunkene Kathedral* (1918; music: Debussy) Ursula, clad in
dark silky pants, moved as the shadow of her more radiant sister, whose
short dress exposed her exquisite legs. The pair dances often dramatized a
"darkness in darkness," with both sisters wearing dark garments and constructing languid arabesques and eerie mirror movements out of the delicate intertwining of their bodies. Ursula, though tinged with "genial dilettantism," disclosed a "morbid, languid decorativeness," a "mondaine-
bizarre and capricious sense of movement" at the "edge of what is artistically
possible." This contrasted well with Gertrud's soft smile, a fragile radiance
slipping through the "nordic fog" (133–134).

The Falke sisters favored conservative-romantic music—Chopin, Schumann, Reger, Rachmaninov, Grieg—and elegantly decorative fantasy costumes designed by Doris Boekmann. The appeal of their aesthetic reached

its strongest intensity in 1920, when Mary Wigman, a friend from the Hellerau and Ascona days, invited them to assist her in the formation of a dance school at the Dresden Opera. But this plan fell apart when political intrigue at the opera prevented Wigman from receiving the anticipated appointment. Soon thereafter, the sisters began to move in separate directions, although in 1922 they did appear together on a special program in Hamburg that also featured Lavinia Schulz and Walter Holdt. Gertrud married a lawyer, Hermann Heller, in 1921 and settled in Leipzig, where he directed the Volkshochschule, but his work as an expert on administrative law required further moves to Berlin and Frankfurt. Because he was a Jewish socialist, he and Gertrud migrated to Madrid in 1933, and when Heller died in 1936, she settled in England, where she worked with Kurt Jooss at Dartington Hall. She devoted herself in later years to dance therapy instruction in Scotland and London, where she died.

Ursula sought to establish herself as a solo dancer; but this ambition proved difficult to attain because of her dark erotic life. She had long loved the sculptor Richard Luksch (1874–1936), under whom she had studied sculpture in 1914. She gave birth to his daughter in 1921 but she did not marry Luksch until 1923 because it took him until then to complete his divorce from his first wife. Because of his financial obligations to his previous wife and children, Luksch could not provide Ursula with the financial security she had craved since 1914. After the birth of her daughter she tried, unsuccessfully, to establish herself in the Berlin film industry. In 1925 she attempted to resurrect her career as a solo dancer by cultivating a more bizarre image. Luksch designed masks for three of her dances. In *Der Prinz* (1925) she wore a very androgynous white mask of vaguely Southeast Asian aspect, but her costume, which included dark, satiny pants, featured a vest with emphatically designated breasts (Figure 3). In *Rosa* (1926) her mask was that of a surprised little girl with ropelike, braided hair, reinforced by a very short, polka-dot dress. For *Die weisse Frau* (1925) she wore a white mask that was actually an eerie caricature of her own face; the rest of her body remained shrouded in a gauzy white cloak, so she moved like a tall, lean Gothic apparition.

Such effects, however, were not enough to sustain the interest of a reliable audience, for her sense of movement lacked dramatic power and always seemed governed by a sculpturesque perception of her body. By 1929 she had formed a partnership with another Hamburg dancer, Gertrud Zimmermann (1895–1962), and opened a new school that incorporated the theories of Laban, but this project was also a failure. In 1932 she and Zimmermann collaborated with Luksch on a most intriguing grotesque dance, *Die grosse und die kleine Dummheit*, which premiered at a Hamburg arts festival. The piece featured an enormously inflated balloon-caricature of Adolf Hitler, who hatched two large eggs, from which emerged Zimmer-

PAIR DANCING 219

mann and Falke as a pair of lascivious, scantily clad, blonde-wigged caricatures of Aryan female beauty (Jockel 17–31). This piece was as much a
macabre critique of the dark sister pair Ursula had constructed with
Gertrud Falke and then with Gertrud Zimmermann as a sociopolitical
satire. After 1933 Ursula ceased dancing in public, and after the death of
her husband, in 1936, she moved to Berlin and taught in an arts academy.
The Falke sisters had only minor artistic interest independent of each other,
for what made them significant was their skill in disclosing the presence of
another dark woman in the female dancer, an insight Ursula seemed to
grasp with hauntingly ominous implication in her eerie Hitler dance. But
the most curious aspect of the Falke sisters was their reluctance to exploit
their strength with any rigor or visionary ambition; they seemed afflicted
with languor, procrastinating gestures, a dilettantish disdain for technical
complexity. Yet this resistance to ambition was perhaps their strongest
defense against the constant temptation to treat dance as primarily a
response to the oppressive economic realities they inherited from their parents and then from the war.

THE SACHAROFFS

Alexander Sacharoff (1886–1963) and Clotilde von Derp (1892–1974)
formed the most enduringly popular dance pair in European history. The
aesthetic that bound them together depended on an atmosphere of
extreme artificiality and refined gender game–playing, which may explain
the couple's great durability. Sacharoff was born into a middle-class Jewish
family in the Ukraine. In 1903 he went to Paris to study painting at the Acad-
emie Julien under Bourgereau; however, when he saw a play in which the
actress Sarah Bernhardt performed a minuet with Coquelin, he decided to
become a dancer. In 1908 he began studying acrobatics in Munich, where
he made friends with such modernist artists as Wassily Kandinsky, Franz
Marc, Marianne Werefkin, and Alexander Jawlensky, for whom he sometimes posed as a rather androgynous figure. His own taste in art inclined
much more strongly toward ancient Greek vase painting and fifteenth-
century Italian masters. He gave his first concert in Munich in 1910, and in
all his early performances he projected the image of an ancient Greek vase
painting figure, donning a kind of tunic-skirt while dancing to music (harps
and string quartet) by Renaissance Italian composers (Palestrina, Monteverdi, Di Lassos) or a waltz by Johann Strauss. In both movement and costume he strove toward adrogyny, which seemed to suppress all muscularity
of expression. In 1912–1913 he danced with the Rita Sacchetto ballet company. Critics, according to Brandenburg, "found that the feminine part
seemed masculine and the masculine feminine, and in fact Sacharoff moved
with wonderful lightness; he even wept with his partner in his hands, without

making us think that because of this action he wanted to step too closely to a bad comedy not of his own invention." For her part, Sacchetto sputtered in "incoherent and idle attitudes of a costumed doll" (148).

Meanwhile, Clotilde von Derp was shaping her own career as a dancer. Born in Berlin to an aristocratic family, she moved with her mother to Munich in 1900, where she studied ballet and violin. Like Sacharoff, she gave her first concert in Munich in 1910, and her success was such that Max Reinhardt invited her to perform an elf role in a pantomime production, which led to her assuming the main role in his spectacular pantomime *Sumurun* in London in 1911. Brandenburg felt that before she teamed with Sacharoff she was a "purely lyrical dancer" with an unusual gift for constructing "rich" bodily rhythms, "song[s] of the blood" that did not seem dominated or determined by musical rhythms: her body appeared moved and freed by the music, not synchronized with it—not, so to speak, married to it (142–143). He regarded her partnership with Sacharoff as a mistake, for she "denied her blood" and intellectuality to pursue an aesthetic that made him look more masculine and forced her to sacrifice her lyrical severity for an excessively sweet femininity (155).

Brandenburg's anti-Semitism somewhat clouded perception of the couple, but as a dance pair they hardly embodied the qualities pervasively associated with a distinctively German impulse in dance. They met in 1913 at an arts festival in Munich and decided to become a dance pair once they had perfected their technique. When the war broke out, Sacharoff moved to Lausanne, with Derp following (1916), accompanied by her mother. The two did not begin dancing together until 1917, entirely in Switzerland. They married in 1919, and the same year in Zurich they made the acquaintance of the wealthy Edith Rockefeller, who offered to sponsor their performance at the Metropolitan Opera in New York early the following year. American audiences, however, showed little enthusiasm for the Sacharoffs' aesthetic. In 1921 they settled in Paris, which became their base during the interwar years, and they performed throughout Europe until 1930, when they embarked upon a successful tour of China and Japan. They repeated the tour in 1934, followed by concerts in Montreal, Detroit, and South American cities. In Spain when Germany invaded France, the Sacharoffs migrated, by way of Portugal, to Buenos Aires, where they remained until 1949, when they returned to Paris. In 1950, while visiting Italy, where they had once enjoyed much success, they met Count Guido Chigi Saracini, who invited them to teach a dance course at his Accademia Musicale Chigiani in Siena. Thus, from 1952 until their deaths they lived in Rome, teaching in Siena and at their own school in Rome at Palazzo Dorio. Although they stopped dancing as a pair in 1956, they remained prominent figures in the Italian dance world, with Sacharoff the subject of art exhibitions featuring his extravagant costume designs (Veroli; Fontaine; Ropa; Vaccarino; Vuillermoz).

The Sacharoffs made an enduring impression as a couple embodying a unified aesthetic, yet the pair performed only a few dances together, and most of these were romantic waltzes they had created in the years 1916 to 1919. Their romantic pair waltzes and chorales had the effect of masking differences between them and of presenting couplehood as the ultimate motive for dance. But despite Brandenburg's contention that she lost her distinctive sense of bodily rhythm through her match with Alexander, Clotilde did retain much of her original style in her solos, and her association with Alexander primarily implied (for him as well as her) a stronger mastery of ballet technique, although neither dancer was ever in any sense a virtuoso. Ballet technique enabled the couple to build a repertoire of movements, which they applied to the construction of virtually all their dances into the 1940s. They introduced no innovations in movement, and Alexander in particular consistently showed a tendency to think out dances as a series of poses, an approach no doubt due to his education in art. His acrobatic training urged him to synchronize all his movements to the music, whereas Clotilde moved much more independently of the music, urged more by the image the music created in her mind than by the rhythms themselves. In other words, she danced not to the music but rather to an idea within herself stimulated by the music, which is why Brandenburg described her style as "intellectual."

Clotilde displayed a more eclectic and modern taste in music than Alexander, who seldom chose anything from the twentieth century, whereas she favored music created during her lifetime: Reger, Schmitt, Pizzetti, Faure, Stravinsky, Scriabin. The couple displayed little narrative imagination and had difficulty developing dramatic structures for their dances. However, Clotilde's body possessed an extraordinarily dramatic and luscious glow, and in spite of her very dark hair her face exuded a hypnotic luminosity and her eyes a haunting, enticing shine. Indeed, perhaps no other dancer of the era owned such a powerful yet delicate repertoire of smiles. The music she chose projected mostly a melancholy or elegiac mood in a minor key, yet she always conveyed the impression that she experienced great pleasure in displaying, moving, and costuming her body. She seemed to suggest that no matter the context, she would feel some mysterious happiness on her own, aristocratic terms, whereas Alexander constantly adopted a more serious aspect, drifting occasionally into pathos even when he danced with her. But for neither of them was dance an expression of struggle or toil. Their art lacked a tragic dimension, just as it lacked kinetic technical innovation, yet all the same it was complex. The Sacharoffs created alluring dances by recombining their rather narrow range of balletic movements and poses in relation to a gorgeous array of costumes, letting their glamorous outfits make old movements new.

Alexander and Clotilde often designed their own costumes, sometimes they collaborated with major figures of the Parisian haute couture: Georges Barbier, Paul Poiret, Hubert de Givenchy, Jeanne Lanvin, René Goetz, Nathalia Goncharova, Marie-Louise Bruyere. All their costumes displayed spectacular colors, luxurious refinement, and a glorification of remote historical fashions (Figure 53). For *Petit Berger* (1917) Clotilde wore a stunning green chiffon minidress decorated with red, yellow, and blue cloth roses, but in *Poeme Printanier* (1917) she danced in a fuller dress printed with an ecstatic multitude of brilliant flowers. In *Danse* (1921) she wore an elegant medieval-Byzantine dress in blue and gold. Even when she donned folk dresses, the designs were so lavishly stylized that folk culture appeared as a charming abstraction rather than as a stable sign of "authenticity." She also liked flaming red costumes, elegantly trimmed with silver or accompanied by black capes and accessories. Sometimes she danced in swirling chiffon trousers, and she never lost her taste for appearing in an eighteenth-century, "half-boyish, half-girlish union of pants and coat," for she looked extremely pretty and radiantly feminine in male garments (HB 142).

Alexander's taste in costume was just as flamboyant: from the time of *Visione del Quattrocentro* (1913), introduced during his work with Sacchetto, he strongly favored sacerdotal, medieval-Renaissance robes and vestments of imperial splendor. He often appeared, especially in pair dances, wearing luxurious pajama-type pants of an exotic nature or Venetian-Pierrot costumes with all sorts of precious details. He loved painting and powdering his face, with *Pavane Royale* (1913) being perhaps his most elaborate masquerade of masculinity, for here he parodied the already fantastic mannerisms of an aristocrat in the court of Louis XIV. *Golliwog's Cakewalk* (1916) was virtually a transvestite performance, even though he wore gaudy puff-trousers, but he really did not cultivate female impersonation. Rather, he sought to show the beauty of "effeminate" masculinity, freed from the conventional markers of modern male identity, the male body completely detached from muscularity and heroic posturing yet nevertheless pleased with itself and not at all constrained in its power to lead the woman.

When he teamed up with Clotilde, Alexander ceased to adopt the ancient Greek look, but Clotilde began to explore it, most notably in *Danseuse de Delphes* (1916), in which she achieved a far more elegant, refined, and yet modern (proto–art deco) look than Isadora Duncan ever did. The Sacharoffs delighted in bizarre hats, shoes, and wigs, with some of their wigs consisting of "hair" sculpted out of gold or silver metal and further ornamented with extravagant garlands of silk flowers and wax fruit.

For their pair dance *Chanson des Oies* (1923), they wore identical furry white duck masks and trim "duck suits"; only Clotilde's little "feather" skirt established a difference between male and female. For *Chanson Negre* (1921), which used a black gospel song as accompaniment, she actually wore, for once, a modern-style dress, with spats, black gloves, a scarf, and a sort of Little Orphan Annie wig, but she attached to her waist a skirt of huge ostrich plumes. One cannot say that she impersonated a black person or even a black way of dancing—rather, she demonstrated how black music disclosed yet another mask of her white femininity (Vuillermoz 33).

Indeed, the great message of the Sacharoffs was that sexual identity, pairing, and marriage itself were all masquerades, the consequences of perfect artificiality rather than "nature." The happiness of a couple depended on elaborate masks and a common balletic rhetoric of movement to disguise powerful differences between them. Brandenburg found this implication so haunting and unsettling that he spent an unusually large number of pages trying to explain it away, for perhaps he grasped intuitively a further implication: that the "happy couple" consisted of two people who were happy together, not two people who were happiest only when they shared the same desire. In the artificial world of the Sacharoffs, no one was happy who was not intensely narcissistic. Perhaps this point was never clearer than in Clotilde's solo interpretation of Debussy's *Le prelude à l'apres midi d'un Faun* (1936). Nijinsky's 1912 interpretation of Debussy's music had provoked much controversy in Paris because of his friezelike presentation of a bacchantic female choir and his own muscular but delicate impersonation of the faun, who, unable to consummate his desire for any of the women, concluded the piece by masturbating in his bower-lair (Nectoux). Clotilde's version was just as daring, especially if one reads it as a commentary on Nijinsky's piece. She wore not an animal-like costume but rather a flimsy white chiton printed with red and black splotches, which gave the effect of violent bloodstains on her torso. Around her shoulders she looped a long purple scarf, and around her head she set a garland of wax grapes. She performed her dance largely by sitting on the floor in a soft spotlight, undulating, writhing, arching, discarding the scarf, and spreading her legs so that the hem of the dress slid down her thighs to display the splendor of her flesh (Veroli 148–149). She passed through her wonderful repertoire of smiles and langorous glances. The dance was a masturbatory glorification of her beauty, of her love for herself, the dominant source of an ecstasy that depended on no one but herself; for as close as she was to the spectator, her pleasure always seemed remote, a secret she alone appreciated. Of course, it is extremely rare to witness a forty-four-year-old woman dancing with such voluptuous pleasure in herself, basking in her own beauty with a brazenness that seems to awaken an outraged urge to violate her—an urge she herself has already anticipated.

YVONNE GEORGI AND HARALD KREUTZBERG

Yvonne Georgi (1903–1975) and Harald Kreutzberg (1902–1968) enjoyed enormous and unprecedented international appeal as a pair from 1928 to 1930, then suddenly went in separate directions because their ambitions were so incompatible. No pair was so interesting to such a large audience, and their appeal lay precisely in their sophisticated synthesis of quite incompatible sensibilities.

Georgi was born in Leipzig, where her father was a prominent physician married to a French-Algerian woman. Yvonne Georgi projected an exotic, Arabic image: sleek, black-haired, smoldering. At school during the war, she endured embarrassments because of her French mother; when (1920), as a result of playing in a pantomime at the home of conductor Arthur Nikisch, she announced her intention to become a dancer instead of a librarian, she faced major skepticism and disappointment from her parents. Perhaps because of a need to overcome serious doubts about the nature of her desires, Georgi was throughout her life intensely competitive and ambitious. She put on her first program of dances in 1920, then went to Hellerau to study the method of Jaques-Dalcroze, which she soon found too gymnastic and lacking in dance expressivity. Having seen Wigman perform in Leipzig, she enrolled at Wigman's school in Dresden, where she easily became a star pupil and a member of Wigman's famous first group, which included Wigman, Palucca, Holm, and Trümpy. But Georgi wanted more. She started producing her own solo programs, which consisted of dances with music, dances with percussion accompaniment only, and dances in silence, as well as cyclical works built around the music of Scriabin, Haas, Milhaud, and Krenek. By 1923 she had learned all she could from Wigman and had embarked on her own path. She accepted Kurt Jooss's invitation to dance in his production of the Tels-Wellesz *Persisches Ballett* (1924) in Münster, and her success prompted the Gera Municipal Opera to appoint her ballet mistress. But she was there only a year (1925) before the Hannover Municipal Opera offered her the position of ballet mistress. Her popularity in Hannover was great, enduring, and, remarkably, achieved through her desire to create distinctly *Ausdruckstanz* ballets using advanced modern music (Figure 54). She lured Mila Cirul and Kreutzberg away from their soloist positions with the Berlin State Opera to dance in her 1926 production of Stravinsky's *Petrouchka* (1911), and at the end of the year, after establishing her own school, she and Kreutzberg put on a concert together containing fourteen pieces. Only two of these were pair dances; nevertheless, he decided not to return to Berlin (Koegler 22–33).

Kreutzberg came from a quite different milieu. His grandfather and father were in the circus and wild animal entertainment business, and his mother strongly encouraged his precocious gift for play-acting and theatrical gestures. He was born in Bohemia, but the family tended to wander: Breslau, Leipzig, Dresden. In 1920, while attending art school in Dresden (Kreutzberg was also a gifted draftsman), he performed a "hashish dance" at a student carnival party. The popularity of this piece was such that he decided to enroll in an amateur course at Wigman's school. His talent impressed Wigman, but she made little use of it, so in 1923 he accepted the invitation of another Wigman student, Max Terpis, to dance in Hannover, where Terpis directed the ballet of the Municipal Opera. Working in a large ensemble made Kreutzberg somewhat nervous, but the opera director, Hanns Niedecken-Gebhard, recognized Kreutzberg's gift for acting and cast him in the small character roles that often make dances memorable. Meanwhile, Kreutzberg formed a partnership with Frida Holst to produce pair dance recitals. Then Terpis accepted appointment as ballet director of the Berlin State Opera and took Kreutzberg with him. In Wellesz's controversial ballet *Die Nächtlichen* (1926), Kreutzberg appeared as Fear, a sinister, dissonant evocation of demonic forces circulating through the city between twilight and dawn. Despite the unpopularity of Wellesz's morbid music, Terpis went in for more gloom with *Don Morte* (1926), a version of Edgar Allen Poe's *The Masque of the Red Death*, employing music by the Austrian composer Friedrich Wilckens (1899–?). In this piece, Kreutzberg danced the role of an eccentric jester, wearing a gold costume and a mask with a bald head. The opera costume shop had difficulty devising a bald wig for him, so he shaved off all of his blond hair. His appearance made such a powerful impression on audiences that he maintained his trademark bald head for the rest of his life. *Don Morte* also initiated the lifelong collaboration between Kreutzberg and Wilckens, who not only wrote numerous pieces for Kreutzberg but also was his accompanist.

With Elisabeth Grube, another dancer at the opera, Kreutzberg and Wilckens produced several dance recitals in Berlin. Kreutzberg's partnership with Grube collapsed when Georgi invited him to Hannover, but the new collaboration stalled almost immediately when, in 1927, Max Reinhardt cast Kreutzberg in Salzburg productions of *Turandot* and *Jedermann*, then as Puck for a New York production of *A Midsummer Night's Dream* (Figure 55). Even in his most serious performances, Kreutzberg cultivated the image of a jester, a medieval fool, a demonic acrobat. When he returned to Hannover in 1928 as a dance instructor, he collaborated with Georgi and Wilckens on a grotesque pantomime, *Robes, Pierre and Co.*, which presented a man falling murderously in love with a show window mannequin and featured dances accompanied by the sound of typewriters, gunshots, and Kreutzberg himself singing a falsetto parody of a coloratura aria (Pirchan 7–31).

Like the Sacharoffs, Georgi and Kreutzberg performed only a few dances together, but their appeal as a pair rested largely on their skill at manipulating the architecture of the concert program so that their solo dances appeared not as autonomous, self-contained pieces but as movements within a larger-scale image of pairing. Unlike the Sacharoffs, Georgi and Kreutzberg eschewed an aura of luxury and concentrated on perfecting an austere, streamlined modernism. Both of them were muscular, athletic dancers who delighted in displaying physical prowess and dexterity, yet they each drifted into melancholy moods, with Georgi especially prone to orgiastic-ecstatic impulses and Kreutzberg never losing touch with the grotesque, the demonic, and the macabre. Kreutzberg occasionally incorporated feminine movements and details into his dances, most obviously in his *Turandot* dance (1927), in which his bald head yielded to the signifying power of a dark Oriental gown and large tassel-earrings, and in *Der ewige Kreis* (1936), in which he wore the medieval masks and costumes of a prostitute and an idle rich woman. Unlike either Sacharoff or Seewitz, Kreutzberg tended to parody feminine movements for grotesque effect, though rarely in his pair dances with Georgi, where they tended to mirror or echo each other's movements. Georgi, however, entertained hardly any doubt about the difference between masculine and feminine; indeed, she almost never wore any sort of trousers, and she avoided any movements or costume effects that destabilized the spectator's perception of her constant, dark, athletic femaleness. She was, therefore, quite unlike Clotilde von Derp, who loved disclosing ever-new aspects of her femaleness. But as a result, in pair dances, Kreutzberg's movements, mirroring Georgi's, appeared more feminine than if she had mirrored his.

Fahnentanz (1928) was a quintessential mirror dance: they wore vaguely centurionlike cap-helmets, tunic-skirts, and large capes, which they waved as flags in great, rapid, swirling movements. They created the impression of ecstatic warriors controlled by a powerful, undulating current that made them echo rather than fight each other. *Hymnis* (1929), with music by Lully, was a much more somber, ceremonial piece: "[T]hrough it Mr. Kreutzberg and Miss Georgi were marvellous counterparts, weaving the dance in two strands, now meeting in unified motion, now parting in motion contrasted; two in one in mated style and suggestion" (Parker 212). *Pavane* (1930, music: Ravel) repeated this effect with even greater gravity, with Georgi and Kreutzberg wearing glowing white costumes as they moved slowly and mournfully through the dark space. Another slow piece, *Persiches Lied* (1928, music: Satie), done in glamorous Oriental costumes, showed the dancers meeting in the space, coiling about each other, striving always to produce matching movements that allowed them to sink to the floor embracing, covered in a veil (Braaksma). All their other pair dances were variations on those described here: they sought to make the couple the source of mirror-echo effects—"complementary patterns" and "reciprocities of motion" (Parker 204). They never presented man and woman in conflict with each other, never created tension through competing configurations of bodily rhythm, and this avoidance (or fear) of conflict greatly diminished the dramatic power of their pair dances. In their 1931 Berlin performance to Gustav Holst's huge symphonic poem *The Planets* (1916), one of the largest pair concerts ever staged, they employed a monumental abstract set consisting of a row of dark, cavelike entrances from which emerged spiraling ramps and towering, slanting walls; these gave the impression that no matter how remotely separated in space the man and woman were, the couple always retained its power to define itself through complementary movement.

But in reality Georgi and Kreutzberg did not complement each other, and in their solo dances the differences between them introduced a dramatic power that their pair dances lacked. Georgi constantly hungered for rapturous excitement. In *Wälzer* (1929, music: Wilckens) she swirled and eddied her sleek body with breathtakingly voluptuous lyricism. In *Salome* (1929)—which, curiously, used music by Cyril Scott rather than the more familiar pieces on this theme by Schmitt or Strauss—she was almost naked and moved with an unapologetic, maybe even vulgar determination to appear sexy. With *Cassandra* (1929), shrouded in a great net-veil, she displayed the ominous, tragic ecstasy she could feel in prophesizing, in dreaming of vast doom. Darker and stranger still was *Tanz des Böses* (1923), in which, accompanied only by crashing gongs, she exulted, convulsively, in the glamor of demonic possession, of unashamed evil and sadism. In *Arabische Suite* (1927), however, she signified an ecstasy derived from exquisite, shimmering, rippling refinements of a delicately fluttering body, while in *Dämmerung* (1929, music: Debussy) she conveyed a melancholy "restlessness subdued to quiet ecstasy" (204). Kreutzberg, for his part, nurtured the image of the jester or sardonic stranger. In *Narrentanz* (1927) he produced a muscular, hyperexpressionist dance in which he held rather than wore a mask and dramatized a passionate spirit of revolt against the masked identity seeking to impose itself on him. In *Drei irre Gestalten* (1928), accompanied only by hallucinatory noises, he adopted an even more Caligariesque expressionism in his clinical impersonations of an idiot, a homicidal maniac, and a paranoiac, solitary inmates of an asylum. Most spectacularly expressionist of all was *Der Engel der Jüngste Gericht* (1928, music: Wilckens), in which he wore an enormous, swirling black cape that concealed his entire body except for his bald head and made him a "figure of darksome splendors, blessing and warning, aloof and drawing nigh" (205). At the end of the dance, he sank to the floor as if he were a demonic body descending into a great, rippling circle of darkness, a pool of undulant blackness. In *Engel der Verkündigung* (1928, music: Wilckens), he was a good angel, in biblical costume, quietly, slowly, and luminously signifying the immanence of divine message. *Der Königstanz* (1928, music: Reger) was altogether more muscular and martial, full of "turbulent, imperious motion" yet somewhat grotesque, with Kreutzberg wearing a weird, pharaoanic wire headpiece and a gold scarf attached to bracelets on both arms, so that the vehemence of his movements seemed curiously restrained, rather than provoked, by the vaguely feminine decorative accessories. With *Caprice* (1929, music: Smetana) he introduced his archetypal incarnation of the carefree, strolling, skipping, lolling, wandering, improvising jester who, in various "vagabond" guises, exerted such endearing appeal for German audiences of the 1930s and 1940s (Parker 200–213; Wille).

Clearly, pair dances alone scarcely explained the enormous international popularity of the Georgi-Kreutzberg team. Between 1929 and 1931 they made four comprehensive tours of both Europe and the United States, where they appeared up and down both coasts and throughout the Midwest as probably the most profitable modern dance act in U.S. history (Pirchan 32–40). No American dancers, including the team of Ted Shawn and Ruth St. Denis, enjoyed such popularity. Yet, unlike the Sacharoffs, Georgi and Kreutzberg did not embody the "happy couple." Their pair dances tended toward the elegiac and ceremonial; they seemed to express a virtuosic, synchronized cheerfulness rather than a stirring or triumphant happiness. In *Potpourri* (1929), for example, they wore polka-dot costumes and goofed around on stage with the pianist, Wilckens, interrupting his efforts to get a dance started with music by hovering over him and inserting their own discordant chords: "[O]ff they flung in staccato steps with that perfect mating of heads and arms, as in a two-fold pattern made one in line and rhythm. . . . Like children, they snatched up sticks, called them bows and arrows, sported with them," until the exasperated pianist crept away with the music and compelled the dancers to follow him off stage (Parker 206–207). But though this sort of humor proved quite delightful, it both concealed and revealed the major limitation of their pair dance aesthetic: their reluctance to build dramatic tension between each other in relation to a source of conflict—the music, the musician, or the man.

Yet it was precisely because they pursued such divergent ambitions that they could not long remain a dance couple, and in 1931 they made their last tour. Georgi always wanted more powerful and commanding opportunities to assert her authority as an artist. In 1928 she accepted appointment as ballet mistress at Braunschweig as well as at Hannover. Then, when the national economic crisis of 1930–1931 severely reduced subsidies to the opera houses, Georgi accepted an invitation from the Wagner Society to choreograph in Amsterdam. In 1932 she married a prominent Dutch journalist and found even grander opportunities for her talent, although she continued to work for Hannover until 1936. Already in 1926 Georgi had published an article in the *Berliner Illustrierte Zeitung* in which she contended that "the modern solo and group dance must conquer the theatre in order to enlarge its field of activity and expand its borders." She complained about the lack of production values and the excessive modesty of concert recital dance culture, which, she believed, had enfeebled public enthusiasm for modern dance. She blamed dancers themselves for their lack of ambition in appropriating the state theatre apparatus, for "it is not true that the expressivity, the intensity of dance in the theatre, be it in a ballet or within an opera, becomes lost" (Koegler, *Yvonne Georgi*, 31–32). The article was in part a veiled criticism of her teacher, Wigman, who favored cultic performance at the expense of large-scale productions and never displayed any enthusiasm for a reconciliation of *Ausdruckstanz* with ballet.

Georgi always distrusted schools, including her own, to recognize and exploit talent to the fullest, for teachers invariably accommodate the limitations of most students rather than the potential of a few. Besides, she wanted to put modern dance culture on a more secure economic foundation than that offered by the fragile school companies, in which, indeed, students paid to dance instead of receiving pay. An elevation in the economic status of the dancer demanded the production of large-scale ensemble pieces sponsored by generously subsidized institutions that could attract top talent in a range of fields—dance, music, design, choreography, administration. Moreover, she wanted dance to attract strong male talent, but how was that possible if dance did not situate itself within the institutionalized emblems of power through which society expected men to fulfill their obligations to it? One might even say that Georgi aspired to become the Wagner of the German dance world, so grandiose was her sense of dance as an institutional power on the European cultural scene. She continued to give solo concerts in Germany and even in New York (1935), but her heart was in the big theatrical productions she produced in Hannover and Amsterdam. Yet progress toward her aim remained slow. She staged over twenty ballets in Hannover and Amsterdam before putting together a company to tour the United States in 1937. But the tour was a disaster that bankrupted her, and in 1938 she accepted an offer to choreograph ballets for a Dutch circus and to direct a huge spectacle celebrating the fortieth anniversary of Queen Wilhelmina's reign. Her success in these endeavors enabled her to form the Ballet Yvonne Georgi in 1939.

By this time, however, disciples of fascism in Dutch culture, led by the artist Hein von Essen and the critic Weremeus Buning, sought to dominate Dutch dance through control of a group called Nederlands Dansliga. For many years, an oversupply of dancers had afflicted Dutch dance with dilettantism. Georgi's productions considerably raised the standards of Dutch dance performance, but voices within the Dansliga contended that she "monopolized" the dance world by her intensely competitive desire to attract the best talent and highest production values, by her "un-Dutch" devotion to Greek mythological themes, and by her subordination of modern dance expressivity to the aims of classical ballet. When the Germans invaded in May 1940, the situation became more ambiguous, for Georgi's husband, Lodewijk Arntzenius, an official of the Concertgebouw concert hall, was sympathetic to Nazism, and the Germans firmly approved of Georgi's aesthetic. With unprecedentedly generous subsidies, the Ballet Yvonne Georgi produced works of a scale and virtuosity never before achieved in Dutch dance history: *Orfeus and Euridice* (1941), *Josefs Legende* (1942), *Carmina Burana* (1944). But when the war ended, Georgi and her husband faced serious stigmatization that compelled them to leave Holland in 1949. With great success she resumed her choreographic duties in Hannover (1953–1970), but a visit of this company to Amsterdam in 1967 awakened bitter criticism of her Nazi collaboration (Koegler, *Yvonne Georgi;* ESG 49–65). Well before the war, her choreography had begun to make ever greater concessions to ballet technique and conventions, and her enthusiasm for Greek mythological themes seems to have subdued her inclination toward unbridled ecstasy. In spite of her taste for modern orchestral music, her ballets never advanced the expressive power of dance beyond what it was in 1930, and certainly none of her ballets of the 1930s and 1940s displayed the innovative imagination of her early group pieces in Hannover, such as *Saudades do Brasil* (1925), *Petrouchka* (1926), *Baby in der Bar* (1928), *Tanzsuite* (1928), *Das seltsame Haus* (1928), and *Robes, Pierre and Co.* (1928).

After the war she achieved even greater acclaim for her ballet choreography in Düsseldorf, Hannover, and Vienna and for television, but this acclaim seemed directed more at her success in mobilizing postwar resources on behalf of dance than at her ballets themselves. It is surprising how meagerly German dance historians have treated her work, especially in the postwar period, even though she significantly raised the standards of German ballet, at least in terms of production values and technical competence. Her turn toward ballet implied a sacrifice of her dark ecstatic impulse; she used modernism and dance to reconcile historical tensions within herself rather than within a society struggling with its past. She displaced the aesthetic of reconciliation from her pair dances with Kreutzberg onto her large-scale ensemble productions, resulting, despite a strong narrative element, in a lack of dramatic power and transformative effect on modern dance art. But the Berlin critic Fritz Böhme had observed as early as 1923 that Georgi had "not yet reached" a "compelling" sense of composition or made the "conquering step" toward artistic triumph (Koegler, *Yvonne Georgi,* 24). The problem was that Georgi was afraid of her own ambition and appetite, afraid of taking that one wild step further that might destroy her in its refusal to reconcile itself with any other step. The intense ambiguity of Georgi's identity left an equally ambivalent legacy, for despite appearances to the contrary it was never her desire to abandon *Ausdruckstanz* for ballet. She more than anyone showed the power of *Ausdruckstanz* to take over ballet and imbue it with an expressionist attitude toward the body.[1]

As for Kreutzberg, he followed a different path altogether. Though he occasionally choreographed theatre productions in Leipzig and Berlin and even appeared with Georgi in a couple of her Greek ballets for Hannover in 1934–1935, Kreutzberg's art flourished most distinctively in his solo concerts. He was always looking for a partner—Elisabeth Grube, Tilly Losch, Yvonne Georgi, Ruth Page, Ilse Meutdner—but his most enduring partnership was with Wilckens, his composer, accompanist, and business manager. With the American dancer Ruth Page (1898–1991), Kreutzberg pursued a pairs aesthetic closely resembling that of his partnership with Georgi. The two teamed up for a tour of the United States in 1933 and were so successful they repeated it the following year and continued on to Japan and China. During the 1920s, Page had exhibited an exuberant modernist spirit that had somehow evolved out of the decorative ballet style imported to America by Adolph Bolm (1884–1951), her teacher, whom she regarded as an "excessive influence" on her expressivity (Page, *Class Notes*, 15). Her *Prelude in Blue* (1926), *Ballet Scaffolding* (1925), and *Flapper and the Quarterback* (1926) were perhaps the most expressionistic-constructivist dances produced in the United States before 1930, and her astonishing *Bolero* (1930, music: Ravel), with its mounting tension achieved through accumulating movements of stationary bodies, was perhaps the most exciting achievement of the Ravinia Opera Company of Chicago (where Page hoped, in vain as it turned out, to create a base for modern dance culture competitive with that of New York). Like Georgi, Page longed to do big theatrical dances, but she displayed limited imagination in the construction of pair dances, with her most notable success in this vein being the violent and quite lurid *Frankie and Johnny* (1938, music: Moss), a WPA project. Here, at last, pair dancing (within an ensemble) was synonymous not with complementary or synchronous movements but with explosive drama.

She regarded Pavlova and Kreutzberg as the "greatest influences" on her career, but Kreutzberg's aesthetic apparently absorbed little of her romantic spirit (Page, *Video Archives*, tape 13). He retained his usual

---

1. Max Dooijes (b. 1919) was a student of Georgi during the war years and later a prominent dance teacher in The Netherlands. When I interviewed him in Amsterdam in February 1992, he spoke of his teacher with great warmth and affection. He described the Wigman-like instruction Georgi gave, her determination to release the unique expressive potential of the student. As he spoke, it became evident that what was most significant about her was her elegant ambiguity, her ability to refine every movement, to make every movement dramatic and alluring enough for ballet without being formed completely out of ballet positions. Georgi had a unique gift for awakening in men a desire to dance expressively in a competitive and demanding way far exceeding that of the lay movement choirs in which so many female expressionist dancers encountered male movement students (Dooijes).

repertoire of solos and refashioned his dances with Georgi to fit Page. For example, in *Bauerlicher Tanz* (1928, music: Wilckens) the couple danced back to back in matching polka-dot costumes with their arms entwined. But in *Bacchanale* (1933, music: Malipiero) he took the same idea and darkened it in a way he never had with Georgi: the couple danced back to back with arms entwined, but Page wore a black dress and Kreutzberg a black shirt and pants, and both wore black elastic bands around their arms and white elastic bands crossing their faces and around their heads (Turbyfill). These bands, first introduced for Kreutzberg's solo *Königstanz* (1927), created the impression of bodies both bound and bandaged, reinforcing the theme of bacchanalian ecstasy as an intense closeness to another body yet a frenzied (wounding?) struggle to face that body. Page began experimenting with elastic bands for her expressionistic solos, and Kreutzberg began devising solos, such as the primeval *Der erste Mensch* (1934, music: Bach), in which he twisted rope around his arms in a more muscled style than elastic bands suggested.

After 1935 Kreutzberg moved decisively toward the perfection of his medieval, vagabond jester image, Eulenspiegel. Georgi inspired his interest in Greek themes, which inspired *Orfeus klagt um Euridike* (1935), a revision of his jester's revolt dance. This time he danced, in chiton and wig, holding the mask of Euridice, although later presentations of the dance featured a mask with more emphatically feminine features than earlier ones. In *Orestes* (1935), with gold rope wig, he struggled again with ropes around his arms. The pathetic Orfeus dance remained in his repertoire for years, but his fame rested on his more grotesque works, such as the medieval *Der ewige Kreis* (1936), in which, with fantastic masks, he presented a death-dance suite of Boschlike impersonations of archetypal Gothic figures. Even in *Der Tod* (1937) he impersonated Death as a lurching, pouncing, acrobatic jester wandering aimlessly across a twilight space like one of the "mad creatures" in his asylum piece. In 1935 he toured the United States yet again, this time with four women, including Ilse Meudtner. Here he introduced his "scenes from Breughel" and his *Nächtliche Habanera* (music: Debussy), in which the four women appeared as ancient skeletons dressed in elaborate black sixteenth-century Spanish costumes with mantillas and fans (Meutdner 30–43). Kreutzberg's appeal in the United States was perhaps only a little less than what it was in Germany, which says much for the power of his aesthetic to cross borders.

Harald Kreutzberg was probably the most popular dance figure in Germany during the 1930s and 1940s, and his success with solo concerts during these years enabled him to live quite comfortably in a Tirolean chalet and to give him the sense that he had accomplished all that he was capable of doing. However, his aesthetic implied more than he intended. In 1943 Kreutzberg appeared with Werner Krauss in Pabst's handsome film *Paracel-*

sus, set in the late Middle Ages. Not surprisingly, he played an acrobatic jester, who winds up assisting the great physician in his escape from the *volk*-estranged authorities. The jester performs a grotesque dance in a tavern, almost a parody of expressionistic dance, creating a hypnotic effect on the male and female tavern patrons and driving them to a lunatic frenzy. When Paracelsus arrives on the scene, he recognizes the dance as a symptom of the plague and prescribes a cure based on his mysterious understanding of the "healthy community" rather than on the impotent academic rationalism of the university doctors. The film presents *Ausdruckstanz* as a sign of disease and communal pathology, but it is doubtful that Kreutzberg was even conscious of this implication. He just wandered into the film and then wandered on, always living entirely in the self-contained world of his solitary jester-self.

The army drafted him in 1944, but the Americans soon captured him on the Italian front; when they eventually released him, he returned to Germany and resumed his international career in the solo mode until 1959, performing mostly the same pieces he had created in the 1920s and 1930s. He also appeared in an excellent film version of *Der ewige Kreis* (1956) ("Harald Kreutzberg"). He was unquestionably the most significant male dancer to emerge from *Ausdruckstanz,* yet his impact on modern dance was far less than that of Vaslav Nijinsky (1888–1950), who in just a few years (1910–1917) had revolutionized the dance world by imposing upon it an overpowering intelligence. Nijinsky was a genius (and a madman) precisely because his mind was too complex to allow dance to construct a quintessential self for the dancer. He pushed bodies toward almost impossibly intricate and contradictory rhythms; he treated dance as the systematic dissolution of the self, the fragmentation of the body into multiple identities, bisexual ambiguities, violently conflicting impulses—as when, in *The Rite of Spring* (1913), the ballet corps had to shift instantly from, say, 5/16 rhythm to 7/8 to 2/4, and the right arms and legs had to move with a different rhythm from the left. Neither Laban nor Dalcroze, on the theoretical plain, could approach Nijinsky in complexity of imagination, in the application of an often impenetrable system of expressivity. By contrast, Kreutzberg seems to have retreated into his jester-self as a way of evading the heroic, almost superhuman expectations associated with an artist such as Nijinsky. The solitary jester figure was comfortably accessible to himself and to his audience; it was, in the iconography of male dance, a touching foil to the remote, unfathomable, and uncontainable god that was Nijinsky.

Group Dancing

Group dancing evolved more slowly than solo or pair dancing, primarily because of the economic complexities involved in setting up performance companies. In Germany, dance performance received subsidies only when affiliated with an opera or school, and even school companies did not begin to receive subsidies until 1925. The problem with school companies was that they depended almost entirely on students, on immature creative talent, which lowered production values in performance. What schools saved in dancer salaries was hardly enough to finance more lavish sets, costumes, lighting, or music. Conversely, professional companies had to pay huge salaries to dancers, which brought the further burden of providing high production values to attract audiences large enough to pay the salaries. The more familiar audiences became with dance art, the more impatient they became with dancers who did not invest adequately in the material quality of their productions, a reality successful solo and pair dancers understood very well.

Professional dance companies could not survive without touring, as no home-city audience for dance was large enough to sustain a professional company in its own theatre; indeed, only school companies owned their own theatres. But touring added heavily to the payroll because it tied up performers over long periods of time; thus, one could not form a professional company without having the resources to outbid other professional companies for the services of talented performers and designers. Moreover, impressive group dances depended on the controlling intelligence of a leader who had strong choreographic and managerial skills and could motivate members of a company to transcend petty differences between them on behalf of a collective aesthetic ambition. Laban grasped the importance of cultivating a "mysterious personality" for himself and his students, but his leadership skills were much better suited to forming an elaborate institutional apparatus, a network of devoted schools, than in creating significant group dances themselves. His student, Wigman, showed far greater imagination in turning cultic performance into an act of choreography, a dramatic event for an audience, probably because of her obsession with thematizing ambiguous relations between group and leader. Even so, her school groups of 1921 to 1929 were always small and always built around her need to show her own skills as soloist within group dances or in a cycle of solo and group sections. As long as modern dance valued individual over group expression, it remained slow to develop a distinctive group aesthetic outside the bankrupt ballet tradition, which in the opera houses constructed ensemble pieces out of mechanical formulas and conventions authorized in St. Petersburg, Copenhagen, Paris, and Vienna.

RITA SACCHETTO

In Berlin, Rita Sacchetto (1880–1959) became one of the first in Germany to form, out of students in her school, an independent dance company, though hers lasted only a couple of years (1916–1918). Born in Munich, she was the daughter of a respected Venetian painter and an Austrian woman. Two of her brothers became painters, and Sacchetto established her own artistic identity through the creation of what she called "dance pictures" (*Tanzbilder*); in these she used famous paintings to model dances, so that it seemed as if music and movement made the paintings come to life. She took ballet lessons and gave her solo debut concert in Munich in 1905, performing sarabandes, gavottes, minuettes, tarantellas, and Oriental dances in which costumes and poses resembled to a remarkable degree well-known paintings by, among others, Gainsborough, Reynolds, Botticelli, Greuze, and Moritz von Schwind. Her success led to an invitation to perform her odalisque dance in a production of Bizet's opera *Djamilah* in Vienna, where such artists as Gustav Klimt, Kolo Moser, and Joseph Hoffmann expressed delight in her art. Sacchetto then began a long (1907–1909) period of touring throughout Germany, Eastern Europe, Amsterdam, Paris, Madrid, South America, and New York. Loie Fuller arranged for her to perform intermezzo dances at the Metropolitan Opera, and in 1910 she gave at the Met an entire dance concert featuring her Botticelli dances, Siamese dance, and a large-scale pantomime called *The Intellectual Awakening of Woman,* which used Grieg's *Peer Gynt* suites and a group of thirty female dancers (Rieger). Later that year she embarked on a tour of Russia, which led to a collaboration with fashion designer Paul Poiret at his private theatre in Paris, where she impersonated a famous painting of the Empress Eugenie wearing her original dress (Ochaim). By 1912 she was back in Munich as Alexander Sacharoff 's partner in a pair dance team (HB 147). But the collaboration was brief, for in 1913 Sacchetto initiated her career as a movie star by appearing in *Odette*.

A 1914 concert in Copenhagen was apparently a "fiasco," but it brought her to the attention of the Nordisk film company, which never had enough female stars for the sensational erotic melodramas that made Danish films competitive on the European market. The Danes had introduced dance into silent film melodramas such as *Afgrunden* (1910), *Vampyrdanserinden* (1911), *Det blaa Blod* (1912), and *Atlantis* (1913), and Danish film companies had even tried to make film stars out of ballet dancers such as Elna Jorgen Jensen. Not without controversy, Nordisk hired Sacchetto to star in films for the astonishing salary of 7,000 kroner per picture, but she made many quite successful films, including *Tempeldanserindens Elskov* (1914), *Madame Destinn* (1914), *Den skonne Evelyn* (1915), *Rovederkoppen* (1915), and *Fyrstinde Bianca a Costa* (1916) (Brusendorff 140–145; Hendig 49–55; Bordwell 203). Sacchetto exuded a dusky, melancholy beauty that seemed even more refined and aristocratic, a "breeze of perfume," when displayed in opulent historical costumes. Although she excluded modern paintings of women from her graceful productions, she was probably the first to use silent film as a model for composing dances. Brandenburg spoke somewhat disparagingly of her "kinodrama," *La Sonambula* (1912), performed with Sacharoff, and in a review of a Budapest concert the Hungarian cultural journal *Nyugat* (9/1, 16 March 1916, 375–376) complained that Sacchetto, excellent film actress though she was, relied too heavily on lavish costumes and theatrical devices designed to accommodate the tastes of movie audiences; consequently, her dances had "nothing to say" and represented a degradation of a Greek aristocratic ideal in which dance was central to the perfection of a highly educated intelligence.

By this time Sacchetto, now residing in a luxurious villa in Berlin-Grunewald, had opened her "ballet school," which actually had less to do with ballet than with pantomime training. Her most important students included Anita Berber and Valeska Gert. Gert caused a minor scandal at a 1916 concert in the Bluthner auditorium when Sacchetto allowed her to perform her *Tanz in Orange* (a lewd parody of ballet steps) and, with Sidi Riha, the homosexual duet *Golliwog's Cakewalk*, which the police regarded as indecent (LF 11–13). Sacchetto, however, remained faithful to the pictorial gracefulness that Gert subverted.

The dance company toured several German cities. In 1917 Sacchetto married the Polish Count Zamoysky and resumed her work in the movies with *Die Nixenkönigen* before returning to Munich to open another school. She was soon touring with a small company consisting of herself and two students, Wally Konchinsky (Valerie Conti [1903–1945]) and Isa Belle. Reviews of her concerts in Berlin, Breslau, and Düsseldorf unanimously reached the conclusion that her dance aesthetic was "kitsch," "unintentionally humorous," full of "empty pretentious poses," very dated, technically crude, and entirely dependent on her personal beauty (*KTP*4, 1920, 117–119). Nevertheless, she always seemed to find an audience; in 1921 alone, she gave 120 performances in Paris. In 1922 her company included the husband of Wally Konchinsky, Jan Pawlikowsky, and the repertoire tended to consist of ornamentally bizarre pair dances performed by different combinations of the three. For example, in the "dream of a young woman," Konchinsky, in white tights with a white veil, danced with Sacchetto, in a black veil and black pants, a curious echo of the black-versus-white theme of the Gert-Riha *Golliwog's Cakewalk*. Sacchetto also created a *Cocaine* dance at the same time (1922) that Berber produced her own, nude *Kokain*.

Through Count Zamoysky, Sacchetto and Konchinsky became acquainted with the intellectual circle around the radical modernist writer-artist Stanislaus Witkiewicz in Zakopane, Poland (Siedlecka 122–126). In 1924 one of the count's friends accidentally shot Sacchetto in the foot, and only this misfortune prevented her from continuing to dance in public, even though she was already forty-four years old; her beauty apparently compensated for all her technical defects and long-faded tastes (LF 15). Still, she continued teaching in Munich, staging pantomime pair dances for Dagmar Helsing and Helge Peters-Pawlinin and opening a school in Krakow in 1928 (Rieger). In 1930 Sacchetto and the Count left Poland to live in her father's homeland, Italy, in the town of Nervi, near Genoa. She remained there until her death, although in the 1930s she worked occasionally in Italian film production. It was easy to sneer at Sacchetto; critics obviously did after she entered the movies, and Berber and Gert made a point of desecrating her gaudy, pictorial historicism. But few dancers enjoyed such popular international acclaim, and the reason for her success lay in her attempts to historicize her beauty; like an old painting, the danced movement of the body suspended time itself and, indeed, turned the present into a luxurious cinematic image of the past.

TWO OTHER EARLY DANCE GROUPS

At the end of World War I, Magda Bauer formed the Münchener Tanz-Drei. Besides Bauer, the group included Erika Skogen and Ellinor Tordis, with the occasional participation of Lucie Heyer and costumes by Hanns Haas. This group's concerts consisted mostly of solos by each member, and the only pieces in which all three appeared were round dances in an exuberant style. The repertoire featured primarily old dance forms (waltzes, rondos, contra dances) in a free and giddy mood, although Bauer devised a piece that told a "Chinese story" in a droll fashion. Apparently, however, her strongest piece was *Gebet und Tempeltanz*, which was actually the creation of

Edith von Schrenck, who was hardly a cheerful or happy dancer. In this piece, to music by Grieg, Bauer included seventeen of her students in a complex set of movement patterns on all sides of the dance space, signifying an archaic temple; movement with, toward, around, and against other dances produced a "flowing polyphony," a "great prayer machinery," indicating a "monolithic, compulsively moving ecstasy"; "bodies made music— it was a racial dance that one had hardly expected of this cool-looking German Blondine" (HB 135; *KTP* 4, 1920, 122). Bauer soon faded from the dance scene, but Heyer remained active as a teacher in Munich, where her methods coincided with *Nacktkultur*. Her interest in ensemble dancing drifted toward lay movement choirs, and at the 1930 Munich Dance Congress, which is the last I hear from her, she presented excerpts from a large, socialistic work called *Die Elemente*, scripted by Edith Grothe.

Another early dance group of Munich, the Münchener Tanzgruppe, actually began in Hamburg; its name had something to do with attracting dance talent from Munich to Hamburg. Supposedly formed by two men, Paul Theodor Et*bauer (1892–?) and Andreas Scheller, it lasted only a few years, from 1920 to 1924, but because of its unusual structure a large number of dancers participated in its innovative activities. The most significant personality was neither Scheller nor Et*bauer but Jutta von Collande, who participated with the group from beginning to end. Most of the dancers came from the school managed by the Falke sisters, but some obtained their education from Laban or unknown sources (Jockel 32–51). Dancers who worked sporadically with the Münchener Tanzgruppe included Elsbeth Baack, Marna Glaan, Grete Jung (1900–?), Frida Holst (1900–1979), Gertrud Zimmermann, Elsa Kahl (1902–?), Laura Oesterreich, Tilli Daul, Manya Haack, Brigitte Artner, Hildegard Troplowitz, and Sigurd Leeder (1902–1981). But some performances of the Münchener Tanzgruppe involved Claire Bauroff, Frances Metz, Marie Müllerbrunn, Ella Knales von Vinda, Beatrice Mariagraete, Roswitha Bössenroth, Gertrud Falke, Anita Nessen, and Edith von Schrenck, and in 1921, Jutta von Collande and Gertrud Zimmermann collaborated on a program with Sebastian Droste, who soon became the partner and husband of Anita Berber. Hans W. Fischer and Hans Brandenburg acted as advisers to the group, and H. H. Stuckenschmidt composed the music, in a decidedly modern vein.

With Münchener Tanzgruppe, the notion of "group" was somewhat complex. It referred to a loose association of dancers who appeared in different combinations on programs of different dimensions at different times. This apparently was Scheller's intention, in spite of the managerial difficulties of achieving this ambition (HB 228). Programs often consisted of solos, duets, and trios, and the Münchener Tanzgruppe even sponsored solo concerts by some of its members, such as Hildegard Troplowitz, who had given solo concerts in Hamburg since at least 1918. Yet the group clearly thrived under the controlling leadership of Collande. Scheller and Et*bauer, who was active as an expressionist artist, designer, art commentator, and dance instructor, created the Münchener Tanzgruppe to produce large-scale ensemble pieces. In January 1921 they presented their first two group works, along with "masculine" ("in the best sense") solos by Ella Knales von Vinda and "Oriental sketches" by Et*bauer. Laura Oesterreich directed the *Galante Pantomime* (music: Winternitz), an exquisite rococo entertainment in which Collande performed the role of a cavalier to Gertrud Falke's baronness; Anita Nessen played the maid, Grete Jung appeared as Polchinelle, and Elsbeth Baack portrayed the baron. A contemporary reviewer felt that in successive performances of this piece, in different theatres, the performers moved toward a refinement that was excessive and unnecessary (Ehlers). Scheller's only choreographic effort, *Faschingsschwank in Wien* (music: Schumann), was a much larger work involving "fifteen or sixteen" dancers who created "whirlpools and streams" of a "collective will" against the "solo personality" of Jutta von Collande: "[S]he seeks the mass, becomes drawn and repulsed by it, and eventually seizes the leadership of it, so that all power finally comes together in a large, happy festival procession" (Hans Fischer, *Hamburger,* 255).

Scheller planned to produce Hans Fischer's "dance play" *Die traurige Prinzess,* with the Falke sisters, Collande, and music by Stückenschmidt, but the insane inflation destroyed all the financing for the project, and it was not until 1922 that another group dance reached performance. By that time, Scheller had departed from the group, and Collande was in control. *Der himmlische Kreisel* (1922) was part of an "astral dance show" conceived by Fischer in collaboration with Collande and Stuckenschmidt and involving girl dancers from the Loheland school as well as an orchestra. By Fischer's own account, the work was a fascinating piece of imaginative ensemble thinking, far in advance of modern dance group productions anywhere else at the time, and it still seems radical today. The thirty-five-minute work used no consistent musical accompaniment but employed gong tones and a montage of passages from Adam, Grétry, and Stückenschmidt. On wobbly legs, a "giant golden sphere" (Et*bauer) tottered and hopped about wildly to the snapping of a clapper while the pianist played tenderly. Suddenly four little girls zoomed in as a scatter of shooting stars, followed by a comet—Manya Haack, dressed in black with a long gold headband trailing behind her. She, too, danced wildly, to music by Adolph Adam, but in an "entirely mature" manner. Then a "violet moon creature" in a bearded mask appeared and made "grasshopper" leaps before Jutta von Collande performed, with "clockwork precision," a dance of the planets with two girls. Lavinia Schulz and Walter Holdt depicted the "immensity of Sirius" as a wildly rotating shimmy, with a nebula of Loheland girls forming an undulating orbit. Finally came the pantomime of the "abduction and liberation of the sun," which appropriated ideas from the Japanese Noh theatre. Two "winter demons" snatched the frail, trembling orbit of the sun (Collande); then a sorcerer (Andre Luksch) summoned the demons, who wore double-coned or horned masks, and engaged them in a bizarre dance in which they used their voices to strengthen the rhythm of their movements. A gate opened with the blare of a trumpet fanfare, and the sun emerged to dispel the sorcerer and his demons. With Gretry's music, the sun summoned all the other dancers into a great, final dance of bodies flowing in space (Hans Fischer, *Hamburger,* 263–266). This piece depicted collective movement as a cosmic principle, but it was a rare example of collectivity wherein different musics, different choreographic styles, and different theoretical perspectives interacted to produce a single work.

The Münchener Tanzgruppe never again attempted a work of this scale, although Scheller apparently had this sort of aesthetic in mind when he formed the group. Financial problems plagued the company, in spite of the consistent success of its concerts in Hamburg. Under Collande the group seldom, if ever, produced any dances requiring more than four dancers, as was the case even before Scheller left (*KTP* 8, 1920, 221–222). Collande's idea of "group dance" implied different combinations of dances featuring herself in relation to different combinations of dancers, so that any one dance—solo, duet, trio, or quartet—had a distinct context in an ever-shifting program accommodating the ambitions of "other" performers. She disclosed a peculiar fondness for the music of the French opera composer Andre Gretry (1741–1813), but Brandenburg observed that only she knew how to dance to it (229). Perhaps for this reason, as much as for economic ones, she was hesitant to work on a larger scale. But within the modest realm of duets, trios, and quartets, she was quite inventive. For example, in *Primavera* (1920), which she danced with Claire Bauroff and Maria Müller-brunn, the dancers moved to the music of three separate harps until, finally, one figure dominated the other two (HB 230). Of another trio, set to the music of Leoncavallo, a reviewer (*KTP* 8, 1920, 221) remarked delightedly that Collande, Troplowitz, and Zimmermann transformed themselves, in response to sharp rhythmic differentiations, from gray, yellow, and red peacock-feathered puppets into beautiful human beings embodying inspiration (Collande), feeling (Troplowitz), and temperament (Zimmermann).

No one seems to know what happened to Jutta von Collande after 1924. It is a haunting enigma. She seems to have obtained power over many people, yet group works provoked anxiety in her, and in her small ensemble pieces she was able to thematize the problem of constructing a group that did not devalue the individuality of its members. In her dances she suggested that an emancipated idea of the group nevertheless depended on the controlling power of an individual within the group rather than on the synchronizing power of music. But in a larger sense, she treated the Münchener Tanzgruppe as a constellation of bodies orbiting around her, but not in the same trajectory, to form a single, unified sphere of energy: the larger group was a magnate that attracted people because of its opportunities for performance individuality, but Collande was at the center because she knew how to build a sense of communal identity entirely out of combinations of twos and threes. Gretry's music was important because it compelled dancers to trust Collande rather than the music and to place the body rather than the music at the center of this constellation of disparate desires. Her sudden disappearance hardly indicates the failure of her strategy; on the contrary, it implies the failure of economic systems to conceive of power and groups in anything but aggregate terms.

VERA SKORONEL

Perhaps no dancer of the Weimar era was as aggressive in the pursuit of an emphatically modernist group aesthetic as Vera Skoronel (1906–1932), yet she displayed a strongly ambivalent attitude toward the abstraction conventionally associated with modernism. She was astonishingly precocious. Her father was the scientist Rudolf Lämmel, whose *Der moderne Tanz* (1928) contains the most detailed account of her aesthetic. Born in Zurich, she studied with Laban at age thirteen and then, in Zurich, with Laban's student, Suzanne Perrottet; in 1921 she enrolled at the Loheland school but the following year shifted to Dresden to study under Wigman. At age eighteen she accepted an offer to direct the dance activities in Oberhausen, where she formed her first group. When in 1925 financial difficulties forced Oberhausen to suspend its dance program, Skoronel joined forces with another Wigman student from Switzerland, Berthe Trümpy (1895–1983), in managing an opulent school in Berlin. A Gothic-medieval aura permeated Trümpy's dances; in her Christmas piece of 1926, a choir of female dancers in silver gowns performed with silver swords and lighted candles, and in *Verkündigung* (1927) Trümpy was a girlish, "sweet," and melancholy Madonna to Skoronel's rather cubistic-abstract and Oriental angel (RLM 172–173).

Trümpy was an excellent teacher and administrator who grasped the necessity of bestowing bourgeois seriousness and respectability on dance studies, an ambition that, she felt, required the establishment of a rigorously developed state dance academy presided over by a "scholarly nondancer" (Freund 27). She needed someone to give her school a strong artistic identity, and that task fell to Skoronel, a dramatic-theoretical thinker whose movement imagination revealed a physicist's delight in formal abstraction. In the solo *Kriegrrhythmus* (1924), she introduced the "throwing, cutting, independent" arm movements for which she became famous. But this "stringent" warrior dance, with its Balinese and Singhalese influences, also conveyed a "tender" and "animal-like innocence," a strange "purity" of "unconscious culture" that had "nothing to do with militarism" (146–147). *Quadrat* (1924) began with a solo by Skoronel, performing angular, broken movements as if in the grip of a fanatical demon. She sank to the floor, and the space became silent and dark; the lights returned to reveal a "stiff wall of human bodies," their dark arms upraised. The human wall drew closer and closer to Skoronel's inert form with "heavy waltz steps," until the entire group slowly sank around the lifeless body. Both the concept and choreography of the dance seemed astonishingly simple, yet it dramatized well a mysterious tension between the convulsed, "possessed" solo dancer and the "stiff" group, with the group submissive not to the wild dancer or to a strange music but to a powerfully inert body.

For the more abstract and ambitious *Tanzspiel* (1926), Skoronel devised a detailed written scenario to articulate the elaborate complexities of the piece and had the Trümpy school orchestra perform music specially composed to enhance particular effects of the scenario. Here the group had no visible leader, although Skoronel herself danced in it. Indeed, the group contained no characters, only "figures" such as the Id, the Mirror Being, the Two Lengths, and the Dancing Stage Wings, but these referred more to the abstract tunic costumes worn by the dancers than to the representation of differentiated motives for action. The piece, in three parts, dramatized the dynamic geometry of abstract movement categories. Lines and rows of bodies metamorphosed into whirlpools, spirals, triangles, diagonals, quartets, double duets, diagonals within circles, canons, and fugal patterns. Yet movement within a single configuration contained its own categories of dynamics: the elasticity of the line operated in relation to notions such as "crescendo," "mirroring," "syncopation," and "extension." Musical rhythms shifted abruptly, and different sections of the group moved to different rhythms; for example, one pair of dancers might move only its head and shoulders while a second pair moved its arms and a third moved its legs; one section might make hacking movements with the arms while another created undulations. Skoronel furthermore imposed emotional categories on the movement, so that arms moved "softly" or "mockingly," "violently" or "sweetly," "grotesquely" or with "melancholy." She concerned herself with the smallest bodily details: how the eyes should dance, when to smile, the vibration of the fingers, the melody of breathing (150–156) (Figures 56–57).

A dance for her was a matter of constructing a unique relation between these abstract categories of movement. She first enunciated this approach at age fifteen in a novel (never published), "Asja und Skule" (1919), about two female friends seeking ecstatic power through an intensely intellectual love of dance (161–162). Dance implied the mathematization of space, movement, and body, and group dance was the most powerful expression of this mathematization because it offered the greatest possibilities for combining categories of movement or signification. Skoronel associated ecstatic freedom with "absolute" formal abstraction, and, in an unpublished manuscript from 1932, she explicitly linked abstraction with mechanization. By "mechanization" she did not mean imitation of or reference to machines; rather, she proposed the treatment of the body as an "instrument, which no longer displays human features" but moves according to an absolutely "pure harmony" that has "no content" and "nothing more to express" (MS 40). In an earlier article, she observed that with the "absolute dance," "form and content do not exist," and "superhuman ecstasy does not lie in the human psychic zones of joy and sorrow, but actually in the cosmic experience of the infinite—in abstraction" (Freund 73). In the *Kinetographie*, Laban sought to identify all possible abstract categories of human movement, but he was unable to apply these categories systematically in the creation of dances: he had a dictionary but could not form any sentences or syntax. Skoronel showed far greater power in thinking out dance abstractly, yet she relied on conventional writing (scenarios and theoretical essays) and stick-figure drawings to formulate her dances; she did not move toward any system of computation tables or logarithms to optimize the mechanization of movement.

In other words, Skoronel betrayed a measure of ambivalence toward her own abstractionism. This ambivalence surfaced overtly in *Legende des Weissen Waldes* (1927), a "dance fairy tale in four scenes," with "figures" such as a Sorceress, the Child of the White Forest, the Creatures of the White Forest, twelve Black-and-White Knights, four Water Sprites, and the Demon. The various dances making up the piece contained the complex combinations of movement categories already apparent in *Tanzspiel*, but this time movements constructed a semipantomimic narrative about the awakening of the solitary Child of the White Forest, the failure of the Knights and Prophets to protect the Child from the Demon, the rescue of the Child by the Sorceress, and, in a final test of "innocence," the Child's attempt to dance without sinking on the surface of a black lake. Silence accompanied several of the dances, but even more innovative was the imaginative use of lighting in the choreography. For example, spotlights showed only the arms of dancers (branches of "trees") undulating in a world of darkness; indeed, during some moments no dancers at all appeared on the stage, and one only saw the movement, the intensification or fading, of light. At one point, dancers moved in darkness; the lights came up suddenly and glaringly, then went out, conveying the impression that no one could see the whole dance, not even the dancers, who, like the Child, are blind to the world, even to themselves. The relation between the Child and the Prophets and Red Flowers was somewhat similar to that of the inert body and the synchronized wall of bodies in *Quadrant*, whereas the relation between the Demon and the Knights followed the model of a wild, turbulent, polyrhythmic group dominated by an explosively moving leader, who pressured the group to explore and feed off all tensions within it without ever dissolving into individuals. But the appearance of the Sorceress, "accompanied by four Guards," complicated group-leader relations, for she performed an "angular-pantomimic" dance that inspired neither the fanatical rhythm of the Demon-group dances nor the trancelike tread of the Child-group dances. The pantomimic leader produced a slow, heavy rhythm, a steady, triumphant motion that soon dominated the movement of all groups and marked the Child's dance on water.

Few dances, including Wigman's, theorized leader-group relations with such sophistication and with such ambivalence over the ultimate authority of inert, abstract, or pantomimic bodies to lead, to mold bodies into groups. Yet Skoronel herself claimed that the "aim of the group dance (insofar as it has an aim) is the complete equality of given tensions: mass, group, soloist, leader. The harmonic, melded unity of all poles, even the strongest contrasts, is the basis of the new group dance" (RLM 169). As director of the speech and movement choirs of the Berlin Volksbühne, Skoronel applied these theoretical concepts on a larger scale in *Erweckung der Masse* (1927) and *Der gespaltene Mensch* (1927), in which, apparently, groups of women in dark tunics and bare legs moved in tension with a group of bare-chested men in black trousers. Here she pursued the gendered dynamics by which one group leads another or consolidates competing groups.

One might say that, through abstractionism, Skoronel sought to transcend the erotic themes or dynamics of erotic desire that exclusively female ensembles hesitated to explore, at least in an overt, romantic fashion. Nevertheless, eroticism pervaded her aesthetic. In *Tanzspiel,* some female dancers wore boyish haircuts and vaguely masculine (long-sleeved) tunics. Skoronel was herself a small, lithe, muscular woman who liked to be photographed performing aggressive, thrusting, surging movements that, when incarnated by such a pretty body, exerted strong erotic appeal for male spectators. Abstraction was not for her the end of eroticism; rather, she eroticized abstraction, attempting to make the desireability of the female body manifest in angular, hacking, squatting, or pumping movements. But the attempt succeeded only partially. Fritz Böhme, dance critic for the *Deutsche Allgemeine Zeitung,* observed that Skoronel's formalism resembled ballet technique, with emphasis on arm rather than leg movements, and strove toward an "ideal of objectivity" based on mechanization of movement. But the result was a "pedantic" pleasure in exactness of execution not far removed from that displayed in the revue dances of the Tiller Girls (28 October 1926). In a review of *Erweckung der Masse* (27 March 1927), he complained that although the movement choirs performed expertly, the piece as a whole seemed guided by a force external to the "masses" themselves: "The movements are externally directed, not centered inwardly. The piece certainly contains symmetry, asymmetry, and polarities, but these lack an inner, living, spatial necessity. Everything appears calculated, predetermined. . . . The 'awakening of the masses' does not unfold; it is given, imposed, ordained" by formal design.

Later the same year (5 October 1927), Böhme offered some deeper insight into the limitations of Skoronel's abstractionism. He remarked that she seldom sank into herself; instead, through her exaggerated, rushing movements, she projected a powerful will to test and exceed the "limits of bodily possibilities." But no matter how great her will, "she cannot overcome these limits," and "she will never reach the power of Wigman's gestural language," for "her dances continually show gestures of cutting, striking, shaking, annihilating, destroying." Without serious "content," such a dance aesthetic produced a "sort of agitation gone demonic." In Paris, André Levinson, a reactionary supporter of ballet, commented (1929) more favorably on the "turbulent agitation" of a "nearly tragic" aesthetic that did not strike him as German at all—perhaps Slavic. Skoronel "attacked" dances with "relentless exasperation," moved with "vehemence," turned "in a rage upon herself," "projected with force a steeled arm and fist," "stamped with anger" to embody "a young Fury prostrated by her paroxysm" (500). But in Berlin critical approval remained restrained. A reviewer for the *Steglitzer Anzeiger* (237, 9 October 1930) said of a solo concert by Skoronel that she knew "only two degrees of movement—the excited, convulsed leap and the ecstatic rotation," and as a result all of her pieces were too long.

In a 1929 article for *Schrifttanz*, Trümpy responded to criticisms of excessive abstraction in modern dance by arguing that Germans were a more intellectual than physical people and that therefore a distinctly German dance culture depended on intellectualism and abstraction. Russian-style ballet technique had emerged from a unique cultural context, she wrote, but in Germany ballet was a completely dead art, and efforts to promote a "healthy sensuality" in German dance based on pantomimic principles were misguided (VP 11–12). However, Trümpy's article actually somewhat confused the issue of dance's cultural identity, for Skoronel's mother was Russian, so her inclination toward abstraction and ballet-type formalism perhaps owed as much to Slavic heritage as to Germanic intellectualism (assuming the validity of Trümpy's own cultural distinctions). Skoronel died suddenly and mysteriously (of leukemia?), and when the Nazis took power Trümpy found it expedient to merge her school with the Günther school in Munich, where Maja Lex pursued a formalistic notion of the group that was far less "turbulent" and "vehemently" intellectual than Skoronel's.

HANS WEIDT

A much more conventional and overtly politicized perception of group dancing appeared in the work of Hans Weidt (1904–1988), who was an agent of the Communist Party. Born into a Hamburg working-class family, his father an alcoholic social democrat, Weidt was twelve when a folk-dance group stirred his interest in dancing. However, he had no money to study dancing, and when, as a teenager, he started working as a gardener, he found it difficult to arrange hours for dance lessons. In 1921 he studied briefly under Sigurd Leeder and then under Olga Brandt-Knack (1885–1978), both Laban students and ardent social democrats. But the poverty-stricken Weidt struggled to save money and find time for his passion, and in 1923 his participation in communist-led agitations completely radicalized his political beliefs in favor of a revolutionary transformation of society. In his solo debut concert in Hamburg in 1925, he presented dances depicting "the worker," "the lady beggar," "the new beginning," "on the dock," "rebellion," "the sick boy," "faces in the street," all subjects seldom introduced by bourgeois dancers. Further peculiarities of the concert were Weidt's use of Chopin compositions to accompany these unromantic themes and the use of a trumpet to perform the music (Weidt had made friends with an orchestral trumpet player who provided accompaniment for no fee).

Despite the ambivalent critical response to this concert, he decided to pursue a career as a dancer. He gathered about him a group of unemployed youths "from all classes," mostly male, who practiced in a factory studio and performed at communist-sponsored events. Yet financial difficulties constantly subverted his ambitions. Then Brandt-Knack, ballet mistress of the Hamburg State Opera, gave him the lead role in a ballet, *Der Gaukler und der Klingelspiel* (1928), enabling him to become conscious of his own capacity to sustain large-scale dance forms. Theatre director Erwin Piscator attended a performance of the Worker's Dance Group and was so impressed that he invited Weidt to work on theatrical productions in Berlin. There Weidt became acquainted with leading artists of the left: Friedrich Wolf, Erich Mühsam, Stefan Wolpe, Ludwig Renn, Ernst Busch, Helene Weigel. To support himself he gave dance lessons and taught physical education at *Nacktkultur* camps and communist youth societies, but his living circumstances remained hard. In 1930 he danced the role of the Dark Leader in Margarethe Wallmann's huge dance drama *Orfeus Dionysos*. Though in Hamburg he had performed some duets with Lotte Lobstein, he definitely preferred the company and collaboration of men, and he viewed his female students as narcissistic dilettantes (Weidt 15). He presented himself as a hopelessly unromantic working-class ugly duckling, incapable of inspiring desire in bourgeois women, but he was actually quite good-looking, enjoyed nudism, and delighted in opportunities to display his muscular physique in dances. He choreographed movement choirs in Piscator's production of Friedrich Wolf's *Tai Yang erwacht* (1929), and through Wolf, Weidt became indoctrinated into communist ideology, joining the party in 1931.

His party connections enabled him to form Die Roten Tänzer, a company that soon comprised forty-five dancers and produced the most overtly propagandistic dance in Weimar Germany, notably in *Passion eines Menschen* (1931, in collaboration with Ludwig Renn), *Tanz des Arbeitslosen* (1930), *Arbeiterkampflieder* (1931), *Potsdam* (1932), *Das Gas wird von Arbeiter gemacht* (1932), and *Tanz der Gefangenen* (1933). However, the audience for these efforts consisted largely of the already converted, and only the red press viewed them with much favor, although Fritz Böhme, soon to become a Nazi sympathizer, expressed enthusiasm for Weidt's aesthetic. The production of *Potsdam,* which clearly satirized right-wing political figures such as Hitler, Hugenberg, and von Papen, got Weidt arrested in January 1933. Theatre director Karl-Heinz Martin, for whom Weidt had originally conceived *Tanz der alten Leute* (1931) as part of a failed production of Alfred Döblin's play *Die Ehe,* arranged for Weidt's release, whereupon the Communist Party arranged for him and his group to participate in the Moscow Olympiade in May 1933. The Russians welcomed him effusively, but they regarded his dance aesthetic as insufficiently "militant": "Our attempt to shape themes of the worker movement with the expressive possibilities of the new artistic dance . . . was at that time still hard to understand, all the more in a country in which the classical ballet played so great a role" (Reinisch 48–49).

Weidt returned to Hamburg, but the police were waiting at the dock to arrest him, so he stayed on the ship and made his way to Paris, where he had friends, party connections, and opportunities through the House of Culture. He renamed himself Jean Weidt, starred in short dance films of Dukas' *The Sorcerer's Apprentice* (1933) and Ravel's *Bolero* (1934), and formed a new dance group, Ballet Weidt, which performed mostly at party-sponsored rallies. The French bourgeois press reacted more appreciatively to his aesthetic than had Weimar critics, but the French police considered him a foreign subversive and took steps to have him deported. In 1935 he therefore accepted another invitation from the exiled Piscator to work again in Moscow, where he seriously began to study ballet technique at the Bolshoi. Although ballet technique offered exciting possibilities for *Ausdruckstanz,* the ballet productions themselves seemed tediously "conventional" and lacking in modernist revolutionary spirit. Thus, in January 1936, Weidt journeyed to Prague to work with the avant-garde theatre director E. F. Burian and the Liberated Theatre of Voskovec and Werich. Life continued to be hard for him, and he had to construct a pseudonymous identity to avoid deportation by the vigilantly anticommunist police. Eventually, however, he succeeded in strengthening his connections to the party in Paris, where he returned in 1937. There he cultivated many influential friends: Jean Cocteau, Louis Aragon, Arthur Honegger, Pablo Picasso, Charles Dullin, Jean-Louis Barrault. A newly formed Ballet Weidt, following an itinerary shaped by the party, performed in Paris, Marseilles, Cannes, and

Corsica, often in support of fund-raising efforts to defeat the fascist forces in the Spanish Civil War. Weidt also pursued a romance with a communist French woman, who gave birth to a son in 1939, but his German identity, so he claimed, estranged her from him, and when the Germans invaded France he never saw them again.

He sought to escape persecution by fleeing to North Africa, but by 1942 Casablanca was under Vichy control, and Weidt's life became even harder. He spent terrible months in an Algerian concentration camp until a new commandant permitted him to dance for soldiers at the Algiers Opera House. When the British captured Algiers, he danced for them, too—mostly his solo worker dances from the Weimar days. He then joined the British army and participated, as a member of a construction brigade, in the Allied invasion of Italy. Upon his discharge in 1946 he returned to Paris, where he founded yet another group, Ballet des Arts, comprising six men and six women. In 1947 the company produced *Die Zelle,* winner of the gold medal at the international ballet competition in Copenhagen. But in spite of successful tours of Holland and Belgium, the group suffered from continually inadequate financing. Weidt could not resist an offer of generous subsidies from the communist government in East Berlin, to which he made his final migration in 1948. There Weidt became a highly respected teacher and choreographer of ideologically correct ballets for opera companies, but his work during the many ensuing years of stability lacked both the innovation and the utterly distinct political expressivity of his fugitive years before the war (Weidt; Reinisch)

Weidt's perception of group dancing was virtually antithetical to that of Skoronel: political content entirely dominated his thinking about bodily movement, and matters of form and technique always remained subordinate to the projection of a correct spirit, which acknowledged that "dance is struggle" on behalf of an oppressed class of people (Reinisch 185–191). In his memoirs and polemical statements, he scarcely reflected on dance at all; instead, he discussed his hard struggle to live as a dancer with a communist perspective. His autobiography devoted more pages to his few dismal months in the concentration camp than to any phase of his artistic career. Dance was for him a way to achieve a higher class identity, which, however, he assumed was impossible for him to achieve independently of the Communist Party. From his debut concert on, he thought of his work as ballet, because ballet resonated with a grandeur and dignity of identity denied the working class. But his aesthetic before 1939 actually had little to do with ballet in any rigorous sense, and even in relation to *Ausdruckstanz* he was hardly an auspicious innovator in the realm of movement dynamics. He claimed to free dance from the prettified mythic images of bourgeois female dancers, yet his own dances borrowed heavily from the stereotyped poster imagery of downtrodden social types and heroically victorious workers. He asserted that his dances included movements he had learned as a gardener, but in reality none of his dances presented any insightful relation between laboring and aesthetic movements, despite the enormous and quite unexplored potential for expressivity in constructing such a relation. Slow, ponderous movements and huddled bunching of female bodies signified the oppressed masses; gaping mouths and outstretched arms signified suffering. Drooping, cowering, cringing, plodding movements characterized further aspects of oppression. The heroic side of the struggle, represented mostly by bare-chested males, entailed militant flexing of muscles, strident stepping, uplifted faces, vigorous swinging of arms, confrontational stances, and lunging rushes.

For Weidt, a group implied a synchronized, uniform identity for several bodies, and although he sometimes contrasted different groups he showed little awareness of contradictions within a group; nor did he disclose a sophisticated perception of leader-group dynamics: the destiny of a group derived not from any force within it nor from the force of a mesmeric, lonely individual nor even from any distinct music but always from a conventional, archetypal image of "hunger" or "the worker" or, perhaps, "the red flag." One of Weidt's most interesting works, *Passion eines Menschen* (1931), with spoken narrative by Ludwig Renn, music by Stefan Wolpe, and masks by Erich Goldstaub, derived its imagery from a "novel" in woodcuts by the Flemish expressionist-socialist artist Frans Masereel. This piece followed a simple iconographic narrative: workers in a factory suddenly find themselves laid off, and, when they protest, the police persecute them. One of the workers, Klaus, kills a police spy who attacks Klaus's mother in a bar where she sells flowers. In jail Klaus meets his true "comrades" while "women lament over their men." The court regards Klaus as a political murderer, and the workers' efforts to save him from execution are in vain; however, his death provokes a revolutionary upheaval (Reinisch 165). Narrative content sustained interest in this and most of Weidt's other dances, and as long as the story dominated movement choices, movement retained a crudely pantomimic identity almost completely devoid of irony. To insure that his audience "got" the story, he even inscribed it into the program: *Eine Frau* (1930, music: Heyken)—"once she was a mother, but the war took everything from her. Now she must work again, as if she were thirty. Her life is worry and work"; *Strassentänzer* (1931, music: Erben)—"China—it could be Berlin—he always dances with consuming ecstasy. For what? For the street? For pleasure? For a pair of coins?" A more curious work was *Potsdam* (1932), in which narrative development remained subordinate to an abstract aim, the construction of a group piece that had no leader, even though it showed the leaders of the Weimar Republic. Hitler, Hugenberg, Hindenburg, and von Papen, wearing caricatured masks, danced as unified group to hit tunes of 1932. They moved in an amusing, courtly-bizarre style that was "not directly ridiculous" but "incredible" and so perverse as to imply a dreadful "danger" in such a unified group of leaders.

Although Weidt revived the dance in Paris, his aesthetic never again moved in this intriguing direction. He loved using masks in his group works, yet most were eerie caricatures of archetypal expressions of oppression, elderliness, and deprivation. However, in the solo *Indian-Romantik* (1934) and the group *Kampftanz* (1934), supposedly based on Sioux Indian tribal dances, he explored opportunities to display heroic male nudity, and he made a very handsome model for nude sculptures by Niko Eekman in 1937. In his choice of music, he showed an enthusiasm for contemporary composers, as long as they possessed correct political credentials: Arthur Berger, Stefan Wolpe, Hanns Eisler, Wolfgang Erben, Alban Berg, Josef Kosma. Yet the music he loved best was by that most bourgeois and romantic of all composers, Chopin. If it is difficult to take him as seriously as he wished, it is because he never seriously acknowledged any struggle within himself to form the personality he valued so highly. Personality for him always emerged from without, as a struggle to rise from the depths. Ambiguities of bodily movement and sexual identity seemed obstacles to the approval of the great party of revolutionary men who understood his constant hunger to find a better place to sleep, a better home.

HERTHA FEIST

Weidt expressed much gratitude for the help given him during his years in Weimar Berlin by Hertha Feist (1896–1990), although, curiously, her own students seemed reluctant to show her any gratitude at all (Reinisch 35; Peter 37). Her bourgeois socialism produced an image of group identity far removed from Weidt's archetypal "masses." She was the younger sister of Fritz Böhme's first wife. Böhme, in an unpublished 1947 manuscript, gave an enchantingly vivid description of Feist dancing nude only for him in the golden twilight of a grove in the Grunewald in the summer of 1915: she asked him to close his eyes until she said open them, and when he opened them he saw a glorious female body approaching him, improvising the most complex movements, stretching, folding, trembling, kneeling, rising up on tiptoes, twisting, spiraling, rotating, arching, turning her breathing into music, until she suddenly disappeared into the shadows (Böhme, "Laban," 1–5). Nudity and the "purest" expression of the healthy body constituted dominant features of Hertha Feist's aesthetic. Yet she had many teachers whose incompatible influences led to a set of works that somehow did not live up to the summer afternoon vision of her described by Böhme.

She studied first with Dalcroze at Hellerau (1914), then with Bode and a Mensendieck teacher in Munich (1915); Böhme recommended that she study with Olga Desmond in Berlin (1917), where she made her debut in

1919 with a baring of her breasts. Finding Desmond's instruction unsatisfying, she went to Stuttgart to study under Laban, whom she soon followed to Mannheim and then to Frankfurt, Lübeck, Bremen, Gleschendorf, and Hamburg, appearing in grandiose productions of Laban's *Der schwingende Tempel* (1921), *Agamemnons Tod* (1922), and *Faust II* (1922) and participating in his countercultural pastoral-communal lifestyle (Schuftan 32; Peter 36). By 1923, however, she decided it was time to go her own way. She therefore returned to Berlin to establish her own school and to teach a class at Carl Diem's sports academy. Feist was especially successful at integrating the study of gymnastics, sport activity, nudism, and dance. No other dance school in Germany attracted such a large number of male students, although few of hers entertained professional ambitions. She continued to collaborate with Laban on Berlin performances of his *Lichtwende* (1923), *Prometheus* (1924), *Dämmernde Rhythmen* (1925), and *Don Juan* (1926), in which she danced the role of Donna Elvira; of course, her pedagogy emphatically promoted the doctrines of Laban. She involved herself in curious projects, such as the dances for a production of Klaus Mann's play *Anya and Esther* (1926), with music by Klaus Pringsheim and costumes by Lotte Pritzel, and some sort of dance in connection with the showing of an American sound film, *Hands* (1929), containing music by Marc Blitzstein. However, her most provocative work was the bizarre group dance *Die Berufung* (1928), performed by her Novembergruppe with strong support from the social democratic cultural apparatus. With this piece she toured Germany, Poland, Switzerland, and England. In 1930–1931 she danced in the controversial Laban-Jooss *Tannhäuser-Bacchanal* at Bayreuth (Cameron). But with the beginning of the Nazi era, her work as a choreographer came to an end. Her last ensemble piece was an ambitious production of Glück's *Iphigenie in Aulis* on the steps of the Pergamon Museum in May 1933. Soon thereafter the Nazis appropriated her school building and compelled her to move to smaller quarters. She always had many students, but all her choreography, even after the war ended, consisted of reconstructions of Renaissance dance forms. In 1943 she moved to Celle, then Hannover, where she taught (1952–1965) at the Volkshochschule. Eventually she became an adept of the Rosicrucian Order, for which she created her last dance, in 1965, to consecrate the Golden Temple of the Rose Cross in Bad Münder (Peter, "Hertha Feist," 37).

Like Jutta von Collande, Hertha Feist cultivated an elaborately complex image of the group that achieved complete expression not in any one piece but in relations between pieces or between dancers from different schools. Just as she desired to integrate dance, gymnastics, and sports, so she welcomed opportunities to merge people from different institutions into a single work. But this inclination to merge forces conflicted with her deeper urge to achieve maximum purity of expression. Indeed, she experienced some difficulty in naming her desires. A 1925 program proclaimed: "WE ARE NOT A DANCE COMPANY. NOT BALLET! Our dance work is spiritualized gymnastics"; however, the program also announced itself as the work of the Tanzgruppe Hertha Feist ("Hertha Feist"). She experimented with lengthy concerts containing as many as fourteen or fifteen dances, but the organization of the dances—solos, duets, trios, ensembles—conformed to a grand structure so that different pieces by different dancers seemed to be part of a single large work, with each dance a kind of commentary on the previous one. Moreover, Feist tended to impose a formal color scheme on the order of dances. Thus, a 1925 concert opened with an ensemble sword dance, in which the movement choir wore gray; the ensuing prayer dance, for solo male, was yellow, as was the seventh dance, a female solo on the theme of "the powerful." The third dance, a female duet, was in green, the fourth dance a female solo in white, and the fifth a female solo in blue; a female trio was in red, and the piece concluded with movement choir in a spectrum of colors.

Feist worked closely with Lotte Auerbach and Seraphine Kinne in producing concerts featuring the three of them, and she gave solo concerts as late as 1933, but she liked best to assert herself within a large, complex group, and she did not mind turning her own or another dancer's solo into a trio or ensemble piece. Early in 1927 she began including an ensemble of eight men in her concerts for "battle" dances, but she apparently had difficulty devising dances in which the sexes interacted, for the male dances consistently appeared separately. That was an especially odd feature of her choreography, because in the classroom or in outdoor arenas she liked to have groups of male and female dancers exercise together and perform gendered thesis-antithesis patterns of movement. Even in these cases, however, the male and female groups rarely actually merged; males became integrated only if females greatly outnumbered them. Though she encouraged nudism for both sexes, Feist liked having the men exercise nude or nearly nude while the women wore tunics. In her dances, however, nudity was negligible, despite the unforgettable beauty of her nude dance for Böhme in 1915 and her association with Olga Desmond.

In 1926 she and her school group started participating in concerts sponsored by the Social Democratic Party, performing her solo "Dionysian dance," Auerbach's "elegy," and ensemble pieces on the themes of summoning, struggle, and joy. *Ein Frühlings Mysterium* (1927) was a huge choral-dance work, with music by Heinz Tiessen (conductor: Jascha Horenstein) and a script by Bruno Schönlank, the radical socialist author of *Der gespaltende Mensch* (1927), another grand hymn to class solidarity. Vera Skoronel supervised the choreography for this work, in which Feist coordinated the movements of her own students with those of children's, youth, and drama groups of the SDP.

Her most significant piece was *Die Berufung* (1928), a "dance poem in four round dances and a prelude," with orchestral music (now lost) by Edmund Meisel, costumes by Thea Schleusner, and masks by Wolfdietrich Stein. *Die Berufung* was an ensemble piece about the merging of ensembles. Feist differentiated each group by color, with each female group having a female leader: violet (Auerbach), green (Kinne), black (Anna Fligg), gray (Hertha Boethke), orange (Eva Becher). The silver group, however, was male and led by Feist herself. After a prelude establishing the control of the silver group over the space, the first round presented the "dance of isolated animal-like humanity," in which the five color groups danced independently of each other until the appearance of the silver leader, who imposed unity through oppression. The second round depicted the awakening of the groups to the perception that their obsession with preserving the purity of their colors had allowed the silver leader to dominate them. The third round showed the emerging strength within the color groups, their struggle against the silver leader, the appearance of the "dark forms," and the defeat of the dark forms by the silver group. The final round opened with a "bacchanal of groups," which led to strife between the groups, the return of the silver group, the partitioning, immobilization, and annihilation of the groups into an amorphous mass, and the summoning (*Berufung*) of two kinds of controlling, balancing forms from the mass.

Feist saw the piece as dramatizing the evolution from chaos to community, but critics, not without good reason, tended to find the piece filled with obscurity. Richard Biedrzynski, in the *Deutsche Zeitung* (7 March 1928), observed that Feist had sacrificed dance power for visual power: "movement drama is not dance drama." Nevertheless, he contended, "the new as such is always stronger than what has already succeeded," and Feist had "raised movement in space to a symphony in colors." But Böhme was already convinced that Feist was not sure what identity she wanted for herself, her group, or her dances (*Deutsche Zeitung*, 22 November 1927). Even *Die Berufung* underwent several radical revisions, at least one of which identified the different groups not by color but by species: hippopotamuses, rain worms, polyps, and "greedy, lewd, coquettish creatures." In the Volksbühne version, the silver group did not wear masks, but most of the other groups did. The silver group wore Buck Rogers–type capes and astro-suits that made no distinction between the female leader and the male group; the color groups wore costumes of a style that prevailed in the Dark Ages (Figure 58). John Schikowski in *Vorwärts* (18 November 1927) and a reviewer for the *Tägliche Rundschau* (17 November 1927) both asserted that Feist showed greater strength in handling grotesque or burlesque moods than melancholy or demonic themes, a serious defect in Böhme's mind. Feist's decision to use color rather than species groups was obviously an effort to encourage a more serious attitude toward her message, which in any case was hardly a model of purity of expression ("Hertha Feist").

Although *Die Berufung* fascinated audiences, Feist abandoned the highly uncertain direction it entailed and instead concentrated on integrating with other groups guided by Laban (1930–1931), Dorothea Albu (1930), the social democrats (1932), and Jutta Klamt (1934). *Iphigenie in Aulis* (1933), with Max von Schillings conducting a full orchestra performing Wagner's updating of Glück's music, was an immense outdoor production that apparently involved movements very difficult to execute on the great marble steps of the Pergamon Museum, but knowledge about this piece remains scant. With Jutta Klamt in 1934 she created an eight-woman piece, *Botschaft,* with a score by the Croatian composer and theorist of "astral music" Josef Slavensky. By 1935, however, she had only one male dance on her programs, a duet fool's dance, and the following year she had no male dances at all, for she had no male students (though female students remained plentiful). Meanwhile, she wrestled with a theme that had preoccupied her since 1921, writing an essay on the "relation between body culture and art." Here she differentiated gymnastics from dance, contending that dance focused on the whole body and its emotional relation to time and space whereas gymnastics focused, in a mechanical manner, on parts of the body independently of feelings. By 1936 she had conceded the futility of integrating dance and gymnastics and proposed that dance ultimately achieved purity of expression by recovering the archaic spirit of the folk dance. At Nazified concerts she performed waltzes, mazurkas, tarantellas, humoresques, contra dances, and even dance forms from the time of the Renaissance, though nothing larger than trios; however, her taste in music did not entirely coincide with this direction, for she especially favored the music of Bach and Scriabin. Nazism clearly diminished her power to attract men toward dance and toward herself, but even before the Nazis took over she seemed to have experienced a great disillusionment over her failure to create anything as mysteriously naked and pure as the dance she performed for Böhme in the woods. The source of this disillusionment lay not within a pathological social reality or malfunctioning perception of group identity but within her own body, about which it is so difficult to decide whether it was seriously beautiful or merely good. As Schikowski remarked (*Vorwärts,* 18 November 1927), she projected strength, rigor, and elegance, "lightly shadowed by a frail cloud of melancholy."

JUTTA KLAMT

Like Skoronel and Wigman, Jutta Klamt (1890–1970) associated modernity of expression with an "absolute" or "abstract" perception of dance, free of all pantomimic signification; like Feist, she equated ecstatic modernism with a redemptive sense of purity. In 1925, Karl Grabe remarked: "Her dance comes from the depths of the most painful experiences and sinks into the depths, seeking one final expression, one final release of inner energy. A tragic seriousness pulses in her dances" (Stefan 93). Grabe compared her images of the human form to the great tragic heroines of Friedrich Hebbel and the paintings of Ferdinand Hodler. But despite her devotion to modernist aesthetics, hardly any other artist of modern dance was more enamored of Nazism or committed to the ideals of the Third Reich. She came to dance fairly late, and apparently the most painful experience of her life—the death of her mother, when Klamt was twenty—triggered in her an intense hunger to dance and to free the body from a terrible burden. She was completely self-taught, though she taught herself slowly; she did not give her debut concert, in Berlin, until January 1919. In 1920 a reviewer for the *Berliner Börsen-Courier* commented that "it is always like moonlight around her rich, silver blondness . . . a gravestone under bending cypress branches . . . Gretchen in prison . . . the often too pleasantly guided hands flutter palely away from the gray veil. . . . Everything elemental becomes soft, like in a dream . . . remains finally the timid smile of a sweet passivity." The writer recommended that she move more in the startling direction of her "nearly grotesque," black-wigged idol dance (*KTP* 4, 1920, 116–117).

But the grotesque did not suit her; if anything, her aesthetic became more somber. She opened a school in Berlin in 1920, and it became one of the most successful in Germany over the next two decades. In 1923 she collaborated with the Berlin Philharmonic in a huge, dark, tragic dance-drama, *Der Aufschrei*, in which she sought to purge her aesthetic of all pantomimic movement: "[T]he individual will of the leader does not command; the group breathes, sways, and lives as one in a closed totality. Effects are achieved only through the rhythm of forms and colors, sound and movement curves. . . . Line and color are the chief bearers of expression" (Stefan 93). *Tänze der Nacht* (1924) was an even darker and more lugubrious ensemble piece, in which dark-costumed dancers moved like shadows on a lunar stage that might as well have been lit by candles; it was as if Klamt sought to eclipse altogether the glowing blondness that dominated every perception of her body. In 1925 she married Joachim Vischer, who became her partner in the management of the school, and this circumstance seems to have infused her thinking with greater radiance, although she continued to pursue a stark, abstract, modernist notion of dance.

Her modernism was evident in the design by Cesar Domela, a De Stijl artist, of a 1928 brochure describing her school. The cover showed a black circle, on beige background, penetrated by two vertical lines, a black one from the top and a red one from the bottom; a third, black line touched the circle from the right but did not penetrate it. The penetrating lines did not meet directly in the middle of the circle; rather the red line veered perpendicularly to the right to meet the unyielding black line. On each side of the circle appeared in red block letters the words "BERLIN" and "JUTTA KLAMT SCHULE" (Broos 91). The design created a bold sense of dance and dance study as a radically abstract conflict between elemental geometric forces, between line and curve, between relative powers seeking to penetrate the closed, inner, circular zone of connection. However, neither the curriculum for Klamt's school nor her aesthetic adopted the extreme purity of abstraction projected by Domela's design. For Klamt, abstraction entailed freeing the body from impersonation and narrative motives for movement: the body's expressive power became visible only when a story did not distract, interfere with perception. This attitude assumed that particular gestures, positions, or movements were inherently expressive of particular emotions or conditions, regardless of context (Freund 42–47). Ever since the death of her mother, Klamt had regarded dance as a way to free herself from an oppressive story, from the dominating account of someone else's life. Dance was freedom because it made the body into a symbol of those innately healthy emotions that narrative logic suppresses by compelling the body to read the self in the life of another person. Such thinking bestowed a predominately therapeutic value on dance.

In the early 1930s, Klamt and her husband became enthusiastic about National Socialism, and when Hitler assumed power they launched a body culture journal, *Kontakt,* which promoted a Nazi ideology of body consciousness by extolling the therapeutic significance of dance. In the first issue (January 1933, 33–40), Fritz Böhme repudiated ecstasy as the aim of modern dance. He claimed that an international, individualistic pursuit of ecstasy led to an excessive, constraining formalism that estranged dance from national and racial sources of identity, from a cultural bond between "blood and movement." The new task of modern dance was to develop a uniquely "German movement language" that elevated unifying social-communal identity over the futile search for a mythic and ecstatic individuality. Heide Woog echoed this point in the following issue (1/2 May 1933, 22–24): "The demand now resounds: away with all individuality—only then is it possible for us to grasp the urgent concept of mature life." Later (September 1933, 48–50) a director of a women's auxiliary of the Nazi Party in Thüringen proposed that "the dance of German woman must consciously free itself from sultry oriental mysticism, it must free itself from the libidinous ecstasy of religious hysteria ending in negro dances." Dance, she asserted, referred to the "rhythm of a noble life," the image of "a pure deep soul, the protector of everything good, the high moral power of a clear spirit, a strong will to struggle, which will trample the demons of life," and the "heart of the mother," whose "wings spread over all suffering" (C. Richter, 49).

In 1936, Klamt published *Vom Erlebnis zum Gestalten*, which attempted to explain the educational process or values that symbolically manifested the body's inner sources of energy as deindividualized, *Volk*-defined forms of bodily expression. She employed a mystical, aphoristic, therapeutic rhetoric of restoring strength and health to the female body—"a people gains its full strength through obedience to nature" (11)—but the breath-centered "German gymnastic" technique she promoted was a version of the contraction-and-release themes developed by Wigman and cultivated even in the United States by Martha Graham. Klamt spent most of the book describing the inner condition that motivated the dancer—it was always an image of strength and health modeled after an idealized racial identity given by "nature" and "the people." Her disdain for serious theory and intellectual challenge did not allow her to get beyond vacuous, inspirational platitudes, and she wound up reinforcing the comfortable belief that dance was for people with small brains; this conclusion probably did not worry her, for "[i]ntellectualism, which overwhelmed our concept of education, also began to transform the feminine racial ideal into an aberrant image" (17).

But in one sense, Klamt remained faithful to the image of modernist abstraction embodied by Domela's brochure design of 1928. She contended that two geometric forces dominated the body's relation to space: the line and the curve. The line symbolized will, desire, striving, release, whereas the curve, the circle, symbolized bond, fulfillment, completion, finality, unity (91–94). All dance entailed struggling combinations of lines and curves. But Klamt warned that strong dances could not emerge from a purely formal, rationalized perspective; one must always stay "obedient to a higher will" signified by an idealized racial identity. The photos in the book provided images of this identity, yet a curious tension marked them. Those pictures taken outdoors showed smiling women dancing alone or in duets or trios on grassy hills before a vast expanse of sky, across which moved masses of radiant white clouds. The camera viewed the bodies from a low angle to emphasize the sky rather than the earth. But pictures taken indoors conveyed an altogether darker mood, with women in dark garments performing in subdued light. Klamt apparently favored ensemble dances in which trios or even larger masses of bodies moved, in friezelike fashion, in columns and circles, traversing the performance space in different configurations of implosion and radiation, rupture and reformation, canon and countercanon. Here the camera tended to view the bodies from a point higher than eye level. The effect is of a mysterious cultic milieu in which the most differentiating feature of a dancer is her *blondness*. The somewhat somber frontispiece portrait of Klamt herself with her eyes closed, as if in a trance, dramatizes this mysterious blondness even more powerfully than the indoor images of dancers.

Yet her dances of the 1930s disclosed more a religious than a fascist aura, as in *Ex profundis* (1930), *Sieghaft* (1933), *Tanz der Andacht* (1934), *Religiöse Tänze* (1934), *Tanz der Stille* (1935), and *Gemeinsames Ziel* (1935). In the latter piece women wore dark, satiny, abstract tunics or gowns and moved as if belonging to a strange, modern cult rather than to an undisguisedly fascist community (Figure 59). In the outdoors pictures, of course, the dancers project a generic, heroic image of health glorified by the Nazis. But these images were so generic that one had to read Klamt's text to situate them unambiguously within Nazi ideology. Klamt does not seem to have used specifically Nazi insignia or iconography in her dances; her distaste for narrative-pantomimic dancing prevented her from placing bodily expressivity within the context of a "story" about people who represent Nazi ideals and the struggle to validate them. Curiously, then, Nazism was an extension of her modern, personal struggle to escape entrapment within a story she did not and could not make herself.

During the Third Reich, Klamt and her school prospered from favors and privileges granted by the Nazi hierarchy, but even though the cultural landscape changed substantially after the war, Klamt continued to teach in Berlin, at the Free University, until 1968, when she retired to Switzerland to form another school, which still operates. She proved that modernist abstraction and Nazi ideology could coexist, as long as both modernism and Naziism remained subordinate to her larger therapeutic ambition. But the embrace of Nazism had much less auspicious consequences for Manda van Kreibig (1901–1990), whose aesthetic drifted toward the bizarre-grotesque rather than the tragic. After beginning dance lessons with Isadora Duncan at the age of five, she studied ballet under Heinrich Kröller in Munich and movement under Bode, but her early dances were grotesque travesties of ballet technique. In 1921 *Elegante Welt* (10/21, 12 October, 32) reported on a solo concert in Berlin in which she appeared in fantastic clown and ballet costumes designed by Munich artist Fritz Schaefler. She performed, with "mathematical exactness," an American Indian dance, a jazz dance, a dance in a "luxury nightclub," a comic dance of contrasts between balletic grace and a grotesque parody of gracefulness, and a dance concerning a "fury over a lost coin," which used music by Beethoven. Kreibig was ballet mistress at Darmstadt (1925–1928), Nuremberg (1928–1929), and Braunschweig (1929–1930) and participated in the dance experiments of the Bauhaus (1927–1929), from which emerged her most notable ensemble piece, *Farbentanze* (1929; music: Kuntzsch). In this work, six dancers applied ideas about the movement of colors and geometric forms Kreibig had gained from her collaboration with Schlemmer in Dessau. The resulting suite of dances combined ballet positions with extremely abstract visual designs that presented the dancing body as a genderless, robotic expression of formal absolutism. In 1929 she suffered a severe stage accident that ended her career as a dancer. She joined the Nazi Party in 1931, but despite the strong influence of party officials she was unable to secure a serious position. Poverty-stricken, she retreated to San Remo, Italy, where she lived with relatives in complete obscurity and dependency until her death (DS 164–167, 174–176, 323; Mueller, "3. Deutscher Tanzerkongress," 21).

Another dancer who embraced Nazism was Heide Woog, whose abstractionism developed more in relation to sound than to visual or geometric forces. In 1923–1924 she led a dance group in Duisberg, which, according to a review in *Hellweg* (4/4, 23 January 1924, 71), produced images of "healthy femininity" leading to "nothing serious." Woog went off on her own and created a two-hour dance concert consisting of a single work, *Der lebende Tempel* (1924, music: Toch). In this piece she danced to speech, music, and an assortment of noises (devised by Karl Gothes), producing an odd tension between pantomimic drama and counteractive, antinarrative abstraction in which "a restlessly pulsing play of forms triumphs over theory and dogma" (*Hellweg*, 4/8, 20 February 1924, 143). This uncertainty about whether to pursue narrative or abstraction apparently fed a further ambivalence toward the ecstatic objective for dance. A reviewer for *Die Schallkiste* (3, 11 April 1928, 10) declared that the demonic and the ecstatic were the "power source of every dance" in contemporary culture, but Woog displayed this realization only "in moments" where a "free play of the body" struggled against constraints whose deepest cause was to be found perhaps in conflicts with theorems, but perhaps also in psychic regions. The boyish bravado which so happily fit her image of an Ephebe overturned her efforts to project the image of an innocent girl, "leading to a stiffness" that was "no longer restraint" but "dance in chains." Woog's uncertainty about the relation between narrative and abstraction, between ecstasy and stability, may therefore have derived from deeper ambiguities regarding her sexual identity.

She had a school in Mühlheim, where, like Klamt, she placed great emphasis on breathing as the basis for releasing "inner" and "healthy" sources of energy (Woog). Unlike Klamt, though, Woog enjoyed inserting explicitly Nazi symbols and iconography into her dances. *Deutsche Mythe* (1934), performed at the Duisburg Municipal Theatre, was a monumental, three-part "festival play" on the theme of "leadership and heroism" for speech and movement choirs, with music by Bernhard Zelter and text by Richard Euringer. The piece showed the aimless plodding of leaderless, suffering masses of humanity, "sunk in darkness," until the appearance, in a mysterious spotlight, of "The One," who moved with "somnambulistic certainty" and used his hypnotic aura to draw ever greater numbers of alienated, isolated individuals into a single, ecstatic, glorious community. Thus unified by the hypnotic leader, the community in the third part of the drama performed spectacular round dances, marches, acrobatic stunts, battle dances, unfurling swastika flags, and surging choral images of human masses forged into the might of SA, Hitlerjugend, Wehrmacht, and "people's storm" units (MS 142–143). *Weihe* (1936), introduced at the International Dance Competition in Berlin, presented another glorification of Nazi unity, though with less concession to narrative order. It is difficult to say that Woog favored narrative at the expense of abstraction, for even *Deutsche Mythe* moved from narrated, pantomimic movement to an almost complete abstraction of humanity into formal designs modeled on and around the dominating symbols of Nazism, such as the swastika, the searchlight, the Hitler salute, and the stormtrooper pose and strut.

RUDOLF STEINER

A different order of therapeutic mysticism prevailed in the movement theory of Rudolf Steiner (1861–1925), whose ideas exerted little impact on the German dance scene as a whole but nevertheless sustained an enduring cult of "anthroposophy," the appeal of which has by no means diminished since his death. Steiner coined the term "eurhythmics" to describe his approach to the perfection of bodily expressivity, although this word, derived from ancient Greek, had long been in use among Germans (Herder, Goethe) to categorize the study of aesthetic movement; Steiner's longtime associate and eventual wife, Marie von Sivers (1867–1948), has sometimes received credit for introducing the name (Veit 46–49). Eurhythmics, however, was but a small facet of a vast, comprehensive philosophy that sought to identify the conditions of salvation in a modern world wherein old religious doctrines had lost their credibility. Anthroposophy was a sort of holistic, Christian-Nirvanic-Dionysian search for the forms of thought, feeling, and action that connected the body to a cosmic sense of purpose. Steiner left hardly any area of life unexamined by his thinking; his complete writings (1954–1984) spanned 350 volumes and covered science, medicine, education, art, social planning, architecture, anthropology, theatre, and literature. But despite its stress on mobilizing mystical forces within the body and the cosmos, anthroposophy always presented itself as a theory of consciousness rather than an expression of religious faith.

Born in the Croation region of Austria-Hungary, Steiner began his career as an academic, specializing in the studying and editing of Goethe's scientific writings; his doctoral dissertation (1891) constructed a philosophy of freedom. While a lecturer at Wilhelm Liebknecht's Worker's School in Berlin in 1901, he turned his attention to the problem of identifying a new spirituality as pursued by the Theosophical Society of that city. For the next twelve years Steiner gave an enormous number of lectures throughout

Europe in which he explained the affinities between Christian and ancient religions, the mystical significance of organic forms, and the reform of intellectual development. The lecture was his medium; probably no one ever gave as many lectures on as many subjects as he did. Like Laban, he was a prodigious teacher but a weak scholar who expended his mental energies on innumerable lectures rather than on impressive research. He always conveyed a sense of analytical authority by introducing categories, concepts, and definitions, but he did not apply them with any systematic rigor—he preferred to move on to a new topic rather than lose his audience, often naive, in theoretical complexities. In 1913 he broke with the Theosophical Society and formed his own anthroposophical cult, with headquarters in Dornach, near Basel, where he supervised (1913–1921) the building of the famous anthroposophical temple, the Goetheanum, a huge wooden structure set among woods and orchards and made up of cavernous rooms modeled after organic forms, such as caves, shells, and cellular tissues. He gained adherents throughout Europe, perhaps because he showed the compatibility of mysticism and scientific rationalism; indeed, he disapproved of submission to unconscious powers, arguing that spiritual renewal depended on full consciousness of one's perceptions, feelings, and actions. When in 1922 the Goetheanum burned down, he immediately launched plans to build a new one in concrete and succeeded in raising funds from adepts around the world. But he did not live long enough to see it (Kugler).

Steiner had no formal training in dance, and he did not begin his adventures in "eurhythmic art" until 1912, when, in Munich, he collaborated with a nineteen-year-old dance student, Lory Smits, on exploring relations between vowel sounds and movements. Eurhythmics, according to Steiner, revealed "harmonic" connections between sound patterns in speech and the movement of the body. Whereas Klamt and Woog emphasized breathing as the primal sign of the body's inner power, Steiner stressed words. He remarked in 1908, "the word, which intones the soul, the logos, was there in the beginning, and the word so guides evolution until finally being emerges which can also appear. What finally appears in time and space was first there in spirit" (Veit 42). Music derived from tonal and rhythmic principles already embedded in speech, so spoken language disclosed the deepest, most secret bodily responses to sound. Movement made sound visible, and eurhythmics treated language as a "cosmos" of sound units, beginning with vowels and consonants, then words, syntactic structures, punctuation, sentences, meter, rhyme, alliteration, metaphor, hyberbole, recitation, and declamation, all of which corresponded to specific movement choices or combinations of movements. An elaborate process of symbolism bestowed emotional values upon sound units and structures, which then became associated with particular colors, organic and inorganic forms, creatures, planets, and abstract conditions (e.g., active or passive). For example, the letter

U (indigo) signified a sinking or deepening motion (arms bending parallel before the chest), whereas the letter T (yellow-red) signified a striking or pushing gesture. Letters were elements of a sound "scale," and different combinations of letters—words—produced different "chords" and rhythmic "intervals."

Not surprisingly, this approach, when applied to all the variables of speech, led to enormous complexities, which neither Steiner nor any of his adepts was able to put into helpful charts or tables. But Steiner's aim was not to provide a rigorous system of correspondences; rather, he sought to suggest complexities that encouraged people to become highly conscious of sounds and movements and to realize that even the slightest utterance or movement could reverberate with significance. In reality, his approach was too complex for his lecture-style language, which suited a writer with so many interests besides the almost incidental theme of eurhythmics. But, as Laban eventually discovered with the *Kinetographie,* the lecture style became hopelessly inadequate in accounting for all the expressive variables of the dynamic body. Steiner therefore relied heavily on drawings, many done in colored chalk, to describe movement possibilities and correspondences, especially for ensemble pieces. A great many of these drawings traced the image of movement without showing the body or bodies and thus transmitted a powerfully mysterious level of abstraction (Steiner). Few images have ever conveyed so persuasively the perception of movement as a mystical phenomenon. But these chalk sketches on slate backgrounds were an extension of Steiner's lecture style, and they emblematized a metaphysical dimension that scarcely seemed to correspond to the physical reality of actual bodies moving in specific times and spaces.

In spite of the implied complexity of the cosmic-word concept, the dance culture of the anthroposophists consistently projected an aura of simplicity. Steiner never stressed virtuosity of movement, nor did he push toward any professionalization of performance. He promoted a level of performance that strengthened the cultic identity of those already initiated into the mysteries of anthroposophy; an appeal to the uninitiated audience for professional dance and theatre held practically no interest for him, although he did not hesitate to give public demonstrations of eurhythmics throughout Europe. He regarded bodily movement as primarily a lyrical rather than dramatic action, "song made visible," which is to say that he and his adepts overwhelmingly favored "flowing" bodily movements and movements of the body in space. The body curved; arms and shoulders undulated; rows of bodies pulsed and surged; groups swelled or rippled into spirals, serpentine coils, arabesques; circles metamorphosed into stars, flowers, anemones, swirling disks, and intimations of stirring cosmic and "organic" forms. Both bodily and group movement were dominated by the image of waves, currents of water. The welter of tonal and rhythmic tensions in speech and language implied by Steiner's invocation of the "cosmic word" actually had little counterpart in tensions within or between moving bodies. But this lack of rigorous correspondence between theory and practice hardly troubled his adepts, for the arcane, convoluted mysteries defining the sound-world of speech signified a motive for movement rather than a system of it: indeed, the more complex the system became, the more it signified a mystery to which the body responded with a pliant flow of energy rather than with a compatible or congruent manifestation of complexity.

Eurhythmic dancers favored long, flowing costumes—robes, chitons, gowns, capes, veils—following images of ancient Greek maenads, sacerdotal Egyptians, or Romanesque-medieval figures, except that Steiner imposed a cryptic color symbolism on the fabrics. Steiner had staged "mystery plays" since 1889, when he directed his own adaptation of a Goethe fairy tale. He subsequently staged, for festival-cultic occasions, productions such as Eduard Shure's *Eleusis* (1907), scenes from Goethe's *Faust* (1915–1916), and Shakespeare's *Midsummer Night's Dream* (1923), in which he applied some eurhythmic principles. He also staged fairy-tale dramas of his own composition: *Die Pforte der Einweihung* (1910), *Die Prüfung der Seele* (1911), *Der Hüter der Schwelle* (1912), and *Der Seelen Erwachen* (1913). However, strictly eurhythmic performance evolved slowly. Steiner spent several years testing his ideas with Lory Smits, and during World War I, when the anthroposophists expended much of their energy on constructing the Goetheanum, resources for performance remained scarce. Thus, after an initial demonstration in Munich in August 1913, Steiner gave no more demonstrations of eurhythmic art until August 1918. The fantastically cavernous Goetheanum was able to provide a most appropriate setting to support Steiner's claim that "every artistic dance derives originally from the old art of temple dances, those cultic dances which were performed in the temples of the old high cultures" (Fröböse 35). In the 1913 recital, featuring the movements of Lory Smits and two other women, bodies moved entirely to the sound of recited poetry by Goethe and Brentano. But by 1918, Steiner was including musical accompaniments, composed by adepts, that sometimes underscored the speaking of poetry by Goethe, Hebbel, Morgenstern, Meyer, or Nietzsche. From 1919 to 1923, Steiner gave demonstration recitals in Dornach, Zurich, Paris, Amsterdam, Oxford, Prague, and numerous German cities, with Tatiana Kisseleff as his star dancer and Marie von Sivers as his chief reciter.

It is difficult to determine how many people actually performed in the group dances or how the dances on any program differed from each other; most dances bore the titles of the poems that accompanied them, and most documentation of the concerts focused on the concept of eurhythmics rather than on the execution of the concept. (Photo documentation is unusually scant in relation to the abundant documentation of Steiner's eurhythmic drawings and watercolors.) In her memoirs, Kisseleff recalled the initial—and not altogether friendly—reception of public (not cultic) audiences, which tended toward bewilderment, and she observed that even within the Anthroposophical Society many people disliked Marie von Sivers's portentous manner of reciting poetry (Veit 69–72).

Shortly before Steiner's death, Else Klink (b.1907) began studying at the newly founded Eurhythmeum in Stuttgart under one of Steiner's protégés, Annmarie Dubach-Donath (1895–1972). After two years (1927–1929) at the Goetheanum, Klink accepted an invitation to work at the Steiner institute in The Hague; she remained until 1935, when she returned to Stuttgart to direct the activities of the Eurhythmeum (Veit 77–110). While Steiner was alive, male adepts apparently functioned as musicians and scenic artists on eurhythmic performances, and women did the actual performing. But when von Sivers and Klink assumed greater authority within the Anthroposophical Society, men became more prominent figures in the performance of dances, and music assumed greater significance than words as a motive for movement, although the "cosmic word" still retained theoretical primacy. The Nazis banned the Anthroposophical Society in 1935 but permitted eurhythmic instruction at the Eurhythmeum until 1941, during which time enrollment at the school rose from twenty to eighty students. The Gestapo was ever suspicious of eurhythmics and of Klink, whose dark, "un-Aryan" features led to a scheme in 1937 to replace her with a former Wigman student, Martha Morell, who refused to cooperate. In 1941 the Gestapo finally shut down the school and assigned Klink, her associate Otto Wiemer, and her students to factory labor for the duration of the war. In the immediate postwar era, Klink revived the school at the Eurhythmeum and carried on the cultic performance tradition into the 1980s, by which time Steiner's philosophy had returned to the German cultural scene with perhaps even greater popularity than it enjoyed in the 1920s.

Eurhythmics was obviously more important than nearly all dance histories suggest. Though it did not exert substantial influence on German dance culture or produce any powerful dance personalities, it did establish bodily movement as a redemptive mystery accessible to all people as long as they believed in the anthroposophical philosophy as a whole. Neither an elaborate technique nor a powerful expressivity bestowed value upon eurhythmic dance; rather, eurhythmic dance bestowed an aura of exclusivity upon its humble performers. Such dance always functioned within the context of the temple, of a grandiose synthetic doctrine that separated the initiated from those who were blind to a mystery that transcended the banality of the physical world. Through eurhythmics, dance allowed mystery to become a visible feature of ordinary, daily life.

GERTRUD BODENWIESER

Expressionism presented modernist abstraction as a primal image of inner psychic or spiritual conditions. Klamt and Steiner represented almost antithetical political variants of abstractionism in this key. But expressionism sometimes linked abstraction to heightened conditions of mechanization rather than spirituality. Skoronel insisted that in her case mechanization referred to formal properties of movement rather than to the theme of machines or industrialization, but expressionist performance did not remain entirely indifferent to relations between bodies and machines, as was evident in such prominent dramas as Kaiser's *Gas* (1918–1920), Čapek's *RUR* (1920), Toller's *Die Maschinenstürmern* (1922), and Bronnen's *Anarchie in Sillien* (1924), Max Brand's opera *Maschinist Hopkins* (1929), and Fritz Lang's film *Metropolis* (1927). As late as 1934, one could see in Braunschweig a full-length ballet, *Menschenmaschinen*, by the genial Hungarian composer Eugene Zador (1894–1977). Unlike futurism, however, which glorified machines, expressionism projected a skeptical attitude toward their salvational power, even though, in the theatre at least, expressionism relied extravagantly on new performance technologies to construct its messages.

Dämon Maschine (1924) was probably the most famous "machine dance" performed in Germany during the Weimar era, but its creator, Gertrud Bodenwieser (1890–1959) resided in Vienna. Though she converted to Catholicism early in life, she came from an affluent, cultivated Jewish family influential in financial circles, and she eventually married a Jewish theatre director, Friedrich Rosenthal. From childhood she enjoyed contact with modernist art and music personalities in Vienna; the artists Felix Harta and Franz von Bayros collaborated with her on the designs for some of her early dances. Between 1905 and 1910 she studied ballet under Carl Godlewski, ballet master at the Vienna Royal Opera, but the reactionary insulation of Viennese ballet from virtually any modernist impulse in dance meant that most of her "teachers" were dancers she observed at concerts or learned about through readings and photographs. She matured quite slowly, for she did not give her debut concert, at a modernist art gallery for an invited audience, until 1919. The program contained only six dances, but she received an enthusiastic critical response; yet she did not give her next concert, again presenting only six dances, until two years later. In 1922 she ventured into pair dancing in a recital with Ernst Walt, who was actually a composer, but neither solo nor pair dancing accommodated her ambitions, and the only other dance in which she performed with a man (Curt Hagen) was *Konstrucktivistisches Liebeslied* (1928, music: Poulenc). Group dance was her passion. So in 1923 she formed a school and ensemble in the basement of the Vienna Concert House, which remained her headquarters until 1938 (MacTavish 15–20).

Her school, she asserted, embraced expressionism wholeheartedly and did not focus "one-sidedly" on the cultivation of "gracefulness," nor did it adopt any of the prewar Grecian dance styles as a model for a new dance art. Bodenwieser saw dance as an image of the modern world in which she lived: "I want in my dances struggle, passion, Dionysiacally intensified feeling for life, but also chaos, horror, and degeneration" (Stefan 95). With her ensemble she choreographed an enormous number of pieces, and the company visited an astounding number of European cities, perhaps more than any other Germanic dance group of the era, especially in such countries as Czechoslovakia, Poland, Italy, Rumania, Bulgaria, and Belgium; it also visited New York, France, England, Holland, and gave the first Germanic ensemble productions in Japan (1934). Wherever the Bodenwieser group appeared, it signified a self-consciously modernist attitude toward performance, informed by avant-garde tendencies in the visual arts and an openness to contemporary music. When the Nazis annexed Austria, she knew she no longer had a future in Europe, so she and her husband went into exile, along with several of her students, first to France, where she formed a new group, then to Venezuela and Colombia, for a concert tour that even included performances in a bullfight ring. Her husband stayed behind in France to do radio work, but two years later he disappeared after the Gestapo arrested him. Bodenwieser, at the invitation of one of her students, had traveled to New Zealand and Australia, which became her home for the rest of her life. In Sydney she soon established another school and became one of the strongest personalities in the modern dance scene of Australia and New Zealand, producing about a hundred dance works in less than twenty years.

Though Bodenwieser choreographed an astonishing number of group dances before she left Austria, *Dämon Maschine* remained her most famous achievement and the work upon which perception of her as an avant-garde artist rested. This piece contained all the major features of her dance aesthetic, and her prolific output was perhaps based on her skill in constructing manifold variations of these features. But the piece projected a peculiar relation to abstraction. Originally, *Dämon Maschine* was the second part of a four-part cycle of dances, *Gewalten des Lebens* (1924), whose first part, *Ein Wesen*, dated from her brief partnership with Ernst Walt in 1922. However, the second part attracted so much fascination that the cycle as a whole often became identified as *Dämon Maschine*. Bodenwieser began presenting the second part independent of its context, even though the cycle constituted a dramatic narrative that disclosed an overarching, controlling attitude toward machines. The second part unwittingly showed the power of abstraction to undermine narrative unity, yet Bodenwieser's notion of abstraction was hardly extreme, for she never allowed it to undercut her enthusiasm for decorative theatricality. In the first part, two figures, He and She, wearing light-blue veils, made swinging motions together to "dreamy" music by Debussy. (In group performance, a woman danced the male figure.) According to Bodenwieser, "The body of the woman softly repeats the rhythm of the man. He reaches high and grasps at the stars. But already the half-sunken beings [around the couple] reach with the same desire into the ether. Full of ardor, the man kneels humbly before life. And she with him." With the couple, a "common destiny weaves them into asingle being," and the "great swaying of life urges them toward a final and scarcely intimated abyss" (RLM 181).

The second part, "Dämon Maschine," employed gong and percussion music by Lisa Mayer and showed how machines destroyed the unity of being achieved by the couple. Six dancers turned their bodies into images of machines: gears, levers, pumps, pistons, pulverizers, dynamos. Five of the dancers wore abstractly colored briefs and long-sleeved tops that exposed much flesh and thus reinforced the perception of the body as a machine; the sixth dancer wore a dark, "demonic" uniform, looking somewhat like a robot. Bodies functioned as parts of a single "machine"; they intertwined and joined mechanically through complicated, contortionistic relations among kneeling, squatting, kicking, grasping, thrusting, squirming, hammering, and interlocking, moving from lying to standing positions, from profile to full face. A group was a carnal machine—and quite decorative, too (Renner 53–54) (Figure 60).

The third part presented "the golden calf" (music: Petyrek). Here two bodies formed a single idol, with four arms, a crown, and a "golden aura." Around the idol danced five Corybants: "Lust from tip-toes to finger-tips. . . . Throbbing, ecstasy, frenzy, impotence, collapse. The idol grins victoriously" (RLM 182). In the final part (music: Mussorgski), "the oppressed, the defeated, the confused, the devastated. Frost passes through the column of the outcast. The priestess strides through the group. The glow of reason and good streams through the darkness," in the manner of a painting by Massacio. What probably made the machine dance so popular was its erotic decorativeness. The piece did not, as in revue dancing, rely on chorus-line synchronicity of movement to suggest mechanization of identity and feeling. Rather, bodies formed different patterns of synchronicity and counterpoint with each other to create a pulsing, mutant machine-organism of ecstatic intensity, amplifying both the desireability and the demonic power of female bodies.

The piece was never so abstract that one lost sight of the theatrical imitation of a machine. Bodenwieser always remained devoted to theatrical effects; indeed, she advocated closer relations not between dance and opera-ballet but between dance and the literary theatre (Stefan 58–59). For Karlheinz Martin and Friedrich Rosenthal, she "choreographed" actions and inserted dances into productions of otherwise danceless plays by

Raimund, Wedekind, and Kokoschka, and she designed a dance for Friedrich Kiesler's experimental, spiral *Raumbühne* in 1924. But in spite of her declared distaste for gracefulness, she never detached her theatricality from decorativeness and elegant pictorial effects derived from her familiarity with modernist art trends; these made her dances seem advanced and sophisticated without being especially demanding or disturbing. In her solo "cubistic dance" (1923), she wore a bizarre costume of conical sleeves and pants, but the music was by the American romantic composer Edward MacDowell! Her image of the machine was peculiarly lyrical, drawing on a Viennese tradition of curvilinear beauty exemplified earlier by Grete Wiesenthal; her introductory dance course began with the study of figure-8 spiral movements (Brown 16). She created a huge quantity of charming adaptations of folk, social, and cabaret dances that pleased audiences as much in London or Crakow as in Vienna. These contrasted almost absurdly with her ambitious, mystical-allegorical dance cycles, usually in three parts, such as *Biblische Themen* (1923), *Gotische Suite* (1928, music: Glück), *Schwingungsaustausch* (1930, music: Lorber), *Rhythmen des Unbewussten* (1928, music: Wellesz), *Die grosse Stunden* (1931, music: Tcherepnin), and *Drei Tanzsymbolen* (1933, music: Bortkievich). *Strömung und Gegenströmung* (1928), whose three parts were titled "Mysticism," "Mechanization," and "Decadence," was another machine dance based on Henry Ford's principles of automated factory labor, but this piece provoked less favor than others had, perhaps because it lacked decorativeness. A Rumanian reviewer remarked: "With shining eyes, girls wander happily in pairs. Demonic mechanization emerges. Sucks them into its black-red song. Compels them to convulsive gliding, stamping, and swinging, to pushing and shoving." The orgiastic bacchanal of the "decadence" part ended in paralyzed impotence (MacTavish 37). The narrative for this strange cycle suggested that mechanization arose out of mysticism, out of the mysterious unity of the couple, and destroyed it as well as the couple; mechanization awakened in the body a hunger for a monstrous ecstasy, leading inevitably to decadence, from which no one could expect salvation or a redemptive light.

A recurrent feature of Bodenwieser's group dances was the absence of a leader figure, a major contrast to Wigman's ensemble aesthetic. However, her mystical image of the couple appeared even stranger than most embodiments and was not without a strong homoerotic aura. Bodenwieser liked images of intertwining female bodies—pillars, pyramids, friezes of conjoined or interlocking bodies—which produced a curiously contorted, arabesque view of feminine being as multilimbed, multiheaded, and multimirrored, an effect beautifully captured in popular photographs taken by the D'Ora-Benda studio (Faber, *Tanzfoto*, 66–69). But Bodenwieser especially stressed the looping, cradling, embracing, nudging, plying, rubbing, and prodding of bodies, often in kneeling or reclining positions, with pairs and sometimes trios of dancers, most obviously in *Ich und Du* (1935), *Wiegenlied der Muttererde* (1934), *Tanz mit goldenen Scheiben* (1934), *Die Masken Luzifers* (1936), and *Tanz der drei Schwestern* (1928). For Bodenwieser, the mystical coupling of bodies entailed a lyrical mechanization of movement—ecstasy, one might say, depended on the decorative coupling of mysticism and mechanization.

The intertwining of female bodies also appeared, to a lesser degree, in the work of other dancers in Vienna, such as Ellen Tels and Ellinor Tordis, and in the work of Gisa Geert and Hilde Holger, both students of Bodenwieser. Holger (b. 1905) danced in the first production of *Damon Maschine*, and her ensemble aesthetic relied strongly on the Bodenwieser device of intertwined bodies creating a "single being." This device appeared most emphatically, perhaps, in *Orchidee* (1933, music: Ravel), though it also pervaded her choreography of *Mechanisches Ballett* in 1926, with music by Hirschfeld-Mack. Holger, too, came from a cultivated Jewish family, which brought her in touch with prominent Viennese artists and intellectuals such as Stefan Zweig, Elias Canetti, and Erni Kniepert, and she posed nude for modernist artists such as Felix Harta, Benedikt Dolbin, and Joseph Heu and the photographer Antios (Takvorian 18–19). Yet a peculiar timidity marked her dance aesthetic and her performance productivity. In 1926 she left the Bodenwieser group and formed her own school and ensemble in the Ratibor Palace in Vienna. Unlike Bodenwieser, however, Holger ventured eventually to infuse her mysticism with overtly Jewish themes, which appeared in the solo *Hebräischer Tanz* (1929, music: Weprik), *Kabbalistischer Tanz* (1933, music: Rieti), *Ahasver* (1936, music: Rubin), and *Golem* (1937, music: Wilckens).

Holger's perception of bodily movement owed less to the image of the machine than to the image of the marionette, particularly after she became friends with Richard Teschner (1879–1948), the Viennese designer of masks, figurines, and marionettes. Teschner's eerily exquisite fairy-tale figurines inhabited a fantastic miniature theatrical world ("Figuren-Spiegel") of rococo, *Arabian Nights,* and Indonesian puppet ornamentality. Holger began to introduce masks and historicizing costume details that made her dances appear less abstract, as in her solos for *Javanesische Impression* (1931) and *Golem.* Much of her group work in Vienna was for children, and it was not until she went into exile in 1939 and gave up solo dancing altogether that she disclosed any expansive confidence in group dance to embody her desires. She spent the war years in Bombay, where she formed a school and put on concerts, then (1948) migrated to London, which became her permanent home (her husband, an Indian, was a physician). There she opened another school (1951), which operated continuously into the late 1980s. Unlike Bodenwieser, Holger liked working with male students and dancers, one of whom was the wild English theatre director Lindsay Kemp (b. 1939).

But wildness was precisely what Holger's aesthetic lacked. Her reluctance to push herself beyond the devices of Bodenwieser and Teschner apparently resulted from her sense, throughout her life, of having to move cautiously, with marionette decorum, in societies (rather than close-knit circles) that were permanently foreign to her (including Vienna) and easily capable, as she herself suggested, of "misunderstanding" almost any serious bodily movement of modernity (Takvorian 37).

KURT JOOSS

With Kurt Jooss (1901–1979), expressionist dance avoided both abstraction and influences from modernist art yet explored themes of social alienation and anxiety. Indeed, Jooss acquired an exaggerated reputation as a satiric commentator on (or caricaturist of) social role-playing because he respected traditional narrative models for framing bodily movement. His modernism therefore depended on his situating expressionistically distorted images of contemporary social types within a premodern narrative structure.

Jooss was born on a farm near Stuttgart but never showed any serious interest in farming; even so, a vaguely agrarian-guildish (rather than cultic) notion of community shaped his aesthetic and perception of social reality. At first he considered a career as an artistic photographer, then (1919) focused on singing and drama at the Stuttgart Academy of Music. But "something was missing everywhere, and I no longer believed in my dream of the arts" (Markard 29). He therefore resolved to return to the family farm. However, as soon as he made the vow he encountered Laban in Stuttgart, and although Jooss was, as he put it, "heavy, phlegmatic, and totally without muscles," his "whole being gradually became a part of this art," to the extent that "my body changed." On the farm again, he could think only of dance, and he experienced the most intense suffering of his entire life. Shortly after his father died, Jooss could no longer live apart from dance, so in 1922 he rejoined Laban in Stuttgart and followed him to Mannheim, then Hamburg, where he met Sigurd Leeder, who had collaborated with Jutta von Collande. Early in 1924, Jooss and Leeder formed the only male pair dance couple in German dance, but it was not until 1926–1927 that they actually devised the program "Two Male Dancers," comprising solos and four duets, all apparently grotesque. The composer Marcel Lorber, who worked so closely with Bodenwieser in Vienna, accompanied them on the piano. But the tour collapsed when Jooss injured his knee.

By this time, however, he had other tasks to fulfill. His close connection to Laban recommended him to the innovative opera director Hanns Niedecken-Gebhard in Münster, where in 1924 Jooss had choreographed his first notable ensemble piece, the Tels-Wellesz *Persisches Ballett*, with Yvonne Georgi and Jens Keith. Jooss and Leeder worked with a small corps of six men and ten women on modernistic operatic and dance works by Hindemith, Toch, and Wellesz; Jooss supplemented these pieces with large and small scenarios of his own composition, primarily of a grotesque and satirical nature. After observing ballet schools in Paris and Vienna, Jooss and Leeder began to incorporate ballet technique into their pedagogy and productions, although Jooss continued to regard ballet as "dead from within" (35). In 1927 the city of Essen invited Jooss and Rudolf Schulz-Dornberg to establish a subsidized arts school, the Folkwangschule, with Jooss as director of a dance studio aiming to integrate dance and theatre—"Tanztheater." At Essen he gathered about him a team of collaborators whose talents were manifest at Münster: Leeder, the scenic designer Hein Heckroth (1901–1970), the composer Fritz Cohen (1904–1967), and the Estonian dancer Aino Simola (1901–1971), whom Jooss married in 1929. Jooss further consolidated dance and theatre by working with the conductor Toscanini and Laban on the Paris version of the *Tannhäuser Bacchanale* (1930) and by accepting appointment as ballet director of the Essen Municipal Opera, for which the Folkwang dance company performed all ballets. Then he appeared as a dancer-actor in stage productions of Kaiser's *Europa* (1931) and Shakespeare's *Midsummer Night's Dream* (1931), in which he played Puck. With *The Green Table* (1932), Jooss produced his most popular international work, winning first prize and 25,000 francs at the Concours de Choreographie in Paris.

At this point Jooss detached his dance company from the subsidized theatre and formed the Ballets Jooss, which toured several Rhineland cities, Holland, Belgium, Switzerland, Paris, London. Nazi press and propaganda, however, expressed virulent hostility toward Jooss, primarily because he collaborated with Jews, but because his company enjoyed no subsidies it was not until September 1933 that the Gestapo moved to arrest him—in vain, for Jooss and his entire company of twenty-three persons had sneaked across the Dutch border. In 1934, Lord Elmhirst invited Jooss and his company to make their headquarters in Dartington Hall, Devon, England, where the company remained until 1942, realizing "Jooss's early dream of an academy of the arts in a rural setting" (Coton 56). But financial pressures compelled the company to tour almost continuously from 1934 to 1940 throughout Europe, South America, the United States, Canada, England, and Ireland. Probably no other dance company in the world reached such a large international audience, although the repertoire consisted primarily of works created before 1933. For reasons of national security, the company moved to Cambridge in 1942, and Jooss served in the British Army. The Ballets Jooss returned to Europe and America in 1946 as part of the British Army entertainment services, and Jooss himself became a British citizen in

1947. In 1949 he accepted another invitation from Essen to direct the dance activities of the Folkwangschule; by 1953, however, the city claimed it could not longer fund the company. After a stint at the Düsseldorf Opera (1954– 1956), he devoted himself entirely to teaching until the 1960s, when state subsidies allowed for the establishment of the Folkwangballet. By this time Jooss enjoyed the reputation of a revered master teacher who synthesized *Ausdruckstanz* and ballet through the concept of "dance theatre." His most famous student was Pina Bausch (b. 1940), probably the greatest dance artist to emerge from Germany since the Weimar years. When he retired from the Folkwangschule, in 1968, Jooss continued to lecture and hold master classes internationally; his daughter, Anna Markard (b. 1931), supervised the elaborate documentation of his legacy. At the end of his career he seemed to have no enemies and no serious challenges to his perspective; he was always a "sweet" man, gentle, patient, persistent, friendly, and sensible, free of fanaticism and abundantly blessed with quiet, healthy optimism.

As an artist, Jooss was skeptical of "barbaric *Ausdruckstanz*" and believed by 1924 that "the creative adventures of expressionism lie behind us" (Markard 15). He therefore followed a vision of "New Dance" in which a Platonic sense of order was no longer incompatible with modern bodily expressivity (Coton 30–31). At the heart of Jooss's aesthetic was "a creative compromise between free personal expression and formal compliance with objective, intellectual laws," "a compromise in the noblest sense, which one can likewise designate as axial to the world of art" (Markard 17). For Jooss, compromise meant a synthesis of dance and theatre achieved through a synthesis of *Ausdruckstanz* and ballet. But Jooss's concept of ballet was somewhat ambiguous, for by it he did not mean an elaborately rigid system for automating bodily movement within an extravagantly artificial performance space. He loved the idea of laws governing movement, but he wanted a "gestural training based on natural laws of mimicry and expression," so that movement always appeared "new" and "natural" at every moment of performance (Coton 72).

In practice, this notion of compromise supposed that expressive power derived from the observation and perfection of socially coded bodily movements in daily and ceremonial life. In the rather abstract *Larven* (1925) and *Groteske* (1925), Jooss used masks and eccentric costume details to render bizarrely comic the idealizing gestures and poses of ballet—with, for example, a female dancer performing on pointe pirouettes in a specially constructed dress that made her look like a dwarf, with the other four dancers amplifying the perception of a community unified only through a grotesquely extravagant respect for conventionalized signification of heroism and grace. In these cases, costume largely designated movement as grotesque. But in *Kaschemme* (1926) and *Tangoballade* (1926), costume scarcely departed from what the dancers might actually wear on the street; instead, movements from popular social dances became powerfully exaggerated, with female couples dancing passionately, eyes closed, as in *Kaschemme*, or in a kind of somnambulatory line, as in *Tangoballade*. In *Pavanne* (1929), with its lavish sixteenth-century costumes, Jooss showed that exaggerations of conventionalized decor and movement could operate in a tragic as well as grotesque mood (although the intense sadness of Ravel's music probably dominates perception of any movement it accompanies to such an extent that I think it impossible for anyone to produce a grotesque-comic dance using the piece).

Jooss sought a compromise between abstraction and "naturalness," and this he achieved above all by emphasizing the restoration of conventional narrative strategies as the chief source of value and motivation for dance. As early as 1924 he was willing to assert that "the dance pantomime is the actual theatre form of dance" ("Der grüne Tisch," 22). The exaggerated perfection of socially coded movements transformed the body into a recognizable social type (or caricature) whose actions produced an easily readable story. It was not pantomime so much as the "natural" consequence of exaggerating the social codes signifying various emotions and motives, regardless of their historical context. Jooss did not confine himself to a contemporary image of the world. *The Prodigal Son* (1931), for example, with music by Prokofiev and choreography by Balanchine (originally done for Diaghilev in 1929), presented a vaguely biblical parable about a young man whose acquisition of glory and power leads to his corruption and then his betrayal by his followers. A Mysterious Stranger, who earlier had tried to dissuade the young man from his dream of power, finds refuge for him among a community of harlots, then denounces him to an underworld mob. Alone and penniless, the man journeys wearily back to the home of his father but meets the Mysterious Stranger along the way. This time he repudiates his enigmatic "friend." Here, as in subsequent works, Jooss disclosed an acutely ambivalent attitude toward the pursuit of power and leadership, but he had difficulty constructing an image of community that effectively justified or neutralized his ambivalence.

This ambivalence toward the power and ambition of leaders reached maximum intensity in the great international hit *The Green Table* (1932, music: Cohen), an expressionist satire on political power-brokering inspired, according to Jooss, by the medieval dance of death. The dance drama contained eight scenes showing the triumph of Death over all who followed their leaders to war. The first depicted ten diplomats in formal attire and distorted masks "negotiating" around a green table: "They smile, persuade, flatter, argue, then rage at one another. They threaten and gesticulate wildly with harsh, puppet-like movements which stress the unreality of the emotions to which they pretend. They go through a formula of discussion; they understand, they apologize, they resume their chattering until their mutual hatred impels to a mutual rage. At this point they leave the table, pacing up and down, back and forth, with the agitation of bantam cocks or the wariness of foxes" (Coton 49). This description indicates how Jooss's idea of building dances around socially coded movements actually entailed an almost cartoonish exaggeration of conventional (or "formal") significations to suggest the demonic insincerity of gestural signs, an observation reinforced by archival film footage of the dance and by videotape documentation of the Joffrey Ballet's 1976 reconstruction. Subsequent scenes depicted the call to arms, the farewell, military training, the battle, a brothel, "the dark roads where wander the homeless and stricken refugees," and the return of the ridiculous diplomats. The two major figures were the War Profiteer and Death, who form a macabre partnership that concludes with a chess game won by Death, who gathers up all the pieces along with the Profiteer. Originally played by Jooss himself, Death appeared in all the scenes, "sapping desire, corrupting ability, as he hovers in the background or stalks steadily, mechanically and undeviatingly through scenes of battle, flight, or surrender" (49). Death was played by a nearly naked dancer who had a skeleton painted onto his body and wore a sort of centurion hat, boots, and a black pelvis/rib cage. Though the diplomats looked contemporary, the figures in all the other scenes projected vaguely archaic and definitely premodern images—except for the Profiteer, who wore a bowler and a T-shirt and resembled more a habitué of a boxing gym than a figure from a corporate boardroom. For Jooss, the desire for power entailed the heightened expression of insincerity, which led to catastrophic misunderstandings and conflicts (war). Death, the ultimate power figure, controlled the destinies of societies; a leader was someone whose body moved in accordance with the grand ambition of Death to take everyone with him. This attitude was quite at odds with that of Wigman in the spectacular *Totenmal* (1930), in which the (female) leader established her command over groups (movement choirs) through movements signifying a heroic confrontation with Death rather than a foolish blindness to it.

With *The Big City* (1932), Jooss moved toward a more cinematic narrative style that dispensed altogether with the figure of the leader and the theme of ambition as the measure of identity. Here he presented a complex image of a modern society defined and unified above all through sexual desire: "We see typists and clerks, the newsboy and prostitutes, factory girls and working lads; elegant and would-be-elegant men of leisure, a few tramps and fanatics, a sprinkling of touts, beggars and street vendors walk, loiter, amble or trot briskly along. It is the evening cross-section of Main Street anywhere, made up almost entirely of those whose lives are too formless, or whose pockets are too light, to enjoy solitude or leisure" (Coton 40). In the midst of this crowded scene appear a Young Girl and a Young Worker, lovers, who dance romantically and innocently until the entrance of the Libertine, who casts his suave spell upon the Young Girl and entices her away, leaving the Young Worker impotently enraged. The ensuing scene depicted, with much use of magnified shadows, the Libertine bestowing an expensive gift (a party dress) on the Young Girl in her tenement neighborhood. When the Young Girl departs momentarily to change into the dress, the street urchins display a peculiar capacity to resist the seductive charm of the Libertine and perceive his insincerity. The Young Girl returns and dances with the Libertine into the night while the children and mothers point accusatorially at the couple. The final scene takes place in a dance hall, "where stupid, doll-like youths and girls stamp and contort through graceless motions of a debased kind of ballroom dance" (41). The Girl and the Libertine appear and dance orgiastically. Then the music becomes melancholy, and the ballroom figures metamorphose into proletarian couples, who perform a kind of tragic waltz of futility. The Young Worker enters and dances with different partners, seeking the Young Girl, but in the end he dances all alone; dancers from both classes become mere shadows, while "the maddening stupid rhythm goes on and on, marked by the even stamp and shuffle of the dancing automatons" (44).

This rather rural vision of big city life was, according to Coton, "built on all variations of human locomotion—prancing, shuffling, ambling, gliding, hesitant, bold, furtive—and a style of freely rhythmic and unstressed dance which show[ed] more elasticity but less elevation, little line but plenty of roundness, in comparison with classical Ballet" (44). Moreover, Jooss used "long cross-stage lines and full-stage circles," with "small circles opposed to, or built towards, large circular movements," to suggest "characters moving inside space, rather than against a background" (45). Thus, although Jooss offered a conventionally negative representation of female class mobility through erotic desireability, the movement of an entire social class was signified by intricate circular patterns—especially of multiple couples and trios—rather than by the synchronicity of feeling and action that conventionally signified "class" in theatrical performance. This work indicated that the use of socially coded movements to shape dance was synonymous with the representation of conditions of loneliness, alienation, futility, and disillusionment, an attitude cultivated with even greater intensity in the postmodern dance aesthetic of Pina Bausch.

With *A Ball in Old Vienna* (1932, music: Lanner), Jooss satirized the conventions of the courtly waltz in a nostalgic atmosphere of the 1840s. By exaggerating its movements, he implied that the waltz disguised the desire to assert power over an entire social class: one asserted power over the body of one's partner in a context elaborately contrived to produce this disguise—the ball. For Jooss, dance itself implied an intensely physical "fascination in the actions and reactions of those people, at any social level, who are able to exercise practically unlimited power over others" (53). In *Ballade* (1935, music: Colman) he returned to the tragic, medieval mood of *Pavanne*, full of somberly ceremonial movement, but this time he pitted two couples—King and Queen, Marquis and Marquise—against each other, with a virtually static Queen provoked to a display of "awful power" by a trivial indiscretion of the King and the Marquise. *The Mirror* (1936, music: Cohen), however, told a contemporary story of three men—the Man of Leisure, the Middle-class Man, and the Laborer—comrades during the war, who return to their homes to find expanding misery, poverty, and unemployment. The unemployed Laborer abandons his wife to a life of prostitution; the Middle-class Man attempts to form a political movement uniting bourgeois and proletarian interests, but the workers repudiate him. An encounter with the wife-whore awakens in the Middle-class Man the authority he needs to lead a full-scale revolution against the capitalists. But total chaos results, and the three men, united by pervasive social suffering, find themselves comrades again. *Chronica* (1939, music: Goldschmidt) followed an even more complicated plot, set in the Italian Renaissance, about a stranger who gains the confidence of influential citizens to become leader of a city. However, when he resorts to despotic measures to restore social order, he unwittingly provokes conspiracies, treasons, revolution, madness, and the sacrifice of his life.

In these later works of the 1930s, Jooss apparently wished to test the capacity of dance to construct unprecedentedly complex narratives and psychological states. The narratives became more convoluted, but the movements of the dancers did not: his repertoire of movements included hardly anything beyond the social codes he had already explored in pre-1933 works. It was thus evident that narrative complexity had little to do with choreographic complexity, semantic density, or expressive power, an indication that Jooss's belief in conventional narrative as the force synthesizing dance and theatre was perhaps excessively optimistic. *Pandora* (1944, music: Gerhard) nevertheless constructed another elaborate allegory, in three acts, in which the beautiful but evil Pandora corrupts the People with her mysterious box. Pandora releases all sorts of monsters on the world and persuades the masses to sacrifice their children to the Machine God; a lone Young Man remains ever-faithful to the virtuous but remote Psyche. Only in a context of complete destruction and desolation is it possible for the Young Man to assert power over the People and banish Pandora. But this sort of morality drama, saturated with intricate plot twists, could not disguise a fundamentally ruralistic oversimplification of tensions between leader and group, with "good" authority over the People dependent above all on loyalty to the unerotic visions of innocence cultivated by youth rather than on desire for a magnitude of love that "insincere," conflict-ridden social codes deny people. Jooss was skillful in exposing socially coded movement, but he lacked the imagination, so strong in Wigman, to perceive the power of movement to differentiate bodies, to free bodies from social codes; he failed to create in movement, rather than in a story, a convincing representation of human salvation and freedom.

Like every gifted student of Laban, Jooss attracted many strongly talented dancers (especially men, perhaps to a greater degree than any other Weimar dance personality), including Karl Bergeest (1904–1983), Jens Keith (1898–1958), Rudolf Pescht (1904–1959), Ernst Uthoff (b. 1904), Hans Zullig (b. 1914), Elsa Kahl (b. 1902), Trude Pohl (1907–1975), Lisa Czobel (b. 1906), Frida Holst, and Heinz Rosen (1908–1972). His company contained dancers from Poland, Latvia, Switzerland, France, England, Hungary, Holland, Austria, and the United States (Agnes de Mille collaborated with the Ballets Jooss in New York in 1942); no doubt his devotion to accessible theatrical narrative enhanced his appeal for young dancers wary of the great risks involved in pursuing more abstract or experimental forms of dance, with their smaller and more cultish sense of community. After World War II, when Leeder went to Chile, the doctrine of building dance out of socially coded movement spread further through the international dispersion of Jooss's disciples. But it was in Germany that his influence reached most deeply, for in postwar Germany he appeared almost alone in proposing that dance exposed contemporary social realities by being "about" the very movements that constructed social identities and relations in the world inhabited by the spectator. As he once remarked in *Der Scheinwerfer* (11/12, March 1928, 23): "But the dancer himself . . . experiences the highest human happiness: to rise up out of the pitiful, sorrowful realm of the small, personal quotidian life and to ascend, with body and soul, as a human of flesh and blood, into the heaven of all religions: the eternal fantasy." Thus, even the effort to produce a sober, "objective" critique of the social basis for movement and bodily expressivity carried with it a grandiose hunger for ecstasy.

LOLA ROGGE

The synthesis of *Ausdruckstanz* and theatre through dramatic narrative could take another form than that demonstrated by Jooss. Instead of building narratives out of socially coded movements, modern dance could build them out of idealized or historically coded movements that nevertheless did not derive from either ballet or "nature" as Jooss understood that term. Such a strategy defined the work of Lola Rogge (1908–1990). She was born in Altona near Hamburg and spent virtually her entire career in Hamburg. Her choreographic output was small, but she favored large-scale, ambitious projects, which she liked to revise and perfect. She first studied dance at age twelve under Gertrud Zimmermann, and in 1923 she decided to become a dancer after performing a solo in a school dramatization of poems from Goethe's *West-östlichen Divan*, at which time she encountered a student familiar with Laban's new school in Hamburg. Rogge's parents opposed a career in dance for their daughter, believing that a career in hospitality services was more suitable. Her mother expressed alarm at the sight of bare-chested men in Laban's studio; however, the daughter displayed an even stronger will. She arranged for Jenny Gertz, a Laban disciple devoted to the instruction of children, to give another demonstration, which succeeded in persuading Rogge's parents to let her begin study at the Laban school in 1925. During the war, Rogge's health became delicate as a result of nutritional deficiencies, and she experienced a very sheltered life and education. Yet her dance aesthetic evolved toward a heroic-athletic image of the body, though she did not construct an especially hygienic attitude. One might even say that Rogge showed greater interest in representing a powerful will than in manifesting a healthy spirit.

At the Laban school, where she claimed she "discovered" her body, she became active in the movement choir experiments that contributed so abundantly to Laban's appeal and mystique. In these Laban treated the group as an abstract form, full of elaborate, geometric configurations detached from any conventional narrative context. What excited Rogge about movement choirs was the possibility of becoming a choir leader, who could "carry with her the group dancers, draw them into her sphere" (PS 29). But her sense of community was more cultured than cultic and did not altogether fit the aim of the movement choirs, with their constant, improvised appropriation of new spaces and their frequent indifference toward the idea of an audience. For Rogge, the group was the image of a powerful controlling will, the creation of a leader, whose desires manifested themselves in narrative movement that surpassed the strength of ballet technique or "systems" of modern dance to constrain them. But she first established her own identity as a leader by opening, at age nineteen, a school in Hamburg—the Lola Rogge Laban School, which still exists. Her first students came from elite Hamburg families, daughters of her parents' friends; she innovated by introducing courses whereby employees of major Hamburg firms, such as Shell, Reemtsma, and Deutsche Bank, could study bodily movement through corporate-sponsored cultural and development programs. She also devised schemes that permitted working-class families to take movement courses for very nominal fees, with some subsidiary support from labor unions. In 1928 she initiated regular free days for schoolchildren, who received an entire day of instruction and exercise free. She started doing morning radio broadcasts of gymnastic exercises in 1930.

In 1929, Rogge began collaborating with the Social Democratic Party and Hamburg ballet mistress Olga Brandt-Knack in coordinating lay movement choir activities. This led, in 1931, to her first large-scale ensemble piece for the public, scenes from Albert Talhoff's expressionistic "vision for word, dance, and light," *Totenmal,* a choric memorial to soldiers killed in the Great War. Wigman had provoked much controversy the previous year at the Munich Dance Congress with her own grandiose multimedia version of Talhoff's poem; Rogge's treatment of the material was far less experimental, complex, or spectacular. She confined the action within a small proscenium stage and set the unmasked movement choir against painted expressionist backdrops, whereas Wigman had employed a huge space permitting antiphonal and contrapuntal relations between various masked speech and movement choirs, as well as highly abstract lighting effects achieved partially through a color organ. Rogge herself danced the role Wigman had assumed, the female spirit of life in dialogue with Death, but she apparently stressed the motherly dimension of the role at the expense of the erotic (PS 44–47; Peters 4). Nevertheless, the production received much acclaim; indeed, one can say that Rogge never created a work that was a failure with the public. Her next project, done in 1931 with her students, definitely thematized the identity of the leader by being a choreographed enactment, with original music by Willi Jansen, of the medieval story of the Pied Piper. The same year she married Hans Meyer, a businessman with a great affection for playing the piano. He added his wife's surname to his own and became Hans Meyer-Rogge. When he lost his job with an export firm during the economic crisis of 1930, he assumed significant managerial responsibility for the Rogge school and became a kind of shadowy collaborator with his wife on the creation of her dance works.

Thyll, with original orchestral music by Claus-Eberhard Clausius, appeared in 1933. This long dance drama in four scenes, from a scenario by Meyer-Rogge, depicted the Breughelesque adventures of the Flemish folk hero Thyll, danced by Rogge herself. The vagabond Thyll exerts a charismatic spell over the carnival-like crowd in a late-medieval Flemish town, performing a dance with two swords and other acrobatic feats. Upon learning of his father's death, he seeks his beloved, Nele, but their paths never seem to cross (Rogge constructed a curious, spatially distanced duet between them to signify their attraction to each other without their ever becoming a couple). In a dream Thyll sees the foreign oppressors of his country, then hears the voice of his conscience, which is also "the voice of the people." "Only when farmers and citizens are united, only then will Flanders be free. If Avarice, Envy, and Indifference hinder the work of unification, Thyll must die and with him freedom" (PS 56). When Thyll awakes, he gathers about him an expanding group of insurgents, who march on the town in the most spectacular scene in the drama, the "Geusenmarsch," or march of the Protestant "beggars." Thyll remains outside while the crowd pours into the city. At a patrician ball featuring a children's gavotte and a nobles' pavanne, Thyll sees the disunity produced again by Avarice, Envy and Indifference. He therefore dies of despair—but who can bury the Flemish spirit? "You can sleep, but die?—never!"

Rogge used spoken narration to clarify some actions, such as the appearance of the disunifying vices in black, yellow, and gray. Unlike Jooss, she did not build narrative complexity through exaggeration of socially conditioned movements in daily life. Rather, narrative evolved through movements rooted in athletics, gymnastics, and military maneuvers, although these tended to signify something other than physical prowess or exertion. Rogge's movement style was far less pantomimic than Jooss's but always dramatic. She derived many of her movements from archaic or traditional dance forms, such as the gavotte, the pavanne, the Teutonic sword dance, and various German folk dances; few choreographers displayed as much imagination in making use of march rhythms. Her ensemble movements were consistently choric, faithful to the Labanian concept of the movement choir, which implied all sorts of complex geometric patterns and formal tensions between groups (in circles, countercircles, spirals, converging diagonals, colliding rows, phalanxes) but little development of individuals (or leaders) within groups and little effort to show transformations of groups into new communities. With the disbanding of the Social Democratic Party movement choirs by the Nazis and the subsequent pressure to depict groups in unison formations, Rogge enjoyed little opportunity to explore deeper dynamics or contradictory tensions defining group movement. However, the regime did not intrude much on her completely private school, never even reproaching her for excluding mandatory courses on ideology and race theory from her curriculum.

For the Hamburg State Theatre, Rogge choreographed numerous dance interludes inserted into otherwise strictly dramatic productions, and her school participated regularly in civic festivals held by the city of Hamburg. But these activities seemed incidental to her next big project, *Amazonen* (1935), a three-act dance adaptation of Heinrich von Kleist's monumental tragic drama of female warriors, *Penthesilea* (1808), which already had been turned into an exciting expressionist opera in 1926 by Othmar Schoeck and a luxuriantly eccentric comedy by Ilse Langner (1932). A passionate student of ancient Greek mythology and archeology, Meyer-Rogge wrote the scenario; the music consisted of various compositions by Georg Friedrich Handel, whom Rogge regarded, curiously, as a superior composer of dance music. In the first act, set in the mysterious, cultic female state of the Temple of Diana, the High Priestess bestows the golden bow of power upon the newly elected Queen of the Amazons, danced by Rogge. In the second act the Amazons encounter intruding Greeks, led by Achilles. A great battle ensues, with the outcome decided in a duel between the Queen and Achilles. The Queen wins, and the Greeks become prisoners of the Amazons. In the final act, the Amazons celebrate the festival of roses, the culmination of which entails the marriage of the Queen to Achilles, with whom she has fallen passionately in love. But Amazon law forbids female desire for the male, and the High Priestess demands that the Queen return the bow. When the Queen resists and declares her intention to crown Achilles king, the High Priestess stabs her, and she dies in the arms of her beloved. All the women vacate the scene, leaving "men as the future rulers of the new state."

Rogge's productions established a powerful intersection of erotic desires and aggressive drives. But in Kleist's tragedy Penthesilea mistakenly kills Achilles, then literally dies of a broken heart; in Rogge's work, threats to the authority of the female community came from women themselves (the High Priestess), not from men. The choric movement was monumentally ritualistic, making extensive use of march patterns and rhythms, saluting gestures, and tensions between sinking obedience and triumphant invocation, with mass movements occasionally interrupted by grandiose solos (bow dance) and duets (Achilles/Queen duel) (Figure 61). The dancers wore sleek, art deco versions of Hellenic costumes, with male warriors, in armor, strongly differentiated from the more lightly clad female warriors. Except for the sacred bow, Rogge declined to use any shields, spears, or swords, preferring, apparently, to suggest martial prowess entirely through bodily gesture, although she claimed to seek a "realistic" image of antiquity (PS 87).

Rogge risked a great deal of money on the production, but *Amazonen* proved enormously popular in the Third Reich, impressing high-level officials at the Berlin dance festival of 1935. As Meyer-Rogge remarked: "The tragedy of community differs from the tragedy of the individual in that it places the hero as the basis for action in the people, that is, it identifies the hero with a necessary moral ideal," which reinforces unity of identity rather than accommodates difference (PS 86). However, Rogge's enthusiasm for classical antiquity dated back to her school days, when she wrote papers on excavations at Pompeii, using books in her parents' library (17), and it is doubtful that she paid much attention to Nazi ideology in shaping her dance drama. After performing *Amazonen* in several occupied countries during the war, she was able to revive it with equal success in 1947 and again in the 1950s.

Her next major work, the four-part *Mädcheninsel* (1939), also featured music by Handel and explored much the same domain as *Amazonen*. It functioned as the second part of a trilogy that was to have concluded with a great dance drama about the Trojan War (however, the outbreak of the real European war prevented this from materializing). Meyer-Rogge's scenario depicted the evolution of Achilles into a warrior. The first scene

shows the birth of Achilles to Thetis and Peleus. The oracle prophesies that
Achilles will lead a short, glorious life or a long, peaceful but unremark-
able existence, and Thetis must choose his fate. When representatives of
the underworld arrive with gifts of helmets, shields, and swords, Thetis
determines that Achilles shall not follow the life of a warrior. So he grows
up on an island of girls, wearing girl's clothes and playing girl games.
(Rogge herself danced the role of Achilles.) In one game the girls blindfold him, but suddenly a group of Greek warriors appears, bearing shields
with doves imprinted on them. The girls flee, leaving Achilles alone; when
a soldier removes the blindfold, Achilles sees the warriors and shields,
becomes aroused by their dark challenge to him, and begins to test his
martial prowess in a powerful combat duet with shields between himself
and another soldier. He displays superior instincts as a warrior, and the soldiers express their admiration by bestowing the famous armor on him and
lifting him up onto their shields. The women then return to the scene,
shifting their allegiance from Thetis to Achilles, who boards the ship for
Troy and a glorious doom.

As in *Amazonen*, Rogge relied here on choric movement patterns to sustain dramatic interest, with groups deployed in circles, friezelike rows,
squares, and phalanxes: "The choric movements occurred chiefly through
striding marches or feathery, skipping runs with raised arm gestures" (110).
Not surprisingly, the Nazi-controlled press bestowed lavish praise upon the
work, but Rogge herself saw nothing distinctly fascist in her production,
which she viewed as an account of a figure moved by an "inner necessity,"
destiny, rather than will (109). But this explanation was peculiarly ironic
from a woman for whom group dance was, as Stöckemann repeatedly
asserts, the expression of an "iron will." In any case, she had no trouble
reviving the dance after the war.

The war itself no more disturbed her "will" than had the political up-
heavals of the previous twenty years. Following the surrender, she became
prodigiously active in restoring vitality to the Hamburg cultural scene and
in establishing the prominence of her school within that scene. At the same
time, she raised four children. She produced two more large dance dramas,
Vita Nostra (1950) and *Neue Lübecker Totentanz* (1956), but in these works
she turned for inspiration to images from the late Middle Ages rather than
from classical antiquity. In both of these productions, the medieval image
of Death (a skeleton painted onto the body stocking of a male dancer)
became the power driving and defining the identity of the group. In these
later works it became evident that for Rogge the will, as manifested through
leadership and control over groups, was synonymous with a desire to face
death, a determination to test the strength of the inevitable. Dance drama
was for Rogge the ideal medium for establishing the body (rather than the
state) as the decisive site of conflict between the will and the inevitable. She

came from a deeply respected, almost puritanical, patrician family governed by an ambitious ideal of civic honor and dignity. This sense of honor she brought to dance in perhaps greater degree than any other dance personality of the Weimar era. Yet her art was not without ambiguities in its images of a will, of a body, of entire groups seemingly "undetermined" by the great political turbulence of the times in which they lived.

Theatre Dancing

Though Jooss and Rogge obviously saw *Ausdruckstanz* as moving toward an ultimate identity as dance-theatre, the relation between dance and theatre in the Weimar Republic was in reality a power struggle in which modern dance attempted to appropriate some of the terrain occupied by the established, subsidized institutions for opera, ballet, and literary drama. The attempt succeeded for the most part, but the reason for the appropriation was as much economic as aesthetic. The institutionalization of *Ausdruckstanz* occurred in three large phases. In the first phase (1910–1923), dance established its expressive power and credibility through solo concerts, which revealed the authority of dance to construct distinct artistic personalities. The second phase (1924–1929), marked by the opening of an amazing number of schools, witnessed the expansion of dance as a field of study. But by 1929 it was no longer possible for the schools themselves to provide careers for all their graduates. Moreover, the public had now seen a great deal of dance, and talented dance artists (rather than teachers) believed that, if they were to sustain the interest of audiences, they needed access to greater resources and virtuosity than the schools could offer. Thus, the third phase (1930–1935) entailed a self-conscious competition for subsidized positions within the huge network of publicly funded theatres throughout the nation. The program actually was well underway before 1930, with Laban and Wigman students being especially aggressive in obtaining theatrical positions as choreographers: Olga Brandt-Knack in Hamburg (1922), Skoronel in Oberhausen (1924), Jooss and then Jens Keith in Münster (1924–1925), Georgi in Gera (1925), Max Terpis in Berlin (1924), Anne Grünert in Duisberg (1925), Edith Bielefeld in Karlsruhe (1926), Günther Hess (1903–1979) in Hagen (1925), Lizzie Maudrick in Berlin (1928), Claire Eckstein in Darmstadt (1928), Ellen von Frankenberg in Aachen (1927), Manda van Kreibig in Darmstadt (1925), Ruth Loeser in

Düsseldorf (1929), and Laban himself in Mannheim (1922) and Berlin (1930).

HEINRICH KRÖLLER AND ELLEN PETZ

In spite of the invading action of these and other personalities, the history of *Ausdruckstanz* in the theatre remains obscure and almost absurdly under-documented. Even the history of German ballet during these years is seldom anything more than a listing of names and titles (e.g., Erben), despite the fact that Germany officially possessed the largest system of ballet companies in the world. Yet ballet might just as well have not existed at all, so powerful was the hold of *Ausdruckstanz* on the dance imagination of the time. Powerfully influential dance critics such as Brandenburg, Böhme, Giese, Fischer, Lämmel, and Suhr tended to regard ballet as a dead and distinctly "un-German" art, and it is still something of a mystery as to why the Germans insisted on subsidizing a mode of dance in which they consistently failed to achieve any international or even national distinction. Gifted ballet dancers were hardly lacking, but imaginative choreographers trained in Paris, Italy, or Copenhagen definitely were. Curiously, the whole strategy of *Ausdruckstanz* to take over the ballet companies depended on a reconciliation between modern dance and ballet, with the schools making strenuous efforts to incorporate ballet technique into the curriculum.

The ballet world remained quaintly insulated from the storm of body consciousness that had swept over Central Europe even before World War I. Traditionalists acted as if modern dance advocates were hysterically unreasonable in asserting that ballet's rigid regulation of bodily expressivity emerged from a deeper—and darkly ideological—anxiety toward both modernity and the signifying power of the body. An exception was Heinrich Kröller (1880–1930), ballet director in Frankfurt (1915), Munich (1917–1930), Berlin (1919–1922), and Vienna (1922–1928). He openly promoted the idea that ballet and *Ausdruckstanz* could evolve only in relation to each other, rather than independently, and his susceptibility to at least a modern look on the ballet stage brought him invitations to choreograph in Prague, Stockholm, and Italy (see Mlakar). During World War I, in Munich, he apparently won admiration for his refusal to subordinate group movement to star solos and for his determination to make ballet an art form that conveyed serious meaning rather than a mere display of physical virtuosity (Vettermann, 217). But much more information about his work must surface before a strong statement about his significance can appear. He scored an enormous hit in Berlin in 1921 with his version of Richard Strauss's *Josephs Legende* (Suhr, *Tänzerin*); Strauss himself was so impressed that he persuaded Kröller to give up his duties in Berlin and direct the ballet of the Vienna State Opera.

Kröller collaborated with Strauss on further successes, including *Couperin Suite* (1923) and *Schlagobers* (1924), but he was anything but happy in Vienna. Reactionary elements within the opera, supported in part by conductor Franz Schalk, persistently undermined his efforts to introduce some of the more modernistic (Stravinsky) productions of the Ballets Russes, let alone strategies affiliated with *Ausdruckstanz*. Munich was much more hospitable. There he choreographed bold productions of the Bartók-Balazs *Wooden Prince* (1924), the Krenek-Balazs *Mammon* (1927), and John Alden Carpenter's *Skyscrapers* (1927). But these were "bold" in large part because of their expressionistic or constructivist set designs. It remains unclear how modern Kröller was in his conception of group dynamics or bodily movement, though he freely acknowledged his interest in Laban's ideas about movement choirs. In *Mammon*, for example, he included a most intriguing image of a graceful huddle of women in conventional ballet slippers and tutus menaced by a phalanx of masked, pointing, caped demonic men, while another, smaller group of dwarfish, servile humans crept between these two groups. It therefore seems possible that Kröller created compelling dance theatre by self-consciously making the tension between ballet and the movement choir a dramatic feature of the performance itself.

Another puzzling figure from the world of ballet was the mysterious Ellen Petz (aka Ellen von Cleve-Petz). She studied ballet in Berlin, Budapest, and London, with an interlude at the Mensendieck school in Berlin, and this international education allowed her aesthetic to exude an aura of cosmopolitan refinement, her dancers being "representatives of real aristocratic art," according to a clipping from the *Leipziger Tageblatt* (13 August 1921). As early as 1917, she attracted attention for her taste in luxurious costumes and for her darkly glamorous Amazon solo dance (Török 11). In 1919 she formed the Petz-Kainer Ballet with the expressionist artist Ludwig Kainer, who designed the decor for her productions. In the early 1920s she toured numerous cities in Germany, as well as Budapest and Vienna, with a corps of six female dancers. Kainer's decor introduced Caligariesque distortions of scenic context that were otherwise lacking in ballet culture, and Petz contributed innovative, worldly scenarios, as in *Triumph der Mode* (1920), which depicted the "liberation of Queen Fashion through the tempestuous Prince Fantasy" (*Elegante Welt*, 9/5, 3 March 1920, 7). She moved into more darkly decorative moods with *Eifersucht* (1921), *Phantom* (1921), *Sklavin Reich* (1922), *Groteske* (1922), and *Hiawatha* (1923). Petz apparently liked to keep her dancers on pointe, but she did not have enough performers to stage full-length ballets. So in her concerts she presented several small, entirely original stories (no adaptations) in quite idiosyncratic settings. She always subordinated the display of virtuosity to the necessity of telling a strange story.

But she soon wearied of running a private company and accepted the position of ballet mistress at Dresden. With more than twenty dancers at her disposal, she produced the opulent *Die Elixiere des Teufels* (1925), with music by Jaap Kool and almost lascivious Oriental costumes. Then she attempted a "dance symphony" (1925, music: Resznicek). Even more intriguing was her *Spielzeug* (1928), an abridged version of Tchaikovsky's *Nutcracker* using emphatically geometrized Bauhaus set designs by Oskar Schlemmer (DS 181–183, 325). At Dresden she made Helge Peters-Pawlinin her partner, and in 1929, in Brussels, they produced an even more unusual dance experiment, *La Masque de cuir.* This production employed as decor the projection of scenes from movies starring Ronald Colman and Vilma Banky, who were popular screen lovers between 1926 and 1928. Petz and Pawlinin apparently performed solo/duet dance commentaries on the screen lovers to the accompaniment of music by Mozart (Colman) and Brahms (Banky) ("Ellen Petz"). In subsequent years, Petz's already shrouded career became maddeningly obscure. She resurfaced in 1938, when Queen Elena of Italy and Ethiopia invited her to present dances with a vaguely medieval aura in Rome, but by then her decorative blurring of differences between ballet and *Ausdruckstanz* had led to work about which one must locate still hidden sources of information.

THEORETICAL POSITIONS

As the careers of Kröller and Petz indicate those who attempted to integrate ballet and *Ausdruckstanz* developed vague artistic identities, and their impact was considerably less obvious or even noticeable than that of the hard-core expressionist dancers. Still, by 1929 the appropriation of ballet seemed a necessary facet of modern dance's appropriation of theatre. Moreover, appropriation entailed more than approval of ballet's rigid regulation of bodily expressivity through the classical on pointe "positions"—it entailed the assumption that a greater expressive power for dance depended on its success in constructing sustained, comprehensible narratives of sufficient complexity to test the capacity of the spectator to read kinetic signs. In short, the appropriation of ballet and theatre implied a devaluation of the abstraction and montage aesthetics defining the domain of *Ausdruckstanz.*

Naturally, these aesthetic implications, driven by economic objectives, led to interesting theoretical controversies. As early as 1922, Hans W. Fischer argued that expressionist dance created its own forms of narrative, forms that, because they focused perception on the body rather than on costume or on "objective" systems of movement, were not pantomimic ("Tanztraum"). But this argument did not explain how modern dance

should appropriate established theatrical institutions if the institutionalization of dance depended on narrative values defined largely by ballet. By
contrast, in *Das ekstatische Theater* (1924), Felix Emmel asserted that contemporary literary drama required a new mode of performance in which
speech and gesture emerged out of "rhythms of destiny," an "ecstasy of the
blood" achieved by bringing acting and directing closer to dance and choreographic design, as in his own production of *Der Bogen des Odysseus* (1922)
in Weimar (30–33). However, at the Munich Dance Congress in 1930,
Emmel declared that in the literary theatre dance must serve the aim of the
text and come from within it rather than, as in the work of the Russian directors Meyerhold and Tairov, being imposed upon it. Thus, the incorporation
of dance into the literary theatre would require dramatists to write plays
embodying a strong dance consciousness ("Tanz und Schauspiel"). Gustav
Grund, a lay movement choir director for youth groups in Hamburg, took
almost the opposite position: in both the literary theatre and the opera, the
written text functioned as music that motivated bodily movement. Dance
was not an illustration of the words nor a pantomimic representation of the
word referents; rather, it was a kind of dramatic commentary on the words,
often in tension with them, and therefore did not depend on either the
author or the text for its inclusion in performance (*Die vierte Wand*, No. 3,
1927, 7–10).

At the Magdeburg Dance Congress of 1927, Hans Brandenburg
explained that dance was the "primal cell of all theatre" and that both dance
and theatre should strive toward a common goal or aesthetic identity. He
insisted that modern dance not only had every right to move from the concert podiums to its own deserved zone of the subsidized theatres but even
should constitute an expected element of all literary theatre ("Tanz und
Theater"). Gertrud Bodenwieser in Vienna adopted a more practical attitude. She hardly believed that dance and drama could form a single, unified art form, for the difference between the choreographic and literary
imaginations was far greater than nonpractitioners supposed. But because
choreographic imagination was as significant for performance as literary
imagination, she displayed no hesitation about inserting dances into plays,
even where they were not intended, a strategy rejected by Emmel in his
1930 statement (see Stefan 58–59).

In *Tanzkunst* (1926), Fritz Böhme grasped that modern dance had transformed relations between body, movement, and space to such an extent
that the subsidized theatre could no longer accommodate it; modern dance
required a new architecture altogether. The further evolution of *Ausdruckstanz* depended on freeing it from conventional ideas of a stage and situating it within radically different architectural forms so that the visual dimension of performance no longer remained confined within the picture frame
of a proscenium (198–207). Laban had already expressed this sentiment

with his proposal for a Gothic, cupola "dance temple" (*Die Schönheit*, 22/1, 1926, 2–4; 43–48). But by 1928 it was obvious that new theatre architecture of any sort, let alone specifically for dance, would not appear soon in the Weimar Republic; dance would have to content itself with appropriating a prewar notion of performance space, which implied some form of reconciliation with ballet. At the Essen Dance Congress of 1928, Kurt Jooss offered a distinction between *Tanztheater* and *Theatertanz*. *Theatertanz* referred to dance as an element contained within a larger dramatic narrative, such as Salome's dance in Oscar Wilde's play. *Tanztheater* involved drama created entirely out of and for dance, and it was the strongest basis for dance's appropriation of theatre. Thus, dance theatre, as defined by *Ausdruckstanz*, entailed new forms of danced narrative (scenarios and themes) rather than new relations between the body and space or even new methods of dancing. In another argument, Fred Hildenbrandt claimed that the institutionalization of the modern dance impulse actually meant the appropriation of the acrobatic dancing found in cabarets and revues and of contemporary social dance forms—a not altogether eccentric idea, but one that hardly resonated in the world of "serious" modern dance (*Der Scheinwerfer*, 11/12, March 1928, 24–26). Yet another view came from Rudolf Kölling, first solo dancer of the Berlin State Opera, who contended that as a member of a ballet corps, a dancer had to cultivate a much more complex consciousness of theatrical context than prevailed in modern dance: the dancer had to calculate every bodily movement in relation to every detail of costume, lighting, decor, music, ensemble, and special effect. The ballet dancer worked under much greater pressure than did dancers in the school companies, for "as an opera dancer, one must think of a thousand things, must overcome constraints, master obstacles. Only in this way will we succeed in conquering the theatre" (*Die Schallkiste*, 3/9, September 1928, 7–8).

The influence of Dalcroze no doubt contributed to many dancers' hesitation to "conquer" the theatre. He denounced the pathological effects on the body caused by the exorbitant demands of theatrical dance, especially ballet. Nevertheless, the Hellerau-Laxenburg school, guided by Valeria Kratina (1892–1983), developed its own form of dance theatre favoring open-air productions of dance dramas on themes of classical mythology cherished by Dalcroze himself—although in 1923 Kratina did stage the German premiere of Bartok's *The Wooden Prince* (Chladek, 54–59). In the late 1920s she choreographed the Laxenburg dancers in open-air dance versions of Greek tragedies in the amphitheatre at Syracuse, Sicily. Then, in 1930, she accepted appointment as ballet mistress in Breslau and Karlsruhe (1933–1937), later shifting to Dresden (1938–1944). But in her case, too, a serious assessment of her significance depends on the excavation of some substantial information about her work. Like Lola Rogge, she apparently sought to create a monumental image of classical culture that was free of

both ballet classicism and the excessively feminized Grecian ideal of improvised "naturalness" promoted by Isadora Duncan. Kratina's work suggested
that dance theatre became institutionalized as *Ausdruckstanz* when it
evolved independently of the state theatres, even if she herself eventually
moved on to official positions.

Wigman perhaps believed even more strongly in this position. No doubt
the political intrigues that prevented her from receiving the ballet mistress
position in Dresden in 1920 contributed to her distrust of the official theatres and of dance theatre itself, for her concept of the group was probably
too cultic to flourish within the complex political apparatus of a state theatre. She did choreograph dances for Hans Pfitzner's opera *Die Rose von
Liebesgarten* (1921) in Hannover and for a Dresden production of *A Midsummer Night's Dream* (1922), but obviously she saw no future in this sort of
work. By 1929 she had disbanded her own school group because she felt
she had reached an impasse with regard to further development of expressionist group dancing. She tried to resolve the crisis by producing one of
the largest and most complex group pieces of the century, the controversial
Totenmal (1930), which enjoyed an unprecedented run of ten weeks in
Munich following its premiere at the Dance Congress. The production
entailed an elaborate intersection of personnel and logistical support from
a variety of organizations, as well as a stadiumlike performance space. But if
Totenmal represented the future of expressionist dance theatre, one could
not expect the state theatre system to supply the resources for it without
introducing a radical change in production practices, and subsequently no
one, including Wigman, attempted an ensemble production of similar scale
or complexity. At the Essen Dance Congress of 1928, she gave a lengthy
statement in which she argued that the aims and working methods of expressionist dancing and theatre dancing were so different that expressionist
dance could "conquer" the theatre only through a radical revision of what
theatre is: "We want not only dance in the theatre, but a rhythmically propelled and propelling theatre" (MS 77–82). In practice, she meant that
expressionist dance theatre had to create its own institutions rather than try
to fit into the prewar system, a strategy that was not convincing for some of
her own brightest students, including Yvonne Georgi, Darja Collin, and Max
Terpis, who accepted the necessity of accommodating ballet technique.

However, Margarethe Wallmann (b. 1904), director of the prosperous
Wigman school in Berlin since 1927, attempted to reinforce the complex
mode of production for *Totenmal*. In 1930, in Berlin, she produced the
hugely successful (or, at least, far less controversial) *Orfeus Dionysos* (music:
Glück), a vast and violent dance drama with a scenario by Felix Emmel. It
employed an enormous corps of dancers and musicians (including Ted
Shawn, Hans Weidt, and Mila Cirul) recruited from a variety of sources;
Wallman herself danced the part of Euridice. The piece contained no con-

cessions to ballet technique, even though Wallmann had studied ballet in her native Vienna, but her choreography for the savage tribe of female Furies was so complicated that she required many more rehearsals than a regular full-length ballet. Her group movements avoided synchronized or unison effects and involved convoluted configurations that individualized each dancer, creating a very turbulent image of an ecstatic community in violent contrast to the almost stately composure of the ecstatic couple (see Mueller, "3. Deutscher," 23). For Wallmann, the ecstatic couple was an illusion destroyed by the ecstatic community of Furies, with communal ecstasy reaching its peak in mass violence, in the tearing apart of Orfeus.

Wallmann continued her complex, large-scale group choreography in another violent "mystery play," *Das jüngste Gericht* (1931, music: Handel), which premiered at the Salzburg Festival, where she was an annual participant during the 1930s (Figure 62). Here she situated her apocalyptic vision in a vaguely biblical context inhabited by allegorical figures such as the Rich Youth, the Poor Girl, the Spirit of Darkness, the Activist. The success of this piece urged her to break with Wigman, from whom she had already become somewhat distanced after a difficult experience teaching the Wigman doctrine at the Denishawn school in the United States 1928–1931). With the advent of the Third Reich, Wallmann, who was Jewish, returned to Vienna, where she became ballet mistress of the Vienna State Opera and director of its ballet school. Though she devised intriguing, original ballet scenarios such as *Fanny Elssler* (1934) and *Der liebe Augustin* (1936), her work became distinctly less intriguing than it had been before 1933. In 1939 she migrated to Buenos Aires, where she directed operas at the Teatro Colon, a task she pursued after the war in Rome and Milan, where she still lives.

CLAIRE ECKSTEIN

Another Wigman student who did remarkable work in the theatre was Claire Eckstein (1904–1994). In Munich she met the gifted scenic designer Wilhelm Reinking, whom she soon married, and he recommended her to Heinrich Strohm, director of the opera theatre in Würzburg. Impressed with her extravagant sense of humor, Strohm hired her to choreograph Hindemith's ballet *Der Dämon* (1926), then Kool's *Der Leierkasten* (1927) and Rimsky Korsakoff's *Scheherazade* (1927), for which Reinking did the scenery. Along with stage director Arthur Maria Rabenalt, Eckstein and Reinking moved to Darmstadt, where from 1927 to 1931 Eckstein, in addition to her usual duties for the opera and operetta, staged several comic ballets with a distinctive modernist ambience: Massarani's *Der arme Guerino* (1928), Milhaud's *Le boeuf sur le toit* (1928), Satie's *Parade* (1929), Schmitt's *Ein höher Beamter* (1930), and two ballets for which she herself composed the music: *Soirèe* (1930) and *Die Gestrandeten* (1930). During these years, American dancer Edwin Denby (1903–1983) was her partner-collaborator. However, in 1930 the Berlin Kroll Opera invited Reinking to design *The Barber of Seville*, and this opportunity led to others for him in the city. Eckstein brought several of her Darmstadt pieces to Berlin (1931), but these did not open up possibilities for her in a theatre culture suffering from severe austerity measures. She and Reinking divorced the same year. In 1933 she danced in Berlin cabaret productions of Werner Finck and Erika Mann, but she did not return to choreography until 1942, when she arranged dances for Helmut Käutner's film *Anuschka*, shot in Rome and Prague. Her final choreographies were for two musical films directed by Rabenalt in Yugoslavia in 1954 and 1955. According to Reinking, she could "no longer open herself up without her partner Denby" (176). But what did Denby— or, more accurately, what did the peculiar collaborative environment in Würzburg and Darmstadt, with Reinking and Rabenalt—bring out in her? "She had the gift of being able to observe the movements of people and to arrange these observations into dance-like gestures, in which the bearing and character of these observed persons became strikingly revealed in a lightly caricatured or at least exaggerated form" (63).

It sounds as if she was close to Kurt Jooss in her aesthetic. However, Jooss never achieved the comic intensity that Eckstein brought to grotesque dance, though his caricaturizations of ordinary movements often carried him into the realm of the grotesque. Eckstein caricatured idiosyncratic movements of persons rather than of social classes or of socially conditioned modes of gesture. She exposed the absurdities of individual rather than social identity and therefore also exposed the power of dance to treat social norms as sources of humor rather than anxiety. Moreover, having a designer for a husband, she relied much more than Jooss on complex scenic effects to construct comic perceptions. In *Oben und unten,* Reinking's set depicted a building under construction; the construction workers (in blackface) moved on the stage, on the ramp leading to the second story of the building, and on the second story, handling boards, buckets, and building tools. *Die Gestrandeten* featured a bizarre collection of dancers stranded on a desert island, where they perched on small tables, lounged on pillows of "sand" under a palm tree, sewed, fixed meals, and prayed before an altar. The stage thus became fragmented into idiosyncratic zones defined by individual dancers and their props. *Neues vom Tage* (1929), an opera by Hindemith, was set in the headquarters of a newspaper, with dancers in business suits working at copy desks before a three-story edifice containing rows of cubicles and workers (Rabenalt 441). Offenbach's *Die schöne Galatee* (1929) showed dancers impersonating mannequins in display windows. Eckstein obviously delighted in pieces that used complicated or not particularly danceable costumes; in *Soirèe,* for example, the performers wore elaborate formal garb of the 1890s. She constantly played with Denby's image by out-fitting him in wigs, eccentric makeup, extravagant paddings, and whimsical accessories such as a monocle. Probably no other choreographer of the era was as fond of dances in which dancers wore heeled shoes or laced boots. Many of her dancers were actors, and she sometimes incorporated their voices into her works to create a "sort of sound painting, as if one heard the members of a grand society all speaking and perhaps the ladies laughing but cannot understand any individual" (Reinking 108). It was therefore through the curious movements of the body that individuality revealed itself.

But Eckstein, though entirely theatrical in her attitude toward dance, had little interest in subordinating dance to narrative. She constructed her ballets out of material she had already used for dances in operas and operettas, and her dances for the musical stage seldom had any connection with the libretto story. Reinking suggested that her dances were not ballets at all but "little theatre pieces," in which actions and relations between bod-ies unfolded in strange fragments and the climax resulted from the accu-mulation of idiosyncratic effects rather than from the resolution of an intensifying conflict. Yet Berlin theatre critic Herbert Ihering observed that her dances were "in no way abstract, but immediately, directly critical" in a way that was quite remote from the aesthetic of her teacher, Wigman. In performance, Eckstein exuded an exquisitely radiant smile, a luscious, lav-ish pleasure in masquerade.

LABAN IN THE THEATRE

Laban's contribution to theatre dance was much more ambiguous than Eck-stein's, partly because of his own uncertainty regarding his aims in appro-priating the theatre. His perception of group dynamics was shaped by his work with lay movement choirs, which offered all sorts of opportunities to introduce convoluted rhythmic patterns and bodily entanglements. More-over, movement choirs, with their partially gymnastic foundation, seemed to function best when they appropriated almost any space except the the-atre. Laban was more at home in meadows and groves than on the stage. Nevertheless, serious validation of his grandiose ambitions depended on his success in gaining a critical audience among established theatre circles. He therefore devoted much energy to the production of large-scale dance dra-mas for conventional theatres. In these works he sought to affirm the cred-ibility of his "runic" ideas about bodily movement and to present the move-ment choir aesthetic as an alternative to ballet in forming a modern concept of group dynamics in dance. Laban's work for the theatre hardly lacked ambition, but its impact on both dance and theatre remained obscure, and it is difficult to find insightful documentation for any of his dance dramas. During the 1920s, his group choreographies for conventional theatres in Stuttgart, Mannheim, and Hamburg were largely staged by a student unit, Tanzbühne Laban; productions included *Himmel und Erde* (1921), *Die Geblendete* (1921), *Faust II* (1922), *Der schwingende Tempel* (1923), *Gaukelei* (1923), *Agamemnons Tod* (1924), *Dämmernde Rhythmen* (1924), *Don Juan* (1925), *Terpsichore* (1925), *Narrenspiegel* (1926), *Die gebrochene Linie* (1927), *Ritterballett* (1927), and *Titan* (1928). These works, originated not in the theatre but in the school, and Laban took them to various venues, such as, in Hamburg, the Conventgarten, the Deutsches Schauspielhaus, the Circus Busch, and the Schiller Opera. As ballet director in Hamburg (1923–1925), he blurred the distinction between theatre and school, but the blurring in itself suggested considerable ambivalence about grounding a dance aesthetic within the theatre.

As a choreographer, Laban apparently was innovative without being especially imaginative, guided more by theory than artistic insight. He conducted daring experiments but was reluctant to follow up on them with any tenacity. In *Ritterballet* (music: Beethoven), for example, he put a large number of dancers in vaguely medieval costumes with intricate, emblematic black-and-white motifs; when the dancers moved they created a strange kinetic mosaic or jigsaw puzzle, an extravagantly abstract design that nevertheless retained an archaic aura. In *Die Nacht* (1927, music: Kahn), the men wore fezzes, tuxedos, and tights, the women fezzes, eccentric tutus, or skirts with aprons. Movement appeared calculated to produce striking effects through different combinations of costume motifs; design did not evolve in response to an independent movement scheme. But this approach actually resulted in highly complicated movement patterns that subordinated narrative clarity to abstract relations between body, time, and space. In *Drachentöterei* (1924), the dancers wore costumes faintly reminiscent of fairy-tale Orientalism, but the movements, judging from still photos, were extravagantly, expressionistically angular. For Laban, modernity did not imply an image of contemporary society, even if the movements he employed sprang completely from the time in which he lived; rather, he sought an image of modernity that was ahistorical or, as in his Gothic projects, polyhistorical in the decorative context for bodily movement, with costumes and scenes in which signs of different historical eras intersected.

Yet Laban's choreography often lacked narrative or dramatic drive. In reviews (on deposit in the Leipzig dance archive) of Laban's work as ballet director for the Berlin State Opera (1930–1934), Fritz Böhme observed that Laban's choreography lacked "musicality" and expressive power. Laban apparently had difficulty shaping his material and building emotional structures for his pieces, and his productions suffered from prolixity, from a sense of squandered energy that set up grandiose expectations the work could not sustain. *Don Juan* (1925, music: Glück), with Laban himself as the seductive hero, was three hours long, contained numerous intriguing tableaux, and enjoyed performances in numerous cities; however, the piece failed to move audiences with near the efficiency of innumerable smaller works produced by dancers who had access to far fewer resources. Indeed, the discourse provoked by *Don Juan* seemed almost entirely focused on its scale. In spite of his difficulty in telling a story, Laban believed that a dance theatre built around *Ausdruckstanz* depended on devising original scenarios. However, those of his students who accepted theatre appointments found themselves charged with maintaining a repertoire defined and associated with ballet.

OTHER THEATRE CHOREOGRAPHERS

Lizzie Maudrik (1898–1955), ballet director at the Berlin Municipal Opera (1926–1934) and then the German State Opera (1934–1945), studied ballet under Michel Fokine (1880–1942) in Paris before becoming one of Laban's adepts. At the Municipal Opera she encouraged her large ensemble to adopt techniques of expressionist dance, and she guided a ballet corps composed of many dancers with modern dance backgrounds, including Julia Marcus, Jens Keith, Ruth Abramowitsch, George Groke, and Alice Uhlen. But in a 1929 article she firmly declared that an opera house dance corps must always remain subordinate to theatrical objectives and that the opera house was no place for the cultivation of "abstract" or "absolute" dance (MS 43). Thus, her ambition was to apply expressionist dance techniques to the performance of standard works from the ballet repertoire, as in her immensely successful 1930 version of Delibes' *Coppelia* (1870), in which Julia Marcus danced the role of the mayor and Alice Uhlen that of the doll Coppelia. Later, at the State Opera, Maudrik devised ballets with national-historical themes, such as the rococo *Die Barbarina* (1935) and *Bauerischer Tänze* (1935), which continued to incorporate expressionist attitudes toward bodily movement. But, as with Kröller, much more evidence of her work needs to surface before a satisfactory understanding of her significance is possible.

The same is true of two other Laban-educated ballet directors: Olga Brandt-Knack (1885–1978) in Hamburg (1926–1932) and Ruth Loeser in Düsseldorf (1929–1933). Virtually all of Brandt-Knack's choreography was for mainstream opera production, but she put on concerts consisting of dances from seven or eight operas. These concerts, definitely in a modernist vein, had the effect of establishing her opera dances as independent entities, a view not pursued by Maudrik, who always saw dance in relation to a total, theatrical-narrative context. In Düsseldorf, Loeser presided over a corps of eight to thirteen dancers (including one male) presenting old or classical forms of dance in a sardonically modern style. For example, *Suite I und II* (1930), with music by Stravinsky, consisted of several old dance forms: gavotte, Neapolitan, flamenco, balalaika, march, waltz, polka, gallop. But the dancers wore cocktail dresses, with some of the women impersonating men in tuxedos. Scenery was virtually absent from the bare stage, so perception focused entirely on the tension between old dance steps and modern bodily inflections or distortions. No conventional narrative logic linked one dance to the next; rather, an abstract emotional logic governed the piece, making it closer to a theoretical-critical essay than to a story. However, evidence of Loeser's achievements is even more recessed than that of other theatre choreographers. She, like Brandt-Knack, lost her position because of her left-wing affiliations, not because she repudiated narrative in dance or incorporated modern dance techniques.

Maudrik, who prospered during the Third Reich, remained devoted to the authority of narrative but consistently maintained in print that ballet had no serious significance independent of modern dance techniques, even though the Nazis aggressively promoted the necessity of establishing a "German" idea of ballet at the expense of modern dance. Nazi cultural policy favored ballet because ballet was already so rigorously institutionalized in the theatre: it was easier to administer, to regulate, and to standardize than modern dance. Once ballet had come to dominate dance culture, the government exerted complete control over the destinies of dancers.

Despite the lack of any serious understanding of dance by members of the Nazi hierarchy, dance in the Third Reich managed to achieve some distinction, for it was during this time that Ilse Meudtner, Oda Schottmüller, Marianne Vogelsang, Dore Hoyer, Afrika Doering, Lola Rogge, Maja Lex, Alexander von Swaine, and Helge Peters-Pawlinin established their artistic identities. Of course, these personalities worked independently of the subsidized theatres. One of the most impressive ballet talents of the 1930s, Aurel von Milloss (b. 1906), studied ballet in Budapest and Italy before attending the Laban school run by Hertha Feist in Berlin. In 1928 his relation to Feist ended sadly (for her) when he accepted an invitation from Max Terpis to dance at the Berlin State Opera. Though he gave his first solo concert at the Sturm Gallery in Berlin in 1928, it was not until 1932 in Breslau that he presented his first choreographed ballet, *H.M.S. Royal Oak*, with jazz music by Schulhof. Then his star rose. He became ballet master in Hagen, Duisburg, Augsburg, and then (1934–1935) Düsseldorf, accepting assignments in Budapest and Italy during this period. He was immensely prolific, probably staging more ballets, theatre dances, opera dances, and operetta dances in more theatres than any other figure of the 1930s and 1940s. He favored the modernist music of such composers as Stravinsky, Bartók, Kodály, Roussel, Honegger, Milhaud, Strauss, and Prokofiev, and he enjoyed working on scenic designs with such modernist painters as De Chirico, Prampolini, Casorati, Severini, and Cassandre. In 1936, Milloss accepted appointment as ballet master in Budapest and stayed until 1938, when he moved to Rome, which became his home for the remainder of his long and prodigious career (Taui). His art lacked an innovative dimension, but he brought a sumptuous elegance to his productions, and through grand production values he restored vitality to the depleted classical ballet scene. Yet the heralded ballet culture of the Third Reich apparently offered inadequate scope for his ambitions.

MAX TERPIS

Perhaps the most troubled of the theatre choreographers in Germany during the 1920s was actually a Swiss, Max Terpis (aka Max Pfister, 1889–1958). Originally a student of architecture, he encountered Laban in Stuttgart (1920) and took classes from Laban's protégé in Zurich, Suzanne Perrottet, who urged him to study under Wigman in Dresden. He spent only a single year (1922) with Wigman. Though Terpis came to dance relatively late in his life, no one soared to such national prominence with greater speed. His talent for group movement immediately attracted the attention of Hannover theatre director Hanns Niedecken-Gebhard, who hired him to choreograph *Der Tänzer unser lieben Frau* (1923, music: Stürmer), *Die Nächtlichen* (1923, music: Wellesz), and *Der fliegende Prinz* (1923, music: Paumgarten). Terpis danced the lead role in his own version of Richard Strauss's *Josephs Legende* (1923). His only solo concert, given in Hannover in 1924, featured no musical accompaniment and was a collaborative affair involving solo dances by Kreutzberg, Frida Holst, and Else Rudiger.

The Hannover choreographies brought him to the attention of Max von Schillings, director of the Berlin State Opera, who sought to reform the ballet corps, which numbered nearly a hundred dancers yet failed to achieve anything resembling the seriousness of purpose that Kröller had attempted to provide it in 1919–1922. Terpis held the State Opera position for six years, but his life there was a nightmare of political intrigue and reactionary efforts to undermine his reforms and authority. He produced nineteen ballets at the State Opera, nearly all of which used music by living modernist composers, including Kool, Stravinsky, Kömme, Wilckens, de Falla, Schreker, Prokofiev, Klenau, Benatzky, and Milhaud; Terpis wrote most of the scenarios himself. Scenic designers such as Emil Pirchan and Panos Aravantinos assisted him in creating expressionist-constructivist settings for ballets that largely inhabited the realm of symbolic fantasy; *Die fünf Wünsche* (1929) contained a film sequence shot by Gina Fagg. Because of persistent resistance to his expressionist methods from doyens and classically trained dancers, he could not construct group dances as powerfully or radically as he wished, so he increasingly relied on the talents of a few extraordinarily gifted soloists—Rolf Arco, Rudolf Kölling, Daisy Spies, Walter Junk,

Dorothea Albu. This strategy only aggravated tensions between himself and the majority of the corps, although Schillings and his successor, Heinz Tietjens, continued to support him. But in 1929 Terpis faced a full-scale insurrection, from new music director Otto Klemperer, who accused him of lacking "musicality" and of failing to grasp the nature of theatrical art. Terpis therefore handed in his resignation, and Laban soon replaced him. The next year he retreated into almost monastic seclusion, opening a school in Berlin-Grunewald, which he directed until 1939. He then returned to Switzerland, where he directed numerous operas and stage plays in Bern, Basel, and Zurich throughout the war years. In the last decade of his life, he devoted himself primarily to the study of psychological theory, particularly to problems of color perception and semiotics, on which he even published scholarly articles, although relations between color and movement had preoccupied him in the 1920s (Schede).

Terpis appealed to male theatre administrators because his thinking seemed rigorously disciplined and austerely rational. He seemed capable of creating an atmosphere of sober freedom derived from a synthesis of ballet and modern dance techniques. Thus, a major irony of his career was that his own corps regarded his thinking as too radical (expressionist), when in reality his ideas lacked sufficient respect for excess, flamboyance, and wildness. None of his ballets resonated much with either the public, the critics, or the dance world, in spite of his impressive seriousness and ambition, and useful descriptions of them remain difficult to excavate. Even his almost completely uncritical biographer, Wolfgang Schede, gave only the vaguest descriptions of them, offering only a couple of photographs, and Terpis himself did not discuss any of his ballets, publishing scenarios of ballets that never got produced rather than analyzing those that did. He offered an aesthetic of grandiose restraint and heightened sobriety, as he indicated in a lecture to students around 1932: "Our time has an outspoken inclination toward exaggeration, consumption; it loves the loud, the screaming, the extreme. . . . The dance programs consist largely of grotesques, parodies, problematic spiritual distortions, insofar as they do not exhibit artistic or virtuoso formalisms. . . . It is rarely that one can identify a dance as 'beautiful' or 'elegant,' rarely that a dance displays internally or externally an aristocratic bearing. Today we are immediately ready to identify everything that is 'beautiful' and poetic—that is, harmonic—as kitsch. The ugly, unharmonic, unlogical strike us as interesting" (Schede 101–102).

Terpis pursued what one might call an architectural sense of movement fusing concepts of classical ballet with theoretical categories of modern dance; indeed, "architecture and choreography share the narrowest of affinities" (Terpis, *Farbenspiel,* 102). He tended to build individual movements out of classical concepts supplemented by a distinctly modern enthusiasm for swinging motions, although he showed little interest in pointe technique. For group movements he favored modern theoretical categories, which nevertheless seemed more rooted in architecture and space than in the body. Group movement achieved maximum expressivity through Terpis's notion of "symmetricality": "The ordering of masses in space is symmetrical," he believed, for symmetricality provided the most effective "representation of the idea of power, wealth, strength, and domination" (107). Asymmetrical constructions opened up the world of "fantasy" (which he actually preferred on the narrative level), but these must never transgress "laws and order" established through symmetry (112). Group symmetry occurred through the application of abstract geometrical categories: the circle, the triangle, the square, and the row. Each category contained numerous variations—the circle, for example, included cylinders, half-circles, tunnels, balls, arches, and so forth. Asymmetry intervened when group movement no longer disclosed recognizable geometric categories. Choreography entailed the fusion of abstract geometrical categories with classical ballet positions and with modern notions of swing and pulse.

Terpis's belief in synthesis operated at a further level: he sought to fuse abstract categories of movement with a very literary sense of narrative. He wrote most of the scenarios for his ballets, which primarily projected a fantastic or Gothic atmosphere, and he seemed unable to imagine dance without an elaborate libretto (Terpis, "Wie ensteht," 4). Yet knowledge of his scenarios is so scant that it is difficult to ascertain what he wished to say. *Don Morte* (1926, music: Wilckens), perhaps his most successful work, was a grandiose adaptation of Poe's "The Masque of the Red Death." This piece, which revealed such powerful anxiety toward fleshly pleasures and the body, conveyed the logic of his asceticism: he feared the body and the turbulent emotions it provoked; carefully scripted narrative dance, constructed symmetrically within an elaborate theatre bureaucracy, was the most effective way to regulate the body and the threats to spatial order from impulse and fantasy, which the body "covered up." He loved the extravagant productions of the Ballets Russes when they visited Berlin—these sent him walking alone through the city for hours—but he was incapable of anything so unapologetically lavish and hedonistic. Yet the State Opera (including the corps) probably expected him to come up with some serious competition for the Parisians, a task he could hardly achieve through his own productions of Stravinsky's *Pulcinella* (1925) and *Petrouchka* (1928). In the scenarios for his unproduced dances—*Saul und David* (1930), *Orpheus Lysios* (1936), *Circe* (1936), and *Niobe* (1937)—he revealed perhaps most overtly his greatest desire: to show how dance bestowed upon the body a redemptively priestly identity (*Farbenspiel*, 169–177). But the theatre was never a happy home for such an ascetic attitude.

Mass Dancing

movement Chorus [handwritten annotation]

Because of the difficulties of institutionalizing *Ausdruckstanz* within the sub-sidized theatres, sizable sectors of the modern dance and body culture phe-nomenon pursued strategies of group movement that functioned indepen-dently of the official theatres, whose expectations and conventions set too many limits on bodily expressivity. These sectors promoted the so-called movement choirs. Movement choirs attempted to construct a dynamic image of community that preserved the amateur status of the performers yet transmitted a convincing, almost ritualistic aura of modernity, ground-ing an idealized communal identity in a common appreciation of bodily expressivity. Indeed, these lay productions probably appealed more to per-sons who performed in them than to those who watched them. Much of the pleasure of participating in movement choirs derived from improvisations performed in "appropriated" spaces not usually designated for perfor-mance, and in this sense mass movement escaped the constricting regula-tion of the body associated with literary narratives, although plenty of peo-ple did devise scenarios to celebrate the movement choirs.

Laban has received much credit for introducing the concept of the movement choir in Stuttgart around 1920, but the origins of the genre were actually more obscure and apparently owed more to the theatre than its promoters tended to acknowledge. Part of its appeal derived from the enor-mous publicity generated by the curious, lavish revival of Handel's operas and oratorios, initiated on an annual basis in Göttingen in 1920 and sup-plemented by numerous professional productions in Hannover and Mün-ster starting in 1923. The driving figure behind the Handel productions was Hanns Niedecken-Gebhard (1889–1954), a master of "mass-suggestive effect," according to a review of a 1924 Handel production (Peusch 99–100). Beginning in 1920, Niedecken-Gebhard staged the old operas (and oratorios) in a radical, antihistoricist style in which the chorus moved

Handel Revival [handwritten annotation]

in bold and complex configurations on expressionistically abstract architectural forms such as elevated platforms, stairways, and ramps. With such choreography, the archaic, rococo music and the old stories seemed to awaken a powerfully modern image of dynamic communal identity. No one who examines stills of these and many other Handel productions from this period can fail to observe a sleek, streamlined break with the operatic performance traditions of previous centuries. The chorus did not perform opera dances or pantomime or even choreographed acting—it performed "mass movement," acting as a dynamic, pulsating organism rather than as a mechanically precise corps. More important, the Handel productions showed that mass movement did not exist exclusively apart from theatre, from interior spaces, from elaborate texts, or even from old stories in a highly "domesticated," classical mode. Mass movement appeared to be latent not in the text but in the idea of performance as the foundation for constructing a modern communal identity. Niedecken-Gebhard enjoyed a busy career directing operas in Hannover, Münster, Berlin (1929–1932), and even the Metropolitan Opera in New York (1933); perhaps it is not surprising that he also assumed responsibility for staging some of the most stunning of the Nazi mass spectacles in the 1930s.

Nevertheless, the great majority of movement choir activities occurred outside conventional theatrical spaces, preferably in the open air or in large studios. Mass movement strove more often than not to achieve powerful dramatic expression without being theatrical. Though the Nazis brought mass movement to unprecedented dimensions (largely after 1933), during the 1920s the public consistently identified this aesthetic with left-wing or emancipatory political aims sponsored by the social democrats, the labor unions, the *Nacktkultur* clubs, the gymnastic organizations, and liberal bourgeois cultural and religious associations. At the 1930 Munich Dance Congress, Otto Zimmermann, leader of a Leipzig "proletarian lay group" called Der Tanzring, presented *Achtung! Wir schalten um!,* a "satiric dance play" with jazz music by Hermann Heyer that contrasted idealized communist lay movement with dilettantish, ineffectual, bourgeois lay movement.

Mass movement, however, appealed to a wide range of political ideologies, and it is misleading to assume that the aesthetic inherently embodied a totalitarian vision of communal identity. Laban was obviously the most persuasive spokesman for the aesthetic. By the late 1920s, Laban movement choirs affiliated with dance schools alone numbered nearly one hundred, and the generic concept of the movement choir operated in an even wider range of contexts. At the 1928 Essen Dance Congress, Laban spoke about "the choric artwork," declaring that "the lay dance choir is a rediscovery of a much earlier artistic community" in which mysterious ritual was the foundation of social unity and "the spectator play[ed] a secondary role." The reason the lay choir remained suspicious of theatre was that effective mass movement required large performance spaces that undermined interest in solo or individualistic performances. The pleasure of watching mass movement resembled the joy of watching a "great orchestra" perform; yet "the choric artwork can only be a mirror of our social and ideal will" (MS 88–89). The movement choirs owed as much to gymnastics as to dance techniques, but at the 1930 Dance Congress in Munich, Laban asserted that the value of the aesthetic did not depend on either gymnastic or dance skill. Its value was pedagogic: participation in a movement choir changed the mental, emotional, and physical identity of the performer, enhancing an idealized sense of belonging to an "artistic community" ("Kunstgemein-schaft") (96–98; also Laban, "Vom Sinn"). Laban denounced the undisguised propagandizing of "false" movement choirs, but it was perhaps impossible for the aesthetic to thrive outside of an overt political stance as long as its value resided largely in the power of indoctrination. Mass movement evolved primarily through teachers in classrooms.

Laban himself loved to improvise endlessly with lay choirs. He delighted in devising increasingly convoluted rhythms and configurations of a large group of bodies. Mass movement did not imply synchronized or unison movements; Laban liked to see how a group could maintain unity of identity while containing all manner of different, individualized movements (Figure 63). Mass movement activity resembled Dalcrozian rhythmic gymnastics in its seemingly infinite capacity for improvised variations and for Laban, at least, it became even more exciting without music or text. The improvisational dimension revealed how membership in a group heightened individual freedom. It may seem difficult to comprehend how a powerful sense of communal unity could arise out of improvisation and the abandonment of a guiding, prescribing text, especially because the movement choir leaders, including Laban, did not theorize their methods at all lucidly or systematically (for communal identity was a "mysterious" phenomenon). But the secret of the mass movement improvisational aesthetic lay, I believe, in its gymnastic foundation. An excellent American book by Bonnie and Donnie Cotteral, *Tumbling, Pyramid Building and Stunts for Girls and Women* (1931), explains (often with photographs and stick-figure diagrams) numerous rolling, balancing, and mounting positions by which bodies in pairs or trios may support each other to create a lively image of bodily interdependence. These include, among many others: the wheelbarrow, the camel walk, the eight-legged animal, the saddleback, the horse and rider, the Jack in the box, the Andy over, the Indian wrestle, the churn the butter, the wring the dish rag, the Siamese twins, the human bar, the archway, the merry-go-round, the treadway, the skin, the snake, the opening of the rose, the opening of the double rose, and thirty distinct pyramid constructions for between six and fourteen girls. Although performance of these stunts entailed rhythmic "counts," music was completely optional and used apparently only for competitive demonstrations. Most significant, a group could combine stunts with almost infinite variety, and maneuvers designed for pairs or trios could be combined within a larger group to produce a more complex effect.

Of course, one may question what such mathematically driven improvisation says in a deeper sense, other than revealing the intricate coordination and physical trustfulness defining the ideal group. For this reason, Laban subordinated gymnastic aims to the more complex task of constructing a dramatic, emotion-laden, mystical message. This task required not only stunts but symbolically loaded gestures, so that the meaning of group movement derived from semiotic analysis, from a self-conscious manipulation of signs rather than positions. However, the movement choirs seemed unable to produce a solid theoretical apparatus such as Delsarte had introduced in the nineteenth century, and even Laban became distracted by an obsession with "objectifying" movement to the point of draining it of all content. The most powerful source of emotion (and therefore meaning) is conflict. But the movement choirs resisted situating conflict within the group, so afraid were they of undermining their utopian image of the community. (It was a mistake Wigman managed to avoid in her generally small group works.) Consequently, the movement choirs tended to associate conflict with a force external to the group: prudery, capitalism, fascism, communism, technology, industrialization, urbanization, and so forth, often designated more by implication than by any serious embodiment and against which the group appeared as a liberating antidote, a utopia in microcosm.

SIGNIFICANT THEORISTS OF MASS MOVEMENT

In Hamburg (1922–1927) and then in Halle (1927–1933), Jenny Gertz (?–1966), a Laban student, achieved unrivaled distinction for her movement choir work with children and teenagers, male and female together. Most of her students came from the proletariat, and for several years she maintained close connections with both the Social Democratic Party and the Communist Party, but in the early 1930s she drifted more decisively toward communism. Nudity was central to her pedagogic method, and photographs of her nude students performing outdoor movement choir improvisations are among the most beautiful images of group action produced during the Weimar Republic. Equally unique was her dramatic use of speech to develop bodily expressivity. She would require her students to respond in an imaginative, sometimes complex, but seldom uniform fashion to almost surrealistic commands: "run loudly," "become big very quickly, then slowly become very small again," "be a very small package on the floor, tightly bound," "be noisy people when two cars have collided," and so forth.

The children often inserted their own voices to make the "sound" of a movement. Gertz could combine these tiny body dramas into larger structures, and children themselves might lead the group (Losch 81–87). In collaboration with her friend Rose Mirelmann, Gertz did produce such "choric dramas" for young people as *Schwarz-Rot* (1930) and *Revolutionspiel* (1932), propagandistic celebrations of communist idealism. But the Gestapo shut down her school and compelled her to seek exile in Prague, where Mira Holzbachova, another student of Laban, was a prominent communist dancer. Just before the Germans invaded Czechoslovakia, Gertz migrated to England, where she continued to teach children's dance until 1947, when she returned to Halle.

Otto Zimmermann forged a much more "determined" relation between speech and movement than prevailed in Gertz's free-spirited pedagogy. He directed Der Tanzring, a communist movement group in Leipzig, which had witnessed a very turbulent period of red mass spectacles in the early 1920s (Pfützner). For the 1929 Festival of Speech and Movement Choirs in Leipzig, Zimmermann took spoken words from the Internationale and assigned to them specific physical, unison movements. For example, the words "clean table" produced "from sideways position left, right arm swinging wide to the left side in pumping motion"; "power to the oppressed" provoked "right arm stretches spaciously right and sidewards through the space, making a right-pathed circle"; "armies of slaves, awake!" meant "stride forward toward the spectating masses, great lifting movement of both hands deep and high" (Losch 338). But this sort of synchronicity of word and movement appealed to people for whom group solidarity was incompatible with internal variation and, indeed, improvisation. Yet this strategy tended to prevail in the production of large-scale dramatic works written for movement choirs, such as Bruno Schönlank's, staged by Vera Skoronel and Berthe Trümpy at the Berlin Volksbühne (1927–1928), whose movement choir contained seventy persons.

By contrast, Martin Gleisner (1897–1983), an actor under Max Reinhardt and from 1922 on a close associate of Laban, acknowledged that the power of group identity depended on "structured work" and advocated a position between text-driven performance and full improvisation (VP 43–46). From 1925 he directed a Laban-school in Jena with a social democratic–communist orientation: "[T]he movement choir, through the creation of group artworks, is in the strongest sense *social*" but must not exclude "the bizarre, the dark, the grotesque," for the path to freedom allows the layman "to express everything that is within him" (*Gymnastik*, October 1926, 150–151). Gleisner's book, *Tanz für alle* (1928), explained (not very systematically) his pedagogic-aesthetic approach. He sought to create an inherently socialistic form of group dance unique to the movement choir, which entailed deemphasizing gymnastic devices. He wanted a dance form designed explicitly for performance at festivals of a political character. To achieve this aim, he followed a twofold strategy. First, to establish the social identity of group movement he drew upon old folk dances, especially round dances, and repudiated contemporary social dances, for "the ballroom of our days is a symbol of the anarchistic, bourgeois society of our time" (Gleisner 73). Second, he sought to transform labor-related motions such as sweeping or digging into dance elements and thus to collapse the difference between labor and dance. He also liked to have as many as five discrete groups interacting with each other in a wide-open space, in different modes of movement, until they became one group.

All of Gleisner's "choric artworks" appeared at political festivals, but the documentation on them has largely disappeared, so it is difficult to say what sort of "structured" message he transmitted. *Rotes Lied* (1929), created to commemorate the fortieth anniversary of the German Workers' Singing Federation in Berlin, was probably his most visible work. It was a vast production performed for more than 40,000 spectators in a football stadium. The hour-long piece required separate speech, song, and movement choirs, with a full orchestra playing sections of Beethoven's Eroica Symphony and Tchaikovsky's Pathetique Symphony, as well specially composed marches and folk dances by Alexander Levitan. The speech choir contained 50 speakers, while the singing choir numbered 2,000 and the movement choir 1,000. The choreography "was not illustrative, but rhythmically defined" because the narrative was so abstract. The three-part structure apparently described the power of the group to survive destruction and disintegration and reemerge triumphantly in ecstatic folk dances or monumental marches with red banners (Losch 331–333).

As a socialist and a Jew, Gleisner obviously had no future in the Third Reich, so he migrated to Holland, where he became prominent as a leader of often huge socialist movement choirs, publishing a Dutch translation of his book (1934) and working with the Flemish dancer Lea Daan. In Antwerp, Gleisner and Daan collaborated on a group movement piece, *People and Machines* (1936), and then produced a film of it, a fragment of which still exists. Images show men and women in worker and peasant garb, respectively, making heavy, lurching, swaying movements in synchrony to signify "toil," but the sexes do not make the same movements. The film fragment does not make clear what sort of music Daan employed. What makes the film unusually compelling is its use of cinematic technique. The camera moves in close to the dancers, films them at low angles from the side and the back, from high angles, and with low angle tracks and pans. The mass bodily movement techniques are designed to be seen from great distances in large spaces, but the camera brings the spectator in close, conveying a peculiar feeling of heroic, monumental physicality and, at the same time, a sense of oppression. It is a rare example of uniquely cinematic rhythms in which camera movement and editing "dance" with the movement of dancers themselves rather than merely watching them, an effect that only Hollywood's Busby Berkeley had mastered at that time. Eventually Gleisner emigrated to the United States, where he specialized in teaching movement expressivity to older people.

The socialist aesthetic of *People and Machines* was obviously remote from the Catholic-socialist aesthetic of the *massatooneel*, which entirely dominated the movement choir phenomenon in Holland and Flanders, where lay public productions were favored on a scale the Germans would hardly have considered revolutionary. The Dutch Catholic girls' association, De Graal, for example, staged *Pinksterzegen* (1931) with 10,000 girls divided into nine movement choirs of 250 to 4,800 girls each and each choir, representing such things as "seraphs and cherubs," "Grail cadettes," and "October and the Komsomol children," assigned specific, bold colors (Van der Poel 25). The Brussels *Credo!* (1936), directed by Lode Geysen for the Flemish Catholic Socialist Federation, involved 20,000 performers in a stadium filled with 150,000 spectators. The Dutch-Flemish lay choirs also employed Soviet-inspired constructivist scenography and complex, spectacular scenic technology, which, German socialists tended to feel, undermined the original focus on the body as the source of communal identity. Moreover, distinguished Dutch and Flemish authors such as Henriette Roland Holst, Martinus Nijhoff, and Michel de Ghelderode, composed the texts for movement choirs, and these inscribed the integration of speech, song, and movement with such monumental "structure" that the improvisational pleasure of the German movement choir scarcely emerged (Boon; Van der Poel; Roland Holst) (Figures 64–65). In Holland and Flanders, the socialist movement choir enjoyed a prosperity (or grandeur) in the 1930s that it never had enjoyed in Weimar Germany, but for an improviser like Gleisner the Catholic vision of utopia, immensely inclusive though it was, perhaps excluded too much "the bizarre, the dark, and the grotesque."

TOTENMAL

The validation of the movement choir aesthetic seemed assured when various of Laban's students incorporated it into theatrical or professional productions. Rogge, Jooss, Skoronel, Feist, Loeser, Knust, and Laban himself produced professional stage works that applied movement choir technique, even though public performance was a secondary aim of this concept. Ironically, the most ambitious and complex use of the movement choir came from a Laban student who displayed little confidence in it as an expression of modernity, Mary Wigman. In 1930, at the Munich Dance Congress, she premiered *Totenmal*, a work of spectacular ambiguity and fascination. The eight-part "dramatic choral vision for word, dance, and light," written by the

Swiss expressionist Albert Talhoff, called for six separate choirs representing, respectively, the spirits of fallen soldiers (two choirs) and their wives, mothers, sisters, and lovers. The eight parts, or "compositions," included five "halls" and three interludes, with each hall signifying emotional conditions—calls, forgetfulness, expulsion, echoes, and devotion. Of the six choirs, one, the Celebration Choir, consisted of two parts: one part spoke within the halls, and the other part, situated around two "light altars," spoke in close proximity to a color organ. A female dance choir (Tanzender Chor I) and a male dance choir (Tanzender Chor II) never spoke and only danced. A Speech-Orchestral Choir, like the Celebration Choir, contained voices of both sexes. Both of these choirs occasionally spoke in unison or broke into as many as ten groups of voices; one of these groups, for example, consisted of a boy choir. The Instrumental Choir, which played percussion instruments and music (drums, cymbals, bells) composed by Talhoff himself, sometimes spoke or screamed. From out of these choirs came eight figures who spoke numerous solo verses. Another five figures danced without speaking; these included a male Demon and a female Dance-Play figure, performed by Wigman.

It is not clear from Talhoff's text what the total number of voices was for either the choirs or the groups within them. Some of the groups appear to have consisted of voices from more than one choir. The idea, apparently, was that neither the language nor the voices that spoke it belonged entirely to any one community. It was a very complex perception of voice. However, Talhoff's text offered no great distinctions among the voices spoken within it. The strongest distinction within the text was that between Talhoff's language and the quoted language of the actual letters written by soldiers who had died.

In this huge dance, literary language did not construct characters in any way that we might expect from a dramatic text. Instead, Talhoff's expressionistic verse turned the bodies that spoke into abstractions. Whether in a choral or a solo mode, the speaking body projected an anonymous, generic identity. The language created different communities of voice that nevertheless spoke the same types of language and (pacifist) sentiments. No single body seemed powerful enough to express any sentiment unique unto the speaker; each body (and voice) seemed but a fragment of a larger, more abstract communal identity. Despite the communality of desires signified by the interlocking choirs and solo speakers, the dominant mood of the piece was one of profound loneliness, of the living (both genders) separated irrevocably from the dead (male) and vice versa. The distribution of speech among so many choirs, groups, and soloists produced an extremely complex, antiphonal sound world. Wigman treated this sound world as a musical accompaniment to dance movements. Though the choirs and speakers were by no means static, the piece strongly differentiated between their movements and those of the dancers. Choirs swayed, undulated, or extended their arms but otherwise never moved with the freedom or complexity ascribed to the Demon or the two Dance Play figures. Just as the realm of the dead was immutably "other" than that of the living, so speech remained in tension with movement. Because, however, the text motivated the dance, one must assume that, in this case, language "controlled" movement or shaped it according to its own rhythms. But the text did not make clear how bodily movement "translated" the spoken language that accompanied it. The free verse wildly shifted rhythms from speaker to speaker. For example:

SPEECH AND GESTURAL FIGURE II:

No!!
from the ten million dead
              the dead
              the dead
for you it is the path out of hate and need assigned
all their peoples
make them holy
holy
beacons of this planet (*Darkness.*)

CELEBRATIONAL CHOIR:

And no one guesses
that now at last before God and the world
without question
and for murder
hammer of death
falls on all those of this earth—!

INSTRUMENTAL CHOIR:

VOICES:

    oh save
        save
    the light of the world!
        light of the world!
                the world
world
            (Talhoff 71)

To intensify the anonymity and abstraction of the body, all the performers wore eerie masks designed by Bruno Goldschmidt. But whereas the costumes and masks of the males were identical, those of the females were differentiated according to eight archetypal, "feminine" emotions. Mask type determined movement type. Performing before the various choirs was a lone, unmasked woman (Wigman) who attempted, unsuccessfully, to resurrect the dead through dance. Speech did not issue from her or her counterpart, the shrouded male Demon. The choirs and figures recited Talhoff's verse lamentations for the dead and messages from the dead, and they occasionally exhorted the audience not to forget the dead. Integrated into Talhoff's language were fragments of actual letters written by English, French, and German soldiers who died in World War I. The solo speakers of these fragments were male and invisible, speaking in chanting, *Sprechstimme* style, individually, from concealed booths.

The sixth composition concluded when Wigman, having apparently revived the dead by persuading the male movement leader to imitate her gestures, became separated from her partner by a sinister male Demon (masked), who compelled her, through dance, to retreat into the shadows. The final (eighth) composition did not involve bodily movement at all: the male and female speech choirs stood rigidly with arms upheld while a color organ bathed the scene in blazing red light and the Celebration Choir thunderously exhorted the audience to believe that God's love will triumph over destructive human impulses toward war. The final "Amen" produced a strange ending. The lone woman appeared to have danced herself to death trying to revive the dead. Yet the sign for triumph over death was a tableaulike image of monumental stasis, with a multitude of bodies frozen in the almighty refulgence. In the end, light and sound were dynamic, not the bodies.

In *Totenmal,* speech signified a kind of "deadness" but not death itself. Death here had a "demonic" male *body*, which *danced*. The (male) dead themselves appeared statically uniform, but Death was dynamic. The dance of Death was indeed of such power that it vanquished the woman dancer, overshadowed the dance of Life. Yet it was the woman's dance that invited or provoked the appearance of Death. Wigman thus represented Death as a kind of male shadow of the feminine body: dance does not conquer death but drives the dancer toward it, "heroically." The dance culminates in complete stasis, with the male and female bodies of the speech choirs standing perfectly still, the woman dancer and movement choirs absent, and the dynamic configuration of bodiless light accompanied by bodiless dead voices. If we can't see the woman, we can't see death; we can only see the dead, that final condition in which language, speech, and voice are all coordinates of a triumphantly immobile, rather than invisible or repressed, body. Death is movement toward a final stasis.

Dance, then, is not a release from death—it is an exposure of it. Movement makes us see that which is otherwise hidden from us: namely, the view that death is *in* life rather than opposed to it. For the feminine body, death is "masculine" insofar as it is demonic, a figure of desire, another body exposed by the dancer's effort to use her body to bring things to life. The lone dancing body of the woman motivates a multiplicity of other bodies that are communal, male and female, speaking and moving, historical yet archetypal, dead yet alive, physical and metaphysical, choric yet suffused with a profound sense of loneliness, abandonment. These bodies are masked, for the other is in itself the mask of identities hidden within the body that is most naked, the unmasked body of the lone woman dancer. By keeping her face unmasked and by wrapping the rest of her body in a medieval-like gown, Wigman effectively dramatized the perception of the "real" or "authentic" body as an intensely death-conscious vortex of tension between exposure and concealment. The chief sign of loneness is naked-ness (of the face); the chief sign of otherness is speech; and the chief sign of the dissolution of difference between lone being and the others is move-ment (KT; Manning 148–160; Prinzhorn, "Grundsätzliches").

Totenmal was probably the most controversial dance work produced dur-ing the whole of the Weimar Republic. It provoked a turbulent critical response throughout the country and fascinated audiences during a ten-week run in Munich; some haunting film footage survives. The idea of com-munity signified by the elaborate interlocking of choirs and groups seemed fantastically complicated and saturated with a political ambiguity further intensified by Wigman's unresolved dramatization of tensions between the solo body and the group. Few people were ready to acknowledge that com-munal unity was an illusion, a matter of masks and generic identities; few people were ready to acknowledge that Death was somehow behind the illu-sion of unity. But what most touched many spectators was Wigman's monu-mentally tragic sense of an absent, vanished, or dead maleness, which left the curious impression of a world bereft of heroic identity except for the lone and abandoned female figure.

The political significance of the piece lay in its power to divide audiences rather than unite them. In *Schrifttanz* (3/3, November 1930), Alfred Schlee, one of the journal's editors, declared that *Totenmal* had "brought disrepute upon the idea of the ritual theatre" and that Wigman had "wasted her tal-ents on this amateurish creation." "At a time when a number of theatres are fighting for their survival, one single work consumed the amount of money which would have secured a theatre's budget for an entire year" (VP 87). Josef Lewitan, editor of *Der Tanz* (3/8, August 1930, 15) condemned the piece as "unworthy" of Wigman and asserted that "for dance art and dance evolution *Totenmal* offers virtually nothing" in "times of direst need," when 100,000 marks might well serve a less "dilettantish" project. But Friedrich Muckermann, a Catholic priest who had addressed the Dance Congress as a proponent of lay movement choirs within the Church, praised *Totenmal* for its powerful Christian sentiment (*Der Gral*, 24/8, May 1930, 675). Hans Brandenburg also endorsed the work (*Der Tanz*, 3/6, June 1930, 5), but he was in a delicate position, having already prophesied (*Schrifttanz*, 3/1, April

1930) that the piece would inaugurate a new form of dance theatre and choric art. In *Der Ring* (3/36, 623–628), a "conservative cultural journal" (as it described itself on the masthead), the great psychologist Hans Prinzhorn wrote possibly the most detailed description of a Weimar-era dance performance ever published. Prinzhorn condemned the production for being underrehearsed and relying on a tedious, painfully naive text, then systematically criticized all the multimedia performance elements. Yet he praised Wigman's "dramatic" choreography and dancing, which he said were in tension with the stereotyped message of the text: through movement, Wigman freed perception from "schematized" concepts of action within social reality. He complained that the whole production offered an inadequate understanding of the war's significance and provided no insight into the value of the sacrifices made by all the soldiers who died in it. Prinzhorn blamed Talhoff's script for nearly all of the problems, but when, under the auspices of the Social Democratic Party, Lola Rogge staged sections of the text in Hamburg in 1931, in a far less ambitious or innovative manner, the press response was uniformly enthusiastic.

Wigman never again attempted such a grandiose dance, but neither did anyone else. (Her student Margarethe Wallmann did attempt complicated choric dances, though not an interlocking image of community, in *Orfeus Dionysos,* also performed at the Congress.) From Wigman's perspective, the problem with *Totenmal* was logistic: inadequate rehearsal time, an inadequate performance space, inadequate technical support, and, worst of all, inadequate talent within the choirs. *Totenmal* exposed the limit of the movement choir and of mass dancing generally to signify communal identity. From then on, a large, inclusive representation of community depended less on complexity of group movement and bodily expression and more on the technological complexity of a huge visual design.

THE DANCE CONGRESSES

The big dance congresses in Magdeburg (1927), Essen (1928), and Munich (1930) were remarkable and complex manifestations of mass dancing. The Magdeburg Congress, in conjunction with the great International Theatre Exposition in that city, was organized largely by Rudolf Laban, Hanns Niedecken-Gebhard, and Oskar Schlemmer. The event attracted about 300 people, but Laban and his disciples overwhelmingly dominated the proceedings. Wigman and her disciples refused to attend because Laban declined to offer them an opportunity to perform. Laban hoped the congress would further his aim of uniting all German dance organizations and institutions under a single federation, but achieving this on paper proved to have considerably less dramatic consequences than he anticipated. Nevertheless, the congress was quite successful insofar as it gave

Ausdruckstanz unprecedented media visibility. An intellectual-theoretical aura pervaded to a greater extent here than in the subsequent congresses. The Jena monthly journal *Die Tat* (19/8, November 1927) devoted an entire issue to publishing the bulk of the proceedings, and the journals *Schrifttanz* and *Der Tanz* emerged directly out of the congress.

The controlling theme of the congress was the institutionalization of *Ausdruckstanz*. Nearly all the papers and discussions focused on the historical, aesthetic, technical, and organizational difficulties of integrating modern dance into the theatre, the state educational apparatus, and large-scale institutional structures. Impressive lectures addressed dance music (E. Wellesz), dance criticism (H. W. Fischer), dance in the theatre (H. Brandenburg, H. Niedecken-Gebhard, M. Terpis), dance psychology (A. Loos, H. Liebermann), and modern dance as a historical phenomenon (A. Levinson, F. Böhme, W. Howard, O. Bie). Oskar Schlemmer discussed abstract relations between dance and costume and presented models of experimental stages designed by the Bauhaus in Dessau; Laban showed films of his movement choir experiments; and Lothar Schreyer, Gertrud Schnell, Paul Et*bauer, and Gustav Klamt, among others, held a complicated dialogue on the nature of choreography. Unlike other congresses, this one featured extensive exhibition of costumes and set designs, reinforcing the perception of dance as an art defined more by fantasy than by the reality of the body.

But perhaps the most interesting feature of the congress was the series of open meetings conducted to identify the goals of a unified dance federation and the methods for achieving the goals. Some participants, including Berthe Trümpy, Charlotte Bara, and Olga Brandt-Knack, did not believe that modern dance would benefit much from a close affiliation with the theatre, the state, classical ballet, or even lay education. In other words, not everyone agreed that it was in the best interest of dance to construct a broad united front or to accommodate a wide variety of constituencies. Nevertheless, diverse sectors within dance culture expressed a willingness to support each other and to promote new ideas and new values for dance within existing cultural institutions. Laban dominated the congress performance scene with stagings of *Titan, Die Nacht,* and *Ritterballett,* and Vera Skoronel presented her mass dance *Die Erweckung der Masse.* Two evenings offered solo and ensemble pieces from twenty performers, including Hertha Feist, Harald Kreutzberg, Hilde Strinz, Josepha Stefan, Rudolf Kölling, and Ingeborg Roon. Curiously, *Die Tat,* in its eighty-eight-page report, did not discuss the dance performances at all, though it published most of the lengthy lectures.

Fritz Böhme coordinated the Essen Congress with help from Alfred Schlee, Kurt Jooss, and Ludwig Buchholz. This time Mary Wigman was present, along with Yvonne Georgi, Gret Palucca, Hanya Holm, and Rosalia Chladek. Wigman had formed (March 1928) a new dance federation,

Deutsche Tanzgemeinschaft, to compete with Laban's Magdeburg federation, so no one expected the congress, which attracted about 1,000 participants, to produce an image of professional, aesthetic, or political unity. Panels focused on the themes of dance in the theatre (again), dance notation, dance pedagogy, and (again) the theory of lay dance culture. Unlike Magdeburg, Essen attempted, mildly, to situate dance modernism within an international context. Andrè Levinson, from Paris, was on hand again to defend the classical ballet tradition, as was the Javanese dancer Rodan Mas Jodjan. A special Sunday program offered "national" dances from England, Russia, Germany, Java, and Sumatra. The congress hoped to have the Soviet scholar Alexei Sidorow present a slide lecture on Russian modern dance, supplemented by performances of several Moscow modern dance groups, but at the last minute Soviet authorities refused to issue visas. These performances probably would have been the most exciting features of the congress, for knowledge of Russian modern dance during the 1920s was (and still is) frustratingly obscure. Mary Wigman presented her ensemble piece *Die Feier,* Terpis and Kröller presented ballets designed for the official theatres, and the Essen Municipal Theatre dancers, under Jooss, performed Honegger's *Die siegreiche Horatier* and Milhaud's *Salat.* An evening of solo dances included work by Kreutzberg, Chladek, Skoronel, Georgi, and Edgar Frank.

Patricia Stöckemann has spoken unfavorably about this congress, claiming that panelists brought nothing new to the discussion platform and bogged down in "formal things like the length of training time for dance teachers and dancers and the repeated demand for a [state-subsidized] dance academy . . . an artistic stagnation was obvious" (MS 75; also 72–90). From my perspective, the congress's atmosphere of stagnation resulted from the complete failure to address aesthetic issues or to present any analyses of actual performances. When theoretical discourse focuses exclusively on mundane details of pedagogic method, dance notation, and bureaucratic procedure in the theatres, one senses that dance is no longer an art or even a pleasure but an almost incidental aspect of career maneuvering.

The 1930 congress in Munich, jointly organized by Wigman, Laban, Böhme, Brandenburg, and several others, achieved an unprecedented and still unsurpassed scale in dance history. It attracted 1,400 participants from several countries and from numerous schools and theatres across Germany. Scholarly presentations were virtually absent, with only a few lectures on the old themes of dance in the theatre (Emmel, Brandenburg) and lay dance culture (Laban, Gleisner), although Böhme spoke perceptively about the social identity of the dancer. Joseph Lewitan, in *Der Tanz* (July 1930, 2), complained acidly about the lack of academic reflection, which at a medical congress would seem "grotesque." The major administrative objective of the congress was to formulate accreditation standards for dance academies.

This task proved unexpectedly easy to carry out, probably because it was not difficult to agree on broad categories of instruction—the real (undiscussed) problem was to identify values for dance, domains of meaning. But the great achievement of the congress lay in the huge number of performances from an astonishing variety of artists. Almost everybody of significance in the world of Central European modern dance appeared: Wigman, Laban, Kröller, Chladek, Maudrik, Gertz, Eckstein, Kratina, Loeser, Wallmann, Kraus, Palucca, Brandt-Knack, Klamt, Skoronel, Heide Woog, Dorothee Günther, Mila Cirul, Manda van Kreibig, Ellinor Tordis, to name only about half of the German groups, along with dancers from Holland, Czechoslovakia, Yugoslavia, Hungary, Austria, Poland, Bulgaria, and the United States. A special program featured solo pieces by thirty-five young dancers.

Stöckemann has also complained about this congress, saying that its "failing artistic impulse had a directly frightening and disillusioning effect . . . even the protagonists of the modern dance had hardly anything new to present" (MS 91). But this view seems to derive from the belief that the congress should have displayed a more urgent awareness of contemporary political realities or perhaps a more aggressively avant-garde image of dance, such as Schlemmer and the Bauhaus designers introduced at Magdeburg. If, however, one examines closely many of the works performed at the congress—as I have tried to do throughout this book—the impression emerges of substantial innovation and diversity within the world of modern dance. The congress did not exist to unify dance as a major power broker in the national cultural scene; on the contrary, it served to reveal the impossibility of unifying dance. The congress showed that the more dance expanded in a general, inclusive sense, the more it became fragmented into an enormous program of untheorized performances that supposedly spoke for themselves. The dancing body inescapably constructed patterns of difference, not structures of unity, despite the obsession with bureaucratic rhetoric emanating from nearly everyone who spoke.

NAZI CONCEPTS OF MASS MOVEMENT

A fourth congress, planned for Vienna, never materialized because of the Nazi takeover. Instead, Goebbels authorized the organization of German Dance Festivals, held in Berlin in 1934 and 1935. These were autumnal rather than summertime affairs and completely devoid of scholarship, lectures, or even panel discussions. Performances alone would purportedly reveal a uniquely German dance aesthetic. But these gatherings were much smaller in scale than the Munich Dance Congress. Georgi, Wigman, Kreutzberg, Maudrik, Kratina, Laban, Palucca, and Günther contributed pieces to the 1934 festival, held in conjunction with a large museum exhibit on dance in art, but the following year only Wigman, Palucca, Kreutzberg,

Maudrik, and Günther returned. Rogge, however, presented *Amazonen;* Helga Svedlund, ballet mistress at the Hamburg State Opera, gave her production of Ravel's *Pavanne;* and Lotte Wernicke, a Berlin lay movement choir director, premiered *Die Geburt der Arbeit* (music: Kessler), a "choric dance play" in six scenes that dramatized the "awakening of humanity and its path to various modes of labor which are the foundation of human community" (MS 159). The Nazi press had criticized some of the 1934 dances, including those by Wigman and Palucca, for being insufficiently or unimpressively German; the 1935 Rogge and Wernicke works were lauded as appropriate examples of "heroic" German bodily movement, but Goebbels apparently disliked *Amazonen* because it was too Greek in its iconography.

The provinciality of the festival strategy was obvious even to Goebbels; he therefore endorsed the idea of an International Dance Competition, sponsored by the government itself, to coincide with the 1936 Berlin Olympics. The newly formed Reichsbund für Gemeinschaftstanz invited participants from Italy, Poland, Holland, Rumania, Greece, Bulgaria, Austria, India, Yugoslavia, Canada, Switzerland, and Belgium. (Martha Graham declined an invitation to attend because she disapproved of Nazi persecution of Jewish dancers.) The competition emphasized dances of a folk-national character, although the German entries (from Palucca, Wigman, Maudrik, Günther, Kreutzberg, and Kölling) displayed almost no connection to folk-dance forms. Laban promoted the lay movement choir concept as a modern form of folk dance, and he planned a large, four-part "choric consecration play," *Vom Tauwind und der neuen Freude,* involving 1,000 lay persons from thirty German cities, for performance in the new Dietrich-Eckart Amphitheatre. The piece derived its inspiration from Nietzsche's *Also sprach Zarathustra.* Harry Pierenkamper directed the first part, "Kampf," employing choirs from Mannheim, Heidelberg, and Frankfurt; Albrecht Knust and Lotte Müller supervised the second part, "Freude," with choirs from nine cities. Heide Woog directed choirs from the Ruhr area in the "Weihe" section, and Lotte Wernicke led the entire ensemble in "Besinnung." As Marie Luise Lieschke, Laban's chief assistant for lay movement education, explained: "We have grown out of the I-and-You era into the We era—but not so that we are merely 'masses': we are a people's community [Volksgemeinschaft], led by the Führer, and our lay dance is education in this sense: to lead and become led" (*Wir tanzen,* 7). But when Goebbels, along with 20,000 others, attended a dress rehearsal of the production, he (apparently alone) expressed deep disappointment, regarding the piece as too "intellectual" and a dilettantish masquerade of Nazism that really had "nothing at all to do with us" (MS 166). He thus compelled the withdrawal from the competition of both the consecration play and Rogge's *Amazonen.* From this point on, Laban's relations with the regime became progressively colder, with Rudolf Bode rising to favor as the leader of movement education.

At the Olympic Games themselves, Carl Diem, coordinator of the entire event, had arranged for the performance of a gigantic festival spectacular, *Olympischer Jugend,* following the 1 August 1936 opening ceremony, watched by 100,000 persons. Directed by Hanns Niedecken-Gebhard, it was a nocturnal event in five scenes. It began with the tolling of the huge Olympic bell and the appearance of 2,500 girls, age ten to twelve, in white dresses, followed by 900 young men in different-colored gymnastic uniforms, then 2,300 teenage girls. Under powerful spotlights these huge groups performed an immense round dance choreographed by Dorothee Günther and Maja Lex to music by Carl Orff. Günther and Lex juxtaposed large, marching phalanxes of dancers against flowering, swirling circles of girls. The second scene, "Anmut der Mädchen," choreographed by Palucca, employed the teenage girls in a vast waltz, followed by a solo waltz, which Palucca danced herself. The music was again Orff's, after Palucca decided she could not dance to the excessively modern piece offered by Werner Egk. In the third scene, male athletes marched with flags from many nations, circling around bonfires and singing hymns composed by Egk. The fourth scene drifted into a tragic mood, commemorating heroic struggle and sacrificial death for one's country. For this scene, Kreutzberg designed a weapon dance for sixty male dancers carrying shields, all of whom "died" in the end; Wigman followed with a lamentational dance for dead heroes involving about sixty female dancers. Again, Egk composed the music for these pieces. The final scene, "Olympischer Hymnus," entailed the singing by everyone in the stadium of the "Ode to Joy" section of Beethoven's Ninth Symphony while the great spotlights, introduced by Albert Speer, panned across the field and soared upward in a stunning colonnade to the heavens.

None of this stirring spectacle appeared in Leni Riefenstahl's film masterpiece, *Olympische Spiele* (1938), because she and her cameramen did not think they had enough light to shoot the scenes (Downing 83). Instead, she inserted outdoor shots of nude female dancers, undulating "eurhythmically," as she put it, under a cloud-dappled sky. These images of bacchanalian dancing bodies served as the transition from the mythic, male world of classical athletic competition to the lighting of the Olympic flame (Diem's idea) in the twentieth-century stadium. This very mysterious effect dramatizes the unity of the athletic body to nature much more powerfully than the stadium spectacle. But *Olympische Jugend* dramatized far more vividly the integration of the athletic body into a vast image of community in which all bodies were minute compared to the great movement of the whole.

The assumption persists that, because a fascist government endorsed and promoted *Olympische Jugend,* mass movement and dancing are inherently expressions of totalitarian ideology (e.g., Manning, 195–201). However, the piece contained no Nazi iconography and glorified youth and Olympian

Thingspiel

aspiration as the foundation of an international sense of community. *Olympische Jugend* treated athletic competition as a political ideology unto itself, to which all other ideologies remained subordinate, if not altogether eclipsed. Still, the relation between mass movement and totalitarianism demands clarification, for the Nazis obviously adopted lay movement choir techniques in the production of numerous propaganda spectacles, especially with the curious genre known as the *Thingspiel*, which flourished between 1933 and 1937. The *Thingspiel* derived its name from the *Thing*, or outdoor judgment space, designated by pagan-Teutonic tribes to decide communal problems. However, the *Thingspiel* was an expressionistic, multimedia genre designed for open-air performance employing speech choirs, movement choirs, singing choirs, narrators, and elaborate scenographic effects involving banners, marches, loudspeakers, spotlights, and projections. Although the Nazi Party sponsored nearly all performances of *Thingspiele*, the productions functioned at the civic-amateur level, often entailing thousands of performers supervised by SA and SS officials. The *Thingspiel*, "which frequently assumed the character of an oratorio," was apparently a genuinely popular genre: the Nazis built amphitheatres to perform the works in 62 cities but could not accommodate the demand for nearly 500 (Eichberg 139).

The texts for *Thingspiele* came from authors close to expressionism, including Richard Euringer, Eberhard Wolfgang Möller, Kurt Heynicke, Max Halbe, Heinrich Zerkaulen, Heinrich Lersch, Gustav Goes, Heinrich Harrer, Max Ziese. In the *Thingspiel*, the protagonist was always "the people" (embodied by choirs), who struggled, with simple, heroic pathos, against the evil inflicted by capitalism, bolshevism, Judaism, industrialization, unemployment, hunger, the "backstabbing" diplomats who contrived the Versailles Treaty, decadent intellectualism, gangsters, racial impurity, and the foolish, misguided administrators of democracy in the Weimar Republic. The salvation of the people depended on the emergence of the Führer, representatives of the SA or SS, or potent symbols of Germanic or Aryan heritage. Menz (340) contends that the *Thingspiel* represented the "revolutionary" phase of the Third Reich, which emphasized the socialism in National Socialism (although a faction around Alfred Rosenberg and opposed by Goebbels stressed reactionary glorification of archaic Teutonic mythology). The revolutionary phase came to an end with the production of *Olympische Jugend*. From that point on the party ceased to sponsor *Thingspiele* and drastically curtailed its authorization of independent productions, although Hans Baumann's *Passauer Niebelungenspiel* appeared as late as 1939. The reason for the policy change remains obscure, but apparently Goebbels felt the party could not maintain sufficient control over the utopian dreams ignited by these productions and over the large measure of improvisation that prevailed within them (Eichberg 147). Such performances did not adequately prepare the people for the impending reality of war.

Antecedent The *Thingspiel* was hardly a uniquely Nazi innovation. Menz (332–333) identifies numerous models for the genre, including Greek tragedy, medieval mystery plays, and the grandiose spectacles of Max Reinhardt; Eberhard Wolfgang Möller claimed that Brecht's *Lehrstücke* provided superb models for *Thingspiele* texts. But Eichberg points to more immediate precedents in the mass theatre of the Social Democrats in the Weimar Republic. Festival or "sacramental" plays, often on a huge scale, appeared at mass events sponsored by labor and socialist organizations in the early 1920s, with Leipzig (1920–1924) being an especially fertile site of innovation (Pfützner). Bertha Lask's *Die Toten rufen* (1923) and Gustav von Wangenheim's *Chor der Arbeit* (1923) and *7000* (1924) were notable examples before the First International Workers' Olympics in Frankfurt in 1925, which saw a vast production of Alfred Auerbach's *Kampf um die Erde*. A workers' festival of gymnastics in Nuremburg (1929) featured *Mach dich frei!* involving 60,000 persons in the spectacular drama of a great proletarian storm troop that "takes up the fight to free all intellectually, economically, socially, and politically enslaved people from their bondage." Yet another festival play, created by Robert Ehrenzweig for the Second Workers' Olympics in Vienna (1931), used 5,000 performers and dramatized the "revolutionary awakening" of the proletariat against "the oppressive ages of industrial servitude." In the final "storm of enthusiasm uniting the masses, the golden idol [of capitalism] sinks away, and from the platform come the lanterns of freedom—at first single torches in a chorus of joy, then bands and streams of light, which surround the high circle and expand and swell through the marathon gate to the accompaniment of the Internationale sung by 65,000. The torch procession, through the Prater to city hall, is joined by the audience" (Eichberg 143–144).

All these productions plainly resembled the *Thingspiel* in their open-air deployment of marches, flags, loudspeakers, speech and movement choirs, narrators, generic identities, expressionistic language of pathos and euphoria, torches, gigantic emblems, protagonization of "the people," audience participation, and narratives focused on the struggle of the masses to overcome abiding indignities (Rühle 35–40; Bartetzko, 133–143). On the formal level, then, the *Thingspiel* was scarcely revolutionary. But even after it waned, around 1936, the Nazis continued to stage vast mass spectacles similar to the awesome 1934 party rally documented so ominously in Riefenstahl's famous film *Triumph of the Will* (1935). With the success of *Olympische Jugend*, Niedecken-Gebhard, still busy staging Handel operas, became probably the most significant director of mass spectacles in the Reich, supervising the gigantic nocturnal Olympic Stadium celebration (1937) of Berlin's seven hundredth anniversary. This event involved 5,000 schoolchildren and 7,000 members of the army, Gestapo, Labor Service, SS, Nazi women's auxiliary groups, and Hitler Youth, along with 360 dancers performing folk dances, death dances, waltzes, sword dances, harvest dances, and soldier dances choreographed by such people as Berthe Trümpy, Marianne Vogelsang, and Reich folk dance expert Erich Janietz (Figure 66). In 1938, Niedecken-Gebhard produced *Volk in Leibesübungen* for an athletic festival in Breslau, this time calling on Dorothee Günther, Marta Welsen, Berthe Trümpy, and Günther Hess to handle choreographic assignments; the piece concluded with a triumphant entry march of flag-bearing army troops under an immense dome of light. *Glückliches Volk* (1938), presented at the Berlin stadium, showed an idealized, Biedermeier world of graceful, waltzing women (300 of them) protected by an ever-vigilant, heroically disciplined military. *Triumph des Lebens* (1939), the last of the mass spectacles, was staged in a Munich stadium and again paired "manly strength" and "womanly grace" in gigantic folk dances and marches involving 1,000 girls and several thousand uniformed men. The pieces were choreographed by Günther, Peters-Pawlinin, Trümpy, and instructors from the Elisabeth Duncan school; Maja Lex and Harald Kreutzberg performed solos, and, as usual, the thing concluded with a monumental hymnic surge of humanity toward the swastika (MS 146–149).

Goebbels favored these productions because they adopted the model of the 1934 party rally in Nuremburg, which in itself was an enormous elaboration of the Nazi performance aesthetic before 1933. This aesthetic did not tell stories of struggle and revolution but stressed the *reality of the moment.* The mass spectacle did not merely imagine utopia but embodied it through manifestations of power and perfection embedded in, rather than signified by, the act of performance: the mystic figure of the leader, gigantic emblems (eagle and swastika), torches, bonfires, spotlights, flags and drums, loudspeakers, dramatic uniforms, the continuous movement of countless bodies across a vast space, and sudden moments of reverential stillness. Individual bodily movements were simple (march-step, salute), synchronized, and unisonal yet nevertheless capable of creating complex designs, such as an enormous, swirling swastika produced by streams of torch-bearing columns. But on a formal level, mass movement on this scale did not differ significantly from the lay movement choirs of Laban and Gleisner. The appeal of mass movement lay in its power to turn simple action into a large-scale, transformative end in itself, a destiny rather than a referent of an imaginary existence. Laban's improvisations with movement choirs shared this reverence for action with the militarized, machine-precise synchronizations of the Nazi mass performance aesthetic, for action in this sense strengthened and ultimately expanded the identity of any group. The totalitarian identity of mass movement therefore does not reside inherently in the formal qualities of such movement in itself but in the content of the movement, in those symbols and emblems imposed upon the movement that identify action with a "total" vision of community; the symbol, not the movement, subsumes all difference. The same mass movement devices can make a swastika or a star; totalitarianism is not inherent in either. However, the swastika rather than the star became a totalitarian symbol because it urged people to act on behalf of a community that invariably valued sameness over difference.

Left: Figure 47. Mila and Elia Cirul performing *Tentation,* Paris, 1935. Photographer unknown, from AI 21.

Right: Figure 48. Niddy Impekoven performing *Der gefangene Vogel,* ca. 1919. Photograph by Hanns Holdt, Munich, from HB, plate 99.

Figure 49. Gret Palucca performing one of her famous leaps, Dresden, ca. 1927. Photograph by Charlotte Rudolph, from a contemporary postcard.

Figure 50. Gret Palucca dancing. Drawing by Wassily Kandinsky, from *Tanzkurven zu den Tänzen der Palucca* (1925).

Figure 51. Valeska Gert in a typically impudent pose, Munich, ca. 1922. Photograph by Hanns Holdt, from Fritz Giese, *Körperseele* (1924), plate 75.

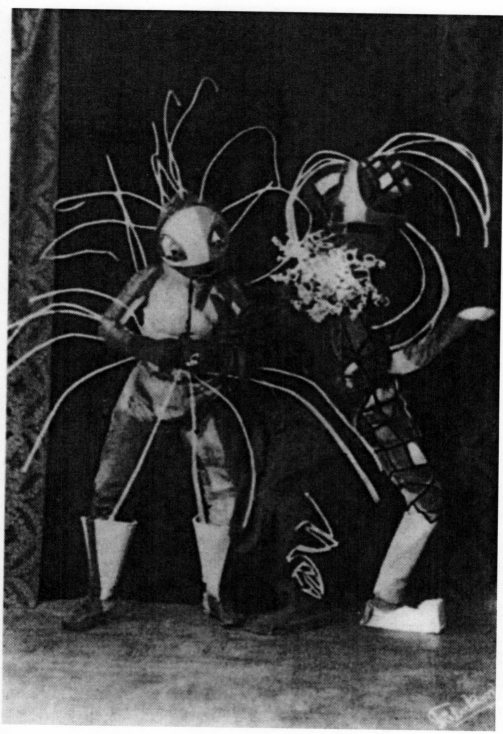

Figure 52. Walter Holdt and Lavinia Schulz performing as "Tobaggan" and "Springvieh," Hamburg, ca. 1922. From Hamburg Museum für Kunst und Gewerbe.

Figure 53. Clotilde von Derp and Alexander Sacharoff, ca. 1917. Photographed by Hugo Erfurt and G. Puschtivoi, from HB, plates 48 and 55.

Left: Figure 54. Yvonne Georgie, Hannover, 1926. From a contemporary postcard.
Right: Figure 55. Harald Kreutzberg as the Master of Ceremonies in Gozzi's *Turandot*, Berlin, 1927. From Emil Pirchan, *Harald Kreutzberg* (1941), plate 20.

Figure 56. Vera Skoronel. Photo by Suse Byk, from RLM, plate 39.

Figure 57. A scene in Skoronel's *Tanzspiel*, 1927. Photo by Suse Byk, from RLM, plate 43.

Top: Figure 58. Scene from Hertha Feist's *Die Berufung,* Berlin, 1927–1928. Photo by Suse Byk, from RLM, plate 5.
Bottom: Figure 59. Unidentified dance performed by students of Jutta Klamt, Berlin, ca. 1928. Photo from the Joan Erikson Archive of the Harvard Theatre Collection.

Figure 62. Convoluted configuration of group movement, with individualized bodies of group members, in Margarethe Wallmann's dance drama *Das jüngste Gericht*, Salzburg, 1931. From the Theatre Collection of Cologne University.

FACING PAGE:
Top: Figure 60. Gertrud Bodenwieser's *Dämon Maschine* (1924). Photograph by D'Ora Benda, from Faber, *Tanzfoto* (1991), 69.
Bottom: Figure 61. A scene from Lola Rogge's *Amazonen* (1935), with Gerti Maack, as Penthesilea, leading the Amazons. Photo by Estorff-Volkmann, from Stöckemann, *Lola Rogge* (1991), 88.

Figure 63. Mass movement. Students
from the Margarete Schmidts school in
Essen, 1927. From RLM, plate 64.

Figure 64. Image of ecstatic mass movement in the Flemish *massatooneel. Tota Pul-
chra es!*, Moorslede, 1935. From Jozef
Boon, *Spreekkoor en massatooneel* (1937).

Top: Figure 65. Flemish mass movement. *Het werk onzer handen!,* Antwerp, 1935. From Jozef Boon, *Spreekkoor en massatooneel* (1937).
Bottom: Figure 66. Spectacle celebrating "Berlin in seven hundred years of German history" at Olympic Stadium in Berlin, 1937. From the Theatre Collection of Cologne University.

Figure 67. An example of Jaap Kool's effort to integrate movement notation with music notation, here for a dance by Grit Hegesa. From Kool, *Tanzschrift* (1927), 24.

Figure 68. The "shadows" section of Mary Wigman's *Der Weg* (1932). Photo by Albert Renger-Patzsch, from MWB 83.

TÄNZE DER FALKE·SCHULE

Figure 69. Poster designed
by Ursula Falke announcing
dances performed by stu-
dents of the Falke sisters'
school in Hamburg, 1917,
from Hamburg Museum für
Kunst und Gewerbe.

Figure 70. A woman dancing
while wearing glasses. Expressionist painting by Hugo
Scheiber, Berlin, ca. 1928,
from Darany, *Hugo Scheiber.
Leben und Werk* (1982).

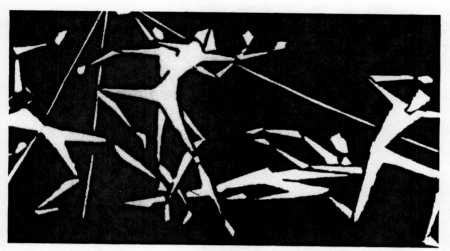

Figure 72. Luise Grimm's
woodcut *Tanzszene*, Berlin,
1923. From Ruthenberg,
Luise Grimm (1985), 52.

Figure 73. Mary Wigman and
her dance group. Charcoal
drawing by Luise Grimm
(1924), from Ruthenberg,
Luise Grimm (1985), 59.

FACING PAGE:
Figure 71. Erika Vogt. Painting in "Neue Sächlichkeit" style by Fritz Uphoff, Worpswede, 1930, from Küster, *Kunstwerkstatt Worpswede* (1989), 159.

Figure 74. *Jazz* (1931). Woodcut by Frans Masereel, from Galerie Bodo Niemann, Berlin.

Figure 75. *The Break-down* (1926). Painting by John Bulloch Souter, from Bourne Gallery, London.

Figure 76. Toni Freeden cradling the steel sculpture of her head by her husband, Rudolf Belling, Berlin, 1925. From Nerdinger, *Rudolf Belling* (1981), 205.

Figure 77. Dancers rehearsing in the Himmelssaal of the Atlantis House in Bremen, 1930. From Golücke, *Bernhard Hoetger* (1982), 97.

Figure 79. *Study of Russian dancers*, Vienna, 1926.
Photograph by Rudolf Koppitz, from Faber, *Tanzfoto*
(1991), 61.

FACING PAGE:
Figure 78. An example of the dramatic athletic pho-
tography of Gerhard Riebicke, Berlin, ca. 1930. From
Wick, *Hunde vor der Kamera* (1989), 80.

Left: Figure 80. Experimental dance. Photograph by Marta Vietz, Berlin, ca. 1931, from Frecot, *Marta Astfalck-Vietz* (1991), 21.
Right: Figure 81. Dore Hoyer, Dresden, 1934. Superimposition photograph by Edmund Kesting, from Galerie Bodo Niemann, Berlin.

FACING PAGE:
Top: Figure 82. Olga Gzovska, performing her Salome dance, Prague, 1912. Photograph by Frantisek Drtikol, one of a series documenting the entire dance and published as a folio, from Museum of Applied Art, Prague.
Bottom: Figure 83. Untitled photograph by Frantisek Drtikol, Prague, 1928. From Birgus and Brany, *Frantisek Drtikol* (1988), plate 68.

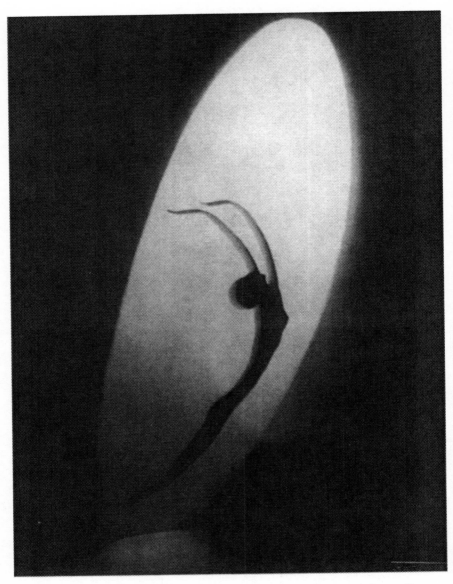

Figure 84. *Composition* photograph by Frantisek Drtikol using paper figure, Prague, 1930, from Birgus and Brany, *Frantisek Drtikol* (1988), plate 83.

Music and Movement

The power of music to motivate unusual, aesthetically interesting bodily movement is a strange, hardly understood neurophysiological phenomenon, and the idea that bodily movement "means more" when accompanied by music has dominated dance culture throughout the world since prehistoric times. But exact relations between music and movement are unstable and subject to all sorts of cultural relativism. To an unprecedented degree in dance history, the Weimar era exposed numerous complexities and ambiguities in relations between music and movement, without, however, producing any transformative theoretical perspective on the problem. Of course, Dalcroze proclaimed that music, particularly rhythm, determined and regulated movement, and Dalcroze's disciples in Europe were multitudinous. But Dalcroze was merely a starting point, for many dancers decided to explore the "independence" of bodily movement from music. No doubt the expanding gymnastic culture assumed much responsibility for encouraging these explorations. Yet in some ways the Weimar dance culture made music more significant than ever by revealing the mysterious capacity of the body to engage in dialogue with that power of expression that seems to have no body, no image at all.

Modern dance displayed an ambivalent attitude toward modern music. The vast majority of modern dancers favored classical music from the previous century, especially works from the romantic repertoire and especially in the years before 1923, when solo dancing prevailed considerably over group dancing. In a survey of more than two hundred European dance concert programs between 1910 and 1926, I discovered a strong preference for the following composers: Grieg, Schumann, Chopin, Tchaikovsky, Brahms, Schubert, Mozart, and Dvořák. The Dutch dancer Tilly Sylon compiled an instruction list of 375 "Dalcroze dances" dominated by these

same composers ("Gertrud Leistikow"). Modern (or living) composers in
the repertoires of most European dancers before 1925 included Rachmaninoff, Scriabin, Moszkowski, Cyril Scott, Schmitt, Debussy, Ravel, Granados,
Satie, and Sibelius. Modern music during this period was vaguely synonymous with an "exotic" coloring or "foreign" mood. Dances on the solo program rarely lasted more than four minutes, and *the length of the music determined the length of the dance.* One never finds a single dance accompanied by
music from different composers, although in the early 1920s, Wigman and
others began experimenting with "cycles" comprising different dances using
different pieces of music. Solo dancers probably favored nineteenth-century
composers partly because their music was cheaper than contemporary
music, which required royalty payments. Few dancers ever collaborated
closely with a composer; Grit Hegesa's long partnership with Jaap Kool was
completely unique. Even when, after 1925, dancers became bolder in seeking music in an aggressively modern idiom (Bartók, Haba, Wellesz, Stravinsky, Milhaud, Hindemith, Slavensky, Prokofiev), they tended to use works
that had been composed independently, not specifically for dance. The
major exceptions here were Gunild Keetman's work for Dorothee Günther
and Maja Lex, Friedrich Wilckens's collaboration with Harald Kreutzberg,
and Fritz Cohen's compositions for Kurt Jooss. Max Terpis favored original
ballets by modern German composers, but he wrote nearly all the librettos
himself and thus felt no great inclination to maintain a close working relation with any composer or, for that matter, to build movements out of the
music. As a result, critics complained that his dances lacked "musicality."

Moreover, composers, even those who were enthusiastic about dance,
generally did not feel comfortable with the idea of collaborating with
dancers. Egon Wellesz (1885–1974) was one of the busiest composers of
dance and theatre music, but he liked being a free agent who could shape
the libretto as well as the score. Music was "modern" for most dancers
because of its rhythmic rather than harmonic complexity, and for that reason it was practically impossible to find a dance accompanied by atonal or
twelve-tone music. Indeed, scarcely any dancer showed the boldness of
Janine Solane (b. 1912), who, for her 1932 solo debut concert in Paris,
danced a single large work, *L'Abandon celeste,* entirely to the music of Wagner. Ellinor Tordis in Vienna perhaps approached her by creating several
dances in 1922–1924 using piano transcriptions for sections of Bruckner's
Seventh Symphony. From a harmonic perspective, the modernist composer
who most appealed to dancers was probably Scriabin, whose difficult piano
pieces emphatically identified ecstatic experience with richly chromatic
chord structures rather than driving rhythms.

Overwhelmingly, the preferred instrument of accompaniment was the
solo piano, even for ensemble pieces, for this instrument provided the
cheapest means of achieving maximum tonal coloration and rhythmic

strength. Exceptions were rare: Alexander Sacharoff used two harps, Lili Green supplemented the piano with a violin or soprano voice, and Lavinia Schulz was accompanied by a solo saxophone. Anita Berber was apparently the first to dance to gramophone records, around 1925, and Gertrud Leistikow experimented briefly with street organ accompaniments in the late 1920s. But in any case, dancers who used accompaniments other than the piano restricted them to one or two dances on a program. Of course, the Günther cult, under the influence of Keetman and Carl Orff, constructed its own orchestra of wood flutes and percussion instruments; even more unique, Günther and Lex completely integrated music-making into the dance, so that the playing of instruments was no less important than pure bodily movement to the choreography. Conventional orchestral accompaniments for *Ausdruckstanz* appeared more frequently after modern dance developed affiliations with the subsidized theatres, which could afford to finance large royalties and rehearsals for a large set of musicians. Orchestral accompaniments elevated the prestige of dance as a cultural institution but invariably subordinated bodily expression to often conventional narrative expectations.

The great bulk of Weimar orchestral music for modern dance has long since disappeared from the stage, the concert hall, and the recording studio; a few of Hindemith's works occasionally appear on disk, but Egon Wellesz's dance compositions of the 1920s have suffered decades of unjust neglect. Jaap Kool wrote several fine orchestral dance compositions during the decade, but his later sympathy with Naziism seems to have kept him in oblivion in both Holland and Germany. No German composer in a modernist vein appealed as much to dancers as a variety of foreign modernists: Bartók, Stravinsky, Ravel, Schmitt, Prokofiev, Satie, Malipiero, Milhaud. Germany possessed greater resources than any other country to sponsor original dance orchestral music, yet no German achievements in this domain have matched the greatest works that Diaghilev, with no help at all from the state, managed to inspire in such composers as Ravel, Stravinsky, and Prokofiev. Indeed, the most popular German ballet music of the 1920s, Strauss's *Josephs Legende* (1914), was actually a commission from Diaghilev. But Diaghilev exerted such magnetism and awakened such intense ambition precisely because he had no serious competitors in Paris and could present the Ballets Russes as the ultimate opportunity for the marriage of new music and new dance. In Germany, however, no city, no theatre, and no personality could ever become established as "ultimate," because Germans regarded power as an expansive rather than concentrative phenomenon. Dance established its own authority when its value did not depend on music that enjoyed a life apart from the dance and that often subordinated the dancer's intention to the composer's. It was a matter of getting musicians to follow dancers instead of dancers following musicians.

Folk tunes and tunes from social dance forms, such as the tango and the habanera, appeared in dance concerts before World War I, and jazz music accompanied dancers as early as 1919 in the revues and cabarets; Kool had experimented with "blues" pieces for Hegesa during the war in Rotterdam. Jazz, however, tended to inspire gimmicky dances of a satirical nature that exposed the eccentric currents of ecstasy circulating within cosmopolitan night life; examples include H. H. Stückenschmidt's shimmy for Lavinia Schulz and Walter Holdt in *Die Ungeheuer vom Sirius* (1922), Wilhelm Grosz's music for Yvonne Georgi's *Baby in der Bar* (1928), and Gertrud Boden-wieser's *Jazzbandparodie* (1932). Jazz functioned as a category of light music with little capacity to urge the body into dark, tragic, mysterious, or monumental moods, although Kool, who authored an excellent treatise on the saxophone (1931), revealed a strong gift for blues invention and melancholy handling of social dance forms. The waltz remained the dominant social dance form in the repertoires of modern dancers, and not surprisingly: the vast majority of dancers were women and thus were expected to represent a connection between lyricism and feminine grace, which the waltz supplied more conveniently than perhaps any other musical genre. Yet Sibelius's somber and haunting *Valse triste* (1899) was a favorite among female dancers throughout Europe into the 1930s; the film actress Lil Dagover (1897–1980) made a deep impression when she danced this piece in a tight black evening gown (rather than a ballroom waltz dress) on a bizarre program of "Phantastisches Theater" in Berlin in 1919 (Ola Alsen in *Elegante Welt*, 8/19, 10 September 1919, 21).

Although the musical taste supporting the German dance culture may appear somewhat conservative, the relations between bodily movement and musical design showed an unprecedented experimental dimension. Some dancers, such as Clothilde von Derp and Mila Cirul, made dark or melancholy dances out of bright pieces of music; others, such as Julia Marcus and Valeska Gert, made comic dances out of dark compositions. The weird movements and costumes of Lavinia Schulz and Walter Holdt made any piece of music sound bizarre and alien. Dancers such as Ellen Tels and Hertha Feist would move rapidly to slow music or slowly to fast music. In Gertrud Leistikow's exquisite *Gnossienne*, Satie's music floats with hypnotic slowness, but the arms of the dancer undulate rapidly while the head, the torso, and the legs move far more slowly than the music. Wigman showed that deep tones do not necessarily accompany sinking motions, nor do notes in the high register signal the elevation of the body. Anita Berber revealed how soft or gentle music could accompany movements of extreme violence, and Charlotte Bara delighted in using music of grandeur to accompany movements of great delicacy. Jutta von Collande's preference for Gretry's music was significant insofar as it pleased her to demonstrate that she and no one else could persuasively dance to it. Niddy Impekoven sought to escape her pubescent, "imprisoned bird" image by dancing, with a kind of virginal voluptuousness, to the music of Bach. A more mysterious figure, Edith von Schrenck, loved the rapturous romanticism of Rachmaninoff and Scriabin, but their music did not send her rushing across the stage—instead, she contorted her body ecstatically within a very constricted portion of the performance space. Stranger still, in Hamburg, Erika Milee (b. 1907), a graduate (1928) of the Laban school and dancer for Kurt Jooss, produced a curious dance for the ghettoized Jüdische Kulturbund before receiving a teaching invitation that allowed her to migrate to Paraguay in 1939. *Ein Tag bei den Mickeymäusen* (1937), a "pantomimic revue" in ten scenes, depicted domestic scenes from the life of the Disney cartoon character Mickey Mouse and his family, but the music consisted of European folk melodies (Jockel 88–89).

These examples and many others I could retrieve from previous discussions indicate persistent *tensions* between music and the dancing body in the dance culture of the Weimar era, and in these tensions stir the aesthetics of the grotesque. In spite of all the rhetoric in the dance and gymnastic schools about restoring "harmony" to the body, a great many of the exciting dances of the era disclosed a deep distrust toward conventional harmonic order. Dance partially established its independence from music by setting ecstasy in tension with harmony.

But harmony proved less of a determinant of dance than did synchronization. The belief that musical rhythms regulate bodily rhythms is virtually universal. Dalcroze proposed a "natural" relation between musical and bodily rhythms, and for that reason he gave rhythm almost total power to motivate and define bodily movement. Performing a 3/4 waltz step to a 4/4 musical rhythm was a feat that dancers of the era (indeed, any era) found incredibly difficult to imagine. Dalcroze himself, in his obsession with composing exercises, stumbled across the underlying problem when he discovered how *unnatural* it was for the body to accommodate rapidly shifting musical rhythms, as when, for example, the meter (not to mention the tempo) shifts every measure or even every few measures from 3/4 to 5/4 to 4/4 to 3/8 to 6/2 to 3/16—an effect favored by Stravinsky. This observation strengthened the perception that synchronization depended on *sustained* musical rhythm, which habituated the body to such a degree that it actually constrained bodily expressivity and freedom.

To free the body from music, Wigman and many others devised dances accompanied entirely by percussion instruments—various drums, tambourines, gongs, cymbals, triangles, woodblocks. Detached from harmonic structures, sonic designs would *follow* bodily rhythms rather than determine them. Percussion sounds (rather than rhythms) stripped music of its power to blind or to weaken visual perception. In an article for a 1931 issue of *Schrifttanz*, Hanns Hasting, the percussion composer for Wigman, declared that harmony, as an increasingly discredited sonic quality that creates a "sense of spaciousness," "is not a valid expression for dance," because dance produces an impression of space that is more "fluid, intangible, and imaginary" (VP 73–74). What he meant in a cruder sense was that the percussionist had to watch the dancer very carefully to know when to strike the drum or gong and could not simply count beats to structure the space of the music.

Because dance seemed to challenge the authority of music to regulate bodily movement, composers themselves began to review the conditions under which music was appropriate for dance. In *Tanz in dieser Zeit* (1926), Paul Stefan gathered a valuable collection of statements from nine composers (80–91). Friedrich Wilckens maintained that effective dance music entailed an emphatic, controlling rhythm and a distinctive melody but not harmonic, contrapuntal, or rhythmic complexity, for "while the ear can easily follow rapid tempos and abrupt changes of musical rhythm, the eye is not capable of following too complicated movement rhythms" (82)—definitely a synchronist perspective. But Alfredo Casella contended that dance music was not defined by the intentions that created it, that any music was danceable, and Vittorio Rieti echoed him, claiming that music was danceable to the extent that a dancer discerned a way to move to it. Ernst Krenek, after supposing that "dance without music is unthinkable," settled for the view that music amplified the dramatic effect of performance. Erwin Schulhoff confessed that the composition of dance music was for him an "erotic concept," for writing dance music meant thinking deeply about the body; but the image of the body intensified most through the use of percussion sounds, which he categorized as "masculine" (drums), "feminine" (tambourines), or bisexual (cymbals, triangle, ratchet, whip, gong, Japanese wood drum). Schulhoff further proposed that modern dance music had no life independent of dance performance. But Felix Petyrek argued for a distinction between "pantomimic" music, which was "programmatic," and "dance" music, which was "absolute" and defined by abstract musical categories, chiefly rhythm. Heinz Tiessen reinforced this view: "[T]he more suggestive the rhythm, the stronger the fusion of music and dance" into an "organic totality." Egon Wellesz straightforwardly declared: "The are no special laws of dance composition"; though "the composer who writes for dance must have a clear optical vision of dance," knowledge of the choreographic process must not override purely musical considerations. Jaap Kool, however, argued that a dancer danced not only the rhythm (assigned to the feet and legs) but also the melody (assigned to the arms and upper body), and this "symmetrical construction of the body" required music of similar symmetricality: "a too finely differentiated ambience is unplastic."

Both Kool and Wellesz reflected elsewhere on the identity of dance music. At the Magdeburg Congress of 1927, Wellesz, in a lengthy speech,

linked the relation between dance and music to large cultural and historical processes that had evolved toward the present moment, when the identity of dance music was completely "subjective" and governed by an intricate
complex of psychological variables. The work of Laban, Wigman, and
Niedecken-Gebhard was revelatory in showing unprecedented possibilities
of bodily expressivity that rendered all previous models of dance music
composition obsolete. For Wellesz, modern dance music implied above all
complex rhythmic contrasts that pushed both music and dance toward ever
greater complexity of expression. This complexity was necessary to achieve
the synthesis of will and drive, which the nineteenth-century ideal of civilization had separated (*Die Tat,* 19/8 November 1927, 597–604).

Kool's perspective was more anthropological than historical. He sought
the identity of dance music in an "original" but repressed relation between
sound, rhythm, and movement ascribed to prehistoric and primitive cultures, as indicated in his little book *Tänze der Naturvölker* (1921). In *Tänze
und Tanzszene* (1920) he treated dance as an exotic form of bodily expression that benefited from music influenced by exotic (chiefly Asian)
rhythms and harmonies. Kool's interest in jazz derived from his belief that
this form of music emanated from a buried, primitive notion of pulse. In a
brief article on the composition of social dance music, he asserted that the
appeal of a dance tune depended on what one "does *not* hear": "the most
important thing is, so to speak, what lies behind the music": namely, the
"nerves," the "energy," the "tension," which disturb the "inner" stability of
the body and urge it to move, though not necessarily in agreement with
the "external" rhythms of the music (*Tanzsport Almanach 1924,* 89–94). A
couple of years later, in a statement on "noise instruments," he observed
that the difference between tones and noises became blurred when one
examined the acoustic properties of percussion instruments; the primeval
power of percussion instruments—"mystic drums"—to blur distinctions
between tonality and noise was the foundation of ecstatic release from the
"demon and Moloch of our time," rationality, with its sharp distinctions
between identities (Stefan 77–79). Kool supported this view by composing
a concert piece for 28 drums.

By 1929, however, Alfred Schlee, an editor with the Viennese music publisher Universal Edition, perceived that dance and music seemed to move
in completely different directions, neither of which was healthy for the
other: musicians buried themselves in the notes, dancers buried themselves
in "expression," and neither paid sufficient attention to the audience perspective. In a 1929 article for *Schrifttanz,* a Universal Edition publication, he
saw technology as the solution to the conflict: mechanical instruments,
gramophone recordings, film models, and a new collaboration between
composer, dancer, and engineer (VP 69–72). Among many other musical-
theatrical activities, Schlee (b. 1901) worked with Wigman, Georgi, and

Niedecken-Gebhard, edited for publication compositions by composers prominent in the modern dance empire (Bartók, Grosz, Wellesz, Kool, Schulhoff, Wilckens, Milhaud, Krenek), composed percussion pieces for Georgi and piano dances for Ruth Abramovitch, and played the piano accompaniment for Oskar Schlemmer's *Triadic Ballet* in Paris in 1932 (Oberzaucher-Schüller). He thus enjoyed influential status in both the dance and music worlds. Yet his idea of mechanizing musical accompaniments to accommodate dance expressivity went nowhere. Some composers did write unmechanized music that attempted to evoke machines or sound like them, and more than a few choreographers created dances about humans turned (alas, of course) into machines (Rode 270–271). Such was, one might say, the legacy of synchronism in the uneasy relation between music and dance.

Dance theorists showed less inclination than composers to define the identity of dance music. In promoting the independence of *Ausdruckstanz,* they found it expedient to push the issue of music to the periphery of consciousness. Thus, in *Tanzkunst* (1926), Fritz Böhme explored numerous categories of dance, cultural-historical contexts for dance, and pedagogical problems of dance without even mentioning music. Brandenburg devoted only two pages to dance music in *Der moderne Tanz,* simply stressing the need for dance to maintain its independence (222–223). Lämmel, in his *Der moderne Tanz,* had even less to say about music, as his major aim was to establish the arbitrariness of music in relation to the expressive rhythms of the body. The controversy that reverberated in the music world between proponents of opulently sensuous music for dance (Franz Schreker, Alexander Zemlinsky) and proponents of undecorative, "functional music" (*Gebrauchsmusik*), many of whom were students of Schreker (Hindemith, Krenek, Wilckens, Schulhoff), scarcely seemed to exist for the dance theorists. In *Körperseele* (1924), Fritz Giese, coming from a gymnastic orientation, spent a mere three pages discussing "musicality," which he largely defined as a "bridge" to discovery of unique sources of rhythm within the body: dance "musicality" resided within the body, not the music (143–145).

Frank Thiess, in *Der Tanz als Kunstwerk* (1923), devoted somewhat more attention to the issue. He suggested that dance and music emerged simultaneously from a common origin: rhythm. They were like two siblings who, despite being quite different, nevertheless enjoyed an affinity for each other. This affinity manifested itself through "structural parallelism," whereby dance was a response to music, not an illustration or translation of it. The same piece of music could produce entirely different dances of equal artistic value: for example, Lucy Kieselhausen's "tender and perfumed" version of Mozart's "Gavotte joyeuse" and Rony Johansson's "grotesque," satyr-like version. One could imagine many other versions of the same music. Nor did Thiess (unlike "hundreds" of other critics) object to pantomimic dramas accompanied by music with no programmatic content of any sort. Indeed, because artistic dance was a response to music, not a child of it, music was "not necessary" at all for dance (37–42).

By 1923, this assertion hardly seemed radical, for "silent dances" appeared on concert programs almost simultaneously with the advent of the percussion orchestras in Hellerau and in Laban's Ascona camp. Alexander Sacharoff introduced a silent dance in Munich in 1913, and Wigman's first solo dance, at Ascona in 1914, was silent. By the mid-1920s numerous dancers included a silent piece in their repertoires, and the appeal of silent dances continued into the 1930s, although by then it took considerable imagination to provide any more surprises using this concept. Laban loved to improvise with unaccompanied movement choirs, yet in the concert hall group silent dances remained extremely rare. Ironically, group silent dances tend to sustain attention longer than solos. In *Der tanzende Mensch* (1921), devoted entirely to the theme of musicless dance, Fritz Böhme contemplated the significance of music more seriously. He argued that cultural and historical pressures conditioned a person to expect music with dance and to expect dance to obey music. With music dominating perception, the ear learned to process acoustic signs more quickly and confidently than the eye processed visual signs. This argument implied that behind the obedience to music resided a deep, culturally determined fear of looking intensely at the body. But if dance was to achieve an artistic identity of its own, such as music already possessed, then the body must display a power of expressiveness that owed nothing to music. Unfortunately, Böhme's language remained entirely on a cloudy theoretical plain; he did not demonstrate the authority of his speculations by analyzing any dance performances, silent or otherwise. But Böhme dedicated his pamphlet to Hertha Feist, who in 1915, we should recall, had improvised her unforgettably mysterious nude dance for him in the silent twilight of the summer woods.

HILDE STRINZ

Perhaps the most fanatical advocate of the silent dance was Hilde Strinz (1902–1927), who inspired strong admiration from Böhme. After studying ballet for several years, she presented her first solo concert in Berlin in 1921 with a program accompanied entirely by music of romantic composers (Grieg, Schumann, Beethoven, Liszt). But already she sensed the limitations of music in releasing the "inner tones and melodies of the body." She searched for revelatory teachers, but none seemed radical enough; the strongest dance influence in her life was apparently Pavlova. Wigman, seeing Strinz's great potential, tried without success to keep her as a student. For the most part, Strinz developed her aesthetic alone and in isolation, though she showed up at the Magdeburg Congress in 1927: "a woman travels a bitter path of sorrow when she ventures out and becomes a creator." She did not present her second concert until 1925, earning money in the interim by dancing in cabarets in Dresden, Leipzig, and Berlin. At the second concert, also in Berlin, she used no musical accompaniment but titled her dances with abstract categories of musical form (adagio, scherzo, polonaise, minuet, waltz, two-voice melody). The third Berlin concert, in 1926, was also musicless and even more abstract. Here she performed two four-part cycles of dances, with each cycle following the four-movement structure of a musical sonata. Thus, the four movements of *Tanzstück Nr. 2* were: 1) allegro, with great swinging power; 2) adagio, sunk and burdened; 3) allegretto, light but with energy; 4) finale, rising out of the depths, quietly, rhythm with quickening feet. Her "four dances in red, with restrained passion to dance" carried even more abstract designations of their identities (*Fantasie Nr. 1, 2, 3, and 4*). For her final Berlin concert, in February 1927, Strinz formed an ensemble of seven women to present group dances without music. The concert was not entirely silent, for in a couple of the dances she employed a drum. This time she followed classical sonata form less rigidly. A "pathetic dance piece" contained five movements: majaestoso, adagio, march, scherzo-trio-da capo, and finale. The "unsung songs" contained three movements, including a choir with solo "voice" and a "night song," but *Chorodie* was in one movement, with drum and group choir.

Strinz's willingness to use abstract musical structures as models for dance structures did not really compromise her determination to detach dance from music; her ambition was to free dance from the *sound* of music and to advance dance as visual music. Her aesthetic had barely reached articulation when she died of a heart attack in 1927. But she left behind a strange collection of notes, aphorisms, and theoretical pronouncements, which Böhme published as a way of commemorating her eerie achievement. She regarded her body as a kind of orchestra—the right arm was a violin, the left a cello, the right leg a flute, the left a bass—but melody was in the movement. She admitted the use of percussion instruments in dance as long as the player danced while striking them. But in that moment when the dancer achieved "ecstasy itself"—the "aim, climax, and conclusion" of all dance—the dancer must cease to make any sound, for ecstasy was a "sleep-like plunge" into silence. "Dance is the unknown goal of all action." She disliked ensemble pieces in which the group moved in unison, for the group, like her body, was an orchestra, with each dancer able to function momentarily as a soloist. The strongest dancer was the "conductor," "the center, the magic element," whose "leading power . . . brings the group to ecstasy." "Artistic dance is no amusement or diversion or a form of *womanly* surrender through melting into music. It is surrender, but the surrender of a creator to dead space, which he wants to bring to life. Through the will, strength rises out of the body, without the stimulation of a third party (here music)." She added, "I have no desire for women's kisses, I have no desire for love of men." Music "disturbed" her "concentration," for to concentrate meant to "breathe the world pulse" from which "the world emerges."

Strinz cultivated curious ideas about the visual aspect of dance: "There is only *one* mask for the artist—that is his pure [naked] face." She liked saturating a cycle of dances with variations on a single color, such as her "four dances in red." "Brown: the mystic, unreal color, which never appears in the rainbow. Color of distance. It creates the atmosphere of space between signs of endless becoming." She preferred to dance in a long, satiny, somewhat medieval gown, but the other women in her group performed with bare arms and bare legs. For Strinz, the tension between dance and music led to a profoundly tragic, death-driven conflict over the real identity of the self: "I could sink away entirely without a sound and tomorrow perhaps everything would be extinguished. I have so many people inside me, it makes me sick. Therefore I love best being centric" (Böhme, *Hilde Strinz*).

DANCE AS WRITING

The use of spoken words to accompany dance was the subject of an article on "Worttanz" in *Schrifttanz* (2/3, August 1929, 52–54) by E. F. Burian, a Czech avant-garde theatre director and advocate of jazz in the theatre. Burian proposed that spoken words possessed the power to move the body uniquely because they were a unique acoustic phenomenon, and anything acoustic was "impossible without space." His thinking derived from the efforts of the Czech composer Leoš Janáček to notate the melodies of common speech. A polyphonic dance composition, according to Burian, contained three components: word dynamics, body dynamics, and text content. The dancer responded to the acoustic dimension of the word, not to its semantic value; the dance was not a redundant illustration of the text, as too often occurred in pieces involving movement choirs and speech choirs. Group dances accompanied by "group words" introduced the "especially rich" possibility of polyrhythms in the dance, whereby, for example, some dancers within the group move to one tempo or beat (2/4) while others move to another (7/4) or yet another (3/2). Such complexity was extremely rare in ensemble pieces, although Laban, for one, tended to explore polyrhythmic complications without any accompaniment at all. Of course, polyrhythmic music was (and still is) itself extremely rare. Burian did not clarify whether the spoken word should come directly from the dancer or from speakers external to the dance, for the "word dance" was not in any sense sung with a trained voice. Cilli Wang (54) responded to Burian's ideas by suggesting that success in this venture depended on using words and sentences whose intellectual or semantic density did not "destroy the line of movement"; lyric poetry therefore (and rather predictably) provided the appropriate language for word dancing. Although experiments of this nature remained almost entirely confined to the "choric drama" genre, Burian's article actually indicated that language emerged from peculiar bodily rhythms, rather than the other way around. But for most dancers, language implied *text*, an inscribed configuration of signs rather than an acoustic spatial phenomenon, and music constituted a text with great power to overdetermine the movement of the body.

For some, this overdetermination could be inhibited by treating bodily movement as a text in itself. Dance notation systems therefore functioned as potent evidence of dance's "textuality," particularly in the courts, which did not consider dances copyrighted, according to a 1901 law, unless they existed in a permanent, verifiable format. Dance notation systems date back at least as far as the fourteenth century, and each succeeding century has produced a plethora of methods for "notating" human movement. Even the advent of film and video documentation has not lessened the zeal for writing down dances. Laban's system first appeared in print in 1926, but he had worked on the problem of notating bodily movement since around 1900. By 1930 the Germans generally accepted Labanotation as the most accurate system for recording movement, and it remains the most widely used system in the world. Yet very few Weimar dances actually got notated (nearly all of those that did were notated by Laban disciples), partly because Labanotation is quite difficult and time-consuming to read and learn and partly because it was so expensive to have anyone do it. In a 1929 article for *Schrifttanz*, which Universal Edition originally founded to promote Labanotation, Fritz Klingenbeck pointed out that Labanotation recorded only the movement of the dance and ignored significant variables, such as the physiognomy and personality of the dancer, costume, set design, lighting (VP 43–46; see also 24–42).

Laban used music notation as the model for movement notation: the body was a stave upon which the notater inscribed a complex array of symbols for parts of the body, direction, duration, tempo, frequency, weight, and many other dynamics. But unlike music notation, dance notation, contrary to Laban's expectations, showed no creative potential: dancers disclosed no inclination at all to compose dances on paper before entering the performance space, so Labanotation's chief purpose became to record dances which were already composed. Of course, dancers like Mary Wigman and Dorothee Günther shaped movement concepts in their minds by drawing stick figures and using colored pencils and symbols that (especially with Wigman) were virtually unreadable to anyone but themselves. Some dancers worked from vague scenarios, others (Skoronel, Schlemmer) from abstract geometric forms; Terpis did both. Quite simply, the dance imagination, unlike the musical imagination, resists "textualization" as notation defines it: we don't see the dance until we see the body.

Jaap Kool (1891–1959) offered a composer's perspective on the problem when he published his *Tanzschrift* (1927), in which he introduced a
notation system that (in vain) he believed would make it easier to compose
dances. Indeed, his system was easier to learn and far easier to read than
Laban's. He used a musical stave to inscribe the notation of the movement,
but he set it directly above the stave for the musical notation, so that one
read the dance concurrently with the music. He ascribed musical note values to steps by creating a stick figure whose head designated the note value
for any combination of steps and movements. Direction in space he signified by the placement of the stick figure in relation to spatial values assigned
to lines of the stave. Other dynamics entailed further symbols (Figure 67).
It was an ingenious method that gave a pretty clear image of the movement
(not scenic elements) from measure to measure and even from note to
note. But Kool did not demonstrate its practicality in handling more than
Grit Hegesa's technically uncomplicated solo dances. Once a dance contained two or more bodies, the space of the stave became inadequate to
accommodate all the complexities. Of course, that was always the problem
underlying the tension between music and dance: as an image on the page,
as a text, musical imagination could always fit into the stave, the measure,
the note, a confined space of enormous symbolic density. With dance, however, the body produces signs that refuse to fit into any space other than that
in which it actually moves. In that sense, the dancing body is the clearest
manifestation of reality, the opposite of an inscribed text, which always
refers to something absent.

Dance Criticism

The textualization of dance through inscribed language occurred much more luxuriously in the published discourse on dance in the Weimar Republic than in the various attempts at notation. *Ausdruckstanz* was such a mysterious and deeply stirring phenomenon in Germany that between 1919 and 1935 more writing on modern dance appeared in German than in any other language before or since. The dance (and gymnastic) bibliography from the period is enormous and suggests that, far from being an art that was beyond linguistic control, modern dance functioned as a great provocation to say something—in words. More precisely, the perception that modernity signified itself through dance seems to have inspired deeper excursions into language for explanations of a phenomenon that could create serious misunderstandings about the body as a sign of emancipation. Probably the fact that the overwhelming majority of modern dance bodies were female contributed much to the need for literate, rational explanations of the emancipatory impulse. Because of its very appreciation of the body's power to sustain aesthetic feeling (desire), this impulse always risked being perceived as a threat to the power of language, to sexual morality, and to the authority of institutions such as schools and the theatre to "contain" the body, yet it simultaneously affirmed the body's capacity for ecstasy.

Dance criticism as such, the attempt to articulate meanings for dance, suffered from peculiar limitations resulting from an abiding uncertainty about how to look at dance. The most detailed and accurate descriptions of the dances themselves remain buried in local newspaper reviews, in difficult-to-obtain journals, and in photographs and drawings, not in the books of the leading dance theorists nor in the statements of the dancers themselves. So much of the published discourse on dance focused on the intentions of dance and dancers and on the methods for achieving those intentions that the actual performances and the relation between intention and realization were often overlooked. Dance theorists preferred describing general features of a dancer's personality or style over analyzing particular dances or concerts. They tended to present dance as an abstract category of art rather than a set of often contradictory practices, even within the same dancer; the latter approach might complicate the idealized image of dance the theoretical discourse attempted to construct. Both Fritz Böhme and Rudolf Laban consistently wrote about dance as if it were an image in their minds rather than a reality before their eyes, and many others obviously adopted this habit, as is evident from all the papers given at the dance congresses and even from the bulk of material published in such journals as *Schrifttanz* and *Der Tanz*. When intentions governed the value of dance, the distinction between theory and publicity became blurred, although this blurring probably did not bother the Weimar world as much as it does ours.

The main task of the theorists was to exalt the value of dance and to reveal a great power within the body that modern sensibilities had discovered—and few would deny that they succeeded grandly in fulfilling this task, considering the fantastic expansion of dance culture in the 1920s and the concurrent lack of analytical focus on performance in the published discourse. Much of this discourse assumed a polemical stance against shadowy and often reactionary defenders of prudery, ballet, the exhausted culture of the nineteenth century, and journalistic morality. At the same time, however, it did establish dance as a complex object of theorization, as a phenomenon requiring systematic categorization into genres, styles, forms, and techniques, even if the categories derived from intentions rather than performance realities. But the theoretical discourse evolved in a peculiar fashion. The major general dance histories of the era by Oskar Bie (1906) and Max von Boehn (1925) showed scarcely any interest in modernist challenges to their subject. Until 1920, the vast bulk of published discourse on the new currents in dance appeared in local newspapers and arts journals that today require considerable labor to excavate. Yet dance was by no means a negligible subject simply because it possessed no "voice" coming from an author who saw the art on a large or national scale. Indeed, the press, in the formative years of *Ausdruckstanz* (1910–1923) seemed positively eager for information about dance; the enormous amount of commentary from numerous cities quoted or reprinted in Adorée Villany's *Tanz und Pseudo-Moral* (1912) indicates the volume of writing on dancers and performances still buried in archives, assuming old copies still survive. Gabi Vettermann's brief investigation of dance reviews in Munich newspapers from 1906 to 1930 reveals a rich, hitherto unexplored source of information about dance.

The focus in dance research on the period 1928–1932 has created the misleading impression that this was the "exciting" period of *Ausdruckstanz*.

But this focus has resulted in large part because information about the earlier period is so difficult to access. Actually, the earlier period was no less exciting and in many ways was more mysterious because it was not yet the object of complicated institutional politics. Even people of the 1928–1932 era, with all their exaggerated brooding at the congresses about "crisis" and "stagnation" in dance culture, seemed to sense that something had been lost from those earlier years. Moreover, the history of *Ausdruckstanz* has been constructed and transmitted orally for the most part, from teacher to student, with most of the teachers left to tell the story having been students themselves in the 1928–1932 period. These oral histories concentrate, anecdotally, on biographies, on pedagogic methods, and on intentions and aspirations, not on performance realities; rarely do they offer a scholarly perspective that derives from detached curiosity about "what actually happened." After all, people who make history often misremember it, and, as Freud observed, the unconscious discloses itself only to those for whom it is other.

The press was for many years uncertain how to classify its discourse on dance. Was dance an art? A sport? A form of theatre? A social phenomenon? Because of this uncertainty, commentary on dance appeared in a wide range of journals with subjects including art, theatre, gymnastics, social reform, sexuality, body culture, *Nacktkultur*, education, film, music, and cultural overview. Journals devoted specifically to dance as an art did not appear until around 1920, with the Berlin-produced *Der Tanz* (1919), *Illustrierte Tanz-Zeitung* (1920), *Konzert, Tanz und Presse* (1920), *Tanz und Welt* (1922), *Terpsichore* (1923), and the Dresden-produced *Mask und Palette— Illustrierte Zeitung für Theater, Tanz, Film* (1920). But these all lasted only for a few issues and are now extremely difficult to procure. The gymnastic and body culture journals that began to proliferate after 1922 tended to enjoy much longer lives. *Tanz und Gesellschaft* (1926), out of Potsdam, *Moderne Tanzkunst* (1929–1931), out of Vienna, and *Der Bewegungschor* (1928), out of Hamburg, did not last long either, nor did *Körperrythmus und Tanz* (1929), edited by the Klamts in Berlin, which became *Tanz und Gemeinschaft* (1929–1930) before the Klamts launched *Kontakt* (1933–1934) with a National Socialist orientation. Even the Laban-oriented *Schrifttanz* (1928–1931), from Vienna, one of the outstanding modernist journals in Europe, could not survive the economic crisis. *Singchor und Tanz* (1928–1935), a movement choir journal out of Mannheim, and *Gymnastik und Tanz* (1926–1943), from Dresden, fared better, but *Der Tanz* (1927–1943), with its trade rather than scholarly focus, remained the most successful of the dance journals initiated in the Weimar era.

Yet all these journals accounted for only a tiny portion of the dance bibliography of the era. One of the appealing features of the journalistic discourse is precisely its inclination to treat dance not as a clearly defined specialization but as an ambiguous phenomenon that roamed across disciplines and could claim the interest of people with other modernist agendas. In this respect, the journalistic discourse represented dance as a power that integrated the aesthetically expressive body into a culture that already seemed overspecialized. Ola Alsen, in *Elegante Welt*, chattily reviewed dance concerts as if they were luxurious examples of elite fashion and pretexts for glamorous photographs. In *Der künstlerische Tanz* (1922), Werner Suhr, a *Nacktkultur* enthusiast, denounced such "trivialization" of dance, but for a young person at the time, dance could seem alluring because it offered both the masks of social mobility and the nakedness of "natural" beauty, and therefore offered a unique freedom.

Dance theory emerged out of journalism insofar as the major theorists shaped their voices as journalists rather than as scholars in academia (although important thinkers such as John Schikowski, Rudolf Lämmel, and Fritz Giese possessed doctorates). But dance as an art showed a curious capacity to undermine clear distinctions between journalistic and theoretical language. Paul Nikolaus (1894–1933), whose *Tänzerinnen* (1919) contains many valuable details about dancers of the wartime era, was a leading cabaret personality in Berlin. Werner Suhr (1900–?) began as a publicist for the *Lebensreform* movement before becoming an editor of *Der Tanz* (1927–1937); after World War II he published books on marketing strategy and salesmanship. Fred Hildenbrandt (1892–1940) was a Berlin newspaper reporter whose little books about Niddy Impekoven (1922) and Valeska Gert (1928) and picture album of female dancers, *Tänzerinnen der Gegenwart* (1933), indicated the extraordinary degree of instability female dancing could inflict on male desire. Leopold Wolfgang Rochowanski (1885–1961) was an ecstatic Viennese publicist for expressionist art and literature, friendly with the flamboyant Ernst Schertel and author of *Nackte Inspirationen* (1921); his *Der Formwille der Zeit in der Angewandten Künste* (1922) and *Der tanzende Schwerpunkt* (1923) and his contribution to the Berber-Droste *Tänze des Lasters, des Grauens und der Ekstase* (1922), associated dance movement with the most radical images in expressionist art. These few writers typified the hodgepodge of backgrounds that apparently qualified various persons to make pronouncements about dance.

HANS BRANDENBURG

The first major book on *Ausdruckstanz* was the enormously popular *Der moderne Tanz*, by Hans Brandenburg (1885–1968), which appeared in 1913, with subsequent, expanded editions in 1915, 1917, and 1921. It remains one of the finest books on modern dance ever published, and no other book produced during the era achieved its critical authority, even though, obviously, it did not examine most of the era's significant achievements. The success of Brandenburg's book established the commercial value of the wave of dance books to follow and served as a model for representing modern dance as a historical force. Brandenburg, unlike Bie or Boehn, treated (in a few pages) the whole history of dance up to 1912 as but a prelude to the powerful, Dionysian achievements of the solo dancers who emerged just before World War I. He situated dance within a complex social context that had reached the conclusion that ecstatic experience of freedom depended on inner powers of the body, not on the materialistic accumulation of things. Yet the book's great achievement was its detailed, materialistic descriptions of dance performances.. He supplemented the text with numerous photographs and drawings, many by his wife (Dora Brandenburg-Polster), which further strengthened the perception of dance as a reality and established the necessity of vivid photographs for any book on dance. Dance was for him a reality that tested the authority of his perceptions and his capacity to articulate them. His most significant contribution as a dance theorist was to embed theory in performance, so that the aim of theory—to provide a systematic explanation of the body's modern, ecstatic potential—always emanated from material reality rather than a metaphysical ideal. But this example proved difficult for other theorists to emulate, with Laban being perhaps the most "metaphysical" of them all. At Ascona, Brandenburg wrote a kind of choric dance-drama, *Der Sieg des Opfers* (published in 1921), which Laban planned to produce in 1914, but the war prevented the project from happening. In the 1921 edition of *Der moderne Tanz*, Brandenburg aggressively favored Laban's ideas over those of Dalcroze yet still grounded critical intelligence in the reading of performance signs rather than the linguistic-diagrammatic signs and symbols of metaphysical idealism.

After 1921, Brandenburg never produced another book on dance. He resided in Munich, where he reviewed dance concerts for journals and newspapers, acted as adviser to the Münchener Tanzgruppe, participated in the dance congresses, and pushed for stronger theatricalization of dance art ("Zur Einführung!"). But he showed no inclination to expand his initial view of dance modernity to include the busy dance culture of the 1920s. Instead, he published literary studies of Schiller and Hölderlin (1924) and pursued a career as a novelist with *In Jugend und Sonne* (1917), *Das Zimmer der Jugend* (1920), *Traumroman* (1926), and *Das Zaubernetz* (1944). He achieved considerable success with *Pankraz der Hirtenbub* (1924), an idyllic tale of an alienated mountain boy's gradual integration into a skeptical village community. His sympathy for National Socialism apparently stemmed from the real condition of communal integration that both Naziism and theatre performance embodied. Dance absorbed him to the extent that it embodied a tranformative historical force and always anticipated new forms of culture. At the conclusion of *Der moderne Tanz*, he remarked (236) that "the 'modern dance' is already history; this book is the only one in which it will be inscribed and in which at the same time its broad material sense is recognized. . . . [T]he flowering of the solo dance, which constitutes [this history], that dance, although it reaches into the Dionysian communal feeling . . . is in spite of great talents which are still here and yet to come, apparently past; but it was perhaps just a late-blooming of a dying individualistic culture." The modern dance as he described it was "perhaps but a transition to a new social and super-social group and theatre art, whose realization calls us into a dawning era"—which, presumably, was not in reality either the Weimar Republic or the Third Reich.

HANS W. FISCHER

Brandenburg was a friend of Hans W. Fischer, and for a couple of years (1920–1921) they worked together to support the ventures of the Münchener Tanzgruppe, based in Hamburg, where Fischer lived. Fischer (1876–1945) began his literary career with dramas about the mythic aura of technology, including *Flieger* (1913) and *Der Motor* (1919). Brandenburg regarded Fischer's epic poem *Das Schwert* (1920) as the finest piece of literature about the Great War. By 1920, Fischer was reviewing dance and theatre productions for the *Neue Hamburger Zeitung,* and *Hamburger Kulturbilderbogen* (1924) compiled his vivid descriptions of the lively dance and theatre culture in Hamburg during the early years of the republic. In *Das Tanzbuch* (1924) he organized his thinking about dance around abstract categories—folk dance, the female dancer, the absolute dance, the group dance, and so forth—rather than, as Brandenburg had done, around dance personalities. His thinking on the abstract level, however, was not especially original or insightful; his writing was much less verbose than Brandenburg's but also much less "demonic." Moreover, *Das Tanzbuch,* like his Hamburg book, contained no pictures (instead, he appended the scenarios for three of his "dance plays"). Thus, Fischer did not ground the idea of dance very deeply in the mechanics and materiality of specific performances or pieces.

His major strength as a critic lay in his skill at associating a distinct message with a dancer's personality and style of dancing, even if he did not analyze particular performances or contradictions within the style. For example: "Valeska Gert dances the world of the cabaret, the bar, the loft, the circus, and the operetta, in short, all the amusements of civilization, behind whose glowing arc-lamps menaces the desolate darkness of sordid streets . . . constructed with fantastic certainty of instinct and given with diabolical joy" (57). On Sent M'ahesa and Ruth St. Denis: "How far removed is her studied boredom from the exoticism of Ruth St. Denis! [St. Denis] does not exude the contrived aura of incense clouding an art studio, but the fragrance of the jungle, the menagerie, and even the cabaret, with its mixed blood attractions—wildness, conjuring, insolence, captivation, intimidation, and a bit of the cheap bazaar" (45). Nikolaus and Suhr had already introduced this technique of ascribing meanings to personalities rather than to dances, but Fischer's literary skill surpassed theirs. His chief contribution to theory was to associate the voice of the spectator with a vivid, metaphorical language of meaning rather than with the analytical language that exposes the techniques used in making meaning.

But Fischer's hugely popular *Körperschonheit und Körperkultur* (1928), containing nearly 200 photographs, revealed a fundamental tension within him. He masterfully described numerous categories of sport and athletic activity in great technical detail and from the athlete's perspective without, however, describing the personalities of athletes, who consistently remained generic identities—the rower, the motorcyclist, the swimmer. But when, in the second half, he focused on categories of dance, he reverted to his convention of ascribing meaning to personalities rather than to dances or even dance techniques. Unlike the theoretical categories for sport, the theoretical categories for dance seemed empty of meaning in themselves, entirely dependent on personalities to bestow value on them. Some chapter-categories, such as those for folk dance and social dance, contained no discussion of personalities, but the curious, journalistic blandness of his writing in these sections perhaps inadvertently disclosed that these categories of dance did not produce distinctive personalities. The value of any category of dance derived from its power to reveal an interesting personality.

Fischer could describe well the personalities issuing from dance, but he lacked the temperament to describe differences in value between generic movement techniques and techniques unique to the dancer and performance. All along he sensed that abstract categories of dance possessed their own meanings, but he could not identify them persuasively. His literary inclinations perhaps dominated his perception: he saw the referent, not the sign; he saw what Gert signified, not how she signified; he saw what the dance evoked in his imagination, not the dance. Probably this affection for the imaginary urged him toward the mythic image of the body advanced by National Socialism. He upheld this image himself in *Götter und Helden* (1934), and in *Lachendes Heimat* (1933) he compiled wit and humor ascribed to the healthy disposition of an idealized Nordic race. With *Menschenschönheit* (1935), a large, luxurious production with nearly 400 illustrations, Fischer explored "the secret of beauty" in the human body, examining images of (mostly female) bodies from cultures and eras around the world in an effort to identify the abstract, generic, "natural" values of the "well-created body," which transcends all cultural difference. What made bodies beautiful, he concluded, was neither nature nor culture but will, the conscious act of disciplining the body to fulfill the image of an ideal, of an imaginary identity. Though the ideal itself was subject to cultural relativism, the will was not—the will was relative only to personalities and therefore only to bodies, not to cultures. "The stronger the will to beauty is, the stronger it forms a [beautiful] manifestation" (72). In this sentence lies the limitation in Fischer's mode of theorizing: the will to manifest beauty becomes confused with the will to see the manifestation; the generic category of the will collapses the difference between sign and referent; though Fischer's assertion about the relation between will and beauty seems correct, his language does not.

ERNST BLASS AND RAINER MARIA RILKE

Fischer's difficulties in theorizing meaning formation in dance and bodily expression perhaps explain the increasing tendency toward metaphysical idealism in German dance theory—the tendency, that is, to define the value of dance according to the intentions, or will, that created it. Ernst Blass devoted the first half of *Das Wesen der neuen Tanzkunst* (1921) to identifying the abstract categories defining the "being" of a new dance art; these included the marionette, the animal, breathing, and leaping. The new dance art achieved being as the power of breathing (as taught at Loheland) moved the body away from the lifelessly mechanistic precision of the marionette archetype to natural animality and then to the ecstatic hurling of the body into space. In the last part of the book, he very briefly described the personalities of four dancers (Wigman, Impekoven, Bara, Gert). Yet the strongest section of the book described a completely "imaginary jazz cabaret," a sort of short story in which a character named Madeleine Travers, "a genie of public dancing," performs a wild dance with a bear, a nude dance, and then an "incredible march," a "storm, " a "titanic attack" (21–26). These imaginary dances, rather than those of real dancers, served to illustrate the abstract categories defining the new dance art. Certainly this approach suggested that dance was something more imagined than seen.

Yet Blass's theory of the new dance actually represented the self-conscious response not to dance itself but to theories of the body by two great poetic minds: Heinrich von Kleist and Rainer Maria Rilke (14). Kleist, in his disturbing essay-short story "Ueber dem Marionette Theater" (1807), had argued that the perfect, sublime movement of a body resulted from forces external to it—gravity and the manipulations of the invisible marionetteer. A dance achieved complete purity and perfection insofar as the dancer possessed no will—indeed, no consciousness. Will, as a manifestation of distorted self-perception, was the source of imperfect movements and actions. Rilke, in an essay on puppets written in 1914 and published in 1921 as *Puppen* in collaboration with the figurine-maker Lotte Pritzel, sought to differentiate the doll or hand puppet from the Kleistian marionette. For Rilke, the marionette, a figure of fantasy, could awaken artistic imagination because of its potential for perfect movement. But the "soulless" doll was the object of a child's rather than an artist's imagination because it was incapable of perfect movement. It remained subordinate to the will of an unformed or ungrown body—the child's. The child grabbed and discarded the doll, squeezed, caressed, and neglected it, knowing that it possessed no serious value independent of its owner. The doll helped the child to grow by being an estranging and somewhat sinister image of a body without a will.

On the face of it, Rilke seemed to disagree with Kleist over the relation between will and the beauty of human movement, but he described the doll with such melancholy delicacy that he implied that the idea of "growing" a will, which enabled humans to achieve perfectability of their actions, was an illusion (cf. Lüders). For Blass, a "new dance art" detached the concept of will from the manifestation of perfectability: modern dance embodied a powerful will whose object was not perfection but movement, a "ceaseless" condition of becoming rather than a state of being implied by the notion of perfection. However, the evidence to support this theory came more from the imagination than from performance realities; apparently dance had yet to "become" what will (imagination) could make it.

FRANK THIESS

The perception begins to emerge that the voice of dance theory was distinctly male; women appeared disinclined to publish books or even Rilkian essays that examined dance abstractly, as a philosophical, metaphysical, or cognitive problem. This perception intensified with *Der Tanz als Kunstwerk* (1919; 1923) by novelist Frank Thiess (1890–1977). Thiess classified abstract aesthetic principles by which a critical evaluation of dance as artwork was possible. These principles included movement, rhythm, line, color, music, costume, lighting, nudity, space, and decorative properties. These principles designated differences between dance and pantomime, between tragic and comic dance, and between "beautiful," "nonbeautiful" (grotesque), and "ugly" dances. In his rambling, excessively informal style of writing, Thiess made numerous valuable references to the performance styles (rather than performances) of various dancers (Kieselhausen, Hegesa, Bara, Johansson, von Derp) who remain too much in the shadows of dance history. He supplemented his text with twenty-four photos of solo female dancers. But despite categorizing dance art around aesthetic principles (rather than around personalities or generic dance forms), Thiess was neither systematic nor deep enough for the categories. He continually introduced an aesthetic principle or device without explaining its inherent semantic or cognitive significance. Instead, he merely fell back on a rather conventional rhetoric of "harmony," "beauty," and "structure," for "the borders of the non-beautiful are much narrower for this art than for other arts" (102). He was at his best when illustrating a principle by reference to a dancer's style:

> Ronny Johansson danced a grotesque in black and yellow. Perhaps the best of her dances, in any case, wonderfully instructive for those who want to see the immanent comedy in dance. For what was comic here? Did she make faces? Roll her eyes? Wiggle her ears? None of that. Her face had a quiet, cunning, lurking expression, as if she expected something pleasurable, but which she actually did not wish to invite. . . . She moved neither crookedly nor with bent legs, nor did she wear Turkish pantaloons and slippers or an otherwise ridiculous dress; instead, she wore a costume which in each and every line supported her movements . . . But her movements were of brain-burning choppiness, of such cunning, delighted attenuation, grotesquely angular and so splendidly mis-defined, tightened, and knotted by each other, that one begins to laugh without knowing why . . . startled by the terrible seriousness with which she constructs each attitude (74–75).

Although he insisted that "rhythmic movement and it alone is primary in dance" (45), Thiess did not describe bodily movement well (compared with decorative effects). His significant achievement in his book was to show how performance elements other than movement governed the power of dance to embody meaning. Thiess went on to publish many novels but not any more statements on dance; he articulated the perspective of a cosmopolitan spectator who brought to dance a set of general aesthetic principles dominated by ideals of beauty, ideals that became inadequate in relation to the complexities and ambiguities of *Ausdruckstanz* in the postwar years.

FRITZ GIESE

The presentation of dance as something more imagined than seen was by no means exclusive to theorists with literary inclinations. Fritz Giese (1890–1935) appeared to be a complete rationalist, boasting an impressive background in quantitative psychology, which he taught at the university in Halle. Though he published novels and literary sketches, including the bizarre *Der Mond der Toinette* (1920), he was in fact a stupefyingly productive scholar deeply preoccupied with how seemingly humble changes in the daily lives of individuals led to large-scale social transformations. *Körperseele* (1924) dealt with body culture generally, allowing Giese to shift freely from gymnastics to dance in his theory of bodily expressivity. He derived his numerous categories for describing "body souls" from psychology, social science, and aesthetics, but his focus always remained on the techniques and attitudes that allowed everyone to appreciate the body as a sign of salvational power, without which a stifling of life occurred (149). Giese always thought in terms of *types*—types of body, types of personality, types of pedagogy, types of culture, types of dance—and although typological thinking was by no means a weakness, his statistically biased focus on average identity prevented him from examining very insightfully the ambiguities of performance realities. Only very occasionally did he refer to the work of dancers, and he did not analyze their dances: "I come to the last type in the spectrum [of dance types]—to the idea dance. In this zone we find only the most complete of all [dance] representatives. Here Wigman emerges—but always guided more expressively than intellectually; here one finds occasionally Sent M'ahesa, then Hedwig Nottebohm and Valeska Gert, with Laban" (181).

The 88 photographs in the book provided far stronger evidence of the body in performance than Giese's language. But Giese's aim was to analyze pervasive psychological or cognitive conditions defining perception of the body as an expressive sign; he wanted to explain how types of dance possessed inherent semantic value independent of the idiosyncrasies associated with individual personalities. He therefore wrote copiously about types of dances. For example, in his rather convoluted discussion of nude dancing as a type, he remarked, as no one else ever did:

> There is still one problem [with nude dancing]: namely the question of how a man should perform it. It is physiologically very difficult to handle and hard to make him carry [a dance] into complete nudity. But with that, his dance immediately loses the unerotic dimension [the asexual stage of objective pleasure], for each special concealment must only emphasize what it conceals [i.e., the penis—K. T.]. We know well that this situation will have little influence on the female spectator. Woman is total, never specially effected by observation of the strange. But the idea of the nude dance must still collapse, and one moves on to the question of whether the male body, from an aesthetic standpoint, may appear naked in a dance or satisfy aesthetically (174).

Though Giese's explanation of why male nude dancing was virtually nonexistent may seem hopelessly obscure, no one else showed the slightest inclination even to imagine such a category. Therein lay the chief advantage of cognitive categories: they established possibilities for dance culture that neither history nor performance had yet included. Moreover, the subordination of types and categories to a cognitive definition of the body permitted Giese to show, as so few other theorists dared to do, that the body of the dancer shaped the meaning of dance quite as much as movement, music, or scenic elements did.

However, an analytical system built around types invariably locates values in intentions rather than in performance realities, and in spite of the typologist's affection for average or aggregate identities, metaphysical idealism dominates perception: "The ideal always grows out of the ordinary" (142). The weakness of his method was perhaps most obvious in his discussion of the "androgynous dance" he associated with Clotilde von Derp, Alexander Sacharoff, Sent M'ahesa, Joachim von Seewitz, and Hedwig Nottebohm. Here he seemed completely uncertain of what these "male-female" bodies intended to represent by their dancing, and so he drifted into an absolutely abstract idea of the human body—an ideal "asexuality," a "neutrality" of being, a suprahuman "objectivization" of movement, a "bisexual romanticism" (180–181). Giese hesitated to make body type entirely responsible for this typological confusion, but his reluctance to analyze differences in the performances of the androgynous dancers left completely obscure the degree to which movement either neutralized the sexual identity of the dancer or manifested a bisexual desire of one sex to inhabit the other.

The reductivist economies of typologies may make the world accessible to everyone, but they wind up concealing differences behind the illusion of a total, unified system for assigning identities to the body. Consider, for example, the "shadows" section of Wigman's cycle *Der Weg* (1932). In this group piece, all the dancers wear white robes and hoods that completely conceal their bodies (Figure 68). Only spectators who knew that Wigman only used female dancers could tell for sure the sex of the performers. Otherwise the spectator would have to identify the sex of the dance or dancers from the movement. But what happens when an all-male or mixed-sex group performs the same movement in the same neutral costumes? Wigman seemed to suggest that only movement, not bodies, can transcend sexual difference. But for Giese, bodies always projected the force of a social type that imposed a unifying, social identity upon human movements. He published more body culture books—*Weibliche Körperbildung* (1922), *Männliche Korperbildung* (1924), *Geist im Sport* (1925), *Girlkultur* (1925)— that explained, in the typological method, how people could create a strong, healthy society by devoting modest portions of the day to the cultivation of their bodies through participation in exercise, sports, nudism, or bodily recreations. However, his own workaholic lifestyle led him to a premature demise.

RUDOLF LÄMMEL

Rudolf Lämmel, the father of Vera Skoronel, was a physicist with a professorial position in Dornburg. He published books on mass education (1923), the theory of relativity (1925), intelligence testing (1923), and "social physics" (1925) before serving on a state commission examining dance schools for accreditation. His *Der moderne Tanz* (1928), an overview of "the new dance" for the years 1923 to 1927, was hardly comprehensive but nevertheless the most inclusive theoretical treatment of the subject after Brandenburg's book.

For Lämmel, the meaning and identity of dance derived above all from the specific educational background of the dancer, not from pervasive cultural or psychological pressures. He therefore devoted the first half of his book to teachers of pedagogical methods for developing bodily expressivity: Mensendieck, Dalcroze, Kallmeyer, Menzler, Wigman, Laban, Bode, Trümpy, and so forth. He described how these methods prepared bodies to explore "restless technical possibilities" of corporeal expressivity (67). Dance interested Lämmel to the extent that it moved beyond ethical, social, or hygienic problems and discovered hitherto unrecognized signifying powers of the body. Distinctive teachers struggled against stabilizing or even retarding cultural-historical forces to free the body from culturally conditioned fears of it. Thus, for him, the value of dance depended not so much on body type or movement in itself but on the body's relation to space, on its authority to define and establish its control over space through movement (68). Awareness of body-space relations depended almost entirely on teacher-student relations (rather than on dancer-spectator relations) and varied from teacher to teacher.

In the second half of the book, Lämmel examined the work of numerous dancer-teachers and the significance of such formal categories of dance as the movement choir, the revue, the social dance, the dance accompanied by noise, and dance in film. He mentioned all sorts of dancers about whom we would otherwise know nothing, including Helmi Nurk (Bremen), Anne Grünert (Duisburg), Karin Schneider (Graz), Olga Suschitzky (Vienna), Marion Herrmann (Oldenburg), Frances Metz (Munich), and Gertrud Volkenesen (Hamburg). The most detailed and valuable sections of the book described the works and teachings of Vera Skoronel and Berthe Trümpy. The implication was that pedagogic methods produced not types of dancers but distinct dance personalities and that a distinct personality resulted from a struggle to overcome methodological limitations and "through new creations prepare the path of further evolution" (144). Lämmel expanded the idea of "performance reality" to include what happened in the school-class studio, which he described much more effectively than concert performances. Still, he included a hundred pages of theatrical photographs that more than any other publication showed the glamorous presence of modern dance, as both an art and an education, throughout Germany. Lämmel, perhaps unable to resolve the problem of defining the space of dance, published nothing more on the subject and devoted himself to exploring the nature of scientific imagination, publishing books on

Galileo (1929), Newton (1957), race theory (1936), and "the modern scientific world image" (1932).

FRITZ BÖHME

The theorist with the greatest presence in Weimar dance culture was probably Fritz Böhme (1881–1952). Of all the theorists, he disclosed the strongest attachment to metaphysical idealism. He studied literature and art history at the university in Berlin; he did free-lance journalism from 1902 until 1915, when he decided that dance was his compelling subject. He contributed dance criticism to several Berlin newspapers and periodicals, including *Libelle* (1918), a now extremely rare journal devoted entirely to dance. In 1919 he assumed the editorship of the feuilleton section of the *Deutsche Allegemeine Zeitung (DAZ)*, and in this paper his dance reviews appeared almost daily for many years. During the Weimar era, Böhme was a driving force in the organization of dance associations, dance congresses, dance criticism, dance journals, dance education forums, and dance performance opportunities. His longer and more intellectual articles appeared in such heavyweight cultural journals as *Die Tat, Ethos,* and *Der Scheinwerfer.* Meanwhile, he personally amassed the largest library of writings on Weimar dance ever assembled. In 1933 he joined the Nazi Party, supposedly because he thought his influence would ameliorate the hostility the Nazis generally tended to project toward modern dance. His great ambition during the Third Reich was to establish a national academy of dance and a national archive for dance history, seeded by his own immense personal archive. The government procrastinated on the formation of the academy, and in 1943 a British air attack completely destroyed Böhme's great archive (Manuel, "Wegbereiter").

Böhme's most interesting writings on dance consisted of his innumerable reviews for the *DAZ*, but these remain very difficult to obtain; even the Böhme collection of the dance archive in Leipzig possesses only a limited selection of them. They exerted far less influence than his theoretical publications, yet until more of them surface, understanding of his thinking about dance will remain quite incomplete. Only in the reviews can one grasp his response to dance as a performance reality, for in his widely disseminated theoretical works he detached dance from performance more completely than any other theorist. As an object of theory, dance preoccupied him as a sign of dynamism (rather than stability) in the cultural-historical structure of societies. He liked to paint the big picture of the "situation" of dance and dancers for any given era, particularly his own. Dance was a dynamic historical force because it embodied an ideal, and therefore he analyzed dance ideals rather than dances, historical situations of dance rather than dance performances, even though probably no one in Germany had seen more dance performances than he.

In "Materialien zu einer soziologischen Untersuchung des künstlerischen Tanzes" (*Ethos* 1, 1925–1926, 274–293), he introduced vague conditions for identifying the status of dance in terms of social structures, such as professionalization, choreography, affiliation with other arts. At the Magdeburg Congress in 1927, he discussed "the dancer of our time," asserting that the function of the dancer was to bring a powerful sense of "rhythm in being" to an era dominated by "mass organization and mechanization" without succumbing to the temptations of military drill and mechanized mobilization of the body (*Die Tat*, 19/8, November 1927, 580–588). In "Der Radius des Tanzkunstwerks" (*Der Scheinwerfer*, 11/12, March 1928, 14–15), he declared that dance art was above all "the expression of an era, the attempt through movement and gesture, to realize, along with sculpture, music, architecture, and literature, the lines of this our epoch." For *Schrifttanz* in 1928 he briefly explained, by reference to eighteenth-century contributions, how an era's efforts to notate its dance art signified the "final crowning" of its achievements in dance (VP 30–32). In *Kontakt* (1/3, September 1933, 33–40), he suggested, with help from language of the Führer himself, that the "ecstatic moment" of a "new German dance art" arises out of the "rhythm of [the dancer's] blood, out of the breath of his race," and in a 1936 essay, after politely proposing that the difference between folk dance and art dance did not entail an ideological conflict, he concluded that the "social responsibility of the dancer in the present" involved immersion in "the National Socialist movement and the honorable and passionate surrender to the work of our leader Adolf Hitler" (MS 123–125).

Perhaps Böhme's most substantial publication was *Tanzkunst* (1926). Here he covered almost every aspect of dance art since its mysterious origins—without, however, analyzing a single dance. The language of the book always remained focused on "the meaning of the situation" associated with untested categories of dance. For example: "Ecstatic dance cannot advance to artistic refinement, but only to a natural, organically grown expression. It lacks the conscious will to form of an artist, lacks the conscious and cool affinity for material laws, the sense of material limits, which is necessary to contour forms and artistic expression. The spirit of ecstasy is latent and objectified will in the artwork" (59). However, the truth of this assertion depends on analysis or, at least, an example of something designated as ecstatic dance. *Tanzkunst* consisted almost entirely of language in this aphoristic style, making no concessions at all to the materiality of performance itself except for the twenty-four photographs that decorated the book. Although the book today makes rather dull reading, the Weimar dance culture appreciated it precisely because it treated every abstract category of dance (ecstatic dance, ballet, movement choir, folk dance, nude dance, and so forth) as a dynamic historical force in itself, independent of performance realities and therefore defined by intentions and ideals. These, Böhme knew through long experience as a newspaper reviewer, conflicted with the intensely material but ephemeral "historical situation" of specific bodies moving in specific ways in specific spaces at specific times. He did not describe the pleasures of dances; he described his anticipation of "the dance" as something yet to come.

CRITIQUES OF GERMAN CRITICAL WRITING

With dance theory continually drifting toward metaphysical idealism, it was not surprising that dance criticism, responses to dances themselves, unfolded informally and abundantly in a highly idiosyncratic, fragmented fashion from a multitude of perspectives. Taken together, this body of criticism implied that, contrary to much of the theorizing, the value of dance, as a performance reality, was quite relative and that dance had little power to unify either perception or the language used to articulate its value. Laban probably assumed that the development of an accurate dance notation system would have the effect of getting people to see dance more acutely and uniformly, but this possibility soon proved an illusion.

At the 1927 Magdeburg Congress, Hans W. Fischer spoke on the theme of dance criticism. He observed that dance criticism was no longer "completely dilettantish," despite the proliferation of "pseudo-critical" dance picture books distracting the public from a deeper level of discourse. He focused less on principles of dance criticism than on the qualifications of the dance critic, who could not shift from opera, theatre, or ballet reviewing as easily as editors seemed to think. "One must be born to dance criticism," he asserted, and the born critic viewed art as an "eternally new beginning." This value remained obscure when dogmatic principles and distinctions prevented, for example, the critic from appreciating Wigman's use of a cabaret device in an otherwise somber dance or from regarding social dance forms as seriously as ballet, which Fischer believed "no longer has a future." Stable critical principles could not accommodate the dynamism of modern dance culture. Already, critical language had become banalized by the misuse of such words as "absolute" and "cultic." The critic must bring to dance an "instinct" for "eruptions" or "blossomings": "One can not push the borders far enough, raise the challenge high enough, or fix the responsibility strictly enough. Because in the field of dance, so much is in flux, so much still unclarified and controversial" (*Die Tat*, 19/8, November 1927, 591–596). Alfred Bratsch adopted a more cynical tone in a 1931 article on dance criticism for *Schrifttanz*, stating that most dance criticism served journalistic objectives before it served the

needs of dance, and he accused dancers of perpetuating journalistic standards by their willingness to confuse criticism with publicity. Moreover, he
did not think critics who were close to the dance establishment produced
superior criticism: "Just those 'non-dancing' artistic people whom we may
say really ought to be rejected as critics could be allotted an important task
because their judgment is not yet corrupted by close familiarity" (VP
77–79). However, in the increasingly crowded and competitive dance community itself, leading representatives devoted more energy to establishing
standards for school accreditation than to raising the level of performance
criticism; yet without a theory of performance values, standards for accreditation would continue to rest upon idealistic rhetoric defined by nebulous
intentions rather than measurable results.

The most powerful, detailed examination of any dance during the era
surely was psychologist Hans Prinzhorn's negative review of Wigman's
Totenmal in 1930 for *Der Ring*, a right-wing journal of cultural-political
analysis that otherwise paid no attention to dance. Prinzhorn, who was
actually a close friend of Wigman, analyzed numerous performance elements in the piece—movement, costume, music, lighting, text, scenography, choreography—and contemplated their significance in relation to
Wigman's artistic-ideological intentions, which he regarded as defective
and incapable of provoking the intensity of feeling the creators expected
of the spectator ("Grundsätzliches"). But dance and performance analyses
of this magnitude or intensity did not often appear, even in the dance journals. For that matter, no published review of a German dance book ever
achieved a magnitude comparable to that of Frits Lapidoth's enormously
detailed review of J.W.F. Weremeus Buning's *De Wereld van den dans* (1922)
in the Dutch theatre journal *Het Tooneel* (9/4, September 1923, 51–57).
Nor was any German monograph on a dancer as precise in describing its
subject's dances and their meanings as Joe Jencik's 1930 book on Anita
Berber, published in Czech. Moreover, Jencik's *Tanecnik a snobove* (Dance
and Snobbery, 1931) offered a much more scintillating and persuasive
analysis of the psychosocial and historical pressures defining dance as an
art than the German theorists ever did; even if he did not analyze many
dances, he nevertheless showed how movements of the dancing body in its
diverse manifestations exposed class distinctions and estrangements from
normative attitudes toward bodily expressivity in different social contexts.
But Jencik (1893–1945) lived extensively in the world of theatrical performance, dancing and choreographing ambitious modernist productions for
the National Theatre in Prague, appearing in films, leading a jazz revue
group (the Jencik Girls), collaborating with the cabaret duo of Voskovic
and Werich, and staging plays (*Narodni divadlo*, 192–193; ES 245–249).
Still, he managed to publish several theoretical-historical articles for
Divadlo, the leading Czech theatre journal, as well as some autobiographi-

cal novels, including the eerily beautiful *Omyl Mea Mara Indry* (1944), about the ambiguous sexual identity of a dancer. In other words, Jencik did not accept a concealed class distinction between the bodily world of performance and the intellectual world of criticism and theory. He traveled freely between both worlds, untempted by the redemptive claims of metaphysical idealism.

It would seem, from all the fog enshrouding the domain of theory, that dance possessed considerable power to challenge the authority of conventional scholarly and critical language. Perhaps Blass was right: to articulate accurately one's responses to dance, one should turn to the language of poetic imagination and value dance by its power to awaken such language. Not surprisingly, the metaphorical image of the dancer appeared frequently in the poetry of the era, most recklessly, perhaps, in Curt Corrinth's ecstatic prose-poem *Potsdamer Platz* (1919) (cf. W. Roth). But aside from these often stirring metaphorical images and the somewhat vapid odes to dancers such as Niddy Impekoven, Grete Wiesenthal, and Lili Green, the most imaginative use of literary language to reveal dance appeared in the Berber-Drost *Tänze des Lasters, des Grauens und der Ekstase* (1922) (see Chapter 6 herein).

Another interesting figure, Alfred Richard Meyer (1882–1956), cultivated the life of an aesthete-connoisseur in Berlin, publishing exquisite, rare editions of his own poems, beginning with *Vicky* in 1902. In 1910 he began to publish many of his writings under the name and persona of Munkepunke, a dandyish, cosmopolitan fellow who constantly indulged in witty word games. Meyer-Munkepunke drifted into the turbulent orbit of expressionism, producing, as was the habit of the expressionists, a great abundance of poems in a multitude of small editions, as well as a little book about Charlotte Bara (1921). After 1933 he became an officer of the Nazi Chamber of National Literature; when the war ended, he devoted himself to translations of literary works (Raabe 329–337; Josch). As Meyer-Munkepunke, he published several poems about dancing and dancers, which he collected in *Tanzplakette* (1913) and *Grit Hegesa* (1920). *Tanzplakette* satirically equated individual poems with different social dances or with "posters" for dancing, such as "Tango," "Foxtrot," "Maxie," "Voo-Doo," and so forth: "The new dance, the pouch dance of the kangaroo." A curious feature of the poems was that Meyer kept the right side of the margin even instead of the left. For example, in these lines from "Foxtrott":

> I trot, you trot, we trot.
> You trot before me, I trot after you.
> Two bodies are exactly determined to become one.
> But a wall of space always keeps us separate.
> We stamp, heavy falling hammer blow, clap-clap the beat of the melody
> (Meyer, *Grosse Munkepunke*, 107).

The effect is of words piling into a "wall of space" from uneven starting points instead of "flowing" from an even starting point. Thus, with these poems, Meyer indicated the power of dance to subvert the conventional order and rhythms of poetic language. In *Grit Hegesa*, the disturbance of linguistic order was much more radical, as Meyer inscribed his responses to Hegesa's *Groteske* and *Der Samurai:*

> High over Tohuwabohu of a thousand street organs
> Suddenly a green floating boat,
> Somehow an even-membered triangle:
> Black pompon, pompon, pompon.
> Pythagoras, Pythagoras, how do you do it!
> a^2+b^2—must have a circle first—to be able to fly
>
> . . . .
>
> Wild street organing over me and in me with all rainbow colors.
> "Meyer, you will never in this life get beyond fourth grade!"
> Said my mathematics teacher Frank sourly: "Once more: a^2+b^2"
>
> . . . .
>
> A momang! I won't prick you, you meadow green girl!
> You black point—o holy Archimedes!
> I place myself on it and raise this earth off its angles.
> Jaap Kool, organ your heavenly festival a little more!
> Corn in the chimes. I shoot. Myself.
>
> (113)

Here Hegesa's grotesque dance inspires a vision in which both linguistic and natural order become subverted, as the dancing body urges the poet to imagine principles of grammar, poetic "rhythm," mathematics, physics, geometry, acoustics, time, and perception itself colliding—or perhaps "dancing"—in a wildly delighted manner.

PAUL VAN OSTAIJEN

The deepest, most radical, and most ecstatic language provoked by German modern dance came not from a German but from a Flemish poet, Paul Van Ostaijen (1896–1928), an intellect of great, captivating brilliance. He was an intensely cosmopolitan figure who had an almost unsurpassed knowledge of modernist movements (expressionism, futurism, surrealism) in a wide range of European arts (literature, painting, film, theatre, dance, music). In his first volume of poems, *Music Hall* (1916), he indicated that the rhythm of modernity achieved its ripest expression not through technology (as the futurists believed) but through a complex multiplicity of sensations that fragmented the identity of the modern body. Life was modern

to the extent that it was a collage of competing rhythms, moods, and fragments of images. In subsequent works, he accommodated the presence of
machines by appropriating printing technology, the resources of typography, to "materialize the word" and construct more radical manifestations of
collage. He suspended words in the white space of the page; he alternated
rhythms of phrases by varying spaces between words and by making idiosyncratic use of italics and boldface. He "enlarged" words by capitalizing
them and used different typefaces to create new "images" for words. Stabilizing margins disappeared; quoted language from a variety of sources
(newspapers, advertisements, neon signs, popular songs, foreign lan-
guages) abounded. Words appeared on the page in "columns," "clusters,"
or "planes," and it is sometimes quite difficult to know the order in which
to read them.

All these devices of collage construction encouraged the perception that
modern identity entailed a shattering of syntactic unity and the logic associated with understanding signs. This materialization of the word, this physicalization of the signifier, gave "body" to the word and freed it from having
to depend on its referent to achieve any expressive power. The collage strategy allowed the poem to signify the presence of many disparate voices
within one body, that of the poet or reader. The introduction of nonlinear,
simultaneous pressures on the perception of the reader developed the idea
that the body contained "other" voices. Otherness was not external to the
body but inside it. Modern poetic language fragmented the body of the
reader by representing the fragmented body of the poet/speaker. What
made a body modern was its capacity to appear as a collage of other voices
within itself. But in pursuing this strategy, Van Ostaijen actually detached
poetic language from the body in that these poems were unspeakable; he
constructed a radical difference between the spoken and the written word.
It is extremely difficult to translate accurately the complex range of visual
signs defining the texts. Moreover, Van Ostaijen stressed the contradictory
status of the voice of the modern body by titling a number of word-collages
"songs" or "tunes." Writing remained music, projected a voice, even when
nobody could speak it. Yet Van Ostaijen never drifted into the nonsense language or purely sonic poetry explored by the futurists or dadaists: he always
gave primacy to words, semantically decipherable units, but expanded their
meanings by portraying them as icons, dynamic forms, bodies in movement.
In 1925 he gave a memorable lecture in Brussels on "operating instructions
for poetry," asserting that the expression of ecstasy is the dominant aim of
"lyrical emotion"; poetry achieves this aim when the "transcendent word" is
no longer reducible to either its sound or sense but has become an "organism" that lives independently of both the conscious and unconscious desires
that use it (*Verzameld Werk II*, 369–379).

Between 1919 and 1921, Van Ostaijen wrote several poems that introduced especially intriguing relations between dance and writing. During
the years 1918 to 1920 he lived rather marginally in Berlin, where the revolutionary implications of modernist art became apparent to him and where
he experienced his first serious encounters with modern dance. He composed "Gnome Dance" (Gnomendans) in Berlin in 1919, but the piece,
which he produced in both Dutch and German versions, did not appear in
print until 1934 (VW II, 157–159; 255–258). Compared with later poems it
was fairly conventional, with a stable left margin and no startling typographic
effects other than an absence of punctuation. Yet it is strange all the same.
The poem describes the "dance" of celestial lights during the "night adagio
of the erotic." Here the concept of collage operates through a tension
between the complex, alliterative (though unrhymed) "gnomic" rhythms
("Kreuze kreuzen Kreisen wirbeln") connecting words and the fantastic
images ("Waltz of the Earth's orbit waltz of the global spheres") evoked by
the words. The poem inscribes a monumental, indeed cosmic, vision of the
night sky ("lights dance in shards") moving in response to erotic impulses.
Glowworms and "millions of kissing stars" create a great "cage" in which a
multitude of beings of "humid" and "yellow-green lights . . . fall." The poem
is three-fourths over before the reader discovers that the voice of the body
that "speaks" belongs to that of "we gnomes," whose "sperm is violet." The
"dance" of the gnomes consists of "always falling" bodies within an ever-
expanding "cage." This falling into oblivion provokes an orgasmic exhilara-
tion. Thus, dance becomes the ambiguous sign of both the body's freedom
and its fall from the stars. Dance signifies the cosmic movement of erotic
desire from celestial heights to "gnomic" depths.

In Antwerp in 1920, Van Ostaijen assembled a collection of poems under
the title Feesten van pijn en angst (Feasts of Fear and Agony, 1976). This project
required printing technology to reproduce his own handwriting of the
poems. He wrote words in different sizes and at different angles. His handwriting changed from poem to poem, with the pressure of the pen bolder
or softer, but not necessarily in relation to the mood of the poem. Furthermore, he wanted to vary the "color" of words by varying the color of ink used
to print them. Word colors would change from poem to poem, but each
poem would present a complex of different-colored words. Printing technology, however, was not sufficiently advanced to accommodate these
demands, and Van Ostaijen was never able to produce a desired version of
the text. For him it was handwriting, rather than the voice, that disclosed
the most naked relation between language and the body.

Three poems in this collection contained unique perceptions of dance.
The longest poem, "The March of the Hot Summer," employed a spectacu-
lar range of typographic and orthographic devices to make words "dance."
The poem is stupefyingly complicated in its formal organization and

deployment of violent, even shocking, erotic imagery (menstruation, masturbation, sadomasochism, exhibitionism, mass orgasm). I merely indicate here that, for the poet, words "danced" when they appeared on the page as if they were simultaneously falling into a great space yet marching toward the reader. Written words "move" erotically like the bodies to which they refer because they look like organisms, spermatozoa, trembling in the hot white space of the page. It is in just such a spewed, fragmented fashion that language exists inside the body.

"Barbaric Dance" is equally perverse. The first part of the poem describes the reptilian dance of a woman from the perspective of "the desirous body," a male spectator or possibly partner, who exhorts her to "make your gender dance," for in dancing she dispels "dream and death," "Snakes and Doves together." In the second part, however, the voice of the poem shifts to that of the dancer herself—"me who partners him who observes"—the dancer speaks while she dances. That is, she says what her dance doesn't say: "WATCH the thinking of my feet." She speaks thoughts and feelings that no one can see in either her dance or her body, and "according to the law which is and does not speak/this is being."

> Over the white shivering of my arms
> I throw
> the shimmer
> of my
> eyes

For this reason—"my body is to itself a light and a darkness"—she observes:

> NOBODY
>   understands me

Yet in the third part, she claims: "I am happy . . . So very solitary in my dancing I am not lonely." "Naked warm and fresh," she plunges a dagger between her breasts, and the implication is that words are like daggers in their power to penetrate the body. She dies "because my dance is dying," and dance dies when the spectatorial "partner" manages to "enter" the body of the dancer, get "inside" it, and read in it signs hidden from the other by the dance itself. The dancer obviously welcomes this penetration, but what is more significant is that the poem as a whole suggests that language is both in and other than the body. Here the idea of collage develops around a seemingly simpler strategy: poetic language constructs the subjectivities defining distinct bodies (male spectator and female dancer), which actually inhabit a single, divided body, that of the poet or the reader. Dance is the provocation for this inscribed collage of subjectivities and signifies depths of desire because of its power to provoke "barbaric," violently erotic, and obviously bisexual tensions between subjectivities that lie deep within the body and are visible only through the inscribed, "organic" word (*VW II; Feasts*, 25–31).

When the word calls attention to itself—when, freed of syntactic laws, the "body" of the word becomes visible—the body of the writer or reader becomes fragmented. In the final poem of the collection, "Fear, A Dance," the poet remarks, "All becoming is being undone/in the All-Being Word." When the being of the word manifests itself, through its iconic properties, the being of the speaker becomes "undone," fragmented, shattered. For this reason the word is a source of anxiety, a great fear. Words that have life, intense physicality, "bodies," are also intimations of death. In this poem, the poet impersonates the voice of a dancer who is himself, dancing the "dance of the self." But the objective of the poem is to treat a specific emotion (fear) as a dance "performed" by words. Dance and language are "within" each other:

> To dance is
>
>   to be full-bellied
>
> of the seed
>
>   of the word
>
> While bodies which
>
>   are dancing away
>
>   falling
>
>   matter
>
> are dancing WORD-ward
>
>   are now reality of undone things.

Dance, then, emerges as an explosive sign of fear of the "Incarnate LOGOS"; "my dancing body" objectifies "my for fear of the word fearful body." More precisely, fear of the word is fear of the body, fear of erotic desires, the erotic "FLAME," which gives "life" to all objects yet makes them "fall." The freedom of the modern identity depends on a modernist freeing of the word. This freedom is ecstatic insofar as it is the modernist dancing/writing of fear that frees the modern identity from fear of the word, the body, death. Freedom from fear thus becomes the "final" sign of the modern identity (*VW II; Feasts*, 69–76).

In *Bezette stad* (Occupied City, 1921), ostensibly an image of Antwerp life during the German occupation, Van Ostaijen published other wild poems about dance written in Berlin. But his message was already clear. Most practitioners of modern dance perceived dance as a condition of freeing the body from constraints imposed upon it by language, by oppressive communication codes. Dance was movement away from language (e.g., Baxmann). Van Ostaijen, however, perceived dance as movement toward the "free" word, toward an emancipatory language that was not "other" than the body but deep inside it. No one in Germany recognized so clearly the capacity of dance to undermine the stability of language and thus the stability of differences between dancer and spectator, male and female, word and body. And though his poems did not describe "real" dances, no one in Germany acknowledged so well what Blass had only intimated: that dance, as a manifestation of bisexuality, required a radical theoretical perspective on the meaning of the body in which critical and poetic language were embedded in each other.

Dance as Image

Dance was as much a self-contained image as a performance reality or a construct of metaphysical idealism. A vast dance iconography flourished throughout Europe in the years 1910 to 1935 in painting, the graphic arts, sculpture, and photography. Indeed, the great majority of people during the era encountered dance far more through pictures of it or of dancers than through dance performance itself, and images of dance assumed considerable importance in awakening or intensifying the desire to dance in many women. (The few men who became dancers seemed motivated entirely by experiences with dance performance, although many men—as well as women—who did not become dancers collected pictures of dance and dancers.) Dance iconography deserves a book of its own, but some reflection on the aesthetics of selected dance imagery may prove valuable here in illustrating the perception of dance as an ecstatic phenomenon.

From the artistic perspective, dance was an appealing subject because it encouraged the display of superior skill in dramatically depicting dynamic-kinetic tensions within the human body, even if the image was a portrait. But from the dance perspective, the image was crucial in shaping the identity of dance itself. Dance could not rely on performance or on serious criticism or even on the mystical language of metaphysical idealism to expand its authority within the cultural sphere, for in more ways than one, as we have seen, it was difficult to "see" dance clearly and without misperception. Dance culture appropriated dance imagery in its struggle to overturn lingering nineteenth-century perceptions of dance as either a rigidly deterministic regulation of the body (ballet) or a morally dubious pleasure in the body associated with marginalized and even stigmatized classes of women. But in achieving this aim, the dance iconography also introduced ambiguities that made dance more mysterious than anyone intended. It was not enough for the dancer to have the right body or sufficient talent; the dancer must like being in a picture and must constantly think of the image as a decisive power in his or her destiny.

As early as 1910, such contrasting dancers as Grete Wiesenthal and Adorée Villany understood this principle and its application above all through photography. Not every dancer showed the willingness, the eagerness, of Grit Hegesa or Anita Berber to appear in paintings, drawings, photographs, and movies, but the pact that dance made with the image implied an unprecedented measure of respect for narcissism, for the pleasures (rather than the old anxieties) of being looked at "always." Dancers and dance schools produced postcards, many of which received national distribution, and bold, innovative posters were also necessary to construct a modern image of dance. (I have not yet discovered a German dancer who could match American Ruth St. Denis in the extravagantly luxurious pictorial beauty of her printed programs between 1918 and 1921.) Dancers expected to sign photographs and postcards of themselves for spectators and even for other dancers (witness the huge album of pictures collected by Yetty Thom from the time she was a Wigman student in 1927 until well into the 1940s). Posters from 1910 to about 1924 tended to feature a distinctive, often expressionistically drawn image of the dancer's body, but after 1924 posters relied more on distinctive, often constructivist typographical effects in a collage relation to a small photograph of the body (if a body even appeared in the image). This change probably occurred because after 1924 group concerts became more pervasive than solo concerts, and great uncertainty prevailed about the images groups should project (Figure 69). In the early 1930s, the Orami cigarette company in Dresden began attaching small photos of dancers to cigarette packs in the manner of trading cards. The success of this ploy was such that this company and others published elegant albums of complete photo series in *Das Orami-Album* (1933), *Der künstlerische Tanz* (1933), and *Tanzbühnen der Welt* (1934).

GRAPHIC ARTS

Unlike photography, the painting and drawing of dance did not always entail the conscious collaboration of dancers. In general, expressionist artists tended to represent dance (ubiquitously designated by female bodies) as a primeval or archaic impulse emanating from nature, from paradise, from intense colors and emotions concealed behind merely empirical images of natural phenomena; Emil Nolde and Ernst Ludwig Kirchner were perhaps the most powerful creators of this perspective on dance. However, artists of the so-called New Objectivity, which emerged around 1924, tended to represent dance "realistically," as a symptom of the urgent rhythms defining modern urban life and a sign, often, of the dark, lurid, even morbid forces guiding the urbanization of the body; Otto Dix and Karl Hubbuch were but two of many powerful creators of this perspective.

But the distinction between expressionism and New Objectivity was not altogether as solid as many supposed, nor was the difference between the two in their perception of dance. For example, in "Salome," his lascivious series of color drawings done in 1930, Leo Putz (1869–1940) used expressionist devices to show how the primeval archetypal image of the dancer embedded a feminine sadistic desire to tempt, taunt, tease, and torment both the male and female spectator (Poetter 44–47). In Berlin, the Hungarian painter Hugo Scheiber (1873–1950) employed aggressive expressionist effects in numerous pictures of dancers to show dance as the strongest manifestation of ecstatic energies latent in the city rather than in nature, as in his turbulent 1927 image of a woman dancing in the most peculiar circumstance of wearing glasses (Figure 70) (Schmidt). By contrast, Fritz Uphoff, educated in the utopian milieu of the Worpswede colony, used the extremely precise techniques of realist New Objectivity in painting his idealized 1930 image of the dancer Erika Vogt (one of many portraits he did of her) (Figure 71). Here the platinum-haired, bronze-skinned dancer seems to move delicately, as if under a remote spell, toward an unexpected ecstasy, despite the black wall or void that presses in on her: "from the invisible background radiates a hidden light like a quiet hope" (Küster, *Kunstwerkstatt*, 158). In his fascinating 1918 portrait of the Bremen dancer Marna Glahn (aka Glaan), the Communist Heinrich Vogeler (1872–1942), another Worpswede artist, shows the head and shoulders of the dancer rising out of a waterfall and bushes, with nude female bodies flowing out of her head and dancing in the sea above her. However, the expression on her face does "not mirror happiness as present, but as a shimmer of hope," as a "sign of unfulfilled dreams" (Hoffmeister 14). Thus, the rising body of the dancer appears between the empty idyll of nature and the nude utopia of which women dream.

In Vienna in 1919, Professor Franz Cizek (1865–1946) at the Academy of Applied Arts began teaching "kineticism," which fused expressionist, cubist, futurist, and constructivist aesthetics to represent the movement of objects and the dynamic properties of forms and spaces. The image of the dancing body was for Cizek the key to achieving this synthesis (or "simultanism") of aesthetic styles. Dance had long attracted him; in 1912, he had even turned down an offer to teach at Dalcroze's new school in Hellerau. Soon he became friends with the writer and arts publicist L. W. Rochowanski, who himself performed expressionist dances in Vienna, Prague, and Krakow with his wife, Katja Kandinsky, during the war years (Markhof 49). Rochowanski published a book, *Der Formwille der Zeit in der angewandten Künste* (1922), that featured numerous illustrations of works exhibited by Cizek's students in Vienna. It was an exciting collection of paintings, drawings, sculptures, and designs that showed the ecstatic movement of abstract forms, colors, lines, and human figures through space, "the turning and surrounding of the body" (23). Buildings, mountains, storms, and typography undulated, swirled, and plunged like dancing bodies; nude dancing bodies "radiated" waves of rhythmic patterns in pencil, paint, wood, clay.

These works came from thirty-five students, most of whom were women, including Trude Fischl, Franziska Kantor, Irmgard Lang, Herta Müller-Schulda, Gertrude Neuwirth, Johann Scheibner, Heinz Reichenfelser. Though many of these students subsequently pursued quite obscure lives, their achievements here suggested the great potential of the dancing body, as a "kinetic form," to awaken an ecstatic artistic imagination in a wide range of personalities. One of Cizek's students, Harry Täuber, designed sets and lighting for Anita Berber and Sebastian Droste when they visited Vienna in 1922 (Berber). Another very gifted student, Erika Giovanna Klien (1900–1957), designed a wild cubo-expressionist-constructivist poster-kiosk to announce "Anita Berber dances" (1924); with her "simultaneous structures," "Klien developed entire dramas in an image" (Markhof 21). Her enthusiasm for dance remained strong; she did numerous drawings of dancers, an exhilarating dance frieze (1924), designs for a "kinetic marionette theatre" (1924), even kinetic designs for bank notes. After Elisabeth Duncan visited the Cizek classes in 1923, Klien decided to study under her, then accepted (1926) an offer to teach at the new Duncan school in Klessheim. The American modernist art collector Katherine Dreier arranged to have some of Klien's works displayed in 1926 at the International Exhibition of Modern Art in New York. When in 1929 she migrated to the United States, where she taught art at exclusive private schools for girls in New York and Chicago, Klien maintained her connection to the Duncan school in New York and devised dance dramas for her own students, although she faced continual resistance from school administrators. Even though her art evolved toward geometric dynamism, she never abandoned her perception of the kinetic dancing body as the commanding sign of, as she put it, a propulsive tension "between abstraction and eroticism" (Markhof 22).

In Berlin, Luise Grimm (1900–?) displayed an altogether different expressionism in her representation of dance. She had taken lessons in *Ausdruckstanz*, but a stark Christian mysticism pervaded her art. *Tanzszene* (1923), a woodcut, depicted bodies of dancers as naked forms of light in a black void; a female dancer leaps toward the pinnacle of a pyramid of light that has the effect of hurling the male dancers away from it: "the thin, delicate bodies look like marionette figures" (Ruthenberg 51) (Figure 72). In 1924, Grimm saw Mary Wigman's group dance in Berlin, and she did several woodcuts, drawings, and ink sketches of the group. One image was especially fascinating (Figure 73). Here four ghostly figures stand in a strange swirl of plantlike shadows. The faces of the standing figures are of varying size; it appears as if they are not on the same plane, even though they stand next to each other. One of the faces resembles Wigman, another Georgi. Before the standing figures moves a faceless woman, but Grimm signifies her movement through the swirl of her dress—her arms, torso, and head remain rigid. She seems to dance for the standing figures, but the eyes of these women are closed, with the Wigman and Georgi faces bearing faintly Oriental expressions. In this image, dance appears as the creation of alien beings from an eerie world of shadows, the mysterious ritual of foreign creatures who can move blindly, without eyes, and can see beautiful movement without opening their eyes (53–61).

However, no German artists of the dance, not even Schlemmer and his adepts at the Bauhaus, represented dance with the extreme level of abstraction achieved by several of the De Stijl artists in Holland between 1916 and 1928, beginning with Theo Van Doesburg's (1883–1931) still vaguely figural paintings *Dance I* (1916) and *Dance II* (1916), and then the much more abstract stained-glass windows of these works (1917). With *Rhythm of a Russian Dance* (1918) Doesburg had virtually eliminated the body altogether from the image and reduced the movement of the dance to conjunctions of differently colored vertical and horizontal lines. Elegant costume designs by Piet Zwart from 1920, though much more figural, nevertheless indicated the authority of costume to impose rectilinear order on the curvilinear languidity of the dancing body. But perhaps the most radical De Stijl image of dance was the *Mechanical Dancing Figure* (1920–1923) of Vilmos Huszar (1884–1960). The artist constructed a male robotic body entirely out of wooden blocks and intended the figure to dance in a completely automated theatre using, according to Huszar, "electro-mechanical or coloristic-cinematographic means." However, the debut performance of the "plastic drama" in 1923 actually resembled a kind of shadow play (Troy 649–650). Dance, as the De Stijl artists defined it, referred to jazz or popular dances and to traditional ethnic dances of Indonesia, not to modern dance. Jazz and Balinese dances came from "primitive" peoples and therefore did not suffer from the pathological pretensions of European art, as Piet Mondrian (1872–1944) remarked in 1926: "All modern dances look dull next to [Josephine Baker's] powerful, sustained concentration of speed" (645).

Dance for De Stijl artists motivated an art "conceived with reference to a primitive means of expression that the artist sought to transpose into abstract, mechanistic terms" (644). The tenth anniversary issue of *De Stijl* (VII) in 1927 contained an article by Valentin Parnac describing a performance of his dance *Epopée* at the Meyerhold Theatre in Moscow in 1925. In this work, Parnac sought to eliminate all curved lines from choreography and to develop "the tendency towards denaturalization [of the body] . . . based on the contrast of horizontal and vertical movement"

(Jaffé 188–189). By this time, however, Van Doesburg had moved toward what he called "elementarism," the signification of abstract kinetic power through diagonal lines rather than through the "pure" vertical-horizontal conjunctions demanded by Mondrian, who subsequently left De Stijl over this issue. In 1928, Van Doesburg made stunning application of his diagonal aesthetic in the radically sleek design of the Cafe Aubette cinema-dance theatre in Strasbourg, whereas Mondrian moved toward the purified rectilinearity of "Broadway Boogie Woogie" (1942). But another Dutch artist with only a tentative connection to De Stijl, Willem Van Leusden (1886–1974), did a series of drawings of dancers in 1926–1927 that severely abstracted the body (rather than the movement) of the dancer to a complex of triangles and circles, triangles and spheres, or triangles and cones (Adelaar 102). Yet one should remember that the Dutch fascination with "primitive" dance did not necessarily lead to a repudiation of expressionism, for the artists affiliated with the modernist arts journal *Wendingen* pursued a much more mystical image of form and the body, which Jaap Kool, among others, articulated in articles on Balinese dance, the Ballets Russes, Grit Hegesa, and Gertrud Leistikow.

In 1933 Helene von Taussig published a book of twenty-four charcoal drawings of Harald Kreutzberg dancing. These minimalist motions studies attempted to establish bodily movement rather than physiognomy as the salient feature of Kreutzberg's dance persona (although the dancer's bald head assumes a very assertive presence in all the drawings). In plate 9 the artist assigned a vaguely feminine identity to the dancer by making his hips wide and curvaceous; in plate 24 his body seems peculiarly Negroid. The main fascination of the drawings lies in Taussig's effort to show how movement individuates the body—or, at least, how a peculiar physiognomy produces peculiar forms of movement. This approach differentiated Taussig's images from Kandinsky's purely geometric images of Palucca. Taussig strove to create, in a few broad strokes, a complex image of intense muscular nudity, emotional turbulence, and rapturous action. Kreutzberg leaps, runs, twists, his arms spread, thrusting, or propelling; he exists in a white void, as if every movement were the negation of an inescapable emptiness. The artist designated movement by using lines of two thicknesses, fat and thin, with each thickness given a variety of weights, determined by the degree of pressure exerted on the charcoal as it moved across the paper. She further complicated the images by setting strokes describing bodily features in different directions, so that it appears as if powerful dance movement occurs when the body is somehow divided by contradictory energies. A heavy thin line may contradict a light fat line, but the thin line may designate only the bald head, whereas the fat line may construct the torso and leg, thus conveying the sense that most of the body is less clearly definable than the head. Movement challenges the definability of the body. The desirability of the male body for the female artist depends on this display of contradictory energies released through dance. But this desire is perhaps visible only through a reductivist pleasure in abstraction.

In Germany, however, the dancing body appeared perhaps too volatile, too pervasive, and too saturated with erotic connotations to lead the visual imagination toward the extreme, ascetic abstractionism of De Stijl. The German dance culture compelled perception to focus on the body itself, not on the abstract forms that "transcended" the body and therefore constituted a "pure" vision. For De Stijl, dance was a "problem" of imperfect bodily form, which the artist solved by striving toward a rectilinear utopia of "absolute equilibrium." The convoluted instability of expressionism was a more appropriate aesthetic for disclosing the emotional disturbances, the distortions of desire, and the sheer perceptual violence provoked by the body and its impulse to dance. The expressionist image of dance achieved its rawest intensity in the work of the Flemish artist Frans Masereel (1889–1970), whose "novels in woodcuts" remained popular in Germany after the publication of *Die Idee* (1920). His almost lewd woodcut of *Jazz* (1931) shows three looming, demonic black musicians in tuxedos urging a nude white woman to dance with orgasmic ecstasy (Figure 74). Here the crude, dark force of the "primitive" is what drives the female body to uncontrolled freedom and vulnerability, but the message achieves conviction through the bold, expressionist juxtaposition of burning whiteness and surging blackness. Yet despite its racism, this image of dance never elicited the controversy associated with *The Breakdown* (1926), by the English artist John Bulloch Souter (1890–1971) (Figure 75). In this painting, Souter applied the realist techniques of New Objectivity to the image of a nude white woman dancing to the saxophone of a single tuxedoed black man. Unlike the woman in Masereel's picture, Souter's incandescent woman dances not wildly but slowly, as if in a trance, yet ecstatically. The musician gazes not at the woman but out toward the spectator, and the implication is that jazz and dance together allow man and woman to cross racial barriers and form a new and mysteriously intimate (or trusting) sort of couple, each immersed in separate aspirations. The space common to them both is defined by the broken monumental statue upon which the musician sits. The collapsed classical order represented by the heroic statue has been replaced by a new order of symmetry: the music of black maleness achieves cool equilibrium with the dance of white femaleness. This beautiful painting from England, with its cool, rational rejection of primitivism and cautious curiosity about a new mode of romanticism to replace the fallen classical ideal of power, entailed an erotic image of dance that neither expressionism nor New Objectivity in Germany, no matter how "rawly" or intensely they saw dance, presented with such nakedness or disturbing detachment.

SCULPTURE

In the field of sculpture, the Berliner Georg Kolbe (1877–1947) predominated in the representation of dance. A proponent of nudism and gymnastic culture, he depicted nearly all of his dancers in nude poses beginning around 1912. His style was a sort of heroic, athletic expressionism emphasizing the supple, rounded rhythms of the muscles, the pliant mass of the dancing body. Dance movement suffused the body with curvatures of exquisite smoothness and obedience to internal rhythms. Kolbe's unambiguously healthy image of dance appealed to a large public and private audience, yet he was clearly a modernist in his search for an unusual, dramatic curve to the body's thrust toward freedom. One of his nude dancers stood before the Mies van der Rohe pavilion at the international modern art exposition at Barcelona in 1929. In both his sculpture and his graphic work, Kolbe tended to see dance rather than the dancer, so his image of the kinetic body made few concessions to the expressive realities of particular bodies. But the Nazis also found his image of the dancing body congenial to their cultural program. His 1925 statue of the beautiful Edith von Schrenck displayed the same heroic idealism as his more generic works, even though the aesthetic of this tragic dancer, loaded with the image of bondage and cramped flesh, completely contradicted his hygienic, emancipated view of dance.

Another Berliner, Oswald Herzog (1881–?), cultivated a much more abstract curvilinearity in his representation of dance. In 1914 he produced *Ecstasy,* a sculpture of a dancing maenad in which the nude figure of the dancer, attached to the base only by the toes of one foot, seemed to shoot into space with shocking exuberance. In subsequent sculptures of the war years, Herzog intensified his abstraction of the dancing body's curvatures so that stone moved with an organic freedom and bodies looked like strange, strong plants, shaped by the rhythms of wind, water, and molecular plasticity. In *Plastik—Sinfonie des Lebens* (1921), he asserted that "rhythmic dynamism is the law of world order" and that "dynamism is the source of all bodiliness [Körperlichkeit]" (12); moreover, "the abstraction of eroticism comes through the fusion of forms" (7). This attitude led to an image of the dancing body—seen, for example, in *Geniessen* (1920)—as "absolute" in its curvilinearity as the De Stijl artists were in their rectilinearity (cf., Kuhn, *Der Cicerone,* 8/9, April 1921, 245–252). Yet another Berlin sculptor, Rudolf Belling (1886–1972), achieved more powerful expression of organic curvilinearity, but dance was not his preferred subject. In 1923, however, he married a dancer, Toni Freeden, who apparently specialized in experimental, mechanical ballets. Belling's 1925 polished steel sculpture of her head was remarkable in bestowing a dancelike flow of metallic movement through the masklike, robotic face, the domed skull, and the wave of her hair. A curious photograph shows the dancer cradling this image of herself with possessive affection (Nerdinger 194–195; 204–205) (Figure 76).

In Vienna, Lotte Pritzel created decorative wax dolls of incredible rococo refinement. These became popular during the First World War and remained so throughout Europe and America in the Weimar era. The figures were always thin, lithe, undulating with movement, and luxuriously costumed and ornamented, with haunting, ethereal, worldly facial expressions that somewhat contradicted the innocence usually associated with dolls. She constructed numerous dance dolls, a few of which were even "supposed to be accompanied by music and song, and dance entirely in circular movement" (*Arts and Decoration*, 24 December 1925, 45). Most peculiar, though, was the effort of four such contrasting dancers as Anita Berber, Niddy Impekoven, Grit Hegesa, and Herta Hornbach (a grotesque "fashion" dancer in Berlin) to include "Pritzel-doll" dances on their programs in 1919.

The market for decorative figurines of dancers expanded enormously in the 1920s with the evolution of carving, foundry, and glazing technologies that permitted the manufacture of extremely refined representations of the human body. A large number of artists in Germany, France, and Austria specialized in the production of these objects. The great majority of the figures had bodies formed out of ivory and bronze, which the artist cold-painted, tinted, or gilded and then set on an onyx or marble base. But some pieces featured bodies of painted porcelain or tinted glass. Female dancers predominated overwhelmingly. Many bodies were nude, but the majority wore glamorously exotic costumes or sleekly elegant contemporary fashions. The figures idealized (and sometimes satirized) dance as a luxurious, exquisite expression of the body's seductive plasticity, vitality, and vulnerability. They represented bodily movement with a breathtaking realism and refinement that was exuberantly modern yet the very antithesis of the abstraction associated with expressionism and other "isms." As Arwas has remarked, "they seemed about to come alive" in an "unnervingly" fanciful way (6). The variety of movements, poses, costumes and color effects depicted was astonishing and indicated a constant, even "addictive," appetite for discovering ever more decorative rhythms for the body.

In Paris, the Rumanian Dimitri Chiparus (1888–1950) was perhaps the most prolific producer of figurines; his dancers wore glamorously ornamental costumes of an oriental or antique type. But in Berlin, Ferdinand Preiss (1882–1943) was perhaps the greatest of all the figurine makers. During the 1920s his firm enjoyed a large global market, with England being an especially strong importer of the highly distinctive Preiss-Kassler product. "Preiss figures are the epitome of grace and elegance, the faces pretty but with character, the costumes colorful but restrained" (Arwas 244). Before the war Preiss tended to put his figures in the garb of classical antiquity, but after 1920, when he intensified the realism of the representation, he dressed them in suavely tasteful contemporary fashions and cultivated a maddeningly exquisite athletic eroticism in which the sleek bodies looked both wholesome and impossibly refined (Arwas 161–207; Catley 256–283). He apparently relied for his models not on dancers themselves but on pictures from books, magazines, and newspapers. In Munich, however, dancer Lo Hesse modeled for Walter Schnackenberg and Constantine Holzer-Defanti (Arwas 110–111; 213–215). Much more perversely erotic dance figurines came from Dorothea Charol (1895–?) in Berlin and Bruno Zach in Vienna. Zach cultivated a glossy image of the proud, haughty, high-heeled dominatrix or Amazon in shiny black latex or with a riding crop. In these curious works one observes in the dance pose the perfect, sadomasochistic image of the modern, emancipated female as a new species of aristocrat, the born ruler of strange, dark desires (223–231; Catley 303–307).

DANCE ARCHITECTURE

Even though no country in the world was as active as Weimar Germany in providing opportunities to observe modern dance, this art form, which, more than any other activity, calls attention to the expressive power of the body, produced almost no architecture designed specifically for it. Thus, dance culture constantly found itself having to accommodate, invade, or appropriate spaces intended for other modes of performance. Many dancers devised innovative studios, and these often had considerable pedagogical value for dancers themselves, but they seldom drew serious audiences for dance. Unlike cinema and sports, for example, dance was unable to move architectural imagination in a new direction, and though this situation indicated a measure of failure on the part of architecture to explore new relations between bodies and buildings, the consequences for dance were even more disappointing. Dancers rarely got out of the habit of seeing dance in a proscenium frame, with nearly all movement seen in relation to a frontal projection of the body. However, one performance space in particular attracted the interest of several personalities in the Viennese modern dance movement: the Raumbühne, constructed inside the Vienna Concert Hall in 1924. Its designer, Friedrich Kiesler (1890–1965), earlier had composed manifestos advocating "electromechanical" and "optophonetic" theatres and had close ties with the Bauhaus people, the futurist F. T. Marinetti, the De Stijl group in Holland, and the Russian constructivists. The Raumbühne was a giant spiral stage of iron and wood crowned by a large staging area accessible only by a pair of ladders, but action could occur anywhere on the spiral ramps. The audience surrounded the performance space but did not move, as Kiesler had proposed in his 1922 scheme for a "railway theatre." For Kiesler, the spiral was the dominant sign of a modern spirit because of its power to convey a sense of movement. The weakness of the proscenium stage, he contended, was that it encouraged audiences to see drama as image rather than as movement. His spiral stage was therefore a "naked" performance space insofar as it dispensed with scenic and pictorial elements in favor of complex opportunities for movement and relations between bodies. The Viennese press displayed a lack of confidence in the Raumbühne to accommodate plays (Frischauer's *Im Dunkel* [1924], Goll's *Methusalem* [1922]) written with the proscenium in mind, but Kiesler hoped the spiral stage would inspire a new kind of drama that was not so dependent on enervating talk. Such was not the case; early in 1925, Kiesler accepted an offer to work on an exhibition in Paris, and in 1926 he pursued an invitation to work on an exhibit in New York, where he spent the rest of his life.

Without its inventor to supervise its fortunes, the Raumbühne quickly became a conventional (proscenium) performance space and then disappeared. However, the Viennese press did appreciate several dance performances given in the Raumbühne in October 1924. Toni Birkmeyer and his partner, Tilly Losch, produced a somewhat puzzled response, perhaps because they both seemed so deeply attached to the world of ballet whereas the space was so utterly alien to ballet culture. Losch swung up the steps to the upper platform, but Birkmeyer never moved beyond the middle level of the ramp, and this choice signified an "unreachable" distance between male and female bodies that otherwise moved to the same rhythm. Gisa Geert attracted a larger measure of critical approval when she performed a series of solo dances in the Raumbühne. She emphasized a notion of diagonal movement that pressured the body to move in a line up and down the ramps but nevertheless limited its freedom because the ramps were too narrow to permit movement trajectories outside of those forming the spirals. In other words, the Raumbühne seemed no different from the proscenium stage in its ability to signify the freedom of the body from environmental constraints. Group dances would appear to reinforce this point. But when Gertrud Bodenwieser's all-female dance group, which leased a studio in the Vienna Concert Hall, gave a performance in the space in late October 1924, the critics were apparently charmed. The "grotesque" piece, *Film ohne Leinwand*, took advantage of the space's peculiar features by incorporating acrobatic and gymnastic movements. Such movements enhanced the dynamic interaction of bodies and space precisely because they accommodated, rather than submitted to, the interruptions in movement flow and concentration established by the ramps, spirals, ladders, and elevations. Bodenwieser's group performed in the space two months later for Karlheinz Martin's production of Wedekind's *Franziska* (1912), but by then the Raumbühne had been largely dismantled to fit into the proscenium frame of the Raimund Theatre (Lesák, esp. 111–163).

The Raumbühne is an excellent example of how a modern performance space amplifies anxiety toward a modern performing body that resists being framed, not only by a proscenium but also by a literary, text-driven imagination contained by the same frame. The Raumbühne dance concerts generated considerable public interest, but the idea of modern spaces for modern performances threatened to subvert an intricate institutional apparatus, governed above all by the authority of texts and authors, for controlling the body, performance, and sexual difference. The greatest resistance to modernist performance spaces came not from audiences but from within the institutions of theatre culture itself. Kiesler became involved in a noisy public dispute with Dr. Jakob Moreno-Levy (1892–1974), a psychiatrist, over the origin of the spiral theatre concept. In 1926 both men left for New York, and neither revived the idea of a spiral stage (Moreno-Levy's scheme was a "therapeutic" space for performers only). Ironically, after designing the De Stijl modernist Film Guild movie theatre in Manhattan (1928), department store show windows (1929), and the experimental Space House (1933) (Stern 258, 354), Kiesler spent much the rest of his career trying to make modernist opera scenery fit into proscenium stages.

A quite different, but no less modern, approach to architecture for dance performance was the Himmelssaal (Heaven's Hall) of the Atlantis House in Bremen (1930) (Figure 77). This fascinating building was the work of a very complex personality, Bernhard Hoetger (1874–1949). Though his family background was decidedly humble, Hoetger achieved astonishing mastery and success in a wide range of arts. Beginning as a sculptor, he branched out into graphics, painting, furniture design, ceramics, publishing, and architecture. In 1914, supposedly under the spell of the primitive expressionist paintings of Paula Modersohn-Becker (1876–1907), Hoetger moved from Darmstadt, where he was a professor of art, to Worpswede. After designing his own house there, he received invitations to design cafes, hotels, gardens, and monuments in the Bremen-Worpswede area, and for these he applied an increasingly idiosyncratic, dramatic expressionist style that fused modernist and pre-Christian Nordic aesthetics. Hoetger was remarkably eclectic, absorbing influences from Paris, Italy, Egypt, black Africa, expressionism, art deco, and ancient Teutonia. Modern dance appealed to him, and one of his early sculptures, done in Paris, is an exhilarating figurine of the American dancer Loie Fuller (1901). In 1917 he became friends with Sent M'ahesa, who performed works in an Egyptian style, and he produced at least two dramatic sculptures of her, an Egyptian-expressionist head (1917) and a Nordic-expressionist nude (1922).

In 1918 Hoetger made the acquaintance of the Bremen trading tycoon Ludwig Roselius, and the two of them devised plans for renovating an alley in downtown Bremen, the Böttcherstrasse. Hoetger's first building was the Paula Modersohn-Becker house (1927), a fantastic, expressionist brick castle that honored the work and life of this artist, who, like Hoetger, actually discovered her artistic identity in Paris. The second building in the Böttcherstrasse project was the Atlantis House (1929–1931), the purpose of which, according to Roselius, was to remind Germans of their origins in an archaic Nordic culture inhabiting the great plain between the North Sea and the Baltic. In the Atlantis House, architecture strove to link modernism with the recovery of a primordial racial identity, but the result was a strange brick building that combined expressionist monumentality, art deco ornamental effects, and pre-Christian symbolism (above the entrance to the building was a huge crucifix, but the body on the cross was not Jesus but a rather demonic Odin). As Thiemann (29) has observed, moving through the building was like moving through the compartments of a great ship. A stunning, futuristic spiral stair tower, studded with starlike light holes and encased in a glass mosaic cylinder, connected the three floors. The Himmelssaal was on the second floor, between the first floor reading room and the third floor museum.

Figure 77 depicts this room, designed exclusively for dance performances. In spite of its small size and the absence of fixed seating for spectators, the space nevertheless conveyed a monumental atmosphere through its bold contrast between curving lines, smooth surfaces, and cryptic symbolism: cross, glass-imprinted arrows, spears, and discs (one of which, not visible in this picture, was suspended like a gong at the other end of the room). The glass walls of the arcing dome permitted sunlight to pervade the performance space, but the room contained no provision for the use of theatrical lights (or scenery) other than the rows of fixed lamps on each side of the hall; on the left side (not seen), the lamps glowed within glass globes, which further contained intricate wire netting to filter the light. The Himmelssaal projected the aura of a cult temple suffused with mystical light: "a space of meditation, of devotion to something invisible, yet in light. Hoetger is here the adept of abstraction. It makes the cult space ideology-free, but grounded in brotherliness" (Thiemann 29; see also Golücke 94–99; Küster, *Kunstwerkstalt,* 58–83). The swirling linearity and planar emptiness of the room made it an ideal space for modern dance performance. The space invited people to dance within it, to move with unexpected freedom. The three women in the 1930 photograph (probably from Estonian Helmi Nurk's company) seem to "belong" to the space to a degree that is unusual in modern dance photography. By far the majority of modern dancers preferred to have their pictures taken in photography studios, in nature, or in a space without context, as in Figure 1, rather than in the spaces in which they actually performed their dances, because they felt that modern movements did not really belong on proscenium stages designed for bodily movements that were not modern. Figure

77 shows a remarkable unity of modern bodily movement and modern architecture, and this unity requires no more (or less) in the way of scenic context.

But to say that the Himmelssaal was "ideology-free" is somewhat misleading. Critics favorable to the International Style condemned the building for its reactionary mysticism and its eagerness to associate modernism with the politics of cultural fragmentation, with the localization of identity, with provincialism. The Nazis were even less appreciative, despite Hoetger's initial enthusiasm for their program and his scarcely concealed anti-Semitism. In 1935, Hitler himself declared the Böttcherstrasse complex so repulsive that he thought it should be torn down, and Roselius, whose global business interests were important to the Nazis, had to make passionate appeals to the city council to prevent the annihilation of the "temples." In 1937, Hitler agreed to let the buildings stand as examples of "Bolshevist" artistic corruption as long as Roselius affixed placards explaining why such architecture was decadent and anti-German. By 1938, Hoetger was on the list of "degenerate artists," and his life became even more difficult and reclusive. (Today the Böttcherstrasse buildings are a major, delightful tourist attraction.) Hoetger's eclecticism, his openness to so many "foreign" (and feminine?) influences—luridly satirized in Paul Masdack's biographical novel, *Der schwarze Magier* (1924)—undermined his capacity to develop a distinctly Nordic mode of expression that was recognizable to the Nazis. The Himmelssaal was a powerfully and seductively unique space for dance performance; no one from the dance world itself showed the capacity to envision, let alone realize, a dance space even remotely as satisfying. Perhaps, then, an eclectic (rather than "pure") imagination, a Hoetgerian will to absorb ever more categories of artistic expression, is necessary to create the context best suited to allowing bodies to move with a uniquely modern freedom.

CINEMA

For various technical, economic, and aesthetic reasons, dance did not appear often in films. Rita Sacchetto, Jenny Hasselquist, and Grete Wiesenthal had performed in movies before 1920, and in 1919 Mary Wigman made a mountain film, now lost, in Switzerland. Anita Berber made a heap of films but not many in which she danced, although she and Droste supposedly made in Vienna of film of their "dances of vice, horror, and ecstasy." Eight-year old Maryla Gremo performed her curious expressionist dances in the Murnau productions of *Satanas* (1919) and *Sehsucht* (1919), and Murnau directed further films that featured characters who were dancers but played by actors (Conrad Veidt, Sasha Gura). For the Berlin premiere of *Nosferatu* (1922), Elisabeth Grube devised a live dance prologue, *Die Serenade*, with original music by Hans Erdmann (*Friedrich Wilhelm Murnau*, 215–216, 221). In 1920, Laban prepared a fairy-tale dance film for production by the Universum Film Aktiengesellschaft (UFA) studio in Berlin, but this project soon seemed too risky for studio executives of the inflation era and had to be abandoned. He later (1928) planned a film to explicate his system for notating dance, but this project also failed to reach the screen. UFA eventually produced *Wege zu Kraft und Schönheit* (1925), which included documentary footage of several prominent dancers. But the paucity of dance imagery on the cinema screen (rather than before it) is nevertheless disappointing, especially because what little documentary footage remains of Wigman, Laban, Impekoven, Jo Mihály, Gert, and Kreutzberg, is tantatalizingly mysterious. Documentary fragments of Hellerau students in 1913 undulating outdoors through colonnade shadows and bands of luscious sunlight are among the most hypnotic and luminous images of the moving body I have ever seen.

In *Der sichtbare Mensch* (1924), the Hungarian expatriate screenwriter Béla Balazs (1884–1949) grasped that film possessed the unique capacity to reveal the "melody of physiognomy" in a "scientific" manner, through close-ups (or "microphysiognomy" of the body) and "rhythmic" editing of multiple views or angles of the body. Moreover, because "the physiognomy of men [sic] is more intense when they are silent," all-dance films in the silent era of pantomimic acting would seem as feasible in the studio environment as Laban had imagined in 1920 (Balazs 61–65, 80–81, 207). Film speeds, however, were not high enough to allow for the filming of dances in their concert environments; more often, dances on film required a daylight environment, which actually gave the bodily movements a beautiful luminosity. Hans Pasche, in *Die Schallkiste* (3/9, September 1928, 10), urged dancers to use the new synchronized sound technology to produce dances directly for the screen, as demonstrated by a short dance film featuring Dorothea Albu of the Berlin State Opera ballet. But neither the dance nor film worlds explored this possibility. Thus, despite the prodigious dance talent in Germany, dance in film never appeared as anything more than an interlude in a larger, nondanced narrative context.[1]

1. Sladan Dudow's film *Kuhle Wampe* (1932), a Communist Party production with a script by Bertolt Brecht and Ernst Ottwalt, contains an amusing scene in which an unemployed worker, sitting at the kitchen table of his Berlin apartment, reads aloud to his wife a newspaper article on Mata Hari. The newspaper language describes in lurid and almost lascivious detail Mata Hari's body and the movements of her nude dances in Berlin. As the husband reads on obsessively, the wife somberly studies another section of the paper containing advertisements for meat products, so that the male voice becomes juxtaposed with newspaper images of sausages and chops and prices. Without showing any dance at all, the film manages to construct a powerful perception of dance as a luxurious erotic fantasy of flesh that is in some way

Most dancers seemed to grasp that dance on the screen was not the same as dance on the stage and that dance in film achieved expressive power only when the camera did not merely watch the dance but "danced" as well, became an integral component of the movement. Fritz Böhme thought film could achieve dancelike properties when it moved toward dynamic abstractionism, as in the montage editing or "reflecting color music" of "absolute" films or animations by Walter Ruttmann, Hans Richter, or Oskar Fischinger ("Materialen," 25). Of course, in such films, dance was no longer the work of the body. One dancer who well understood how to use film technology on behalf of bodily movement was Leni Riefenstahl (b. 1902), whose *Triumph of the Will* (1935) and *Olympia* (1938) remain among the most seductive cinematic representations of physical beauty and strength in film history. She herself starred in the immensely successful *The Blue Light* (1931), with a scenario by Balazs about a mountain girl shunned by villagers who believe her skill at climbing the rugged cliffs to reach the remote crystal cave of the "blue light" awakens fatal desires in men. Riefenstahl did not dance in this silent film, but she moved through treacherous, sublime nature with a poise, rhythm, and physical precision unique to a dancer. No other director of the era treated the camera as if it were the partner of the body, entailing a fluid tension between the desire of the camera to get closer to the body, and the desire of the body to get closer to the camera.

One of the most prominent examples of this tendency to regard dance, sports, and gymnastics as a unified and unifying ideology of body culture was Wilhelm Prager's 1925 film, *Wege zu Kraft und Schönheit*, written by a physician, Nicholas Kaufmann, in consultation with several professorial advisers. Because the federal government owned a controlling interest in UFA, which produced the film, one does not hesitate to suggest that the film represented official state advocacy of the "modern body culture" it showed. After its initial run in theatres, *Wege zu Kraft und Schönheit* appeared in classrooms and club halls everywhere in Germany. However, because it contained several scenes depicting women performing nude gymnastics, it had difficulty reaching audiences abroad, particularly in England and the United States, both of which banned theatrical exhibitions of the film. The film for the most part contained documentary footage celebrating various sports, athletic prowess, exercise techniques, modern dance forms, and outdoor pleasures. These were interspersed with fanciful reenactments of Greco-Roman sport and beauty culture (performed by students and teachers of the Deutsche Hochschule für Leibesübungen). Among the numerous athletes depicted were Else Döbler (swimming), Nedo Nadi (fencing),

---

responsible for a condition in which people desperately struggle for flesh to eat. It is a very witty juxtaposition of desire with hunger.

Rocky Knight (boxing), Rinjiro Degouchi (jiu-jitsu), Helen Wills (tennis), and Babe Ruth (baseball). Dancers included Mary Wigman, Rudolf Laban, Tamara Karsavina, Jenny Hasselquist, and Niddy Impekoven, and politicians associated with sport culture included Prime Minister Lloyd George of England, Benito Mussolini, and the Crown Prince of Norway. The film also contained didactic sequences, some involving animated diagrams, describing correct posture, the unhealthy effects of corsets, ergonomic factors, and so forth.

The message of the film was obvious: a revitalized national German identity depended on heightened, modern body consciousness in the spectator, a consciousness one could achieve by choosing to pursue one or more of the activities depicted. Nude women from the Hedwig Hagemann girl's school in Hamburg demonstrate, by a placid, sparkling lake, some of the Mensendieck movement techniques as more gentle, less competitive alternatives to the other activities, but the appearance of nude women here and in the Greco-Roman scenes dominates perception of the film as a whole. One wants to see more of this activity or wants to see the nude women doing more; more than enough documentation establishes the other choices. But on the whole the film presents dance, sport, and gymnastics as equally attractive "paths to strength and beauty" without acknowledging the differing aims (and gender politics) motivating the choice to pursue one mode of body culture over another. The viewer must discern these differences according to the image of the body projected by each of the modes. Yet by lumping dance, sport, and gymnastics together, the film makes an integrated idea of body culture into a national sign of individual and societal freedom.

PHOTOGRAPHY

Modern dance culture emphatically preferred photography as the medium for transmitting the new image of dance. The emancipatory authority of modern dance achieved its most convincing representation when aligned with the expanding expressive capacity of photographic technology, which also had a stake in modernism insofar as its own ambition to attain the status of art was concerned. Moreover, although photography supposedly "documented" the "reality" of dance by "scientific" means not associated with painting, dancers had discovered by 1910 that this technology actually was much more efficient in idealizing dance than in documenting it realistically. Nevertheless, the material reality of the body achieved optimum representation through a medium thought of, rightly or wrongly, as the most technologically advanced way to construct the most material image of the world. Of course, dancers (though not always dance) appreciated the attention paid to them by gifted artists. In Vienna, Max Pollak (1886–1970), possibly "the first etcher to turn his attention to the dance as a subject," did numerous refined mezzotint portraits of Joachim von Seewitz, Ellen Tels, Mila Cirul, Ronny Johansson, Tatjana Barbakoff, Maria Ley, Anne Osborn, and Russian dancers within the Tels circle (*Max Pollak*, 37; also, *The Studio*, 86/369, 15 December 1923, 343–345). Felix Harta (1884–1967) was another Viennese whose expressionistic portraits of theatrical personalities included many dancers. But although the fine arts could bestow a distinctive cultural status on dance, photography allowed the dancer greater control over the image.

Before the war, photography of dance took place largely in the photographic studio rather than the dance studio, and studios specifically for dance imagery operated in several German cities as well as in Vienna. Rudolph Dürhkoop (1848–1918), in Hamburg and Nuremburg, photographed Laura Oesterreich and the Falke sisters. In Munich, Hanns Holdt (1880–1972) photographed Edith von Schrenck, Niddy Impekoven, Jutta von Collande, Mary Wigman, Gertrud Leistikow, the Sacharoffs, and Sent M'ahesa, and Hugo Erfurt (1874–1948) photographed the Wiesenthal sisters and Clotilde von Derp in Dresden. Other photographers of dancers cited in Brandenburg, Suhr, and Nikolaus included Wanda von Debschitz-Kunowski (Munich), Stephanie Held-Ludwig (Munich), Elisabeth Morsbach (Munich), Ani Riess (Berlin), Franz Löwy (Vienna), and others in Berlin, Leipzig, Vienna, and Mannheim. After the war, with technology that did not require such long exposure times and with the inspiring success of gymnastic and *Nacktkultur* photo imagery, photographers moved from their studios to the native sites of dance. A number of new photographers found dance a congenial subject for experimentation, including Hans Robertson, Steffi Brandt, and Suse Byk in Berlin, Albert Renger-Patzsch (1897–1966) in Essen, Gertrud Hesse in Duisburg, Anny Breer in Hamburg, and, in Vienna, Josef Trcka (1893–1940) and Rudolf Koppitz (1884–1936). The Merkelbach studio in Amsterdam did numerous images of German dancers (Georgi, Impekoven) in addition to its Dutch clientele. Gerhard Riebicke (1878–1957), in Berlin, was perhaps the most prominent photographer of athletes and *Nacktkultur* after 1923, partly because of his skill in finding dramatic images for athletic action (Figure 78). Umbo (aka Otto Umbehr, 1902–1980) studied (1921–1923) at the Bauhaus in Weimar before working as a magazine photographer in Berlin, where he developed an interest in the improvisations of rehearsal photography.

But highly contrived studio photography of dance and dancers by no means disappeared, with Vienna remaining the site of the most artificial constructions of the dance image. There the Studio D'Ora—operated (1907–1925) by Madame D'Ora (aka Dora Kalmus, 1881–1963) and Arthur Benda (1885–1969), who rose to international prominence through society and high fashion photography—placed the bodies of

dancers (Berber, Tels, Impekoven, Bodenwieser) in highly recessed interior
spaces, completely sealed off from the world visible through the viewfinder
(Figure 26), although Madame D'Ora's aesthetic moved radically out of the
studio after 1945 (Faber, *Madame D'Ora*, 188–190). Her students Edith
Barakowics and Edith Glogau perpetuated her studio style, publishing dramatically contrived dance photographs in Schertel's erotic journals. The
artificiality of the photo studio allowed for a more overt linking of dance
with erotic desires that are "visible" only when protected from the glare of
the world beyond the viewfinder, as was evident in Koppitz's homoerotic
1926 study of two nude female Russian dancers (Figure 79). The nude photographs of Claire Bauroff and Mila Cirul taken by another Viennese, Trude
Fleischmann (1895–1990), presented the dancers' bodies as mostly luminous organisms isolated in darkness and unwilling to gaze at the spectator
(Schreiber 118–122). In the 1930s yet another Viennese studio, Manasse,
run by Olga (1896–1969) and Adorjan Wlassics (1893–1946), created possibly the most contrived dance images of all using trick photography and
processing techniques to produce amusingly erotic collage-fantasies (Faber,
Montrierte).

Before 1920, dance photography emphasized the dancer rather than the
dance and was a genre of portrait rather than action photography, although
as early as 1908 Roland Jobst, in Vienna, had produced quite lyrical outdoor action pictures of Grete Wiesenthal, and Laban had achieved some
remarkable action images at Ascona in 1914 (Faber, *Tanzfoto*, 30–31;
Wolfensberger 109–115). Pre-1920 photography focused on the glamour
and attractiveness of the dancer and dramatized the personality through
calculated "dance" poses before scenographic backdrops. But the need for
ensemble pictures after 1920 compelled photographers to look more carefully at movement as the source of interest in the dance image (Barche and
Jeschke). Hugo Erfurt began taking pictures of leaping dancers around
1920 and discovered that, by cropping out the floor in the image, he could
create the impression of the dancer suspended high in space, an effect soon
repeated ubiquitously. In his photographs of Wigman from 1914 to 1922,
he captured her turbulent movement by occluding her face, and he seemed
to favor the airborne movement.

But his pictures of her were never as dramatic or expressive as the many
Wigman images taken in 1926 by another Dresden photographer, Charlotte Rudolph (?–1971), probably the most well-known of all dance photographers of the era. Rudolph stressed the darkness and heaviness of Wigman's art, its innovative attachment to the earth, and she saw Wigman's face
in the dance, glowing hieratically through the darkness. Rudolph understood how dance introduced dynamism into photography: she varied the
distance between the camera and the dancer, and she defined the photographer's task as selecting those movements of a dance that revealed the

dimensions of its expressive power and of the dancer's personality, an attitude she described in a 1929 article for *Schrifttanz* (VP 79–81). In 1926, Rudolph published photographs to accompany a small collection of bizarre prose poems, *Träume und Maske,* by a Dessau woman, Hilde Doepp. These showed Doepp in trancelike pantomimic poses, but the camera moved close to her so that it saw only the upper portion of her body. This desire to move in on the movement and reveal dance above the legs achieved even stronger representation in Suse Byk's photographs of Valeska Gert, which appeared in Fred Hildenbrandt's 1928 book on the dancer.

Around 1930 in Vienna, Arthur Benda of the D'Ora Studio, in response to homoerotic dances of the Bodenwieser group in which pairs of dancers coiled around each other on the floor, began taking high-angle shots of the bodies, giving a view of the dance not seen by the spectator in the concert hall. Yet the device of photographing dance from unusual angles remained extremely rare in the dance photography of the era, although Degas, in painting, had extensively explored such views of dance in the 1870s. This device occasionally appeared in photographs of movement choirs, and Lola Rogge apparently saw its expressive potential in the mid-1930s (Figure 61). Rudolph sometimes placed dancers before white backgrounds (instead of the dark, curtained walls which ostensibly foregrounded the body) to intensify the sense of the dancer's expanding the space around the body. Her most famous photos, perhaps, were of Palucca's leaps against white backdrops, upon which the dancer projected her soaring shadow (Figure 49). The leap, however, was common to Palucca's aesthetic, not to *Ausdruckstanz* in general, and as an image of freedom it appealed more to photographers than to people preoccupied with modern dance. In Berlin, from 1928, Lotte Jacobi (1896–?) used the white background for an even more spacious effect. She cultivated the friendship of her subjects and preferred relaxed, informal photos that showed the dancer rehearsing or improvising in a studio while incidental afternoon shadows crept up the walls; she did not attempt to freeze the body with absolute precision, allowing the movement to blur the image slightly and to reveal the dance's capacity to circumvent the precisional authority of technology (Jacobi 7–12).

A fascinating experiment occurred in Prague when Viteszlav Nezval and Karel Teige published *ABECEDA* (1926), which consisted of 25 poems, each four lines long and each assigned to a letter of the Czech alphabet. On one page appeared the letter and the poem, and on the facing page appeared an image of the dancer Milca Mayerova (1901–1977) "performing" the letter (Primus 154–162). Mayerova even performed these poses live at various Prague poetry readings (Nezval 147). Strangely enough, this little book was the first attempt to construct a dance photographically, as a sequence of images possessing a self-contained rhythm—the "alphabet dance," a material conjunction of letter, word, body, movement, and photo image. Before this time only Adorée Villany had shown a serious interest in sequential photography of dance (1908–1910), though Baron De Meyer did create a photoreconstruction of Nijinsky's *Afternoon of the Faun* in 1912. But despite examples from gymnastic photography, sequential imaging to produce a photographic dance never developed in Germany, or elsewhere for that matter, presumably because dancers lacked interest in such literary notions of the dance text.

In 1932, Marta Vietz (aka Astfalck-Vietz, 1901–1994) compiled a photo album called *Der schwarze Tänzer,* which became a gift for her father. The album contained sixteen photographs of a black male dancer, nude or nearly nude, performing different movements that, seen in sequence, added up to a dance. One of the photographs depicted the dancer in a startlingly rapacious embrace of a white woman. After an apprenticeship period as a lab assistant and nude model in a photo studio, Vietz became active in Berlin as a photographer, mostly from 1926 to 1932 (Frecot). Because she had considered becoming a dancer herself, she began with self-portraits, adopting dance poses for the camera. She experimented with veils, scrims, low-angle (foot) lighting, backlight silhouetting, shadows, off-center positioning, and nudity, all of which suffused the images with a curiously improvised narcissistic eroticism. The pictures quickly found publication in Ernst Schertel's erotic magazines, although Vietz apparently did not know who published them. Dancers such as Daisy Spies, Sabine Ress, May Carlstedt, Lene Ludwig, and Henri, the former partner of Anita Berber, posed for Vietz (Peter). She did not just photograph dancers or dances; she created dance in the photo studio; through an erotically tinged process of playing around with the body, pose, lighting, props, and camera, she produced images of dance as an experiment in self-seduction (Figure 80).

At the Bauhaus (1927–1929), Albert Braun, T. Lux Feininger (b. 1910), and Erich Consemueller (1902–1957) used multiple exposures, overexposures, multiple shadows, dynamic lighting effects, and occasional odd angles to construct the image of dance experimentation (Figures 36–38). By 1930, however, the Hungarian Gyula Pap (1899–1984), a Bauhaus student from 1920 to 1925, had forsaken such formalist abstraction for an eerie, mystic, totemic image of the body in his shots of masked dances performed on the roof of the Itten school in Berlin (Haus 479–482). In Dresden the painter Edmund Kesting (1892–1970) began, after much experimentation with assemblages and collages, to make photos of Wigman students (Marianne Vogelsang, Dore Hoyer) in 1929 using techniques of superimposition. Here the dancing body appeared in conflict with itself or its image, as if photo technology exposed an invisible shadow within the body (cf., Klaus 56–67). This technique, which Kesting used into the 1940s, encouraged him to move closer with the camera to the dancer, so that the signification of dance often came through the tensions between hands, arms, and face. He produced numerous superimposition images of the tragic dancer Dore Hoyer (1912–1967), whose violently dramatic (and suicidal) aesthetic, which evolved in the 1930s through solos based on incredibly detailed written scenarios and pictographs, made her the most significant artist of expressionist dance in the 1940s and 1950s (Figure 81) (Peter, *Dore Hoyer*). With Kesting, photography did not expose dance so much as dance exposed the act of seeing it as a technological drama, although his superimposition technique never reached the dazzling complexity of Maurice Tabard in Paris.

In 1937 the Dresden expressionist Hans Grundig (1901–1958) painted a portrait of Hoyer before a desolate country road at twilight. It was possibly the most melancholy portrait of a dancer created during the Third Reich, for it showed what no photograph did: a luminously sensitive young person utterly alone and unable to move freely in a huge, empty space of gathering darkness. By this time Siegfried Enkelmann (1905–1978), who had inherited the large Robertson studio in Berlin in 1933, dominated dance photography. He specialized in highly dramatic compositions and relied on intricate lighting designs to produce an effect of pictorial grandeur, which, although unique to the photographic medium, tended to drain the image of the dancelike spontaneity that was visible even in the photography of the prewar period (*Siegfried Enkelmann*).

One of the greatest of all dance photographers was the Czech expressionist Frantisek Drtikol (1883–1961), whose photographs of the 1920s frequently appeared in German art, erotic, and photography journals. Drtikol's images inspired my own interest in the history of *Ausdruckstanz*, so some comment on his way of seeing the dancing body seems relevant. Drtikol began his career in Prague under the spell of Czech symbolism, and his early photographs (portraits, landscapes) show the influence of a decorative, mystical painterly style. Dance and female nudity obsessed him. In 1912 he did a series of twelve photographs depicting Olga Gzovska performing her *Salome*, a "meloplastic" dance drama, in which she "eliminated all the burden of jewelry and ostentatious splendor of royalty, dressing only in flying veils of butterfly colors, tightly bound around her body, a gold tiara in her hair, and long earrings of ancient origin. All attention centered on her face, arms, and legs" (Siblik, *TNZ*, 16). But Gzovska's pantomimic dance, which shifted from the nudity of her female servant to her own nudity and which was performed against a background that shifted from light to dark, had a transformative effect on Drtikol's photography. The "original connection between dance and religious action and ceremony" made the body appear too complex for painterly techniques and moved him toward a more emphatically photographic style, for here "dance nakedly guides us from the beauty, depths, and abysses of the human soul to unnatural desires and pleasures" (Kroutvar 6) (Figure 82).

Drtikol had no interest in photographing dance outside the studio, and the outdoor rhythmic gymnastics program of the Sokol organization influenced his work only in a curiously indirect way. In 1914 he began photographing Ervina Küpferova, a dancer at the National Theatre and director of a Dalcroze school. With her he explored the same biblical image of the dancer that he had explored with Gzovska; he used different costumes and poses, yet Gzovska's smoldering spirit still seems present. After service in the war, Drtikol reestablished himself as the leading portrait photographer in the new Czech Republic. In 1919 he married Küpferova, and for the next several years of their unstable marriage she was the dominant model in his dramatic nude, harlequin, and biblical images of dance, which included further reprises of the Salome theme. But it was only after Küpferova left him in 1926 to pursue her career in Russia that Drtikol moved toward an ecstatic vision of the dancing body. In hundreds of oil print and bromide images constituting a single, gigantic series, he evolved a mystical photo iconography of the modern body in an ambiguous relation to its freedom and movement. He put nude female bodies in tension with abstract geometrical shapes: ramps, hoops, spheres, blocks, waves, pillars, arcs, arches, disks, intersecting or colliding planes, crevices, poles, ropes, and curving floors (Figure 83). Stunning contrasts between light and shadow prevailed not only between the body and its environment but within the body, so that often only a portion of the dancing body was visible—the rest remained in shadow. As the "barbaric dancer" of Van Ostaijen's poem remarked: "My body is to itself a light and a darkness." Some images looked at only a part of the dancer's body, such as the legs or the left arm and torso; others decentered the body in the image to show the degree to which the body adapted to abstract geometrical forms, light, and shadow.

Drtikol did not use dancers as models, yet the women moved like dancers insofar as their movements projected no functional value, existing entirely to signify an inner condition of freedom and power. Nevertheless, no matter how freely the body seemed to move in the image, it always remained hemmed in and defined, not by nature but by abstract geometrical forces, by a "dangerous proximity to death" (Kroutvar 5). The proud, athletic bodies and movements of these shadow-veiled female figures linked the image of the modern Salome to Dalcrozian gymnastics in a manner that was largely invisible to the multitudinous disciples of the doctrine. Yet large numbers of these images circulated throughout Germany as postcards. Drtikol continued in this vein until 1931. But in 1930 his photography became more abstract; he dispensed with the live model altogether and began using extremely stylized paper sculptures of the female body, which danced through a much more cosmically nebulous space toward an ecstatic light (Figure 84). The dancer's body seemed almost insectoid, with arms like antennae, outstretched toward ecstasy. Ecstatic movement not only revealed the "dark" desires of the body, it transformed the body into an alien being dancing alone in a new world of technologically defined abstraction. But by 1935, Drtikol felt he had pushed the "photo-puristic" image of the dancing body to the limit of abstraction. He therefore abandoned the practice of photography and devoted the rest of his life to teaching and theosophical mysticism (Birgus; Farova; Klaricova).

Ecstasy and Modernity

More than any other dance imagery of the era, Drtikol's photography dramatized the controlling impulse of *Ausdruckstanz:* that the body was the vortical source of power in achieving a synthesis of mysticism and modernity and that in this synthesis ecstasy became reality in an expanding technorational culture. The body, with its seemingly infinite inner conditions of desire and energy, established the limits of both abstraction and materialism. As an abstract concept, the new dance signified the most powerful (and therefore ecstatic) claim of the body, fusing mystical transcendence of material illusions and modern fearlessness in looking at human identity with optimum nakedness and materiality. As a material phenomenon, the female dancing body boldly signified that movement toward a modern condition of freedom entailed an ambiguous and often dangerous acknowledgment of erotic desires "buried" deep "inside" the body, desires that were as old as Salome and always a motive for speculation on the dynamics of excess. But ecstasy does not come without excesses: to grasp the mysterious force of the German dance culture, one must write excessively about it. To write excessively about the body culture is to focus on the achievements of peculiar personalities, not on abstract, supracorporeal theoretical perspectives on "the body" purporting to transcend individual bodies. A modern attitude toward the the body implied recognition of it as a site of endless, untranscendable difference. The body emerged as the dominant sign of a personality. A body's identity was not the ideologically determined product of this or that school or theoretical construction; rather, a body appeared as an organic form through which competing, even contradictory theories or reflections about it intersected to disclose a unique identity: difference. The image of it constructed by the German dance culture may indeed assume greater responsibility than performance realities for any perception of excess ascribed to the body's movement toward a modern condition of ecstasy. But the motivating power of the image depends precisely on the magnitude of performance realities that test the authority of the image, and these were considerable, excessive, on a scale never imagined before or since.

Like Russian ballet, *Ausdruckstanz* drew its energy from mystical images of the body associated with the East, with vast, imperial spaces "beyond" home—"The world-state is the body," as Novalis cryptically observed in 1800 (Novalis 5). In this vision of a mythic, imperial space without borders and beyond restraining distinctions between the inner and other, the beauty of human movement always produced a different, estranging, foreign identity. The great irony of *Ausdruckstanz* and indeed of German body culture as a whole is that in striving to make the body an emblem, even a basis, for great social unity, it wound up making the body a dominant sign of difference, otherness, distinction, heroic imagination, and tension between contradictory inner desires and the entirely external concept of unity itself. But the motivating vision of unity is less important than the historical reality. The ultimate achievement, then, in the ecstatic surge of a people, a nation, a race toward modernity, was necessarily the emergence of a cultural empire—with the body as its emblem of sovereignty—which accommodated excessively strange or diverse ways of allowing the body to "speak."

The German body culture that emerged at the end of the Wilhelmine era was imperial insofar as it sought, excessively, to appropriate minds, spaces, and institutions on a national scale, even though it had no centralized authority nor any coherent system for consolidating its goals and achievements other than a mystical belief in the body as a salvational force. It is therefore difficult to construct a grand thesis that establishes a clear positive or negative relation between body culture and the rise of the Third Reich or between body culture and the expansion of European democracy. Fascist and other totalitarian political systems fear the instabilities of perception provoked by the nudity or movement of modern bodies; for the Nazis, the solution to finding a powerful value for human identity within inescapable conditions of modernity depended on subordinating bodies to a "higher" concept of communal-national identity that transcended the corporeal differences within it. For them, the body created a unified identity to the extent that it was "the same," a reproduceable form whose power lay in evoking a strong feeling of not being alone. They therefore created a culture for the body (rather than a body culture) that glorified uniforms, drill, synchronized movement, and the sheer quantity of bodies moving in step. Weimar body culture was to "blame" for Nazism insofar as it ascribed to bodies so many complicated, differentiating significations that only a totalitarian state could dream of containing them. Moreover, by making the body a material sign of modernity, the body culture revealed that modernism was itself a surge of irrationality, not, as often supposed, a grand assertion of rationalist abstraction and consequent liberation from ancient, pathological anxieties over the flesh. Other industrialized countries did not embrace body culture as passionately as Weimar Germany because they feared the power of modern bodies to undermine a unified national perception of modernity as an expression of rationalist abstraction and logical organizations of identity derived from "higher" categories of signification.

Body culture emphatically presented itself as an expression of modernity, and modernity carried with it an aura of unprecedented freedom of desire and action. Moreover, especially in the realms of *Nacktkultur* and dance, body culture tended to perceive modernity and freedom in relation to expanded capacities for ecstasy. But ecstasy is possible only through the perpetration of excesses, and wherever excesses appear, limits and boundaries thrive to mark off the difference between what is excessive and what is "enough." Because of the differentiating presures of excesses, political power within the empire of ecstasy dispersed in a fragmented fashion toward cultic organizations of identities. The empire of ecstasy consisted largely of a great constellation of competing schools, individuals, societies, and performances, and its appeal rested upon its power to align ecstasy with modes of difference rather than with modes of unity (in spite of the glib moralizing and nationalistic rhetoric with which body culture often justified itself). That was the great, unintended revelation of the German body culture: it showed how, as soon as the body became an intense focus of perception, it also became a dominant sign and source of difference, of "otherness," in relation to an ecstatic destiny that could never be the same for any other body. The body was an empire in itself.

The modernity of the body manifested itself above all and in the most convincing degree through the expression of two passions: love of nudity and love of bodily movements that were an end in themselves. The beauty of bodily movements achieved its most articulate representation not in sports or gymnastic culture but in the sprawling German dance culture, wherein the capacity to "see" the body in a new, emancipated dimension depended on freeing perception from the premodern attitudes toward the body codified by ballet culture. Women drove this dance culture; men were largely spectators of it. Perhaps this sexual difference, which did not apply to *Nacktkultur,* constitutes a major failure of the dance culture, a failure that probably could have been avoided only to the extent that women disclosed as intense a desire to see men dance as to see themselves dance. But this sexual difference was not peculiar to Germany, even though the dance culture was; it does not belong to the peculiar historical and cultural circumstances defining Germany. Why, then, was Germany the favored site of both *Nacktkultur* and modern dance? The answer, I believe, has something to do with mysterious and as yet unidentified features of the German language itself, with the ways in which language constructs consciousness and thereby establishes some kind of inner or metaphysical space within the body. We simply do not have the theoretical or technical apparatus to understand how this construction occurs. What we do know from the evidence of history is that an ecstatic body culture emerges because a people prefers to see the body as profoundly strange and to experience deep pleasure in the strangeness.

REFERENCES

The following bibliography does not contain many periodical articles cited completely in the main text, nor a great many other articles from the era.

Adelaar, Dick, Jos van Asperen, and Michiel Roding. *Willem van Leusden*. Utrecht: Kwadraat, 1990.

Adolphi, Max, and Arno Kettmann. *Tanzkunst und Kunsttanz*. Stuttgart: Graphische Kunst-und Verlagsanstalt, 1927.

Abraham, Anke, and Koni Hanft. *Maja Lex*. Hürth-Hermühlheim: Stohrer, 1986.

Akademie der Künste.Mary Wigman 1886–1973. Exhibtion list. Berlin: Akademie der Künste, 1986.

Akademie der Künste der Deutschen Demokratischen Republik. *Mary Wigman. Sprache des Tanzes*. Berlin: Akademie der Künste, 1989.

Alexander, Gerda. "Eutonie." In Moscovici, 39–58.

Alexander, Gerda, and Hans Groll (eds.). *Rosalia Chladek. Tänzerin, Choreographin, Pädagogin*. Vienna: Österreicher Bundesverlag für Unterricht, Wissenschaft und Kunst, 1965.

Alsen, Ola. *Er und Sie*. Munich: Drei Masken, 1928.

Altmann-Loos, Elsie. *Mein Leben mit Adolf Loos*. Edited by Adolf Opel. Berlin: Ullstein, 1986.

Amort, Andrea. "Ausdruckstanz in Österreich bis 1938." In *Ausdruckstanz*, 383–396.

Andritzky, Michael, and Thomas Rauthenberg (eds.). *"Wir sind nackt und nennen uns Du."* Giessen: Anabas, 1989.

Anke, Abraham, and Koni Haft. *Maja Lex*. Düsseldorf: Graphische Werkstatt, 1986.

d'Annunzio, Gabriele. *Notturno*. Rome: L'Oleandro, 1934 [1916].

Anz, Thomas, and Michael Stark (eds.). *Expresionismus. Manifeste und Dokumente zur deutschen Literatur 1910–1920*. Stuttgart: Metzler, 1982.

Appia, Adolphe. *Oeuvres Complètes*. Vol. 3. Edited by Marie L. Bablet-Hahn. Montreux: L'Age d'Homme, 1988.

Archives Internationale de la Danse. Special issue devoted to "La Techniques de la danse." (1 November 1935).

Artus, Hans-Gerd. "Denkend vergleichen. Ist das Mensendieck-System der Körperbildung noch aktuell?" *Tanzdrama* No 10 (1990), 8–13.

Artus, Hans-Gerd, and Maud Paulissen-Kaspar. "Gesetzmässige Bewegung als Grundlage tänzerischer Erziehung." In *Ausdruckstanz*, 233–247.

Arwas, Victor. *Art Deco Sculpture.* New York: St. Martin's Press, 1992.

Ausdruckstanz. Edited by Gunhild Oberzaucher-Schüller. Wilhelmshaven: Noetzel, 1992.

Bach, Rudolf. *Das Mary Wigman-Werk.* Dresden: Reisser, 1933.

Bachmann, Marie-Laure. *La Rhythmique Jaques-Dalcroze.* Neuchatel: La Baconnerie, 1984.

Balázs, Béla. *Theory of the Film.* Translated by Edith Bone. New York: Dover, 1970 [1952, 1949, *Der sichtbare Mensch*, 1924].

Bakker, Noortje, and Maureen Trappeniers. *Jan Sluijters 1881–1957.* 's-Hertogenbosch: Noordbrabants Museum, 1981.

Barche, Gisela. "Als der siebte Schleier fiel." In Köhler and Barche, 356–362.

Barche, Gisela, and Claudia Jeschke. "Bewegungsrausch und Formbestreben. Der Ausdruckstanz in der Photographie 1900–1937." In *Ausdruckstanz*, 317–346.

Bartetzko, Dieter. *Illusionen in Stein. Stimmungsarkitektur in deutschen Faschismus.* Reinbek bei Hamburg: Rowohlt, 1985.

Baxmann, Inge. "Dance as a Language and Utopia in the Roaring Twenties." *ballett international* (February 1989), 13–18.

Behr, Shulamith, David Fanning, and Douglas Jarman (eds.). *Expressionism Reassessed.* Manchester: Machester University Press, 1993.

Bell-Kanner, Karen. *The Life and Times of Ellen von Frankenberg.* Chur: Harwood Academic, 1991.

Berber, Anita, and Sebastian Droste. *Die Tänze des Lasters, des Grauen und der Ekstase.* Vienna: Gloriette, 1922.

Berchtold, Alfred. "Emile Jaques-Dalcroze et son temps." In Martin, *Emile Jaques-Dalcroze*, 27–158.

Bergman, Einar. *Diktens värld och politikens.* Lund: Natur och Kultur, 1967.

Bernhard, Oskar. *Handbuch der Lichttherapie.* Vienna: Springer, 1927.

———. *Heliotherapie in Hochgebirge.* Stuttgart: Enke, 1911.

Bie, Oskar. *Der Tanz.* Berlin: Bard, 1923 (1906).

Bie, Richard. "Eros, Tanz und Emanzipation der Frau." *Der Scheinwerfer* 1/11–12 (1927), 7–10.

Birgus, Vladimir, and Antonin Brany. *Frantisek Drtikol.* Prague: Odeon, 1988.

Blass, Ernst. *Das Wesen der neuen Tanzkunst.* Weimar: Lichtenstein, 1921.

Bloch, Alice. *Harmonische Schulung des Frauenkörpers.* Stuttgart: Dieck, 1927.

Blümner, Rudolf. "Tanz und Tanz, oder Kunsttanz und Tanzkunst." *Der Sturm* 17/4 (1926), 50–56.

Bode, Rudolf. *Angriff und Gestaltung. Ein Beitrag zu politischer Leibeserziehung.* Berlin: Widukind, 1939.

———. *Aufgaben und Ziele der rhythmische Gymnastik.* Munich: Verlag der aerztliche Rundschau, 1913.

———. *Ausdrucksgymnastik.* Munich: Beck, 1925.

————. *Energie und Gestaltung.* Goslar: Blut und Boden, 1939.

————. *Expression-Gymnastics.* Translated by Sonya Forthal and Elizabeth Waterman. New York: Barnes, 1931.

————. *Die Grundübungen der körperlichen Bildung.* Kassel: Bärenreiter, 1931.

————. *Musik und Bewegung.* Kassel: Bärenreiter, 1930.

————. *Neue Wege in der Leibeserziehung.* Munich: Beck, 1923.

————. *Der Rhythmus und seine Bedeutung für die Erziehung.* Jena: Diedrichs, 1920.

Boehn, Max von. *Der Tanz.* Berlin: Volksverband der Bücherfreunde, 1925.

Boer, Jacobien de. "Dansmaskers voor Florrie Rodrigo." Article in unidentified Dutch art journal of the late 1980s, 16–20.

Böhme, Fritz. "Laban." Unpublished manuscript deposited in German Dance Archive, Cologne. Quoted in Peter, "Hertha Feist," 34.

————. "Materialien zu einer soziologischen Untersuchung des künsterlischen Tanzes." *Ethos* 1 (1925–1926), 274–293 (reprinted in *Tanzdrama* 9 [1989], 23–26).

————. "Der Radius des Tanzkunstwerks." *Der Scheinwerfer* 1/11–12 (1927), 14–17.

————. "Die Raumlehre der tänzerische Bewegung." *Gymnastik* 1/9 (October 1926), 133–142.

————. *Der Tanz der Zukunft.* Stuttgart: Delphin, 1926.

————. *Der tanzende Mensch.* Leipzig: Backhaus, 1921.

————. *Die Tänzerin Hilde Strinz.* Berlin: Kinetischer Verlag, 1927.

————. *Tanzkunst.* Dessau: Dünnhaupt, 1926.

————. *Über Totenmal.* Munich: Chorische Bühne, 1930.

————. "Vom Tänzer unserer Zeit." *Die Tat* 19/8 (November 1927), 580–588.

————. "Wachsen und Gestalten." *Kontakt* 1/3 (September 1933), 33–40.

Boon, Jozef. *Spreekkoor en massatooneel.* Sint Niklaas: Van Haver, 1937.

Bordwell, David. *The Films of Carl-Theodor Dreyer.* Berkeley and Los Angeles, 1981.

Bosso, Gastone. "Dei Sakharoff e della danza." *Scenario* 1/5 (4/6) (June 1932), 34–36.

Braaksma, Marja. Dance reconstructions of Leistikow's *Rote Groteske* and *Gnossienne,* Wigman's *Schwingende Landschaft* and *Hexentanz,* the Georgie-Kreutzberg *Persisches Lied,* and the Page-Kreutzberg *Arabian Nights.* In *Ein ewiger Kreis.* Videotape. Amsterdam:V van Laban, 1991.

Bragaglia, Anton. *La bella danzante.* Rome: Nuova Europa, 1936.

————. "La danzatrice Sonja Markus." *Scenario* 1/6 (4/7) (July 1932), 25–28.

————. "Di Gisa Geert e dei mimi d'ogni tempo." *Scenario* 2/11 (November 1930), 583–587.

————. *Jazz Band.* Milan: Corbaccio, 1929.

————. *Scultura vivente.* Milan: L'Eroica, 1928.

Brandenburg, Hans. *Der moderne Tanz.* Munich: Müller, 1921 (1913, 1915, 1917).

————. *Das neue Theater.* Leipzig: Haessel, 1926.

————. "Tanz und Theater." *Die Tat* 19/8 (November 1927), 605–609.

————. "Zur Einführung!" *Die Tat* 19/8 (November 1927), 569–572.

Brandstetter, Gabriele. "Psychologie des Ausdrucks und Ausdruckstanz. Aspekte der Wechselwirkung am Beispiel der 'Traumtänzerin' Madeleine." In *Ausdruckstanz,* 199–211.

————. *Tanz-Lektüren. Körperbilder und Raumfiguren der Avantgarde.* Frankfurt am Main: Fischer, 1995.

Braun, Edward (ed.). *Meyerhold on Theatre.* New York: Hill and Wang, 1969.

Breuhaus, Fritz August. "Kabaretts und Tanz-Paläste." *Innen-Dekoration* 31 (1920), 75–105.

Brinkman, Els. *De Brandung 1917–1926.* Rotterdam: Stichting Kunstpublicatins, 1991.

Broos, Kees, and Paul Hefting. *Dutch Graphic Design. A Century.* Cambridge, MA: The MIT Press, 1993.

Brown, Carol. "The Stylistic Contribution of the Work of Gertrud Bodenwieser to the Ausdruckstanz Movement." In Grayburn, 14–18.

Brusendorff, Ove. *Filmen.* Vol. 3. Copenhagen: Universal, 1940.

Bücher, Karl. *Arbeit und Rhythmus.* Leipzig and Berlin: Teubner, 1909 (1896).

Buckle, Richard. *Diaghilev.* New York: Atheneum, 1979.

————. *Nijinsky.* Harmondsworth: Penguin, 1975 (1971).

Buergel Goodwin, Ida and Henry. *Jenny Hasselqvist.* Stockhom: Hökerbergs, 1918.

Bukh, Niels. *Grundgymnastik.* Berlin: Teubner, 1925.

Buning, J.W.F. Weremeus. *Dansen en danseressen.* Amsterdam: Querido, 1926.

————. "Een gesprek met Edith von Schrenck." *Spel en dans* (November 1925), 49–51.

————. *Tooneel en dans, kronieken en kritiken.* Maastricht: Boosten en Stols, 1925.

————. *De wereld van den dans.* Amsterdam: Querido, 1922.

Buonaventura, Wendy. *Serpent of the Nile: Women and Dance in the Arab World.* New York: Interlink, 1994.

Burghardt, Wilhelm. "Der männliche Tänzer." *Die Schönheit* 22/2 (1926), 69–81.

Burian, Emil Frantisek. *O nové dvadlo 1930–1940.* Prague: Akciové Tiskárny, 1946.

————. "Worttanz." *Schrifttanz.* Vol. 3 (August 1929), 52–54.

Buschbeck, Axel. "Rosalia Chladek." Dissertation. Universität Wien, 1973.

Catley, Bryan. *Art Deco and Other Figures.* Woodbridge, England: Antique Collectors' Club, 1978.

Cavicchioli, Giovanni. "Incontro con Mary Wigman." *Scenario* 1/10 (November 1932), 30–34.

Chipp, Herschel (ed.). *Theories of Modern Art.* Berkeley and Los Angeles: University of California Press, 1968.

Chladek, Rosalia. "Von Hellerau bei Dresden nach Laxenburg bei Wien." In *Ausdruckstanz*, 35–70.

Clotilde et Alexandre Sacharoff. Exhibition catalogue. Paris: Brunoff, 1922.

Cluzel, Magdeleine. "Paul Swan." In Cluzel, *Presences.* Paris: Maisonneuve, 1952, 1–31.

Combes, André. "A partir du *Metropolis* de Fritz Lang: La *Gestalt* de masse et ses espaces." In Claudine Amiard-Chevrel (ed.). *Théâtre et cinéma années vignt. Une quête de la modenité.* Vol. 2. Paris: L'Age d'Homme, 1990, 178–224.

Corrinth, Curt. *Potsdamer Platz.* Munich: Müller, 1919.

Coton, A. V. *The New Ballet. Kurt Jooss and His Work.* London: Dobson, 1946.

Cotteral, Bonnie and Donnie. *Tumbling, Pyramid Building and Stunts for Girls and Women.* New York: Barnes, 1931.

Cunz, Rolf (ed.). *Deutsches Musikjahrbuch.* Vol. 1. Essen: Schlingloff, 1923.

Daan, Lea, and Martin Gleisner. *Mens en maschinen.* Film fragments shot in Antwerp, 1936, on videotape deposited with An-Marie Lamprechts, Leuven.

Daffner, Hugo. *Salome: Ihre Gestalt in Geschichte und Kunst.* Munich: Schmidt, 1912.

Daly, Ann. *Done into Dance.* Bloomington: Indiana University Press, 1995.

Darany, Georges. *Hugo Scheiber. Leben und Werk.* Basel: Edition Inter Art Galerie, 1982.

Delius, Rudolf. *Mary Wigman.* Dresden: Reissner, 1925.

———. *Tanz und Erotik.* Munich: Delphin, 1926.

Desmond, Olga. *Rhythmographik.* Adapted by Fritz Böhme. Leipzig: Breitkopf und Härtel, 1919.

Diehl, Oskar. *Mimik im Film.* Munich: Müller, 1922.

Diem, Carl. *Ausgewählte Schriften.* Vol. 2. Sankt Augustin: Richarz, 1982.

———. *Dokumente zum Aufbau des deutschen Sports.* Sankt Augustin: Richarz, 1984.

Dierker, Herbert, and Gertrud Pfister (eds.). *"Frisch heran! Brüder, hört ihr das Klingen!" Zur Alltagsgeschichte des Berliner Arbeitersportsverein Fichte.* Dudelstadt: Mecke, 1990.

Divoire, Fernand. *Pour la danse.* Paris: Saxe, 1935.

Doepp, Hilde. *Träume und Maske.* Dessau: Dion, 1926.

Dooijes, Max. Personal interview with Max Dooijes in Amsterdam, 26 February 1992.

Dorno, Carl. *Physikalische Grundlagen der Sonnen-und Lichttherapie.* N.p.: 1927.

Downing, Taylor. *Olympia.* London: British Film Institute, 1992.

Dreier, Katherine. *Shawn, the Dancer.* New York: Barnes, 1933.

Dumont, Herve. *Geschichte des Schweizer Films 1896–1965.* Translated by Corinne Siegrist, et al. Lausanne: Schweizer Filmarchiv, 1988.

Duncan, Isadora. *Isadora (My Life).* New York: Award, 1968 [1927].

Dutoit-Carlier, Claire-Lise. "Jaques-Dalcroze, createur de la rythmique." In Martin, *Emile Jaques-Dalcroze,* 305–412.

Eberhardt-Offenbach, Hugo. "Messe-Stände auf der Frankfurter Messe." *Innen-Dekoration* 31 (1920), 237–250.

"Edith von Schrenck." *Propria Cures* 34/4 (7 October 1922), 49–51.

Eichberg, Henning. "The Nazi *Thingspiel:* Theater for the Masses in Fascism and Popular Culture." *New German Critique* 11 (Spring 1977), 133–150.

Eichstedt, Astrid, and Bernd Polster. *Wie die Wilden. Tänze auf der Höhe ihrer Zeit.* Berlin: Rotbuch, 1985.

"Eine Hamburger Weinstube." *Innen-Dekoration.* 31 (1920), 298–301.

Eldorado. Homosexuelle Frauen und Männer in Berlin 1850–1950: Geschichte, Alltag und Kultur. Berlin: Fröhlich und Kaufmann, 1984.

"Ellen Petz." Dossier of clippings and programs related to Ellen Petz in the German Dance Archive in Cologne.

Emmel, Felix. *Das ekstatische Theater.* Prien: Kampmann und Schnabel, 1924.

———. "Neue Sachlichkeit im Tanz." *Tanzgemeinschaft* 2/3 (1929), 3–4.

Endler, Franz. *Das Walzer Buch.* Vienna: Kremagn und Scherian, 1975.

Enkelmann, Siegfried. *Tänzer unserer Zeit.* Munich: Piper, 1937.

Enyeart, James. *Bruguière: His Photographs and His Life.* New York: Knopf, 1977.

Essen, Dini von. *Dans en opvoeding.* Pamphlet inserted into dance program. Amsterdam: N.p., 1932.

Essen, Hein von. *Van maskers, gemaskerden en maskermakers.* Pamphlet version of article that appeared in *De Hollandsche Revue* (15 March 1932).

Ettlinger, Karl. "Sent M'ahesa." *Tanzdrama* 14 (1991), 32–34 (originally published in 1910).

"Expressionismus in Tanz und Bild." *Elegante Welt* 8/11 (1919), 4.

Faber, Monika. *Madame D'Ora. Wien—Paris.* Vienna: Brandstätter, 1983.

———. *Die montrierte Frau. Aktphotographien des Atelier Manassé aus den 20er und 30er Jahren.* Vienna: Brandstätter, 1988.

———. *Tanzfoto. Annäherungen und Experimente 1880–1940.* Vienna: Österreiches Fotoarchiv im Museum moderner Kunst, 1991.

Fárová, Anna. *Frantisek Drtikol. Photograph des Art Deco.* Munich: Schirmer/Mosel, 1986.

Fárová, Anna, and Daniela Mrázková (eds.). *Drtikol.* New York: Robert Miller Gallery, 1984.

Feudel, Elfriede (ed.). *Rhythmik. Theorie und Praxis der körperlich-musikalischen Erziehung.* Munich: Delphin, 1926.

Fiedler, Leonhard, and Martin Lang (eds.). *Grete Wiesenthal.* Salzburg and Vienna: Residenz, 1985.

Fischer, Hans W. *Hamburger Kulturbilderbogen.* Munich: Rösl, 1923.

———. *Körperschönheit und Körperkultur.* Berlin: Deutsche Buch-Gemeinschaft, 1928.

———. *Menschenschönheit.* Berlin: Deutsche Buchgemeinschaft, 1935.

———. *Das Tanzbuch.* Munich: Langen, 1924.

———. "Tanzkritik." *Die Tat* 19/8 (November 1927), 591–596.

———. "Tanztraum und Tanzspiel." *Die Tat* 14/7 (October 1922), 527–534.

Fischer, Lothar. *Anita Berber. Tanz zwischen Rausch und Tod 1918–1928 in Berlin.* Berlin: Haude und Spener, 1988 (1984).

———. "Getanzte Körperbefreiung." In Andritzky and Rauthenberg, 106–123.

Fontaine, Jelena Hahl. "Alexandre Sakharoff a Monaco e il solidalizo con Kandinskij." In Veroli, 42–49.

Frecot, Janos (ed.). *Marta Astfalck-Vietz.* Berlin: Berlinische Galerie, 1991.

Frentz, Hans. *Niddy Impekoven und ihre Tänze.* Freiburg: Urban, 1929.

———. *Weg und Entfaltung Niddy Impekovens.* Leipzig: Weibezahl, 1933.

Freund, Liesel. *Monographien der Ausbildungsschulen für Tanz und Tänzerische Körperbildung.* Charlottenburg: Alterthum, 1929.

Friedrich Wilhelm Murnau. Edited by members of the Deutsche Kinemathek. Munich: Hanser, 1990.

Fritze, Benno. "Albert Talhoffs *Totenmal.*" *Teatret* 31 (1930–1931), 28.

Fröböse, Eva. *Rudolf Steiner über Eurythmische Kunst.* Cologne: Dumont, 1983.

Froning, Hubertius. *E. L. Kirchner und die Wandmalerei.* Recklinghausen: Bongers, 1991.

Gagnebin, Henri. "Jaques-Dalcroze, compositeur." In Martin, *Emile Jaques-Dalcroze,* 159–288.

Garafola, Lynn. *Diaghilev's Ballets Russes.* New York: Oxford University Press, 1989.

Gay, Jan. *On Going Naked.* Garden City, NY: Garden City Publishing, 1932.

Gentges, Ignatz. *Tanz und Reigen.* Berlin: Bühnenvolksbund, 1927.

Gert, Valeska. *Die Bettlerbar von New York.* Berlin: arania, 1950.

———. *Ich bin eine Hexe.* Munich: Schneekluth, 1968.

———. "Mary Wigman und Valeska Gert." *Der Querschnitt* 4/5 (1926), 361–363.

———. *Mein Weg.* Leipzig: Devrient, 1931.

———. "Der neue Tanz." *Der Scheinwerfer* 11/12 (March 1928), 11–13.

———. "Tanzen." *Schrifttanz* 4/1 (June 1931). Reprinted in Preston-Dunlop, 13–16.

"Gertrud Leistikow." Dossier of clippings, programs, photographs, and pedagogic materials related to Gertrud Leistikow in the Netherlands Dance Institute.

Gertz, Jenny. "Tanz und Kind." *Die Schönheit* 22/2 (1926), 49–61.

Giese, Fritz. *Geist im Sport.* Munich: Delphin, 1925.

———. *Girlkultur.* Munich: Delphin, 1925.

———. *Körperseele.* Munich: Delphin, 1924.

———. *Männliche Körperbildung.* Munich: Delphin, 1924.

Giese, Fritz, and Hedwig Hagemann. *Weibliche Körperbildung und Bewegungskunst.* Munich: Delphin, 1922.

Giraudet, A. *Mimique. Physionomie et gestes.* Paris: Librairies-Imprimeries Réunies, 1895.

Gleisner, Martin. *Dans voor allen.* Amsterdam: Uitgave van de Arbeiders Jeugd Centrale, 1934 (*Tanz für alle,* 1928).

Goldmann, Otto. *Nacktheit, Sitte und Gesetz.* Dresden: Die Schönheit, 1924.

Goll, Yvan. *Sodom Berlin.* Translated by Hans Thill. Berlin: Rotbuch, 1985 (1929).

Golücke, Dieter. *Bernhard Hoetger.* Worpswede: Worpsweder Verlag, 1982.

Gordon, Mel. "Lothar Schreyer and the Sturmbühne." *The Drama Review* 24/1 (T85) (March 1980), 85–102.

Gorsen, Peter. "'Lebensreform' und 'Alternativkultur.' Notizen über Beschädigungserfahrungen." *Neue Rundschau* 94/3 (1983), 56–66.

Graham, Cooper C. *Leni Riefenstahl and Olympia.* Metuchen, NJ: Scarecrow Press, 1986.

Graeser, Wolfgang. *Körpersinn.* Munich: Beck, 1927.

Grayburn, Patricia (ed.). *Gertrud Bodenwieser 1890–1959.* Sydney: University of Sydney, 1990.

Green, Lili. *Einführung in das Wesen unserer Gesten und Bewegungen.* Berlin: Oesterheld, 1929.

"Grit Hegesa." Dossier of clippings, photographs, programs related to Grit Hegesa in the Netherlands Dance Institute.

Grund, Gustav. "Maskentanz." *Hellweg* 6/40 (1926), 692–693.

———. "Opernbühne und neuer Tanz." *Singchor und Tanz* 45/3 (1928), 27–28.

———. "Tanz und Theater." *Die vierte Wand* 3 (1927), 7–10.

"*Der grüne Tisch.* Choreographie: Kurt Jooss." *Tanzdrama* 15 (1991), 22–26.

Günther, Dorothee. *Einführung in der Deutsche Mensendieckgymnastik.* Leipzig: Hachmeister und Thal, 1928.

———. *Gymnastik Gundührngen in eigner Zeichenmethode.* Munich: Delphin, 1925.

———. *Gymnastik Grundübungen nach System Mensendieck.* Munich: Delphin, 1926.

————. *Mädchen-Reigen. Ein Gemeinschaftstanz, entworfen für die Festspiel "Olympische Jugend" der 11. Olympiad, Berlin 1936.* N.p.: 1936.

————. *Rhythmische Grundübungen im Bewegungslauf dargestellt.* Munich: Delphin, 1926.

————. *Der Tanz als Bewegungsphänomen.* Reinbek bei Hamburg: Rowohlt, 1962.

Haags Gemeente Museum. Archive list of works by Jaap Kool deposited in the museum (curator Frits Zwart). Fax communication, 26 June 1992.

Hagemann(-Boese), Hedwig. *Über Körper und Seele der Frau.* Leipzig: Grethlein, 1927.

Hagen, Wilhelm. "Rhythmus und Körperbildung." *Die Tat* 14/10 (January 1923), 755–764.

Häger, Bengt. *The Swedish Ballet.* New York: Abrams, 1990.

Hällström, Raoul af. *Siivekäät jalat.* Helsinki: Kustannososkeyhtio Kivi, 1945.

"Harald Kreutzberg." Dossier of photographs, programs, articles, and clippings related to Harald Kreutzberg in the Netherlands Dance Institute.

Haselbach, Barbara. "Harald Kreutzberg." In *Ausdruckstanz,* 123–132.

Hatvani, Paul. *Salto Mortale.* Heidelberg: Saturnverlag, 1913.

Haus, Andreas. "Die Präsenz des Materials—Ungarische Fotografen aus dem Bauhaus-Kreis." In Hubertus Gassner (ed.). *Wechsel Wirkungen. Ungarische Avantgarde in der Weimarer Republik.* Marburg: Jonas, 1986, 472–489.

Hauser, Nancy Mason. *Hanya Holm. Portrait of a Pioneer.* Video. Princeton, NJ: Princeton Book Company, 1988.

Havelaar, Just. *The Etchings of Hein von Essen.* Amsterdam: Paris, 1929.

Heidegger, Martin. *Being and Time.* Translated by John Macquarrie and Edward Robinson. New York: Harper and Row, 1962.

Hendig, Arnold. *Fremede fugle i dansk film.* Copenhagen: Athene, 1951.

Heller, Reinhold (ed.). *Art in Germany 1909–1936: From Expressionism to Resistance.* Munich: Prestel, 1990.

Herrlich, Lotte. *Edle Nacktheit.* 3 vols. Dresden-Weinböla: Aurora, 1920.

————. *In Licht und Sonne.* Dresden-Weinböla: Aurora, 1924.

————. *Der Kinderakt und Anderes.* Hamburg: Heldt, 1928.

————. *Das Kind am Wasser.* Wuppertal-Barmen: Plaut, 1932.

————. *Neue Aktstudien.* Hamburg: Heldt, 1923.

————. *Rolf: Ein Lied vom Werden.* Kettwig-Ruhr: Lichtkampf, 1924.

————. *Seliges Nacktsein.* 2 vols. Hamburg: Heldt, 1927.

————. *Das Weib.* Rudolfstadt: Greifenverlag, 1928.

————. *Der weibliche Akt.* Hamburg: Seggern, 1928.

Herzog, Else, and Hermann Schreiber (eds.). *Tanz-Sport Almanach 1924.* Berlin: Mörlin, 1924.

Herzog, Oswald. *Plastik. Sinfonie des Lebens.* Berlin: Kunstheim Twardy, 1921.

Heun, Walter. "Die Elisabeth Duncan-Schule." In *Ausdruckstanz,* 224–232.

Hildenbrandt, Fred. *Briefe an eine Tänzerin.* Stuttgart: Seifert, 1922.

————. *Tänzerinnen der Gegenwart.* Zurich and Leipzig: Fussli, 1931.

Hilker, W. Franz. "Aus der Geschichte der gymnastischen Bewegung." *Gymnastik* 1/4 (April 1926), 48–54.

Hirschbach, Denny, and Sonia Nowoselsky (eds.). *Zwischen Aufbruch und Verfolgung. Künstlerinnen der zwanziger und dreissiger Jahren.* Bremen: Zeichen und Spuren, 1993.

Hofer, Karl. *Tanz*. Leipzig: Verlag des Kreises Arndt Beyer, 1922.

Hoffmeister, Christine. *Heinrich Vogeler. Die komplex Bilder.* Worpswede: Worpsweder Verlag, 1980.

Holdt, Hanns. *Niddy Impekoven.* Folio of photographs. Berlin: Mörlin, 1920.

Holtmont, Alfred. *Die Hosenrolle.* Munich: Meyer und Jessen, 1925.

Homage to Free Dance in Germany. Two-part television program directed by Petra Weisenburger and Jean-Louis Sonzogni. Paris, Cologne, Lisbon, 1991.

Howe, Dianne S. "The Notion of Mysticism in the Philosophy and Choreography of Mary Wigman 1914–1931." *Dance Research Journal* 19/1 (1987), 19–24.

Hurok, Sol (ed.). *Trudi Schoop and Her Comic Ballet.* New York: Nicholas Publishing, 1938.

Huyssen, Andreas. "The Vamp and the Machine: Sexuality and Technology in Fritz Lang's *Metropolis.*" *New German Critique* 8 (Winter 1981–1982), 221–237.

Ibel, Rudolf. "Die deutsche Tänzerin." *Der Kreis* 9/12 (1932), 692–696.

Ilbak, Ella. *Otsekui hirv kisendab.* Lund: Eesti Kirjanike Kooperativ, 1952.

Impekoven, Leo. *Niddy Impekoven.* 16 copper drawings. Berlin: Reiss, 1920.

Impekoven, Niddy. *Die Geschichte eines Wunderkinds.* Zurich: Rotapfel, 1955.

——. *Werdegang.* Dresden: Huhle, 1922.

Ingber, Judith Brin. "The Gamin Speaks: Conversations with Gertrud Kraus." *Dance Magazine* (March 1976), 45–50.

——. "The Vienna Years 1927–1939." *Dance Research Journal* 13/2 (1981), 25–31.

Internationales Tanz Adressbuch. Leipzig: Bockhaus, 1922.

Isenfels, Paul. *Getanzte Harmonien.* Stuttgart: Dieck, 1926.

——. *Gymnastik als Lebensfreude.* Stuttgart: Dieck, 1926.

Jacobi, Lotte. *Theater and Dance Photographs.* Woodstock, VT: Countryman Press, 1982.

Jacobs, Artur. "Arbeiternot, Kulturnot und die Erneurung durch den Rhythmus." *Die Tat* 14/9 (December 1922), 641–664.

Jaffé, H.L.C. *De Stijl 1917–1931.* Cambridge, MA: Harvard University Press, 1986.

Jannario, Don. "Revyer." *Scenisk Konst* 7 (1915), 21.

Jansen, Wolfgang. *Glanzrevuen der Zwanziger Jahren.* Berlin: Hentrich, 1987.

Janssen, Volker (ed.). *Der nackte Mann in der Fotografie. Bilder aus der FKK-Bewegung der 20er Jahre.* Berlin: Fotokunst Verlag, n.d.

Jaques-Dalcroze, Emile. *Rhythm, Music and Education.* Translated by Harold F. Rubenstein. New York: Barnes, 1921.

Jelavich, Peter. *Berlin Cabaret.* Cambridge, MA: Harvard University Press, 1993.

Jencik, Joe. *Anita Berberova.* Prague: Terpsichora, 1930.

——. "Kokain.Versuch einer Analyse des Tanzes Anita Berber." *Schrifttanz* 4/1 (1931), 10.

——. *Tanecnik a snobové.* Prague: Terpsichora, 1931.

Jockel, Nils, and Patricia Stöckemann. *"Flugkraft in goldene Ferne . . ." Bühnentanz in Hamburg seit 1900.* Hamburg: Museum für Kunst und Gewerbe, 1989.

Johnson, Donald. *The Nudists.* Spokane: Outdoor American, 1959.

Jordan, Karl-Heinrich (ed.). *TanzSzene Berlin 1925–1934.* 10 vols. Audio cassetes. N.p.: Bobsette, 1990–1991.

Jowitt, Deborah. *Time and the Dancing Image.* Berkeley and Los Angeles: University of California Press, 1988.

"Julia Tardy-Marcus." *Tanzdrama* 14 (1991), 14–15.

Juffermans, Jan. *Jan Sluijters.* Mijdrecht: Tableau, 1981.

Junk, Viktor. *Handbuch des Tanzes.* Stuttgart: Klett, 1930.

"Jutta von Collande." Dossier of clippings, programs, advertisements related to Jutta von Collande and the Münchener Tanzgruppe in the German Dance Archive in Cologne.

Kaes, Anton. "*Metropolis;* City, Cinema, Modernity." In Timothy O. Benson (ed.). *Expressionist Utopias.* Los Angeles: Los Angeles County Museum of Art, 1993, 146–165.

Kaes, Anton, Martin Jay, and Edward Dimenberg (eds.). *The Weimar Republic Sourcebook.* Berkeley and Los Angeles: University of California Press, 1994.

Kallmeyer, Hedwig (Hede). *Künstlerische Gymnastik; harmonische Körperkultur nach amerikanischen Systems Stebbins-Kallmeyer.* Berlin: Kulturverlag, 1910.

Kandinsky, Wassili. "Tanzkurven zu den Tänzen der Palucca." *Das Kunstblatt* 10/3 (1926), 117–120.

Keetman, Gunild. *Elementary First Acquaintance with Orff-Schulwerk.* London: Schott, 1974

Keetman, Gunild, and Carl Orff. *Musica poetica. Orff Schulwerk.* 10 phonograph records. Münster: Harmonia Mundi, 1963.

Kernspecht, W. "Das tänzerische Aktbild." *Das Photofreund.* 8/19 (1928), 355–357.

Kersting, Hannelore. "Maler der Bauhaus—Aspekte." In Hannelore Kersting and Bernd Vogelsang (eds.). *Raumkonzepte: Konstuktivistische Tendenzen in Bühnen- und Bildkunst 1910–1930.* Frankfurt am Main: Städtische Galerie, 1986, 149–200.

Ketterer, Roman Norbert. *Das Werk Ernst Ludwig Kirchners.* Lugano: Galerie Ketterer, 1980.

Kieser, Klaus. "Ausdruckstanz im Opernhaus." In *Ausdruckstanz,* 443–451.

Kirchner, Ernst Ludwig. *Drawings and Pastels.* New York: Alpine Fine Arts, 1982 (1979).

Klaricová, Katerina. *Frantisek Drtikol.* Prague: Panorama, 1989.

Klatt, Fritz. "Schöpferische Schwingungen." *Der Leib* 2/2 (January 1921), 34–53.

Klamt, Jutta. *Körperrhythmus und Tanz.* Charlottenburg: Jutta Klamt-Gemeinschaft, 1929–1930.

———. *Vom Erleben zum Gestalten.* Berlin: Dorn, 1936.

Klaus, Werner. *Edmund Kesting.* Leipzig: VEB Fotokinoverlag, 1987.

Klingenbeck, Fritz. *Die Tänzerin Rosalia Chladek.* Amsterdam: Veen, 1936.

Klooss, Reinhard, and Thomas Reuter. *Körperbilder. Menschenornamente in Revuetheater und Revuefilm.* Frankfurt am Main: Syndikat, 1980.

Koch, Adolf. *Körperbildung/Nacktkultur.* Leipzig: Oldenburg, 1932 (1924).

———. *Nacktheit, Körperkultur und Erziehung.* Leipzig: Oldenburg, 1929.

———. *Das Nacktkulturparadies von Berlin.* Leipzig: Oldenburg, 1933.

Koeber, F. W., and R. L. Leonard. *Das Tanz-Brevier.* Berlin: Eysler, 1913.

Koegler, Horst. *The Concise Oxford Dictionary of Ballet.* London: Oxford University Press, 1982.

———. "In the Shadow of the Swastika. Dance in Germany, 1927–1936." *Dance Perspectives* 57 (1974), 1–48.

———. "Laban." In Karl Corino (ed.). *Intellektuelle im Bann des Nationalsozialismus.* Hamburg: Hoffmann und Campe, 1980, 165–179.

———. "Tanz in den Abrund. Berliner Ballett um 1930." In Wolfgang Haus (ed.). *Theater in Deutschland 1928–1948*. Berlin: SFB-Werkstatthefte, 1981.

———. *Yvonne Georgi*. Velber bei Hannover: Friedrich, 1963.

Köhler, Michael, and Gisela Barche (eds.). *Das Aktfoto*. Munich: Bucher, 1985.

Kölling, Rudolf. "Arbeit des Tänzers an der Oper." *Die Schallkiste* 3/9 (September 1928), 6.

Kool, Jaap. "Productieve oog en de groteske dans van Grit Hegesa." *Wendingen* 2/3 (1919), 15–21.

———. *Tänze der Naturvölker*. Berlin: Fürstner, 1921.

———. *Tanzschrift*. Bordeaux: Duvignau-Canet, 1927.

———. *Tänze und Tanzszene*. Berlin: Fürstner, 1920.

———. "Tanzmusik." In Herzog and Schreiber, 89–94.

Die Körperkultur im Film. Dresden: Giesecke, 1925.

Kothes, Franz-Peter. *Die theatralische Revue in Berlin und Wien 1900–1938*. Wilhelmshaven: Heinrichshofen, 1977.

Kränich, Friedrich. *Bühnentechnik der Gegenwart*. 2 vols. Munich and Berlin: Oldenburg, 1933.

Krasovskaya, Vera. *Nijinsky*. Translated by John Bowlt. New York: Schirmer, 1979 (1974).

Kröschlová, Jarmilla. *Vyrazovy tanec*. Prague: Orbis, 1964.

Kroutvar, Josef. "Der Tanz als Inspiration bei Frantisek Drtikol." Manuscript paper, 1991; abridged version appears in Faber, *Tanzfoto*.

Krull, Edith, and Werner Gommlich. *Palucca*. Berlin: Henschel, 1964.

Kuckhoff, Adam. "Tanz und Nacktheit." *Die Tat* 19/8 (1927), 643–644.

Kugler, Michael. "Von der 'Rhythmischen Gymnastik' zu den 'Realisationen.'" In *Ausdruckstanz*, 71–94.

Kugler, Walter. *Rudolf Steiner und die Anthroposophie*. Cologne: Dumont, 1991.

Kuhn, Alfred. "Die absolute Plastik Oswald Herzogs." *Der Cicerone* 8/9 (April 1921), 245–252.

Der künstlerische Tanz. Dresden: Eckstein-Halpaus, 1933.

Küster, Bernd. *Das Barkenhoff Buch*. Worpswede: Worpsweder Verlag, 1989.

———. *Kunstwerkstatt Worpswede*. Worpswede: Worpsweder Verlag, 1989.

Kuxdorf, Manfred. "Expressionism and Dance." In Behr, Fanning, and Jarman, 147–159.

Laban, Rudolf. "Aus einem Gespräch über das Tanztheater." *Die Tat* 14/9 (December 1922), 676–680.

———. *Choreographie*. Jena: Diederichs, 1926.

———. *Gymnastik und Tanz*. Oldenburg: Stalling, 1926.

———. *The Mastery of Movement*. Plymouth: Macdonald and Evans, 1980 (1950).

———. "Der Tanz als Eigenkunst." *Zeitschrift für Aesthetik und Allgemeine Kunstwissenschaft* 19 (1925), 356–364.

———. "Das tänzerische Kunstwerk." *Die Tat* 19/8 (November 1927), 588–591.

———. "Das Tanztheater." *Die Schönheit* 22/1 (1926), 3–4.

———. "Tanztheater und Tanztempel." *Die Schönheit* 22/1 (1926), 42–48.

———. "Titan: Ein Bewegungschor und eine Forderung." *Der Kreis* 5/1 (1928), 30–32.

———. "Vom Sinn der Bewegungschöre." *Die Schönheit* 22/1 (1926), 84–91.

————. *Die Welt des Tänzers.* Stuttgart: Seifert, 1920.

Laban, Rudolf, and F. C. Lawrence. *Effort: Economy of Human Movement.* Plymouth: Macdonald and Evans, 1979 (1947).

Lagerweij-Polak, E. J. "Dans-en toneelmaskers van Hildo Krop." *Jong Holland* 6 (1988).

Lämmel, Rudolf. *Der moderne Tanz.* Berlin: Oestergaard, 1928.

Lang, Erwin. *Grete Wiesenthal.* Berlin: Reiss, 1910.

Lania, Leo. *Der Tanz ins Dunkel. Anita Berber.* Berlin: Schulz, 1929.

Lapidoth, Frits. "Een Nederlandsch boek over danskunst." *Het Tooneel* 9/4 (September 1923), 51–57.

Lazzarini, John and Roberta. *Pavlova.* New York: Schirmer, 1980.

Leppin, Paul. "Tanz und Erotik." *Das Leben* 1 (1917), 7–11.

Lesák, Barbara. *Die Kulisse explodiert. Friedrich Kieslers Theaterexperimente und Architekturprojekte 1923–1925.* Vienna: Löcker, 1988.

Levinson, André. "Aus der Formen-und Gedankenwelt des klassichen Tänzers." *Die Tat* 19/8 (November 1927), 572–580.

————. *La danse d'aujour d'hui.* Paris: Ducharte et Van Buggenhoudt, 1929.

————. "The Modern Dance in Germany." *Theatre Arts Monthly* 13/2 (February 1932), 143–153.

Lex, Maja. "Brief and den Tanz." *Der Tanz* 8/10 (1937), 2–3.

Lexova, Irena. *Ancient Egyptian Dances.* Translated by K. Haltmar, New York: Dance Horizons, 1974 (1935).

Liess, A. *Carl Orff—Idee und Werk.* Zurich: Atlantis, 1955.

"Lili Green." Dossier of clippings, programs, photographs, drawings, and notes related to Lili Green in the Netherlands Dance Institute.

Loesch, Ilse. *Mit Leib und Seele.* Berlin: Henschel, 1990.

Lothar, Rudolph. "Jazz." In Herzog and Schreiber, 84–88.

Lüders, Eva M. "Kleist, Rilke und der Tänzer." *Deutsche Vierteljahrschrift für Literaturwissenschaft und Geistesgeschichte* 42/4 (October 1968), 515–552.

Lustig, Dorine. Inventory of Items Concerning Gertrud Leistikow Deposited in the Netherlands Dance Institute, 1991.

MacTavish, Shona Dunlop. *Gertrud Bodenwieser.* Bremen: Zeichen und Spuren, 1992.

Magriel, Paul. *Pavlova: An Illustrated Monograph.* New York: Holt, 1947.

Maletic, Vera. *Body-Space-Expression: The Development of Rudolf Laban's Movement and Dance Concepts.* Berlin: Mouton de Gruyter, 1987.

————. "Wigman and Laban: The Interplay of Theory and Practice." *Ballet Review* 14/3 (1986), 86–94.

Mammen Gesellschaft, Jeanne (ed.). *Jeanne Mammen 1890–1976.* Berlin: Berlinische Galerie, 1978.

Mamontowicz-Lojek, Bozena. *Terpsychora i lekkie muzy. Taniec widowiskowy w Polsce w okresie miedzywojennym (1918–1939).* Warsaw: Polskie Wydawnictwo Muzyczne, 1972.

Manning, Susan. "An American Perspective on Tanztheater." *The Drama Review* 30/2 (1986), 57–79.

————. "Body Politic: The Dances of Mary Wigman." Ph.D. dissertation, Columbia University Press, 1987.

————. *Ecstasy and the Demon: Feminism and Nationalism in the Dances of Mary Wigman.* Berkeley and Los Angeles: University of California Press, 1993.

————. "German *Rites:* A History of *Le sacre du printemps* on the German Stage." *Dance Chronicle* 14/2 (1991), 129–158.

————. "Lotte Goslar: Interview." *Tanzdrama* 5 (1988), 18–21.

Manning, Susan, and Melissa Benson. "Interrupted Continuities: Modern Dance in Germany." *The Drama Review* 30/2 (1986), 30–45.

Manor, Giora. *The Life and Dance of Gertrud Kraus.* Tel Aviv: Hakibbutz Hameuchad, 1978.

————. "Der Weg zu den Wurzeln. Anfänge des Ausdruckstanz in Eretz Israel." *Tanzdrama* 13 (1990), 7–11.

Markard, Anna and Hermann. *Jooss.* Cologne: Ballett-Bühnen-Verlag, 1985.

Markhof, Marietta Mautner. *Erika Giovanna Klien 1900–1957.* Vienna: Museum moderner Kunst, 1987.

Martin, Frank (ed.). *Emile Jaques-Dalcroze.* Neuchatel: La Baconnière, 1965.

Martin, John. "The New Dance and Its Influence on the Modern Stage." *The Drama* 19/2 (November 1928), 36–39.

————. *Ruth Page.* New York and Basel: Dekker, 1977.

Mata Hari. *The Diary of Mata Hari.* Translated by Mark Alexander. North Hollywood: Brandon House, 1967.

Max Pollak: In Retrospect 1886–1970. Santa Clara, CA: Triton Museum of Art, 1973.

McNeill, William H. *Keeping Together in Time: Dance and Drill in Human History.* Cambridge, MA: Harvard University Press, 1995.

Melzer, Anabelle. *Latest Rage the Big Drum: Dada and Surrealist Performance.* Ann Arbor: UMI Research Press, 1983.

Mensendieck, Bess. *Anmut der Bewegung im täglichen Leben.* Munich: Bruckmann, 1929.

————. *Bewegungsprobleme, die Gestaltung schöner Arme.* Munich: Bruckmann, 1927.

————. *It's up to You.* New York: Mensendieck Main School, 1931.

————. *Körperkultur des Weibes.* Munich: Bruckmann, 1906 (*Körperkultur der Frau.* Munich: Bruckmann, 1924).

————. *Standards of Female Beauty.* New York: Schob and Wisser, 1919.

Menz, Egon. "Sprechchor und Aufmarsch. Zur Entstehung des Thingspiels." In Horst Denkler and Karl Prümm (eds.), *Die deutsche Literatur im Dritten Reich.* Stuttgart: Reclam, 1976, 330–346.

Menzler, Dora. *Harmonische Gymnastik.* Leipzig: N.p.: 1914.

————. *Körperschulung der Frau.* Stuttgart: Dieck, 1925.

————. *Die Schönheit deines Körpers.* Stuttgart: Dieck, 1927 (1924).

Merrill, Frances and Mason. *Among the Nudists.* Garden City, NY: Garden City Publishing, 1931.

Merritt, Russell. Personal communication, Goethe Institute, San Francisco, 16 February 1994.

Meudtner, Ilse. *". . . tanzen konnte man immer noch."* Edited by Dietrich Steinbeck. Berlin: Hentrich, 1990.

Meyer, Alfred Richard. *Charlotte Bara.* Berlin: Meyer, 1921.

————. *Grit Hegesa. Eine Huldigung.* Berlin: Meyer, 1919.

————. *Der grosse Munkepunke.* Hamburg and Berlin: Hoffmann und Campe, 1924.

————. *Tanzplakatte*. Berlin: Meyer, 1913.

Mlakar, Pia and Pino. "Eine Gedenkstunde für Heinrich Kröller (1880–1930)." *Das Tanzarchiv* 28/7 (1980), 382–394.

————. "Vom Ausdruckstanz zum modernen Ballett." In *Ausdruckstanz*, 452–459.

Molkenbur, Norbert, and Klaus Hörhold. *Oda Schottmüller.* Berlin: Henschel, 1983.

Molnár, Antal. "Rita Sacchetto." *Nyugat* 9/1 (16 March 1916), 375–376.

Money, Keith. *Anna Pavlova, Her Life and Art.* New York: Knopf, 1982.

Morris, Hugh. *Facts about Nudism.* New York: Padell, 1935.

Moscovici, Hadassa K. *Vor Freude tanzen, vor Jammer halb in Stücke gehen. Pionierinnen der Körpertherapie.* Frankfurt am Main: Luchterhand, 1989.

Mosse, George L. *The Crisis of German Ideology. Intellectual Origins of the Third Reich.* New York: Schocken, 1981 (1964).

Mück, Hans (ed.). *Baumeister, Schlemmer und die Üecht-Gruppe.* Stuttgart: Matthaes, 1989.

Mueller, Hedwig. "Ausdruckstanz und Nationalsozialismus." In *Ausdruckstanz*, 460–470.

————. "Dritte Deutscher Tänzerkongress." *Tanzdrama* 13 (1990), 17–29.

————. "Die Form zu ändern wagen. Die Tanzgruppe Maja Lex." *Tanzdrama* 18 (1992), 5–7.

————. "Mary Wigman: Lebenslauf." *Tanzdrama* 8 (1989), 23–25.

————. *Mary Wigman. Leben und Werk der grossen Tänzerin.* Berlin: Quadriga, 1986.

Mueller, Hedwig, and Patricia Stöckemann (eds.). *". . . jeder Mensch ist ein Tänzer."* Giessen: Anabas, 1993.

Národní Divadlo. Edited by Vladimir Procházka. Prague: Akademia, 1988.

Nectoux, Jean-Michel. *Afternoon of a Faun. Mallarmé, Debussy, Nijinsky.* New York: Vendome Press, 1989.

Neelsen, Lotte. *Entwürfe auf der Tanzkunst.* Hamburg: Heldt, 1924.

Nerdinger, Winfried. *Rudolf Belling.* Berlin: Deutscher Verlag für Kunstwissenschaft, 1981.

Nezval, Vitezslav. *Aus meinem Leben.* Translated by Eckhard Thiele. Leipzig: Reclam, 1988.

Nicodemus, Katja. "'Das Hätte liegt im Bette'" (Julia Marcus). *Die Tagezeitung* (16 January 1995), 16–17.

Niedecken-Gebhard, Hans. "Bedeutung des Tanzes für das Kulturtheater." *Die deutsche Bühne* 19/6 (1927), 109–110.

Nikolaus, Paul. *Tänzerinnen.* Munich: Delphin, 1919.

————. "Tanz und Tanz-Kritik." *Die neue Schaubühne* 2/11 (1920), 310–312.

Novalis [Friedrich von Hardenberg]. *Fragmente und Studien. Die Christenheit oder Europa.* Stuttgart: Reclam, 1984.

Oberzaucher-Schüller, Gunhild. "Schlee. Ein Musikverlager mit Tanzvergangenheit." *Tanzdrama* 18 (1992), 8–10.

Obst, Milan, and Adolf Scherl. *K Dejinám ceské divadelni avantgardy.* Prague: Naklada Telstvi Ceskoslovenské Akademie ved, 1962.

Ochaim, Brygida Maria. "Die getanzten Bilder der Rita Sacchetto." *Tanzdrama* 14 (1991), 22–25.

Odom, Selma Landen. "Wigman at Hellerau." *Ballet Review* 14/2 (1986), 41–51.

"Olga Desmond." Mimeograph essay, ca. 1926–1928, on deposit at the Leipzig Tanzarchiv.

Oppler, Ernst. *Gertrud Falke in Radierungen.* Leipzig: Seemann, 1920.

Das Orami-Album Berühmte Tänzerinnen und Tänzer. Dresden: Orami Cigarette-Fabrik, 1933.

Orff, Carl. *Das Schulwerk.* Translated by Margaret Murray. New York: Schott, 1978 (*Dokumentation.* Vol. 3. Mainz: Schott, 1976).

Ostwald, Hans. *Berliner Tanzlokale.* Berlin: Seemann, 1905.

———. *Kultur-und Sittengeschichte Berlins.* Berlin-Grunewald: Klemm, 1924.

———. *Sittengeschichte der Inflation.* Berlin: Neufeld und Henius, 1931.

Otto, Werner. "Die Hellerauer Schulfeste von 1912 und 1913." In Horst Seeger (ed.). *Musikbühne 76.* Berlin: Henschel, 1976, 143–169.

Page, Ruth. *Notes on Dance Classes around the World.* Brooklyn: Princeton Book, 1984.

———. *Page by Page.* Edited by Mark Wentlink. New York: Dance Horizons, 1978.

———. *Video Archives.* 112 tapes. Chicago: Thea Flaum Productions, 1990.

Pallat, Ludwig, and Fritz Hilker. *Künstlerische Körperschulung.* Breslau: Hirt, 1923.

"Palucca. Zum Geburtstag einer Meisterin." *Tanzdrama* 18 (1992), 20–25.

Pander, Oswald. "Mary Wigman und die neue Choreographie." *Der Kreis* 2/2 (1925), 1–6.

Parker, Horatio Taylor. *Motion Arrested.* Edited by Olive Holmes. Middletown: Wesleyan University Press, 1982.

Parmelee, Maurice. *Nudism in Modern Life.* Mays Landing, NJ: Sunshine, 1941 (1927).

Pasche, Hans. "Tanz-Lehrfilme im Tonfilm-Verfahre." *Die Schallkiste* 3/9 (September 1928), 10.

Pastori, Jean-Pierre. *A corps perdu. La danse nu au XXe siècle.* Lausanne: Favre, 1983.

Paul Leni. Edited by Hilmar Hoffmann and Walter Schobert. Frankfurt am Main: Deutsches Filmmuseum, 1986.

Percival, John, *The World of Diaghilev.* New York: Harmony Books, 1979 (1971).

Peter, Frank-Manuel (ed.). *Dore Hoyer.* Berlin: Hentrich, 1992.

———. "Helge Peters-Pawlinin." *Tanzdrama* 9 (1989), 12–13.

———. "Hertha Feist." *Tanzdrama* 13 (1990), 34–37.

———. "'Mitgift war mir ja wurscht.' Die Photographin Marta Astfalck-Vietz (1901–1994)." *Tanzdrama* 26 (1994), 8–10.

———. "Nicht 'Weltanschauung,' sondern Heiterkeit schelchthin. Ein Nachruf auf Claire Eckstein." *Tanzdrama* 26 (1994), 22–27.

———. *Valeska Gert.* Berlin: Fröhlich und Kaufmann, 1985.

———. "Wegbereiter des modernen Tanzes. Der Tanzpublizist Fritz Böhme." *Tanzdrama* 9 (1989), 22.

Peter-Fuhr, Susanne. "Zum Rhythmischen in der Erziehung. Symposium zum Erinnerung an Elfriede Feudel." *Tanzdrama* 18 (1992), 26–27.

Peters, Hugo. *Revolution und Nacktkultur.* Dresden: Die Schönheit, 1919.

Peters, Kurt. *Lola Rogge.* Hamburg: Das Tanzarchiv, 1964.

Peusch, Vibeke. *Opernregie. Regieoper. Avantgardistisches Musiktheater in der Weimarer Republik.* Frankfurt am Main: tende, 1984.

Pfister, Gertrud (ed.). *Frau und Sport.* Frankfurt am Main: Fischer, 1980.

Pfützner, Klaus. *Die Massenspiele der Arbeiter in Leipzig (1920–1924)*. Leipzig: Hofmeister, 1960.

Pirchan, Emil. *Harald Kreutzberg. Sein Leben und seine Tänze*. Vienna: Frick, 1950 (1941).

Poetter, Jochen. *Leo Putz. Zeichnungen und Bilder aus dem Spätwerk*. Munich: Museum Villa Stuck, 1981.

Pollack, Heinz. "Das erzieherische Moment der neuen Tänze." In Herzog and Schreiber, 119–125.

———. *Die Revolution des Gesellschaftstanz*. Dresden: Sibyllen, 1922.

Prager, Wilhelm. *Wege zu Kraft und Schönheit*. Film on videotape. Berlin: UFA, 1925.

Preston-Dunlop, Valerie and Susanne Lahusen (eds.). *Schrifttanz. A View of German Dance in the Weimar Republic*. London: Dance Books, 1990.

Prevots, Naima. *Dancing in the Sun: Hollywood Choreographers, 1915–1937*. Ann Arbor: UMI Research Press, 1987.

———. "Zurich Dada and Dance: Formative Ferment." *Dance Research Journal* 17/1 (1985), 3–8.

Primus, Zdenek. "Fotografie und Fotomontage." In Primus (ed.). *Tschechische Avantgarde 1922–1940*. Hamburg: Kunstverein in Hamburg/Museum Bochum, 1990, 124–162.

Pringsheim, Klaus. "Der Unfug der neudeutschen Tanzkunst." *Der Querschnitt* 10/9 (September 1930), 623–628.

Prinzhorn, Hans. "Grundsätzliches zum *Totenmal*, zum kultischem Stil und zum Unternehmertum des Feierns." *Der Ring*. 3/36 (1930), 623–628.

Pudor, Heinrich. *Babel-Bibel in der modernen Kunst*. Berlin: Baumgärtel, 1905.

———. *Der Einfluss des Lichtes auf den menschlichen Organismus*. Langensalza: Gesundes Leben, 1905.

———. *Die Entstehung der Sprache*. Leipzig: Pudor, 1905.

———. *Die Frauenreformkleidung*. Leipzig: Seemann, 1903.

———. *Das Geschlecht. Bisexualitat*. Berlin-Steglitz: Pudor, 1906.

———. *Hygiene der Bewegung*. Langensalza: Beyer, 1906.

———. *Die internationalen verwandschaftlichen Beziehungen der jüdischen Hochfinanz*. Leipzig: Pudor, 1933.

———. *Katechismus der Nacktkultur*. Berlin-Steglitz: Pudor, 1906.

———. *Nackt-Kultur*. 3 vols. Leipzig: Pudor, 1907.

———. *Die Steinachschen. Verjüngsversuche und die natürliche Verjüngen durch Nacktkultur*. Dresden: Die Schönheit, 1920.

Rabenalt, Arthur Maria. "Der Ausdruckstanz und das Theater der Zwanziger Jahre." In *Ausdruckstanz*, 431–442.

Reiho, Bertta. *Luonnollinen lükunta*. Helsinki: Söderström, 1945.

———. *Rytmillinen lükunta*. Helsinki: Söderström, 1948.

Reinisch, Marion (ed.). *Auf der grossen Strasse. Jean Weidts Erinnerungen*. Berlin: Henschel, 1984.

Reinking, Wilhelm. *Spiel und Form*. Hamburg: Christians, 1979.

Renner, Gabriele. "Gertrud Bodenwieser. Ihre choreograpische und didaktische bedeutung fur den Freien Tanz." Dissertation, Universität Wien, 1981.

Rhodes, David. "The Body and the Dance: Kirchner's Swiss Work as Expressionism." In Behr, Fanning, and Jarman, 133–146.

Richards, Erwin. "Das Recht der Tanzschulen." *Der Tanz* 3/7 (1930), 18–19.

Riefenstahl, Leni. *Memoiren.* Munich: Knaus, 1987.

Rieger, Claudia. "'Lebende Bilder' und 'Bewegte Plastik.'" In *Ausdruckstanz*, 367–376.

Robinson, Jacqueline. *L'aventure de la danse moderne en France (1920–1970).* Paris: Bougé, 1990.

Rochowanski, Ludwig Wolfgang. *Der Formwille der Zeit in der angewandten Kunst.* Vienna: Burgverlag, 1922.

———. *Der tanzende Schwerpunkt.* Vienna: Amalthea, 1923.

Rode, Susanne. "Tanzmusikalische Experimente nach der Jahrhundertwende." In *Ausdruckstanz*, 254–277.

Rohden, Hedwig von, and Louise Langgaard. "Berufs-Ausbildungsstätte Loheland-Gymnastik." Special issue of *Gymnastik* 3/5–6 (1928).

———. *Gymnastik/Sport/Schauspiel.* Fulda: Loheland, 1928.

Roland Holst-Van der Schalk, Henriette. *Over dramatische Kunst.* Rotterdam: Brusse, 1932.

Rollier, Auguste. *Die Heliotherapie der Tuberkulose.* Berlin: Springer, 1913.

Ropa, Eugenia Casini. "La primavera apparizione sulla scena di Clotilde e Alexandre." In Veroli, 50–54.

Rothe, Wolfgang. "Sport und Literatur in den Zwanzigerjahren." *Stadion* 7/1 (1981), 131–151.

Rothschuh, Karl E. *Naturheilbewegung Reformbewegung Alternativbewegung.* Stuttgart: Hippokrates, 1983.

Rühle, Günther. *Zeit und Theater,* Vol. 3. Berlin: Propyläen, 1974.

Ruthenberg, Peter (ed.). *Luise Grimm. Zeichnungen und Druckgraphik 1919–1979:* Berlin: Kunstamt Kreuzberg, 1985.

Rydberg, Olaf, and Will Grohmann. *Die Tänzerin Palucca.* Dresden: Reissner, 1935.

Schab, Günter. "Leni Riefenstahl," *Hallesche Zeitung* (12 May 1923).

Schäfer, Rolf Helmut (ed.). *Yvonne Georgi.* Braunschweig: N.p., 1974.

Schaik, Eva van. *Max Dooijes.* Amsterdam: Stichting van de Toekomst, 1990.

———. *Op gespannen voet. Geschiednis van Nederlandse teaterdans vanaf 1900.* Haarlem: De Haan, 1981.

Schede, Wolfgang. *Farbenspiel des Lebens.* Zurich: Atlantis, 1960.

Scheier, Helmut. "Ausdruckstanz, Religion und Erotik." In *Ausdruckstanz*, 166–180.

Der Scheinwerfer. 1/11–12 (March 1928), 3–41. Special issue devoted to dance.

Scheper, Dirk. *Oskar Schlemmer. Das Triadische Ballett und die Bauhausbühne.* Berlin: Akademie der Künste, 1988.

Schertel, Ernst. *Bedürfnis und Begierde. Moral und Mensch.* Leipzig: Parthenon, 1931.

———. *Das Blut der Schwester.* Publicity brochure. Munich: Wende-Film, 1922.

———. *Der erotische Komplex.* 3 vols. Leipzig: Parthenon, 1932.

———. "Der Erwecker." *Eos* 1/1, Ausgabe A ("Ekstatik"). Berlin: Wende, 1918, 22–41.

———. *Der Flagellantismus als literarisches Motiv.* 4 vols. Leipzig: Parthenon, 1929–1932.

———. "Gibt es hypnotischen Tanz?" *Die Umschau* 30/2 (9 January 1926).

———. *Irrgarten der Leiber.* Leipzig: Parthenon, 1928.

———. *Die Katakomben von Ombas.* Munich: Wende, 1917.

————. *Magie. Geschichte/Theorie/Praxis.* Prien: Anthropos, 1923.

————. *Magie der Leiber. Ein Prolog.* Munich: Wende, 1921.

————. *Nacktkultur und Religion.* Leipzig: Parthenon, 1930.

————. "Der neue Tanz." *Soma* 1 (1926), 18–22.

————. "Pornographie als Kulturfaktor." *Asa* 3 (1931), 65–71.

————. *Schellings Metaphysik der Persönlichkeit.* Inaugural Dissertation, University of Jena. Leipzig: Quelle und Meyer, 1911.

————. *Die Sünde des Ewigen, oder dies ist mein Leib.* Berlin: Wende, 1918.

————. *Tanz, Erotik und Bessessenheit.* Leipzig: Parthenon, 1928.

————. "Tanz, Erotik und Okkultismus." *Erster Asa-Auswahlband.* Leipzig: Parthenon, 1928, 1–8.

————. "Tanz und Hysterie." *Zweiter Asa-Auswahlband.* Leipzig: Parthenon, 1928, 161–165.

————. "Tanz und neue Bildung." *Soma* 4 (1926), 105–106.

————. "Tanz und Ueberschwang." *Soma* 10 (1926), 272–275.

————. *340 mal. "Thema eins" in Wort und Bild. Sitte und Sünde.* Berlin: Pergamon, 1930.

————. "Das Traumland der Bühne." *Dritter Asa-Auswahlband.* Leipzig: Parthenon, 1928, 1–3.

————. *Das Weib als Göttin.* Leipzig: Parthenon, 1928.

————. *Weltwerdung.* Munich: Wende, 1919.

Schikowski, John. *Geschichte des Tanzes.* Berlin: Büchergilde Gutenberg, 1926.

————. *Der neue Tanz.* Berlin: Volksbühnenverlag, 1924.

Schlemmer, Oskar. *Idealist der Form.* Edited by Andreas Hüneke. Leipzig: Reclam, 1990.

Schlemmer, Oskar, Laszlo Moholy Nagy, and Farkas Molnár. *The Theater of the Bauhaus.* Translated by Arthur S. Wensinger. Middletown: Wesleyan University Press, 1961 (1925).

Schmidt-Linsenhoff, Viktoria. "'Körperseele.' Freilichtakt und Neue Sinnlichkeit." *Fotogeschichte* 1/1 (1981), 41–59.

Schnackenberg, Walter. *Ballett und Pantomime.* 22 colored plates. Munich: Müller, 1920.

————. *Kostüme, Plakate und Dekorationen.* Munich: Musarion, 1920.

Schoop, Trudi. *Won't You Join the Dance?* Palo Alto, CA: National Press Books, 1974.

Schreiber, Hans. *Trude Fleischmann. Fotografin in Wien 1918–1938.* Vienna: Wirtschafts-Trend Zeitschriften, 1991.

Schrenck, Edith von. *Mappe,* with lithographs by Ottheinrich Strohmeyer. Munich: Platenius, 1919.

Schrenck-Nötzing, Albert von. *Die Traumtänzerin Magdeleine G. Eine psychologische Studie über Hypnose und dramatische Kunst.* Stuttgart: Enke, 1904.

Schreyer, Lothar. *Expressionistisches Theater.* Hamburg: Toth, 1948.

————. *Zwischen Sturm und Bauhaus.* Edited by Brian Keith-Smith. Stuttgart: Heinz Akademischer Verlag, 1985.

Schrode, Thomas. "Kostüm und Maske im Ausdruckstanz." In *Ausdruckstanz,* 294–305.

Schröder, Heribert. *Tanz und Unterhaltungsmusik in Deutschland 1918–1933.* Bonn: Verlag für Systematische Musikwissenschaft, 1990.

Schuftan, Werner. "Der Dritte Deutsche Tänzerkongress." *Singchor und Tanz* 47/13–14 (15 July 1930), 210–214.

———. *Handbuch des Tanzes*. Mannheim: Deutscher Chorsängerverband und Tänzerverbund, 1928.

Schumann, Gerhard. *Palucca. Porträt einer Kunstlerin*. Berlin: Henschel, 1972.

See, M. "Tänzer, Choreograph und Regisseur in der Zeitwende. Zu Heinrich Kröllers 40. Todestag un 90. Geburtstag am 25 Juli 1970." *Neue Zeitschrift für Musik*. 81 (1970), 445–454.

Seiss, Margarete. *Körperbildung in der Mädchenschule*. Berlin: Herbig, 1930.

Seitz, Josef. *Die Nacktkulturbewegung*. Dresden: Die Schönheit, 1923.

Selden, Elizabeth. *The Dancer's Quest*. Berkeley: University of California Press, 1935.

Seydel, Renate, and Allan Hagedorff (eds.). *Asta Nielsen*. Munich: Universitas, 1981.

Shawn, Ted. "Germany's Newest Genius. An American Dance Leader Interviews Margarete Wallmann, Mary Wigman's Lieutenant." *The Dance Magazine* 14/1 (August 1930), 15, 21.

Shead, Richard. *Ballets Russes*. Secaucus, NJ: Wellfleet Press, 1989.

Shelton, Suzanne. *Ruth St. Denis*. Austin: University of Texas Press, 1990 (1981).

Siblik, Emanuel. *Tanec. Mimo nás i v nás*. Prague: Nakladatelstvi václav Petr, 1937.

———. *Tanec. Novéhp zivota*. Prague: Zatisi, 1922.

Siedlecka, Joanna. *Mahatma Witkac*. Warsaw: Slowo, 1992.

Siegel, Marcia. "A Conversation with Hanya Holm." *Ballet Review* 9/1 (1981), 5–30.

———. "*The Green Table*. Sources of a Classic." *Dance Research Journal* 21/1 (Spring 1989), 15–21.

Skerl, Lucie. *Anleitung für den Gymnastikunterricht in den Schulen*. Berlin: Teubner, 1926.

Skoronel, Vera. "Mary Wigmans Führertum." *Tanzgemeinschaft* 2/2 (1930), 4–6.

Smith, David Calvert. *Triumph of the Will*. Richardson, TX: Celluloid Chronicles Press, 1990.

Snyder, Allegra Fuller, and Annette Macdonald. *Mary Wigman, 1886–1973: "When the Fire Dances between the Two Poles."* Videotape. Pennington, NJ: Princeton Book Company, 1991.

Soden, Kristine von. *Die Sexuelberatungsstellen der Weimarer Republik 1919–1933*. Berlin: Hentrich, 1988.

Sokol. *Základy rytmického telocviku sokolského*. Prague: Sokol, 1929.

Solane, Janine. *Pour une danse plus humaine*. Paris: Vautrain, 1950.

Sorrell, Walter. *Hanya Holm*. Middletown: Wesleyan University Press, 1979 (1969).

Stadler, Edmund. "Jaques-Dalcroze et Adolphe Appia." In Martin, *Emile Jaques-Dalcroze*, 413–460.

———. "Theater und Tanz in Ascona." In Harald Szeeman (ed.). *Monte Verita. Berg der Wahrheit*. Milan: Electa, 1979, 126–135.

Stebbins, Genevieve. *Appendix to Society Gymnastics*. New York: Werner, 1895.

———. *Delsarte System of Dramatic Expression*. New York: Werner, 1896.

Stefan, Paul (ed.). *Tanz in dieser Zeit*. Vienna: Universal Edition, 1926.

Stenzig, Bernd. *Worpswede-Moskau*. Worpswede: Worpsweder Verlag, 1989.

Stern, Richard A. M., Gregory Gilmartin, and Thomas Mellins. *New York 1930*. New York: Rizzoli, 1987.

Stöckemann, Patricia. *Lola Rogge*. Wilhelmshaven: Noetzel, 1991.

————. "Niddy Impekoven. Geburtstag eines Wunderkinds." *Tanzdrama* 11 (1990), 26–28.

Stuckenschmidt, Hans Heinz. *Zum hören geboren.* Munich: Piper, 1979.

Suhr, Werner. "Der entfesselte Tanz." *Deutsches Musikjahrbuch.* Vol. 3 Essen: Reismann-Grone, 1925, 240–245.

————. *Das Gesicht des Tanzes.* Egestorf: Lauer, 1927.

————. *Der künstlerische Tanz.* Leipzig: Siegels Musikalienbibliothek, 1922.

————. *Der nackte Tanz.* Egestorf: Lauer, 1927.

————. *Die Tänzerin Ani Schwaninger und die Josefslegende.* Freiburg: Muth, 1924.

Surén, Hans. *Deutsche Gymnastik.* Berlin: Oldenburg, 1925.

————. *Der Mensch und die Sonne.* Stuttgart: Dieck, 1925 (1924).

Suritz, Elisabeth. "Der 'plastische' und 'rhythmo-plastische Tanz' im Russland der Zehner und Zwanziger Jahre." In *Ausdruckstanz,* 405–420.

Sutter, Esther. "Gret Palucca." In *Ausdruckstanz,* 116–122.

"Die Tagungen des Tänzerkongresses. München 19.–25. Juni 1930." *Der Tanz* 3/8 (August 1930), 4–16.

Takvorian, Rick, and Denny Hirschbach. *Die Kraft des Tanzes. Hilde Holger. Wien, Bombay, London.* Bremen: Zeichen und Spuren, 1990.

Talhoff, Albert. *Totenmal.* Stuttgart: Deutsche Verlags-Anstalt, 1930.

Die Tanzbühnen der Welt. Dresden: Eckstein-Halpaus, 1933.

Die Tat. Special issue devoted to the Magdeburg Dance Congress. 19/8 (November 1927), 569–645.

Taui, Gino. "Aurel von Milloss." *Enciclopdia dello Spettacola.* Rome: Casa Editrice le Maschere, 1960, 586–593.

Taussig, Helene von. *Der Tanzer Harald Kreutzberg.* Vienna: Kunstverlag Wurthe, 1933.

Teige, Karel. "Die Aufgaben der modernen Fotografie." *Fotogeschichte* 9/32 (1989), 55–60 (originally published in 1931).

————. *Film.* Prague: Bubenec, 1925.

————. *Liquidierung der "Kunst." Analysen, Manifeste.* Translated by Paul Kruntorad, Frankfurt am Main: Suhrkamp, 1968.

————. "Ueber die Fotomontage." *Fotogeschichte* 9/32 (1989), 61–70 (originally published in 1932).

Tepp, Max. *Gertrud und Ursula Falke. Tänze.* Lauenberg: Saal, 1924.

Terpis, Max. "Das Opernballett." *Tanzdrama* 7 (1989), 24–25 (first published in 1926).

————. *Tanz und Tänzer.* Zurich: Atlantis, 1946.

————. "Wie entsteht ein Ballett?" *Die Schallkiste* 3/9 (September 1928), 4.

Thiemann, Eugen. *Hoetger.* Worpswede: Worpsweder Verlag, 1990.

Theobald, Christiane. "Wechselwirkung zwischen Komposition und Ausdruckstanz in der neuen Musik." In *Ausdruckstanz,* 248–253.

Thiess, Frank. *Der Tanz als Kunstwerk.* Munich: Delphin, 1923 (1920).

This Nude World. Film directed by Michael Mindlin from a story by Jan Gay. New York: Vision Pictures, 1932.

Thom, Yetty. Scrapbook-diary, 1927–1945, on deposit with Wilfried van Poppel, Amsterdam.

Toepfer, Karl. "Nudity and Modernity in German Dance, 1910–1930." *Journal of the History of Sexuality* 3/1 (July 1992), 58–108.

———. Review of Dirk Scheper, *Oskar Schlemmer: Das Triadische Ballett*. In *Theater Three* 8 (Spring 1990), 116–122.

———. Review of Susan Manning, *Ecstasy and the Demon*. In *The Drama Review* 38/3 (T143) (Fall 1994), 187–192.

———. "Speech and Sexual Difference in Mary Wigman's Dance Aesthetic." In Laurence Senelick (ed.). *Gender in Performance*. Hanover, NH: University Press of New England, 1992, 260–278.

Török, Alphons. *Tanzabende*. Vienna: Der Merkur, 1918.

Traber-Amiel, August. *Der Tanz als Weg zur neuen Kultur*. Berlin: Theaterverlag Eduard Bloch, 1924.

Troy, Nancy J. "Figures of the Dance in De Stijl." *Art Bulletin* 66/4 (December 1984), 644–656.

Turbyfill, Mark. *The Art of Ruth Page*. N.p: n.d. (1934).

———. *Ruth Page, Harald Kreutzberg*. N.p.: 1934.

Ueberhorst, Horst. *Frisch, frei, stark und treu. Die Arbeitersportbewegung in Deutschland 1893–1933*. Düsseldorf: Droste, 1973.

——— (ed.). *Geschichte der Leibesübungen*. Vol. 3, Parts 1 and 2. Berlin: Bartels und Wernitz, 1980–1982.

Ullmann, Lisa (ed.). *Rudolph Laban. A Vision of Dynamic Space*. Philadelphia: Laban Archives/Falmer Press, 1984.

Ungewitter, Richard. *Nackt*. Stuttgart: Ungewitter, 1920.

———. *Nacktheit und Aufstieg*. Stuttgart: Ungewitter, 1920.

———. *Nacktheit und Kultur*. Stuttgart: Ungewitter, 1907.

———. *Nacktheit und Moral*. Stuttgart: Ungewitter, 1906.

——— (ed.). *Der Zusammenbruch. Deutschlands Wiedergeburt durch Blut und Eisen*. Stuttgart: Ungewitter, 1919.

Vaccarino, Elisa. "I Sakharoff per immagini. Analisi di un'estica." In Veroli, 55–61.

Van Collem, Anton. "Eenige dansen van Gertrud Leistikow." *Wendingen* 2/3 (1919), 21–24.

Van der Poel, Dirk. *Leekenspel*. Rotterdam: Brusse, 1933.

Van Ostaijen, Paul. *Feasts of Fear and Agony*. Translated by Hidde Van Ameyden van Duym. New York: New Directions, 1976.

———. "Gebruiksaanweijzing der lyriek." In Van Ostaijen. *Music-Hall*. Edited by Gerrit Borgers. Amsterdam: Bakker, 1982, 161–178.

———. *Verzameld Werk*. 4 vols. Antwerp and The Hague: Bakker/Daamen/De Vries-Brouwers, 1963 (1954).

Van Vechten, Carl. "The New Isadora." In Van Vechten, *Merry-go-round*. New York: Knopf, 1918, 307–317.

Vavra, Otakar. *Zamysleni reziséra*. Prague: Panorama, 1982.

Veit, Wolfgang. *Eurythmie. Else Klink*. Stuttgart: Urachhaus, 1985.

"Vera Skoronel." Dossier of clippings related to Vera Skoronel in Leipzig Tanzarchiv.

Vernon, Doremy. *Tiller's Girls*. London: Dobson, 1988.

Veroli, Patrizia. "'La vita che abbiamo danzato': itinerio attraverso la vita e l'arte dei Sakharoff." In Veroli, 15–41.

————— (ed.). *I Sakharoff. Un mito della danza fra teatro e avanguarie artistiche.* Bologna: Bora, 1991.

Vettermann, Gabi. "Tanzkritik als Spiegel der soziokulturellen Situation von Tanz." In *Ausdruckstanz,* 212–223.

Villany, Adoreé. *Tanz-Reform und Pseudo-Moral.* Paris: Privately printed, 1912.

Vuillermoz, Emile. *Clotilde et Alexandre Sacharoff.* Lausanne: Editions Centrales, 1933.

Waagenaar, Sam. *Mata Hari, niet zo onschuldig.* Bussum: Van Holkema en Warendorf, 1976.

Wang, Cilli. "Der Tanz nach gesprochenem Wort." *Schrifttanz* 3 (August 1929), 54.

Warstat, Willi. *Der schöne Akt.* Berlin: Hackebeil, 1929.

Wege zu Kraft und Schönheit. Promotional brochure. Berlin: UFA (Universum Film Aktiengesellschaft), 1925.

Wege zu Kraft und Schönheit. Film by Wilhelm Prager. Berlin: UFA, 1925.

Weidemann, Magnus. *Körper und Tanz.* Rudolstadt: Greifenverlag zu Rudolstadt, 1925.

Weidt, Jean. *Der Rote Tänzer.* Berlin: Henschel, 1968.

Weimarer Republik. Edited by Kunstamt Kreuzberg and the Institut für Theaterwissenschaft der Universität Köln. Berlin: Elefanten Press, 1977.

Weiss, Sheila Faith. "The Race Hygiene Movement in Germany 1904–1945." In Mark Adams (ed.). *The Wellborn Science.* New York: Oxford University Press, 1990, 8–68.

Weissenböck, Jarmilla (ed.). *Der Figurenspiel. Richard Teschner.* Vienna: Böhlau, 1991.

Weissenböck, Jarmilla, and Andrea Amort (eds.). *Tanz in 20. Jahrhundert in Wien.* Exhibition catalogue. Vienna: Österreiches Theatermuseum, 1979.

Wellesz, Egon. "Tanz und Musik." *Die Tat* 19/8 (November 1927), 597–604.

Wels, G. "Das Teatro San Materno." *Das Werk* (February 1929).

Welzien, Lenore. "Vom Rhythmus zur Bewegung—von der Bewegung zum Tanz. Interview mit Rosalia Chladek." *Tanzdrama* 11 (1990), 18–23.

Wiederanders, Max. "Das 'Lustspiel-Haus' in München." *Innen-Dekoration* 33 (1922), 107–111.

Wiener, Hans, as told to John Martin. "The New Dance and Its Influence on the Modern Stage." *The Drama* 19/2 (November 1928), 36–39.

Wigman, Mary. *Deutsche Tanzkunst.* Dresden: Reissner, 1935.

—————. *Kompositionen.* Überlingen: Seebote, 1925.

—————. *The Mary Wigman Book, Her Writings.* Edited by Walter Sorrell. Middletown: Wesleyan University Press, 1973.

—————. *Die sieben Tänze des Lebens—Tanzdichtung.* Jena: Diedrichs, 1921.

—————. *Die Sprache des Tanzes.* Stuttgart: Battenberg, 1963.

—————. "Der Tänzer und das Theater." *Blätter des Hessischen Landestheater* 7 (1929–1930), 49–58.

Wille, Hansjürgen. *Harald Kreutzberg und Yvonne Georgi.* Leipzig: Weibezahl, 1930.

Winther, Fritz and Hanna. *Der Heilige Tanz.* Rudolfstadt: Greifenverlag, 1922.

—————. *Körperbildung als Kunst und Pflicht.* Munich: Delphin, 1919 (1914).

—————. *Lebendige Form.* Karlsruhe: Braunsche Hofbuchdruckerei, 1920.

—————. *Der rhythmische Mensch.* Rudolfstadt: Greifenverlag, 1922.

Wobbe, Eva. "Ausdruckstanz im Spiegel der Zeitschrift *Der Tanz.*" Magisterarbeit. Ludwig Maximillians Universität (Munich), 1988.

————. "Die Gymnastik." In *Ausdruckstanz*, 25–33.

Wolfensberger, Giorgio J (ed.). *Suzanne Perrottet. Ein Bewegtes Leben*. Bern: Benteli, 1990.

Woog, Heide. "Mein Weg zum Tanz." *Deutsches Musikjahrbuch*. Vol. 3 Essen: Reismann-Grone, 1925, 238–240.

————. *Ueber Atmung und ihre Bedeutung für die neuzeitliche Körperbildung*. Pamphlet produced by the Heide Woog School, Mühlheim, 1929..

Wysocka, Tacjanna. *Wspomnienia*. Warsaw: Czytelnik, 1962.

Zivier, Georg. *Harmonie und Ekstase. Mary Wigman*. Berlin: Akademie der Künste, 1956.

INDEX

Abel, Hermann, 81
Abramowitsch, Ruth, 211, 295, 328
Abt, Lisa, 159
Adolphi, Max, 2, 67–68, figs. 17–19
Agadati, Baruch, 193
Alastair, 212
Albu, Dorothea, 254, 298, 372
Allen, Maud, 158
Allerhand, Ruth, 155n
Alsen, Ola, 337
Altmann, Elsie, 157, 199
androgyny, in dance, 345
Ansermet, Ernst, 16
Antios, 269
Appia, Adolphe, 16
Aragon, Louis, 247
architecture, relation to dance, 367–71
Arco, Rolf, 297
Argentina, La (Antonia Merce), 158
Arntzenius, Lodewijk, 230
Arp, Hans, 108
Artner, Brigitte, 238
art and dance, 358–81. *See also* graphic arts; sculpture; cinema; architecture; photography
asexuality, in dance, 345
Auerbach, Alfred, 318
Auerbach, Lotte, 252
Aurel, Rita, 43, 200–201
Avnon, Naftali, 144

Baack, Elsbeth, 238
Bach, Johann Sebastian, 166, 180, 184, 325

Baer-Frissell, Christine, 119
Baker, Josephine, 362
Balanchine, George, 273
Balazs, Béla, 286, 372–73
Ball, Hugo, 108
ballet, relation to modernist body culture, 18, 80, 74–96, 244, 285, 287
Ballets Russes, 286, 299, 323, 363
Balluff, Willy, 47
Banky, Vilma, 287
Bara, Charlotte, 53, 171–75, 179, 312, 324, 342, fig. 45
Barakovic (Barakowics), Edith, 60, 376
Barbakoff, Tatiana, 206, 375
Barbier, Georges, 222
Barrault, Jean-Louis, 247
Barrison, Gertrud, 159–60
Bartók, Béla, 120, 138, 286, 289, 296, 322, 323, 328
Bauer, Magda, 237–38
Bauhaus, 5, 67, 105, 135–45, 367, figs. 4, 35–38. *See also* Schlemmer, Oskar; Schreyer, Lothar
Baumann, Hans, 317
Baur, Helga, 66
Bauroff, Claire, 54, 58, 238, 240, 376, fig. 13
Bausch, Pina, 272, 275
Bayros, Franz von, 265
Becher, Eva, 253
Becher, Johannes R., 187
Beckmann, Max, 78
Belle, Isa, 236

Halbe, Max, 317
Haller, Hermann, 75
Hallman, Adolf, 82
Hammer, Trude, 55
Handel, George Frideric, 121, 166, 180, 280, 281, 291, 300–302
Hard, Nina, 27
Harrer, Heinrich, 317
Harta, Felix, 96, 265, 375
Hasselquist, Jenny, 53, 150, 153, 371, 374
Hasting, Hanns, 112, 325–26
Hatvani, Paul, 208
Hauptmann, Gerhart, 201
Hausmann, Raoul, 108
Hauth, Emil van, 169, fig. 44
Hebbel, Friedrich, 255, 263
Heckel, Erich, 216
Heckroth, Hein, 271
Hegesa, Grit, 43, 53, 67, 153, 167–71, 322, 342, 351–52, 359, 363, 366, figs. 42–44, 67
Heidegger, Martin, 31
Heiner, Emmy, 118
Held-Ludwig, Stephanie, 375
Heller, Hermann, 218
Hellerau, 16, 119–21, 140, 250, 360, 372
Helsing, Dagmar, 237
Herion, Ida, 2–5, 55, 67–68, figs. 1–2, 17–22
Herrlich, Lotte, 48–51, 58, 60, fig. 12
Herrlich, Rolf, 49, 50–51, 60, 105
Herrmann, Marion, 346
Hertel, Lucie, 159
Hertig, Jutta, 203
Herzog, Oswald, 365
Hess, Frida, 211
Hess, Günther, 284, 318
Hesse, Gertrud, 375
Hesse, Lo, 213–14, 367
Heu, Joseph, 269
Heyer, Hermann, 301
Heyer, Lucy, 55, 237
Heynicke, Kurt, 317
Hildenbrandt, Fred, 43, 183, 213, 289, 337
Hillig, Hugo, 75
Himmelssaal (experimental dance space), 369–71
Hindemith, Paul, 138, 140, 271, 291, 322, 323
Hitler, Adolf, 201, 218–19, 247, 249, 348, 371
Hodler, Ferdinand, 255

Hoetger, Bernhard, 369–71, fig. 77
Hoffmann, Kitty, 60
Hoffmannsthal, Hugo von, 160
Holdt, Hanns, 375, figs. 39, 48, 51
Holdt, Walter, 136, 214–16, 239, 324, fig. 52
Holger, Hilde, 269–70
Hollaender, Felix, 182
Holm, Hanya, 109, 156, 186, 224, 312
Holst, Frida, 225, 238, 277, 297
Holzbachova, Mira, 304
homoeroticism (female), 208, 216. *See also* Bloch, Alice; Bodenwieser, Gertrud; Günther, Dorothee; Hagemann, Hedwig; Hellerau; Loheland; Tels, Ellen
Honegger, Arthur, 247, 296, 313
Horenstein, Jascha, 252
Hornbach, Hertha, 366
Hötzel, Elsa, 140, 212
Hoyer, Dore, 189, 296, 378–79, fig. 81
Hubbuch, Karl, 360
Hugenberg, Alfred, 247, 249
Huszar, Vilmos, 362
Hutten, Fred van, 211

Ihering, Herbert, 293
Ilbak, Ella, 164
imagery of dance, 4–5, 104–5, 358–81
Impekoven, Niddy, 43, 118, 182–86, 191, 204, 324–25, 351, 372, 374, 376, fig. 48
Inyoka, Nyota, 158
Isenfels, Paul, 4–5, 67–68, 105, figs. 2, 20–22
Issachenko, Claudia, 164

Jacobi, Lotte, 377
Jacobs, Artur, 126–27
Jacobs, Dore, 123
Janáček, Leo, 331
Jansen, Willi, 279
Jaques-Dalcroze, Émile, 15–21, 29, 83, 99, 108, 110, 118, 119–25, 128, 142, 164, 167, 194, 217, 224, 233, 250, 289, 321, 325, 346, 380, fig. 5
Jawlensky, Alexander, 219
jazz, 210–11, 301, 324, 331, 341, 362, 364
Jencik, Joe, 84–86, 89, 350–51
Jensen, Elna Jorgen, 236
Jobst, Rudolf, 160, 376
Johansson, Ronny, 178, 199, 328, 342–43, 375
Jolson, Al, 201

WEIMAR AND NOW: GERMAN CULTURAL CRITICISM

Martin Jay and Anton Kaes, General Editors

Breinigsville, PA USA
02 February 2011
254701BV00006B/7/A